September 13–16, 2016
Vienna, Austria

I0054882

**Association for
Computing Machinery**

Advancing Computing as a Science & Profession

DocEng '16

Proceedings of the 2016 ACM Symposium on
Document Engineering

Sponsored by:
ACM SIGWEB

Supported by:
Adobe, APA IT, FXPAL, HP, & Xerox

Association for Computing Machinery

Advancing Computing as a Science & Profession

The Association for Computing Machinery
2 Penn Plaza, Suite 701
New York, New York 10121-0701

Notice to Past Authors of ACM-Published Articles
ACM intends to create a complete electronic archive of all articles and/or other material previously published by ACM. If you have written a work that has been previously published by ACM in any journal or conference proceedings prior to 1978, or any SIG Newsletter at any time, and you do NOT want this work to appear in the ACM Digital Library, please inform permissions@acm.org, stating the title of the work, the author(s), and where and when published.

ISBN: 978-1-4503-4438-8 (Digital)

ISBN: 978-1-4503-4680-1 (Print)

Additional copies may be ordered prepaid from:

ACM Order Department
PO Box 30777
New York, NY 10087-0777, USA

Phone: 1-800-342-6626 (USA and Canada)
+1-212-626-0500 (Global)
Fax: +1-212-944-1318
E-mail: acmhelp@acm.org
Hours of Operation: 8:30 am – 4:30 pm ET

Printed in the USA

Welcome from the Symposium and PC Chairs

It is both an honor and a pleasure to hold the 16th ACM Symposium on Document Engineering, DocEng 2016, at the TU Wien, Austria, organized by the Computer Vision Lab (CVL). DocEng is the leading international ACM symposium for researchers, practitioners, developers, and users to explore cutting-edge ideas and to exchange techniques, tools, and experiences in the domain of document engineering. It aims at bringing together researchers in the fields of computer vision, multimedia technologies, image processing, image analysis, information and systems analysis, electronic publishing, business process analysis, and business informatics. The symposium is intended as convention of renowned experts in all areas of document engineering of both academia and industry to present and discuss recent progress and advances in the fields of: document models and structures, document representation and standards, distributed documents, collaborative documents and the sharing economy, document internationalization, multilingual representations, document authoring tools and systems, document presentation (typography, formatting, layout), automatically generated documents, content customization, variable printing, documents for mobile devices, web document processing and interaction, document repositories, massive collections of documents, digital libraries and archives, secure document workflows, collaborative authoring and editing, culture-dependent layouts, and many more.

Our call for papers attracted submissions from 27 countries (Australia, Austria, Brazil, Canada, China, France, Germany, Greece, India, Indonesia, Iran, Italy, Japan, Korea, Macao, Malta, Netherlands, New Zealand, Romania, Russian Federation, Slovakia, Spain, Switzerland, Tunisia, United Kingdom, United States, Vietnam). All papers were carefully reviewed by a minimum of three Program Committee members, upon which decisions for acceptance were based on correctness, presentation, technical depth, scientific significance and originality. The Program Committee accepted 11 of 35 reviewed full paper submissions (31%) and 12 of 36 reviewed short paper submissions (33%) for oral presentation, for a combined acceptance rate of 32%. A further 10 short paper submissions were accepted for poster presentation.

This year's program includes a Doctoral Consortium as a special session for the fourth time, where doctoral students in their second year or later present their dissertation project and get feedback from a panel of senior researchers as well as from the general audience. This session, called ProDoc@DocEng, is intended to provide students with constructive criticism and helps them in formulating their research question, deciding about methods and approaches to use, and creating further ideas. This is one of the key ways in which we support the future generation of researchers in Document Engineering.

A true highlight of this year's DocEng are the valuable and insightful keynote talks:

- *Design Is Not What You Think It Is,* Peter Bil'ak, founder of the Typotheque design studio and Lecturer at the Royal Academy of Arts in The Hague, Netherlands

- *Research Infrastructures, or How Document Engineering, Cultural Heritage and Digital Humanities Can Go Together,* Günter Mühlberger, from the University of Innsbruck, Austria

The Proceedings of DocEng 2016 contain the papers in the same order as they were presented at the conference, grouped by their corresponding thematic session. In putting these Proceedings together, many people played a significant role which we would like to acknowledge: First of all, our thanks are due to the authors who contributed their work to the symposium. Secondly, we are grateful for the dedicated work of the 60 members of the Program Committee for their effort in evaluating the submitted papers and in providing the necessary decision support information and the valuable feedback for the authors. We also thank Sonja Schimmler for organizing the first day with two tutorials and two workshops, Cerstin Mahlow for coordinating ProDoc@DocEng, Charles Nicholas for chairing the Birds of a Feather session, and Ethan Munson for his support regarding the Student Travel Awards. We also thank the Steering Committee and in particular Steven Simske for their support.

Finally, we are grateful for the support of the hosting university TU Wien, the Vienna Convention Bureau, our sponsor ACM SIGWEB, and the generous industry support of HP, Fuji-Xerox Palo Alto Laboratory (FXPAL), Adobe, APA-IT, Xerox, and Austrian Airlines. Many thanks to our local support team consisting of Florian Kleber, Stefan Fiel, Markus Diem, Fabian Hollaus and Katharina Pois, who made this symposium possible and took care of all practical tasks involved in planning DocEng 2016. Special thanks go to Markus Diem who designed and maintained the conference website and took care of the publicity together with Fabian Hollaus, and all members of the CVL who helped in organizational matters. We hope that these Proceedings, in following the tradition of all DocEng conferences, will not only impact on the readers' current research, but will also represent important archival material for years to come. We wish all participants a pleasant stay in Vienna and many fruitful scientific contacts.

Robert Sablatnig
DocEng 2016 Symposium Chair
TU Wien, Austria

Tamir Hassan
DocEng 2016 Program Chair
HP Labs, Austria

Table of Contents

Session 13: Text Analysis III: Summarization
Session Chair: Dick Bulterman *(Centrum Wiskunde en Informatica, Amsterdam)*

Session 14: Applications and Security
Session Chair: David F. Brailsford *(University of Nottingham)*

Session 16: Visual Document Analysis
Session Chair: Steven J. Simske *(HP Labs)*

DocEng 2016 Symposium Organization

Symposium Chair: Robert Sablatnig *(TU Wien, Austria)*

Program Chair: Tamir Hassan *(HP Labs, Austria)*

Workshop and Tutorials Chair: Sonja Schimmler *(Universität der Bundeswehr München, Germany)*

Doctoral Consortium Chair: Cerstin Mahlow *(Institut für Deutsche Sprache, Germany)*

BOF Chair: Charles Nicholas *(University of Maryland, USA)*

Local Chairs: Florian Kleber *(TU Wien, Austria)*
Stefan Fiel *(TU Wien, Austria)*

Publicity Chairs: Markus Diem *(TU Wien, Austria)*
Fabian Hollaus *(TU Wien, Austria)*

Steering Committee Chair: Steve Simske *(HP Labs, USA)*

Steering Committee: David Brailsford *(University of Nottingham, UK)*
Dick Bulterman *(FX Palo Alto Laboratory, USA)*
Matthew Hardy *(Adobe, USA)*
Peter King *(University of Manitoba, Canada)*
Kim Marriot *(Monash University, Australia)*
Ethan V. Munson *(University of Wisconsin-Milwaukee, USA)*
Charles Nicholas *(University of Maryland, USA)*
Maria da Graca C. Pimentel *(Universidade de São Paulo, Brazil)*
Cécile Roisin *(Université Pierre Mendes and INRIA, France)*
Jean-Yves Vion-Dury *(Xerox Research Centre Europe, France)*
Anthony Wiley *(OpenText, USA)*

Program Committee: Apostolos Antonacopoulos *(University of Salford, UK)*
Vlad Atanasiu *(University of Fribourg, Switzerland)*
Steven R. Bagley *(University of Nottingham, UK)*
Helen Balinsky *(HP Labs, UK)*
Jean-Luc Bloechle *(Sugarcube IT, Switzerland)*
Uwe M. Borghoff *(Universität der Bundeswehr München, Germany)*
David F. Brailsford *(University of Nottingham, UK)*
Anne Brüggemann-Klein *(Technische Universität München, Germany)*
Pablo Cesar *(CWI, Netherlands)*
Paolo Ciccarese *(Harvard Medical School/Mass. General Hospital, USA)*
Michael L. Collard *(The University of Akron, USA)*
Niranjan Damera-Venkata *(HP Labs, India)*
Markus Diem *(TU Wien, Austria)*
Angelo Di Iorio *(University of Bologna, Italy)*
Stefano Ferilli *(University of Bari, Italy)*
Stefan Fiel *(TU Wien, Austria)*

Program Committee (continued):

Pierre Genevès *(CNRS, France)*
Gersende Georg *(French National Authority for Health, France)*
C. Lee Giles *(Pennsylvania State University, USA)*
Matthew Hardy *(Adobe, USA)*
Tamir Hassan *(HP Labs, Austria)*
Fabian Hollaus *(TU Wien, Austria)*
Andrew Hunter *(HP Labs, UK)*
Nathan Hurst *(Shutterstock, USA)*
Rolf Ingold *(University of Fribourg, Switzerland)*
Peter R King *(University of Manitoba, Canada)*
Florian Kleber *(TU Wien, Austria)*
Alberto Laender *(Universidade Federal de Minas Gerais, Brazil)*
Monica Landoni *(USI, Switzerland)*
Baoli Li *(Henan University of Technology, China)*
Lei Liu *(HP Labs, USA)*
Marcus Liwicki *(University of Fribourg, Switzerland)*
John Lumley *(jwL Research, UK)*
Cerstin Mahlow *(Institut für Deutsche Sprache, Germany)*
Simone Marinai *(University of Florence, Italy)*
Kim Marriott *(Monash University, Australia)*
Evangelos Milios *(Dalhousie University, Canada)*
Mirella M. Moro *(UFMG, Brazil)*
Ethan V. Munson *(University of Wisconsin-Milwaukee, USA)*
Charles Nicholas *(University of Maryland, USA)*
Ermelinda Oro *(ICAR-CNR, Italy)*
Giorgio Orsi *(University of Birmingham, UK)*
Maria da Graca Pimentel *(Universidade de São Paulo, Brazil)*
Michael Piotrowski *(Leibniz Institute of European History, Germany)*
Stefan Pletschacher *(University of Salford, UK)*
Cécile Roisin *(Université Grenoble Alpes, France)*
Sebastian Roennau *(Ravensburger AG, Germany)*
Robert Sablatnig *(TU Wien, Austria)*
Sonja Schimmler *(Universität der Bundeswehr München, Germany)*
Patrick Schmitz *(UC Berkeley, USA)*
Badarinath Shantharam *(HP, India)*
Ryan Shaw *(University of North Carolina at Chapel Hill, USA)*
Steven Simske *(HP Labs, USA)*
Fouad Slimane *(EDSI Tech, Switzerland)*
Margaret Sturgill *(HP Labs, USA)*
Cheng Thao *(University of Wisconsin–Whitewater, USA)*
Frank Tompa *(University of Waterloo, Canada)*
Fabio Vitali *(University of Bologna, Italy)*
Jean-Yves Vion-Dury *(Xerox Research Centre Europe, France)*
Christine Vanoirbeek *(EPFL, Switzerland)*
Erik Wilde *(Siemens, USA)*
Anthony Wiley *(OpenText, USA)*
Raymond Wong *(UNSW, Australia)*

DocEng 2016 Sponsor & Supporters

Sponsor:

Supporters:

Table Modelling, Extraction and Processing

Max Göbel
Wirtschaftsuniversität Wien
Vienna, Austria
mcgoebel@gmail.com

Tamir Hassan
HP Labs
Vienna, Austria
tamir.hassan@hp.com

Ermelinda Oro
ICAR-CNR
Rende, Italy
linda.oro@icar.cnr.it

Giorgio Orsi
University of Birmingham
Birmingham, UK
g.orsi@bham.ac.uk

Roya Rastan
University of New South Wales
Sydney, Australia
rrastan@cse.unsw.edu.au

ABSTRACT

This tutorial is targeted at academics and practitioners, both within and outside of the Document Engineering community, who are confronted with table processing tasks such as information extraction and conversion, or have an interest in the topic, and wish to deepen their understanding of the state-of-the-art in this field.

1. TOPICS AND GOALS

Tables are of particular interest to document engineers as they contain information in a human-readable, structured form that can relatively easily be made machine-readable. Table processing tasks can thus be split into two major groups:

- **Table understanding,** the more common problem, deals with extracting information from tables and representing it in a known structured form.

- **Table generation** is the reverse of this process: the transformation of data from its structured form into a physical table.

The above tasks can be effectively tackled by separating the actual data from its presentation. Many research groups have proposed methods for doing so in the past and we are currently witnessing a resurgence of this field due to the widespread presence of tabular data on the web. This tutorial will provide a general overview of these methods and be geared to the general academic community without requiring prior experience in this area.

2. STRUCTURE OF THE TUTORIAL

The tutorial will be split into two interactive sessions of approximately equal length; a theoretical and a practical session, with a break in between. Each session will end with a Q&A session.

2.1 Theory

What is a table? Despite their apparent simplicity, tables have proven elusive, and their processing can be surprisingly difficult.

DocEng '16 September 13–16, 2016, Vienna, Austria
© 2016 Copyright held by the owner/author(s).
ACM ISBN 978-1-4503-4438-8/16/09.
DOI: http://dx.doi.org/10.1145/2960811.2967173

We will begin by providing a number of definitions that researchers have used in the past to describe tables. Here are a few examples:

A means of arranging data in rows and columns. [Wikipedia, as of July 2016]

2-D cell assembly for presenting information; A regular, repetitive structure along at least one axis; A datatype determined by either horizontal or vertical index. [6]

While everyone seems to know what a table is, a precise, analytical definition of "tabularity" remains elusive because some bureaucratic forms, multicolumn text layouts, and schematic drawings share many characteristics of tables. [2]

Model-based table understanding. The biggest challenge facing researchers is to *understand* the table and extract the data it holds, as part of an information extraction system. It is commonly recognized that this process consists of three tasks of increasing complexity:

- *table detection:* locating the regions of a document with tabular content;

- *table structure recognition:* reconstructing the cellular structure of a table;

- *table interpretation:* further analysis of the cellular structure of the table; this can include:

  - *functional analysis:* determining the abstract logical relations between the cells of the table; and

  - *semantic interpretation:* rediscovering the semantics of the table in terms of the entities represented in the table, their attributes with corresponding values, and the mutual relationships between such entities.

We present each of these stages in detail, providing an overview of current approaches in the field from both academia and industry. We also describe the formalisms proposed by the tutorial presenters [4] to model the inputs and outputs of each of these stages:

- the *table region model* for table detection;

- the *cell structure model* for table structure recognition; and

- the *functional model* for functional analysis.

The main motivation behind these models is to enable a more principled comparison between different systems and approaches, even when only some of the above tasks are performed. For example, OCR systems generally stop at the table structure recognition stage, but our architecture can also be used to aid and evaluate further processing, e.g. for structured information extraction from tables.

2.2 Practice

ICDAR Table Competition. After the break, we will introduce the ICDAR Table Competition [5], organized by the presenters of this tutorial in 2013. We will focus on the following points:

- why we decided to hold the competition;

- which stages of the process were tested in the competition (table location and table structure recognition) and why;

- comparing the results of various systems using the above models;

- our approach to generating the practice and competition datasets;

- participating systems and their results;

- lessons learned from the competition and future plans for the competition and dataset.

Future research and directions. We will conclude the tutorial by presenting ongoing research in the field. In particular, we will discuss how to integrate the results of the table understanding process into IE systems. Broadly, there are two separate approaches for doing so:

- *Domain-independent table understanding* focuses largely on the logical layout analysis to understand the tables and populate them into a database. [3]

- *Semantic-based table interpretation* is a process of linking elements of a table, e.g. data, header labels, to ontological concepts and instances. These can either be part of existing, general knowledge bases, such as DBpedia, Freebase, WordNet, and Yago, or domain-specific ones, such as bio-medical knowledge bases. [1]

Supported by a case study, we will introduce a scalable and flexible architecture for Big Data processing capable of retrieving PDF documents from the web, and recognizing and extracting semantic data from tables contained in these documents. We will also discuss current challenges in data extraction from very large numbers of tables and the advantages of the proposed architecture.

3. TUTORIAL PRESENTERS

Max Göbel is a researcher at the Department of Information Systems and Operations of the Vienna University of Economics and Business Administration (Wirtschaftsuniversität Wien), where he is work package lead of the DecarboNet project (EU Seventh Framework Programme). His current research interests lie in large-scale knowledge extraction from online media and social networks, including information diffusion, information integration, and system architecture. Previously, he worked at the Information Systems Institute of the TU Wien on machine learning algorithms for web information extraction.

Tamir Hassan has over a decade of experience in document engineering, having written his PhD on information extraction from print-oriented (PDF) documents and having subsequently worked in document image analysis and digital typography, among other areas. He is currently working at HP Labs as a researcher in automated publishing and aims at separating content (not only in tables) from visual presentation, enabling the content to adapt to a variety of different screen and paper sizes.

Ermelinda Oro is a researcher at the Institute of High Performance Computing and Networking of the National Research Council of Italy. She is founder and Chief Scientific Officer (CSO) of Altilia Srl that transforms Big Data into Smart Data by means of its MANTRA Smart Data Platform. Her research interests include big and smart data technologies, web search and querying, data and information extraction and wrapping, document layout analysis and understanding, knowledge representation and reasoning, ontologies, linked data, semantic technologies, natural language processing, deep learning, graph representation and analysis, and social network analysis.

Giorgio Orsi is a Lecturer in Database Systems at the School of Computer Science of the University of Birmingham and co-founder of Wrapidity, a web scraping startup. His current research focuses on Big Data wrangling and automated reasoning, in particular large-scale data harvesting from the web. He is a co-investigator of the EPSRC Programme Grant VADA (Value-Added Data Systems—Principles and Architecture).

Roya Rastan is currently completing the final semester of her PhD in computer science at the University of New South Wales. The focus of her thesis is on extracting and interpreting tabular structure from unstructured documents, especially those in PDF format. Her research interests include text mining, pattern recognition, information extraction and in general applications of NLP and analytical methods.

4. REFERENCES

[1] C. S. Bhagavatula, T. Noraset, and D. Downey. TabEL: entity linking in web tables. In *Proceedings of the International Semantic Web Conference (ISWC)*, pages 425–441, 2015.

[2] D. W. Embley, M. Hurst, D. Lopresti, and G. Nagy. Table-processing paradigms: a research survey. *International Journal on Document Analysis and Recognition (IJDAR)*, 8:66–86, 2006.

[3] D. W. Embley, M. S. Krishnamoorthy, G. Nagy, and S. Seth. Converting heterogeneous statistical tables on the web to searchable databases. *International Journal on Document Analysis and Recognition (IJDAR)*, 19(2):119–138, 2016.

[4] M. Göbel, T. Hassan, E. Oro, and G. Orsi. A methodology for evaluating algorithms for table understanding in PDF documents. In *Proceedings of the ACM Symposium on Document Engineering (DocEng)*, pages 45–48, 2012.

[5] M. Göbel, T. Hassan, E. Oro, and G. Orsi. ICDAR 2013 Table Competition. In *Proceedings of the 12th International Conference on Document Analysis and Recognition (ICDAR)*, pages 1449–1453, 2013.

[6] D. P. Lopresti and G. Nagy. A tabular survey of automated table processing. In *Selected Papers from the Third International Workshop on Graphics Recognition (GREC '99), Recent Advances*, pages 93–120, published 2000.

Document Engineering Issues in Malware Analysis

Charles Nicholas
Computer Science and Electrical Engineering
University of Maryland, Baltimore County
Baltimore, MD 21250 USA
nicholas@umbc.edu

Robert Brandon
Computer Science and Electrical Engineering
University of Maryland, Baltimore County
Baltimore, MD 21250 USA
robe1@umbc.edu

ABSTRACT

We present an overview of the field of malware analysis with emphasis on issues related to document engineering. We will introduce the field with a discussion of the types of malware, including executable binaries, malicious PDFs, polymorphic malware, ransomware, and exploit kits. We will conclude with our view of important research questions in the field. This is an updated version of last year's tutorial, with more information about web-based malware and malware targeting the Android market.

1. INTRODUCTION

Malware analysis has become an important field within the general area of cybersecurity. Skilled malware analysts are in high demand, and they are employed in cybersecurity firms, financial institutions, intelligence and law enforcement agencies, and other large organizations.

For many years, most malware was written for the Windows OS and the x86 architecture. Windows is still an important malware target, since so many PCs run it, but in recent years the amount of malware targeted to the mobile telephone, especially the Android, has grown enormously. Although it focuses on Windows XP, we have found that Sikorski's "Practical Malware Analysis" [1] is still the best single resource for this area.

2. TOOLS AND TECHNIQUES

In the tutorial we will present an overview of the field of malware analysis, with emphasis on topics we believe to be of special interest to the Document Engineering community. Teaching materials for Android malware are starting to become available, but for our purposes we will focus on the Windows environment, since that platform is more likely to be more familiar to more people.

Malware on the Windows platform is often, but by no means always, found in executable binaries. Malware can be examined in static form, e.g. by inspection of the PE header and the system call import table. Windows provides tools for such activity, and many third party tools do so as well. IDA is a powerful disassembler, which allows the analyst to examine a suspect binary in a variety of forms, including raw assembly code and call graphs.

Basic IDA functionality can be augmented with plug-ins written in C or Python.

Malware can also be studied in dynamic form, that is, by running it and seeing what happens. OllyDbg is one of several powerful debuggers available for the Windows platform, which has gained a following among malware analysts. Dynamic analysis is usually done from the safe confines of a virtual machine, running under the auspices of VMWare, for example.

Some collections of malware specimens are available to researchers, and these will be used as examples as appropriate. Alas, there is no shortage of malware to be studied, since malware production is easily automated. Collecting malware specimens for analysis is an important sub-area, and anti-virus companies for example devote much effort to this.

As time permits, we will discuss recent and ongoing work in malware analysis-in-the-large, which (to us) refers to finding patterns and trends in collections of malware. Malware specimens can be subjected to cluster analysis, based on static and dynamic characteristics. Malware attribution is and will remain a difficult problem, for reasons which we will explain.

3. AUDIENCE PARTICIPATION

Tutorial participants are welcome to bring their own laptops. We recommend installing a virtual machine platform such as VMWare or Virtual Box, with virtual machines running Windows and Linux. Participants that have IDA Pro (the free version 5.0) and OllyDbg installed, as well as Microsoft's System Tools suite, may be able to run some examples with us. However, participants that choose to leave their laptops at home will be at no disadvantage.

Charles Nicholas is a professor of computer science at UMBC. Robert Brandon is a Ph.D. candidate in computer science at UMBC, with many years of practical malware analysis experience.

4. REFERENCES

[1] M. Sikorski and A. Honig. *Practical Malware Analysis.* no starch press, 2012.

DocEng '16 September 12-16, 2016, Vienna, Austria

© 2016 Copyright held by the owner/author(s).

ACM ISBN 978-1-4503-4438-8/16/09.

DOI: http://dx.doi.org/10.1145/2960811.2967174

Document Changes: Modeling, Detection, Storage and Visualization (DChanges 2016)

Gioele Barabucci
Cologne Center for eHumanities
Universität zu Köln
Köln, Germany
gioele.barabucci@
uni-koeln.de

Uwe M. Borghoff
Institute for Software Technology
Universität der
Bundeswehr München
Neubiberg, Germany
uwe.borghoff@unibw.de

Angelo Di Iorio
Department of Computer
Science and Engineering
Università di Bologna
Bologna, Italy
diiorio@cs.unibo.it

Sonja Schimmler
Institute for Software Technology
Universität der
Bundeswehr München
Neubiberg, Germany
sonja.schimmler@unibw.de

Ethan Munson
Department of EECS
University of
Wisconsin-Milwaukee
Milwaukee, WI, USA
munson@uwm.edu

ABSTRACT

The DChanges series of workshops focuses on changes in all their aspects and applications: algorithms to detect changes, models to describe them and techniques to present them to the final users are only some of the topics we investigate. The workshop is open to researchers and practitioners from industry and academia.

This year, we would like to focus on the application of change-tracking and diff algorithms to documents that are collaboratively edited via the web.

We will also follow up on the discussion of DChanges 2015 about algorithms and interfaces to better understand and exploit detected changes, and about standards for modeling and transmitting changes. Particular attention will also be given to the use of diff, change tracking, and versioning techniques in the field of digital humanities.

CCS Concepts

• **Information systems → Version management;** • **Applied computing → Version control;** • **Software and its engineering → Software configuration management and version control systems;**

Keywords

applications; change analysis and interpretation; change detection; change tracking

1. INTRODUCTION

The goal of the DChanges series of events is to share ideas, common issues and principles about models and algorithms

DocEng '16 September 12-16, 2016, Vienna, Austria
© 2016 Copyright held by the owner/author(s).
ACM ISBN 978-1-4503-4438-8/16/09.
DOI: http://dx.doi.org/10.1145/2960811.2967169

for change tracking and detection, versioning, collaborative editing and related topics.

This is the fourth edition of the workshop. The previous ones were quite successful and generated lively and fruitful discussions among participants. This edition will follow up on these discussions and will report on recent progress in the area.

The main topic of this year's edition is the application of diff algorithms to documents that are collaboratively edited via the web. Creating documents via web interfaces is becoming the standard in many environments, from academic papers to office documents. And not only textual documents are edited online, but also photos, music, videos and huge bodies of knowledge like Wikipedia. This poses new challenges to the way version control tools work, as they are mostly based around a no-longer applicable view of what "local files" inherited from source control. Is the research in the field of document changes ready to deal with these new forms of collaboration? How can the evolution of these documents be visualized? Are new algorithms and tools needed?

We will also follow up on the discussion of DChanges 2015 about how changes are interpreted and visualized, and – as a basis – about standards for modeling and transmitting changes. All previous editions, in fact, made evident the need for novel interfaces for dealing with changes.

Another important topic, we would like to follow up on, is the use of diff, change tracking, and versioning techniques in the field of digital humanities.

Updated information about DChanges 2016 will constantly be available at http://diff.cs.unibo.it/dchanges2016/.

2. PROGRAM

The program picks up the structure of DChanges 2013 [1, 2], 2014 [3, 4] and 2015 [5, 6]. Such a continuity is a key aspect of our vision, a crucial step towards the creation of a more connected community of researchers.

At the time of preparation of this summary, we have not

finalized the program, yet. We plan to have three main sessions: a first series of presentations on research topics, a second series of short reports on work-in-progress, and finally, a round-table discussion.

2.1 Presentations on Research Topics

The first part of the workshop is a session devoted to the presentation and discussion of research papers. We are currently selecting research papers that represent well the topics of DChanges and show where the research is leading.

All presented papers will be included in the proceedings of the workshop published by ACM.

2.2 Short Reports on Work-in-Progress

The second series of talks will focus on work-in-progress: we would like to give participants a chance to report on their current work in an informal setting. Our vision is that people from industry and academia will exchange their views in an open session.

2.3 Round-Table Discussion

The main part of the workshop will be an open forum, in which participants can briefly introduce their research interests and recent achievements relevant to the workshop. The goal is twofold: fostering research collaboration and eliciting topics and suggestions for future research directions.

A summary of the round-table discussion will be published online at http://diff.cs.unibo.it/dchanges2016/ soon after the conclusion of the workshop.

3. PEOPLE

The workshop is organized by the same group of people as last year: Gioele Barabucci, Uwe M. Borghoff, Angelo Di Iorio, Sonja Schimmler and Ethan Munson.

An international program committee helped the organizers getting in touch with the researchers, selecting the best submissions, and improving them.

The organizers thank them all: Serge Autexier (DFKI Bremen), Martin Dias (Université Lille 1), Anne Etien (Université Lille 1), Boris Konev (University of Liverpool), Pascal Molli (Université de Nantes), Sebastian Rönnau (Ravensburger GmbH), Yannis Tzitzikas (University of Crete), Fabio Vitali (Università di Bologna), Andreas Winter (Carl von Ossietzky University Oldenburg) and Loutfouz Zaman (York University).

4. REFERENCES

[1] BARABUCCI, G., BORGHOFF, U. M., DI IORIO, A., AND MAIER, S., Eds. *DChanges 2013: Proceedings of the International Workshop on Document Changes: Modeling, Detection, Storage and Visualization, Florence, Italy, September 10, 2013* (2013), CEUR Workshop Proceedings, 1008.

[2] BARABUCCI, G., BORGHOFF, U. M., DI IORIO, A., AND MAIER, S. Document changes: modeling; detection; storing and visualization (DChanges). In *ACM Symposium on Document Engineering 2013, DocEng '13, Florence, Italy, September 10–13, 2013* (2013), S. Marinai and K. Marriott, Eds., ACM, pp. 281–282.

[3] BARABUCCI, G., BORGHOFF, U. M., DI IORIO, A., MAIER, S., AND MUNSON, E., Eds. *DChanges 2014: Proceedings of the 2nd International Workshop on Document Changes: Modeling, Detection, Storage and Visualization, Fort Collins, CO, USA, September 16, 2014* (2014), ICPS, ACM.

[4] BARABUCCI, G., BORGHOFF, U. M., DI IORIO, A., MAIER, S., AND MUNSON, E. Document changes: modeling, detection, storage and visualization (DChanges 2014). In *ACM Symposium on Document Engineering 2014, DocEng '14, Fort Collins, CO, USA, September 16–19, 2014* (2014), S. J. Simske and S. Rönnau, Eds., ACM, pp. 207–208.

[5] BARABUCCI, G., BORGHOFF, U. M., DI IORIO, A., MAIER, S., AND MUNSON, E., Eds. *DChanges 2015: Proceedings of the 3rd International Workshop on Document Changes: Modeling, Detection, Storage and Visualization, Lausanne, Switzerland, September 08, 2015* (2015), ICPS, ACM.

[6] BARABUCCI, G., BORGHOFF, U. M., DI IORIO, A., MAIER, S., AND MUNSON, E. Document changes: Modeling, detection, storage and visualization (dchanges 2015). In *ACM Symposium on Document Engineering 2015, DocEng'15, Lausanne, Switzerland, September 08–11, 2015* (2015), C. Vanoirbeek and P. Genevès, Eds., ACM, pp. 227–228.

Future Publishing Formats

Michael Piotrowski
Leibniz Institute of European History
Alte Universitätsstraße 19
55116 Mainz, Germany

piotrowski@ieg-mainz.de

ABSTRACT

The familiar PDF-based scholarly publishing workflow—which emulates even earlier paper-based workflows—has been surprisingly resistent to change. However, it is becoming increasingly clear that it no longer meets the requirements of a quickly evolving scholarly, technical, and political environment, which includes the trend towards open access publishing, reproducible research, mobile devices, linked open data, and many other developments. This workshop approaches scholarly publishing from a document engineering perspective and focuses on the question of document formats for submission, review, publication, and archival of scholarly publications. We will discuss the current state of scholarly publishing from a document engineering point of view, with the explicit goal of identifying potential alternatives to the current workflow.

1. INTRODUCTION

There is currently much discussion and research about open access, alternative publishing models, semantic publishing, peer review, data sharing, reproducible science, etc.—in short: the future of scholarly publishing. Not incidentally, both candidates for ACM president in the 2016 General Election have stressed the importance of publishing for ACM and the need to further enhance the Digital Library. The wide interest in advancing scholarly communications is also evidenced, for example, by the founding of FORCE11,[1] the *Future of Research Communications and e-Scholarship Group*, which also organizes a conference series on this topic (FORCE,[2] previously called "Beyond the PDF").

The DocEng community defines document engineering as "the computer science discipline that investigates systems for documents in any form and in all media," and states that document engineering "is concerned with principles, tools and processes that improve our ability to create, manage, and maintain documents".[3] Thus, the future of scholarly publishing is clearly of interest for document engineering research; but it is also a topic that directly concerns document engineers as scholars and authors.

---

[1] https://www.force11.org
[2] https://www.force11.org/meetings/force2016
[3] http://doceng.org/

DocEng '16 September 12–16, 2016, Vienna, Austria

© 2016 Copyright held by the owner/author(s).

ACM ISBN 978-1-4503-4438-8/16/09.

DOI: http://dx.doi.org/10.1145/2960811.2967170

DocEng 2013 in Florence featured a workshop, organized by Michael Wybrow [5], entitled "Reimagining Digital Publishing for Technical Documents," which focused on designing and evaluating better layout approaches and interaction techniques for allowing people to read, annotate and edit technical documents in adaptive, dynamic contexts. Beyond that, the document engineering community, however, currently does not seem to be at the forefront of these developments. This is surprising given its roots in electronic publishing, and given how much it could bring to the table. The workshop therefore tries to stimulate the discussion on scholarly publishing in the document engineering community.

2. TOPICS AND GOALS

Scholarly publishing involves a myriad of aspects—academic, social, legal, technical, commercial, typographic, etc.—, which are interconnected in numerous ways. This workshop focuses on the question of *document formats* for submission, review, publication, and archival of scholarly publications. This list illustrates that the format (or formats) used for representing scholarly documents determines how a document can be processed and manipulated in all stages of the publishing process. The submission format, in particular, determines how authors may create documents and which tools they have at their disposal. The emergence of numerous *lightweight markup languages* in recent years indicates that many authors feel a need for alternative document formats. Such formats are increasingly used in places where previously LaTeX, Microsoft Word, and PDF would have been used. Examples include Markdown, Org-Mode, reStructuredText, and AsciiDoc. Many such formats were originally only intended for documenting code or creating Web pages, but people are now working on extending the applicability of such formats to scholarly articles. For example, due to its support for including live code, Org-Mode[4] is becoming popular in the context of reproducible research; Scholarly Markdown[5] is a project to make Markdown suitable for scholarly publications—Leijen [3] presented an authoring system for Scholarly Markdown at DocEng 2015; RASH, Research Articles in Simplified HTML [1, 4], is a markup language defined as a subset of HTML+RDFa for writing scientific articles, which has already been adopted as a submission format by a number of conferences.

The workshop thus has two main goals: On a higher level, we will look at the current state of scholarly publishing from a document engineering point of view. On a more practical level, the goal is to identify potential alternatives to the current ACM publication workflow. Points to be discussed thus include:

1. Identification of issues

---

[4] http://orgmode.org
[5] http://scholarlymarkdown.com

- What are the main issues with the current PDF-based workflow?

- What are the areas that need immediate improvement, and what are longer-term improvements to aim for?

2. Potential alternatives

- What are alternative publishing formats and markup languages for use in the domain of scholarly publishing?

- What role could semantic publishing approaches play, such as nanopublications [2], Linked Open Data, etc.

- How can the idea of single-source publishing made viable for scholarly publishing?

3. Evaluation

- What are the benefits and downsides of individual publishing formats?

- What are the evaluation criteria for alternative publishing workflows from an author's perspective?

- What evaluation criteria need to be considered from the perspective of document engineering research and experience?

- What are the implications of alternative approaches for authoring, submission, review, and archival?

3. PROGRAM

This workshop is intended as a workshop in the original sense of the word, i.e., a working session, not a "mini conference." The workshop is opened by an introductory presentation and followed by small group discussions on the questions listed above and a plenary session aiming at building consensus for future publishing formats in the document engineering community.

The workshop is organized by Michael Piotrowski, head of the Digital Humanities research group at the Leibniz Institute of European History in Mainz, Germany. He holds a PhD in computer science from Otto von Guericke University, Magdeburg, and an MA in computational linguistics from Friedrich–Alexander University, Erlangen.

4. REFERENCES

[1] A. Di Iorio, A. G. Nuzzolese, F. Osborne, S. Peroni, F. Poggi, M. Smith, F. Vitali, and J. Zhao. The RASH framework: Enabling HTML+RDF submissions in scholarly venues. In S. Villata, J. Z. Pan, and M. Dragoni, editors, *Proceedings of the ISWC 2015 Posters & Demonstrations Track*, Aachen, 2015. CEUR. URL http://ceur-ws.org/Vol-1486/paper_72.pdf.

[2] P. Groth, A. Gibson, and J. Velterop. The anatomy of a nanopublication. *Information Services and Use*, 30(1–2):51–56, 2010. doi: 10.3233/ISU-2010-0613.

[3] D. Leijen. Madoko: Scholarly documents for the Web. In *Proceedings of the 2015 ACM Symposium on Document Engineering*, pages 129–132, New York, NY, USA, 2015. ACM. doi: 10.1145/2682571.2797097.

[4] S. Peroni, D. Shotton, and F. Vitali. Faceted documents: describing document characteristics using semantic lenses. In *Proceedings of the 2012 ACM symposium on Document engineering (DocEng 2012)*, pages 191–194, New York, NY, USA, 2012. ACM. doi: 10.1145/2361354.2361396.

[5] M. Wybrow. Reimagining digital publishing for technical documents. In *Proceedings of the 2013 ACM Symposium on Document Engineering*, DocEng '13, pages 285–286, New York, NY, USA, 2013. ACM. doi: 10.1145/2494266.2494324.

Research Infrastructures, or How Document Engineering, Cultural Heritage, and Digital Humanities Can Go Together

Günter Mühlberger
Digitisation and Electronic Archiving (DEA)
University of Innsbruck
Innsbruck, Austria
guenter.muehlberger@uibk.ac.at

ABSTRACT

Research Infrastructures (RIs) are one of the key concepts in Horizon 2020, the European Commission's Research programme. A budget of EUR 2.7bn is available for projects under the RI programme. The talk will describe some of the main characteristics of RIs and introduce the H2020 Recognition and Enrichment of Archival Documents (READ) project which is dedicated to setting up a highly specialized service platform and making available some of the state-of-the-art technology in pattern recognition and document engineering, namely Handwritten Text Recognition, Automatic Writer Identification, and Keyword Spotting. Archives and libraries, as well as humanities scholars and the general public will be enabled to use the service platform which will improve access to cultural heritage, advance research in humanities and encourage a broad audience to investigate their personal family history.

Keywords

Research Infrastructures; Archival Documents; Document Analysis

1. SHORT BIOGRAPHY

Günter Mühlberger received his Ph.D. in 1996 with a dissertation on Johann Wolfgang von Goethe. Since 1992 he worked as research assistant and lecturer at the Department for German Language and Literature. Since 1995 his professional focus is on Digital Humanities, Digital Libraries and digitisation technologies. From 1998 he initiated and managed several national and international projects (LAURIN, Books2u!, reUSE, METADATA ENGINE, ...). From 2008–2012 he was member of the executive board of the FP7 project IMPACT and sub-project leader for Text Recognition. He is member of the Executive Board of the Europeana Newspaper project as well as advisor for the Austrian Ministry of Infrastructure and Science ("Kulturpool") and member of the Austrian Centre for Digital Humanities.

DocEng '16 September 12-16, 2016, Vienna, Austria

© 2016 Copyright held by the owner/author(s).

ACM ISBN 978-1-4503-4438-8/16/09.

DOI: http://dx.doi.org/10.1145/2960811.2967146

A General Framework for Globally Optimized Pagination

Frank Mittelbach
LaTeX3 Project
Mainz, Germany
frank.mittelbach@latex-project.org

ABSTRACT

Pagination problems deal with questions around transforming a source text stream into a formatted document by dividing it up into individual columns and pages, including adding auxiliary elements that have some relationship to the source stream data but may allow a certain amount of variation in placement (such as figures or footnotes).

Traditionally the pagination problem has been approached by separating it into one of micro-typography (e.g., breaking text into paragraphs, also known as h&j) and one of macro-typography (e.g., taking a galley of already formatted paragraphs and breaking them into columns and pages) without much interaction between the two.

While early solutions for both problem spaces used simple greedy algorithms, Knuth and Plass introduced in the '80s a global-fit algorithm for line breaking that optimizes the breaks across the whole paragraph [16]. This algorithm was implemented in TeX'82 [15] and has since kept its crown as the best available solution for this space. However, for macro-typography there has been no (successful) attempt to provide globally optimized page layout: all systems to date (including TeX) use greedy algorithms for pagination. Various problems in this area have been researched (e.g., [1, 11, 9, 2]) and the literature documents some prototype development. But none of these prototypes have been made widely available to the research community or ever made it into a generally usable and publicly available system.

This paper presents a framework for a global-fit algorithm for page breaking based on the ideas of Knuth/Plass. It is implemented in such a way that it is directly usable without additional executables with any modern TeX installation. It therefore can serve as a test bed for future experiments and extensions in this space. At the same time a cleaned-up version of the current prototype has the potential to become a production tool for the huge number of TeX users world-wide.

The paper also discusses two already implemented extensions that increase the flexibility of the pagination process: the ability to automatically consider existing flexibility in paragraph length (by considering paragraph variations with different numbers of lines [8]) and the concept of running the columns on a double spread a line long or short. It concludes with a discussion of the overall approach, its inherent limitations and directions for future research.

DocEng '16, September 12 - 16, 2016, Vienna, Austria
Copyright is held by the owner/author(s). Publication rights licensed to ACM.
ACM 978-1-4503-4438-8/16/09. . . $15.00
DOI: http://dx.doi.org/10.1145/2960811.2960820

CCS CONCEPTS

•**Applied computing** → **Format and notation;** *Publishing;*

KEYWORDS

typesetting; macro-typography; pagination; page breaking; global optimization; automatic layout; adaptive layout

ACM Reference format:
Frank Mittelbach. 2016. A General Framework for Globally Optimized Pagination. *DocEng '16, Vienna, Austria, September 12 - 16, 2016.*
DOI: http://dx.doi.org/10.1145/2960811.2960820

1 INTRODUCTION

Pagination is the act of transforming a source document into a sequence of columns and pages, possibly including auxiliary elements such as floats (e.g., figures and tables).

As textual material is typically read in sequential order, its arrangement into columns and pages needs to preserve the sequential property.[1] An algorithm that undertakes the task of automatic pagination therefore has to transform the textual material into individual blocks that form the material for each column and arrange for distributing auxiliary material across all pages (thereby reducing available column heights) in a way that it best fulfills a number of (usually) conflicting goals.

This transformation is typically done as a two-step process: by first breaking the text into lines forming paragraphs and this way assembling a galley (known as hyphenation and justification or h&j for short) and then as a second step by splitting this galley into individual columns to form the pages.

However, separating line breaking and page breaking means that one loses possible benefits from having both steps influence each other. So it is not surprising that this has been an area of research throughout the years, e.g., [20, 2, 8]. The algorithm outlined in this paper implements some limited interaction to add flexibility to page-breaking phase.

The remainder of the paper is structured as follows: We first discuss general questions related to pagination, give a short overview about attempts to automate that process and the possible limitation when using a global optimization strategy for pagination. Section 2 then describes our framework for implementing globally optimizing pagination algorithms using a TeX environment. Section 3 then discusses details of the algorithms we used and gives some computational examples. The paper concludes with an evaluation of the algorithm quality and an outline of possible further research work.

---

[1]There are applications where this is not the case or not fully the case, e.g., in newspaper layout, where stories may be interrupted and "*continued on page X*", but in this paper we limit ourselves to formatting tasks with a single textual output stream.

1.1 Pagination rules

Rules for pagination and their relative weight in influencing the final result vary from application to application, as they are often (at least to some extent) of an aesthetic nature, but also because depending on the given job some primary goals may outweigh any other. It is therefore important that any algorithm for this space is configurable to support different rule sets and able to adjust the weight of each rule in contributing to the final solution.

The primary goal of nearly every document is to convey information to its audience and thus an undisputed "meta" goal for document formatting is to enhance the information flow or at least avoid hindering or preventing successful communication of information to the recipient. An example of a rule derived from this maxim is the already mentioned requirement of keeping the text flow in clearly understandable reading order.

Other examples are rules around float placement: to avoid requiring the reader to unnecessarily flip pages, floating objects should preferably be placed close to (and visible from) their main call-out and if that is not possible they should be placed nearby on later pages (so that a reader has a clear idea where to search for them). For the same reason they should be kept in the order of their main call-outs—though that, for example, is a rule that is sometimes broken when placement rules are mainly guided by aesthetic consideration.

Other rules are more aesthetic in nature, even though they too originate from the attempt to provide easy access to information, as violating them will disrupt the reading flow to some extent: avoid widows and orphans (end or beginning line of a paragraph on its own at a column break), do not break at a hyphenated line or have a heading followed by a minimal number of lines of normal text. An example from mathematical typesetting is to shun setting displayed equations at the top of a column, the reason being that the text before such a formula is usually an introduction to it and that would look odd at the bottom of a column on its own.

Rules like the above have in common that they all reduce the number of allowed places where a column break could be taken, they all generate unbreakable larger vertical blocks in the galley. Thus finding suitable places to cut up the galley into columns of predefined sizes becomes harder and greedy algorithms often run into stumbling blocks (no pun intended) where the only path they can take is to move the offending block to the next column, thereby leaving a possibly huge amount of white space on the previous one.

The second major "meta" goal, especially in publishing, is to make best use of the available space in order to keep the costs low. If we look only at formatting a single text stream (no floats) then it is easy to see that this goal stands in direct competition with any rule derived form the first meta goal. It is easy to prove that a greedy algorithm will always produce the shortest formatting if the column sizes are fixed and all document elements are of fixed size and need to be laid out in sequential order. So in order to satisfy both goals one needs to allow for either

- variations in column heights,
- variations in the height of textual elements, or
- allow non-sequential ordering of elements.

In this paper we look in particular at the first two options. The last bullet is usually not an option for text elements, except in the case of documents with short unrelated stories that can be reordered or texts that are allowed to be split and "continued". As these form their own class of documents with their own intrinsic formatting requirements [10, 7, 3, 4] they are not addressed in this paper. There is, however, also the possibility to introduce a certain amount of additional flexibility through clever placement of floats (such as figures or tables) as this will change the height of individual columns.[2]

A variation in column height (typically by allowing the height to deviate by one line of text) is a standard trick in craft typography to work around difficult pagination situations. To hide such a change from the eye of the reader, or at least lessen the impact, all columns of a page and in two-sided printing a double spread (facing pages in the output document) need the same treatment.[3] It is also best to only gradually change the column heights to avoid big differences between one double spread and the next.

The second option involves interaction between the micro- (line breaking of paragraphs, formatting of inline figures etc.) and the macro-typography phase (pagination of the galley material), either by dynamically requesting micro-typography variants during pagination or by precompiling them for additional flexibility in the the macro-typography phase. Examples are line breaking with suboptimal spacing (looseness setting in TEX's algorithm [14, 8]) or font compression/expansion (hz-algorithm, [6]) within defined limits. Other examples are figures or tables that can be formatted to different sizes.

1.2 Pagination strategies and related work

While TEX already introduced global optimization for micro-typography in the '80s [16], pagination in today's systems is still undertaken using greedy algorithms that essentially generate column by column without looking (far) ahead.

Already in his PhD thesis [21] Michael Plass discussed applying the ideas behind TEX's line-breaking algorithm to the question of paginating documents containing text and floats. Since then a number of other researchers have worked on improved pagination algorithms, e.g., Stephan Wohlfeil addressed optimal float placement for certain types of documents in his PhD thesis [22] and with Anne Brüggemann-Klein and others [1] using dynamic programming based on the Knuth/Plass algorithm with a restricted document model. Charles Jacobs et al. [12] explore the use of layout templates that can be selected by an optimizing algorithm also based on Knuth/Plass to best fulfill a number of constraints. Paolo Ciancarini et al. [2] present an approach (again based on Knuth/Plass) in which the micro- and macro-typography is more tightly coupled by delaying the definite choice of line breaks and instead offering to the pagination algorithm a set of options per paragraph modeled as a flexible glue item.[4]

---

[2] In this paper we do not address the question of optimization through float placement but assume that floats are either absent or their placement being predetermined or externally determined. The class of documents for which this can be assumed is rather large, so the findings in this paper are relevant even with this restriction in force.

[3] Also the paper for printing should be thick enough, so that the text block on the back is not shining through, as that would be a dead giveaway.

[4] Using glue has the advantage that the complexity of the pagination algorithm stays low compared to the approach outlined in this paper, but the disadvantage that other aspects of the fully formatted paragraphs are unavailable to the pagination algorithm, e.g., that for certain formatting the available breaks may be of different quality. Also if the pagination requests that a paragraph format itself to a certain height, say, 3.5 lines, it can only fulfill that request to the nearest line number and as these errors accumulate, it is possible that the optimal solution is missed.

So why has no production system, whether it be TeX or any other, started to use a global optimizing pagination algorithm up to now?

The answer is at least twofold: On one hand, due to the fact that pagination has to deal with unrelated input streams, the problems in this space are much harder than those in line breaking even though superficially they have a lot in common. As a result most of the research work so far has focussed on experimenting with certain aspects only (with the possible exception of the work carried out by Jacobs et al.) and was less concerned in providing a production-ready solution initially. On the other hand typesetting requires much more than pagination and any generally usable system implementing a new pagination needs to either also provide all the features related to micro-typography (which is a huge undertaking) or it needs to integrate into an existing system like TeX or any commercial engine.

On the commercial side, the complexity of full or even only partial optimization was so far probably considered too high compared to any resulting benefits, and the open source TeX system (while offering most aspects needed for high quality typesetting[5]) is monolithic and so optimized for speed that it is very difficult to extend or replace some of its algorithms.

As a result what we have to date are only prototypes discussed in the research literature but not available anywhere.

1.3 Downside of applying global optimization

While globally optimizing the pagination to further automate the typesetting process sounds like a good idea, there are a number of issues related to it that need to be taken in consideration and require further research.

First of all global optimization means that any modification in the document source can result in pagination differences anywhere in the document. This is already now a source of concern for TeX users experiencing situations where *deleting* a word results in a paragraph getting *longer* or being broken differently across columns.

By optimizing the pagination such type of problems are moved from the localized level of micro-typography to the overall document level—just consider a book revision where a few misspellings are corrected and instead of regenerating a handful of photographic plates for these pages the publisher has to generate a fully reformatted book.[6]

But there are also problems related to the interaction between globally optimized pagination and automatically generated (textual) content. If such generated content depends on the pagination, for example, if a text "see figure 3 on the following page" changes to the much shorter text "see figure 3 on page 7", then this generates feedback loops between micro- and macro-typography, i.e., it might change the formatting, which might change the generated text, which might change the formatting etc. It is not difficult given an arbitrary pagination rule set, to construct a document for which there is no valid formatting possible under its conditions. While such situations can already occur with pagination generated by greedy algorithms, they are far more likely if global optimization (especially with variant formatting for higher flexibility) is used.

2 A GLOBALLY OPTIMIZING FRAMEWORK USING TeX

As the open source program TeX by Don Knuth is undisputedly one of the best typesetting systems in existence when it comes to micro-typography or math typesetting, it is a natural candidate for any attempt to implement improved pagination algorithms as all other aspects of typesetting are already provided with high quality and due to its large user base there are immediately many people who could benefit from an improved program.

Unfortunately the original program [15] is of monolithic design and highly optimized so that modifying its inner working has proven to be a serious challenge. There have been a number of such attempts though and three of them have established themselves in the world-wide community: pdfTeX is an engine written by Hàn Thế Thành as part of his PhD [6] that was the first engine directly generating PDF output and it also provided a number of micro-typography extensions, such as protrusion support and font expansion (hz-algorithm). These days this TeX-extension has become the default engine in most installations, i.e., the program being called, when people are processing a TeX file. The other two (still more or less under active development) are X⒥TeX [5] and LuaTeX [17].

The interesting aspect of LuaTeX is that it combines the features of a complete (and in fact extended) TeX engine with a full-fledged Lua interpreter that allows the execution of Lua-code inside of TeX with full access to the internal TeX data structures and with the ability to hook such Lua-code at various points into most TeX algorithms, enabling the code to modify or even to replace them. As Lua is an interpreted language there is no need to compile a new executable whenever some Lua code is modified, all it needs is the base LuaTeX engine to be available (which is a standard engine in all major TeX distributions such as TeXlive 2015).

Thus, even while LuaTeX is still somewhat unstable (version 1.0 is expected in fall 2016) it can serve as a very versatile testbed for developing algorithms that can be directly tried and used by a large user base. For this reason the framework described in this paper is based on this program.

2.1 High-level workflow

The framework presented here consists of four phases and uses LuaTeX for the reasons outlined above:

Phase 1 (preprocessing) The document, which consists of standard TeX files, is processed by a TeX engine without any modification until all implicit content (e.g., table of content, bibliography, etc.) is generated and all cross-references are resolved.

Phase 2 (galley generation) The engine is modified to interact with TeX's way of filling the main vertical list (from which, in an asynchronous way, TeX later cuts column material for pagination).

In particular, whenever TeX is ready to move new vertical material to the main vertical list this material is intercepted and analyzed. Information about each block (vertical height, depth[7], stretchability if any and penalty of a breakpoint) is then

---

[5]For a discussion of TeX's limitations and failures see [18] and for an update 23 years later [19].

[6]The solution in that case, would be to introduce explicit pagination commands in strategic places to keep the pagination unchanged, even if through the algorithm's eyes it is no longer optimal.

[7]In TeX boxes (such as lines of text) have both a vertical height and a vertical depth which is the amount of material that appears below the baseline, e.g., the vertical size of descenders of letters such as "p" or "g". The total vertical size of boxes is then the sum of height and depth. This distinction is important when filling columns with material,

gathered and written out to an external file. If possible, data is accumulated, e.g., several objects in a row without any possibility for breaking them up are written out as a single data point to reduce later processing complexity.

The modification is also able to interpret special flags (implemented as new types of "whatsit nodes" in TeX engine lingo) that can signal the start/end or switch of an explicit variation in the input source. This information is then used to structure the corresponding data in the output file for later processing.[8]

The second modification to the engine is to intercept the generation of paragraphs targeted for the main galley prior to TeX applying line breaking[9]:

- For each horizontal list that is passed to the line-breaking algorithm the framework algorithm then determines the acceptable variations in "looseness" within the specified parameter settings.[10]
- For each possible variation it then does a paragraph breaking trial to determine the exact sequence of lines, vertical spaces and associated penalties under a specific "looseness" value.
- The results of each trial is externally recorded together with the associated "looseness" value of the variation.
- Finally, instead of adding a vertical list representing the formatted paragraph on the main vertical list, a single special node is passed so that the paragraph material is not collected again by the first modification described above.

As the result of this phase the external file will hold an abstraction of the document galley material including marked up variations for each paragraph.

Phase 3 (pagination) The result of phase 2 is used as input to a global optimizing algorithm modeled after the Knuth/Plass algorithm for line breaking that uses dynamic programming to determine an optimal sequence of column and page breaks throughout the whole document. Compared to the line-breaking algorithm this page-breaking algorithm provides the following additional features:

- Support for variations within the input: This is used to automatically manage variant break sequences resulting from different paragraph breakings calculated in phase 2, but could also be used to support, for example, variations of figures or tables in different sizes or similar applications.

- Support for shortening or lengthening the vertical height of double spreads to enable better columns/page breaks across the whole document.
- Global optimization is guided by parameters that allow a document designer to balance the importance of individual aspects (e.g., avoiding widows against changing the spread height or using sub-optimal paragraphs) against each other.

Details of the algorithm are described in section 3.

The result of this phase will be a sequence of optimal column break positions within the input together with length information for all columns for which it applies. Also recorded is which of the variants have been chosen when selecting the optimal sequence.

Phase 4 (typesetting) This phase again uses a modified TeX engine that is capable of interpreting and using the results of the previous phases. For this it hooks into the same places as the modifications in phase 2, but this time applying different actions:

- To begin with, the vertical target size for gathering a complete column will be artificially set to the largest legal dimension so that by itself the TeX algorithm will not mistakenly break up the galley at an unwanted place due to some unusual combination of data.[11]
- Whenever TeX gets ready to apply line breaking to paragraph material for the main vertical list the modification looks up with which "looseness" this paragraph should be typeset and adjusts the necessary parameters so that TeX generates the lines corresponding to the variation selected in the optimal break sequence for the whole document determined in pagination phase 3.
- While TeX is moving objects to the main vertical list the algorithm keeps track of the galley blocks seen so far and when it is time for a column break according to the optimal solution it will explicitly place a suitable forcing penalty onto the main vertical list so that TeX is guaranteed to use this place to end the current column or page. Again as a safety measure other penalties seen at this point that should not result in a column break will be either dropped or otherwise rendered harmless so that TeX's internal (greedy) page-breaking algorithm is not misinterpreting them as a "best break" by mistake.
- Finally, whenever TeX has finished a column (due to the fact that we have added an explicit penalty in the previous step) we will arrange for the correct target dimensions for the current column according to the data from pagination phase 3. This is done immediately after TeX has decided what part of the galley it will pack up for use in its "output routine" (which is a set of TeX macros) but before this routine is actually called.[12]

The result is a paginated document with optimized column breaks across the whole document.

---

because the depth of the last line is not taken into consideration when determining the total size occupied by the material (while the depth of all other lines is). This reflects the fact that columns and pages should align on the baseline of the last text line regardless of whether or not such a line has descenders.

[8] This interface could be extended at a later stage to support controlling of the algorithm used in the pagination phase 3 from within the document, e.g., to guide or overwrite its decisions locally.

[9] Paragraph variations in other places, e.g., inside float boxes, marginal notes, footnotes, etc. are currently not considered. Thus, those objects always have their natural (fixed) dimensions. Extending the framework in that direction would be possible but would considerably complicate the mechanism without a lot of gain, so this was considered secondary in the first prototype version.

[10] It is not enough to check if TeX could build a paragraph with a specific setting of looseness, as TeX uses a fairly naive approach that would always result in the last line containing only a single word or even only part of a single word whenever the paragraph is lengthened. It is therefore important to first manipulate the paragraph material to prevent this from happening and ensure that "loosened" paragraphs are visually acceptable to the human eye. In the typesetting phase 4 the same manipulation has to be applied when typesetting any paragraph variation.

---

[11] As long as the calculation for deciding on a column break used by TeX and the one used by the algorithm deployed in phase 3 are exactly the same this is actually not necessary. However, requiring a 100% correspondence is not a useful restriction, so this is a safety measure against deliberate or unintentional differences in this place.

[12] This way the engine modifications are largely transparent for the TeX macro level and the modification will work with some small adjustments with any macro flavor of TeX, e.g., LaTeX, plain TeX, etc.

2.2 Notes on the workflow phases

The preprocessing phase 1 is necessary to generate all implicit content so that it will be considered in the following phases. Without this phase the page-breaking step in phase 3 would base its evaluation on wrong input.

Phases 2 (galley generation) and 4 (typesetting) will require a modified/extended TeX engine. The workflow uses the LuaTeX engine for this purpose as it internally provides a Lua interpreter to implement the modifications as well as the necessary callbacks into the TeX algorithms so that the new code can easily take control and provide the necessary changes.

The algorithm used in the pagination phase 3 is also implemented in Lua. As this phase is executed without any direct involvement of a TeX engine processing the source document, this code could have been written in any computer language (and could probably be faster, depending on language choice and implementation). Nevertheless, the use of Lua was deliberate, as it allows to use the LuaTeX engine[13] in all phases and this means that the workflow can be executed using a standard TeX installation, i.e., is out of the box available for the millions of LaTeX-users and other TeX flavors without the need to install any additional software programs[14].

While the typesetting phase 4 claims that the result is a globally optimized formatted documented, it doesn't actually claim that it is a correctly formatted document and as explained in section 1.3 this may in fact not be the case. The mechanisms available in LaTeX will detect this situation, but the framework currently makes no attempt to resolve this problem if it arises. Depending on the exact nature of the issue a further run through phases 2–4 might resolve it. However, if the formatted result oscillates between two or more states then manual intervention is necessary.

3 AN ALGORITHM FOR GLOBALLY OPTIMIZED PAGINATION

In the following we discuss a slightly simplified version of the algorithms used in the pagination phase 3 of the framework.

The base algorithm is a variation of the Knuth/Plass algorithm for line breaking [16] suitably changed and adjusted for the pagination application.[15] In particular it uses a somewhat different object model to account for the pagination peculiarities and to support the extensions.

While the double spread extension (section 3.3) has no natural application in line breaking, the variation support extension (section 3.4) could be in theory incorporated back into a line-breaking algorithm: individual variation paths would become alternate words or phrases and a global optimizing line-breaker would then pick and choose among them, to best satisfy other requirements, such as

desired number of lines, number of hyphenated words, tightness of white-space, etc. This would, for example, support and simplify the approach outlined by Yusuke Kido et al. on layout improvements through automated paraphrasing [13].

3.1 The base algorithm

The input for the pagination algorithm is modeled as a list of objects $x_1, x_2, \ldots, x_m$ where each x_i is either a "text" block t_i that will always be present in the final paginated document (e.g., textual material) or a "breakpoint/space" block b_i at which the galley may get split during pagination. If a break happens at b_i then that block gets discarded (in particular it doesn't contribute to the height of the columns on either side of the break).[16] In addition all directly following breakpoint blocks $b_{i+1}, b_{i+2}, \ldots$ will also be discarded.

Usually a text block represents a single line of text in the galley. However, if there is no legal breakpoint between two or more lines[17], then all such lines and any intermediate spaces are combined to form a single text block. In a similar fashion consecutive vertical spaces in the source will be combined into a single breakpoint block as the galley can only be broken in front of the first of such spaces. If, however, a space in the source is followed by an (explicit) penalty, then this starts a new breakpoint block to represent the additional breakpoint. Thus, without loss of generality, we can assume that the block sequence alternates between single text blocks and one or more consecutive breakpoint blocks.

Each block x_i has an associated height $\mathcal{H}_{x_i}$, stretch $\mathcal{S}_{x_i}^+$ and shrink $\mathcal{S}_{x_i}^-$ component that describe the block's contribution to the galley and in case of breakpoint blocks also an associated penalty $\mathcal{P}_{b_i}$, indicating the quality when breaking at this block.

Additionally, each text block t_i has an associated depth component $\mathcal{D}_{t_i}$ that holds the size of the descenders in the last line of the block. This value is not directly incorporated into the $\mathcal{H}_{t_i}$ as it should not participate in height calculations if t_i is the last block before a break as explained earlier. For breakpoint blocks $\mathcal{D}_{b_i} = 0$.

For $i < j$ a "candidate column" $col_{i,j}$ is defined to be the material between the two breakpoints b_i and b_j i.e., it consists of the sequence of all blocks $x_{after(i)}, \ldots, x_{j-1}$ where $x_{after(i)}$ is the first text block with an index greater than i (as all breakpoint blocks are dropped after a break). The natural height of its content is

$$\mathcal{H}_{col_{i,j}} = \sum_{k=after(i)}^{j-2} (\mathcal{H}_{x_k} + \mathcal{D}_{x_k}) + \mathcal{H}_{x_{j-1}} \ ,$$

its depth is $\mathcal{D}_{col_{i,j}} = \mathcal{D}_{x_{j-1}}$, its stretch is $\mathcal{S}_{col_{i,j}}^+ = \sum_{k=after(i)}^{j-1} \mathcal{S}_{x_k}^+$ and its shrink $\mathcal{S}_{col_{i,j}}^-$ is defined in the same way.

If C_k is the target height for column k in the final document, then the quality measure $Q_{i,j}^k$ for $col_{i,j}$ as a candidate for this column is defined to be

$$Q_{i,j}^k = \begin{cases} \infty & \text{if } \mathcal{H}_{col_{i,j}} - \mathcal{S}_{col_{i,j}}^- > C_k \\ f(C_k, \mathcal{H}_{col_{i,j}}, \mathcal{S}_{col_{i,j}}^+, \mathcal{S}_{col_{i,j}}^-, \mathcal{P}_{b_j}) & \text{otherwise} \end{cases} \tag{1}$$

---

[13]LuaTeX can be run as a standalone Lua interpreter by calling it under the name `texlua`.

[14]Lua code is interpreted and available in form of ASCII files. It can therefore be easily provided as part of the standard TeX distributions or (with older installations) manually downloaded and installed.

[15]On a very high level of abstraction one can build an object correspondence between the algorithms as follows: words in Knuth/Plass correspond to paragraphs in pagination; hyphenation points in words to lines that allow column breaks; spaces between words to (stretchable) vertical spaces between paragraphs or other objects on the galley. However, while words or partial words have only a width that is relevant for the Knuth/Plass algorithm, objects for the pagination algorithm have both a height and a depth as we see later and both need to be separately accounted for.

[16]In the remainder of the paper we therefore usually talk about "the breakpoint b" rather than "the breakpoint at breakpoint block b" if there is no confusion possible.

[17]For example, if widows and orphans are disallowed, then a three-line paragraph would have no legal breakpoint and thus would form a single block. Other examples are multi-line equations or code fragments that are marked as unbreakable in the source.

If $Q_{i,j}^k = \infty$ then there is no way to squeeze the material into the available space. Otherwise the function f is used to provide a measure for how well the content sequence fills the column, e.g., how much space is left unused.

For its precise definition many possibilities are available[18], provided the function has no dependencies on breakpoint choices made earlier, or if it does, only needs to look back through a fixed number of earlier breakpoints to ensure applicability for dynamic programming.

If $Q_{i,j}^k \leq q$ for some customizable parameter q we call $col_{i,j}$ a feasible solution for column k in the final document (if all columns have the same target height it would be a feasible solution for all columns) otherwise an infeasible one that we ignore[19].

The goal of the algorithm can now be formulated as the quest to find the best sequence of breakpoints $b_0, b_2, \ldots, b_n$ through the document such that all Q_{b_{k-1},b_k}^k are feasible and

$$D_{b_0,\ldots,b_n} = \sum_{\ell=1}^{n} Q_{b_{\ell-1},b_\ell}^\ell \qquad (2)$$

is minimized (with b_0 and b_n representing start and finish of the document, respectively). D is called the *demerits* of the solution.

To solve this, it is not necessary to calculate $Q_{i,j}^k$ for all possible combinations of k, i and j because $Q_{i,j}^k = \infty$ implies $Q_{i,j+1}^k = \infty$. Furthermore, if $b_1, \ldots, b_k$ and $b_1, b_2', \ldots, b_{k-1}', b_k$ are two breakpoint sequences ending at the same place, the algorithm only needs to remember the best of the two partial solutions, because extending the sequences to b_{k+1} means adding $Q_{b_k,b_{k+1}}^{k+1}$ so the relationship between the extended sequences will stay the same.

The algorithm therefore loops through the sequence of all x_i thereby building up all partial breakpoint sequences $b_0, \ldots, b_k$ that are possible candidates for the best sequences, i.e., applying the pruning possibilities outlined above. For this we maintain a list active nodes $A = a_1, a_2, \ldots$ where each a_i is a data structure that represents the last breakpoint b_k in some candidate sequence plus some additional data.[20] This list is initialized with a single active node representing the document start.

While looping through x_i we maintain information about total height, stretch and shrink from the start of the document up to x_i. In the data structure for an active node a we record the column number k that ended in this node and the total height, stretch and shrink from the start of the document to $b_{after(a)}$ so that calculating, for example, $\mathcal{H}_{col_{a,b_j}}$ becomes a simple matter of subtracting the total height recorded in a from the total height at b_j.

D_a is defined to be the smallest demerits value that leads up to a break at a, i.e., $D_a = D_{b_0,\ldots,b_k}$ for some sequence of $k+1$ breakpoints with $break(a) = b_k$. Recording this value in a's data structure makes it easy to prune those that cannot become part of the final solution and to arrive at equation (2) eventually, as we have $D_{a'} = D_a + Q_{b_k,b_{k+1}}^{k+1}$ for a newly created active node a' at breakpoint b_{k+1}.

Whenever we encounter new possible candidate sequences we compare them and add corresponding active nodes for the best of

them. And when it becomes clear that a particular sequence can no longer lead to the best solution the corresponding active node will be removed again.

The overall algorithm then works as follows: We start by initializing the active list with a single node representing the start of the document. For $i = 1, \ldots, m$ we then do:

Case $x_i = t_i$: We update the totals seen so far by adding $\mathcal{H}_{t_i}, \mathcal{S}_{t_i}^+$ and $\mathcal{S}_{t_i}^-$, respectively. The depth $\mathcal{D}_{t_i}$ is not yet added at this point.

Case $x_i = b_i$: A possible breakpoint. In that case we loop through all active nodes $a \in A$ and evaluate $Q_{a,b_i}^{column(a)+1}$ to see how well it works to form the column $column(a) + 1$ with the material between a and b_i, i.e., col_{a,b_i}:

  If $Q \leq q$ we remember col_{a,b_i} as one feasible way to end column $column(a) + 1$ at b_i.

  Otherwise, if $q < Q < \infty$ we consider col_{a,b_i} an infeasible way to end the column and ignore it.[21] By suitably ordering the active nodes we can be sure that all further active nodes will also have $q < Q$. Thus, as long as $\mathcal{P}_{b_i}$ is not a forced break we can end the loop through the active nodes prematurely, which will speed up the algorithm considerably.

  Otherwise, if $Q = \infty$ we remove the active node as it is too far away and can't form a feasible solution with this or any later breakpoint.

  In either case, if $\mathcal{P}_{b_i}$ is a forced break we also remove the active node a as it cannot form a column with a later breakpoint. That's why we can't end the loop prematurely in case of forced breaks. Then we move to the next active node unless the loop ended prematurely above.

Once all active nodes are processed we determine $b_{after(i)}$ so that the total height, stretch and shrink from the beginning of the document to this breakpoint can be calculated for any newly created active nodes associated with b_i.

We then look at all the newly collected candidate solutions ending in b_i and for each different column k we select the best (having the smallest value of $\sum_{\ell=1}^{k} Q$) and record a new active node for it. Infeasible candidate solutions with $q < Q \leq \infty$ will normally be thrown away at this point unless they are the only way to proceed, i.e., if without one of them the active list would end up being empty.

Finally we update the totals seen so far by adding the new height and the previous depth ($\mathcal{H}_{b_i} + \mathcal{D}_{x_{i-1}}$), and the stretch and shrink $\mathcal{S}_{b_i}^+$ and $\mathcal{S}_{b_i}^-$. This has to happen after generating new active nodes as the material is not part of the current column if a break is taken at b_i.

Finally, after having processed x_m which is the last node in the document and supposed to be a forcing breakpoint, we have only active nodes left that correspond to x_m (but possibly to different columns/pages). Out of those we select the one with the smallest D_a as the best solution. From this active node we can move backwards through the active nodes that lead to it, to obtain the complete breakpoint sequence of the optimal solution.[22]

---

[18] Our prototype currently uses the "badness" function that is also used by TeX's greedy algorithm for page breaking. However, this could be altered and made more flexible.

[19] There are cases where it is necessary to consider infeasible solutions as well but these are boundary cases that we ignore for the discussion here.

[20] Again it is convenient later on to talk about "the breakpoint a" instead of "the breakpoint b that is associated with the active node a" if there is no possible confusion.

[21] Exception: if the current break is forced and we haven't seen a feasible solution so far, we need to keep best of the infeasible ones, as otherwise the active list would be empty afterwards.

[22] From an implementation point of view this means that we can't throw active nodes away when they get removed from the active list as their info may still be necessary in this step.

3.2 Complexity and search space

In the algorithm as described the quality function Q is used both to obtain the final solution (by minimizing $\sum Q$) and to limit the search space as any candidate column with $Q > q$ will be disregarded. The alternative would be to use individual cutoff constants for different axes of the search space, as this may be more a natural way for a user to customize the relative weight of different variable features to the overall solution while easily being able to state that a candidate with a certain feature out of bounds is always infeasible regardless of the "quality" of other features.

Technically though the two ways are identical as it is always possible to provide a definition for f that results in the same behavior, so it is more a matter of user interface style than anything else.

If the column heights vary throughout the document, then the complexity of the base algorithm is of order $O(m^2)$ where m is the total number of blocks x_i in the document. If the algorithm would calculate all $col_{i,j}$ then this would be $m(m-1)/2$ computations, so this gives us an upper bound. However, since many of them will be naturally infeasible, the number of calculations actually needed to be carried out can be reduced a lot, making the problem computable even for larger values of m.

The main loop has to be executed for each block and for $x_i = b_i$ which can be assumed to happen about half of the time and one needs to calculate col_{a,b_i} for all $a \in A$ at this point. Now the number of active nodes a with $column(a) = k$ in that list is bounded by the first line in equation (1) as active nodes get deactivated, once they are too far away from the current breakpoint, i.e., more than C_k plus any available shrink in the material. So assuming the column target height C_k is bounded (which it better be in a real life scenario) as well as the ability for material to shrink, then maximum number of active nodes a with $column(a) = k$ will be smaller than $c \cdot n$ with c as small constant and n the number of breakpoints possible in material of height C_{max}.

However, due to the variation introduced by the ability of material to stretch and shrink the active list will not just contain nodes related to a single column, but over time will grow and contain nodes related to different columns. If we assume, for example, that there is $\pm 5\%$ flexibility generally, then after looking at breakpoints for roughly 20 columns worth of material, we may find active nodes ending at column 19 (material was always stretched) or 21 (material was always compressed) beside those for column 20 which would be the natural length. Thus, with m growing the length of A will grow proportionally to it and even though that factor of growth would be very small it will give us a complexity bound of $O(m^2)$.

But there is a very common subclass of layouts in which the situation is much better: if the target column heights C_k are equal for all columns or all columns after a certain index and if the quality function Q only depends on general characteristics such as a common column size[23], then it is possible to collapse different feasible solutions for a given breakpoint to one even if they are for different columns. This will reduce the search space that the algorithm has to walk through considerably, and the complexity will be reduced to $O(m)$ as now the maximum length of the active list is bounded by a constant.

3.3 Double spread support

Providing support for shortening or lengthening the columns of a double spread means that if the active node a represents a column break for the last column k on a double spread, then the calculation of $Q_{a,b}^{k+1}$ in the main loop needs to be done 3 times with different values for $C_{k+1} + variation$ and we can only deactivate a once Q is ∞ for all different column heights. Furthermore, for column $k+1$ we now need to generate a new active node for each combination of $k+1, C_{k+1} + variation$ for which there exists a feasible candidate.

On the other hand, if such a new active node a' has been created for column $k+1$, then whatever height has been used for column $k+1$ needs to be reused when evaluating $Q_{a',b'}^{k+2}$ for some breakpoint b'. And the same happens for all further columns of that spread. Thus the target height as input to f is no longer just depending on the current column but also on the situation on previous column(s). It can be varied if we are starting a new spread or it needs to be whatever the previous column was if we are on any other column of the spread.

To support this efficiently, we extend the active node data structure to keep track of the type of column T_a that will start at a (i.e., a function of k) and the amount of height adjustment V_a that should be used on that column.[24] Then, at the point in the algorithm where we are generating new active nodes from feasible candidates we check the type of column that has started by the current active node a and ended at the current breakpoint as follows:

- If $T_a =$ last, then the next column has flexibility and can be run a line long or short. We model this by generating at this point not one but three new active nodes that are identical except for the variation amount V_a to be used on the next column: this is set to 0, or $\pm baselineskip$, respectively.
- If on the other hand $T_a \neq$ last, then the variation amount is predetermined by the value specified in the active node a that was used in the feasible candidate. For each group of feasible candidates (with the same value of k and V_a) we therefore generate a single new active node a' and set $V_{a'} = V_a$.

It is important to reiterate that the above means that partitioning of the feasible candidates in groups is not just based on the values for column k but on k and V_a (the latter only if $T_a \neq$ last) and that for each such group one needs to generate a new active node (or a set of active nodes).

In case C_i is constant partitioning needs to happen only on T_a and V_a which reduces the complexity but still means that, compared to the base algorithm, a noticeable number of extra active nodes need to be generated and processed.

The only other modification that is still needed, is to extend the definition of the quality function Q from equation (1), as it now needs to incorporate the value of V_a:

$$Q_{i,j}^{k,V_a} = \begin{cases} \infty & \text{if } \mathcal{H}_{col_{i,j}} - \mathcal{S}_{col_{i,j}}^- > C_k + V_a \\ f(C_k, \mathcal{H}_{col_{i,j}}, \mathcal{S}_{col_{i,j}}^+, \mathcal{S}_{col_{i,j}}^-, \mathcal{P}_{b_j}, V_a) & \text{otherwise} \end{cases} \tag{3}$$

---

[23]This is the case for Q in the base algorithm as it only takes C_k as column related input. In the double spread extension the variant height V_a and implicitly the column type T_a (which is a function of k) are additional inputs to Q and so individual active nodes need to be maintained for any combination of their values. Here collapsing could happen for all columns that share the same type and the same height variation value.

[24]Think of T_a as recording "column x out of y" so that each column is identifiable and we can test if we are in the last column of a spread.

The check whether or not the material fits the column is adjusted to include the height variation and the function f is extended to accept V_a as input, so that deviations from the norm ($V_a \neq 0$) can be appropriately penalized by adding to the value returned by Q.

3.4 Variation support

Support for variants in galley material (e.g., paragraphs with different line breaks resulting in different number of lines, or in a different distribution hyphenation points) is handled by introducing new types of control elements c_i in the input stream that signal "start", "switch" and "end" of a variation set. Start and switch controls have an associated penalty $\mathcal{P}_{c_i}$ that is used to penalize the choice of that particular variation.

One difficulty introduced by variations is that they provide different amounts of material along their variation paths. Thus the distance from the start of the document to any breakpoint b after the variation block is no longer a single well-defined value. Instead it depends on the route through which b has been reached. By supporting multi-path variations as well as variations within variations this can get arbitrarily complicated. In the algorithm this is resolved by manipulating the data stored in active nodes: essentially by pretending that the document has started on an earlier or later point. This way it becomes transparent for the calculation of $col_{a,b}$ through which variation paths b has been reached.

The paths from all variation sets are uniquely labeled, so that every possible way to move from the start to the end of the document can be uniquely described by simply concatenating the path labels.[25]

The active node data structure is extended to record in $path(a)$ the cumulated path through all variations up the break point associated with a.

For variation support the main loop of the base algorithm is then extended as follows:

Case $x_i = c_i$ **with** $type(c_i) = \texttt{start}$ This signals the start of a variation set. We make a copy of the active node list $A_{saved} \leftarrow A$ and we also file away the totals $\bar{H}_{start}, \bar{S}^+_{start}, \bar{S}^-_{start}$ from the beginning of the document to the current position for later use. A label L for the current variation path is chosen and $P = \mathcal{P}_{c_i}$ is saved as the penalty to add to the demerits in case this path is chosen. Then we proceed with the next block x_{i+i}.

Case $x_i = c_i$ **with** $type(c_i) = \texttt{switch}$ In this case we reached the end of a variation path. All nodes currently in the active node list A are either on the current variation path (because they have been only recently created) or they are from before the variation block, but we have evaluated the breakpoints on the variation path against them.

So we update all $a \in A$ by appending the label for the finished variation to the path in each a, i.e., $path(a) \leftarrow path(a);L$ and add P to $demerits(a)$.

If this is the first variation in the variation block we save the totals from the beginning of the document to the current point in $\bar{H}_{first}, \bar{S}^+_{first}, \bar{S}^-_{first}$ for later use.

Otherwise we also update the totals stored in all $a \in A$ with the height difference between the current and the first variation path, i.e., $\bar{H}_{first} - \bar{H}_{c_i}$, etc. This way later on $\mathcal{H}_{col_{a,b}}$ for some breakpoint b after the variation block can still be simply calculated by subtracting the totals at b from the totals at a, i.e., the calculation is transparent to the path by which b was reached.

Finally we save away the updated active node list A. We then restore the context we were in before the first variation, i.e., $A \leftarrow A_{saved}$ and we restore $\bar{H}_{start}, \bar{S}^+_{start}$ and $\bar{S}^-_{start}$ as the current totals. We then select a new label L and set $P \leftarrow \mathcal{P}_{c_i}$ for the next variation path. Then we proceed to x_{i+i}.

Case $x_i = c_i$ **with** $type(c_i) = \texttt{finish}$ The end of the variation block has been reached. We update the active node list as described in the switch case and then combine it with the active node lists saved earlier. This will then form the complete new active node list going forward.

All that remains to do otherwise, is to restore the totals to the values at the end of the first variation (as the active nodes in all other variations have been adjusted to pretend this is correct). These values have been previously recorded as $\bar{H}_{first}, \bar{S}^+_{first}, \bar{S}^-_{first}$.

Starting from the final active node a when finishing the algorithm, we arrive at the optimal solution for the whole document by determining the list of active breaks that lead to this node and examining all selected variation paths as recorded in $path(a)$. The latter is an integral part of the solution as many variation blocks will end up between two chosen breakpoints, yet it is important to know which path was used in the construction since we have to replicate that decision in the typesetting phase 4.

3.5 Complexity of the extensions

It is easy to see that both extensions do not change the overall complexity of the algorithm, i.e., it stays $O(m^2)$ in the general case and $O(m)$ if the column height is constant after a certain point.

In the double spread case the maximum length of the active list will have an additional factor of $3 \times$ *number of spread columns* due to the variability when starting a new spread and the fact that we need distinguish active nodes for different columns on a spread.

The situation with variation blocks is worse, as the number of active nodes depends on the number of paths through the variation sets seen along the way. The number of different paths through variations $v_1, \ldots, v_\ell$ is $\prod_{i=1}^{\ell} w_i$ with w_i being the number of "ways" through variation set v_i. Thus this is exponentially growing in ℓ, but fortunately ℓ is bounded by the number of breakpoints that can fit on a single column. therefore this product is actually also of complexity $O(1)$ though unfortunately with a much larger constant if we have columns with many variable paragraphs; see section 3.6.

In case of constant column heights C_i, the overall complexity is $O(m)$ for the base algorithm, because it is possible to collapse all active nodes associated with breakpoint b into one, regardless of the column they did end. This limits the maximum length of the active node list so that it becomes a constant in the complexity calculation. This argument also holds true for the variation set extension (with the small practical problem that the actual constant is fairly large).

In case of the double spread extension we have dependencies between different columns, therefore a solution for column one is not necessarily a solution for all other columns. Nevertheless,

---

[25] The precise method is of no importance, as long as it is possible to exactly reconstruct the selection made to achieve the best solution. In the prototype implementation sequential numbers for both the variation sets and the individual paths within have been used. For example, $1-2;2-2;3-1$ means that the second path was taken in in the first and second variation set, while the first path was taken in the third variation set.

Table 1: Document performance using different algorithm extensions

	document		active list		paragraphs		available looseness[a]					vertical badness[b]		
	columns	blocks	max	average	total	variable	-1/0	-1/1	-1/2	0/1	0/2	good	bad	ugly
Alice in Wonderland	72				833							69	0	**2+1**
base	–	6947	37	12								*no solution*[c]		
+ spread	–	6947	432	122								*no solution*[c]		
+ variations	–	9498	598	54		111	6	15	0	89	1	73	1	–
+ variations, spread	70[d]	9498	7076	488								71	1	–
Call of the Wild	78				340							64	1	**9+4**
base	–	9148	9	2								*no solution*[c]		
+ spread	78	9148	263	134								78	–	–
+ variations	78	14970	263	67		139	11	3	0	124	1	78	–	–
+ variations, spread	78	14970	3156	704								78	–	–
Grimm's Fairy Tales	236				1041							212	6	**6+12**
base	–	27908	22	4								*no solution*[c]		
+ spread	234[d]	27908	485	319								234	–	–
+ variations	238[d]	59111	437	90		441	10	50	21	318	42	238	–	–
+ variations, spread	236	59111	5532	1030								236	–	–
Pride and Prejudice	316				2127							292	8	**7+9**
base	318[d]	34645	39	14								318	–	–
+ spread	316	34645	486	347								318	–	–
+ variations	320[d]	56861	633	70		483	10	51	6	397	19	320	–	–
+ variations, spread	316	56861	7596	837								316	–	–

[a] A count of paragraphs that can be affected by setting specific looseness values. For example, the column of -1/2 counts all paragraphs that could be shortened by one line and extended by up to two lines.
[b] Badness of columns: "good" means the column material is stretched within the specified limits ($b < 2000$); "bad" means a noticeable stretch ($2000 \leq b < 4000$) and "ugly" means that the space in the column is stretched more than 3.4 times its available flexibility ($4000 \leq b$) or is infinitely bad in TeX's eyes ($b = 10000$) indicated by the second value.
[c] The pagination algorithm ran out of options (active list empty) and produced one or more overfull columns as an emergency fix.
[d] The optimized solution has a different number of columns compared to the default LaTeX solution.

collapsing is also possible with the only difference, that we have to keep the best feasible candidate for each combination of T_a and V_a in the running. Again this makes the length of the active node list independent from m so that the overall complexity of the algorithm drops to $O(m)$.

3.6 Computational experience

To gain experience with the behavior of the algorithm and its extensions it was tested on different types of documents. Several example documents and the respective findings are listed in table 1. The documents are "Alice's Adventures in Wonderland" by Lewis Carroll, "Call of the Wild" by Jack London, "Fairy Tales" by the brothers Grimm translated into English by Edgar Taylor and Marian Edwardes and "Pride and Prejudice" by Jane Austen.

All documents have been set in two columns with a width of 8 cm. Each column could hold 46 lines of text and the paragraph requirements have been fairly strict: no widows or orphans and only a small amount of flexibility (+1pt) for the paragraph separation. This means that in each column one could gain a flexibility of up to 2 lines (but only when there are 8 or more paragraphs in the column and we accept a stretch of up to 3 times the nominal value which corresponds to a badness of 2700).

The first row for each document in the table gives the results when processing the document using the standard LaTeX pagination, i.e., a greedy algorithm and in all cases there are a large number of

bad column breaks that would require manual attention (between 4% (Carroll) and 16% (London) of all columns).[26]

The base algorithm (i.e., optimizing across the whole document but without adding any additional flexibility through an extension) shows a maximum active list length of 37, 9(!), 22 and 39, respectively. As a column with 46 lines would have at most that many breakpoints, these values are in line with expectation, i.e., the inherent galley flexibility only contributes a very small factor, so the maximum possible size is never reached in documents of that length. The very low value for London is due to the fact that this document has very long paragraphs (average of 4 per column) and thus is unable to build up any significant flexibility that makes the active list grow towards its boundary. It is therefore also not surprising that the base algorithm doesn't find a solution (except with Austen), as the number of alternatives to consider are not high enough to resolve all obstacles resulting from widows and orphans.

When applying the spread extension the length of the active list gets bounded by $46 \times 3 \times 4 = 552$ so again the observed maxima of 432, 263, 485 and 486 are in line with expectations. It may appear surprising that this flexibility does not result in a solution for Carroll, but this is due to the fact that this document contains an unbreakable object of nearly the height of a column, so that it requires a much higher amount of flexibility to move this out of a break position.

---

[26] If we take out the flexibility between paragraphs the number of issues rises up to 40% of all columns when using the greedy algorithm.

As discussed in section 3.5, the factor by which the active node list can increase in case of paragraph variations is basically the product $\prod_{i=1}^{\ell} w_i$ where the w_i is the number of different ways one can get through the variation set v_i and ℓ is the number of variation sets in the current column. The majority of the variation sets in the text by Carroll and London have $w = 2$ and only a few 3. Grimm and Austen on the other hand have 113 and 76 variation sets with $w = 3$ or 4, respectively. However, Carroll's paragraphs are much shorter on average, thus more fit on a page and larger values for ℓ are likely. So seeing a factor of 16, 30, 20 and 16, respectively for the four documents again fits with expectation.

With the double spread extension we vary the column height by one line and given 46 lines per column introduce an additional flexibility of roughly $\pm 2.2\%$. The important aspect is that in contrast to variation sets this flexibility will be available on all columns and thus the change in the active node list length should be fairly uniform across all documents. In contrast the paragraph variation extension will only make a noticeable difference in that length when several variable paragraphs are close together. Again we can observe this difference: with the spread extension the average and the maximum are fairly close to each other, while the average length when applying paragraph variations is noticeably smaller.

When running the algorithm in its current prototype implementation with both extensions applied we can see an increase of a factor of 15 to 150 compared to a run using standard LaTeX. While this sounds large, we have to realize that, this means less than 2 seconds per page for a globally optimized document. When the author started to work with TeX, processing time for a single page was often 30 seconds and more so global optimization, even with additional bells and whistles added, has become a workable option.

4 CONCLUSION AND FURTHER WORK

The main contribution of this paper is the definition and implementation of a general framework for experimenting with globally optimized pagination algorithms. This framework will enable researchers to quickly test out new strategies for pagination and make them available to a larger audience with ease.[27]

Experiments with a base algorithm for globally optimized pagination have shown that the relative performance hit, compared to a greedy algorithm, is neglectable with today's powerful computer systems (i.e., processing time increases by a factor of < 8 which means 10 instead of 1.3 seconds for a document such as Austen). However, with many documents (that do not contain enough flexible vertical space) the algorithm will run out of alternatives to optimize and thus manual correction, just like with the greedy algorithm, will still be necessary.[28]

We also presented two methods for adding additional flexibility to the pagination process: The approach of running columns on double spreads one line short or long and the use of variants in the text. The letter was implemented by automatically providing all paragraph variants (i.e., paragraphs formatted with different numbers of lines), whenever this can be done without compromising the quality on the micro-typography level beyond a specified tolerance.

When applying the algorithm with the extensions we add enough additional flexibility to fully optimize (nearly) every document without any manual intervention.[29] And the price to pay is acceptable if it avoids hours of iterative tinkering that are otherwise necessary when manually optimizing the results of a greedy algorithm.

The base algorithm outlined in this paper does not handle additional auxiliary input streams such as floats (which of course raises the complexity further). As there are quite different models possible (some of them touched upon in section 1.2), such work should be provided as extensions to the base algorithm, to enable easy comparison between different approaches.

REFERENCES

[1] A. Brüggemann-Klein, R. Klein, and S. Wohlfeil. Computer science in perspective. Chapter On the Pagination of Complex Documents, pages 49–68. Springer-Verlag New York, Inc., New York, NY, USA, 2003.

[2] P. Ciancarini, A. Di Iorio, L. Furini, and F. Vitali. High-quality pagination for publishing. Software—Practice and Experience, 42(6):733–751, June 2012.

[3] N. E. S. Enlund. Electronic Full-Page Make-Up of Newspaper in Perspective, pages 318–323. Gutenberg-Gesellschaft, Internationale Vereinigung für Geschichte und Gegenwart der Druckkunst e.V., Mainz, Germany, 1991.

[4] G. Gange, K. Marriott, and P. Stuckey. Optimal guillotine layout. In Proceedings of the 2012 ACM Symposium on Document Engineering, DocEng '12, pages 13–22, New York, NY, USA, 2012.

[5] M. Goossens. The XƎTEX Companion: TeX meets OpenType and Unicode. Switzerland, January 2010. http://xml.web.cern.ch/XML/lgc2/xetexmain.pdf

[6] Hàn Thế Thành. Micro-typographic extensions to the TeX typesetting system. Ph.D. thesis, Faculty of Informatics, Masaryk University, Brno, Czech Republic, Oct. 2000.

[7] T. Harrower. The Newspaper Designer's Handbook. Wm. C. Brown Publishers, Dubuque, 1991.

[8] T. Hassan and A. Hunter. Knuth-Plass revisited: Flexible line-breaking for automatic document layout. In Proceedings of the 2015 ACM Symposium on Document Engineering, DocEng '15, pages 17–20, New York, NY, USA, 2015.

[9] A. Holkner. Global multiple objective line breaking. Master's thesis, School of Computer Science and Information Technology, RMIT University, Melbourne, Victoria, Australia, 2006.

[10] A. Hurlburt. The grid: A modular system for the design and production of newspapers, magazines, and books. Van Nostrand Reinhold, New York, 1978.

[11] C. Jacobs, W. Li, and D. H. Salesin. Adaptive document layout via manifold content. In Second International Workshop on Web Document Analysis (wda2003), Liverpool, UK, 2003.

[12] C. Jacobs, W. Li, E. Schrier, D. Bargeron, and D. Salesin. Adaptive grid-based document layout. Association for Computing Machinery, Inc., July 2003.

[13] Y. Kido, H. Yokono, G. Topić, and A. Aizawa. Document layout optimization with automated paraphrasing. In Proceedings of the 2015 ACM Symposium on Document Engineering, DocEng '15, pages 13–16, New York, NY, USA, 2015.

[14] D. E. Knuth. The TeXbook, volume A of Computers and Typesetting. Addison-Wesley, Reading, MA, USA, 1986.

[15] D. E. Knuth. TeX: The Program, volume B of Computers and Typesetting. Addison-Wesley, Reading, MA, USA, 1986.

[16] D. E. Knuth and M. F. Plass. Breaking Paragraphs into Lines. Software—Practice and Experience, 11(11):1119–1184, Nov. 1981.

[17] LuaTeX development team. LuaTeX Reference Manual. Version 0.95, June 2016. http://www.luatex.org/svn/trunk/manual/luatex.pdf

[18] F. Mittelbach. E-TeX: Guidelines for future TeX extensions. TUGboat, 11(3):337–345, Sept. 1990.

[19] F. Mittelbach. E-TeX: Guidelines for future TeX extensions — revisited. TUGboat, 34(1):47–63, Mar. 2013.

[20] F. Mittelbach and C. Rowley. The pursuit of quality: How can automated typesetting achieve the highest standards of craft typography? In C. Vanoirbeek and G. Coray, editors, EP92—Proceedings of Electronic Publishing, '92, International Conference on Electronic Publishing, Document Manipulation, and Typography, Swiss Federal Institute of Technology, Lausanne, Switzerland, April 7-10, 1992, pages 261–273, New York, 1992. Cambridge University Press.

[21] M. F. Plass. Optimal Pagination Techniques for Automatic Typesetting Systems. PhD thesis, Stanford University, Department of Computer Science, Stanford, California 94305, June 1981. Report No. STAN-CS-81-970.

[22] S. Wohlfeil. On the Pagination of Complex Book-Like Documents. PhD thesis, Fernuniversität Hagen, Hagen, Germany, 1998.

---

[27] The framework will eventually become part of the standard TeX distributions.

[28] There is still a huge advantage: the number of issues will be noticeably smaller and resolving them normally doesn't require an iterative process, which is the case with the greedy algorithm.

---

[29] It is certainly possible to construct documents that cannot be optimized even then. But for most documents even using just one of the extensions will be sufficient.

Aesthetic Measures for Document Layouts: Operationalization and Analysis in the Context of Marketing Brochures

David Schölgens, Sven Müller, Christine Bauer, Roman Tilly, Detlef Schoder
Department of Information Systems and Information Management, University of Cologne
Pohligstr. 1 – 50969 Cologne – Germany
{schoelgens; mueller; bauer; tilly; schoder}@wim.uni-koeln.de

ABSTRACT

Designing layouts that are perceived as pleasant by the viewer is no easy task: it requires a wide variety of skills, including a sense for aesthetics. When numerous documents with different content need to be created, one of the bottlenecks is to manually create appealing layouts for each document. Thus, automation for aesthetic layout creation is becoming increasingly important. Prerequisite for this automation are algorithms to measure aesthetics. While the literature proposes basic theoretical fundamentals and mathematical formulas as aesthetic measures, researchers have not operationalized these measures yet.

This paper presents the challenges associated with and the lessons learned from operationalizing 36 aesthetics measures derived from the literature for the context of marketing brochures. We measured the aesthetics of 744 brochure pages from 10 major retailers and found very strong and highly significant correlations between at least 11 of the aesthetic measures, which represent five latent aesthetic concepts. Still, most of the measures were found to be independent in our sample, and they cover a wide range of different aesthetic concepts. Nevertheless, our results suggest that retailers optimize some of these measures more than others. In terms of the aesthetic measures, retailers seem to design brochure pages in the same way regardless of which category products on this page belong to or if it is the first, last, an odd, or an even page. We propose to consider the quality values of aesthetic measures derived from our analysis of the measured brochures as target values for automated document layout creation for aesthetic marketing brochures.

Keywords

Aesthetic measures; aesthetics; document layout; layout arrangement; marketing brochures.

1. INTRODUCTION

A document has to be visually appealing and aesthetically pleasing to serve as an effective means for communication or sales [3]. Consequently, aesthetics is a key factor in document layout creation. While the various facets of aesthetics are studied in philosophy and arts [16], this paper focuses on the aspects of aesthetics that are relevant in document layouts: we consider aesthetics in terms of layouts that are perceived as pleasant by the viewer and adapt them in the context of marketing brochures.

Being able to create document layouts automatically is becoming increasingly important. A particularly interesting application domain is the creation of layouts for personalized documents in which the content is tailored to consumer needs, goals, knowledge, interests, or other characteristics [31]. Personalization leads to a high number of documents with differing content, and thus, each personalized document needs a particular layout [3, 13]. Creating different layouts for every personalized documents is time consuming and costly, particularly when done manually by designers. Consequently, automation of aesthetic layout creation is necessary, which requires automatable algorithms enabling information systems to measure aesthetics.

Within the field of document engineering, various authors have introduced and/or discussed measures for measuring the aesthetics of documents in general [2, 3, 11, 24] or specific application domains, such as newspapers [5, 6, 17], digital photo albums [4], screen design [18–20, 27], and websites [28, 30].

However, to date, an operationalization (adaption and practical implementation) of the discussed aesthetic measures is actually missing. Only Zain et al. [30] presented a small study for six measures of Ngo et al. [20], and Altaboli and Lin [1] investigated the effect of Ngo et al.'s [20] symmetry and unity on visual aesthetics in the context of one website.

We contribute to closing this research gap by adapting and implementing aesthetic measures in the context of marketing brochures. We expect high benefits from the automated layout creation of individualized documents, especially in this context. We report the challenges and lessons learned from operationalizing the provided measures for the context of marketing brochures. Furthermore, we apply our implemented solution to measure the aesthetics of 744 marketing brochure pages. This enables us to derive findings concerning the interplay of aesthetic measures and redundancies. In addition, our analysis provides interesting insights into the aesthetics of brochures for 10 major retailers in Germany. In doing so, we provide a target quality values for marketing brochures that may be particularly useful for automated document creation. Additionally, we discuss in detail the limitations of prior work, identifying future key research threads within the field of aesthetic measures.

The remainder of the paper is structured as follows: We present an overview of related work on aesthetic measures in Section 2. Section 3 describes our methodological approach for operationalizing aesthetic measures based on the literature and the measurement of marketing brochures for 10 major retailers. We report the challenges we encountered when operationalizing the aesthetic measures in our system in Section 4 and provide details on the lessons learned and our solutions. Afterwards, in Section 5, we report the results from our analysis of the marketing brochures.

ACM 978-1-4503-4438-8/16/09…$15.00
DOI: http://dx.doi.org/10.1145/2960811.2960821

After offering a critical discussion of our findings and suggesting potential future avenues of research in the field in Section 6, we conclude with a summary of the main contributions in Section 7.

2. RELATED WORK

Basically, there are three main strands of research on the concepts related to and approaches for aesthetic measurement, which go back to Ngo [18], Harrington et al. [11], and Vanderdonckt [27].

Ngo [18] named and defined 13 aesthetic measures that are relevant in the context of screen design: namely, balance, equilibrium, symmetry, sequence, cohesion, unity, proportion, simplicity, density, regularity, economy, homogeneity, and rhythm. In Ngo et al. [19] and Ngo et al. [20], these 13 measures were specified in more detail, and formulas and some empirical data were provided.

Harrington et al. [11] presented nine aesthetic measures for documents in general without a specific field of application: alignment, regularity, uniform separation, balance, white-space fraction, white-space free flow, proportion, uniformity, and page security. Balinsky [2] and Balinsky et al. [3] referred to the approach by Harrington et al. [11] and provided a more detailed discussion of symmetry, alignment, and regularity. Additionally, Riva et al. [24] built their work on Harrington et al. [11] and Balinsky et al. [3] and introduced two ways to calculate the alignment of a page.

The result of each measure described by Ngo et al. [19] and Harrington et al. [11] is a score ranging from 0 (bad) to 1 (good). Ngo et al. [19] and Harrington et al. [11] proposed a combination of the measures to compute an overall aesthetic quality score.

At almost the same time, Vanderdonckt [27] provided a list of 30 aesthetic measures for interactive applications. This work differentiated five categories: namely, physical techniques, composition techniques, association and dissociation techniques, ordering techniques, and photographic techniques. While both Ngo [18] and Harrington et al. [11] focused on the layout arrangement of a given set of objects – as we also do in our work – the work by Vanderdonckt [27] goes beyond that. First, in contrast to our approach, Vanderdonckt [27] also considered steps like object design and creation in the value chain that precede object arrangement as part of the aesthetic measurement task. For instance, Vanderdonckt [27] discussed aesthetic measures concerning photographic techniques. In our work, though, we did not consider object design and creation as variables in the process of document design; rather, we considered these issues as static, which goes in line with Ngo [18] and Harrington et al. [11]. Second, Vanderdonckt [27] took into account measures that go beyond arrangement, such as consistency, which characterizes how well visual appearance meets the subject of the placed objects. A closer look at Vanderdonckt's [27] presented aesthetic measures with respect to the arrangement of objects shows strong similarities to the aesthetic measures by Harrington et al. [11] and Ngo et al. [19] (e.g., balance, symmetry, regularity, alignment, proportion, economy, simplicity, unity). In other words, in terms of object arrangement, we consider the aesthetic measures by Harrington et al. [11] and Ngo et al. [19] as the roots.

Based on the literature on aesthetic measures, several authors have discussed application scenarios in various application domains. For instance, Chao and Lin [8] provided a template-based approach for capturing the layout of an existing page for reuse with different content. Strecker and Hennig [26] adapted some aesthetic measures to provide a flexible grid-approach for creating layouts in the context of newspapers. In addition, de Oliveira [9, 10] referred to aesthetic measures, especially homogeneity, as a requirement for an item-placement algorithm for layout creation.

Lin [15] presented the concept of a "document layout design engine" but without constraints regarding the aesthetic measures of the layout. Some works [13, 23] have considered document formatting and creation as a constrained optimization problem. While the abovementioned research focused on the subject of layout and document creation, Altaboli and Lin [1], Zain et al. [29], and Purchase et al. [22] dealt with layout evaluation in the context of websites. Furthermore, a recent master thesis [14] used the aesthetic measures presented by Harrington et al. [11] and Ngo et al. [20] to investigate the influence of a few aesthetic measures on figures, including, for example, clarity and readability in the context of magazines.

Even though much of the work has engaged aesthetic measurement, especially in the context of layout and document creation, empirical validation and analysis of the interplay between the aesthetic measures are still missing [19]. We call on this research gap and present empirical validation in the context of marketing brochures and analyze the statistical relationship of the aesthetic measures in the form of their correlations.

3. METHODS

As already mentioned, Harrington et al. [11], Ngo et al. [19], and Vanderdonckt [27] introduced a set of aesthetic measures for layouts in the context of documents in general, screen design, and interactive applications. It is necessary to consolidate and discuss the suggested aesthetic measures for two reasons. First, the authors presented different numbers of aesthetic measures. This could be due to the different contexts for which the measures were suggested and the different levels of granularity; as a result, a one-to-one assignment between the aesthetic measures is impossible. Second, even though the authors sometimes use the same term, they describe different concepts, or vice versa, they use different terms for the same concept.

As Ngo et al. [19] provided the most detailed descriptions and formulas for calculating the aesthetic measures, we used this work as a starting point for explicating the theoretical foundations for our work in Section 4. Then, we analyzed Harrington et al.'s [11] aesthetic measures to complement the list of measures taken from Ngo et al. [19].

We took an iterative approach to operationalize the aesthetic measures. Challenges that occurred during the implementation informed our modification of the aesthetic measures, which we describe in Section 5.

We developed a tool in Java to calculate quality values for the 36 aesthetic measures. Brochures taken from the retailers' websites (PDF representations of printed brochures) were used as input for the aesthetic measurement tool. During the import process, double pages were automatically split into two single pages. After the import, categories and margins were manually set at the page level, whereas retailer names were set at the brochure level. Afterwards, objects – typically consisting of a headline, sub-headline, image, description, and price – were marked with rectangular or polygonal shapes (see Figure 1). The aesthetic measurement is based on those shapes.

We measured 37 brochures with a total of 744 pages from the period August 2014 to September 2015 for 10 major retailers in Germany and divided them into 14 categories. Table 1 shows the distribution of the measured brochure pages across the retailers and categories. All pages of all brochures were used.

In Section 5, we provide details about our statistical analysis methodology along with the results.

Figure 1. Marked positions in measured brochure

Table 1. Distribution of brochure pages

Category	Aldi South	Edeka	Lidl	Media Markt	Netto	Obi	Real	Rewe	Rossmann	Saturn	Σ
Car							3				3
Building Supplies	14			2	16	1					33
Office	7						1				8
Decoration	5						1				6
Electronics & Computers	12			40			28			19	99
Garden/Plants	4					8					12
Household	35	4			16	1	34	9	56		155
Domestic Appliances	2			7	4	3	8			5	29
Clothes	32				2		19	1			54
Food	39	35	24		68		64	55			285
Travel	4							2			6
Miscellaneous	4	1		1			1	6			13
Toys	3				3		5	1			12
Sports	17				1		11				29
Σ	178	40	24	48	96	28	176	74	56	24	744

4. CHALLENGES AND SOLUTIONS FOR THE AESTHETIC MEASURES' OPERATIONALIZATION

Ngo et al. [19], Harrington et al. [11], and Vanderdonckt [27] used different terminology in the context of layout assessment and measurement, which is partly due to their different fields of application. Like Ngo et al. [19], we use the term "object" for a content element that is placed on a page. The "layout" is the smallest bounding rectangle that wraps all the arranged objects on one page. A "page" includes the layout and the surrounding white space, as well the margins at all four edges.

Although Ngo et al. [19] and Harrington et al. [11] provided detailed theoretical foundations, we had to overcome some challenges when implementing their aesthetic measures in a software solution. First, while Ngo et al. [19] and Harrington et al. [11] provided formulas for some aesthetic measures that we could implement right away, other measures were described only theoretically. As a result, we had to create the formulas ourselves based on the theoretical foundations given (e.g., alignment, white-space free flow). Secondly, Harrington et al. [11] discussed the aesthetic measures in a generic way (without tying it to a specific application context), and Ngo et al. [19] provided the measures specifically for screen design. Using those measures in a different context – namely, for brochures – required adapting some measures to fit the brochure-specific characteristics and context (e.g., density, white-space fraction) because there seem to be differences between screen design and printed brochures.

Essentially, adapting the aesthetic measures to brochures required us to define two comprehensive settings that affect multiple aesthetic measures (Section 4.1) and eight measure-specific settings that refer to one single aesthetic measure each (Section 4.2). Eleven measures could be adapted straightaway (Section 4.3). We will provide a brief overview of the adapted measures.

In the aesthetic measurement literature provided by Harrington et al. [11] and Ngo et al. [19], several aesthetic measures consist of two or more sub-measures (e.g., balance, regularity, symmetry). To provide more detailed information and results, we worked with sub-measures and also present findings on the sub-measure level.

Therefore, we split 10 aesthetic measures into sub-measures for a total of 36 disjunctive (sub-) measures not counting those that only represent the median of two sub-measures (an overview of all measures is shown in Table 2).

4.1 Comprehensive Settings

For the software implementation, we had to define two comprehensive settings, which refer to (1) tolerance levels and the (2) concept of dividing objects along the x- and/or y-axis.

4.1.1 Tolerance Levels

The content objects' positions were measured on a pixel basis. Thus, it would have been necessary – for instance, to get accurate alignment points – to measure the positions of the objects very precisely. As this is very costly, we used a tolerance level to simplify measurement complexity such that positions, edges, and areas are regarded as congruent.

As the limited resolution of the human eye allows for imprecision in positioning and alignment, our approach is viable. In short, for the human eye, two alignment points that are relatively close together but mathematically not exactly aligned are still perceived as aligned [3].

The introduction of tolerance levels was not only relevant in alignment calculations but also in the calculation of other aesthetic measures with respect to object positioning and size (i.e., alignment, economy, regularity, simplicity, and unity). As a tolerance level, we used 5% of the layout's width or height in pixels. For the comparison of object sizes in regard to economy and unity, we used 5% of an object's width and height.

4.1.2 Dividing Objects Along the X- and/or Y-Axis

For calculating some of the aesthetic measures (e.g., balance, symmetry), it is necessary to allocate each placed object to one quadrant or one side (i.e., left, right, top, and bottom) of the page, respectively. This is challenging when one object spans multiple quadrants. In such cases, there are basically three options for implementation: (1) dividing the object and partially attributing the object segments to multiple quadrants, (2) attributing the object to the quadrant in which the object has the most pixels, and (3) attributing the object to all quadrants in which it has pixels. We decided to use the first approach because the second and third approaches would require filling the available space in quadrants, sides, or pages more than 100%.

The first approach, which divides objects along the vertical centerline of the page and partially attributes them to the left and right sides of the page, was introduced by Harrington et al. [11] in the calculation of balance. An object that spans the left and right sides of a page is divided along the vertical centerline of the page. The left part of the object belongs to the left side of the page and the right part belongs to the right side [11].

When implementing the various aesthetic measures, we learned that division along the vertical centerline is not sufficient for some aesthetic measures (e.g., sequence). Accordingly, we augmented the concept by division along the horizontal centerline. We use this concept in balance, rhythm, sequence, and symmetry calculations.

4.2 Measure-Specific Settings

4.2.1 Alignment

Harrington et al. [11] discussed the aesthetic measure alignment. This measure's objective is to have as few alignment points as possible. A histogram-based approach for alignment calculation is proposed by Harrington et al. [11]; however, concrete formulas were not provided. The alignment point computation can be based on either left and right edges of the placed objects or their vertical centerlines. For polygonal shapes, we used the bounding rectangle for alignment calculation.

To gain more precise results, we divided alignment into four sub-measures: Alignment.top, Alignment.bottom, Alignment.left, and Alignment.right. Those sub-measures indicate how well aligned the individual edges are. The overall alignment quality is the arithmetic mean of the four sub-measures.

4.2.2 Density

Ngo et al. [19] described the concept of density in the context of screen design. It deals with how much of the available space is covered by objects. Ngo et al. [19] assumed that 50% is the optimal density level, which means that half the page is covered by objects. This assumption may be reasonable in the context of screen design, but the analysis of our data sample of marketing brochures shows that 20% white space is a more realistic condition. Our data sample has an average white space of 14.15% with a maximum of 41.93% and a minimum of 3.4%. Due to our measuring approach, it was inevitable that we marked pixels of white space between images and text blocks as content. Thus, we suggest rounding up that 14.15% to 20% to get a common formula that is appropriate if the marked white space can be captured as white space. Thus we set a density level of 80% as the optimum, which means that a layout achieves the highest possible density score if 80% of a page is covered by objects. To allow for a comparison, we implemented two alternatives: Density50 and Density80.

4.2.3 Page Security

The page security measure indicates that small objects should not be placed near the edge of a page because they seem to "fall off" the page [11]. Since this effect may be greatest at the bottom edge, Harrington et al. [11] recommended weighting the four edges differently. In addition to Harrington et al.'s [11] recommendation, our implementation normalizes the distance by half of the page's total width (on y-axis: height) to get a quality value between 0 and 1. To penalize elements that are placed closer to a problematic edge, weighting is applied in an exponential manner. For the top, left, and right edge, we used 1 as the exponential factor. For the lower edge, which is the more problematic case, we used 2 as the exponential factor.

4.2.4 Proportion

The proportion measure describes how pleasing a given height-to-width ratio is [19]. Whereas Ngo et al. [19] named five different "good" ratios – namely, square, square root of two, golden rectangle, square root of three, and double square – Harrington et al. [11] only mentioned the golden rectangle. Our implementation considers all "good" ratios named by Ngo et al. [19] and Harrington et al. [11], and all of them are considered equal. Proportion is calculated as the arithmetic mean of the two sub-measures of Proportion.object and Proportion.layout. They represent the width and height ratio of all objects respectively to the ratio of the layout.

4.2.5 Regularity

Regularity describes how evenly the content objects are distributed over a page. The regularity concept, according to Ngo et al. [19], consists of two aspects: Regularity.alignment, which focuses on minimizing the number of alignment points, and Regularity.spacing, which considers the number of different spacing distances between the arranged objects [19]. Regularity was calculated as the arithmetic mean of those two values [19].

For two reasons, we detached these aspects and divided them into two sub-measures. First, this approach allows us to provide more detailed insight into aesthetic measures and their interrelation. Second, a badly aligned layout with plenty of different alignment points could reach a relatively high regularity score if the number of different spacing points is close to 0. To consider the sub-measures as isolated measures, each sub-measure's quality value has to range from 0 to 1. Ngo et al.'s [19] formula for more than one arranged object does not handle the case of 0 spacing values, which occurs when two or more objects are arranged diagonally, without overlapping horizontal or vertical ranges. Since Ngo et al. [19] only counted vertical and horizontal spacing values, a setting where elements do not overlap horizontally and vertically would lead to 0 spacing values and subsequently to a regularity spacing quality greater than 1. For this case, we set the quality value of Regularity.spacing to 1.

While it is straightforward to determine the number of different spacing distances in a grid-based layout, for less structured layouts, it is not. Therefore, we counted all distances between two objects' edges. If one object's edge had more than one opposite edge of other objects, we counted all of these edges irrespective of their distances (see also Section 6.5).

4.2.6 Sequence

Sequence deals with how well the object arrangement facilitates eye movement, which starts in the upper-left corner and ends in the lower-right corner in the Western culture [19]. Since, according to perceptual psychologists, big objects attract the eye more than small objects, placing most of the information in the upper-left corner facilitates the reader's eye movement [19].

We implemented two versions of the sequence aesthetic measure. The first version, Sequence.w (weighted), was implemented according to Ngo et al.'s [19] approach. In this approach, the summed areas in one quadrant were multiplied by the quadrant's weight, with the upper-left quadrant's weight being 4, the upper-right quadrant's weight being 3, the lower-left quadrant's weight being 2, and the lower-right quadrant's weight being 1. We criticize that when using this approach, the upper-left quadrant has the highest value for the weighted area almost every time because the content area is multiplied by 4. Thus, it is possible that in this quadrant has less content as the other quadrants but is still seen as an optimal arrangement. Therefore, we implemented the second version, Sequence.nw (non_weighted), without multiplying the areas with the quadrants weight, and we want to compare both approaches in this paper. The weighting in the second version is still used for ordering the quadrants.

4.2.7 Symmetry

The symmetry measure describes how well objects are mirrored along an axis. This measure consists of three sub-measures, namely Symmetry.x, which compares the left and right side; Symmetry.y, which compares the top and bottom; and Symmetry.radial around a central point [19]. While Ngo et al. [19] described the calculation in detail, they did not mention their normalization approach. In our work, we normalized the x-values with the quadrants width and the y-values as well as the angle with the quadrants' height. We use height to normalize the angle only because we consider integer values (pixels) for steps in the x- and y-direction. The overall symmetry score is calculated with the arithmetic average of the three sub-measures.

4.2.8 White-Space Fraction

The aesthetic measure white-space fraction indicates that about half of a page should not be covered by objects and thus be white space [11]. While this 50% ratio may be a good target ratio in other fields of application, according to the considerations we explained in the description of density, 20% white space is a more realistic condition for our data set. Therefore, we modified Harrington et al.'s [11] aesthetic measure white-space fraction to the target ratio of 20% white space. In order to enable a direct comparison of the two possibilities of implementation, we implemented both of them. Accordingly, our Wsf50 measure has a quality value of 1 if 50% of the page is covered by objects, whereas the Wsf20 measure sees 80% of the page covered by objects as the optimum.

4.3 Adapted Measures without Modifications

4.3.1 Centered Balance

Harrington et al. [11] presented the aesthetic measure balance, which consists of left-right balance (see NgoBalance.x below) and centered balance (CBalance). CBalance describes how the visual weight of all arranged objects meets the visual center of the page, which lies slightly above the geometric center of the page [11]. CBalance is the arithmetic average of the sub-measures in the horizontal direction (CBalance.x) and vertical direction (CBalance.y).

4.3.2 NgoBalance

The aesthetic measure NgoBalance represents Ngo et al.'s [19] balance measure. NgoBalance compares the total weights of two page sides [19]. The sub-measure NgoBalance.x describes how balanced the left and the right sides of a page are. The sub-measure NgoBalance.y does the same in the vertical direction. The weight of a page side depends on the placed objects, their visual weight, and their distance from the page's geometrical center [19].

4.3.3 Cohesion

The aesthetic measure cohesion, introduced by Ngo [18] and further specified by Ngo et al. [19, 20], describes how cohesive the page is by evaluating the similarity of used aspect ratios. Therefore, the objects', layout's, and page's aspect ratios are put into relation with each other. Based on Ngo et al.'s two components in the formula for cohesion [19], we split the cohesion measure accordingly into the sub-measures Cohesion.page and Cohesion.objects. In the context of Cohesion.page, the aspect ratio of the layout is compared to the aspect ratio of the page. Within the scope of Cohesion.objects, the objects' aspect ratios are put into relation with the aspect ratio of the layout. The cohesion measure is calculated as the arithmetic mean of the two sub-measures.

4.3.4 Economy

The economy measure favors layouts with as few different object sizes (compared based on height and width) as possible to keep the layout clean and simple [19].

4.3.5 Equilibrium

The aesthetic measure equilibrium [19] requires that the center of the layout – or, more precisely, the center of mass of the arranged objects – coincides with the physical center of the page. As we did with the symmetry measure, we divided the equilibrium measure into Equilibrium.x and Equilibrium.y, splitting the horizontal and vertical part of the measure calculation. The overall equilibrium score is calculated as the arithmetic average of the two sub-measures.

4.3.6 Homogeneity

Homogeneity deals with how evenly the objects are distributed among the four quadrants of the page [19]. If all quadrants contain an equal number of objects, the homogeneity score is at its maximum [19]. To handle content that overlaps several quadrants, based on the calculation example in Ngo et al. [19], we counted this object as 1/(number of overlapped quadrants). At the end, we multiplied the number of objects on the page and within the quadrants with an integer factor of 2, 3, and/or 4 (depending on how many quadrants were overlapped) to get whole-number integers for the number of objects in the quadrants.

4.3.7 Rhythm

The rhythm measure describes how harmonic and structured a layout appears. This measure considers the variation in object arrangement horizontally (Rhythm.x) and vertically (Rhythm.y) as well as the variation in object dimensions (Rhythm.area) [19]. The overall measure is calculated with the arithmetic mean of these three sub-measures.

4.3.8 Simplicity

The simplicity measure [18] integrates two parts: (1) the number of horizontal and vertical alignment points and (2) the number of objects placed on a page.

4.3.9 Uniformity

The uniformity measure describes how well the objects' densities match the average page density, whereas variance in visual density is referred to as non-uniformity [11].

4.3.10 Unity

The aesthetic measure unity measures how well the arranged objects are perceived as "one piece" [19]. This measure was divided into two sub-measures: Unity.form describes how well the objects are related in size, and Unity.space takes into account the ratio of the white space in the layout and the white space on the page. Less white space in the layout leads to a better Unity.space quality value since the arranged objects are more closely packed together. The overall unity score is the arithmetical mean of the two sub-measures.

4.3.11 White-Space Free Flow

The white-space free flow (WsfFlow) aesthetic measure's objective is to minimize the amount of trapped white space, which cannot be reached by vertical or horizontal lines, starting from one of the four edges of the page [11].

5. RESULTS

5.1 Measure-Specific Results

In our first analysis, we examined the distribution of the aesthetic measures' quality values. We considered the quartiles that describe how 25%, 50%, 75%, and 100% of the quality values of the brochure layouts are distributed. The 50% values represent the median, indicating that half of the layouts have a higher quality value and the other half have a lower quality value. The range between 25% and 75% is called the interquartile range (IQR) and represents the size of the range for which 50% of all quality values are distributed around the median. The results are presented in Table 2.

The following measures have a low IQR ($\leq .05$) and are close to a quality value of 1 (median $\geq .92$, marked bold in Table 2): CBalance (median: .9419; IQR: .0228), CBalance.x (.9885; .0150), CBalance.y (.9208; .0328), Cohesion.page (.9791; .0306), Equilibrium (.9800; .0190), Equilibrium.x (.9884; .0150), Equilibrium.y (.9750; .0295),· Proportion.layout (.9459; .0457), Rhythm.area (.9471; .0453), Sequence.w (1.0; 0.0), Wsf20 (.9919; .0121), and WsfFlow (.9979; .0073).

A high IQR value ($\geq .25$, underlined in Table 2) was found for Alignment.bottom (.2517), Alignment.top (.2507), Density80 (.3398), Homogeneity (.2591), Regularity.spacing (.2500), Sequence.nw (.5000), Unity (.2613), Unity.form (.4167), and Unity.space (.3029).

Low quality values (median $\leq .1$, underlined in Table 2) were found for Homogeneity (.0168) and PageSecurity (.0742).

5.2 Correlation Groups

We analyzed the correlation between the aesthetic measures. First, we applied the Anderson-Darling test [21] to each of the aesthetic measures to determine whether they follow normal distributions. The null hypothesis (i.e., the measure is normally distributed) was not supported for any of the measures. Hence, we assumed that all measures are not normally distributed. To account for this fact, we used non-parametric Kendall's τ [7] and Spearman's ρ [25] to assess correlations. In contrast to other measures of correlation (e.g., Pearson's r), Kendall's τ and Spearman's ρ do not require variables to be normally distributed [7, 25].

Kendall's τ is more restrictive than Spearman's ρ, generally yielding lower correlation values [7]. In our analysis, we considered only those (pairs of) metrics that were strongly correlated ($|\tau| \geq .8$ and $|\rho| \geq .8$ are generally assumed to be indicative of strong correlations [12]) with a high level of significance ($p \leq .001$) to be able to identify aesthetic measures that represent latent aesthetic concepts.

We identified five groups of aesthetic measures that correlate among each other, with each of these correlations being very strong (τ and $\rho \geq .8$) and highly significant ($p = .001$). Figure 2 represents the correlation factors of Kendall's τ (red) and Spearman's ρ (blue).

Regularity.alignment is strongly correlated with Alignment. Still, very strong correlations between the sub-measures of alignment could only be found with Spearman's ρ and, then, only between the sub-measures on the same axis.

Equilibrium and NgoBalance correlate very strongly. Their sub-measures Equilibrium.x and Equilibrium.y correlate with the corresponding NgoBalance.x and NgoBalance.y, respectively. On

Table 2. Quartiles of aesthetic measure quality values (bold: high median/low IQR, underlined: high IQR/low median; italic: main measures; non-italic: sub-measures)

	0%	25%	50%	75%	100%	IQR
Alignment	.2659	.5217	.6058	.6993	1.0000	.1775
Alignment.bottom	.0127	.4277	.5791	.6794	1.0000	.2517
Alignment.left	.0188	.6121	.7231	.8218	1.0000	.2097
Alignment.right	.0152	.5918	.7215	.8180	1.0000	.2262
Alignment.top	.0110	.4300	.5805	.6808	1.0000	.2507
NgoBalance	.4935	.8830	**.9219**	.9528	.9991	.0698
NgoBalance.x	.4308	.9213	**.9545**	.9787	.9999	.0574
NgoBalance.y	.2937	.8367	.9004	.9524	1.0000	.1157
CBalance	.7992	.9294	**.9419**	.9523	.9960	**.0228**
CBalance.x	.8288	.9797	**.9885**	.9947	1.0000	**.0150**
CBalance.y	.7530	.9024	**.9208**	.9352	.9998	**.0328**
Cohesion	.5382	.7465	.7920	.8301	.9992	.0837
Cohesion.objects	.1871	.5136	.6076	.6905	1.0000	.1769
Cohesion.page	.7511	.9604	**.9791**	.9910	1.0000	**.0306**
Density50	.0669	.2040	.2599	.3449	.8386	.1409
Density80	.1672	.5101	.6497	.8499	.9999	.3398
Economy	.0400	.1250	.2000	.2500	1.0000	.1250
Equilibrium	.8446	.9694	**.9800**	.9883	.9995	**.0190**
Equilibrium.x	.8286	.9797	**.9884**	.9947	1.0000	**.0150**
Equilibrium.y	.7707	.9587	**.9750**	.9882	1.0000	**.0295**
Homogeneity	.0000	.0000	.0168	.2591	1.0000	.2591
PageSecurity	.0014	.0419	.0742	.1357	.9926	.0938
Proportion	.6333	.8733	.8992	.9243	.9965	.0511
Proportion.layout	.7444	.9243	**.9459**	.9701	.9999	**.0457**
Proportion.object	.3924	.7940	.8559	.9034	.9965	.1094
Regularity	.1667	.5357	.6250	.7045	1.0000	.1688
Regularity.alignment	.0000	.5000	.6000	.6875	1.0000	.1875
Regularity.spacing	.0833	.5000	.6429	.7500	1.0000	.2500
Rhythm	.6055	.7512	.7934	.8501	.9962	.0988
Rhythm.area	.6585	.9207	**.9471**	.9660	.9967	**.0453**
Rhythm.x	.4740	.6745	.7462	.8225	1.0000	.1481
Rhythm.y	.4475	.6205	.6850	.7927	.9967	.1723
Sequence.nw	.0000	.0000	.2500	.5000	1.0000	.5000
Sequence.w	.2500	1.0000	**1.0000**	1.0000	1.0000	**.0000**
Simplicity	.0566	.1500	.2000	.3000	1.0000	.1500
Symmetry	.6020	.7421	.7895	.8406	.9974	.0984
Symmetry.radial	.4275	.6852	.7574	.8270	.9963	.1419
Symmetry.x	.4865	.7676	.8380	.9191	.9996	.1515
Symmetry.y	.4275	.7248	.7960	.8662	.9974	.1414
Uniformity	.5942	.8420	.8847	.9145	1.0000	.0725
Unity	.0844	.3589	.4890	.6202	1.0000	.2613
Unity.form	.0667	.2500	.4286	.6667	1.0000	.4167
Unity.space	.0000	.3761	.5130	.6791	1.0000	.3029
Wsf20	.9266	.9851	**.9919**	.9972	1.0000	**.0121**
Wsf50	.1293	.3664	.4522	.5708	.9739	.2044
WsfFlow	.9172	.9927	**.9979**	1.0000	1.0000	**.0073**

the x-axis, we found a strong correlation with CBalance.x; this did not apply for CBalance.y. Based on our data, we did not find any strong correlation between the sub-measures of the different axis. Only with Spearman's ρ we did find a correlation between the main measures Equilibrium and Equilibrium.y as well between NgoBalance and NgoBalance.y and between those two main measures and Rhythm.area.

Rhythm and Symmetry also correlate very strongly based on Kendall's τ. Expanding this group using Spearman's ρ, we identi-

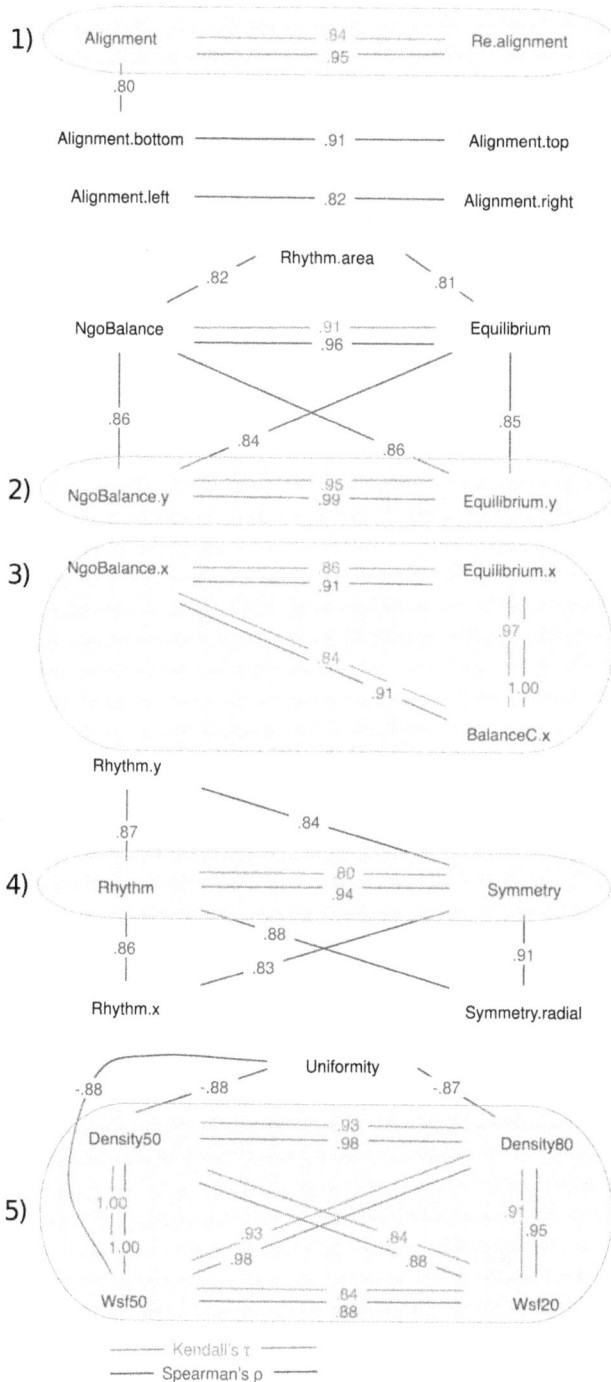

Figure 2. Correlations by Kendall's τ (red) and Spearman's ρ (blue); marked groups of measure concepts

fied correlations with respect to the sub-measures Rhythm.x and Rhythm.y as well Symmetry.radial. Very strong correlations to the other sub-measures Symmetry.x, Symmetry.y, and Rhythm.area were not found.

The largest group of inter-correlating aesthetic measures consists of Density50, Density80, Wsf20, and Wsf50. All four measures correlate very strongly with each other. Using Spearman's ρ, Uniformity also correlates with three of these measures (i.e., Density50, Density80, and Wsf50).

5.3 Retailer, Category, and Page Type

To investigate whether the quality values of the aesthetic measures differ across retailers, we compared the quality values for the pages of each retailer. From Table 1, we see that retailers represent only a few product categories. Accordingly, to exclude effects from the product categories' characteristics, in a second step, we compared the retailers by only considering pages of a particular product category. Thus, we compared retailers by using only pages of the three largest product categories separately: electronics and computers, food, and household.

In all three categories, we found that the retailer Aldi differs from the other retailers. Interestingly, its IQR is frequently larger and/or its median is shifted from those of the other retailers. This especially applies for Alignment.bottom, Alignment.left, Alignment.right, Alignment.top, Economy, PageSecurity, Regularity.spacing, Simplicity, Uniformity, and Unity.space.

Compared to the other retailers, Rewe and Rossmann have better quality values in the household category for Density50, Density80, and Wsf50 and worse quality values for Uniformity (cf. negative correlation as presented in Section 5.2). Rossmann has worse quality values for Simplicity in the household category.

In the food and household categories, Edeka has lower quality values in comparison to the other retailers in the measures Economy, PageSecurity, Regularity.spacing, Unity.form, and Unity.space. Edeka's brochures did not contain pages in electronics and computers.

Comparing the aesthetic measures, no significant differences were found for the different product categories or between first, last, odd, or even pages.

6. DISCUSSION

From our results, several conclusions can be drawn with respect to the single measures, relationships between the measures, and the design specifics of retailers. Furthermore, the implications of our modifications during the operationalization are discussed. We point out that our findings may be limited to the scope of marketing brochures and further characteristics of our sample data, such as evaluated retailers, categories, etc.

6.1 Discussion Regarding Single Measures

We found that some measures have a notably small IQR and that some have a notably large IQR. Those measures with a small IQR are interestingly also close to a quality value of 1. One explanation for the small IQR may be that designers have created the layouts by explicitly optimizing for this measure. It may also be "easy" to achieve a high quality value for these dimensions. Another explanation could be that the respective measure concepts are inappropriate to distinguish layouts properly.

High IQR of a measure may be a result of the difficulty to comply with the measure (e.g., because a measure contradicts another one) or designers' unfamiliarity with or ignorance of the respective aesthetic concept. Furthermore, a measure's concept could also be misunderstood or realized in a wrong way, which would thus lead to a measure with less explanatory power.

Except the measures with high variance (i.e., Alignment.bottom, Alignment.top, Density80, Homogeneity, Regularity.spacing, Sequence.nw, Unity, Unity.form, and Unity.space), every other measure leads to similar quality values for all 744 layouts. Thus, we surmise that the designers of the analyzed retailer brochures optimized the layouts in the same way regarding the evaluated measures.

Given the low quality values (close to 0), it seems that the measures PageSecurity and Simplicity are not so important for designers. An alternative explanation could be that these measures contradict other measures. However, our correlation analysis did not identify any negative correlations for these two measures.

6.2 Discussion of Correlations

Uniformity was the only measure identified to have strong negative correlations with the other measures. However, the negative correlation of Uniformity with Density50, Density80, and Wsf50 reflects the fact that designers have to balance an optimal Uniformity quality level and bad quality values of the latter measures or vice versa.

Furthermore, we found groups of measures that have strong correlations between each other. We assume that measures that make up such groups all represent the same aesthetic concept, whereas a different group of measures represents a different aesthetic concept.

The very strong correlations of the measures Density50, Density80, Wsf20, and Wsf50 (measure Concept 5 in Figure 2) are intuitive: density measures the amount of content, whereas white-space fraction measures the amount of white space, which is the inverse and can be derived from the density. In fact, these four measures only differ in the target value for the amount of content, which we will further discuss in Section 6.3. Based on this, we propose to use either density or white-space fraction.

In the same correlation group (i.e., Density50, Density80, Wsf20, and Wsf50), we also presented Uniformity (cf. Figure 2). Using Spearman's ρ for computing the correlation factors, Uniformity correlates with all measures in the group except Wsf20. Examining the scatter plots revealed missing examples for the following cases in our sample: only a few layouts in our data sample have a density close to 50% or 100% (max: 96.6%; min: 58.07%), thus leading to no measured quality values for uniformity close to 0 and quality values of 1 for Density50 and Wsf50. Taking such layouts into account, the gap in the scatter plot could be filled and the correlation found would probably be strong. Another factor that has to be taken into account is that we operationalize uniformity by calculating the visual weight based on a content object's area. We suggest investigating further on this measure integrating luminance, color, etc. to calculate the visual weight. With the current operationalization and based on our findings, we do not suggest that uniformity belongs to the same aesthetic concept (measure Concept 5) as density and white-space fraction, but it might be conceivable when considering also luminance, color etc. for the visual weight.

Furthermore, as their names already suggest, we found a very strong correlation between Alignment and Regularity.alignment (measure Concept 1 in Figure 2). In fact, the computation of these measures is very similar. Against this background, we propose to substitute the calculation of Regularity.alignment by the Alignment concept that considers all four edges as described in Section 4.2.

The next group of strongly correlating measures that we found is the one between NgoBalance and Equilibrium, NgoBalance.x and Equilibrium.x, as well as NgoBalance.y and Equilibrium.y. We find clear similarities between the formulas of NgoBalance and Equilibrium and their sub-measures. Where NgoBalance uses Euclidian metrics to calculate the distance between object and center of a page, Equilibrium analyses the x- and the y-axis separately; besides this difference, these measures are calculated the same way. Due to the similar formulas and the strong and significant correlations, we propose to consider them as one measure concept for each axis or for the main measure (measure Concepts 2 & 3 in Figure 2). Interestingly, we could not identify a strong correlation between NgoBalance and its sub-measures; the same applies for Equilibrium. We conjecture that one sub-measure balances the quality value of another one.

For the x-axis, we could identify a strong correlation of NgoBalance.x and Equilibrium.x with CBalance.x. The formula of CBalance sums up all center positions on the x-axis and weights them before they are related to the center of the page; this procedure is very similar to the one of NgoBalance and Equilibrium. Therefore, we suggest subsuming CBalance.x under the same concept as NgoBalance.x and Equilibrium.x (measure Concept 3 in Figure 2). In contrast to the x-axis, only weak correlations were found concerning CBalance.y (CBalance.y/NgoBalance.y: $\tau = -.36$, $p = .001$; CBalance.y/Equilibrium.y: $\tau = -.38$, $p = .001$). Probably this could result from the fact that the visual center lies slightly above the geometric center of the page. Here further investigations have to be done, e.g. with another data set.

The strong correlation found between Rhythm and Symmetry form the fourth group. The formulas of Rhythm take values for x, y, and area into account; symmetry uses in addition to x and y values for width, height, angle, and distance. This might be reason why their sub-measures do not correlate but their combination in the main measure correlates (measure Concept 4 in Figure 2).

6.3 Discussion of Page Specifics

Interestingly, we found that the brochures of Aldi are distinct in some measures (cf. Section 5.3) compared to the other retailers' brochures. Delving into details reveals that Aldi uses a lot more full-page images in their brochures than other retailers do. In many cases these images span over a double page while products are only placed on one of the two pages. Furthermore, while Aldi places on average only 3.44 products on a page, overall brochures place 8.59 products on a page (with a maximum of 23.61 products on Rossmann pages). This may explain the differences in the measures.

Furthermore, one cause for the lower quality values of Edeka brochures for Economy, Homogeneity, PageSecurity, Regularity, Simplicity, and Unity may arise from the fact that Edeka arranges products in an entangled way in its brochures, not following a grid-based approach. Additionally, with 13.98 products on average, Edeka presents a relatively high amount of products per page. In fact, those pages may seem complex, overloaded, and confusing, which would explain the rather low quality values.

Interestingly, our data sample does not suggest any significant differences in the layouts of different page types. We assumed that we would find different quality values, for instance, for the first or the last page because these are more prominent and try to attract customers' attention. However, this was not the case given the measures under investigation.

Furthermore, it appears that designers use the aesthetic concepts in the same way over all brochure pages irrespective of the page type or the product category presented. Against this background, we propose: In order to automatically generate layouts that are aesthetically perceived as similar to those we evaluated, the aesthetic measures' quality values of the measured brochures can be considered as target values for the aesthetic layout creation of marketing brochures.

6.4 Discussion of Our Operationalization

With regard to the four possible directions for alignment, the quality values for the alignment of left and right edges was slightly better than for the top and bottom edges. Still, we could not find any evidence that designers would prioritize top and left edges. If products are sized the same in a grid-based approach, then the left and right and top and bottom edges will align naturally. In such a case, it would be sufficient to evaluate only one direction for both the vertical and horizontal axes. Still, for cultural reasons, we suggest further investigating all four directions because, for instance, in the Western culture, the left edge may be more important than the right edge, whereas the opposite is true in Arab cultures.

Furthermore, from our data set, we see that retailers optimize for a white space of about 20% and content density of about 80%. Accordingly, for our data sample, it was useful to adapt the target value for white space to 20% and content to 80% for the density measure to achieve better quality values. Still, the level may depend on the context for which the layouts are created. In addition, further in-depth research is necessary to determine consumers' aesthetic preferences.

Comparing our two approaches for page security, we found that the version that corresponds to Ngo et al. [19] leads to a quality value of 1 for almost all layouts. As a result, this measure can hardly be used to distinguish different layouts. The approach we proposed leads to quality values ranging from 0 to 1, with most layouts achieving values from 0 to 0.5. Although this approach yields worse overall quality values, it is better suited to differentiate between the layouts. Therefore, we suggest using our approach or a third "intermediate" approach that uses less heavy weights.

6.5 Future Avenues of Research

For the measures centered balance and uniformity, Harrington et al. [11] proposed using visual weights. In our study, we operationalized the content's area as a factor for the visual weight. Thus, a text block has the same visual weight as a dark image. We suggest exploring color, luminance, etc., as additional dimensions for calculating visual weight in a more detailed study. We expect interesting insights from such a study, whereas we believe that our approximation does not have large impact on the results, and if so, then the visual weights would only affect those two measures. Additionally, we suggest introducing visual weight to conceptualize density, NgoBalance, white-space fraction, and uniformity instead of using only the area concept because a text's density may appear less than that of an image. For instance, Ngo et al. [19] proposed this for NgoBalance in their future research.

The calculation of different spacing sizes (n_spacing) in regularity was described in Ngo et al. [19] only for the horizontal and vertical directions. As described, we measured the content shapes as polygons. Using our approach, we can additionally have diagonal distances, for example, between a ski and a ski pole that are positioned parallel in a diagonal direction. What size has to be used? If they were not positioned parallel but convex, which size has to be used for the spacing? This aspect needs to be discussed in more detail. In our study, we restricted the measurement to horizontal and vertical distances by using the bounding rectangles for polygons as an approximation. Another aspect for the calculation of n_sizes is the case in which an object has a connection to another object through a small gap between two other elements (e.g., the header of a page has a small connection to the footer through the gap between the two columns). In our paper, we counted every connection regardless of the size of the gap. However, using a minimum size threshold for the gap is also a conceivable alterna-

tive. This would probably match with the viewer's visual perception, but this notion needs to be researched.

In our study, we treated all pages as single pages regardless of whether they were used in a double-page design. Some of the marketing brochures used one background image for the whole double page, thus, connecting those pages. In the context of double pages, it would be interesting to apply the measures to a double page instead of examining both pages independently. This becomes especially necessary if content objects overlap both pages. Measures that would be particularly affected in this context are page security, symmetry, and NgoBalance. For page security, the left edge of a right page would have to be weighted differently than the left edge of a left page.

Our weighting of the edges for page security seems to be a good starting point. Still, future research could also investigate the effects of cultural aspects regarding the aesthetic measures. Cultural characteristics may impact alignment (cf. Section 6.1), CBalance, page security, and sequence. The optical center in CBalance may need to be adapted, for example, in cultures where scripts are written from bottom to top. Furthermore, for the measure page security, reading direction may influence the weights needed for the different page edges. In cultures that read from right to left, it may be preferable to place most information in the upper-right corner and adjust the sequence of the quadrants. Thus, sequence would have to be adapted.

7. CONCLUSION

Automating the creation of aesthetic layouts is an increasingly important topic. First, however, automatable algorithms that enable information systems to measure aesthetics are required. While the literature has proposed basic theoretical fundamentals and mathematic formulas for aesthetic measures, an operationalization of those measures and empirical validation had not been published yet.

Against this background, the present paper provided four main contributions. First, we adapted and implemented the aesthetic measures in the context of marketing brochures. We reported the lessons learned and also provided solutions for how to adapt and modify the fundamentals and formulas so they can be meaningfully applied in practice.

Second, we measured a set of 744 marketing brochure pages for 10 retailers along the 36 aesthetic measures as described in the literature. The results suggest that the measures are applicable and the analysis provides interesting insights into designers' operationalizations of the aesthetic concepts in practice. For instance, we identified that there are some measures for which all retailers' brochures achieve rather high quality measures, some for which all retailers have low quality measures, and only nine measures with high IQR. As the achieved quality values per aesthetic measure show a rather coherent picture among the analyzed retailers, we propose to consider this "aesthetic profile" as target values for aesthetic layout creation for marketing brochures. This target values may be particularly useful for automated document creation.

Third, we presented five groups of measures that have very strong correlations between each other and may thus be consolidated as each group appears to represent the same aesthetic concept.

Fourth, we outlined the limitations of prior work. To overcome these limitations, we discussed future key research threads within the field of aesthetic measures. As aesthetics is a key factor in automated document layout creation, aesthetic measures and their operationalizations are a challenging but important topic. We need to address these measures to be able to provide automatable algorithms that can measure and create layouts that are aesthetic. Only then will we be in a position to automatically design document layouts that are perceived as visually appealing and aesthetically pleasing by the viewer.

8. REFERENCES

[1] Altaboli, A. and Lin, Y. 2012. Effects of Unity of Form and Symmetry on Visual Aesthetics of Website Interface Design. *Proceedings of the Human Factors and Ergonomics Society Annual Meeting* 56, 1, 728–732.

[2] Balinsky, H. Y. 2006. Evaluating Interface Aesthetics: Measure of Symmetry. *Proc. SPIE* 6076.

[3] Balinsky, H. Y., Wiley, A. J., and Roberts, M. C. 2009. Aesthetic Measure of Alignment and Regularity. In *DocEng '09. Proceedings of the 2009 ACM Symposium on Document Engineering.* ACM, New York, NY, 56–65. DOI=10.1145/1600193.1600207.

[4] Bergmann, F. B., Manssour, I. H., Silveira, M. S., and de Oliveira, J. B. S. 2013. Automatic Layout Generation for Digital Photo Albums: A User Study. In *Proceedings of the 15th International Conference on Human-Computer Interaction: Users and Contexts of Use - Volume Part III.* HCI'13. Springer-Verlag, Berlin, Heidelberg, 117–126. DOI=10.1007/978-3-642-39265-8_13.

[5] Buhr, M. 1995. *Aesthetics of Newspaper Layout - and a Survey on Architecture Determining Algorithms,* Computer Science Department, Aarhus University, Denmark.

[6] Buhr, M. 1996. *Newspaper Layout Aesthetics Judged by Artificial Neural Networks.*

[7] Capéraà, P. and Genest, C. 1993. Spearman's ρ is larger than kendall's τ for positively dependent random variables. *Journal of Nonparametric Statistics* 2, 2, 183–194.

[8] Chao, H. and Lin, X. 2005. Capturing the Layout of Electronic Documents for Reuse in Variable Data Printing. In *Proceedings of the 2005 Eight International Conference on Document Analysis and Recognition (ICDAR'05)*, 940. DOI=10.1109/ICDAR.2005.68.

[9] de Oliveira, J. B. S. 2008. Two Algorithms for Automatic Document Page Layout. In *DocEng '08. Proceedings of the eighth ACM Symposium on Document Engineering.* ACM, New York, NY, 141–149. DOI=10.1145/1410140.1410170.

[10] de Oliveira, J. B. S. 2009. Two Algorithms for Automatic Page Layout and Possible Applications. *Multimedia Tools and Applications* 43, 3, 275–301.

[11] Harrington, S. J., Naveda, J. F., Jones, R. P., Roetling, P., and Thakkar, N. 2004. Aesthetic Measures for Automated Document Layout. In *DocEng '04. Proceedings of the 2004 ACM Symposium on Document Engineering.* ACM, New York, NY, 109–111. DOI=10.1145/1030397.1030419.

[12] Henn, M., Weinstein, M., and Foard, N. 2009. *A critical introduction to social research.* SAGE, Los Angeles.

[13] Hurst, N., Li, W., and Marriott, K. 2009. Review of Automatic Document Formatting. In *DocEng '09. Proceedings of the 2009 ACM Symposium on Document Engineering.* ACM, New York, NY, 99–108. DOI=10.1145/1600193.1600217.

[14] Kivelä, I.-M. 2012. Aesthetic Measures for Automated Magazine Layout on Tablet Devices. *Aalto University School of Science Department of Media Technology: Master thesis.*

[15] Lin, X. 2006. Active Layout Engine: Algorithms and Applications in Variable Data Printing. *Computer-Aided Design* 38, 5, 444–456.

[16] McWhinnie, H. J. 1968. A review of research on aesthetic measure. *Acta Psychologica* 28, 363–375.

[17] Meissner, M. 2007. *Zeitungsgestaltung.* Journalistische Praxis. Econ, Berlin.

[18] Ngo, D. C. L. 2001. Measuring the Aesthetic Elements of Screen Designs. *Displays* 22, 3, 73–78.

[19] Ngo, D. C. L., Teo, L. S., and Byrne, J. G. 2002. Evaluating Interface Esthetics. *Knowledge and Information Systems* 4, 1, 46–79.

[20] Ngo, D. C. L., Teo, L. S., and Byrne, J. G. 2003. Modelling Interface Aesthetics. *Information Sciences* 152, 25–46.

[21] NIST/SEMATECH. 2016. *e-Handbook of Statistical Methods: 1.3.5.14. Anderson-Darling Test.* http://www.itl.nist.gov/div898/handbook/eda/section3/eda35e.htm. Accessed 21 March 2016.

[22] Purchase, H. C., Hamer, J., Jamieson, A., and Ryan, O. 2011. Investigating Objective Measures of Web Page Aesthetics and Usability. In *Proceedings of the Twelfth Australasian User Interface Conference.* AUIC 2011 117. Australian Computer Society, Darlinghurst, Australia, 19–28.

[23] Purvis, L., Harrington, S. J., O'Sullivan, B., and Freuder, E. C. 2003. Creating Personalized Documents. In *DocEng '03. Proceedings of the 2003 ACM Symposium on Document Engineering.* ACM, New York, NY, 68. DOI=10.1145/958220.958234.

[24] Riva, A. D., Seki, A. K., de Oliveira, J. B. S., and Manssour, I. H. 2010. Two New Aesthetic Measures for Item Alignment. In *DocEng '10. Proceedings of the 2010 ACM Symposium on Document Engineering.* ACM, New York, NY, USA, 263–266. DOI=10.1145/1860559.1860619.

[25] Salkind, N. J. and Rasmussen, K., Eds. 2007. *Encyclopedia of Measurement and Statistics.* SAGE Publications, Thousand Oaks, Calif.

[26] Strecker, T. and Hennig, L. 2009. Automatic Layouting of Personalized Newspaper Pages. In *Operations Research Proceedings 2008*, B. Fleischmann, K.-H. Borgwardt, R. Klein and A. Tuma, Eds. Springer, 469–474. DOI=10.1007/978-3-642-00142-0_76.

[27] Vanderdonckt, J. 2003. Visual Design Methods in Interactive Applications. *Chapter* 7, 187–203.

[28] Vasilyeva, O. and Lin, A. C. H. 2011. A Theoretical Framework For Understanding Aesthetic Experiences In Relation To Website Design And Utilitarian Outcomes. In *PACIS 2011 Proceedings.* Queensland University of Technology, Brisbane, Australia.

[29] Zain, J. M., Tey, M., and Goh, Y. 2011. Probing a Self-Developed Aesthetics Measurement Application (SDA) in Measuring Aesthetics of Mandarin Learning Web Page Interfaces. *CoRR* abs/1101.1606, 31–40.

[30] Zain, J. M., Tey, M., and Soon, G. Y. 2008. Using Aesthetic Measurement Application (AMA) to Measure Aesthetics of Web Page Interfaces. In *Fourth International Conference on Natural Computation, 2008. ICNC '08.* IEEE, Jinan, 96–100. DOI=10.1109/ICNC.2008.764.

[31] Zimmermann, A., Specht, M., and Lorenz, A. 2005. Personalization and Context Management. *User Modeling and User-Adapted Interaction* 15, 3-4, 275–302.

METIS: A Multi-faceted Hybrid Book Learning Platform

Lei Liu[1], Rares Vernica[1], Tamir Hassan[2], Niranjan Damera Venkata[3], Yang Lei[1],
Jian Fan[1], Jerry Liu[1], Steven J. Simske[4], Shanchan Wu[1]

HP Labs

[1] Palo Alto, CA, USA; [2] Vienna, Austria; [3] Tamil Nadu, India; [4] Fort Collins, CO, USA
({lei.liu2, rares.vernica, tamir.hassan, niranjan.damera-venkata, ylei, jian.fan, jerry.liu, steven.simske,
shanchan.wu}@hp.com

ABSTRACT

Today, students are offered a wide variety of alternatives to printed material for the consumption of educational content. Previous research suggests that, while digital content has its advantages, printed content still offers benefits that cannot be matched by digital media. This paper introduces the Meaningful Education and Training Information System (METIS), a multi-faceted hybrid book learning platform. The goal of the system is to provide an easy digital-to-print-to-digital content creation and reading service. METIS incorporates technology for layout, personalization, co-creation and assessment. These facilitate and, in many cases, significantly simplify common teacher/student tasks. Our system has been demonstrated at several international education events, partner engagements, and pilots with local universities and high schools. We present the system and discuss how it enables hybrid learning.

Keywords

Hybrid Learning; Printing; Automated Publishing; Education

1. INTRODUCTION

With the advent of portable devices such as tablets and e-readers, reading online content for educational, learning, training or recreational purposes has become a very popular activity. Compared to printed material, readers of digital content are offered several levels of interactivity; for example, users may read additional or supplementary online content related to a specific part of the e-text that they have difficulty understanding or wish to explore more; they can add annotations; zoom in on a picture, or play a video embedded in the content. Despite these advantages, printed media still provides other benefits that cannot be matched by digital [5]. Some of the advantages of printed material include: 10-30% faster reading rate [11], lack of distractions, no device compatibility or Internet connection issues, cost effectiveness and, most importantly, the fact that print is still the medium preferred by the majority of students [2]. Instead of eliminating these benefits, we believe that learning should be based on print and enhanced by the use of technology, rather than replaced by it.

To leverage the benefits of reading of both printed and digital content and provide further enhancements to the reading experience, we present METIS, a multi-faceted hybrid book learning platform with the following advantages:

- As an integrated system, METIS provides an easy digital-to-print-to-digital book creation and reading service, which leverages the benefits of learning with both media types.

- Using its inbuilt layout engine, METIS automatically lays out and paginates the content, ensuring a publication-quality appearance.

- Everyone learns differently. To provide the most appropriate reading content for each student, the system offers a personalized book generation service that adapts to each individual's learning profile.

- Interactive book enhancement offers readers multiple content interaction, exploration and annotation capabilities.

- METIS has the capability to automatically extract key concepts from each book chapter. Readers are able to define the relations among these concepts and receive reviews and comments from other peer readers. Such comments and reviews may further help the reader and enhance the book reading experience

2. HYBRID BOOK GENERATION

We provide several functions to help users to generate their own books in METIS, where they have the ability to define the book title, select the cover image, automatically generate the book index and table of contents, etc. In this paper, we will focus on a few advanced book generation features that enhance the book reading experience in multiple facets: layout, personalization, co-creation, and assessments. We also refer the reader to the live demonstration[1] and other videos[2] of METIS.

2.1 Automated Book Layout

The layout framework is one of the core components of the METIS system. The input to the layout framework is a stream of content, which is composed of text, images, and other multimedia elements that need to be laid out. Given this input, the layout framework produces a static, paginated layout of the content, which is output both as PDF for print and HTML for on-screen print preview. The HTML preview additionally includes UI elements for interaction, such as the TOC, images, page flipping, page scrolling, drag-and-drop content, overlay content and external sidebars.

---

[1] http://www.hpmetis.com
[2] https://www.youtube.com/channel/UClYVVdFa4x-9n6d7dUzv01A

Table 1: Personal profile attributes

Book Type	Affinity	Attention span	Complexity
1	Video	10 min	15
2	Video	20 min	25
3	Wiki	10 min	15
4	Wiki	20 min	25
5	Video & Wiki	10 min	15
6	Video & Wiki	20 min	25

In the current version of the METIS system, we have integrated two automated layout engines. The Aero engine [15] leverages native web browser rendering to rapidly render content and apply scoring functions. The JPDM engine [3] uses a probabilistic document model to select the template and optimize the layout according to the content.

A book is generated by the teacher or instructor as follows: (1) The user searches, filters, and selects content, (2) the user selects a layout engine and customizes its execution, (3) the layout framework merges the selected content and provides it to the layout engine, and (4) the layout engine generates the online (HTML) and print (PDF) versions, which are stored in the user's account.

2.2 Personalized Book Generation

Everyone learns differently. Providing the learning content that best fits each individual learner's learning profile is a challenging and important task. Traditionally published content fails to consider this aspect of learning, and provides every learner the same core content (e.g. workbook) and resources. This results in reduced learning efficiency and can result in the learner losing interest.

METIS makes use of a new concept to generate personalized books for an augmented learning experience, which also keeps the core content identical from student to student, but provides different supplementary learning resources based on each reader's learning profile. In the current system implementation, we consider three attributes defined in Table 1 to describe each reader's learning profile, which could be further expanded in the future. In the table, "Affinity" denotes various media formats, "Attention span" denotes the length of concentration while reading and "Complexity" indicates the reading skill of each learner. Also, although our system has the ability to create a personalized book for each individual, we currently generate a fixed number book types (we use 6 as an example in this paper) and assign each reader to the most appropriate book type based on her profile. The purpose is to optimize the usage of computing and storage resources. This trade off is especially helpful in cases with a high volume of readers.

In the current system, each newly enrolled reader is first assigned a default profile and a corresponding book type. While they continue reading in our system, their learning profiles are dynamically updated. Using the new profile attributes, the system automatically recalculates and assigns the most appropriate book type periodically.

2.3 Enabling Co-Creation

In general, readers make annotations to record information that they will need to learn/review at a later time. However, the result of doing so is much more than the production of a passive *external* information store, as the action of creating annotations itself is part of the memorization process and results in the creation of a form of *internal* storage. Furthermore, the creation of annotations eases the load on the working memory and thereby helps people resolve complex problems.

Figure 1: Interactive book consumption

In the METIS reading platform, we provide a novel interactive book enhancement experience in a hybrid learning environment. Our system allows different users who read the same page to create, manage and share their annotations in real-time. These annotations cover different types of learning resources, such as web links, videos, images, comments, articles, etc.

Our system allows users to create annotations at different stages when playing different roles. For example, a user can create the annotations when creating her own reading materials during the content creation phase; such annotations correspond to the content she wants readers to focus on. On the other hand, a user can also create annotations when she reads the created content as a learner to note any portion that she may wish to emphasize at a later time or share with others for discussion or peer-teaching purposes. We also support editing, deleting, moving and resizing any of the annotations.

2.4 Enabling Assessments

Assessing educational achievement and providing feedback to learners is crucial to academic success. METIS enables classrooms and school systems to incorporate concept mapping in formative and summative assessments. Our technology provides two types of automation and support for the wide-scale adoption of concept mapping for assessing student understanding. First, teachers have the capability to embed Q/A to any page. Secondly, METIS has the capability to auto-generate a set of key concepts for each chapter; learners then connect these terms and build a diagram that shows their understanding of how pairs of concepts are related. Furthermore, reviews and comments from other peer learners may help the learner and enhance the reading experience.

3. HYBRID BOOK CONSUMPTION

METIS provides a digital and print learning environment for content consumers. It allows them to easily update reading material, make annotations, and obtain additional learning resources that best align with the individual. In this section, we discuss and demonstrate some of the features for content consumption.

3.1 Interactive Book Consumption

As discussed in Section 2.1, a layout framework is used to generate books that can be consumed interactively in the browser. When a book is read by the student, the cached version of the previously laid out book is retrieved together with the additional UI elements required for content interaction. When the interactive elements are updated, these are stored and associated with the book.

Figure 1 shows two screenshots of the browser-based interactive book consumption UI. The two screenshots show the same content rendered using two different layout engines. Additionally, the screenshots also display various UI elements to enable interactive consumption. These elements are: (1) automatically generated table of contents (left side), (2) scroll bars (next to book pages), (3) automatically generated table of images (center) and (4) notes side-

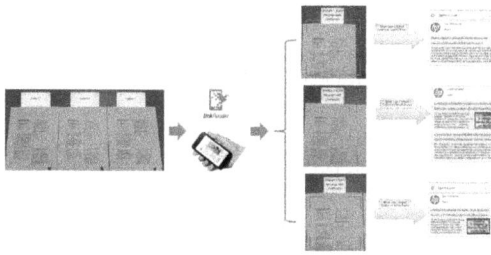

Figure 2: Personalized learning with HP LinkReader

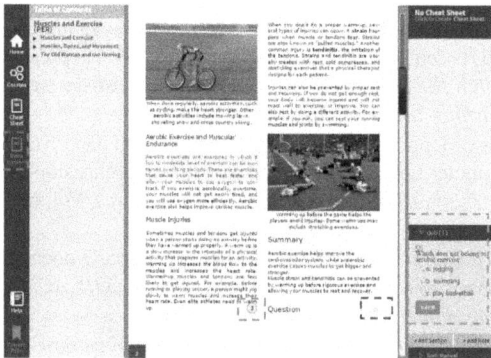

Figure 3: Student reader view

bar (right side, discussed below). Navigation is also possible using the mouse and keyboard.

The user can interact with the notes sidebar by dragging and dropping. Content can be selected from the page and dragged on to the notes sidebar to create a note. The selected content can contain text or other multi-media elements. Once on the notes sidebar, the copied content is fully editable. Colored markers are used to match the note to the location where the text was originally selected on the page. Additionally, sections can be used to organize the notes, and notes can be ordered using different criteria. Finally, note collections can span across books, and a note-only view (with printing options) is also available.

3.2 Personalized Book Consumption

The personalized book can be made available in both print and/or digital formats. The core content is identical for every reader; the HP LinkReader app[3] enables readers to access additional supplementary learning material digitally by scanning the printed page. The reader is then led to customized learning resources that best fit each individual profile (see Fig. 2). When using the digital version of the core content, the "extra content" feature of the METIS reader interface can be used to access this supplementary material.

The METIS reader interface is shown in Figure 3. Book type 1 is assigned to the reader in this example based on her reading profile. Supplementary learning resources allocated to this type of reader will appear in a pop-up window after clicking the icon in the green rectangle as illustrated in Figure 3.

For a more immersive experience, we have also developed a METIS client for the HP Sprout computer, which uses the inbuilt projector to project the supplemental content on top of the physical printed book. Due to space limitations, we refer the interested reader to our video demonstration.[4]

---

[3]https://mylinks.linkcreationstudio.com/

[4]A video demonstration of our HP Sprout client is available here: https://www.youtube.com/watch?v=GPxZI1mB01s

3.3 Co-Creation Experience

The embedded annotation resources that are created in Section 2.3 by the book creator are available to all readers. In addition, different users who read the same page can create and share their annotations with others, allowing for a real-time co-creation experience.

While reading, users can add annotations to any page using the context menu. The recommendation engine [6, 8, 7] helps users create annotations. A user can select content from the book and trigger the recommendation service (Figure 4, step 1). These recommended resources can then be used to create the annotation by simply dragging and dropping the elements onto the page (Figure 4, step 2). Our system has the ability to automatically detect the location of the query box and extract the annotation attributes, such as title, URL, etc. (Figure 4, step 3). After creation, the user can access the annotation at a later time by simply clicking the "Extra Content" button in the left side bar. By simply clicking the annotation area, the previously saved annotation resources are displayed (Figure 4, step 4).

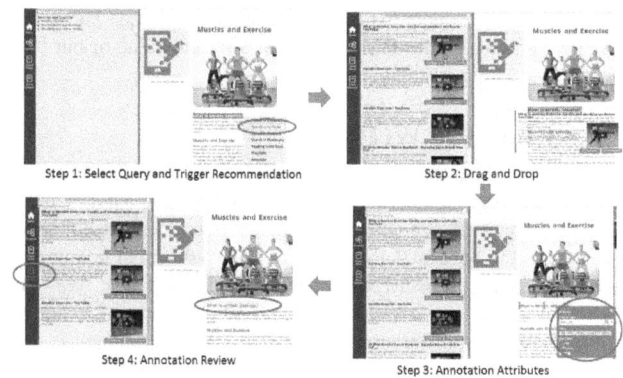

Figure 4: Creating an annotation via recommendation

3.4 Interacting with Assessments

METIS provides two types of assessment modules: assessments created by the content author and concept map based peer-review assessments. Assessments created by the content author appear in the right sidebar (see Figure 3, orange-dashed rectangle). Readers can answer these embedded questions and submit their answers by pressing the "Submit" button. A notification is automatically sent to the teacher.

For concept map based peer-review assessment, we first automatically extract key concepts for each book chapter; readers can then access such concepts at the end of each chapter to perform the peer-review assessment by clicking the gold star icon in Figure 3 to build and define concept relations based on their understanding.

In order to make the scoring of these open-ended diagrams scalable for a large set of people (a large local class or an online learning scenario like a MOOC), every reader does not only build their own concept map based on their understanding but also reviews the concept maps of other learners (by assigning ratings and providing comments). In the end, each learner is evaluated in two ways: (1) their understanding of the book concepts (average review ratings from peer-reviewers), and (2) their ability to provide meaningful and constructive review comments to others (average ratings of review comments they provided). A video demo of this feature is available.[5]

---

[5]https://www.youtube.com/watch?v=fnEebreN1HI

4. EVALUATION

To evaluate the system, we conducted group studies with students and teachers from high schools and universities involving four types of subjects: college students, college teachers, high school students and high school teachers. All these groups of subjects come from diverse institutions. The book content and teachers were chosen to cover multiple subjects as well. Students varied in age, grade, gender and GPA in order to make our survey more objective. Each study involved 8 persons in a two hour session, and begun with a detailed demonstration of METIS' features, followed by an in-depth discussion to identify both successful features and areas for improvement.

Our evaluation showed that the platform was well received from both teachers and students. Teachers preferred METIS for its ability to easily customize course materials, the interactivity with paper, the personalization via supplementary content and the recommendation engine for content creation. Students liked the interactivity with other electronic learning resources, the ease in making annotations and the system's support of students learning together. Furthermore, as the printed books were lighter than conventional textbooks, their carrying load was significantly reduced. These focus group studies confirmed the effectiveness and value of our hybrid book learning system.

5. RELATED WORK

Automatic document layout has been a topic of much research in the document engineering community [4, 9] and METIS uses a layout framework which can integrate different layout engines. As discussed in Section 2.1, we integrated two different layout engines, which are discussed in more detail in [15] and [3].

Other systems for personalized books [12, 10] generate visually different books for different readers, where the same content is not necessarily presented in the same location for each reader. This affects (1) the teachers, who, when teaching the book in class, need a consistent view of the book and (2) the publishers, who are looking to reduce costs when producing the book. To address these problems, the personalized book technology in METIS uses two categories of content: core and supplemental. The core content is laid out identically in all versions of the book, whereas the supplemental content is present at predefined locations.

Previous work on book annotation creation [12] has mainly focused on solving individual exercises alone, empowering students with additional tools to help understand the topic. In the METIS reading platform, we provide a novel co-creation book enhancement experience by allowing different users who read the same page to create, manage and share their annotations in real-time.

To date, most automatically scored assessments use closed-ended questions that are easy to grade, such as multiple choice and fill-in-the-blank types [1, 13]. Open-ended assessments are very revealing and useful to teachers and students, but are generally scored manually. Automating the assessment and feedback mechanisms for open-ended assessment tasks has been especially challenging, and as a result has limited the widespread use of such assessments. In METIS, we provide a novel approach to open-ended assessment, which enables classrooms and school systems to more easily incorporate concept mapping in formative and summating assessments. This active engagement motivates readers/students to think deeper about the topic, brings additional energy to the learning process and has been justified as an effective strategy to learn efficiently and maintain high retention rates [14].

6. CONCLUSION

In this paper, we have presented a multi-faceted hybrid book reading platform to provide an efficient digital-to-print-to-digital book generation and reading service. Our system has capability to enhance the book reading experience in multiple facets, including automated book layout, personalized book generation, co-creation and assessments. The system has been demonstrated in international educational events, partner engagements, and pilots with universities and schools. Its reception has been consistently positive.

7. REFERENCES

[1] A. Abelló et al. LEARN-SQL: Automatic assessment of SQL based on IMS QTI specification. In *Proceedings of the Eighth IEEE International Conference on Advanced Learning Technologies.*

[2] Anne Mangen et al. Reading linear texts on paper versus computer screen: Effects on reading comprehension. In *Internatinal Journal of Educational Research*, Volume 58, 2013.

[3] T. Hassan and N. D. Venkata. The browser as a document composition engine. In *Proceedings of the 2015 ACM Symposium on Document Engineering.*

[4] N. Hurst, W. Li, and K. Marriott. Review of automatic document formatting. In *Proceedings of the 2009 ACM Symposium on Document Engineering.*

[5] Joshua Hailpern et al. To print or not to print: Hybrid learning with METIS learning platform. In *Proceedings of the 7th ACM SIGCHI Symposium on Engineering Interactive Computing Systems.*

[6] Lei Liu et al. LearningAssistant: A novel learning resource recommendation system. In *Proceedings of the 2015 International Conferene on Data Engineering.*

[7] L. Liu. Semantic topic-based hybrid learning resource recommendation. In *Proceedings of the 2015 Workshop on Topic Models: Post-Processing and Applications.*

[8] L. Liu, J. Liu, and S. Wu. Image discovery and insertion for custom publishing. In *Proceedings of the 2015 ACM Conference on Recommender Systems.*

[9] S. Lok and S. Feiner. A survey of automated layout techniques for information presentations.

[10] M. S. Pera et al. Personalized book recommendations created by using social media data. In *Proceedings of Web Information Systems Engineering.*

[11] J. M. Noyes and K. J. Garland. Computer- vs. paper-based tasks: are they equivalent? In *Ergonomics*, Vol. 51, No. 9, 2008.

[12] Peter Baumgartner et al. Living Book–An interactive and personalized book. In *Proceedings of the 2002 International Conference on Advances in Infrastructure for e-Business, e-Education, eScience, and e-Medicine on the Internet.*

[13] V. Pieterse. Automated assessment of programming assignments. In *Proceedings of the 10th Koli Calling International Conference on Computing Education Research.*

[14] M. Prince. Does active learning work? a review of the research. In *Engeering Education '04.*

[15] R. Vernica and N. D. Venkata. AERO: an extensible framework for adaptive web layout synthesis. In *Proceedings of the 2015 ACM Symposium on Document Engineering.*

Digital Preservation Based on Contextualized Dependencies

Nikolaos Lagos
Xerox Research Centre Europe
6 chemin de Maupertuis
Meylan, France
0033(0)476615192
nikolaos.lagos@xrce.xerox.com

Jean-Yves Vion-Dury
Xerox Research Centre Europe
6 chemin de Maupertuis
Meylan, France
0033(0)476615152
jean-yves.vion-dury@xrce.xerox.com

ABSTRACT

Most of existing efforts in digital preservation have focused on extending the life of documents beyond their period of creation, without taking into account intentions and assumptions made. However, in a continuously evolving setting, knowledge about the context of documents is nearly mandatory for their continuous understanding, use, care, and sustainable governance. In this work we propose a method that considers the preservation of a number of interdependent digital entities, including documents, in conformance with context related information. A change that influences one of these objects can be propagated to the rest of the objects via analysis of their represented dependencies. We propose to represent dependencies not only as simple links but as complex, semantically rich, constructs that encompass context-related information. We illustrate how this method can aid in fine-grained contextually-aware change propagation and impact analysis with a case study.

Keywords

Digital preservation; Dependency; Data Governance; Context; Linked Resource Model; Ontology.

1. INTRODUCTION

Corporations, government agencies and other organizations dedicate a big amount of effort for defining document and data governance strategies to help them contend with fast-growing and diverse pools of documents, saved in a variety of formats. The series of managed activities that ensure continued access or renew the usability of documents, and in general digital information, for as long as necessary, is coined digital preservation [1], [2].

Most of existing efforts in digital preservation have focused on extending the life of documents beyond their period of creation without taking into account initial intentions and assumptions made. However, in a continuously evolving setting, knowledge about the context of documents is mandatory for their continuous understanding, use, care, and sustainable governance [3].

Researchers and experts from diverse domains have highlighted the significance of context in digital preservation. Leveson [4] when studying the preservation of software documents (including software programs) argues that there would be significant long-term benefits if specification documents supported wider questions about the reasons why certain approaches were adopted. He proposes recording the context of intended use by creating what he calls intent specifications documents. Johnson [5] notes that poor maintenance is often a contributory factor in software induced accidents. Although many industries already have certification procedures for software maintenance, many companies experience great difficulties in maintaining their software safety cases in the face of new requirements or changing environmental circumstance. Johnson [5] argues that context specification documents would help in that direction by explaining the reasons why any changes were made. Interestingly, the National Library of Australia's Digital Collections has also started using recently what they call "preservation intent statements" i.e. records of the preservation context, including initial intent, for specific classes of digital content, such as digital documents. They argue that this also relates to the concept of "significant properties" i.e. properties that define the (not necessarily strictly quantifiable but observable) qualities that the preserved object has to adhere to, some of these being related to its context [6].

Being able to identify how changes can affect the context of preserved documents is especially crucial in environments that are subject to continual change. Recently, corresponding preservation models consider the separation of preservation from active life as not feasible or desirable [7]. In such cases, to maintain the reusability of complex digital objects and their associated environment, it is necessary to consider risks that can occur due to changes in the environment, to allow determining and performing appropriate mitigating actions.

In this work we propose a method that considers the preservation of a number of interdependent digital entities, including documents, in conformance with context related information. Such entities are assumed to exist within a continually changing environment, which may result in them becoming unusable over time. A major aspect of the methodology is viewing the collection of digital entities as a network of objects where the links between them represent their dependencies. A change that influences one of these objects can then be propagated to the rest of the objects via an analysis of the represented dependencies. We propose to represent dependencies not only as simple links but as complex, semantically rich, constructs that encompass context-related information. In that manner, the corresponding change propagation algorithms take into account the context, encoded in dependency-specific properties.

In the next section we introduce the main concepts we use to represent digital entities, their dependencies, and the corresponding context. In Section 3 we present how dynamic information is recorded and acted upon via a change propagation algorithm that is conditioned on the represented context parameters. A case study is described in Section 4 that demonstrates the advantages of the approach. A review of related work is included in Section 5 and conclusions and directions for future work in Section 6.

2. REPRESENTATION MODEL

As the first step in our methodology we define a model that allows us to represent the preservation ecosystem (i.e. all objects to be preserved and their interconnections) in terms of the corresponding context. To achieve that we define the *Linked Resource Model* (*LRM*), as described in the remaining of the section.

The LRM is an upper level ontology designed to provide a principled way to modelling evolving ecosystems, focusing on aspects related to the changes taking place[1]. In addition to existing preservation models that aim to ensure that records remain accessible, the LRM also aims to model how changes to the context, and their impact, can be captured. It is important to note here that we assume that a change policy governs the dynamic aspects related to changes i.e. natural language descriptions (usually written accounts) of what can change, how and when (e.g. conditions required for a change to happen and/or impact of changes). The properties of the LRM are therefore dependent on the change policy being applied; most of the defined concepts are related to what the policy expects. At its core the LRM defines the ecosystem by means of participating entities and dependencies among them. A set of other properties and specialised entity types are also provided but they are all conditioned on what is allowed/required by the change policy. The main concepts of the LRM are illustrated in Figure 1 and discussed further below[2].

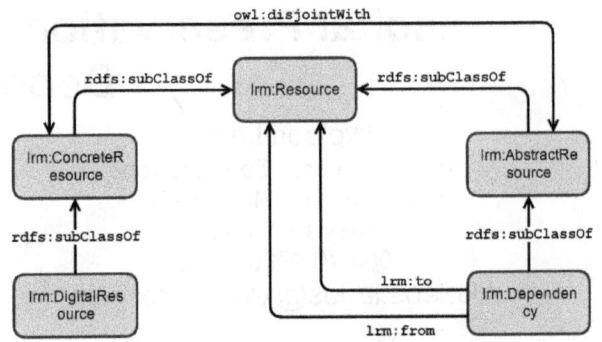

Figure 1. Main concepts of the LRM.

2.1 Resource

The concept of `Resource` in LRM represents any entity in the universe of discourse of the LRM Model. A resource can be *Abstract* (c.f. `AbstractResource` in Figure 1), representing the abstract part of a resource, for instance the idea or concept of a book, or *Concrete* (c.f. `ConcreteResource` in Figure 1), representing the part of an entity that has a physical extension and can therefore be accessed at a specific location (a corresponding attribute called location is used to specify spatial information; for instance for a `Digital-resource`, which represents entities with a digital extension, this information can be the URL required to retrieve and download the corresponding bit stream). A resource (c.f. `lrm:Resource` in Figure 1) can not be both abstract and concrete (enforced by `owl:disjointWith` in Figure 1). The above two concepts can be used together though to describe different aspects of an entity; for example, Don Quixote, as referred by documents talking about the ideas or intentions of the novel, and a corresponding realisation of the novel as a specific book that can be read in the library. To achieve that, the abstract and concrete resources can be related through a specific `realizedAs` predicate.

2.2 Dependency

The core concept of the LRM is that of a *dependency* (Figure 2).

An LRM `Dependency` *describes the context under which change in one or more LRM resources has an impact on other LRM resources.*

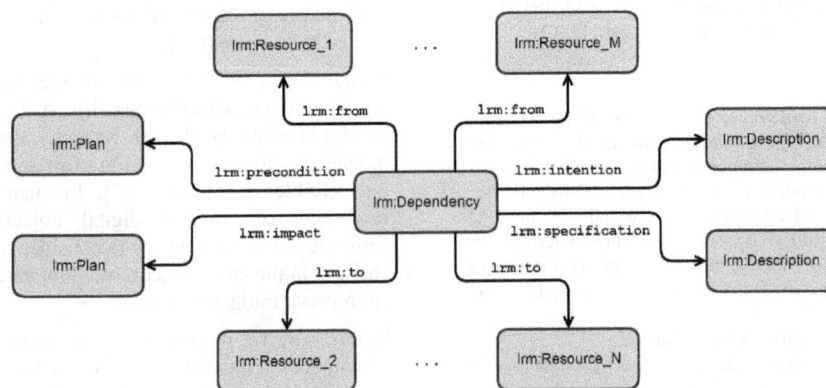

Figure 2. LRM Dependency representation. Properties lrm:precondition, lrm:impact, lrm:intention, lrm:specification can be used to represent the context. Properties lrm:from, lrm:to can be used to represent the directionality of the dependency.

---

[1]The ontology can be downloaded at:
   http://download.xrce.xerox.com/doceng2016/doceng2016_Appendix.zip

[2] For a discussion on the relation of LRM to ontology design patterns see Kontopoulos et al. [8].

Consider a document containing a set of diagrams that has been created using MS Visio 2000, and that a corresponding policy defines that MS Visio drawings should be periodically backed up as JPEG objects by the team that created the set of diagrams in the first place[3]. According to the policy, the team who created the set of JPEG objects should be able to access but not edit the corresponding objects. We should be able to use the classes and properties related to the `Dependency` class to describe each such conversion in terms of its temporal information and the entities it involves along with their roles in the relationship (i.e. person making the conversion and object being converted).

The description of a dependency should therefore minimally include the intent or purpose related to the corresponding usage of the involved entities. From a functional perspective, we expect that dedicated policies/rules further refine the context (i.e. conditions, impacts) under which change is to be interpreted for a given type of dependency. The directionality of a dependency is defined using the `lrm:from` and `lrm:to` predicates (Figure 1, Figure 2).

Explicit classes are also defined for representing conjunctive and disjunctive dependencies (denoted accordingly as `ConjunctiveDependency`, `DisjunctiveDependency`). In the case that a `ConjunctiveDependency` is used then if any of the resources related to that dependency, via the `lrm:from` property, is changed, the dependency is "activated", or in other words the corresponding impact can be computed. Conversely, a `DisjunctiveDependency` is activated only if all resources at the source of the `lrm:from` properties are modified (see also Tzitzikas et al. [10] for an initial introduction to similar concepts)

Of course, this has repercussions on the inference related to the calculation of the impact and corresponding change propagation within the network of dependencies, as explained in section 3.1.

2.3 Contextualising Dependencies

2.3.1 Intent

The LRM `Dependency` is strictly defined according to the intent underlying a specific change. In the example described in Section 2.2 the intent may be described as "*The work group who created the set of diagrams wants to be able to access (but not edit) the diagrams created using MS Visio 2000. Therefore, the work group has decided to convert these diagrams to JPEG format*".

To enable recording the intent of a dependency, LRM relates any Dependency entity with an entity that describes the intent via a property named `intention`, as illustrated in Figure 2. The intent can be described in a formal and/or informal manner i.e. unstructured text. In LRM, the `Description` class represents informal or formal (i.e. expressed in a formal language) written accounts of information related to an `lrm:Resource`. In addition to what is shown in Figure 2, we specialise the `Description` class into a subclass that we call `Intention` to define the space of all possible intents. The expressed intent implies the following.

1. There is a dependency between the MS Visio and JPEG objects. More specifically, the JPEG objects are depending on the MS Visio ones. This means that if an MS Visio object 'MS1' is converted to a JPEG object, 'JPEG1', and 'MS1' is edited, then 'JPEG1' should either be updated accordingly or another JPEG

object 'JPEG2' should be generated and 'JPEG1' optionally deleted (the use case is not explicit enough here to decide which of the two actions should be performed). This dependency would be particularly useful in a scenario where MS Visio keeps on being used for some time in parallel to the JPEG entities, which are in turn used for back up purposes.

2. The dependency between 'MS1' and 'JPEG1' is unidirectional. Actually, JPEG objects should not be directly modified. If they are, no change to the corresponding MS Visio objects should apply.

3. The dependency applies to the specific work group, which means that if a person from another work group modifies one of the MS Visio objects, no specific conversion action has to be taken (the action should be defined by the corresponding change policy).

Some of the above implications, for instance (2), can be expressed by the directionality of the dependency. We define two properties, `from` and `to`, that indicate the directionality of the dependency, as shown in Figure 2.

Expressing more complex behaviour like the one described in implication (3) requires another type of representation. We define a notion called specification that defines the expected constraints and properties that the dependency should adhere to (in a sense its expected behaviour) in a formal and/or informal manner. To enable recording the specification of a dependency, we relate in the LRM the `Dependency` entity with an entity that describes the specification via a property that we name `specification`, as illustrated in Figure 2. As in the case of intention, we can specialise the `Description` class into a subclass that we call `Specification` and which represents the space of all possible specifications.

2.3.2 Preconditions and Impacts

The LRM model provides also concepts that allow the context to be taken into account in an operational manner by recording when a change is triggered and what is the impact of this change on other entities. Let us take once more the above example: we need to be able to express the fact that transformation to JPEG objects is possible only if the corresponding MS Visio objects exist and if the human that triggers the conversion has the required permissions to do that (i.e. belongs to the specific workgroup). The impact of the conversion could be to generate a new JPEG object or update an existing one. The action to be taken (i.e. generate or update) in that case, would be decided based on the change policy governing the specific operation. Assuming that only the most recent JPEG object must be archived, then the old one must be deleted and replaced by the new one (conversely deciding to keep the old JPEG object may imply having to archive the old version of the corresponding old MS Visio object as well). The precondition(s) and impact(s) of a change operation are connected to the Dependency concept in LRM via `precondition` and `impact` properties as illustrated in Figure 2. These connect a `Dependency` to a `Plan`, which represents a set of actions or steps to be executed by someone/something (either human or software). The `Plan` can be used, thus, as a means of giving operational semantics to dependencies. Plans can describe how preconditions and impacts are checked and implemented (this

---

[3] This example is adapted from a use case described in [9].

could be for example defined via a formal rule-based language, such as SWRL [11]).

2.3.3 *Specialising Dependencies based on Context*

One of the strengths of having the dependency notion represented as a class is that we can use the inference mechanisms of OWL to specialize and extend it, according to the intents, specifications, impacts, and preconditions that define it. Take the example of expressing a dependency that defines that the validation of an XML file is dependent on the XML schema and the impact of the validation activity is having a validation report. We can first define the corresponding XML validation dependency as follows:

ex:XmlValidation rdfs:subClassOf
lrm:ConjunctiveDependency.

To specialise this dependency class according to the specific intents, preconditions, and impacts, we can follow a number of approaches, for instance by specializing the `Description` and `Plan` classes and then connect the dependency to these specialised classes as shown below (in Turtle [12]).

ex:XmlValidationDescription rdf:type owl:Class ;
    rdfs:subClassOf **lrm:Description** .

ex:XmlValidationPreCondition rdf:type owl:Class ;
    rdfs:subClassOf **lrm:Plan** .

ex:XmlValidationImpact rdf:type owl:Class ;
    rdfs:subClassOf **lrm:Plan** .

ex:XmlValidation rdf:type owl:Class ;
   rdfs:subClassOf **lrm:ConjunctiveDependency**;
  owl:equivalentClass [rdf:type owl:Class ;
   owl:intersectionOf (
   [rdf:type   owl:Restriction ;
    owl:onProperty **lrm:intention** ;
    owl:someValuesFrom ex:XmlValidationDescription]
   [rdf:type   owl:Restriction ;
    owl:onProperty **lrm:precondition** ;
    owl:someValuesFrom
ex:XmlValidationPreCondition]
   [rdf:type   owl:Restriction ;
    owl:onProperty **lrm:impact** ;
    owl:someValuesFrom   ex:XmlValidationImpact])].

3. OPERATIONAL ASPECTS

3.1 Interpreting Dependencies

The concepts of `ConjunctiveDependency` and `DisjunctiveDependency` were introduced in Section 2.2. Below we provide an explanation of the interpretation of these two classes in terms of change propagation in the dependency graph.

- Conjunctive dependencies (`ConjunctiveDependency`): all source resources are required together and simultaneously to evaluate the impact of a change on the target resource(s). It

means that if one or several of the sources has changed (and the preconditions are satisfied), then the target resources must change according to the impact;

- Disjunctive dependencies (`DisjunctiveDependency`): the target resource(s) do not need to change if there is at least one source resource that did not change.

These two classes of dependencies and their combination allow for expressing for instance, as illustrated in Figure 3, that the transformation of an XML document depends on an XML parser, on a tree-to-tree transformer and on an XML linearizer; but also the fact that a variety of choices for the source resources are possible: for instance the XML parser can be chosen among several standard ones, having slight performance differences, but providing identical functionality, in terms of what is required for the dependency.

In Figure 3 the composition of dependencies is done through a particular resource of the class D-Connector. D-Connector has no other particular semantics than being a "virtual" intermediate resource that is used to propagate the change information in a homogenous way, and therefore, simplifying the algorithms presented in the following sections.

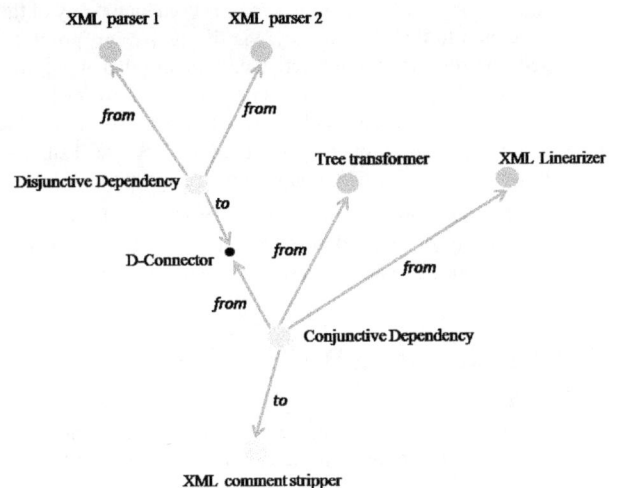

Figure 3. Composition of different dependency types.

3.2 Transactions and Localized Computations

We expect that change propagation can bring about undesirable side-effects e.g. operations that have not successfully terminated can change the state of the actual dependency network in an incorrect way (i.e. the dependency network does not represent any more the actual real dependencies between entities[4]). Furthermore, asynchronous changes may modify the dependency network during change propagation, and therefore may introduce problematic and unpredictable behaviors.

To avoid such issues, we require that the evaluation of the preconditions and the execution of the impacts rely on a transactional, context-aware mechanism that implements a modification to the initial dependency network only if the corresponding conditions evaluate to *true*. Context here corresponds to a specific instantiation of the dependency graph that can be implemented e.g. as an RDF graph[5] or a triple store[6] $.

---

[4] This is a problem: after an unsuccessful evaluation of the operation the state of the dependency network would be altered. This hinders, for instance, reproducibility.

[5] http://www.w3.org/TR/rdf11-concepts/#section-rdf-graph.

[6] https://en.wikipedia.org/wiki/Triplestore

We propose using a nested transaction mechanism[7] adapted to handle triple stores through a stack-like structure, and based on three standard verbs:

- TransactionStart($\mathbb{S}$): Pushes one new entry on the store's stack; each triple addition or deletion will be recorded in this new entry.
- TransactionCommit($\mathbb{S}$): Pops the top level entry out of the stack, and add or withdraw all corresponding triples inside the new top level entry (or updates the ground store if the stack is empty).
- TransactionAbort($\mathbb{S}$): Pops the top level entry out of the stack, and does nothing else (that is, forgets everything about the corresponding triples inside the old top level entry).

Reading the store means that the stack is coherently exploited (scanning the stack from top level down to ground level - the basic store), and is abstracted through the mathematical relation $t \in \mathbb{S}$, where t stands for an RDF triple.

3.3 Context-aware Change Propagation over the Global Dependency Graph

A forward chaining interpretation algorithm can be used to propagate the impact of changes. This is useful when the system is notified of a change to one of the represented resources. In this mode, the change is propagated through the whole representation system by analyzing the dependency graph in a forward fashion.

As preliminaries, we define two functions in Procedure 1 to detect and signal the change of a resource r inside an RDF graph or triple store $\mathbb{S}$, through the use of a particular object called `lrm:changeMarker`. An RDF triple with subject s, predicate p and object o is denoted by `RDF(s, p, o)`.

The first function, denoted `Check-Change($\mathbb{S},r$)`, is a boolean function which checks whether a resource r in a triple store $\mathbb{S}$ has been changed (true) or not (false).

The second function, denoted `Set-Change($\mathbb{S},r$)`, registers that a change has occurred to the resource r in the store $\mathbb{S}$ and inserts the corresponding triple.

---

boolean Check-Change($\mathbb{S}$,r) **is** {**return**
RDF(**lrm:changeMarker**, **lrm:subject**,r) $\in \mathbb{S}$}
void Set-Change($\mathbb{S}$,r) **is** {**set** RDF(**lrm:changeMarker**,
lrm:subject, r) $\in \mathbb{S}$}

Procedure 1: detecting and signaling the change of a resource r inside a store $\mathbb{S}$

As described in section 2, dependencies in LRM are defined according to the *intended usage* of linked resources, which we capture through the property `lrm:intention`, that points to the class `lrm:Intention`. Each dependency instance is therefore associated with a particular intention that is analyzed during the interpretation of the dependency graph. More precisely, a particular dependency will be selected if and only if its intention is compatible with the target intention that characterizes the graph analysis, and which is one of the input parameters. The procedure below (Procedure 2) handles this information through calling the underlying RDF inference mechanism to check for class membership. We note $\mathbb{S} \ni t$ to express that the triple t is inferred from the store $\mathbb{S}$.

// $\mathbb{S}$ is a store, I an Intention descriptor, i is an instance of type Intention, d a dependency instance
boolean Check-Intention($\mathbb{S}$, d, I) **is**
    return RDF(d, **lrm:intention**, i) $\in \mathbb{S}$ **and** $\mathbb{S} \ni$ RDF(i, **rdf:type**, I)

Procedure 2: checking that a dependency is compatible with a particular intention

A recursive method, which combines the two Procedures 1 and 2, as illustrated in Algorithm 1 below, explores the whole dependency graph starting from the changed resource. Cycles are eliminated by memorizing the resources already explored inside a set M. If a resource is already in the set M, this means it will not be considered again, thereby avoiding never-ending cycles to occur. The `precondition` predicate introduced in Section 2.3.2 is used in Algorithm 3 (e.g. `precondition($\mathbb{S}$, d)`) and links a dependency d to a logical property that must be evaluated as true for d to be activated. The impact condition is typically expected to change the context (e.g. the RDF store $\mathbb{S}$), including the target resource(s). In case d has no *to* predicate, the impact condition always evaluates to *true* (or its absence is evaluated as *true*).

---

void FWD-Change($\mathbb{S}$, I, r, M) **is**
// $\mathbb{S}$ is a store, I an Intention descriptor, r a resource
// M is a set to memorize the exploration path
  if ($r \notin M$) {
    set $r \in M$; *// d is a dependency*
    forall d such that RDF(d, **lrm:from**, r) $\in \mathbb{S}$ and Check-Intention($\mathbb{S}$, d, I) **do** {
      TransactionStart ($\mathbb{S}$);
      if precondition($\mathbb{S}$, d) **and** impact($\mathbb{S}$, d) **then** {
        TransactionCommit ($\mathbb{S}$)
        forall tr such that RDF(d, **lrm:to**, tr) $\in \mathbb{S}$ **do**
          Set-Change($\mathbb{S}$, tr)
        forall tr such that RDF(d, **lrm:to**, tr) $\in \mathbb{S}$ **do**
          FWD-Change($\mathbb{S}$, I, tr, M)
      } **else** TransactionAbort ($\mathbb{S}$)
  }

Algorithm 1: propagating the change of a resource

Note that this algorithm handles correctly the composition of dependencies, provided that the preconditions associated with the dependency node check for the disjunctive or conjunctive conditions among the source entities. In the example of Figure 3, a change of the "Parser 1" object will be propagated to the "comment stripper" object (typically, the associated impact would be building a new executable object) only if the precondition attached to the "Disjunctive Dependency" node defined that the "Parser 2" node changed too.

3.4 Context-aware Change Propagation for Targeted Resource (Local) Updating

The forward chaining algorithm presented in Section 3.3 propagates the changes to the whole dependency graph. In Algorithm 2, the idea is to examine a particular resource r and search if it is impacted by one or several changes that may have occurred, exploiting the knowledge stored in the upstream dependency graph, in a backward (BWD) chaining manner. Cycles are handled through the marking mechanism used also in Algorithm 1.

---

[7] https://en.wikipedia.org/wiki/Nested_transaction

```
boolean BWD-Change(𝕊, I, r, M) is
// 𝕊 is a store, I an Intention descriptor, r a resource
// M is a set to memorize the exploration path
  var changed : Boolean = false
  if Check-Change(𝕊, r) then { changed := true }
  else {
    if not (r ∈ M) then {
      set r ∈ M; changed := false;
      TransactionStart (𝕊);
      // d is a dependency
      forall d  such that  RDF(d, lrm:to, r) ∈ 𝕊 and Check-
                   Intention(𝕊, d, I) ∈ 𝕊  do {
        // sr is a resource
        forall sr  such that RDF(d, lrm:from, sr) ∈ 𝕊  {
          if BWD-Change(𝕊, I, sr, M) then changed :=
                                           true
        }
        if changed then  changed := precondition(𝕊, d) and
                                    impact(𝕊, d)
        if changed then break
      }
      if changed then  TransactionCommit (𝕊)
      else TransactionAbort (𝕊)
      unset r ∈ M
    }
  }
  return changed
```

Algorithm 2: examining whether a particular resource has been updated and accordingly propagating updates in the dependency graph

What makes the mechanism powerful, but more complex to handle, is the non-monotonicity of the change computation: local decisions taken during the exploration of the dependency graph may have a global effect, and therefore, may impact future precondition evaluations. Hence, there is a major difference with the forward chaining algorithm: actions associated with each dependency must be undertaken locally during the backtracking process (when preconditions are satisfied), but as they will not be necessarily retained at the end of the process, they must be reversible[8]. To offer this important property, we rely on the nested transaction mechanism described in Section 3.2.

Note that a resource might be impacted by several dependencies; in that case, there is no predefined assumption about the consistency of the result (inconsistency may appear, for instance, if one action

updates the target resource, while another action originating from another upstream graph deletes the resource). The coherence, if any should be ensured, must derive from the structural properties of the dependency graphs[9]. The basic algorithm above applies all relevant actions (regarding the topology and preconditions), regardless of their global consistency or inconsistency (actually, we consider that the behavior of the system for such cases should be detailed at the level of the change management policy).

4. CASE STUDY
4.1 Case Study in Document Governance

We illustrate the advantages of our method over a method that does not take intent and context in general into account with the help of an example. We deal here with the simple task of having two different assemblies of a Visual Studio project, one with (part of) the comments stripped out/transformed[10] and one with all of the comments included in the assembly. The first case is usually happening in a delivery/release setting (when delivering the software to the client we may want (part of) the comments stripped out), while the second in a development setting (the comments are available to the development team). When using Visual Studio, the comments to be rendered are included in corresponding similarly named XML documents[11]. It is also frequent to have another setting where the comments delivered to a client have to follow a format/style that is defined by the policies and or practices of the specific client. Please note, that a partial snapshot of the knowledge base holding the different entities described in this case study formalised in the Web Ontology Language (OWL 2) and serialised in Turtle [12] can be found at Appendix A[12].

4.1.1 Change Cases

Taking into consideration the above requirements we have the following possible change cases.

Case 1. The code changes: Both release and development versions of the assembly have to take this into account.

Case 2. The XML document including the comments changes. In that case we have the following possibilities:

Case 2.1. We want the changes to be visible only to the development team and/or the comments included in the release version to not be impacted. In that case, no change takes place in the release mode, changes take place in the development mode only.

---

[8] Please note that the backtracking algorithm, while qualitatively more complex, is expected to restrict the space complexity of the graph exploration, since it recursively focuses on resources selectively chosen for their relevance regarding a particular intention.

[9] We consider two different levels of consistency: one related to the algorithm: it should provide consistent change management according to the intentions, topology and preconditions associated with dependencies (what we call structural properties). In other words, the right actions must be correctly undertaken during the exploration phase and retained afterward if a global solution is found. A second related to the construction of the dependency graph: the algorithm's results can be consistent only if dependencies are consistently established (e.g. non-contradictory conditions and impacts). Our current approach is to rely on a separate verification mechanism to qualify the dependency network before applying the change

propagation/analysis algorithms, so as to optimize the execution time; however, this is work in progress. We do not necessarily expect the verification process to assess an exact consistency status to any dependency graph, but to detect as much as possible problems. Another approach could be to involve a dependency construction methodology that restrict cases to valid ones, according to a particular generative model.

[10] There are cases where this is an interesting feature, as some comments should not be viewed by the client.

[11] XML documentation files are separate from the DLLs for an assembly. They are just UTF8 XML files. If they are in the same folder as the DLL that they document, and having the same name, then Visual Studio recognizes them and links them appropriately.

[12] Because of the limited space we put this content in Appendix A: http://download.xrce.xerox.com/doceng2016/doceng2016_Appendix.zip

Case 2.2. We want the changes to be visible in the release mode as well. The comments included in the release version are then impacted and changes to both the release and development versions are required.

Case 3. The regulations of the company for comment formatting/styling change. In that case changes to the release version are required but not to the development version.

4.1.2 Participating Entities

It should be obvious from the above list that at least the following objects need to be represented in this case.

Object 1: The DLL files (Here to simplify we will consider only one DLL file). Henceforth noted *DLL*.

Object 2: The XML file holding the documentation for the DLL file. Henceforth noted *XMLOrig*.

Object 3: An XSLT file that holds the transformations that need to be executed to the original XMLOrig so that the resulting XML file that will be included in the final assembly is following the company regulations and/or defines which part of the comments should be stripped out/transformed. Henceforth noted *XSLT*.

Object 4: The resulting XML file after the transformation, noted *XMLTrans*.

Object 5: The rendered object *R*.

For completeness we also represent two different IDEs (*VS1, VS2*) that can be used to render the code and comments. We have to note here that for educational reasons we have greatly simplified this example leaving out a number of other objects that would influence the state of the above entities such as the hardware used.

4.1.3 Dependencies

The dependencies are related to the following three intentions: *render, release,* and *develop* (see also Figure 4). For simplicity we do not include in the Figure the intention related to the transformation of the XML document *XMLOrig* (i.e. transform). Two main dependency types are represented in this example. One related to the generation of the rendering object and one to the transformation of the XML file. Furthermore, the rendering can be sub-classified into rendering for the development team (*rendDevDep* in Figure 4), in which case the *DLL* and *XMLOrig* objects are necessary, and rendering for the client (*rendRelDep* in Figure 4), in which case the *DLL* and *XMLTrans* objects are required. The topology of the resulting dependency graphs is shown in Figure 4.

4.1.4 Context-aware Change Propagation for the Change Cases

Case 1. Code changes imply *DLL* changes, so both release and development versions of the assembly have to take this into account. This is a standard case supported by existing systems and is not detailed further here.

Case 2. XML document changes imply that *XMLOrig* changes.

Case 2.1. We do not want the changes to be propagated in the release mode and/or comments included in the release version are not impacted.

The above change is context-specific where the context is defined by the *develop* intention and the specific topology of the dependency graph. This means that although *XMLOrig* is modified, changes are not propagated to the *XMLTrans* entity, as the intention

release is not compatible with the intention d*evelop*. This is defined in OWL as *ex:Release owl:disjointWith ex:Develop* and following from the fact that *release* is an instance of the *ex:Release* class while *develop* an instance of the *ex:Develop* class. Please note that incompatibility here is defined in terms of OWL-based inconsistency identification. The corresponding dependency graph is shown in Figure 5.

Case 2.2. This is a standard case supported by existing systems and is not detailed further here.

Case 3. This implies that the XSLT object changes.

The above change is also context-specific as the change should only be propagated in the *release* mode. Contrary though to Case 2.1 the XSLT object is not shared between two different intentions. However, such transformation makes sense only if *XMLOrig* is well-formed. If it is not well-formed no change propagation will take place. This constraint is formalised as part of the preconditions of the *xmlTransDep* dependency (an example is included in Appendix A).

4.2 Examples of Use in Other Domains

We have to note here that our method is applicable to different domains. For instance, within the context of the European project PERICLES[13], the same method is used for the preservation of software and/or video-based digital art. In [7], [13] we present an example of a corresponding problem in that domain (in the current paper, when compared to [7], [13], the ontology is much more detailed. It is also the first time we describe the dependency-based change propagation method).

Another example is software versioning. In [14] we present a method for software versioning, which encodes backward-compatibility in the version labels. We believe that this method could be extended by the integration of the dependency-based propagation method presented in this paper and therefore taking into consideration more general context including intent. It is well known that software written to perform the same functionality can be written in different ways. For instance, Cuoq [15] describes two different ways of mixing bits from a pointer p1 with bits from a pointer p2, corresponding to different intents (Table 1 and Table 2).

Table 1. C code mixing some bits from a pointer p1 with bits from a pointer p2 with the intention of assigning either p1 or p2 to r in constant time

```
void * f2(int c, void * p1, void * p2) {
  void * r = p1;
  uintptr_t mask = -c;
  r = (void*)(((uintptr_t)r & mask) | ((uintptr_t)p2 & ~mask));
  return r; }
```

Table 2. C code mixing some bits from a pointer p1 with bits from a pointer p2 with the intention of assigning either p1 or p2 to r as fast as possible without any guarantee on constant time computation

```
void * f1(int c, void * p1, void * p2) {
  void * r = p1;
  if (!c) r = p2;
  return r; }
```

Today, there is no available system that would allow us to keep both variants and version them while keeping explicit the intent-specific semantics into the versioning process. However, this can be a real need for professional software development (e.g. see [16] for a discussion on intents in software development).

---

[13] www.pericles-project.eu/

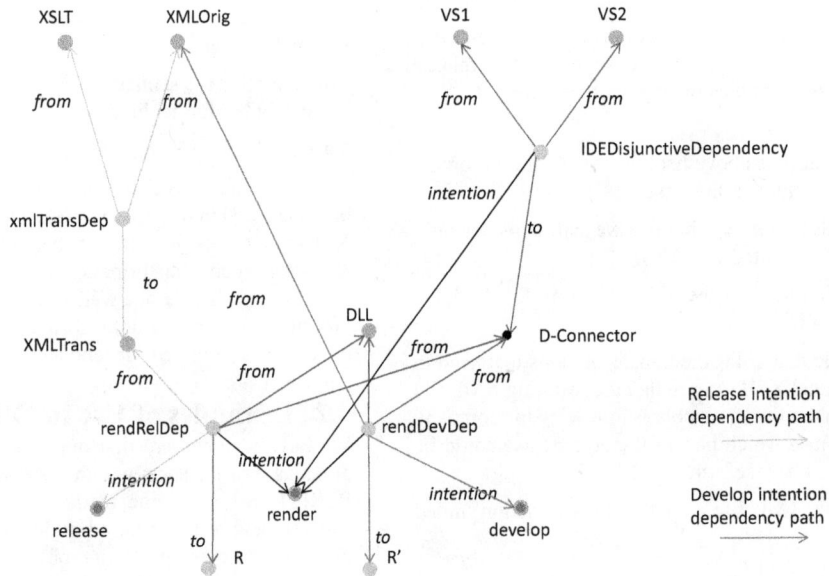

Figure 4. Topology of the dependency graph at time *t* with three different intentions shown: *render*, *release* and *develop*. The dependency instances are *xmlTransDep* (transformation dependency), *rendRelDep* (rendering dependency for release version i.e. the client), *rendDevDep* (rendering dependency for development version i.e. the engineering team). Notice that the dependency paths can be different according to the intention, but also the same intention instances (and in general entities) can belong to different dependency paths (e.g. *render*, *XMLOrig*).

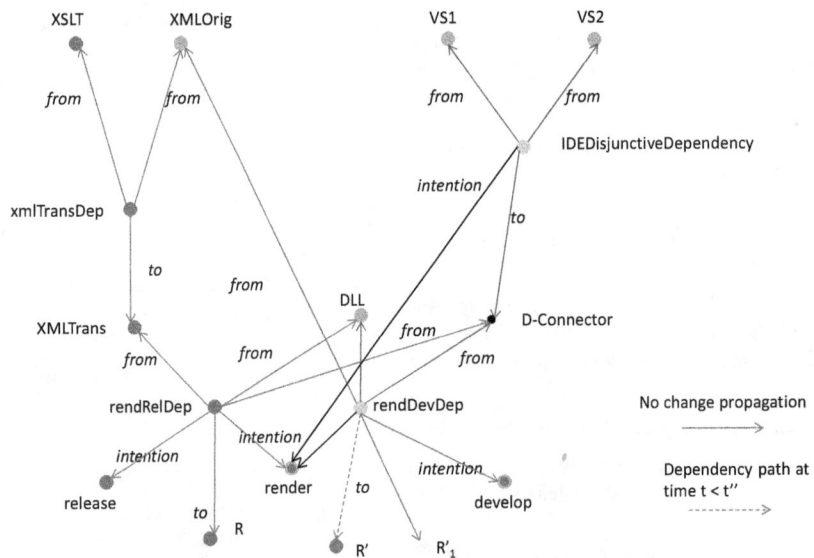

Figure 5. Topology of the dependency graph at time *t''>t* (except for the object *R'* that is kept to highlight the change that happened). Note that only the part of the dependency graph related to the *develop* intention is active for change propagation.

5. RELATED WORK

There are two main streams of work on dependency-based representations for digital preservation. In the first one, dependencies are considered as simple binary relations while in the second one as complex constructs, although in both cases the notion of intention and in general context is not considered.

In the first stream the most important work includes the PREMIS Data Dictionary [18], which defines three types of relationships between objects: structural, derivation and dependency. Derivation and dependency relationships are the most relevant in our setting. A derivation relation results from the replication or transformation of an object. A dependency relation exists when one object requires another to support its function, delivery, or coherence. Examples include a DTD or schema that are not part of the file itself. Objects can be related to events through user-defined dictionaries, and events can in turn be linked to agents that performed those events.

Another widely used model is the Open Provenance Model (OPM) [19] that introduces the concept of a provenance graph, which captures causal dependencies between entities. The most relevant concept from our perspective is process that represents actions performed on or caused by artefacts, and resulting in new artefacts.

Interestingly also in hardware verification and design dependency relations are considered. The closest work is by Casotto [20] where he focuses on the notion of "design intent", which generally refers to what the designer intends in terms of the interaction between components of the design and the designer's expectations regarding acceptable functional behavior. Casotto also refers to "implied design intent", however he models neither of these as an aspect of the dependencies.

In the second stream, the most interesting line of work, and most similar to ours, is from Tzitzikas and colleagues ([21], [10], [17]).

Tzitzikas [21] defines the notions of module, dependency and profile to model use by a community of users. A module is defined as a software/hardware component or knowledge base that is to be preserved, and a profile is the set of modules that are assumed to be known. A dependency relation is then defined by the statement that module A depends on module B if A cannot function without B. For example, a .txt file depends on the availability of a text editor.

Tzitzikas et al. [10] also define the more specific notion of task-based dependency, expressed as Datalog rules and facts. For instance, `Compile(HelloWorld.java)` denotes the task of compiling 'HelloWorld.java'. Since the compilation of the latter depends on the availability of a compiler, this dependency can be expressed using a rule of the form:

```
Compile(X):- Compilable(X,Y);
```

where the binary predicate `Compilable(X,Y)` denotes the appropriateness of Y for compiling X. This formal approach enables various tasks to be performed, such as risk and gap analysis for specific tasks, possibly considering contextual information, such as user profiles.

In addition to the above work, Marketakis and Tzitzikas [17] introduce the notion of *intelligibility* (which seems to be related to the notion of *task* defined in [10]), which allows for typing dependencies. Our approach goes one step further toward genericity, by allowing any kind of dependency specialization, the intelligibility being replaced by the notion of intention, which can be described informally or formally through additional properties. Moreover, LRM offers a much richer topology for dependency graphs through managing dependencies as instances instead of properties. By combining genericity and semantic refinement, we expect a tighter management of consistency criteria, whatever semantics might be potentially involved. Furthermore, we do not constrain ourselves to a specific operational framework (i.e. Datalog) as Tzitzikas et al. do in a part of their work. Another notable difference is that the authors do not make any reference to local computations and the use of anything similar to transactions for defining the computational context (as in our case).

Change propagation and impact analysis have also been traditionally very important in software evolution. Most of the existing work, however, does not take into account contextualised dependencies and/or different intentions. One of the most interesting exceptions is the work presented by Dam et al. [22], where an agent-oriented approach is adopted to perform change propagation for the purpose of software evolution. In this case, the belief-desire-intention (BDI) model is followed, which is actually a way of separating and selecting a plan from the execution of currently active plans. Intentions represent the deliberative state of the agent – what the agent has chosen to do which relates to the execution of a plan. Of course the setting and overall setup is different than ours, but also most importantly, they do not define explicit representation structures for representing the dependencies between different entities. They rather assume that they have a set of plans which have specific goals and the only connection between the entities is encoded within those plans. The context then is defined as an additional or modified goal that can change during the execution of the plan. Constraints on plans are encoded as rules. No change propagation algorithm performing local computation and dealing with transactions, as in our case, is proposed.

6. CONCLUSION

In this paper we have presented a method that allows taking into account initial development and change intentions, as well as relevant context, for document and data governance. To achieve that we view the collection of documents or in general digital entities to be preserved and managed, as a network of entities where the dependencies between them are not simple binary links but complex, semantically rich, constructs that encompass context-related information. Context includes the conditions under which change can have an impact on (part of) the network, definitions of that impact, and links to change and development intents. Our model is extensible, allowing specialising the dependencies and adding more properties if required.

Intent is explicitly represented as a first class citizen in our model. This enables to parameterize dependency interpretation: change interpretation becomes a potentially complex function of intents and relations between them (e.g. by (re)using a specialised ontology). This allows inferences about class membership and classification, or inconsistency identification (as illustrated in our case study) and resolution based on specific context interpretations.

An important aspect of the algorithmic part of our method is that we allow changes that may result in undesirable side-effects e.g. operations that have not successfully terminated can change the state of the actual dependency network in an incorrect way. This is possible thanks to the introduction of a nested transactional mechanism. The same mechanism could be used to enable simulations (e.g. if I change that object, what is the effect on the rest of the objects?), which is an essential aspect of risk analysis.

As illustrated through our case study the advantages of our method when compared to existing ones include: more fine grained change impact calculation and analysis; genericity, as heterogeneous digital objects can be preserved in different contexts; and incompatibility detection via ontology-based reasoning, by specializing/configuring dependencies.

In the near future we would like to extend the inference capabilities presented in this paper with the use of a change impact analysis infrastructure that will allow even more expressivity in the notion of preconditions and impacts. We would also like to apply our methodology in software change management, where intention recording and risk analysis in the face of change are very important.

7. ACKNOWLEDGMENTS

This project has received funding from the European Union's Seventh Framework Programme for research, technological development and demonstration under grant agreement no. 601138

8. REFERENCES

[1] Conway, P. 1996. Preservation in the Digital World. Council on Library and Information Resources, Washington, DC. http://www.clir.org/pubs/reports/reports/conway2/index.html , Accessed: 16 Mar 2016.

[2] Digital Preservation Coalition (2015). Glossary. Digital Preservation Handbook 2nd edition. York, UK. http://www.dpconline.org/advice/preservationhandbook/glossary. Accessed: 16 Mar 2016.

[3] Beaudoin, J. E. 2012. Context and Its Role in the Digital Preservation of Cultural Objects. D-Lib Magazine, 18, 11/12. http://www.dlib.org/dlib/november12/beaudoin/11beaudoin1.html, Accessed: 16 Mar 2016.

[4] Leveson, N.G. 2000. Intent Specifications: An Approach to Building Human-Centered Specifications. IEEE Trans. Softw. Eng. 26, 1, pp. 15-35. http://www.safeware-eng.com/system%20and%20software%20safety%20publications/Intent%20Specifications.htm, Accessed: 16 Mar 2016.

[5] Johnson, C. 2000. Forensic Software Engineering and the Need for New Approaches to Accident Investigation. Proc. 19th Int. Conf. on Computer Safety, Reliability and Security (SAFECOMP '00), Floor Koornneef and Mein van der Meulen (Eds.). Springer-Verlag, London, UK, Draft version: http://www.dcs.gla.ac.uk/~johnson/papers/forensic_se/. Accessed: 16 Mar 2016.

[6] Webb, C., Pearson, D., Koerbin, P. 2013. 'Oh, you wanted us to preserve that?!' Statements of Preservation Intent for the National Library of Australia's Digital Collections. D-Lib Magazine, 19, 1/2. http://www.dlib.org/dlib/january13/webb/01webb.html, Accessed: 16 Mar 2016.

[7] Lagos, N., Waddington, S., Vion-Dury, J.-Y. 2015. On the Preservation of Evolving Digital Content - The Continuum Approach and Relevant Metadata Models. Metadata and Semantics Research, 544, E. Garoufallou, R. J. Hartley, and P. Gaitanou (Eds). Cham: Spring. Intern. Pub., pp. 15–26.

[8] Kontopoulos, E., Riga, M., Mitzias, P., Andreadis, S., Stavropoulos, T., Konstantinidis, K., Maronidis, A., Karakostas, A., Tachos, S., Kaltsa, V., Tsagiopoulou, M., Darányi, S., Wittek, P., Gill, A., Tonkin, E. 2016. Modelling contextualized Semantics. Deliverable 4.4 – PERICLES project, pp.17-19. http://pericles-project.eu/uploads/files/PERICLES_WP4_D4_4_Modelling_Contextualised_Semantics.pdf. Accessed: 11 Jul 2016.

[9] Australian Government Recordkeeping Metadata Standard Version 2.2 Implementation Guidelines. 2011. pp. 52-53.

[10] Tzitzikas, Y., Marketakis, Y., Antoniou, G. Task-Based Dependency Management for the Preservation of Digital Objects Using Rules. Artif. Intel.: Theories, Models and App., pp. 265–74. Springer Berlin Heidelberg, 2010.

[11] Horrocks, I., Patel-Schneider P.F., Boley, H., Tabet, S., Grosof, B., Dean, M. 2004. SWRL: A Semantic Web Rule Language Combining OWL and RuleML. http://www.w3.org/Submission/SWRL/. 15 Mar 2016.

[12] Beckett, D., Berners-Lee, T., Prud'hommeaux, E., Carothers, G. RDF 1.1 Turtle - Terse RDF Triple Language. W3C Recommendation 25 February 2014. https://www.w3.org/TR/turtle/. Accessed: 16 Mar 2016.

[13] Vion-Dury, J.-Y., Lagos, N., Kontopoulos, E., Riga, M., Mitzias, P., Meditskos, G., Waddington, S., Laurenson, P., Kompatsiaris, Y. 2015. Designing for Inconsistency – The Dependency-based PERICLES Approach. In: New Trends in Databases and Inf. Sys. Spring. Inter. Pub., pp. 458-467.

[14] Vion-Dury, J.-Y., Lagos, N. 2015. Semantic Version Management based on Formal Certification. (ICSOFT-PT 2015) – Proc. of the 10th Int. Conf. on Soft. Paradigm Trends. (Eds.) Pascal Lorenz and Marten van Sinderen and Jorge Cardoso. pp. 19-30. Colmar, Alsace, France.

[15] Cuoq, P. When in doubt, express intent, and leave the rest to the compiler. http://trust-in-soft.com/when-in-doubt-express-intent-and-leave-the-rest-to-the-compiler/. 15 Mar 2016.

[16] Khodabandelou,G., Hug, C., Deneckère, R., Salinesi, C. 2014. Unsupervised discovery of intentional process models from event logs. Proc. 11th Work. Conf. on Mining Soft. Repo. (MSR 2014). ACM, New York, NY, USA, 282-291.

[17] Marketakis, Y., Tzitzikas, Y. Dependency Management for Digital Preservation Using Semantic Web Technologies. Int. Journal on Digital Libraries 10(4): 159-77, 2009.

[18] PREMIS Data Dictionary for Preservation Metadata (Official Web Site), The Library of congress, USA. www.loc.gov/standards/premis/. Accessed: 16 Mar 2016.

[19] Moreau, L., Clifford, B., Freire, J., Futrelle, J., Gil, Y., Groth, P., Kwasnikowska, N., Miles, S., Missier, P., Myers, J., Plale, B., Simmhan, Y., Stephan, E., Van den Bussche, J. 2011. The Open Provenance Model core specification (v1.1). Fut. Gen. Comp. Sys., 27, (6), 743-756. http://eprints.soton.ac.uk/271449/1/opm.pdf. 16 Mar 2016.

[20] Casotto, A. 1997. Run time dependency management facility for controlling change propagation utilizing relationship graph. US5634056 A.

[21] Tzitzikas, Y. Dependency Management for the Preservation of Digital Information. Dat. and Exp. Sys. App., pp. 582-92. Springer Berlin Heidelberg, 2007.

[22] Dam, K. Hoa., Winikoff, M. & Padgham, L. 2006 An agent-oriented approach to change propagation in software evolution. Australian Soft. Eng. Conf. (ASWEC 2006), pp. 309-318. Australia. http://ro.uow.edu.au/cgi/viewcontent.cgi?article=1435&context=eispapers. Accessed: 16 Mar 2016.

Schema-aware Extended Annotation Graphs

Vincent Barrellon
Univ Lyon, INSA-Lyon
CNRS, LIRIS, UMR5205
F-69621, Villeurbanne, France
firstname.lastname@insa-lyon.fr

Pierre-Edouard Portier
Univ Lyon, INSA-Lyon
CNRS, LIRIS, UMR5205
F-69621, Villeurbanne, France
firstname.lastname@insa-lyon.fr

Sylvie Calabretto
Univ Lyon, INSA-Lyon
CNRS, LIRIS, UMR5205
F-69621, Villeurbanne, France
firstname.lastname@insa-lyon.fr

Olivier Ferret
Univ Lyon, Lyon 2
CNRS, IHRIM, UMR5317
F-69365, Lyon, France
firstname.lastname@univ-lyon2.fr

ABSTRACT

Multistructured (M-S) documents were introduced as an answer to the need of ever more expressive data models for scholarly annotation, as experienced in the frame of Digital Humanities. Many proposals go beyond XML, that is the gold standard for annotation, and allow the expression of multilevel, concurrent annotation. However, most of them lack support for algorithmic tasks like validation and querying, despite those being central in most of their application contexts.

In this paper, we focus on two aspects of annotation: data model expressiveness and validation. We introduce extended Annotation Graphs (eAG), a highly expressive graph-based data model, fit for the enrichment of multimedia resources. Regarding validation of M-S documents, we identify algorithmic complexity as a limiting factor. We advocate that this limitation may be bypassed provided validation can be checked *by construction*, that is by constraining the shape of data during its very manufacture. So far as we know, no existing validation mechanism for graph-structured data meets this goal. We define here such a mechanism, based on the simulation relation, somehow following a track initiated in Dataguides. We prove that thanks to this mechanism, the validity of M-S data regarding a given schema can be guaranteed without any algorithmic check.

Keywords

Multistructured data model; Validation; Schemas; Graphs.

1. INTRODUCTION

Multistructured (M-S) data models have been a hot topic for over a decade. Correlated to the rise of Digital Humanities, they ground on the fact that a single hierarchy is not always sufficient to represent annotated resources [6], contrasting with the setting of XML-based languages as a standard for scholarly annotations.

DocEng 2016 Vienna, Austria
© 2016 Copyright held by the owner/author(s). Publication rights licensed to ACM.
ISBN 978-1-4503-4438-8/16/09...$15.00
DOI: http://dx.doi.org/10.1145/2960811.2960816

Hence, "multistructured" is then to be understood by comparison with XML: annotating somehow means *structuring* data (a well-formed XML document fits into a tree *structure*); "multi" suggests M-S data models handle multiple, interlaced hierarchical annotations over the same data. Many models have been proposed [18]. However, the enhanced expressiveness resulting from less constrained structural foundations, compared to XML, comes at a cost: M-S models often lack support for tasks like querying or validation which are commonplace in XML.

Indeed, validating highly expressive data is challenging, due to a general trade-off between data models expressiveness and algorithmic complexity. The NEXPTIME complexity of OWL/DL inference [20] will serve as a striking example of how costly the validation of highly expressive graph-structured documents can be. This trade-off is so pregnant and restrictive that it applies to XML [23]. Hence the need for alternative validation strategies for M-S data.

We introduce here "simulation-based validation by construction" for M-S data. Our main results are the following:

- We designed eAG, an expressive M-S data model based on Annotation Graphs (AGs) [2]. We strengthened the AG model in order to address its main deficiencies, like a shared representation for inclusion and cooccurrence and a limited ability to handle composite resources.

- We identified the *simulation* relation, first used for the structural description of semistructured data [5], as a promising mechanism for eAG validation. We designed SeAG, a simulation-based schema model for eAG.

- We defined a coupled representation for SeAGs and eAGs so that, given the representation of a schema, only valid eAGs can be represented: this is "validation by construction". This enables to guarantee the validity of rich M-S data *without algorithmic check*, bypassing the trade-off between expressiveness and complexity, when schema definition can precede annotation.

- We found that the eAG/SeAG model is compatible with classical, *a posteriori* validation. In this case, checking whether an eAG is valid against any schema can be decided in polynomial time ($O(|edges| \cdot |nodes|)$).

- We finally proved that for hierarchical data, SeAG syntactic validation is not less straitening than Relax-NG.

"Validation by construction" can be seen as a special *on-the-fly* validation mechanism. First, we prove the interest of such validation in a (not exclusive) application context. A panorama of M-S models and validation mechanisms follows. Eventually, we formally introduce eAGs and SeAGs.

2. APPLICATION CONTEXT

Among other application fields of M-S data, eAG/SeAG are particularly fit for scholarly digital publishing projects. Four such projects are associated to this work, dealing with Diderot's *Encyclopédie*, Stendhal's *Journaux et Papiers*, Desanti's archive and Flaubert's documentation for *Bouvard and Pécuchet*[1]. Such projects may benefit from a M-S data model supporting on-the-fly validation for two reasons.

Data model expressiveness. Editors are mainly expert humanists; their aim is to express complex and accurate information about the corpus they edit through annotation. They may want to annotate data according to several competing paradigms, resulting in non-hierarchical annotations[2]. For economical reasons, not all editorial projects benefit from technical support, which means editors often face annotation encoding alone. Thus, there is a potential discrepancy between the technicality of annotation and the technical skills of the editors. One (formally elegant) way to bypass this discrepancy is to provide them with very expressive M-S data models, so that non-hierarchical information encoding, that is tricky in XML, becomes straightforward.

Editorial routine. Editorial routines starts with the definition of the *editorial policy*, which sets the nature of the critical enrichments. In XML-based digital publishing projects, *schemas* are a common way to represent this policy. Transcribing the editorial principles into a schema guarantees a certain harmony in annotation – hence the need for a schema-aware M-S data model. Moreover, most XML tools provide the user with content assist (i.e. on-the-fly validation) features, acting as an authoring tool that suggests elements according to the editing context. This feature, that helps commitment into deep annotation, is valuable in a publishing context, where schemas are defined prior to annotation. This is worth translating into the M-S world.

3. RELATED WORKS

XML-TEI is the standard for scholarly publishing. It provides scholars with a modular, versatile and documented schema, and user-friendly XML editors are plenty. Moreover, XML is a natural candidate for annotation. Annotation models need to support: 1. linear characterization (e.g. along *the* reading dimension – if unique), 2. representation of inclusion (e.g. to encode *the* material structure of a text – if unique), 3. of disseminated elements and links. XML does the first two well (in case of uniqueness, above): elements are ordered along the text; nesting represents inclusion.

Still, XML does not suit some common annotation patterns [6]. Overlapping elements are not allowed; links do not have a syntactical representation, so they need separate validation (e.g. with Schematron); non inclusive nesting, frequent in case of multiple annotation, cannot be represented. Some works aim at conforming TEI-XML with more expressive data models [6, 7], but they either fail to tackle some of XML inherent limitations (e.g. *nesting* representing *inclusion*) or lose compliance with XML tools (XSD, XQuery, etc.) [18].

Multistructured data models.

Formally speaking, annotated resources can be regarded as labelled graphs [5]. From there on, the expressive limitations above appear as a consequence of the overly restricted family of graphs upon which XML is based: trees. This formal reasoning gave birth to Competing markup or Multistructured (M-S) data models [18]. The term "multistructured" refers to what *structure* means in XML: in a M-S data model, well-formedness extends from trees to (at least) forests, graphs whose connected subgraphs are trees.

CONCUR [9] precisely enhances SGML to support *forests* of elements. Each tree is defined in a DTD; inside a CONCUR document, the tags explicitly relate to the tree they belong to. MuLaX [11] transposes this philosophy to XML, despite XML documents referring to at most one schema. A MuLaX document is a mix of overlapping elements from disjoint hierarchies; each hierarchy defines a projection, yielding a well-formed XML document that can be validated against a schema. Those solutions, however, do not support cross-hierarchies constraints; self-overlap is also problematic[3]. MSXD [3] implements such constraints. Its formal model is a forest, but unlike the above solutions, the different trees are instantiated in distinct documents. RelaxNG schemas validate each. The relative position of elements from different trees can be constrained by Allen's relations.

Other models rely on well identified and wider graph families like multitrees, where trees may share nodes (TexMecs [12]), multicolored trees (MCT, [13]) or restrained, acyclic polyarchies (GODDAG [22]). Multitrees can be handled by an ingenious grammar-based validation language, dubbed Rabbit/duck Grammar [21]. While checking some crosswise constraints, a Rabbit/duck Grammar extracts hierarchies from the multitree structured document; the extracts are then validated against XML schemas. Rabbit/duck Grammars manage self-overlap.

More expressive standoff, graph-based models, exemplified by LMNL [27], have been proposed. A LMNL document is a layered directed acyclic graph where elements are labelled ranges from a character stream. Since they are text streams themselves, even annotations can be annotated. Creole, a powerful grammar-based schema language, validates LMNL [26]. Annotation Graphs [2] is another model based upon a handy notion of chronology for multimedia corpus annotation. A few RDF-based annotation models have also been proposed, amongst which EARMARK [17], which is built against a dedicated OWL ontology that adds semantics to the logical, directed cyclic graph formalism that RDF is, stands out.

M-S validation : algorithmic complexity.

As detailed above, most M-S validation mechanisms proceed tree after tree, providing the final user with a clumsy modelling tool. MSXD only enables to express weak constraints betwees trees. RdGs, which somehow manages to embrace multitrees, fall short when it comes to validating more general graphs. An explanation to that glass ceiling might be found in time complexity[4]. In general, the more expressive the data model, the higher the complexity for the related processing tasks [23, 15, 14, 20]. This applies, at least, to grammar-based and rule-based validation.

The three main validation languages for XML, namely DTD, W3C XML Schema (XSD) and RelaxNG, are commonly modelled as tree grammars, or tree automaton [15]. Although not equal, the languages that those schemas recognise fit into regular tree lan-

---

[1] The project's Websites are: enccre.academie-sciences.fr ; manuscrits-de-stendhal.org ; archive.desanti.huma-num.fr ; dossiers-flaubert.fr
[2] See [6], ch. 20.

---

[3] Since individual schemas cannot define overlap, an arbitrary number of schemas is required to validate multiple, self-overlapping elements [26]. This also applies to MSXD.
[4] For validation, time- prevails over space-complexity [15].

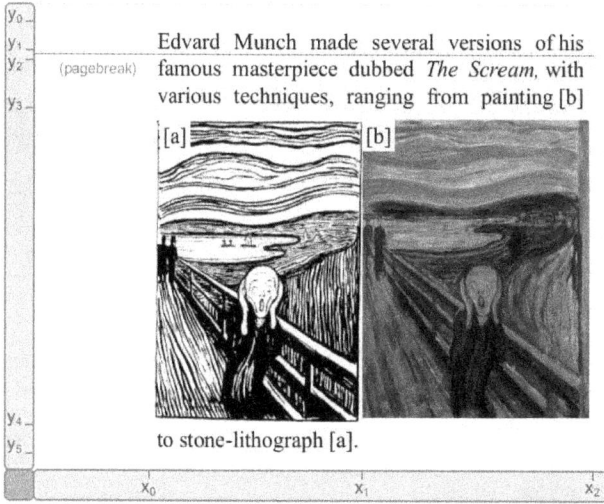

Edvard Munch made several versions of his
(pagebreak) famous masterpiece dubbed *The Scream*, with
various techniques, ranging from painting [b]

[a]   [b]

to stone-lithograph [a].

Figure 1: Document showing overlap, a figure enclosed in text and internal references.

guages[5], for which validation can be done in linear time in the documents' size [14]. Other tree languages may not even be decidable for interpretation [23], which is part of validation in RelaxNG and XSD (see Figure 5).

Little information is available about the complexity of the advanced M-S validation mechanisms. The processing cost of the initial MSXD schema mechanism, combining RelaxNG with Allen's relations, was left undetermined [3]. In the end, it seems not to have been implemented as such [4]: XQuery extensions were designed as surrogates for Allen's relations and cross-hierarchies constraints rather checked by querying the data. Creole, the only consistent schema mechanism validating documents with layered, overlapping annotations, was prototyped using XSLT; despite RelaxNG-inspired optimization, the result was considered "too slow" [26] – no other implementation followed, unfortunately.

RDF-based M-S data models suffer from the same trade-off. OWL reasoners are sometimes used as validators [8, 17]. However, using OWL rules to validate a document is problematic. First, OWL-Full is undecidable and the two main restrictions, OWL-DL and OWL-Lite, perform in NEXPTIME and EXPTIME respectively [20]. Second, OWL rules are not natively interpreted as integrity constraints[6], resulting in a weak validation mechanism [20]. Experimental techniques to by-pass those limitations seem to result in huge execution times [25].

4. PROPOSITION

The above enlightens a trade-off between expressiveness and complexity – trade-off that expresses, to be accurate, *inside the frame of a given validation technique*. For instance, while Brzozowski derivative-based validation [26] runs in linear time for regular tree languages, the same approach does not extend easily to more general graphs. This leads to question the use and tweak of XML and RDF tools for M-S validation, precisely because, as well engineered systems, they are already optimized for their native use.

Simulation [19, 5], is an interesting alternative to rule- and grammar-based descriptive formalisms. A simulation is a relation over (often rooted) directed labelled graphs. Informally, the existence of a rooted simulation of a graph B by a graph A implies that all the paths of B starting from its root have a matching path in A, whose label sequence is identical. Thus, A describes the structure of B, because all the patterns in B somehow have a match in A. Conversely, A behaves as a graph schema: it validates the graphs that contain only patterns defined in A, i.e. that A simulates.

Validation by simulation was first operated for semistructured (S-S) data [24, 1]. The Object Exchange Model (OEM) underlying S-S data is a cyclic, unordered, directed labelled graph. Natively, a S-S database is schemaless; Dataguides [10] or Graph Schemas [5] are inferred from the data. They are graphs that simulate the S-S database, providing a structural description that can be exploited for querying purposes. Simulation check performs in $O(|edges| \cdot |vertices|)$ [19], which is acceptably low for general graph-structured data validation.

Still, despite providing an expressive data model[7] and an appropriate schema mechanism, as far as we know, S-S model was never tuned for annotation. Indeed, it lacks a clear representation of inclusion, a notion of order or a way to index nodes along reading dimensions to support linear annotation; moreover, since Dataguides and Graph Schemas are inferred from the data, they cannot be used as authoring tools.

Still, because the OEM is so general, the principle of a simulation-based validation is not restricted to S-S data but "can be applied easily to any graph-based data model" [10]. We propose here a data model, fine-tuned to comply with simulation-based validation, as we will elaborate.

4.1 Data model: eAG

The data model we propose is extrapolated from Annotation Graphs (AG) [2], hence named extended AG (eAG). It is a standoff markup formalism. The toy document represented in figure 1 will serve to illustrate eAG's expressive power. It is made of one paragraph spanning over two pages, whose text locally refers to parts of a figure. The figure itself, *accidentally*, nests inside the paragraph (without being *part* of it).

An eAG $G = (V, E)$ is a directed, connected and labelled cyclic graph, with edges E and vertices V. It has only one root and one leaf, denoted $rt(G)$ and $lf(G)$ respectively. It verifies all the properties that follow.

Notation. In the following, $v \lfloor e \rfloor v'$ denotes the graph made out of the edge e connecting the node v to v'. $label(e)$ yields the value of the label of e.

First, we define chronologies, that is how locations in composite resources can be made reference to.

Definition 1. A (general) chronology is any ordered set $\langle T, \leq \rangle$. Be then $\mathscr{C}$ a set of strings called "chronometer names". Be $m \in \mathscr{C}$. The reference space associated to m is a unique ordered set $\langle \mathbb{T}_m, \leq_m \rangle$. A chronology over $m \in \mathscr{C}$ is an ordered set $\langle T, \leq_m \rangle$ so that $T \subseteq \mathbb{T}_m$.

Definition 2. (Concatenation) Be $\langle T_a, \leq_a \rangle$ and $\langle T_b, \leq_b \rangle$ chronologies. $\langle T_a \cdot T_b, \leq_{a,b} \rangle$ defines a chronology over $T_a \cup T_b$ iff the following relation $\leq_{a,b}$ defines an order over $T_a \cup T_b$: For any $t, t' \in T_a \cup T_b$, then:
- $t =_{a,b} t' \Leftrightarrow \exists x \in \mathscr{C} \mid (t, t') \in \mathbb{T}_x^2 \wedge t =_x t'$
- $t <_{a,b} t' \Leftrightarrow \exists x \in \mathscr{C} \mid (t, t') \in \mathbb{T}_x^2 \wedge t \leq_x t'$
     or $\nexists x \in \mathscr{C} \mid (t, t') \in \mathbb{T}_x^2 \wedge (t, t') \in T_a \times T_b$.

---

[5]Local tree languages (DTDs) restrict single-typed tree languages (XSD), restricting regular tree languages (RelaxNG).

[6]The Open World Assumption and the No Unique Name feature together allow to assess an assertion is verified, but not that is is not.

[7]Surprisingly, the OEM is referred to as "essentially equivalent to XML" on the Lore project website (infolab.stanford.edu/lore), which was a pioneering OEM DBMS before migrating to XML.

Table 1: Allowed suffixes per label class and the resulting class. "-" stands for "undefined".

↪ suffixed by	$\varnothing$	:In	:Out	:Att	:LinkTo
$l \in \mathscr{L}_\varnothing$	$\mathscr{L}_\varnothing$	$\mathscr{L}_{In}$	$\mathscr{L}_{Out}$	$\mathscr{L}_{Att}$	$\mathscr{L}_{LinkTo}$
$l \in \mathscr{L}_{In}$	$\mathscr{L}_{In}$	-	-	-	-
$l \in \mathscr{L}_{Out}$	$\mathscr{L}_{Out}$	-	-	-	-
$l \in \mathscr{L}_{Att}$	$\mathscr{L}_{Att}$	$\mathscr{L}_{In}$	$\mathscr{L}_{Out}$	-	-
$l \in \mathscr{L}_{LinkTo}$	$\mathscr{L}_{LinkTo}$	-	-	-	-

Example 1. Be $T_1 = \{0,1,2\}$ and $\leq_1$ the order on naturals. Be $T_2 = \{X,Y\}$ and $\leq_2$ the lexical order. $\langle T_1 \cdot T_2, \leq_{1,2}\rangle$ defines a chronology, where $2 <_{1,2} b$ for instance. Now, given $T_3 = \{2\}$ and $T_4 = \{4\}$ equipped with the natural order, $\langle T_1 \cdot T_2 \cdot T_3, \leq_{1,2,3}\rangle$ does not define a chronology (the antisymmetry would not hold), while $\langle T_1 \cdot T_2 \cdot T_4, \leq_{1,2,4}\rangle$ does.

Definition 3. (Inclusion) Be $\langle T_a, \leq_a\rangle$ and $\langle T_b, \leq_b\rangle$ chronologies. We say $\langle T_b, \leq_b\rangle \subseteq \langle T_a, \leq_a\rangle$ iff $\exists (T_1, T_2) \subset T_a^2$ so that $\langle T_1 \cdot T_b \cdot T_2, \leq_{a,b,a}\rangle$ defines a chronology.

Example 2. In Example 1, $\langle T_2, \leq_2\rangle \subseteq \langle T_1 \cdot T_4, \leq_{1,4}\rangle$.

This notion of chronology enables to index a composite, yet continuous content.

Illustration, part 1. Consider the second page in Figure 1. It contains three modules, respectively containing two text lines, a figure, and one line. Be the three chronologies: $\langle T_y, \leq_y\rangle$ based on a vertical descending dimension that is not continuous over page changes, with $T_y = \{y_2, y_3, y_4, y_5\}$ (in ascending order), for the three modules delimitation; $\langle T_x, \leq_x\rangle$ based on an horizontal left-to-right dimension, with $T_x = \{x_0, x_1, x_2\}$, for the figure decomposition into images; $\langle T_c, \leq_c\rangle$, with $T_c = \{41, 83, 84, 129, 130, 154\}$ [8], based on characters (including linebreaks) count, for lines indexation. By double inclusion, we can define a chronology $\langle T, \leq\rangle$ over $T_c \cup T_x \cup T_y$, so that $y_2 < 41 < 83 < 84 < 129 < y_3 < x_0 < x_1 < x_2 < y_4 < 130 < 154 < y_5$.

Definition 4. (References) In an eAG, a reference $ref(v)$ is associated to each node v. For each v, there is a unique reference space $\langle \mathbb{T}_c, \leq\rangle_c$ so that $ref(v) \in \mathbb{T}_c$.

Two references belonging to the same chronology and sharing the same reference space identify a range within the resources to be annotated. Ranges can be annotated by creating two nodes bearing the corresponding references, connected by (at least) a directed, labelled edge. In this simple case, the label constitutes the content of the annotation.

To structure further annotation, we define a label semantics to indicate that an annotation is an element, a link, or is included within another, or is an attribute of another.

Definition 5. (Labels) Be a special character ε [9]. Be $\mathscr{L}_\varnothing$, $\varepsilon \notin \mathscr{L}_\varnothing$, a set of strings that do not contain the character ":". $\mathscr{L}_0 = \mathscr{L}_\varnothing \cup \{\varepsilon\}$ is the set of unsuffixed labels. Additionally, be $\mathscr{S} = \{:In, :Out, :Att, :LinkTo\}$ the set of suffixes. Labels can be iteratively suffixed according to the rules given in table 1. Those rules also define classes of labels, e.g. $\mathscr{L}_{In}$ the set of labels whose last suffix is :In. The set of all labels $\mathscr{L}$ is the union of all the preceding classes.

---

[8] The first line of page 2 starts at character 41, etc.

[9] ε stands for a blank, or void, annotation.

In the following, given two strings l and s, $s \subset l$ denotes the fact that l contains the substring s.

One asset of eAG is a clear distinction between accidental nesting and inclusion representation. We define here inclusion, based upon the :In and :Out suffixes.

Definition 6. (h-equality and dominance). Be $G = (V,E)$ a graph, and $(\{v_0...v_N\}, \{e_0...e_{N-1}\})$ an h-path of G. Be $n, m \in \mathbb{N}$; $0 \leq n \leq m \leq N$.
v_n is said to be h-equal to v_m, denoted $v_n =^h v_m$, iff:
1. $n = m$ or
2. $\forall j \in [n, m-1], label(e_j) \in \mathscr{L}_0 \cup \mathscr{L}_{Att}$ or
3. $v_n \not\geq^h v_m \wedge v_m \not\geq^h v_n$ and $\forall k, l$; $n < k \leq l < m$, $v_n \geq^h v_k \wedge v_n \geq^h v_l \wedge v_m \geq^h v_k \wedge v_m \geq^h v_l$ and $v_k =^h v_l \vee (v_k >^h v_l \vee v_l >^h v_k)$ [see right below].
When $n \neq m$, v_n and v_m are said to border-h-dominate the nodes $v_i, i \in [n+1, m-1]$, denoted $(v_n, v_m) >^h_b v_i$, iff:
1. $\exists l \in \mathscr{L}$; $label(e_n) = l:In$ and $label(e_{m-1}) = l:Out$ and
2. $\forall j < k \in [n+1, m-1], v_j =^h v_k$
   or $\exists (l,m) \in [j, k-1] \times [k+1, m-1]; (v_l, v_m) >^h_b v_k \wedge v_j =^h v_l$
   or $\exists (l,m) \in [n+1, j-1] \times [j+1, k]; (v_l, v_m) >^h_b v_j \wedge v_k =^h v_m$.
Be $x, y \in [0, N]$. v_x h-dominates v_y, denoted $v_x >^h v_y$, iff $\exists n, m \in \mathbb{N}$; $0 \leq n \leq m \leq N \mid (v_n, v_m) >^h_b v_y \wedge v_x =^h v_n$.

Property 1. $\forall v \lfloor e \rfloor v' \subseteq G, v \neq^h v' \wedge v \not\geq^h v' \wedge v' \not\geq^h v$ is equivalent to ":LinkTo" $\subset label(e)$.

Property 2. Be $G = (V,E)$. $\forall v \lfloor e \rfloor v' \subseteq G$ we enforce that:
$label(e) \in \mathscr{L}_{In} \Leftrightarrow (v >^h v')$ and $label(e) \in \mathscr{L}_{Out} \Leftrightarrow (v' >^h v)$

This means that an edge labelled $l:In$ does not go without a h-dominated path ending by an edge labelled $l:Out$.

Definition 7. (h-levels) Be an eAG G. Since G is connected, $\forall v \in V, \exists P = (V_P, E_P) \subseteq G$ a root-to-leaf path so that $v \in V_P$. The h-level of v in P is the biggest subset $N \subseteq V_P$ so that $\forall v' \in N, v' =^h v$. (h-levels direct inclusion) Be a path P, N_x, N_y h-levels in P. N_y is directly included in N_x, denoted $N_x \sqsupset^h N_y$, iff:
1. $\forall (v_x, v_y) \in N_x \times N_y, v_x >^h v_y$ and
2. $\nexists v \in V \mid v_x >^h v >^h v_y$.
(h-levels inclusion) The h-inclusion is the transitive closure of $\sqsubset^h$. It is denoted $\sqsubset^h$.
($\mathscr{P}r$ and $\mathscr{S}c$) An h-level N is primary (secondary), denoted $N \in \mathscr{P}r$ (resp. $N \in \mathscr{S}c$) iff $\forall N' \sqsubseteq^h N, \forall (v, v') \in N \times N'$, if $\exists e$ so that $v' \lfloor e \rfloor v \subseteq G \vee v \lfloor e \rfloor v' \subseteq G$, then ":LinkTo" $\not\subset label(e) \Rightarrow$ ":Att" $\not\subset label(e)$ (resp. ":Att" $\subset label(e)$).

Property 3. Be $G = (V,E)$. We enforce that:
1. For all N h-level of G, $N \in \mathscr{P}r \cup \mathscr{S}c$.
2. For all $N \in \mathscr{S}c, \exists N' \in \mathscr{P}r; N' \sqsupset^h N$.

The above provides us with a definition of inclusion, on which to found a definition of elements and attributes.

Definition 8. (Element, attribute) Be $G = (V,E)$ an eAG. An element (resp. attribute) is a subgraph H of G so that:
1. $H = v \lfloor e \rfloor v' \mid label(e) \in \mathscr{L}_0$ (resp. $\mathscr{L}_{Att}$) or
2. $H = v_1 \lfloor e_1 \cdots e_{M-1} \rfloor v_M$ so that:
   a. $\forall i \in [1, M-1], (v_1, v_M) >^h_b v_i$ and
   b. $\exists N_H \in \mathscr{P}r$ (resp. $\mathscr{S}c$); $v_1, v_M \in N_H$ and
   c. $\nexists H_1 = v_1^1 \lfloor e_1^1 \cdots e_{M_1-1}^1 \rfloor v_{M_1}^1, H_2 = v_1^2 \lfloor e_1^2 \cdots e_{M_2-1}^2 \rfloor v_{M_2}^2$ verifying the above conditions a. and b., with $N_{H_1} = N_{H_2}$ and $e_1^1 = e_1 \neq e_1^2 \wedge e_{M_2-1}^2 = e_{M-1} \neq e_{M_1-1}^1$.

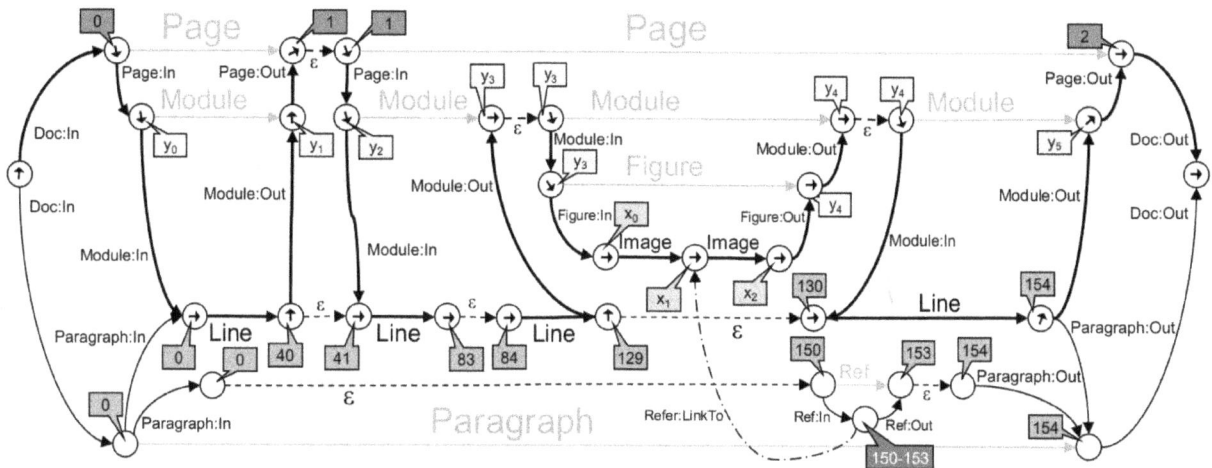

Figure 2: An eAG representing Figure 1 and a way to browse through it (arrows). Grey edges are for reading assistance (they span over the paths defining a structured element). Speech balloons show reference values (shades differenciate between chronometers), from a chronology extending $\langle T, \leq \rangle$ (cf.*Illustration, part 1*) in order to detail the content of Page one and a Ref ("[a]" in the text) between characters 150 and 153.

This defines consecutive elements: two elements A and B are consecutive if, say, $root(B) = leaf(A)$. We can extend that notion to A and B only separated by a series of ε edges. Elements can also include one another, based on the previous definition. We go further and add the following property.

Property 4. Be $A \neq B$ two elements. We enforce that $(lf(A), rt(A)) >_b^h rt(B) \Leftrightarrow (lf(A), rt(A)) >_b^h lf(B)$.

It means that two elements whose roots and leaves are either on the same h-level or on h-levels included one into the other either are *consecutive* (directly or not) or *include* one another. Paths connecting the root of an eAG to its node and made only out of consecutive and inclusive elements will be referred to as "linear annotation paths". An eAG contains several such paths which, individually, represent a given annotation paradigm *à la* XML, since they can be modelled as ordered trees of elements. However, in an eAG, some elements can very well appear simultaneously on several such paths (c.f. *Illustration, part 2*). This means element hierarchies share items: an eAG can be modelled by no less than a multitree. Eventually, because edges whose label contains ":LinkTo" are unrestricted, they can connect any nodes together, which may result in a cyclic graph.

Illustration, part 2. (Linear annotation paths) Figure 2 shows an eAG representing the document illustrated in Figure 1. It contains three competing linear annotation paths. The arrowed path provides a layout-oriented Page description, fragmented into Modules, Lines, Figures and Images. Another identifies a Ref inside the text of the Paragraph. The last path splits Paragraphs into Lines. Lines are *shared elements* with the first path; they are also *the only* shared elements. For instance, the Paragraph *does not* include the Figure element, since there is no h-inclusion between the h-levels where the roots and leaves of the two elements appear.
(Structured element, Link) The Ref element is made out of two edges labelled Ref:In and Ref:Out. It annotates the string "[a]" from inside the text. Graph-wise, it is a structured element, since it contains more than one edge. It is also void, as there is but a node between its two constituting edges; still, this node points towards the second Image on another annotation path by means of an edge suffixed:LinkTo.

Property 5. (Covering chronologies) We enforce that:
1. Be an h-level N. $\exists \langle T, \leq \rangle$ a chronology, $\exists ! c \in \mathscr{C}$ so that $\forall v \in N, ref(v) \in T \cap \mathbb{T}_c$. This defines a sub-chronology $\langle T_N, \leq_N \rangle$ so that $T_N = T \cap \mathbb{T}_c$ and $\leq_N = \leq_c$.
2. Be $(N, N') \in \mathscr{P}r^2$. $N' \sqsubseteq N \Rightarrow \langle T_{N'}, \leq_{N'} \rangle \subseteq \langle T_N, \leq_N \rangle$.
3. Be $v \lfloor e \rfloor v'$ so that $\exists (N, N') \in \mathscr{P}r^2; (v, v') \in N \times N'$ and :LinkTo $\not\sqsubseteq label(e)$. Point 1. or 2. (depending on $N = N'$ or $N' \neq N$) ensure that there is a chronology $\langle T, \leq \rangle$ so that $ref(v), ref(v') \in T$. Then $ref(v) \leq ref(v')$.

Linear annotation only makes sense provided there is a dimension along which the elements flow: in particular, Property 5 means that the structural order in which elements are positioned along a linear annotation path must not contradict the order of the references of their nodes. As a consequence, there is always a covering chronology for a linear annotation path. However, it is possible to annotate a resource without, or against, any chronological order, thanks to the unconstrained edges whose label contains :LinkTo.

Definition 9. (Accidental nesting) Be an eAG G and A, B two elements. B is accidentally nested in A iff there are:
- two linear annotation paths $P_1 = (V_1, E_1), P_2 = (V_2, E_2)$, their covering chronologies $\langle T_1, \leq_1 \rangle$, $\langle T_2, \leq_2 \rangle$ and $N_A \subseteq V_1$, $N_B \subseteq V_2$ the h-levels (in P_1 and P_2 resp.) so that $root(A), leaf(A) \in N_A$ and $root(B), leaf(B) \in N_B$, and
- $c \in \mathscr{C}, \exists N, N'; N \subseteq^h N_A, N' \supseteq^h N_B$ verifying $N \subseteq V_1, N' \subseteq V_2$, and $\exists (v_\chi, v_\phi) \in N^2, (v_x, v_y) \in N'^2$, so that:
1. $ref(v_\chi), ref(v_\phi), ref(v_x), ref(v_y) \in \mathbb{T}_c$
2. $ref(root(A)) \leq_1 ref(v_\chi), ref(v_\phi) \leq_1 ref(leaf(A))$
3. $ref(v_x) \leq_2 ref(root(B)), ref(leaf(B)) \leq_2 ref(v_y)$
4. $ref(v_\chi) <_c ref(v_x) <_c ref(v_y) <_c ref(v_\phi)$.
(Overlap) A and B overlap (with A first) iff the above paths, h-levels, chronometer and nodes exist and verify:
1. $ref(v_\chi), ref(v_\phi), ref(v_x), ref(v_y) \in \mathbb{T}_c$
2. $ref(root(A)) \leq_1 ref(v_\chi) \leq_c ref(v_x) \leq_2 ref(root(B))$
3. $ref(leaf(A)) \leq_1 ref(v_\phi) \leq_c ref(v_y) \leq_2 ref(leaf(B))$.

Example 3. In Figure 2, since the elements Figure and Paragraph are not on the same linear annotation paths, they cannot include one another. However, Figure is accidentally nesting inside the Paragraph.

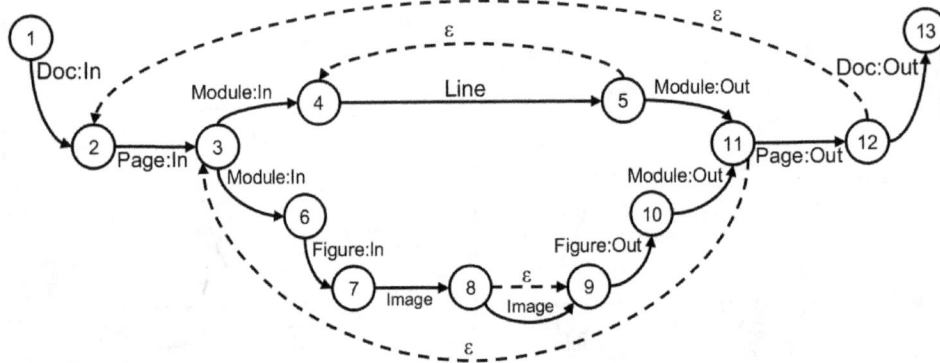

Figure 3: A schema for eAG. It validates the graph from Figure 2, restricted to the arrowed path.

Illustration, part 3. (Linear annotation paths) One can extend the composite chronology $\langle T, \leq \rangle$ defined in *Illustration, part 1* to cover the whole arrowed path in Figure 2, so that for any node v preceding a node v' along this path, $ref(v) \leq ref(v')$.

(Inter-chronometers comparisons) Cross-chronometer assessments can be made on an eAG. First example, because in $\langle T, \leq \rangle$, $x_2 < 130$, we know that from a (top-down) layout point of view, the second image precedes the last Line. (Cross-linear paths comparison) Cross-linear annotation path assessments can also be made, thanks to the notions of accidental nesting and overlap. E.g. Ref is accidentally nested in the last Module, because this Module h-includes the Line delimited by characters 130 and 154, while Ref ranges from character 150 to 153. Then, it is possible to assess that the Ref is located further than the last Image, from a descending layout point of view. The edge labelled `Refer:LinkTo` (which is a link) does not respect the inferred reference order, which is not contradictory with the eAG model.

4.2 Schema model

To sum up, an extended Annotation Graph is a connected, directed and labelled graph whose nodes bear references values. Informally, an eAG is composed of several linear annotation paths sharing items and connected together by :`LinkTo` edges.

We have defined linear annotation paths by some specific properties. Those properties, together with the graph model, define what a *well-formed* eAG is.

Now we define a schema model for eAG. Schemas are a means to define the allowed elements/attributes and their mutual relationships (consecutiveness, inclusion, existence of :`LinkTo` connexions) for the matching eAGs. Since elements, attributes and relationships have a homogeneous edge-based representation, eAG schemas needs be no more than a *graph description* formalism, which simulation is [5].

Definition 10. (SeAG) An eAG schema, denoted SeAG, is a directed, connected, labelled graph with one root and one leaf only. Its labels fall into Definition 5. It verifies Properties 1, 2, 3 and 4. Moreover, two nodes are not allowed to be connected by two edges with the same label.

Definition 11. (Node types) In order to describe the relationship between an eAG and a SeAG, we equip both graphs' nodes with two more values: a type value, and an identifier (see Definition 14). Within a SeAG, for two nodes v, v', we enforce that $type(v) = type(v') \Leftrightarrow v = v'$. Additionally, a type is associated to exactly one chronometer $c \in \mathscr{C}$.

Definition 12. (Simulation) Consider two rooted, directed labelled graphs $A = (V_A, E_A)$ and $B = (V_B, E_B)$. A simulation of B by A is a relation $R \in V_B \times V_A$ so that:
1. $(root(B), root(A)) \in R$ and
2. $(v_B, v_A) \in R \Rightarrow \forall v_B \lfloor e_B \rfloor v'_B \subseteq B, \exists (e_A, v_A) \in E_A \times V_A$ so that $v_A \lfloor e_A \rfloor v'_A \subseteq A \wedge label(e_A) = label(e_B) \wedge (v'_B, v'_A) \in R$. (Node-typed, rooted simulation) A node-typed simulation R verifies the above, plus $\forall (v_B, v_A) \in R, type(v_A) = type(v_B)$.

Example 4. Be A and B two rooted, connected graphs with one leaf. A simulates B implies that for all root-to-leaf path in B, there is a rooted path in A so that the sequences of labels along the two paths are equal. Conversely, given a graph A, building a graph B simulated by A restricts the possible label sequences along paths in the graph B:

Consider the graph A below, where the values in the nodes are their types. It is the Ott automaton [16] representing the regular expression $r = $X:In$(a|b)^*$X:Out. The graph B, whose label sequences along the root to node paths are words from the language of r, is simulated by A.

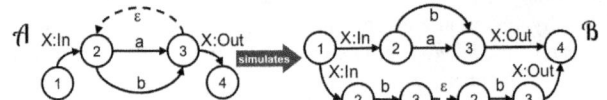

The simulation is easy to decipher here : it is made out of the couples (v_B, v_A) so that $type(v_B) = type(v_A)$.

Definition 13. Be S an SeAG and G an eAG. S validates G iff there is a rooted, node-typed simulation of G by S and $type(leaf(G)) = type(leaf(S))$. In this case, G is called an *instance* of S.

Illustration, part 4. The Figure 3 shows a SeAG. Read as an automaton, it says that:
1. Within a Doc element are one or more Page elements. The backwards ε edge that connects the node typed 12 to the node typed 2 ensures multiplicity.
2. Within a Page are one or more Modules.
3. Modules are defined alternatively as containing either one Line or more (path through nodes typed 3-4-5-11), or containing one Figure (path through nodes typed 3-6-7-8-9-10-11). Alternatives are represented by parallel paths.
4. Within a Figure are either one or two Images. Optionality is represented by the alternative between an element or an ε edge (i.e. by parallel paths, in harmony with point 3. above).

50

Discussion 1. (SeAG expressive power) As illustrated before, based on Ott's linear representation of regular expressions [16], a wide range of composite element contents can be expressed in an eAG: the | operator is represented by two parallel subpaths in the SeAG and the Kleene star operator by a backwards oriented ε edge; any combination is possible.

Importantly, the above automaton interpretation of SeAG only holds because of the well-formedness constraints for eAGs. For instance, the interpretation of the *cyclic* SeAG A in Example 4 as an Ott automaton, i.e. as a means to define an infinite set of *acyclic paths*, would not be correct without Property 5. Indeed, there is at least one cyclic graph that A simulates: A itself, but there is no way a graph structurally identical to A shall be an eAG. Consider A equipped with reference values on its nodes. Property 5, states that edges not suffixed :LinkTo go from nodes with a lower reference value to nodes with a higher one. Since the cyclic subgraph made out of the edges between the nodes typed 2 and 3 contains no :LinkTo, then whatever the reference values of its nodes, it cannot be part of an eAG. Conversely, the cycle in A will only be instantiated by acyclic paths (cf. graph B, Example 4) in the eAGs validated by A.

More generally, eAG data model and simulation-based validation make sense *together*. The following examples illustrate how the definition rules for eAG give sense to the SeAG formalism. First, an SeAG can express that two h-levels share elements: see graph A below. This SeAG does simulate the faulty graph B, where the inclusion semantics is lost (e.g. X:Out is missing), but since *for that reason*, regardless of its nodes references, B is not well-formed (see Property 2), it is not to be considered for validation. However, *A* validates the *well-formed* eAG C, which implements properly multitree annotation with shared items between h-levels.

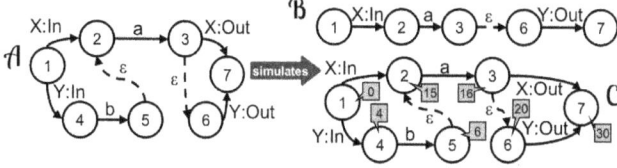

Thanks to the same Property 2 in the eAG data model, an SeAG can contain recursive elements as well :

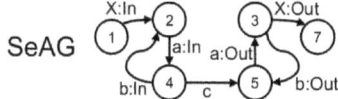

Discussion 2. (Caveats) [5, 1] point out several limitations to simulation-based validation. First, for a given instance graph, several schemas are eligible, since simulation is transitive. This matters greatly when schemas are inferred from the data, but does not when they are predefined.

Second, and more importantly, simulation-based validation as defined by [5] does not enforce the presence of a label. This is true for simulation between two general graphs. Still, this caveat can be bypassed by specifying an appropriate data model. Consider the SeAG A and the graphs B_1 and B_2 below. Even though A simulates both B_1 and B_2, it validates none: B_1 is not well-formed, and $type(leaf(B_2))$ is not equal to $type(leaf(A))$, which contradicts the validation definition.

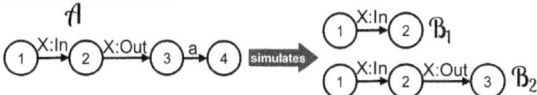

Hence well-formedness and validation rules somehow enforce the presence of labels that simulation does not.

Last, simulation cannot prevent a node from having several outgo-

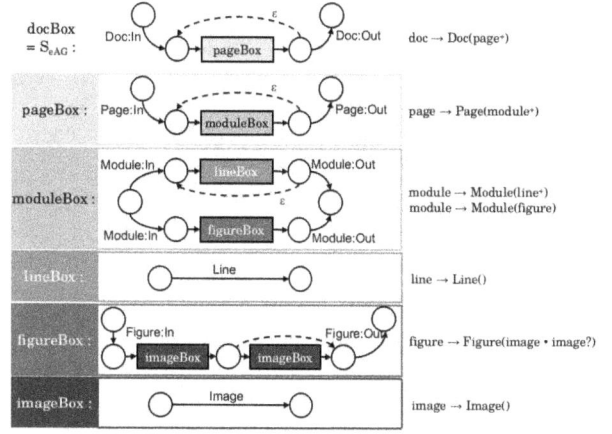

Figure 4: For all $n \in N$ as defined in Figure 5, each nBox representation (middle) and $R_n \subset R$ (right).

ing edges. Said differently, as illustrated in Example 4, even when an SeAG contains one single (cyclic) path, there is no way to prevent the annotator to annotate the same content with several layers all instantiating the same path. Of course, this feature has positive aspects (e.g. self overlap is natively supported). But it means that a hierarchical SeAG will validate multitrees, not trees only.

Still, there is a connexion between simulation and grammar-based validations. An XML document is, syntactically speaking, a tree; a (RelaxNG) schema is a Tree automaton [15], which validates the tree for which there is an "interpretation", as defined in Figure 5. We know there is a way to translate trees into eAGs. For instance, the eAG representing the tree X from Figure 5 is the arrowed path in Figure 2. There is also a way to derive a SeAG from a Tree automaton. Consider an automaton $TA = (S, N, T, R)$, for instance the one from Figure 5. In TA, T is the set of terminals. N is the set of non-terminals, among which are start symbols (S). The elements of R are called production rules. A rule associates a non terminal to a terminal, representing a possible labelled node of a tree, and a regular expressions over N against which the sons of the node shall match.

For our derivation of an SeAG from a TA, we enforce that if there is a rule $r = x \rightarrow X(reg) \in R$ so that *reg* can be expressed as $reg_1 | reg_2$, with no common prefix and suffix between the words in the languages of reg_1 and reg_2, then r must be split into two rules $r_1 = x \rightarrow X(reg_1)$ and $r_2 = x \rightarrow X(reg_2)$. For instance, $module \rightarrow Module(line^+ | figure)$ shall be split into two rules $module \rightarrow Module(line^+)$ and $module \rightarrow Module(figure)$. Then, the derivation of a SeAG S_{TA} from TA[10] defines as follows:
There is a partition of R into sets of rules sharing the same left-hand side. For any $n \in N$, let us call R_n one such subset of R. Then, every $n \in N$ may define what we call a unique Box, denoted nBox. The nBox is a rooted graph that reflects the content of the set of rules in R_n. In the nBox, each $r_i = n \rightarrow T_i(re_i) \in R_n$ is represented by a root-to-node path. If $re_i = \varnothing$, then the path is a single edge labelled T_i. Else, since re_i is a regular expression over N, it can be represented by the Ott automaton made out of the Boxes corresponding to re_i, escorted by two edges labelled T_i:In and T_i:Out. Figure 4 shows the nBoxes for the automaton in Figure 5. By replacing iteratively, in a bottom-up approach, the Boxes contained one in the others, we get a labelled graph which is S_{TA}. One can check that, in the case of Figure 4, this yields the SeAG shown on Figure 3.

---
[10]The following sketch leaves recursive element definition out.

Here comes the interesting point: this example illustrates that, given a tree automaton TA and a tree X so that there is an interpretation of X against TA, the SeAG derived from TA simulates the eAG representation of X[11].

The above provides a sketch of proof for the following connexion between interpretation and simulation for validation:

Property 6. Be a tree X and a tree automaton TA. Be G_X the eAG representation of X; be S_{TA} the SeAG derived from TA. Then, if there is an interpretation of X by TA, then S_{TA} simulates G_X.

4.3 Representation

So far we have introduced extended Annotation Graphs, a cyclic graph data model for multiple annotation of composite resources, along with a schema model, SeAG. Here, we consider the case where a schema is needed to proceed to annotation. We define a matrix representation for SeAG and eAG so that, given the representation of a schema, only valid instances can be represented. This is "validation by construction".

Definition 14. (Identifier sets) Be a graph $G = (V, E)$. There are two countable ordered sets $\mathscr{I}_G$ and $\mathscr{J}_G$ and two bijective functions $id: V \longrightarrow \mathscr{I}_G$ and $id: E \longrightarrow \mathscr{J}_G$ identifying the nodes and edges of G. The ith element of the set $\mathscr{I}_G$, for instance, is denoted $[\mathscr{I}_G]_i$.

Definition 15. Be a graph $G = (V, E)$, $\mathscr{I}_G$ and $\mathscr{J}_G$ two sets of identifiers. Provided G contains no connected subgraph limited to a node and no loop, G can be represented by its incidence matrix $[G]^{\mathscr{I}_G, \mathscr{J}_G}$ so that, $\forall (i, j) \in \mathscr{I}_G \times \mathscr{J}_G$:
$$[G]^{\mathscr{I}_G, \mathscr{J}_G}_{i,j} = 1 \text{ iff } \exists v \lfloor e \rfloor v' \subseteq G; id(v) = i \wedge id(e) = j$$
$$= -1 \text{ iff } \exists v \lfloor e \rfloor v' \subseteq G; id(v') = i \wedge id(e) = j$$
$$= 0 \text{ else.}$$

Property 7. Be a SeAG $S = (V_S, E_S)$. Ordering the sets $\{type(v); v \in V_S\}$, $\{(type(v), label(e), type(v')); v \lfloor e \rfloor v' \subseteq S\}$, provides two special node and edge identifier sets $\mathscr{T}, \mathscr{X}$.

PROOF. In a SeAG, no two nodes have the same type (Def. 11) or are connected by two edges with the same label (Def. 10). Any ordering of the sets is fine. □

Discussion 3. Consider the following SeAG :

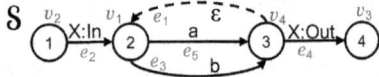

The values v_i are possible identifiers for the nearby nodes, and e_j for edges, so that $\mathscr{I}_S = [v_1, v_2, v_3, v_4]$, for instance. Then, Property 7 means that it is possible to represent the incidence matrix of an SeAG S by indexing lines and columns either on any $\mathscr{I}_S \times \mathscr{J}_S$ or on $\mathscr{T} \times \mathscr{X}$ in particular. For instance, when indexed over $\mathscr{T} \times \mathscr{X}$:

$$[S]^{\mathscr{T}, \mathscr{X}} = \begin{array}{c} 1 \\ 2 \\ 3 \\ 4 \end{array} \begin{array}{ccccc} {}_1\text{X:In}_2 & {}_2a_3 & {}_2b_3 & {}_3\varepsilon_2 & {}_3\text{X:Out}_4 \\ \begin{bmatrix} 1 & 0 & 0 & 0 & 0 \\ -1 & 1 & 1 & -1 & 0 \\ 0 & -1 & -1 & 1 & 1 \\ 0 & 0 & 0 & 0 & -1 \end{bmatrix} \end{array}$$

It is also possible to express a *subgraph* of S in an incidence matrix indexed over the full identifier sets. For instance, below is the incidence matrix over $\mathscr{I}_S$ and $\mathscr{J}_S$ of $H = \{v \lfloor e \rfloor v' \subseteq S; (type(v), label(e), type(v')) = (2, b, 3)\}$, subgraph of S :

$$[H]^{\mathscr{I}_S, \mathscr{J}_S} = \begin{array}{c} v_1 \\ v_2 \\ v_3 \\ v_4 \end{array} \begin{array}{ccccc} e_1 & e_2 & e_3 & e_4 & e_5 \\ \begin{bmatrix} 0 & 0 & 1 & 0 & 0 \\ 0 & 0 & 0 & 0 & 0 \\ 0 & 0 & 0 & 0 & 0 \\ 0 & 0 & 0 & -1 & 0 \end{bmatrix} \end{array}$$

[11]We obliterate the question of node types here. We only compare the bare simulation and interpretation relations.

Definition 16. Given a $n \times m$ matrix $[M]$ of integers, the positive restriction of $[M]$ is the $n \times m$ matrix $[M^+]$ so that $\forall i, j, [M^+]_{i,j} = [M]_{i,j}$ iff $[M]_{i,j} > 0$, else $[M^+]_{i,j} = 0$. The definition of $[M^-]$ the negative restriction of $[M]$ is natural.

Discussion 4. Consider two graphs G and H, $H \subseteq G$ and the incidence matrix $[H]^{\mathscr{I}_G, \mathscr{J}_G}$. Then the positive restriction of $[H]^{\mathscr{I}_G, \mathscr{J}_G}$, read column by column, lists the identifiers of the nodes that are the summits of the edges of H whose identifier matches the one of the column. Conversely, the negative restriction of $[H]^{\mathscr{I}_S, \mathscr{J}_S}$ defined in Discussion 3 is :

$$[H^-]^{\mathscr{I}_S, \mathscr{J}_S} = \begin{array}{c} v_1 \\ v_2 \\ v_3 \\ v_4 \end{array} \begin{array}{ccccc} e_1 & e_2 & e_3 & e_4 & e_5 \\ \begin{bmatrix} 0 & 0 & 0 & 0 & 0 \\ 0 & 0 & 0 & 0 & 0 \\ 0 & 0 & 0 & 0 & 0 \\ 0 & 0 & -1 & 0 & 0 \end{bmatrix} \end{array}$$

Note that the sum of the positive and negative restriction of any incidence matrix gives the incidence matrix.

Definition 17. (Template) Be S a SeAG, G a graph that can be represented by its incidence matrix, and $\mathscr{I}_G$, $\mathscr{J}_G$ identifier sets for G. Consider the block-matrix obtained by replacing each value $s_{i,j}$ of $[S]^{\mathscr{T}, \mathscr{X}}$ by a matrix $[M_{i,j}]$, so that:
- $s_{i,j} = 0 \Rightarrow [M_{i,j}] = [\varnothing]^{\mathscr{I}_G, \mathscr{J}_G}$, where $\varnothing$ is the empty graph, whose incidence matrix is always zero ;
- $s_{i,j} = 1 \Rightarrow [M_{i,j}] = [A]$, where $[A]$ is the positive restriction of the incidence matrix over $\mathscr{I}_G$, $\mathscr{J}_G$ of $H_j \subseteq G$, with $H_j = \{v \lfloor e \rfloor v' \subseteq G; (type(v), label(e), type(v')) = [\mathscr{X}]_j\}$;
- $s_{i,j} = -1 \Rightarrow [M_{i,j}] = [B]$, where $[B]$ is the negative restriction of the incidence matrix over $\mathscr{I}_G$, $\mathscr{J}_G$ of H_j.
This block-matrix is called the expression of G on the template of S, denoted $[G/Temp.S]$.

Example 5. Consider the SeAG S defined in Discussion 3. The expression of S on its own template is:

$$[S/Temp.S] = \begin{array}{c} 1 \\ 2 \\ 3 \\ 4 \end{array} \begin{array}{ccccc} {}_1\text{X:In}_2 & {}_2a_3 & {}_2b_3 & {}_3\varepsilon_2 & {}_3\text{X:Out}_4 \\ \begin{bmatrix} [A_1] & 0 & 0 & 0 & 0 \\ [B_1] & [A_2] & [A_3] & [B_4] & 0 \\ 0 & [B_2] & [B_3] & [A_4] & [A_5] \\ 0 & 0 & 0 & 0 & [B_5] \end{bmatrix} \end{array}$$

with, for instance, $[A_3] = [H^+]^{\mathscr{I}_S, \mathscr{J}_S}$ and $[B_3] = [H^-]^{\mathscr{I}_S, \mathscr{J}_S}$ as defined in Discussion 4.

Definition 18. Be S an SeAG and G, $\mathscr{I}_G$, $\mathscr{J}_G$ a graph containing no subgraph limited to a node and no loop, along with two sets of identifiers. G is said to be fully expressible on the template of S, denoted $G \triangleleft [Temp.S]$, iff the sum of the inner matrices of $[G/Temp.S]$ is equal to $[G]^{\mathscr{I}_G, \mathscr{J}_G}$ the incidence matrix of G, indexed over the same sets as the inner matrices of $[G/Temp.S]$.

Property 8. Be S an SeAG. Then S is fully expressible on its own template.

PROOF. $\forall l \in [0; |\mathscr{X}|[$, the lth column of $[S/Temp.S]$ contains two matrices $[A_l]$ and $[B_l]$. Since they are respectively the positive and negative restrictions of the incidence matrix of $H_l \subseteq S$, which is the union of all the subgraphs $v \lfloor e \rfloor v'$ characterized by the same triple $[\mathscr{X}]_l$ of types and label, $[A_l] + [B_l] = [H_l]^{\mathscr{I}_S, \mathscr{J}_S}$. Since $\mathscr{X}$ is the set of possible triples for S, $\sum_{0 \leq l < |\mathscr{X}|} [H_l]^{\mathscr{I}_S, \mathscr{J}_S} = [S]^{\mathscr{I}_S, \mathscr{J}_S}$. □

Importantly, only schemas define a template. In particular, given an instance G and any identifier sets $\mathscr{I}$, $\mathscr{J}$, since there may not be bijections between those sets and $\mathscr{T}$, $\mathscr{X}$, the notion of template of G is undefined. Still, it is possible to try to express G, not over its own template, *but over the template of a given schema S.*

Let us denote this representation $[G/Temp.S]$. The schema defines the template, that is, the outer matrix of $[G/Temp.S]$, indexed over $\mathscr{T} \times \mathscr{X}$: it restricts the types, the labels between two given types and the paths along which those labels may occur. Be then $[\mathscr{X}]_l \in \mathscr{X}$. Just like above, we can define $H_l = \{v \lfloor e \rfloor v' \subseteq G; (type(v), label(e), type(v')) = [\mathscr{X}]_l\}$, so that $H_l \subseteq G$. Then the inner matrices of $[G/Temp.S]$ are defined just the same way as those in $[S/Temp.S]$, that is: in the lth outer column, on the right outer lines, as the positive and negative restrictions of $[H_l]^{\mathscr{I},\mathscr{I}}$ (see Definition 17).

Interestingly, this approach can be taken for any graph G and any schema S. If the graph contains no edge conforming the schema, then $[G/Temp.S]$ is null. On the contrary, an important result is that provided G is an instance of S, then G is *fully expressible* on $[Temp.S]$. We can even go further:

Property 9. Be a SeAG S and an eAG G. Then S validates G iff $G \lhd [Temp.S]$ and $type(leaf(G)) = type(leaf(S))$ and $type(root(G)) = type(root(S))$.

PROOF. $\Rightarrow$: S validates G, then the types of the two graphs' leafs are equal, by definition of validation. Idem for the roots. The fact that validation implies $G \lhd [Temp.S]$ can be proven just like Property 8, with one more argument. The fact that the sum of the two inner matrices characterised by the same $L \in \mathscr{X}$ yields the incidence matrix of the union of all the subgraphs $v \lfloor e \rfloor v' \subseteq G$ characterised by L holds. Yet, it has to be proven that there is no subgraph $v \lfloor e \rfloor v' \subseteq G$ so that $(type(v), label(e), type(v')) \notin \mathscr{X}$. Since G is rooted and connected, one can check that the presence of such a subgraph shall contradict the existence of a rooted simulation.
$\Leftarrow$: Be $G = (V,E)$, $S = (V_S, E_S)$. $G \lhd [Temp.S]$ implies that $\forall v \lfloor e \rfloor v' \subseteq G$, $\exists L \in \mathscr{X}$ so that $(type(v), label(e), type(v')) = L$, which means $\exists! v_S \lfloor e_S \rfloor v'_S \subseteq S$ so that $type(v_S) = type(v)$, $type(v'_S) = type(v')$ and $label(e_S) = label(e)$. This defines two functions $\delta : V \to V_S$ and $\delta_E : E \to E_S$ so that $\forall v \lfloor e \rfloor v' \subseteq G$, $\exists! (\delta(v), \delta_E(e), \delta(v')) \in V_S \times E_S \times V_S$ so that $\forall x, type(\delta(x)) = type(x)$, $\forall y, label(\delta_E(y)) = label(y)$ and $\delta(v) \lfloor \delta_E(e) \rfloor \delta(v') \subseteq S$.
Additionally, the fact that $type(root(G)) = type(root(S))$ implies $\delta(root(G)) = root(S)$. Then $D = \{(v, \delta(v)); v \in V\}$ is a rooted, node-typed simulation of G by S. $\square$

Illustration, part 5. Consider the eAG B from Example 4. Let us equip its nodes and edges with identifiers, as shown below.

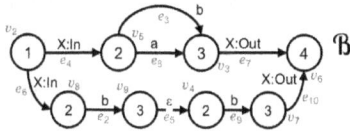

The representation of B in $[Temp.S]$ is:

$$[B/Temp.S] = \begin{array}{c} \\ 1 \\ 2 \\ 3 \\ 4 \end{array} \begin{bmatrix} \text{}_1\texttt{X:In}_2 & \text{}_2 a_3 & \text{}_2 b_3 & \text{}_3 \varepsilon_2 & \text{}_3\texttt{X:Out}_4 \\ [A_1] & 0 & 0 & 0 & 0 \\ [B_1] & [A_2] & [A_3] & [B_4] & 0 \\ 0 & [B_2] & [B_3] & [A_4] & [A_5] \\ 0 & 0 & 0 & 0 & [B_5] \end{bmatrix}$$

with $[B_3]$ the negative restriction of $[H]^{\mathscr{I}_B, \mathscr{I}_B}$, for instance, for $H = \{v \lfloor e \rfloor v' \subseteq B; (type(v), label(e), type(v')) = (2, b, 3)\}$:

$$[B_3] = \begin{array}{c} \\ v_1 \\ v_2 \\ v_3 \\ v_4 \\ v_5 \\ v_6 \\ v_7 \\ v_8 \\ v_9 \end{array} \begin{bmatrix} e_1 & e_2 & e_3 & e_4 & e_5 & e_6 & e_7 & e_8 & e_9 & e_{10} \\ 0 & 0 & 0 & 0 & 0 & 0 & 0 & 0 & 0 & 0 \\ 0 & 0 & 0 & 0 & 0 & 0 & 0 & 0 & 0 & 0 \\ 0 & 0 & -1 & 0 & 0 & 0 & 0 & 0 & 0 & 0 \\ 0 & 0 & 0 & 0 & 0 & 0 & 0 & 0 & 0 & 0 \\ 0 & 0 & 0 & 0 & 0 & 0 & 0 & 0 & 0 & 0 \\ 0 & 0 & 0 & 0 & 0 & 0 & 0 & 0 & 0 & 0 \\ 0 & 0 & 0 & 0 & 0 & 0 & 0 & 0 & -1 & 0 \\ 0 & 0 & 0 & 0 & 0 & 0 & 0 & 0 & 0 & 0 \\ 0 & -1 & 0 & 0 & 0 & 0 & 0 & 0 & 0 & 0 \end{bmatrix}$$

Now compare $[B/Temp.S]$ with $[S/Temp.S]$ as detailed in Example 5. The two matrices share the same outer matrix, which is descriptive of S, they only differ by the values of the inner matrices (e.g. see the value of $[B_3]$ for S in Example 5). Based on Property 9, we can finally conclude:

Given a schema S, the eAGs it validates are the well-formed eAGs model that can be fully expressed in $[Temp.S]$, and whose root and leaf types respect those of S. This means that an instance of S is an eAG *that can be described by* the set of matrix values that fill $[Temp.S]$. From a manufacturing point of view, if the annotator of a resource is given means (through an ergonomic HCI) to define the matrix values corresponding to $[Temp.S]$, in a way that ensures well-formedness, then, by construction, the resulting graph will be valid against the schema. This meets the goal of providing on-the-fly validation for M-S data.

5. CONCLUSION

In this paper, we introduce eAG, an extension of Annotation graphs, along with a novel schema model based upon the notion of simulation. A dedicated representation for eAGs and schemas enables to proceed to validation "by construction": provided a schema, only valid eAGs can be expressed, which bypasses the algorithmic cost of traditional approaches for validation of graph-structured data.

Still, the eAG data model is not restricted to this use case, and simulation-based validation can be adapted to the situations where any eAG $G = (V,E)$ is confronted to any SeAG $S = (V_S, E_S)$. First case, G was made according to a schema $S' = (V_{S'}, E_{S'})$, and the question is whether it conforms to S or not. By transitivity of simulation, S validates G iff S simulates S' so that $(leaf(S'), leaf(S))$ are in the simulation (indicating, *modulo* retyping the nodes of S, a node-typed simulation of S' by S). This checks in $O(|V_{S'} \cup V_S| \cdot |E_{S'} \cup E_S|)$ [19]. Second case, G was not made according to any schema. In this case, node types are irrelevant. An adaptation of SeAG validation is: S validates G iff there is a (general) simulation $D \subseteq V \times V_S$ so that $\forall v \in V$, $\exists! v_S \in V_S$ so that $(v, v_S) \in D$ (the uniqueness of v_S for each v defines a typing of the nodes of G according to S). This checks in $O(|V \cup V_S| \cdot |E \cup E_S|)$. In both cases, this is a reasonable cost for a cyclic graph-based data model.

6. ACKNOWLEDGMENTS

This work is supported by the ARC5 program of the Rhône-Alpes region, France.

7. REFERENCES

[1] S. Abiteboul, P. Buneman, and D. Suciu. *Data on the Web: from relations to semistructured data and XML.* Morgan Kaufmann, 2000.

[2] S. Bird and M. Liberman. A formal framework for linguistic annotation. *Speech communication*, 33(1):23–60, 2001.

[3] E. Bruno and E. Murisasco. Describing and querying hierarchical xml structures defined over the same textual data. In *Proceedings of the 2006 ACM symposium on Document engineering*, pages 147–154. ACM, 2006.

[4] E. Bruno and E. Murisasco. An xml environment for multistructured textual documents. In *Digital Information Management, 2007. ICDIM'07. 2nd International Conference on*, volume 1, pages 230–235. IEEE, 2007.

Tree automaton *TA*

$S = \{\text{doc}\}$ [NB. S is a subpart of N]

$N = \{\text{doc, page, module, figure, image, line}\}$

$T = \{\text{Doc, Page, Module, Figure, Image, Line}\}$

$R =$

    $\text{doc} \rightarrow \text{Doc}(\text{page}^+)$

    $\text{page} \rightarrow \text{Page}(\text{module}^+)$

    $\text{module} \rightarrow \text{Module}(\text{line}^+ \mid \text{figure})$

    $\text{line} \rightarrow \text{Line}()$

    $\text{figure} \rightarrow \text{Figure}(\text{image} \cdot \text{image}?)$

    $\text{image} \rightarrow \text{Image}()$

Interpretation :

An interpretation is a function
$I : T \rightarrow N$ so that :

1. $I(root(Tree))$ is in S and
2. for all maximal subtree of unitary depth

there is $r = t \rightarrow T(RE)$ in R so that:

- $I(T) = t$ and
- $I(T_1) \cdot I(T_2) \cdot .... \cdot I(T_N)$
  is in language of RE.

Tree *X*

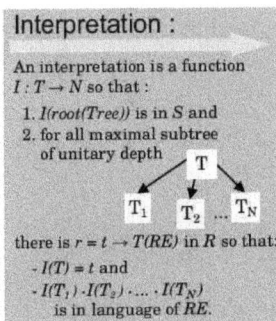

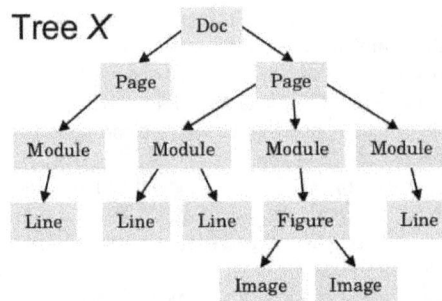

Figure 5: RelaxNG tree automaton-based XML validation mechanism.

[5] P. Buneman, S. Davidson, M. Fernandez, and D. Suciu. Adding structure to unstructured data. In *Database Theory -ICDT'97*, pages 336–350. Springer, 1997.

[6] L. Burnard and S. Bauman. *TEI P5: Guidelines for electronic text encoding and interchange.* TEI Consortium, 2008.

[7] H. A. Cayless. Rebooting tei pointers. *Journal of the Text Encoding Initiative*, (6), 2013.

[8] A. Di Iorio, S. Peroni, and F. Vitali. Using semantic web technologies for analysis and validation of structural markup. *International Journal of Web Engineering and Technology*, 6(4):375–398, 2011.

[9] C. F. Goldfarb and Y. Rubinsky. *The SGML handbook.* Oxford University Press, 1990.

[10] R. Goldman and J. Widom. Dataguides: Enabling query formulation and optimization in semistructured databases. 1997.

[11] M. Hilbert, A. Witt, and O. Schonefeld. Making concur work. In *In Extreme Markup Languages*, 2005.

[12] C. Huitfeldt and C. Sperberg-McQueen. Texmecs: An experimental markup meta-language for complex documents. *URL http://www. hit. uib. no/claus/mlcd/papers/texmecs. html*, 2001.

[13] H. Jagadish, L. V. Lakshmanan, M. Scannapieco, D. Srivastava, and N. Wiwatwattana. Colorful xml: one hierarchy isn't enough. In *Proceedings of the 2004 ACM SIGMOD international conference on Management of data*, pages 251–262. ACM, 2004.

[14] D. Lee, M. Mani, and M. Murata. Reasoning about xml schema languages using formal language theory. Technical report, Citeseer, 2000.

[15] M. Murata, D. Lee, M. Mani, and K. Kawaguchi. Taxonomy of xml schema languages using formal language theory. *ACM Transactions on Internet Technology (TOIT)*, 5(4):660–704, 2005.

[16] G. Ott and N. H. Feinstein. Design of sequential machines from their regular expressions. *Journal of the ACM (JACM)*, 8(4):585–600, 1961.

[17] S. Peroni. Markup beyond the trees. In *Semantic Web Technologies and Legal Scholarly Publishing*, pages 45–93. Springer, 2014.

[18] P.-É. Portier, N. Chatti, S. Calabretto, E. Egyed-Zsigmond, and J.-M. Pinon. Modeling, encoding and querying multi-structured documents. *Information Processing & Management*, 48(5):931–955, 2012.

[19] F. Ranzato and F. Tapparo. An efficient simulation algorithm based on abstract interpretation. *Information and Computation*, 208(1):1–22, 2010.

[20] D. Reynolds, C. Thompson, J. Mukerji, and D. Coleman. An assessment of rdf/owl modelling. *Digital Media Systems Laboratory, HP Laboratories Bristol*, 28, 2005.

[21] C. M. Sperberg-McQueen. Rabbit/duck grammars: a validation method for overlapping structures. In *Extreme Markup Languages*, 2006.

[22] C. M. Sperberg-McQueen and C. Huitfeldt. Goddag: A data structure for overlapping hierarchies. In *Digital documents: Systems and principles*, pages 139–160. Springer, 2000.

[23] M. Stührenberg and C. Wurm. Refining the taxonomy of xml schema languages. a new approach for categorizing xml schema languages in terms of processing complexity. In *Proceedings of Balisage: The Markup Conference*, volume 5, 2010.

[24] D. Suciu. Semistructured data and xml. In *Information organization and databases*, pages 9–30. Springer, 2000.

[25] J. Tao, E. Sirin, J. Bao, and D. L. McGuinness. Integrity constraints in owl. In *AAAI*, 2010.

[26] J. Tennison. Creole: Validating overlapping markup. In *Proceedings of XTech*, 2007.

[27] J. Tennison and W. Piez. The layered markup and annotation language (lmnl). In *Extreme Markup Languages*, 2002.

NCM 3.1: A Conceptual Model for Hyperknowledge Document Engineering

Marcio Ferreira Moreno, Rafael Brandão, Renato Cerqueira
IBM Research | Brazil
Av. Pasteur, 138 and 146
Rio de Janeiro – 22296-903 – Brazil
{mmoreno, rmello, rcerq}@br.ibm.com

ABSTRACT

Most of multimedia documents available today are agnostic to data semantics and their specification language offer little to ease authoring and mechanisms to their players so they can retrieve and present meaningful content to improve user experience. In this paper, we present the main entities of the version 3.1 of the Nested Context Model (NCM), which concentrate efforts at integrating support for enriched knowledge description to the model. This extension enables the specification of relationships between knowledge descriptions in the traditional hypermedia way, composing what we call *hyperknowledge* in this paper. NCM previous version (NCM 3.0) is a conceptual model for hypermedia document engineering. NCL (Nested Context Language), which is part of international standards and ITU recommendations, is an XML application language that was engineered according to NCM 3.0 definitions. The extensions discussed in this paper contribute not only for advances in the NCL specifications, but mainly as a conceptual model for *hyperknowledge* document engineering.

Keywords

Knowledge modeling; Conceptual model; NCM; Hyperknowledge; Document Engineering; Multimedia documents; Hypermedia.

1. INTRODUCTION

The so-called semantic gap [1] is still a challenge in the context of multimedia documents and content meaning. There are two groups of solutions in the literature that attempt to bridge this gap. The first group consists of metadata standards and models (e.g. MPEG-7 [2], Dublin Core [3], and PBCore [4]) that aim to allow searching for material that is of interest to users. They specify descriptors or pre-defined fields to describe low-level aspects of media content (e.g. title, creator, description, etc.). In contrast, the second group gathers solutions that aim at describing high-level concepts and richer semantic relations (specification of ontologies), which are formally defined vocabularies of terms, usually employed by a community of users and machines in a specific domain. RDF (Resource Description Framework) [5] along with its semantic extension RDFS (RDF Schema) and OWL (Web Ontology Language) [6] are among the most used by designers of vocabularies and ontologies to model data relationship and represent structured knowledge.

Generally, document authors have to deal with these two groups of solutions disjointedly, in order to richly relate content and conceptual knowledge in multimedia documents. In the first group, metadata allows the association of descriptions with the content itself, but there is an absence of mechanisms to describe high-level concepts and richer semantic relations among different content. In the second group, existing frameworks and languages to describe ontologies lack full integration with multimedia content and document specifications.

Particularly, the aforementioned solutions do not provide mechanisms to tackle the following document authoring features. First, specification of relationships between knowledge description and multimedia content in the traditional hypermedia way. That is, a document author should be able to specify relationships between knowledge descriptions and hypermedia node interfaces (anchors and properties). Second, specification of interactivity events based on knowledge description. Third, specification of relationships to describe extraction and injection of knowledge from and to the hypermedia nodes described in the multimedia document. Last, but not least, specification of reuse of parts of the multimedia document specifications using knowledge descriptions.

Another explicit drawback of the aforementioned solutions is also related to the multimedia document authoring point of view. In fact, these solutions oblige the use of different technologies to specify the semantics of document presentation. Their approach demands that document authors know specific concepts about metadata or ontology languages/frameworks. Moreover, it is necessary that document authors divide their document specifications (into, at least, the specifications of content relationships, and the specification of document and content semantics), whose presentation semantics can be lost due to further editions and cannot be replicated without domain-specific expert modifications.

To address the limitations found in current solutions, we propose to embrace and model knowledge as a first-class element in a hypermedia conceptual model, composing what we call *hyperknowledge* in this paper. More specifically, we propose that hyperknowledge conceptual models should support the following features:

F1) Specification of knowledge as a first-class element. Conceptual models should provide elements to describe high-level abstraction knowledge, but also consider interoperability support, including the use of RDF/RDFS, OWL or other existing solution as hypermedia nodes;

F2) Specification of relationships between knowledge descriptions and anchors and properties of hypermedia nodes, which can represent: the entire content of a node; time interval of a content or document presentation; region coordinates; segments; etc.;

F3) Knowledge-aware presentation events. Description of presentation anchors with knowledge descriptions. This feature allows that a document author specifies that, for instance, a group of nodes shall be presented every time specific concepts occur, no matter from which hypermedia node;

F4) Knowledge-aware interaction events. Description of interaction events by using not only the traditional hypermedia interfaces, but also knowledge specifications. For instance, enabling a document author to specify that a group of nodes shall be presented every time a user interacts with specific concepts, no matter from which hypermedia node;

F5) Support to reuse of nodes and inference specifications, allowing authors not only to reuse group of nodes that are related to specific knowledge descriptions, but also to specify that concepts can be inferred from content to a knowledge base or to represent F3 and F4 events.

In this paper, we propose to integrate these features in a new version (3.1) of the NCM (Nested Context Model) conceptual model. In its previous version (3.0), NCM focused on the representation and structures of hypermedia documents. It concentrated efforts in the specification of spatio-temporal synchronization relationships. Among existing hypermedia conceptual models, we elected to extend NCM not only due to its historic importance in hypermedia[1], but mainly to take advantage of its intrinsic multimedia modeling and presentation capabilities. These extensions promote an integrated support for describing knowledge and content aspects, with a clear distinction between abstract concepts and media instantiation, inherent from the model. NCM has also prospered through one of its implementations. For instance, NCL (Nested Context Language) [9] is an XML application that was engineered according to NCM 3.0. NCL is part of ITU-T Recommendations for IPTV [9], IBB (integrated Broadcast-Broadband) and DTV services [9], and ISDB-T (International Standard for Digital Broadcasting – Terrestrial) [9].

The NCM extensions discussed in this paper contributes not only to motivate further advances in the NCL specifications, but mainly as a conceptual model for *hyperknowledge* document engineering. Indeed, the choice of using a conceptual model to specify our proposal is based on the significance of these models to document engineering. As Glushko and McGrath state [10], in document engineering, conceptual modeling of documents at a granularity that is implementable is fundamental.

The remainder of this paper is organized as the following. Section 2 provides details of the proposed extensions. Section 3 describes a prototype application. Finally, Section 4 concludes with considerations and reflections, also bringing up a research agenda.

2. KNOWLEDGE MODELING WITH NCM

This section discusses basic concepts of NCM 3.0 and our NCM extensions to enrich knowledge modeling support. These extensions are part of the new version that we are proposing: the NCM 3.1. The main goal is to fulfill the existent gap between rich multimedia presentations and content meaning, by bringing support to the five features discussed in Section 1 to the model and taking advantage of NCM capabilities for specifying n-ary relations.

2.1 NCM 3.0

The foundation of NCM is the usual hypermedia concepts of *nodes* and *links* [7]. The former represents information fragments, while the latter has the purpose of defining relationships among *interfaces* (*anchors* and *properties*) of *nodes*. There are two basic classes of *nodes*: *content node* and *composite node*. A *content node* represents the usual media objects (image, text, video, audio, etc.), while *composite node* is an NCM *node* whose content is a set of *nodes* (*composite* or *content nodes*). A *context node* is an NCM *composite node* that also contains a set of *links* and other attributes [7]. *Context nodes* are useful, for instance, to define a logical structure for hypermedia documents.

A *link* has two additional attributes: A *connector* and a set of *binds*. The *connector* defines the semantics of a relation through an NCM class named *glue*, independently of the components that will be included in the relation [7], and a set of access points, called *roles*. In the set of *binds* of the *link*, each *bind* associates each *link* endpoint (interfaces of *nodes*) to a *role* at the referred *connector*.

Theoretically, *connectors* can represent any type of relation. However, version 3.0 of NCM concentrates efforts in the specification of spatio-temporal synchronization relations through *causal* (causal *glue* that supports *condition*, *assessment* and *action* roles) and *constraint* (constraint *glue* with *assessment roles*) *connectors*. On the one hand, a *condition* must be satisfied in a *causal* relation to execute a group composed by one or more *actions*. For instance, a document author can specify a *connector* that can start (*action role start*) the presentation of one or more *nodes* when the presentation of one or more *nodes* finishes (*condition role onEnd*) or when the property "top" of two or more nodes receives the same value (*assessment role* evaluating property values). On the other hand, on *constraint* relations there is no causality involved. For instance, a *constraint connector* can define that two or more *nodes* must begin (*assessment role begins*) their presentation at the same time and must end (*assessment role ends*) their presentation at the same time. Both types of *connectors* are spotless to specify relations among usual *content nodes* composing a hypermedia document, but are unable to consider interfaces of *knowledge nodes*.

2.2 NCM 3.1

To allow the specification of relations and relationships capable to connect knowledge information, the extensions affect mainly the *link* and *connector* entities, and the *glue* and *role* classes of NCM 3.0. A new *node* subclass, named *knowledge node*, was created to encapsulate knowledge information and to support feature F1 (see Section 1), allowing the new *node* to be used in NCM relationships. Besides the usual *node* interfaces and attributes, the new *node* type also has the attribute *concept* to specify the concept that the *node* instance is representing. Alternatively, the *node* can refer to a concept description, which can be described using simple concepts as in the concept attribute or referring to content specified by existing solutions (e.g. a URL to an OWL or RDF/RDFS description). This is an advantage that is worth highlighting. NCM only defines how *nodes* are structured and related. It does not restrict or prescribe the supported content types of its *nodes*. In other words, NCM 3.1 not only support knowledge modeling, but it is also a model capable of specifying how the extant solutions can be integrated and orchestrated.

Note that with this functionality, NCM 3.1 allows an enhanced interoperability with existing solutions. RDF [5] and OWL [6] only describe binary relations. Binary relations in these languages can

---

[1] NCM was the first hypermedia model to solve the nested context issue pointed out by the historic work of Halasz [8].

connect a participant to another participant or to a value. For instance: Sergio Ramos is a soccer player; Sergio Ramos is a defender. However, there are some cases (as the one in the aforementioned example) where the usual and appropriate method to represent concepts is to use relations that can connect a participant to more than one participant or value. These relations are called n-ary relations [5], which is naturally supported by NCM. W3C is concentrating its efforts on extensions to support n-ary relations on RDF and OWL. Using n-ary relations, the example statements could be more concise and natural, as the following: Sergio Ramos is a soccer player and plays as a defender. Figure 1 illustrates the use of the new structures defined in NCM 3.1, representing n-ary relations. In fact, Figure 1 illustrates the use of our extensions with an example that will be discussed along this section. The idea of the example is, during the presentation of the Champions League final match, each time a player scores a goal, the viewer can interact with the presentation to see goal replays and respective player information.

NCM 3.1 also extends the concept of *context nodes* so it can apply different semantics to a collection of *knowledge nodes*. Two *context nodes* are illustrated in the example of Figure 1. The "Soccer" *context node* is an NCM knowledge base describing events related to the "Soccer" context. The "Champions League" context imports the "Soccer" context to be aware of its concepts. For instance, a concept named "Madrid" in the "Soccer" context could mean different soccer teams (Real Madrid or Atletico Madrid), but in other context could indicate a city located in Spain. This is an aspect of NCM 3.1 to support feature F5 (reuse). Other aspects will be discussed further in this section.

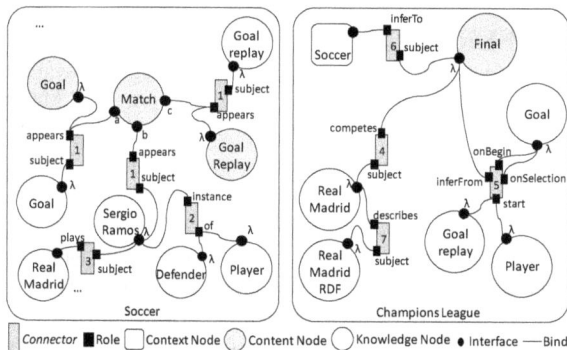

Figure 1. Example using Hierarchy and Knowledge Relations

Knowledge description is usually done with two types of relations. The first is the traditional SPO (subject-predicate-object) as in the *Subject* "Sergio Ramos", the *Predicate* "plays" and the *Object* "Real Madrid". The second can be defined as a hierarchy relation, as in "Sergio Ramos" is an instance of "Defender". In order to represent both types of relations, NCM 3.1 introduces two new types of connectors: 1) *hierarchy connector* with *hierarchy glue* and *roles;* and 2) *knowledge connector* with *knowledge glue* and *roles*. In the same direction, the model extensions also define a *hierarchy link* and a *knowledge link* representing, respectively, relationships that refers to hierarchy and knowledge relations. Figure 1 example illustrates the use of these two new types of connectors (the *knowledge connectors* identified as "*3*" and "*7*", the *hierarchy connector* "*2*"), which use three new types of *role*: *hierarchy role*, *subject role*, and *object role*.

The *hierarchy role* represents a *hierarchy* by using the NCM concept of *classType*, which in this *role* defines the participant function ("parent" or "child") in the relation. In the example of Figure 1, the *hierarchy connector* has two *roles* to define that

"Sergio Ramos" is a "player" and plays as a "defender": role "instance" was defined with the class type "child", and role "of" has the class type "parent".

The *subject* and *object roles* represent, respectively, a *Subject* and an *Object* as in the SPO relations. Returning to our example, the participant "Sergio Ramos" is a subject in a relationship because it is connected to a *subject role*, and it is related with the participant "Real Madrid", which is an object in this relationship by using the *object role* named "plays". Note that the names of *object roles* have semantics, acting as predicates. This occurs when the *object role* describes an *object* using its subclass *knowledge object*.

With these new structures supporting knowledge description and relations, the next step is to integrate these structures with interfaces (anchors and properties) of *content nodes*. This is the support for feature F2, which was done by allowing *content nodes* to be used in the *knowledge* and *hierarchy roles*. In Figure 1, connectors "1" and "4" are referred by *links* that exemplify relationships that allow the model to represent concepts with visual artifacts: 1) "Goal" appears in an *image node* (subclass of *content node*) named "Goal" and in an interval anchor with coordinates (x, y, width, and height) named "a" of the video node "Match"; same relation with "Sergio Ramos" and "Goal replay" and interfaces "b" and "c" of "Match"; 2) "Real Madrid" competes has relation with an anchor "λ" of the video node "Final". In NCM, interfaces with the λ symbol are anchors representing the whole node content (an interval time defined by the node natural begin and end presentation instants).

With the support to specify relations between knowledge and content we can now extend the model to support features F3 (knowledge-aware presentation events) and F4 (knowledge-aware interaction events) by modifying the existing *causal* and *constraint glue* to also support the new *knowledge* and *hierarchy roles*. In Figure 1, causal connector "5" is used in a link to specify that every time that the presentation of concept "Goal" occurs (*condition role onBegin*), the viewer can interact with the "Goal" presentation (*condition role onSelection*) to start (*action role start*) the presentation of the replay and respective soccer player information.

Note, in Figure 1, that the connector "5" also specifies the role "inferFrom", which is an example of the forth type of role created in NCM 3.1: the *inference role*. The inference role completes the support for feature F5 and indicates which participant in the relation shall be considered to infer (defining the inference *direction*, "from" the or "to" the participant) the data according to a knowledge presentation. The link that refers to connector "5" specifies that the presentation occurrence of the concept "Goal" shall be inferred "from" the "Final" video node. Indeed, a critical step when authoring a hypermedia document that describes inter-media synchronization, as the one modeled in the example, is to determine the temporal values of interest to create the anchors. In fact, this step involves a human monitoring the instants that events of interest occur in the content, which is a time-consuming and error prone task. Moreover, if the content is edited in a way that the instants of the event occurrences change, all tasks involved in the step shall be repeated.

Another issue is the repeatability of relationship concepts. In the example, to have the effect of showing each goal replay when "Goal" happens in the "Final" content node, one should not only create new anchors by extracting the temporal information from the "Final" video stream, or by triggering the occurrences in real-time (usual for live events), but also should specify links describing relationships with the created anchors. NCM 3.1 addresses both issues with a hyperknowledge approach. In this direction, in

Figure 1, connector "6" is another example of use of an *inference role*, but this time with the direction "to". In the example, the link refers to connector "6" to specify that a multimedia player shall process the "Final" video node to extract concepts and insert these concepts in the "soccer" knowledge base.

3. PROTOTYPE EXPERIMENTATION

NCM 3.1 has been experimented through a knowledge-aware prototype called c-Learning (http://c-learning.mybluemix.net), where the 'c' stands for cognitive. This Web application uses computational cognitive systems in the cloud to infer concepts, representing it in data structures that reflect our extensions.

The application allows an exploration of topics present in a number of document formats. After uploading a document, users can explore each page of it, getting relevant content suggestions on the same topic or about related topics. The implementation uses NCM context node to group knowledge nodes that are semantic related.

Users can give feedback whether they find a suggestion is relevant or not, promoting curatorship over these suggestions. The relations extracted from these concepts, i.e. hierarchy relations and SPO statements involving participants, are represented in a knowledge base modeled accordingly to the extensions proposed in NCM 3.1.

Finally, another relevant aspect with the c-Learning prototype experimentation is the representation of interpretive trails through the NCM *nodes*. As NCM 3.1 aggregates conceptual knowledge description in the model, the navigation path over knowledge nodes are used to indicate user's interpretation. That is, this interpretive trail can be seen as a representation of the concepts (evidences) that led the user to his/her current mental state.

4. FINAL REMARKS

The NCM extensions discussed in this paper contributes not only to motivate advances in the NCL specifications, but mainly as a conceptual model for *hyperknowledge* document engineering. Indeed, the choice of using a conceptual model to specify our proposal is based on the significance of these models to document engineering. As Glushko and McGrath states [10], in document engineering, the need for conceptual modeling of the documents at a granularity that is implementable is fundamental.

The new structures to support the five features introduced in Section 1 are the main contributions of this paper. It is the first time that this type of support is offered, increasing authors' expressiveness-power, allowing conceptual knowledge to be described and related to content in a single rationale. In addition, authors can use n-ary relationships available in the model to describe rich semantic relations in a more natural form than only binary relations. NCM model does not prescribe content formats and is not tied to a particular media type or domain. That is, any type of content can be modeled as long as the model instantiation provides suitable players for presenting it, which makes NCM 3.1 interesting for interoperability between existing solutions.

It is important to stress out that with the support for the five features, this paper also addresses important issues in the area of hypermedia document authoring. A critical step when specifying inter-media synchronization in these documents is to determine the temporal values of interest to create temporal anchors. This step involves a human monitoring the instants that events of interest occur in the content, which is a time-consuming and error prone task. Moreover, if the content is edited in a way that the instants of the event occurrences change, all tasks involved in the step shall be repeated. Another issue is the repeatability of relationship concepts, which is the effort of expressing similar relationships each time a new event of interest is found. This paper shows how NCM 3.1 addresses both issues with a hyperknowledge document.

The rich support for knowledge modeling also opens the possibility of implementations to integrate inference engines supported by cognitive computing. We are exploring this aspect in the c-Learning prototype application used for validating the proposed extensions. Through the inference roles proposed in NCM 3.1, authors can describe knowledge nodes whose concepts should be automatically inferred by a player. Moreover, authors can define the "direction" of such inference. That is, if concepts will be inferred *from* a content or should be extracted *to* a knowledge base. This integration with inference engines is an aspect that we want to explore further, for example, by automatically prefetching inferred concepts to enrich the user experience in an ongoing presentation.

We defined the following research agenda to guide the next steps regarding the evolution of NCM 3.1: **a)** Instantiation of the conceptual NCM 3.1 extensions in a language such as NCL or other format, e.g. JSON; **b)** design of converters to map knowledge described according to other formats like RDF/RDFS and OWL to NCM 3.1 concepts and its instantiation; **c)** A semantic reasoning system to allow inferring logical consequences from knowledge bases; **d)** a database solution to support storage and retrieval of knowledge, somewhat similar to RDF triplestores; **e)** A semantic query language to allow analytics information derived implicitly and explicitly contextual data, similar to SPARQL; **f)** Finally, to explore the presentation of knowledge base information through the temporal chains in a hypermedia temporal graph (HTG) [11], reflecting the chronological relation between modeled data.

5. REFERENCES

[1] Smeulders, AWM, et al. "Content-based image retrieval at the end of the early years." Pattern Analysis and Machine Intelligence, IEEE Transactions on 22.12: 1349-1380. 2000.

[2] Majidpour J., et al. Interactive tool to improve the automatic image annotation using MPEG-7 and multi-class SVM. In: Information and Knowledge Technology (IKT), 2015

[3] Arakaki FA, Costa PL, Alves RC. Evolution of Dublin Core Metadata Standard: An Analysis of the Literature from 1995-2013. Int. Conf. on Dublin Core and Metadata Apps 2015.

[4] Public Broadcasting Metadata Dictionary Project. PBCore 2.1, http://pbcore.org/, Mar. 2016.

[5] Hartmann T, et al. Evaluating the Quality of RDF Data Sets on Common Vocabularies in the Social, Behavioral, and Economic Sciences. arXiv preprint arXiv:1504.04478. 2015.

[6] W3C Rec. OWL 2 Web Ontology Language. https://www.w3.org/TR/owl2-overview/, Dec. 2012.

[7] Soares, L.F.G; Rodrigues, R. Nested Context Model 3.0. Part 1 – NCM Core. Tech. Report. DI. ISSN 0103-9741. 2005

[8] Halasz, F. Reflections on NoteCards: seven issues for the next generation of hypermedia systems. *Commun. ACM* 1988

[9] Soares, L.F.G. et al Ginga-NCL: Declarative Middleware for Multimedia IPTV Services. In: IEEE Communications Magazine. Vol.48, No.6. June 2010. p74-81.

[10] Glushko, R., and McGrath, T. Document engineering. Cambridge: Mit Press, 2005.

[11] Moreno, M. F., Costa, R. M. R., and Soares, L. F. G. "Interleaved Time Bases in Hypermedia Synchronization." IEEE MultiMedia Magazine, pp. 68–78. 2015.

Using a Dictionary and *n*-gram Alignment to Improve Fine-grained Cross-Language Plagiarism Detection

Nava Ehsan[*]
School of Electrical and
Computer Engineering
College of Engineering
University of Tehran
Tehran, Iran
n.ehsan@ece.ut.ac.ir

Frank Wm. Tompa
David R. Cheriton School of
Computer Science
University of Waterloo
Waterloo, ON, Canada
N2L 3G1
fwtompa@uwaterloo.ca

Azadeh Shakery
School of Electrical and
Computer Engineering
College of Engineering
University of Tehran
Tehran, Iran
shakery@ut.ac.ir

ABSTRACT

The Web offers fast and easy access to a wide range of documents in various languages, and translation and editing tools provide the means to create derivative documents fairly easily. This leads to the need to develop effective tools for detecting cross-language plagiarism. Given a suspicious document, cross-language plagiarism detection comprises two main subtasks: retrieving documents that are candidate sources for that document and analyzing those candidates one by one to determine their similarity to the suspicious document. In this paper we focus on the second subtask and introduce a novel approach for assessing cross-language similarity between texts for detecting plagiarized cases. Our proposed approach has two main steps: a vector-based retrieval framework that focuses on high recall, followed by a more precise similarity analysis based on dynamic text alignment. Experiments show that our method outperforms the methods of the best results in PAN-2012 and PAN-2014 in terms of *plagdet* score. We also show that aligning *n*-gram units, instead of aligning complete sentences, improves the accuracy of detecting plagiarism.

CCS Concepts

•**Information systems** → **Near-duplicate and plagiarism detection**; *Dictionaries; Multilingual and cross-lingual retrieval;* Digital libraries and archives; •**Applied computing** → **Language translation; Document analysis;**

Keywords

Cross-language plagiarism detection; *n*-grams; bilingual dictionaries; text alignment

1. INTRODUCTION

Plagiarism refers to unauthorized use of text, code, music, images, video and ideas [1]. With the rapid growth of documents in

---

[*]Visiting Scholar, University of Waterloo, 2015–16

DocEng '16, September 12-16, 2016, Vienna, Austria
© 2016 ACM. ISBN 978-1-4503-4438-8/16/09. . . $15.00
DOI: http://dx.doi.org/10.1145/2960811.2960817

various languages, the increased accessibility of electronic documents, the availability of translation tools, and the simplicity of cut-and-paste, cross-language plagiarism has become a serious problem, and its detection requires more attention. In automatic cross-language plagiarism detection, the task is to identify and isolate plagiarized text passages within suspicious documents, where each such passage has originated from a source document written in a language other than the one used in the suspicious document. A prototypical example of document plagiarism is depicted in Figure 1, where multiple source documents are used, plagiarized passages are of varying size, and plagiarized text from a source can be re-ordered. In cross-language plagiarism, passages from the source documents are also translated into the language of the suspicious document.

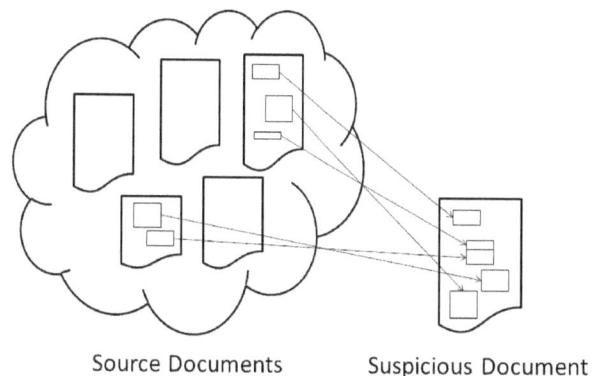

Source Documents   Suspicious Document

Figure 1: Prototypical plagiarism

Given a suspicious document, cross-language plagiarism detection comprises two main tasks: candidate retrieval and pairwise assessment of document similarity [23, 2]. Given a document suspected to include plagiarism, the goal of candidate retrieval is to identify source documents that might contain passages that match fragments of the suspicious document [11]. Assessing pairwise document similarity requires detailed comparison of the suspicious document with each candidate source document in turn to identify the plagiarized fragments precisely. In this paper we focus on this second subtask: given a candidate source document d in language L and a suspicious document d' in language L', determine which fragments of the suspicious document are plagiarized from fragments in the source document.

Most previous methods for isolating plagiarized fragments are based on translating one of the two documents into the language of the other and then applying monolingual techniques [2]. We present an alternative approach that has two steps: a vector-based retrieval framework that focuses on high recall, followed by a more precise similarity measurement based on dynamic text alignment. In the vector-based framework, instead of translating the entire document, we translate selected words and phrases only. For this simpler translation task, lexical knowledge of translation can be taken from any language translation resource. In the second step, only the suspicious fragments identified in the first step are fully translated with a machine translator; these are then aligned to the source document and tested for similarity.

We evaluate the performance in terms of *precision*, *recall*, and *granularity* scores as well as the *plagdet* score, which is a combination of the first three measures, as defined by Potthast et al. [26]. These evaluation metrics are described in Section 4.1. Our method achieves a higher *plagdet* score than the methods with best result in PAN-2012[1] [24] and in PAN-2014[2] [27]. We show that aligning n-grams, non-overlapping runs of n words for a small value of n, instead of aligning complete sentences, improves the accuracy of detecting plagiarism.

The rest of the paper is organized as follows. In Section 2, we review related work. Section 3 describes our two-step approach, followed in Section 4 by a description of the experimental framework and the presentation of our results. Finally, we summarize our conclusions and outline some future work in Section 5.

2. RELATED WORK

Plagiarism detection can use style analysis to detect parts of the text that are inconsistent in terms of writing style (*intrinsic methods*), or it can match suspicious passages in a text to the source(s) for those passages (so-called *external methods*) [1]. Plagiarism research has primarily addressed the monolingual problem, for which the sources are in the same language as the suspicious text. Monolingual external methods have been based on fingerprint indexing [28, 29], string matching [8], using sequences of stopwords [30], vector-based models [15], probabilistic models [3], semantic-based approaches [7], or classification [22].

In cross-language plagiarism detection, the suspicious document or potential source document(s) can be translated into the language of the other document(s) and a monolingual approach can then be applied. Alternatively, a cross-language similarity method can be used [23, 12], in which texts are compared based on extracted features such as individual words (and their translations) or n-grams.

Cross-Language Character N-Gram (CL-CNG) [20] is a syntax-based method that uses overlapping character n-grams of the texts for comparing multilingual documents. This approach is applicable for detecting plagiarism among documents written in languages with similar syntax, but it is ineffective when the languages differ syntactically.

CL-ASA [4], LSI [10] and KCCA [31] use parallel corpora in order to find cross-language similarity. Cross-Language Explicit Semantic Analysis (CL-ESA) [25], which is the cross-lingual generalization of ESA [14], uses comparable corpora for this purpose. Alternative approaches to detect word and phrase translations can be based on multi-lingual dictionaries or thesauri [6].

Barrón-Cedeño et al. [2] compared the performance of a syntax-based approach (CL-CNG), a parallel-corpus-based approach (CL-ASA), and an approach using translation followed by monolingual analysis (T+MA). In their experiments, conducted on the special

[1]http://www.uni-weimar.de/medien/webis/events/pan-12/pan12-web/plagiarism-detection.html
[2]http://www.gelbukh.com/plagiarism-detection/PAN-2014/

case where the suspicious document is an exact copy of a source document, CL-CNG and T+MA outperform CL-ASA. A drawback of full machine translation, however, is that it is computationally expensive. Furthermore, there is a lack of good automatic translators for some language pairs [9]. Franco-Salvador et al. [12, 13] show that their knowledge graph analysis (CL-KGA) using Babel-Net, a multi-lingual semantic network, also outperforms the CL-CNG and CL-ASA methods in detecting plagiarism. They further showed that weighing both the concepts and the relations between the concepts in their knowledge graph, using distributed representation of concepts outperforms the CL-ESA method [13]. We show that our approach outperforms the T+MA approaches presented in PAN-2012 [17] and PAN-2014 [27]. We also show that using a dictionary outperforms using BabelNet in our approach.

3. TWO-STEP RETRIEVAL MODEL

Given a source document d written in language L and a suspicious document d' in language L', let $o_1, ..., o_n$ represent the offsets of the n characters in d and let $o'_1, ..., o'_m$ represent the offsets of the m characters in d'. Let a fragment of a document be represented by a subset of that document's offsets, where the offsets within a fragment are all contiguous. (For simplicity, we use the same notation d to represent a document or its set of offsets.) Our proposed method aims to detect all fragments of the suspicious document, $d'_{f'} \subseteq d'$, that have been plagiarized from source fragments $d_f \subseteq d$. This is depicted in Figure 2, in which four fragments have been plagiarized. Thus, if the first fragment in document d covers offsets $o_i, ..., o_j$ and the corresponding fragment in document d' covers offsets $o'_p, ..., o'_q$, our problem is to detect that $\{[d, o_i], ..., [d, o_j]\} \cup \{[d', o'_p], ..., [d', o'_q]\}$ is an instance of plagiarism.

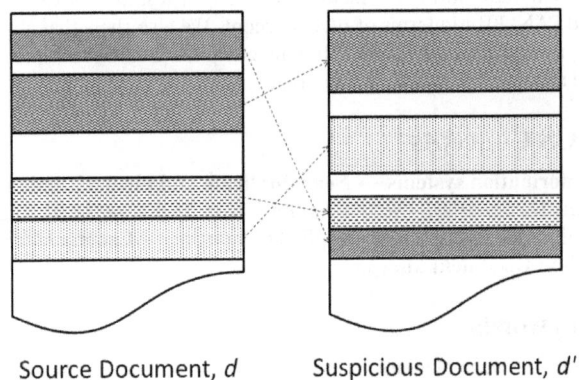

Source Document, d Suspicious Document, d'

Figure 2: Fine-grained plagiarism in a pair of documents

Thus, when comparing two documents for plagiarism, we need to find a matching of segments from the source text with segments from the suspicious one. In a brute-force approach, such a matching can be defined by first partitioning each text into segments and then pairing the segments from each text. If there are N words in the source text and M words in the target text, there are 2^{N-1} and 2^{M-1} possible partitions, respectively, having $O(N)$ and $O(M)$ segments respectively. The number of possible matchings is thus $O(2^{(N+M)}NM)$. Instead of using brute force, the first step in our method tries to find many possibly plagiarized fragments. The aim of the second step is to filter the results by finding alignments between the identified passages and measuring the similarity between aligned fragments more thoroughly. In light of this second step

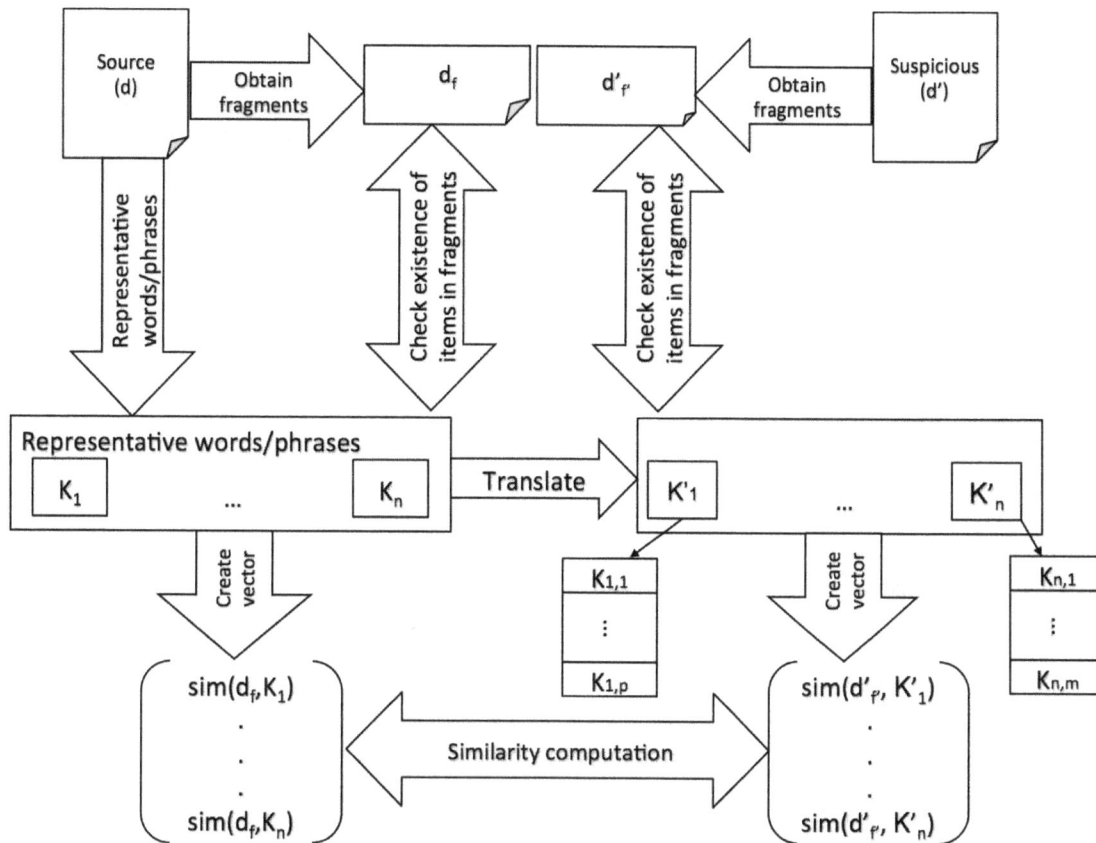

Figure 3: Step 1: Identifying potentially plagiarized fragments

that emphasizes precision, the first step is designed to favour high recall.

3.1 Candidate sentence identification: high recall step

Given a document pair in different languages, we want to identify any plagiarized parts. Rather than translating every word, however, we observe that a sentence in the suspicious document may be a translation of a sentence in the source document if it contains many words that are translations of *representative* terms from the source sentence. We start by identifying terms in the source document that are indicative of its choice of vocabulary. We then isolate fragments of the source document and of the suspicious document, identify which representative terms appear in each source fragment, and identify which *translations* of representative terms appear in each suspicious fragment. Finally we pair source and suspicious fragments when they are sufficiently similar to each other, based on the number of representative words and their translation they have in common. This process is depicted in Figure 3 and described in more detail in the remainder of this section.

3.1.1 Extraction of representative words and phrases

We use two common statistics adopted from information retrieval to select representative terms: term frequency (*tf*) and inverse document frequency (*idf*) [19]. A term's frequency reflects the prominence of that term in a document's vocabulary. This property is even more pronounced for multi-word phrases than for individual words because many complex or technical concepts and product names are expressed with multi-word compounds. Furthermore,

small sequences of words that appear often in a document serve as excellent signatures when identifying plagiarized text.

To build our vocabulary of representative terms, we preprocess a source document by removing punctuation, extra white space, and digits, by converting the text to lowercase, and normalizing diacritic characters; this yields a sequence of consistently generated word tokens. We next include all unigrams (single word tokens, not including stopwords) that have a frequency above half of the maximum frequency of any term in the document. We next include those bigrams (pairs of consecutive word tokens) having a frequency above half of the maximum frequency of any bigram in the document, and all trigrams (triples of consecutive word tokens) appearing more than twice in the document. (We allow extracted bigrams and trigrams to contain at most one stopword each.) Inverse document frequency reflects the selectivity in distinguishing a document's vocabulary from the vocabulary of other documents. Therefore, we also include those unigrams of a document that appear in no other document in the collection.

Finally, we identify additional representative unigrams by adapting a technique from query expansion. More specifically, we use a mixture model for pseudo-relevance feedback [32], available in the Lemur toolkit[3], assuming that each document is relevant to itself. We then include the top 20 such unigrams.

3.1.2 Candidate sentence selection

Having identified a set of representative terms that appear in the source document, we produce a vector space $K_1, ..., K_n$ in the language of the source document and a corresponding vector

---

[3]http://www.lemurproject.org/

61

space of those terms' translations $\mathcal{K}_1', ..., \mathcal{K}_n'$ in the language of the suspicious document. We use a *set* of translations ($\mathcal{K}_i'$) for each term (K_i) instead of relying on one translation only, so that we include paraphrased translations and improve recall. Notably, lexical knowledge for translation can be taken from dictionaries, semantic networks, or any other external language resource.

The next problem is choosing which fragments to test as the smallest detectable unit of plagiarism. In general any sequence of words in the source text might match any sequence of words in the suspicious text. If the texts have N and M words, respectively, this requires testing $O(N^2 M^2)$ pairs and considering translations for each of the $O(N^2)$ sequences. Instead, we split the documents into sentences, recording the position and length of each sentence. We assume that examples of plagiarism involve at least k consecutive sentences, with tuning parameter k. We therefore isolate k-sentence *fragments* from each document, using a sliding window over the sentences of the document. As a result, each fragment is created from a sequence of k consecutive sentences, and two fragments from a document may overlap by as many as $k - 1$ sentences. This is depicted in Figure 4. As a result, we need to test only $O(NM)$ fragment pairs, and we compare only some chosen terms rather than using full translations.

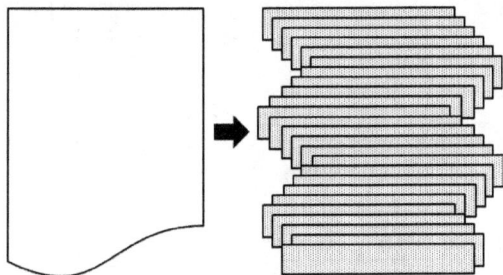

Figure 4: Overlapping k-sentence fragments produced by sliding window

For each fragment d_f in the source document, we create a vector in the space of representative terms by setting $v_{d_f}[K_i]$ to 1 if the term K_i occurs in the fragment and 0 otherwise. Similarly, if *any* of the translations $K' \in \mathcal{K}_i'$ of K_i appears in a fragment identified by $d'_{f'}$ in the suspicious document, we set $v_{d'_{f'}}[K_i']$ to 1. Although the precision decreases by allowing any of the translations, the second step of our approach, described in the next section, has as its goal to improve precision.

Next the representative term vectors for each fragment in the source document are compared to the term vectors for fragments in the suspicious document. d_f will be considered as a potential plagiarism source of $d'_{f'}$ if its representative term vector has maximum similarity to that of $d'_{f'}$ among all term vectors for fragments in document d and that similarity is above a threshold obtained from a training set. Before passing the pairs of potential plagiarism instances to the second step of the algorithm, adjacent pairs are merged if they fall within a fixed proximity threshold in both the source and suspicious documents.

Figure 5 shows one matched pair of fragments consisting of five sentences and eight sentences, respectively, the latter resulting from merging three overlapping windows. The highlighted words in each fragment are the representative words and phrases that indicate that this might be a plagiarized piece of text, with the lighter highlighting indicating those words that match in the other text. Because representative terms in the source document are the only elements being translated, it is not crucial to have high quality ma-

Source fragment:

> Die kontinuierliche Überwachung der legislativen **Arbeit** durch die Wähler, das **Parlament** und die Massenmedien kann durch eine gemeinsame **Datenbank** erleichtert werden, die den Namen des Verantwortlichen in der **Kommission** und des Berichterstatters des Europäischen **Parlaments** **enthält** .
>
> **Ferner** sollte sie Angaben zum **Zeitplan** , zu den Auswirkungen auf den Haushalt sowie zur Rechtsgrundlage umfassen.
>
> Diese **Datenbank** sollte öffentlich zugänglich sein und wäre meiner Meinung nach auch für unsere Kollegen in den einzelstaatlichen Parlamenten von großem Nutzen.
>
> Herr Präsident, ich hoffe, die Kommissionsmitglieder werden bald, vielleicht schon in den nächsten Tagen, Kontakt mit den **Ausschüssen** des **Parlaments** aufnehmen, damit schnellstmöglich mit der Umsetzung des vereinbarten **Zeitplans** und der festgelegten **Arbeitsformen** begonnen werden kann.
>
> Ich glaube, dass mit einer derartigen Änderung der **Verfahren** die Arbeitsweise und der **Legislativzyklus** effizienter, transparenter und verständlicher gestaltet werden können.

Suspicious fragment:

> To make it easier for the electorate, ourselves and the mass media to follow the **legislative** **work** , a common **database** should be set up showing who in the **Commission** and **Parliament** is responsible for a particular proposal.
>
> The **database** should also contain information about the calendar, budgetary implications and legal **base** .
>
> The **database** should be publicly available.
>
> I believe it should prove to be of very great help to our colleagues in the national parliaments.
>
> Mr President, I hope that, no later than in the course of the next few days, the Commissioners will begin to visit Parliaments' committees so that a start can be made as soon as possible on following the agreed **timetable** and **method** of **working** .
>
> About three o'clock in the afternoon during the warm weather Mother would begin skimming the milk, carrying it pan by pan to the big cream pan, where with a quick movement of a case knife the cream was separated from the sides of the pan, the pan tilted on the edge of the cream pan and the heavy mantle of cream, in folds or flakes, slid off into the receptacle and the thick milk emptied into pails to be carried to the swill barrel for the hogs.
>
> I used to help Mother at times by handing her the pans of milk from the rack and emptying the pails.
>
> Then came the washing of the pans at the trough, at which I also often aided her by standing the pans up to dry and sun on the big bench.

Figure 5: A matched pair of fragments detected in the first step, with representative terms highlighted

chine translation between the two languages for this step. There is no need to translate the entire text, and therefore this step of our approach is applicable to languages that have any translation resource. In particular, it is applicable for low-resourced languages but improves as more translations are available for consideration.

3.2 Result filtering: focusing on precision

In the previous step, we retrieved potentially plagiarized, multi-sentence fragments signalled by their use of representative terms. In this step, we translate the suspicious fragments only, using a full machine translation system, and then we filter out those instances that have poor similarity when *all* words other than stopwords are considered. By filtering out false positive detections, the hope is that this step improves the *precision*, and hence the overall performance, of the model.

A plagiarized fragment may omit pieces from the source, but it is likely that at least some of the smallest units of discourse are preserved in their original order. Therefore, for this step of the algorithm, we partition the sentences within a fragment into non-overlapping n-grams (i.e., sub-sentence units consisting of n consecutive words, on average[4]) and try to align such segments in the source fragment with corresponding segments in the suspicious fragment to which it has been paired in the first step. This stage of alignment aims at pairing corresponding segments *without reordering*[5], and it accommodates situations in which a plagiarized text might merge or split segments in the translated document. This is illustrated in Figure 6, where the first segment in the source fragment does not appear in the suspicious one, the second segment is split into two segments in the suspicious fragment, the third and fourth segments are merged into a single segment, and the fifth segment is translated as a single segment in the suspicious document.

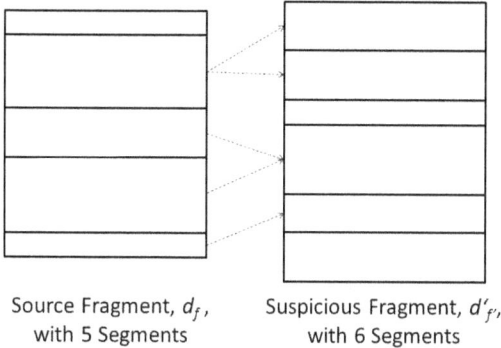

Source Fragment, d_f, with 5 Segments   Suspicious Fragment, $d'_{f'}$, with 6 Segments

Figure 6: Aligning segments within a pair of fragments

The alignment score is obtained by a dynamic programming algorithm based on the one proposed by Ma [18] and using a measure of string similarity *sim*:

$$S(i,j) = max \begin{cases} S(i-1,j) \\ S(i,j-1) \\ S(i-1,j-1) + sim(susp_i, src_j) \\ S(i-1,j-2) + sim(susp_i, src_{j-1:j}) \\ S(i-1,j-3) + sim(susp_i, src_{j-2:j}) \\ S(i-2,j-1) + sim(susp_{i-1:i}, src_j) \\ S(i-3,j-1) + sim(susp_{i-2:i}, src_j) \end{cases}$$

For simplicity, we assume that translations will split or merge at most three segments at a time, and we therefore allow 1-0, 0-1, 1-

---

[4]In fact for a sentence of length s, the number of partitions is chosen to be s/n rounded to the nearest integer, and the final partition may include fewer or more than n terms.

[5]Text rearrangements are accommodated in the first step of the algorithm, described in Section 3.1.

1, 1-2, 2-1, 1-3 and 3-1 alignments. The optimal alignment of the first i suspicious segments and j source segments depends on the alignment score of some sequential prefix of these segments plus a single alignment. $S(i,j)$ represents the similarity from the beginning of the documents to the ith suspicious segment and the jth source segment. The notation $susp_{x:y}$ represents the concatenation of suspicious segments numbered from x to y, and similarly $src_{x:y}$ refers to source segments. We modified the algorithm proposed by Ma [18], to implicitly penalize 1-0 and 0-1 alignments and also to make all scores comparable. To this end, we keep track of the number of alignments obtained so far, and the score in each step is normalized by the number of the alignments. Thus, null alignments (i.e., 1-0 and 0-1 alignments) are penalized because they only increase the count of the alignments but not the similarity score. If the optimal alignment score is above a threshold, that case is reported as a plagiarized case. Finally, complete sentences at the start or end of a fragment having more than half their content in a 1-0 or 0-1 alignment are excluded from the reported suspicious and source cases, respectively.

Figure 7 shows the results of applying the dynamic program to the pair of matched fragments shown in Figure 5. The final pruning step drops the last two sentences of the suspicious text, but keeps all sentences from the source text because more than half of the first and last sentences contribute to the alignment.

4. EXPERIMENTAL FRAMEWORK

Our experiments examine the step-by-step performance of the proposed approach and serve several purposes: (1) evaluating the candidate sentence selection algorithm using three distinct external resources for translation (Section 4.2), (2) evaluating the dynamic alignment algorithm and comparing various levels of granularity for alignment purpose (Section 4.3), and (3) evaluating the effectiveness of determining pairwise document similarity by applying the proposed two step retrieval model (also in Section 4.3).

4.1 Data sets and evaluation metrics

We evaluate our proposed approach using the complete German-English partition of the PAN-PC-12 text alignment corpus[6]. Both the training data set and the test data set include plagiarized documents that are obfuscated by translation from German into English. The training set comprises 305 source and 179 suspicious documents, among which some suspicious documents contain plagiarized text from more than one source document and some source documents are plagiarized in more than one suspicious document, yielding 449 pairs. In the test set there are 263 pairs for which each suspicious document has exactly one corresponding source document. The construction principles of the corpus are defined by Potthast et al. [26], who also define the following evaluation metrics.

Let S and R represent the set of true plagiarism cases and the reported detections, respectively, where $s \in S$ (and similarly $r \in R$) is the union of the sets of offsets in a plagiarized fragment from the suspicious document and in the corresponding fragments from the source document (each offset marked with the document to which it refers). Given source document d and suspicious document d', we say that $r \in R$ *detects* $s \in S$, written as $\delta(r,s)$, if $r \cap s$ includes at least one offset from each document:

$$\delta(r,s) \Leftrightarrow (r \cap s \cap d \neq \emptyset) \land (r \cap s \cap d' \neq \emptyset)$$

The performance of the task is reported as the macro-average *plagdet* score, which is a combination of the macro-average *precision* $\mathcal{P}$,

---

[6]http://www.uni-weimar.de/medien/webis/events/pan-12/pan12-web/plagiarism-detection.html

Source fragment (translated):

the continuous monitoring of the legislative work by the
electorate the parliament and the mass media can be
facilitated by a common database that contains the name
of the person responsible within the commission and the
rapporteur of the european parliament.

it should also include information on the timetable the
impact on the budget as well as the legal basis.

this database should be publicly available and would in
my opinion for our colleagues in the national parliaments of great benefit.

mr. president i hope the commissioners will begin soon
maybe in the next few days contact with the
committees of parliament as quickly as possible to begin
the implementation of the agreed time schedule and established ways of working.

i think that can be made more efficient more
transparent and understandable with such a change in procedures
and the functioning of the legislative process.

Suspicious fragment:

to make it easier for the electorate ourselves and
the mass media to follow the legislative work a
common database should be set up showing who in
the commission and parliament is responsible for a particular proposal.

the database should also contain information about the calendar
budgetary implications and legal base.

the database should be publicly available.
i believe it should prove to be of very
great help to our colleagues in the national parliaments.

mr president i hope that no later than in
the course of the next few days the commissioners
will begin to visit parliaments' committees so that a
start can be made as soon as possible on
following the agreed timetable and method of working.

about three o'clock in the afternoon during the warm
weather mother would begin skimming the milk carrying it
pan by pan to the big cream pan where
with a quick movement of a case knife the
cream was separated from the sides of the pan
the pan tilted on the edge of the cream
pan and the heavy mantle of cream in folds
or flakes slid off into the receptacle and the
thick milk emptied into pails to be carried to
the swill barrel for the hogs.

i used to help mother at times by handing
her the pans of milk from the rack and emptying the pails.

then came the washing of the pans at the
trough at which i also often aided her by
standing the pans up to dry and sun on the big bench.

Figure 7: Aligned 9-grams in the matched fragments from Fig. 5

recall $\mathcal{R}$, and *granularity* $\mathcal{G}$ metrics defined as follows:

$$\mathcal{P}(R,S) = \frac{1}{|R|} \sum_{r \in R} \frac{|\bigcup_{s \in S} (s \sqcap r)|}{|r|}$$

$$\mathcal{R}(R,S) = \frac{1}{|S|} \sum_{s \in S} \frac{|\bigcup_{r \in R} (s \sqcap r)|}{|s|}$$

$$\mathcal{F}_1(R,S) = \frac{2\mathcal{P}(R,S)\mathcal{R}(R,S)}{\mathcal{P}(R,S) + \mathcal{R}(R,S)}$$

$$\mathcal{G}(R,S) = \frac{1}{|S_R|} \sum_{s \in S_R} |R_s|$$

where $s \sqcap r = s \cap r$ if $\delta(r,s)$ and $\emptyset$ otherwise, $S_R = \{s \in S \mid \exists r \in R : \delta(r,s)\}$, and $R_s = \{r \in R \mid \delta(r,s)\}$. Precision, recall, and F_1 (their harmonic mean) are adapted from information retrieval. Granularity is a metric specific to plagiarism detection that reports the average number of reported instances of plagiarism per detected source fragment of plagiarism. These scores are combined into an overall score called *plagdet* and defined as follows[7]:

$$plagdet(R,S) = \frac{\mathcal{F}_1(R,S)}{log_2(1 + \mathcal{G}(\mathcal{R},\mathcal{S}))}$$

---

[7]This measure is used in PAN's plagiarism detection competition.

4.2 Evaluating the performance of candidate sentence identification

In the first step of the algorithm we use the framework described in Section 3.1. We use the training data to tune two parameters. The first one is the number of consecutive sentences to include in each fragment, which represents the smallest detectable unit of plagiarism. The second parameter is the threshold for accepting a pair of fragments as evidence of plagiarism.

Our approach limits candidate fragments to align with sentence boundaries and include at least k sentences. Based on experiments using the training data, we set $k = 5$. (Coincidentally, 5-sentence sliding windows are also used by Franco-Salvador et al. as the fragment size for plagiarism detection [13].) Recall that each fragment from the source and suspicious document is represented as a binary vector $<sim_1, sim_2, ..., sim_n> \in \{0,1\}^n$ as described in Section 3.1. We identify source passage d_f and suspicious passage $d'_{f'}$ as a plagiarism candidate pair if the source passage term vector has maximum similarity to that of $d'_{f'}$ among all term vectors for fragments in document d and their cosine similarity exceeds threshold t, which is set to 0.4 based on the training data. In order to eliminate spurious matches, we also require that the source fragment includes translations of at least three keywords found in the suspicious fragment.

To improve performance with respect to the granularity metric,

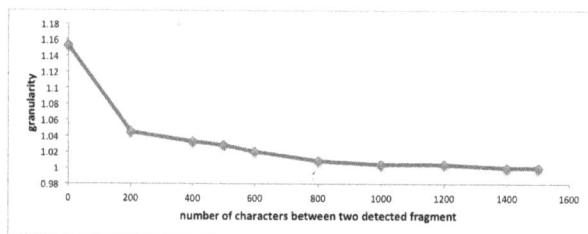

Figure 8: Effect of merging adjacent fragments on the granularity metric

which distinguishes whether an instance of plagiarism is detected as a whole or in several pieces, we merge two adjacent detected fragments to report a single plagiarism case if the number of characters between those fragments in the source and suspicious documents are both below a fixed proximity threshold[8]. Because this threshold is not obtained from training, we measure the sensitivity of the proximity parameter and display the results in Figure 8. Granularity starts at 1.1529 without merging adjacent fragments and decreases to 1 as more characters are allowed to exist between two adjacent fragments. The proximity threshold of 1500 chosen for our experiments falls well within the range that produces a granularity score of 1. The resulting passages are candidate result pairs consisting of five or more sentences each, which are further processed in the next step.

We test three distinct external resources for the translation phase: Google translate[9], BabelNet[10], and dict.cc[11]. Google offers a machine translation service, from which we used the best translation provided to serve as a baseline. BabelNet is a multi-lingual semantic network, in which each node represents a concept and the edges record the semantic relationships between the concepts; concepts and relations are selected from WordNet and Wikipedia [21]. The dict.cc dictionary is a German-English dictionary containing 1,070,884 entries.

Without applying a German stemmer and without splitting compound words, only 28% of the representative terms appear in BabelNet and 43% appear in dict.cc. We therefore apply a lightweight preprocessing step to improve the coverage: we use the jwordsplitter toolkit[12] to split German compounds and a German stemmer based on the algorithm described by Caumanns [5]. We stemmed words from the document and also from dict.cc.

The process of looking up a term is then as follows. We look up each term (unigram, bigram, or trigram) in the original reference work. If a unigram is not found, the stem of the term is looked up (but in the stemmed dictionary for dict.cc). If the term includes multiple words after splitting compounds, each word is treated individually. If all parts of such a term are found in either the original or stemmed reference work, all their translations are recorded. Otherwise we assume that the term is not translated, and the original term is kept as the translation of the term (in case the term is a proper name that is repeated identically in the other language). After applying this preprocessing step, the average percentage of terms found in dict.cc increases to about 81% and in BabelNet increases to about 48%.

Table 1 shows that the approach using Google translation has the highest *plagdet* score at the end of the first step, but the highest recall is achieved by using the dict.cc dictionary with preprocessing. By keeping more translations for each word, we are able to catch paraphrased translations and translations using alternative language resources. The exceedingly low precision of this step and the correspondingly poor *plagdet* score result from not considering the positions of the words, the presence of many possible translations, and the coincidental similarity resulting from the use of common words. In the next step, however, we will eliminate many false positive detections to improve precision.

4.3 Evaluating the two-step approach

The second set of experiments focuses on the filtering step. Since we are looking for text fragments borrowed from another source, the objective is to avoid reporting documents with coincidental similarity between texts.

For this step, we apply the Google translation system to the potentially plagiarized source fragments only. Figure 9 is a stacked graph showing for each document the number of sentences, the number of sentences we translate, and the number of plagiarized sentences. The amount of translation required in our experiments is about 45% of the sentences from the test data, in which approximately 33% of the entire test data sentences are plagiarized. Thus we have significantly reduced the use of an expensive component, and this reduction increases if the suspicious documents include fewer or smaller plagiarized segments.

Those fragments containing randomly common words do not signal plagiarism, and the dynamic alignment algorithm takes into account the position and proximity of the common words. To identify an appropriate threshold to distinguish between true positive and false positive plagiarism detection, we use a subset of our training data, namely 112 cases retrieved from the first step of the algorithm together with their translations. The average similarity scores calculated by applying the second step of the algorithm on this training set is chosen as the threshold.

Table 2 shows the results of the detailed analysis experiment using the dynamic alignment algorithm and how it behaves with both sentence-level and n-gram-level granularity for segments, where n is set to 9 based on runs conducted with the training data. We can see that using n-grams outperforms using sentences by about 4.4%, which is statistically significant (Wilcoxon signed rank test $p < 0.0001$), and running the dynamic algorithm with more items to align was only slightly slower than running the algorithm with sentences instead. The overall score is also compared with the methods of the best results in PAN-2012 [17] and PAN-2014 [27], both of which use monolingual techniques for which the translations of the entire documents of the *source* collection are used. For this experiment, we applied the algorithms described in the earlier papers to the same test collection used for our approach (obtaining slightly different performance results than reported in the original papers on other corpora).

For completeness, we also tested our approach using segments that correspond to elementary discourse units (EDUs), which are clause-like fragments that serve as building blocks of sentences [16]. We hypothesized that since EDUs are semantically coherent lexical units rather than arbitrary sequences of n consecutive words of text, they might be better representatives of the atomic units of plagiarism. EDUs were extracted using the CODRA toolkit[13], requiring 402 minutes to execute for all the candidate fragments identified in the first step of our approach (whereas partitioning into equiva-

---

[8]We could just as well have chosen to measure proximity in terms of numbers of words.

[9]https://translate.google.ca/

[10]http://babelfy.org/

[11]http://www.dict.cc/

[12]https://github.com/danielnaber/jwordsplitter

[13]https://www.cs.ubc.ca/cs-research/lci/research-groups/natural-language-processing/Discourse.html

Table 1: Results of using various translation resources for the first step of the algorithm

External Language Resource	Precision	Recall	Granularity	Plagdet
Google translate	**0.7267**	0.7839	1	**0.7542**
BabelNet (without preprocessing)	0.7067	0.3487	1	0.4670
BabelNet (with preprocessing)	0.5337	0.6379	1	0.5811
Dict.cc (without preprocessing)	0.5733	0.6377	1	0.6038
Dict.cc (with preprocessing)	0.2960	**0.8721**	1	0.4419

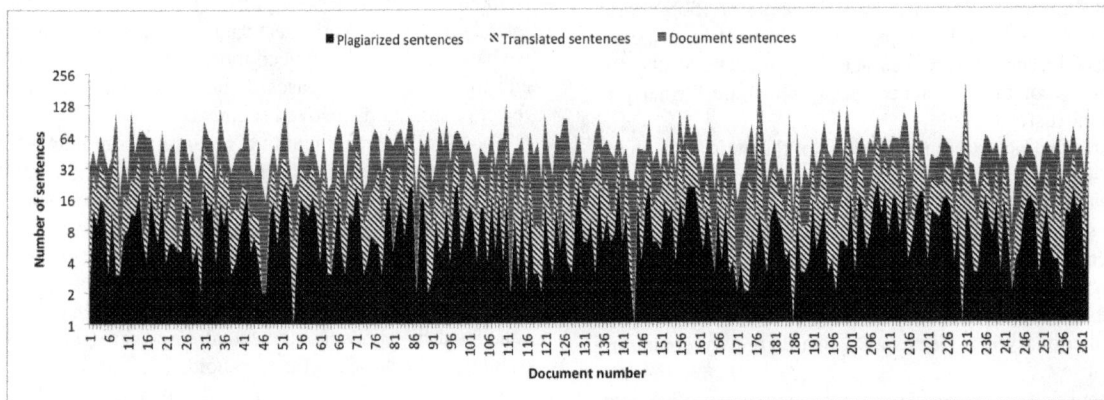

Figure 9: Amount of translation required compared to the number of sentences and the amount of plagiarism

Table 2: Comparing the results of pairwise document similarity assessment

Method	Precision	Recall	Granularity	Plagdet
Best result from PAN-2012	0.8040	0.6976	1	0.7470
Best result from PAN-2014	0.8125	0.7205	1	0.7637
Using dict.cc and sentence granularity	0.8405	**0.8293**	1	0.8348
Using Google translate and n-gram granularity	0.9214	0.7505	1	0.8272
Using dict.cc and n-gram granularity	**0.9301**	0.8193	1	**0.8712**
Using dict.cc and EDU granularity	0.9190	0.8204	1	**0.8669**

lently sized n-grams is essentially instantaneous). Our experimentally chosen value of $n = 9$ for n-gram splitting is, perhaps not coincidentally, fairly close to the average EDU size, which is about 7 for the training data and about 8.6 for the test data. As it turns out, the difference in performance when using EDUs as compared to n-grams is not statistically significant.

To complete our comparison, Table 2 also includes the results from applying our second step to the fragments identified by Google translate in the first step; as expected, the lower recall in the first step results in a lower performance overall. Thus we conclude that using dict.cc in the first step and using n-gram granularity in the second step results in best performance.

5. CONCLUSION AND FUTURE WORK

In this paper we propose a two-step retrieval model for detecting cross-language plagiarized sentences given the source and suspicious documents. The first step selects candidate sentences, with a goal of high recall, and the second step aims to filter out false positive detections with an alignment model connecting similar segments. Lexical similarity cues used in the vector representation of the first step identifies similar fragments which could signal plagiarism. This accommodates rearrangements of plagiarized fragments as well as restricting the dynamic programming algorithm of the next step to highly suspicious regions.

The impact of three distinct translation resources (Google, BabelNet and dict.cc) are evaluated in the first step of the algorithm. The experimental results show that using multiple senses from a dictionary, together with some simple lexical compound-splitting and stemming, outperforms the other resources with respect to *recall* for retrieving potential similarities between sentences of the two languages.

To avoid reporting coincidental similarities as plagiarism, the fragments retrieved in the first step are further processed with a more precise measure using dynamic text alignment. The alignment algorithm is tested with different levels of granularity: sentences, EDUs, and n-grams. Experiments show that using EDUs slightly outperforms using sentence level alignment, but requires significantly more execution time. However, splitting a text into n-gram units performs as well as using EDUs, but with less execution time. The proposed approach outperforms today's best translation and monolingual techniques and cuts translation time significantly.

For further work, we would like to devise a method to apply the same framework without requiring any sentence translation in the second step. Furthermore, our approach should be combined with a high-quality candidate identification mechanism [11] to produce an effective end-to-end system for cross-language plagiarism detection.

5.1 Acknowledgments

The use of computing facilities at the University of Tehran and at the University of Waterloo is gratefully acknowledged. We also thank Miguel Sánchez-Pérez et al. [27] for making their code available.

6. REFERENCES

[1] A. Barrón-Cedeño. On the mono-and cross-language detection of text reuse and plagiarism. In *Proceedings of the 33rd International ACM SIGIR Conference on Research and Development in Information Retrieval*, pages 914–914. ACM, 2010.

[2] A. Barrón-Cedeño, P. Gupta, and P. Rosso. Methods for cross-language plagiarism detection. *Knowledge-Based Systems*, 45(1):45–62, 2013.

[3] A. Barrón-Cedeño, P. Rosso, and J.-M. Benedí. Reducing the plagiarism detection search space on the basis of the Kullback-Leibler distance. In *Computational Linguistics and Intelligent Text Processing*, pages 523–534. Springer, 2009.

[4] A. Barrón-Cedeño, P. Rosso, D. Pinto, and A. Juan. On cross-lingual plagiarism analysis using a statistical model. In *Working Notes for CLEF 2008 Conference; PAN Evaluation Lab: Uncovering Plagiarism, Authorship and Social Software Misuse*, pages 9–13, 2008.

[5] J. Caumanns. A fast and simple stemming algorithm for German words. Technical report, Free University of Berlin, 1999.

[6] Z. Ceska, M. Toman, and K. Jezek. Multilingual plagiarism detection. In *Proceedings of the 13th International Conference on Artificial Intelligence: Methodologies, Systtems, and Applications (AIMSA 2008)*, pages 83–92, 2008.

[7] C.-Y. Chen, J.-Y. Yeh, and H.-R. Ke. Plagiarism detection using Rouge and WordNet. *Journal of Computing*, pages 34 – 44, 2010.

[8] P. Clough and M. Stevenson. Developing a corpus of plagiarised short answers. *Language Resources and Evaluation*, 45(1):5–24, 2011.

[9] V. Danilova. Cross-language plagiarism detection methods. In *the Student Research Workshop associated with Recent Advances in Natural Language Processing, RANLP*, pages 51–57, 2013.

[10] S. T. Dumais, T. A. Letsche, M. L. Littman, and T. K. Landauer. Automatic cross-language retrieval using latent semantic indexing. In *AAAI Spring Symposium on Cross-language Text and Speech Retrieval*, volume 15, pages 18–24, 1997.

[11] N. Ehsan and A. Shakery. Candidate document retrieval for cross-lingual plagiarism detection using two level proximity information. *Information Processing & Management*, 2016.

[12] M. Franco-Salvador, P. Gupta, and P. Rosso. Cross-language plagiarism detection using a multilingual semantic network. In *Advances in Information Retrieval*, pages 710–713. Springer, 2013.

[13] M. Franco-Salvador, P. Rosso, and M. Montes-y Gómez. A systematic study of knowledge graph analysis for cross-language plagiarism detection. *Information Processing & Management*, 52(4):550–570, 2016.

[14] E. Gabrilovich and S. Markovitch. Computing semantic relatedness using Wikipedia-based explicit semantic analysis. In *International Joint Conference on Artificial Intelligence, IJCAI*, volume 7, pages 1606–1611, 2007.

[15] C. Grozea, C. Gehl, and M. Popescu. Encoplot: Pairwise sequence matching in linear time applied to plagiarism detection. In *Working Notes for CLEF 2009 Conference; PAN Evaluation Lab: Uncovering Plagiarism, Authorship and Social Software Misuse*, pages 10 – 18, 2009.

[16] S. Joty, G. Carenini, and R. T. Ng. Codra: A novel discriminative framework for rhetorical analysis. *Computational Linguistics*, pages 904 – 915, 2015.

[17] K. Leilei, Q. Haoliang, W. Shuai, D. Cuixia, W. Suhong, and H. Yong. Approaches for candidate document retrieval and detailed comparison of plagiarism detection. In *Working Notes for CLEF 2012 Conference; PAN Evaluation Lab: Uncovering Plagiarism, Authorship and Social Software Misuse*, 2012.

[18] X. Ma. Champollion: A robust parallel text sentence aligner.

In *LREC 2006: Fifth International Conference on Language Resources and Evaluation*, pages 489–492, 2006.

[19] C. D. Manning, P. Raghavan, and H. Schütze. *Introduction to Information Retrieval*, volume 1. Cambridge University Press Cambridge, 2008.

[20] P. McNamee and J. Mayfield. Character n-gram tokenization for European language text retrieval. *Information Retrieval*, 7(1-2):73–97, 2004.

[21] R. Navigli and S. P. Ponzetto. BabelNet: Building a very large multilingual semantic network. In *Proceedings of the 48th Annual Meeting of the Association for Computational Linguistics*, pages 216–225. Association for Computational Linguistics, 2010.

[22] R. C. Pereira, V. P. Moreira, and R. Galante. A new approach for cross-language plagiarism analysis. In *Multilingual and Multimodal Information Access Evaluation*, pages 15–26. Springer, 2010.

[23] M. Potthast, A. Barrón-Cedeño, B. Stein, and P. Rosso. Cross-language plagiarism detection. *Language Resources and Evaluation*, 45(1):45–62, 2011.

[24] M. Potthast, T. Gollub, M. Hagen, J. Kiesel, M. Michel, A. Oberländer, M. Tippmann, A. Barrón-Cedeño, P. Gupta, P. Rosso, et al. Overview of the 4th international competition on plagiarism detection. In *Working Notes for CLEF 2012 Conference; PAN Evaluation Lab: Uncovering Plagiarism, Authorship and Social Software Misuse*, 2012.

[25] M. Potthast, B. Stein, and M. Anderka. A Wikipedia-based multilingual retrieval model. In *Advances in Information Retrieval*, pages 522–530. Springer, 2008.

[26] M. Potthast, B. Stein, A. Barrón-Cedeño, and P. Rosso. An evaluation framework for plagiarism detection. In *Proceedings of the 23rd International Conference on Computational Linguistics: Posters*, pages 997–1005. Association for Computational Linguistics, 2010.

[27] M. A. Sánchez-Pérez, A. F. Gelbukh, and G. Sidorov. Adaptive algorithm for plagiarism detection: The best-performing approach at PAN 2014 text alignment competition. In *Proceedings of the 6th International Conference of the CLEF Association*, pages 402–413, 2015.

[28] S. Schleimer, D. S. Wilkerson, and A. Aiken. Winnowing: local algorithms for document fingerprinting. In *Proceedings of the 2003 ACM SIGMOD International Conference on Management of Data*, pages 76–85. ACM, 2003.

[29] J. Seo and W. B. Croft. Local text reuse detection. In *Proceedings of the 31st International ACM SIGIR Conference on Research and Development in Information Retrieval*, pages 571–578. ACM, 2008.

[30] E. Stamatatos. Plagiarism detection using stopword n-grams. *Journal of the American Society for Information Science and Technology*, 62(12):2512–2527, 2011.

[31] A. Vinokourov, N. Cristianini, and J. S. Shawe-taylor. Inferring a semantic representation of text via cross-language correlation analysis. In *Advances in Neural Information Processing Systems*, pages 1473–1480, 2002.

[32] C. Zhai and J. Lafferty. Model-based feedback in the language modeling approach to information retrieval. In *Proceedings of the Tenth International Conference on Information and Knowledge Management*, CIKM '01. ACM, 2001.

Relaxing Orthogonality Assumption in Conceptual Text Document Similarity

Xiangru Wang
Faculty of Computer Science
Dalhousie University
Halifax, Nova Scotia
Canada B3H 4R2
xn535650@dal.ca

Seyednaser
Nourashrafeddin
Faculty of Computer Science
Dalhousie University
Halifax, Nova Scotia
Canada B3H 4R2
nourashr@cs.dal.ca

Evangelos Milios
Faculty of Computer Science
Dalhousie University
Halifax, Nova Scotia
Canada B3H 4R2
eem@cs.dal.ca

ABSTRACT

By reflecting the degree of proximity or remoteness of documents, similarity measure plays the key role in text analytics. Traditional measures, e.g. cosine similarity, assume that documents are represented in an orthogonal space formed by words as dimensions. Words are considered independent from each other and document similarity is computed based on lexical overlap. This assumption is also made in the bag of concepts representation of documents while the space is formed by concepts. This paper proposes new semantic similarity measures without relying on the orthogonality assumption. By employing Wikipedia as an external resource, we introduce five similarity measures using concept-concept relatedness. Experimental results on real text datasets reveal that eliminating the orthogonality assumption improves the quality of text clustering algorithms.

Keywords

Wikipedia, Semantic Similarity, Concept Relatedness, Text Clustering

1. INTRODUCTION

Traditional methods usually represent text documents in the "Bag of Words" (BOW) model [1]. Using a Vector Space Model (*VSM*), each document is represented as a vector of dimension equal to the size of vocabulary while each word represents one dimension. To measure document similarity, the dimensions of this space are usually assumed orthogonal. This orthogonality assumption means that words are totally independent of each other. Two documents are thus dissimilar if they do not share common words, while they might have synonyms or related words.

One approach to address this problem is to represent documents in semantic level using external resources such as WordNet [6], MeSH [26], or Wikipedia [4]. The idea behind this approach is that two different words may refer to the same concept, for instance

DocEng '16, September 12-16, 2016, Vienna, Austria
© 2016 ACM. ISBN 978-1-4503-4438-8/16/09. . . $15.00
DOI: http://dx.doi.org/10.1145/2960811.2960813

in Wikipedia. Hence, replacing words by concepts and then representing documents as "Bags of Concepts" (BOC) somewhat relaxes the orthogonality assumption. However, the assumption still exists since two documents are dissimilar if they do not share common concepts in the BOC model.

A semantically enriched similarity is proposed in [9] to relax orthogonality of the BOC model. Given two documents d_A and d_B, represented as BOC vectors, they enrich d_A by the concepts present in d_B but not in d_A. The weight of the newly-added concepts are computed based on their similarities to the concepts of d_A. For this purpose, a concept-concept relatedness is measured from Wikipedia hyperlinks. Cosine similarity is then applied on the enriched representation of documents. The main drawback of this approach is that the weight of a newly-added concept c_B in d_A depends only on the weight of c_B in d_B, the weight of its most related concept c_A in d_A, and the concept-concept relatedness of c_A and c_B. The weights of other related concepts in d_A are thus ignored. In mathematical words, a missing dimension of d_A in concept space is added based on the maximum relatedness of that dimension to the other dimensions of d_A. This means that other pairs of concepts are considered orthogonal. They have demonstrated that this enriched BOC representation performs better than the BOC model in text clustering and classification.

This paper aims at developing conceptual text document similarity measures without relying on the orthogonality assumption. As an external resource, we use Wikipedia to extract concepts of text documents and then represent them in the BOC model. Concept-concept relatedness is also computed based on hyperlinks in Wikipedia. For a pair of documents, we map concepts of one document to concepts of the other document in different ways. Based on the mapping, we then calculate pair-wise document similarities.

It is worth mentioning that Wikipedia concepts are the titles of articles in Wikipedia. Each article is assumed to present one concept.

In our experiments, we compare seven similarity measures including five proposed ones, the cosine similarity in BOW, and the cosine similarity in BOC. We use document clustering to evaluate the similarity measures. Three clustering algorithms are applied on six real text datasets. The experimental results indicate that clustering quality is improved after relaxing the orthogonality assumption.

The rest of this paper is structured as follows. Section 2 reviews related work. Section 3 describes five proposed semantic similarity measures. Section 4 explains about the framework of experiments, the clustering algorithms, and datasets. Section 5 presents the experiments and discussion. Finally, section 6 includes conclusions and future work.

2. RELATED WORK

In this section, we review related research works. First, we review some existing methods for calculating semantic text similarity. After that, we present some researches related to exploiting semantic information in Wikipedia. Then we compare existing Wikification methods. Last, we review works proposed to relax the orthogonality assumption in text document similarity.

2.1 Text Semantic Similarity

The semantic text similarity problem is defined as how to derive the similarity score at the semantic level automatically, given two text documents as input. There have been several word-to-word semantic similarity measures either knowledge-based [25] or corpus-based [23]. A measure which depends on both corpus-based and knowledge-based measures of similarity was developed in [14]. This method was applied on short text and the experiments showed that incorporating semantic information into the similarity measure outperformed the simple lexical matching methods. Another measure modified Longest Common Subsequence (*LCS*) of words to compute the similarity of two texts at both lexical and semantic levels [10].

We investigated the document similarity mainly at a semantic level. By incorporating the semantic similarity among Wikipedia concepts, we propose five semantic similarity measures.

2.2 Semantic Information in Wikipedia

There have been some research works on employing semantic information extracted from Wikipedia in document clustering and classification. The question of what kind of information in Wikipedia can provide more benefit to clustering performance was explored in [7]. They used several vector combinations to represent the document collection including: word vector only, concept vector only, category vector only, word and concept vectors, word and category vectors, concept and category vectors, word and concept and category vectors. Their experiments on three datasets showed that category information is more useful than others in document clustering. However, the study just explored the lexical overlap at a semantic level without considering the relatedness between terms or concepts. In our work, we use the concept vectors and concept-concept relatedness.

The semantic information was captured by representing documents with Wikipedia concepts in the BOC model in [8]. During the clustering process, they utilized Wikipedia to facilitate active learning by measuring the semantic relatedness among concepts to analyze the topic distribution within document groups. Their experiments are based on the orthogonality assumption among terms and among concepts.

A framework was proposed for partitional clustering by integrating Wikipedia concepts into the bag of words model in [18]. By combining clusters from both BOW and BOC, the documents with the same label in the clusterings formed a training set to learn a classifier, which was later used to classify the remaining documents. Their experiments revealed that the BOC model did help if combined with the BOW model, but could not outperform the BOW model by itself. The orthogonality assumption was made in their experiments.

A common observation among these research works is that documents are represented in a space such that the dimensions (words or concepts) are assumed orthogonal.

2.3 Wikification Methods

Given a text document, the wikification task is defined as identifying the most related Wikipedia concepts associated with the text [15]. This task includes two sub-tasks: spotting concepts in text and sense disambiguation. Some research works have been devoted to making the wikification more accurate. By comparing the overlap between a text document and Wikipedia text articles, a list of weighted Wikipedia article titles were extracted in [4]. They also used a machine learning method to perform the sense disambiguation. A dictionary was first built in [7], within which each entry includes preferred Wikipedia concepts and redirected concepts. Then two methods are proposed for concept matching. In this paper, we employ an open toolkit [16] for the wikification task and also for obtaining the concept-concept relatedness.

2.4 Orthogonality Assumption

In the BOW model, we define the orthogonality assumption as assuming that there is no relatedness among terms. This assumption is also extended to the BOC model. To relax this assumption, a method was proposed to measure the pair-wise document similarities by enriching each document with the concepts that have been identified in the other document [9]. This method did not take the connections among concepts fully into consideration and still assumed that concepts were mutually orthogonal.

Measuring the term-term relatedness with the use of WordNet was explored in [22]. They incorporated the semantic information to enrich the document representation as the Generalized Vector Space Model (*GVSM*). Their experiments revealed that by relaxing the orthogonal assumption, their measure could improve the text retrieval performance. However, the method suffers from relatively limited coverage of WordNet compared to Wikipedia [20]. Though their experimental results revealed that embedding semantic information could improve text retrieval, they still need other semantic network models to confirm their conclusion.

In this work, we investigate the use of Wikipedia and integrate its concept relatedness into the BOC model to relax the orthogonality assumption.

3. PROPOSED SEMANTIC SIMILARITIES

In this section, we propose five semantic similarity measures between two text documents. Each document is represented as a vector of Wikipedia concepts. We use "similarity" when referring to documents and "relatedness" when referring to concepts in this work. In the following sections, m is the number of documents and n is the number of concepts extracted from Wikipedia for the whole document corpus. Document a is d_a, document b is d_b, the ith concept of d_a is c_{ai}, the jth concept of d_b is c_{bj}, w_{ai} is the weight of c_{ai}, and w_{bj} is the weight of c_{bj}.

3.1 Single Concept Mapping (*SCM*) Measure

In this section, we explore one simple semantic similarity measure, which searches for the concept pair with the greatest relatedness between two documents to compute the document similarity. In this method, each document is represented as a Wikipedia concept vector. We use *concept frequency-inverse document frequency* (*cf-idf*) [5] as weight.

First, we create a *concept-concept* matrix for a document pair. By searching for the maximum value in this matrix, we select one concept from each document to make a mapping between two concept sets. This measure is defined as below:

DEFINITION 3.1. *Single Concept Mapping: Given two documents and their associated concepts, a single concept is selected*

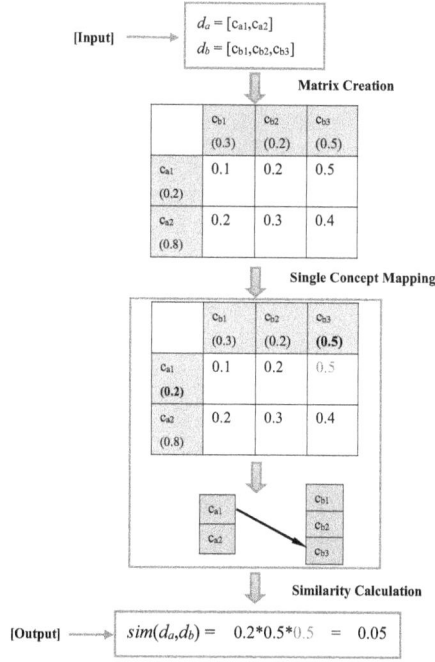

[Input] → $d_a = [c_{a1}, c_{a2}]$
$d_b = [c_{b1}, c_{b2}, c_{b3}]$

Matrix Creation

	c_{b1} (0.3)	c_{b2} (0.2)	c_{b3} (0.5)
c_{a1} (0.2)	0.1	0.2	0.5
c_{a2} (0.8)	0.2	0.3	0.4

Single Concept Mapping

	c_{b1} (0.3)	c_{b2} (0.2)	**c_{b3} (0.5)**
c_{a1} (0.2)	0.1	0.2	0.5
c_{a2} (0.8)	0.2	0.3	0.4

$c_{a1} \rightarrow c_{b3}$

Similarity Calculation

[Output] → $sim(d_a, d_b) = 0.2*0.5*0.5 = 0.05$

Figure 1: *SCM* similarity measure. The measure includes three steps: Matrix Creation, Single Mapping, and Similarity Calculation. By finding the maximum relatedness in the matrix, a single concept of d_a is mapped to a single concept of d_b.

from each document and the selected concepts are mapped to each other to compute the document similarity.

The main steps of this measure are described below and shown in Fig. 1. This method utilizes both concept weights and concept relatedness. Given concept vectors of documents, the time complexity of this method to calculate the pair-wise similarity among documents is $O(m^2 n^2)$. Since each document will contain only a small fraction of the concept set for the entire document corpus, the actual running time will be much smaller in practice.

1. **Matrix Creation:**
   Given a pair of documents d_a and d_b, we assign concepts of d_a to rows and concepts of d_b to columns. In this way, an $I * J$ matrix M is formed, where I is the number of concepts in d_a and J is the number of concepts in d_b. The entry (i, j) of this matrix is represented as $rel(i, j)$, which is the relatedness of c_{ai} to c_{bj}.

2. **Single Concept Mapping:**
   We search for the maximum value $rel(i, j)_{max}$ in M. If there is more than one maximum value in M, we choose the concept pair with the maximum weight product $w_{ai} \cdot w_{bj}$.

3. **Similarity Calculation:**

$$sim(d_a, d_b) = w_{ai} \cdot w_{bj} \cdot rel(i, j)_{max} \qquad (1)$$

3.2 Single Median Mapping (*SMM*) Measure

In this section, we explore another semantic similarity measure, which employs the idea of *median linkage* method in agglomerative clustering. The document representation is the same as in *SCM* measure.

For each document, we first find its median concept. For a concept set, a median concept is defined as the concept with the maximum average relatedness to other concepts. The median can be treated as a representative of a concept set. We map the median of one document to the median of another document to measure the document similarity.

DEFINITION 3.2. *Single Median Mapping: Given two documents and their associated concepts, a single concept is selected from each document as its median concept and the two median concepts are mapped to each other to compute the document similarity.*

The main steps of this measure are described as below and shown in Fig. 2, where c_{am} is the median concept of d_a, and c_{bm} is the median concept of d_b.

1. **Median Searching:**
   For each concept of a concept set, we find its relatedness to the rest concepts of the set and compute the average over those relatedness. Concept with the greatest average relatedness is the median. If there is more than one median of a concept set, we choose the median with the maximum *cf-idf* weight w.

2. **Single Median Mapping:**
   For each pair of documents d_a and d_b, we map c_{am} to c_{bm} to compute the document similarity.

3. **Similarity Calculation:**

$$sim(d_a, d_b) = w_{am} \cdot w_{bm} \cdot rel \qquad (2)$$

where *rel* is the concept relatedness between c_{am} and c_{bm}, and w_{am} and w_{bm} are their weights in the respective documents.

Given concept vectors of documents, the time complexity of this method to calculate the pair-wise similarity among documents is $O(m^2 n^2)$ in the worst case.

3.3 One to One Mapping (*OOM*) Measure

In this method, each document is represented as a Wikipedia concept vector without any weights. By creating a *concept-concept* matrix M for a pair of documents, we map row concept to column concept following a one to one mapping rule.

DEFINITION 3.3. *One to One Mapping: Given two documents and their associate concepts, each concept in the smaller document is mapped to the most related concept in the larger document. The document similarity is then computed by the average relatedness of all concept pairs.*

The main steps of this method are shown in Fig. 3. Due to ignoring the unused concepts in the column vector, this method results in information loss. Given concept vectors of documents, the time complexity of this method to calculate the pair-wise similarity among documents is $O(m^2 n^2)$. Besides, we do not use any *cf-idf* weights in this method because we want to see how important the *cf-idf* is in similarity calculation.

1. **Matrix Creation**:
   We make the document with fewer concepts as the row vectors and the document with more concepts as the column vectors. In this way, an $I * J$ ($I \leq J$) matrix M is formed. The entry (i, j) of M is represented as $rel(i, j)$, which is the relatedness of concept c_{ai} to concept c_{bj}.

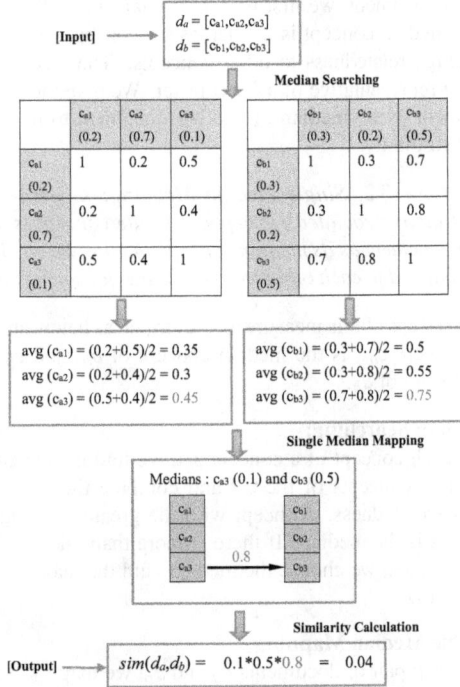

Figure 2: *SMM* similarity measure. In each concept set, we find the concept with the maximum average relatedness to other concepts within the same set, which is called median. The median concept of d_a is mapped to the median concept of d_b in order to compute the document similarity.

2. **One to One Mapping:**
   For each row in M, we first find the column with the maximum value $rel(i)_{max}$ and save it, and then delete that column. Once a column concept is mapped, it cannot be mapped to any other row concept.

3. **Similarity Calculation:**

$$sim(d_a, d_b) = \frac{\sum_{i=1}^{I} rel(i)_{max}}{I} \qquad (3)$$

   where I is the number of rows in M, $rel(i)_{max}$ is the maximum value of each row in M.

3.4 Multiple to One Mapping (*MOM*) Measure

Same as in the *OOM* method, we first create a *concept-concept* matrix M for each pair of documents. We further realize a multiple to one concept mapping procedure on that matrix. Different concepts of one concept set can be mapped to the same concept of the other concept set. The main steps are described below and shown in Fig. 4.

DEFINITION 3.4. *Multiple to One Mapping: Given two documents and their associated concepts, each concept in the document with larger number of concepts is mapped to a concept in the document with smaller number of concepts. Then we take a sum of all the relatedness measures of all the mapped pairs to compute the document similarity.*

1. **Matrix Creation:**
   We make the document with more concepts as the row vectors and the document with fewer concepts as the column

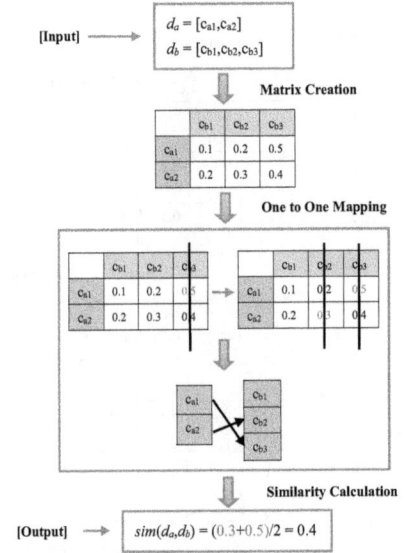

Figure 3: *OOM* similarity measure. Each concept in the smaller concept set is mapped to the non-duplicate concepts in the larger concept set.

vectors. Each concept has its *cf-idf* weight w. In this way, an $I * J$ matrix M is formed, where I is the number of concepts of the document with the higher number of concepts and J is the number of concepts of the document with the smaller number of concepts. The entry (i, j) of the matrix is represented as $rel(i, j)$, which is the relatedness of c_{ai} to c_{bj}.

2. **Multiple to One Mapping:**
   For each row in M, we find the column j with the maximum value $rel(i)_{max}$.

3. **Similarity Calculation:**

$$sim(d_a, d_b) = \frac{\sum_{i=1}^{I} w_{ai} \cdot w_{bj} \cdot rel(i)_{max}}{I} \qquad (4)$$

   where I is the number of rows in M, $rel(i)_{max}$ is the maximum value of each row in M.

This method considers all concepts in the larger concept set. Given concept vectors of documents, the time complexity of this method to calculate the pair-wise similarity among documents is $O(m^2 n^2)$ in the worst case.

3.5 Multiple to Multiple Mapping (*M3*) Measure

In the previous measures, we only use the relatedness of a subset of the concept pairs formed between the two documents. In this measure, we use the relatedness of all possible pairs. We call this similarity measure Multiple to Multiple Mapping (*M3*). The main steps are described below and shown in Fig. 5.

DEFINITION 3.5. *Multiple to Multiple Mapping: Given two documents and their associated concepts, each concept in the first document is mapped to all concepts in the second document. Then we use Eq. (5) to compute the document similarity.*

1. **Matrix creation:**
   We make one document as the row vector and the other document as the column vector. Each concept has its *cf-idf* weight

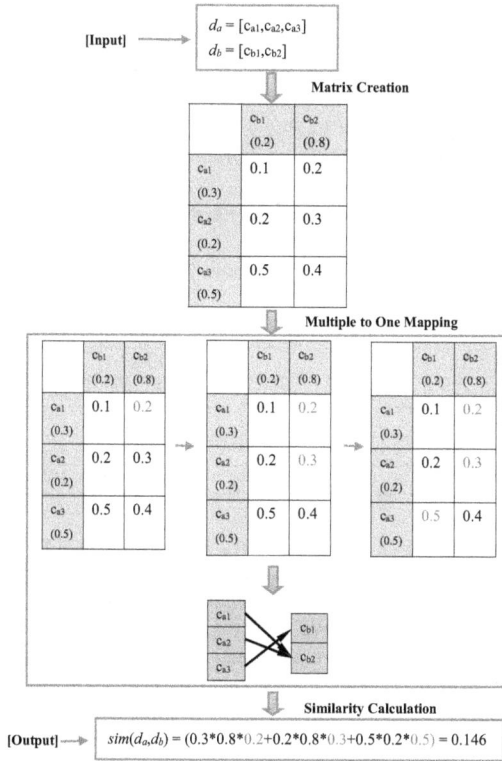

Figure 4: *MOM* similarity measure. Every concept in the larger set can be mapped to one concept in the smaller concept set.

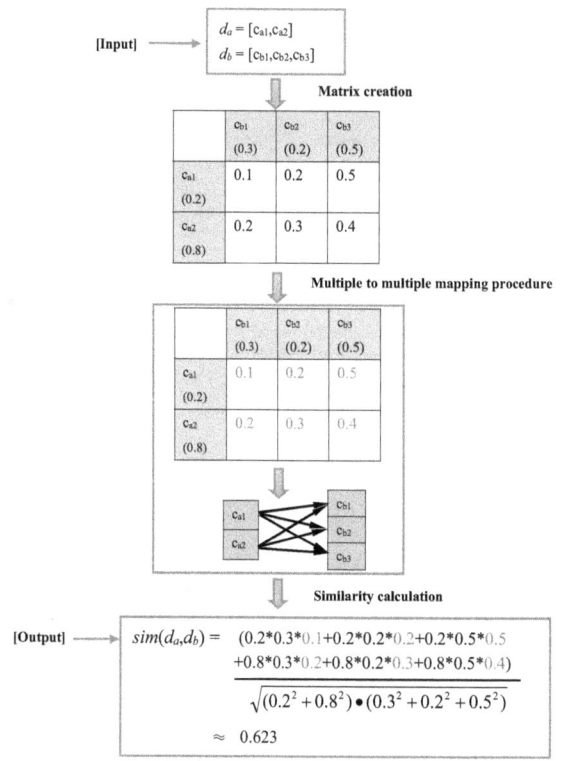

Figure 5: *M3* similarity measure. All the relatedness among concepts are used to compute the document similarity.

w. The entry (i, j) of the matrix is the relatedness, rel_{ij}, of concept c_{ai} to concept c_{bj}.

2. **Multiple to multiple mapping**:
   We use all the relatedness in the matrix to make multiple to multiple mapping.

3. **Similarity calculation**:

$$sim(d_a, d_b) = \frac{\sum_{i=1}^{I} \sum_{j=1}^{J} w_{ai} \cdot w_{bj} \cdot rel_{(ij)}}{\sqrt{\sum_{i=1}^{I} w_{ai}^2 \sum_{j=1}^{J} w_{aj}^2}} \quad (5)$$

The time complexity of this measure is $O(m^2 n^2)$. The similarity measure is symmetric and eliminates the orthogonality assumption among concepts.

This measure can also be presented as an extension of cosine similarity. In cosine similarity based on BOW, words (terms) are treated as independent from each other. Suppose that document d_a is represented by a term vector (t_1, t_2, t_3, t_4), each term weighted with its *term frequency-inverse document frequency (tf-idf)*[1] as w_i. The document d_b is represented by (t_1, t_2, t_3, t_4), each term is weighted by its *tf-idf* as w_i'. The cosine similarity between these two documents is expressed as:

$$\cos(\vec{d_a}, \vec{d_b}) = \frac{[w_1, w_2, w_3, w_4] \cdot \begin{bmatrix} 1 & 0 & 0 & 0 \\ 0 & 1 & 0 & 0 \\ 0 & 0 & 1 & 0 \\ 0 & 0 & 0 & 1 \end{bmatrix} \cdot \begin{bmatrix} w_1' \\ w_2' \\ w_3' \\ w_4' \end{bmatrix}}{\sqrt{\sum_{i=1}^{4} w_i^2 \sum_{i=1}^{4} w_i'^2}} \quad (6)$$

[1] https://en.wikipedia.org/wiki/Tf-idf

The zero values in the matrix of Eq. (6) correspond to the orthogonality assumption. To relax the assumption, the extended cosine similarity of documents d_a and d_b is measured using Eq. (7) and Eq. (8).

$$W = \begin{bmatrix} rel(t_1, t_1') & rel(t_1, t_2') & rel(t_1, t_3') & rel(t_1, t_4') \\ rel(t_2, t_1') & rel(t_2, t_2') & rel(t_2, t_3') & rel(t_2, t_4') \\ rel(t_3, t_1') & rel(t_3, t_2') & rel(t_3, t_3') & rel(t_3, t_4') \\ rel(t_4, t_1') & rel(t_4, t_2') & rel(t_4, t_3') & rel(t_4, t_4') \end{bmatrix} \quad (7)$$

$$\cos(\vec{d_a}, \vec{d_b}) = \frac{[w_1, w_2, w_3, w_4] \cdot W \cdot \begin{bmatrix} w_1' \\ w_2' \\ w_3' \\ w_4' \end{bmatrix}}{\sqrt{\sum_{i=1}^{4} w_i^2 \sum_{i=1}^{4} w_i'^2}} \quad (8)$$

Similarly, the extended cosine similarity can be applied in the BOC model. The entries of matrix W in Eq. (7) contain concept-concept relatedness extracted from Wikipedia. This similarity measure is symmetric and no orthogonality assumption is considered among concepts. The minimum of the extended cosine similarity is zero but its maximum is not 1, compared to traditional cosine similarity.

4. EXPERIMENTAL SETUP

In this section, we first introduce the whole framework of our experiments in Section 4.1. We review characteristics of the datasets used in the experiments in Section 4.2 and the clustering algorithms to evaluate the measures are introduced in Section 4.3.

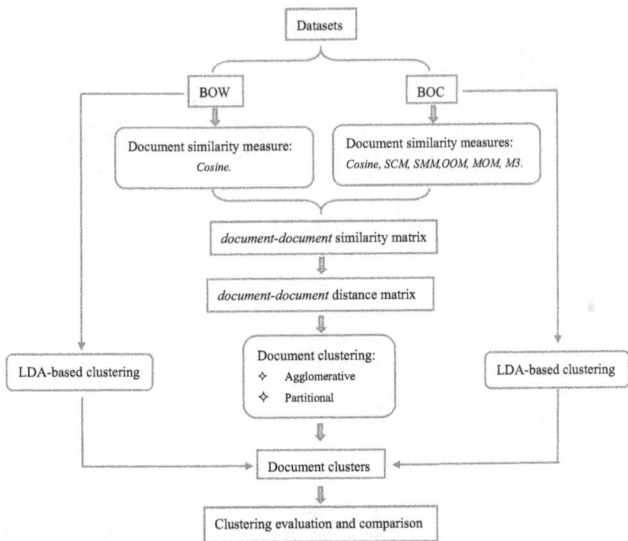

Figure 6: The framework of experiments, which leverages different document similarity measures and different clustering algorithms for document clustering. The proposed similarity measures are not used in *LDA*.

4.1 Framework for Experiments

The framework of our experiments which leverages *SCM*, *SMM*, *OOM*, *MOM*, and *M3* as the semantic similarity measures in document clustering is presented in Fig. 6.

We experiment different document similarity measures on different data representations. We apply *Cosine* similarity to BOW and BOC. We then apply *SCM*, *SMM*, *OOM*, *MOM*, and *M3* to BOC. Documents are clustered by three clustering algorithms including Agglomerative clustering [19], Partitional clustering [3], and *LDA*-based clustering [12] for a comprehensive comparison. Since the proposed measures cannot be used in *LDA*, we run *LDA* on BOC and BOW, separately. Finally, we evaluate and compare the quality of clusterings based on different evaluation measures.

4.2 Datasets

In our experiments, we use four standard document collections, *20Newsgroups*[2], *SMART*[3], *WebKB*[4], and *Reuters-21578*[5].

For efficiency, six small datasets are created from the datasets with different dimensionalities and different numbers of clusters [7]. *Similar-4* from *20Newsgroups* includes four topics of *comp.os.ms-windows.misc*, *comp.sys.ibm.pc.hardware*, *comp.sys.ma-hardware* and *comp.windows.x*. *Diff-5* from *20Newsgroups* includes five different topics of *alt.atheism*, *misc.forsale*, *rec.sport.baseball*, *sci.electronics*, and *talk.politics.mideast*. *Multi-7* from *20Newsgroups* includes seven topics of *alt.atheism*, *comp.sys.ibm.pc.hardware*, *rec.sport.baseball*, *sci.electronics*, *sci.med*, *soc.religion.christian*, and *talk.politics.guns*. *Classic-4* from *SMART* is formed from the scientific abstracts of four topics of *Medical*, *Information retrieval*, *Aerodynamics*, and *Computing algorithm*. *WebKB* contains web pages collected from computer science departments of four universities. We selected only four

out of seven categories of this dataset which includes *student*, *faculty*, *course*, and *project*. *R-754* is created from *Reuters-21578* using 8 classes of *acq*, *crude*, *earn*, *grain*, *interest*, *money-fx*, *ship*, and *trade*. We randomly selected 100 documents from each topic except for topic of *grain* in *R-751* which has 51 documents. A summary of the datasets is shown in Table. 1.

Table 1: Summary of datasets used in our experiments

Dataset	No. of documents	No. of classes	No. of terms	No. of concepts
Classic-4	400	4	4317	1362
Diff-5	500	5	11749	1784
Multi-7	700	7	13236	2583
R-751	751	8	5677	1989
Similar-4	400	4	7980	806
Webkb-4	400	4	9373	1902

As a preprocessing step we remove all the English stop words[6] from documents in the BOW model. We then apply Porter stemming[7] to stem the vocabulary of the collection and reduce dimensionality of the datasets. We finally remove all the non-alphabet characters. Each dataset is represented as a document-term matrix using *term frequency-inverse document frequency*.

To represent documents in BOC, we used the wikification algorithm proposed in [15, 16]. Its web service implementation[8] receives a text document as input and generates a list of Wikipedia concepts as output. Based on the experiments performed in [13], the wikification algorithm has the highest precision compared to the other algorithms publicly available. We finally represent the corpus as a document-concept matrix using *concept frequency-inverse document frequency*. The length of document vectors in both matrices of BOW and BOC is normalized by *L2* norm.

We also compute and store relatedness for all possible pairs of concepts appearing in a document collection using the algorithm proposed in [24]. The web service implementation of the algorithm[9] provides the semantic relatedness between two Wikipedia concepts. The relatedness is calculated from the in-going and out-going links among Wikipedia articles, which is called the Wikipedia Link-based Measure (WLM).

4.3 Clustering algorithms

Among different classes of clustering algorithms, distance-based methods are the most popular ones in a variety of applications [1]. Distance-based clustering algorithms are divided into two categories: agglomerative clustering and partitional clustering. To evaluate the validity of our semantic similarity measures, we apply them to both agglomerative and partitional clustering algorithms.

We used Matlab's statistical toolbox[10] for agglomerative clustering. Seven linkage methods of *average*, *centroid*, *complete*, *median*, *single*, *ward*, and *weighted* are used in our experiments.

For partitional clustering, we chose *Relational k-means* [21], which takes a *document-document* distance matrix as input. We run the *k-means* algorithm for 100 times. The average results of these runs are reported.

The input of agglomerative clustering and *Relational k-means* is a document-document distance matrix. We used the following

---

[2]http://qwone.com/~jason/20Newsgroups/
[3]http://www.dataminingresearch.com/index.php/2010/09/classic3-classic4-datasets/
[4]http://www.inf.ed.ac.uk/teaching/courses/dme/html/datasets0405.html
[5]http://www.daviddlewis.com/resources/testcollections/reuters21578/

[6]http://www.ranks.nl/stopwords
[7]http://tartarus.org/martin/PorterStemmer/java.txt
[8]http://wikipedia-miner.cms.waikato.ac.nz/services/?wikify
[9]http://wikipedia-miner.cms.waikato.ac.nz/services/?compare
[10]http://www.mathworks.com/help/stats/linkage.html?refresh=true

formula to convert a similarity matrix to a distance matrix:

$$dist(d_a, d_b) = e^{-sim(d_a, d_b)} \quad (9)$$

We use Latent Dirichlet Allocation (*LDA*) topic model [2] in our experiments as well. *LDA* is applied on the document collection in both BOW and BOC model, separately. We employed the *Java* implementation of *LDA*, called *JGibbLDA*[11]. The implementation is based on the Gibbs sampling. The number of topics is set as the number of clusters and each document is finally assigned to the topic with the maximum probability.

To analyze the quality of clustering, we used two evaluation measures, *F-score* [11] and *Normalized Mutual Information (NMI)* [27].

5. EXPERIMENTAL RESULTS

In this section, we review and analyze the clusterings obtained by using three clustering algorithms based on the proposed similarity measures and *Cosine* similarity.

5.1 Agglomerative Clustering

The first goal of this experiment is to identify the best linkage method to cluster the datasets. The second goal is to compare the similarity measures based on the best linkage method.

5.1.1 Different Linkage Methods Comparison

In the first experiment, we run the agglomerative clustering algorithm using different linkage methods and similarity measures. The goal of the experiment is to evaluate the performance of different linkage methods. For each dataset, we used different linkage methods and compared the final clusterings.

A comparison performed on *Diff5* dataset is reported in Fig. 7. Different bar groups correspond to different document similarity measures. BOW and BOC employ *Cosine* similarity measure, others use the five similarity measures proposed above. Different bars in each group use different linkage methods for clustering.

To save space, we have not shown the results of other datasets. The main conclusion of this experiment is that the *Ward* linkage is the best linkage method for agglomerative clustering in this work.

5.1.2 Agglomerative Clustering Results Based on Ward Linkage Method

In this section, we compare the proposed similarity measures based on *Ward* linkage agglomerative clustering. For this purpose, we extracted all agglomerative clustering results based on the *Ward* linkage in the previous experiment. A comparison based on *Similar-4* dataset is shown in Fig. 8.

From the results, we can conclude that the BOC model with *Cosine* similarity cannot outperform the BOW model. This observation is consistent with the previous work in [7, 18] such that clustering based on Wikipedia concepts results in a worse clustering compared to using document terms.

The observations based on the BOC model are mentioned below. On *Classic-4*, *Multi-7*, and *Similar-4*, *SCM* generates better clusterings than *Cosine* similarity. On *Classic-4*, *Multi-7*, *Similar-4*, and *Webkb4* *SMM* performs better than *Cosine*. On *Classic-4*, *Diff-5*, *Multi-7* and *R-751*, *OOM* shows better performance than *Cosine*. And on *Classic-4* and *Multi-7*, *MOM* performs better than *Cosine*. This indicates that employing the concept relatedness into the BOC model can improve the clustering performance to a certain extent.

The main observation is that *M3* always results in the best performance by the improvement from 1.99% to 35.39% in *F-score* and from 8.51% to 76.16% in *NMI* value to the baseline (cosine in BOW) on average.

Overall, the experimental results show that a comprehensive concept mapping, which utilizes all *cf-idf* weights and concept relatedness improves the performance of clustering significantly. The *M3* measure always showed a better performance than the other measures.

5.2 Partitional Clustering based on Relational k-means

We ran *Relational k-means* for 100 times. The avarage and standard deviation of these runs are reported in this section.

Same as in agglomerative clustering, we use the similarity measures along with *Cosine* similarity. Document terms are only used in BOW model and the other measures are based on concepts extracted from Wikipedia. We convert all the document similarities into document distances using Eq. (9). The BOW model with *Cosine* similarity serves as the baseline. The experimental results on *Webkb4* dataset are depicted in Fig. 9.

One observation of this experiment is that cosine similarity in BOW outperforms cosine similarity in BOC. This observation has been seen in the agglomerative clustering results. Hence, we con-

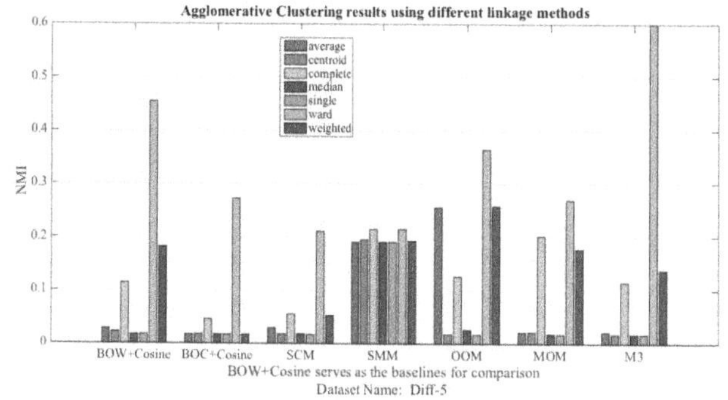

Figure 7: Agglomerative clustering results using different linkage methods and *NMI* as the measure on *Diff-5* dataset. Different bar groups use different similarity measures. BOW with *Cosine* similarity serves as the baseline. *Cosine* and proposed similarity measures are applied on BOC. In each bar group, different colors represent different linkage methods. The light blue stands for *Ward* linkage method, which achieves better performance than the other linkage methods.

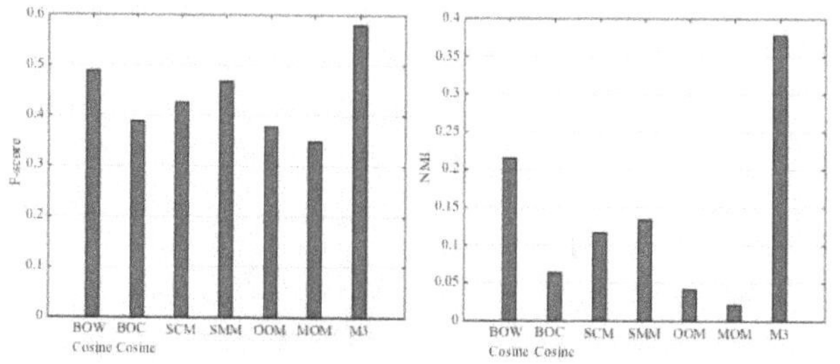

Figure 8: The quality of clusterings in terms of *F-score* and *NMI* obtained from Agglomerative clustering using *Ward* linkage on *Similar-4*. BOW with *Cosine* similarity serves as the baseline. *Cosine* and proposed similarity measures are applied on BOC. *M3* achieves significant improvement in both *F-score* and *NMI* comparing to the baseline.

[11] http://jgibblda.sourceforge.net/

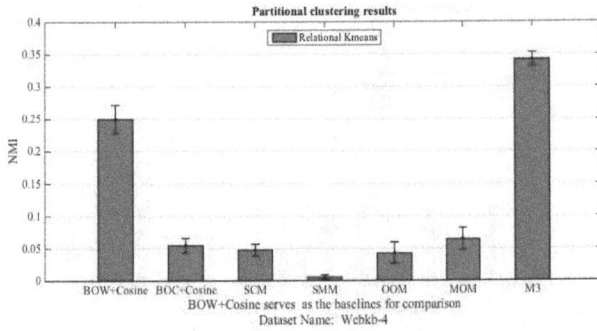

Figure 9: The quality of clusterings in terms of *NMI* obtained from Partitional clustering on *Webkb4*. BOW with *Cosine* similarity serves as the baseline. *Cosine* and proposed similarity measures are applied on BOC. *M3* significantly outperformed other similarity measures.

clude that we cannot simply replace document terms with concepts. The conclusion is consistent with the results obtained in [18].

The clusterings obtained based on the BOC model reveal that the *M3* method outperforms the other similarity measures including the baseline on all six datasets. Besides, *M3* yields smaller standard deviation. This demonstrates that *M3* can generate relatively stable results in our experiments. It is also worth mentioning that *OOM* generates better average results on *Classic-4*, *Diff-5*, and *Multi-7* than the baseline.

5.3 Comparison with LDA-based Clustering

The goal of this experiment is to compare clusterings obtained from agglomerative and partitional algorithms with those obtained from *LDA*. First, *LDA* is run on the BOW model to serve as the baseline in this experiment. Then we run *LDA* on the BOC model to compare the experimental results.

We let *LDA* run for 100 times and each run contains 10,000 iterations. We reported the average and standard deviation over these runs.

The experimental results are shown in Table 2. The best values obtained in terms of *F-score* and *NMI* are shown in bold. By comparing *M3*-based agglomerative clustering and *M3*-based partitional clustering with the *LDA*-based clustering, we observe that *M3* performs better on *Classic-4*. On *Multi-7* and *Similar-4*, *M3* generates better *NMI* scores.

We observe that *LDA* based on concepts always generates the worst results on all datasets. We believe the main reason is that many discriminative terms in a collection do not have corresponding concepts in Wikipedia and are subsequently missed in *BOC*. Since the *Gibbs* implementation of *LDA* is based on frequency count of terms and concepts, *LDA* has a lower performance in *BOC* than in *BOW*.

Another important observation is that *M3* outperforms *LDA* on *Classic-4* in BOW. *Classic-4* includes abstracts in *medical, information retrieval, aerodynamic*, and *computing algorithms*. We believe the reason is that Wikipedia contains more articles about scientific topics than about news or general topics. In this case, *M3* is a suitable measure for semantic similarity.

The experimental results demonstrate that though *LDA* based on words generally produces better clusterings than our proposed approaches, the *M3* measure outperforms *LDA* based on *BOC*.

Based on the observations, we conclude that the *M3* measure has the best performance on scientific documents since the concepts mentioned in the text exist in Wikipedia. On the other hand, if

Table 2: Agglomerative and partitional clustering using *M3* as the semantic similarity measure among documents, and *LDA*-based clustering using bag of words or bag of concepts.

Dataset	Algorithm	*F-score*	*NMI*
Classic-4	**Agglomerative**	0.88	**0.78**
	Partitonal	**0.89±0.01**	0.75±0.01
	LDA (terms)	0.76±0.89	0.67±0.01
	LDA (concepts)	0.47±0.02	0.13±0.02
Diff-5	Agglomerative	0.77	0.60
	Partitonal	0.79±0.01	0.63±0.02
	LDA (terms)	**0.88±0.07**	**0.72±0.01**
	LDA (concepts)	0.57±0.04	0.30±0.04
Multi-7	Agglomerative	0.73	0.65
	Partitonal	0.80±0.02	**0.70±0.01**
	LDA (terms)	**0.86±0.01**	0.66±0.03
	LDA (concepts)	0.26±0.01	0.05±0.01
R-751	Agglomerative	0.72	0.66
	Partitonal	0.72±0.02	0.65±0.02
	LDA (terms)	**0.80±0.01**	**0.66±0.01**
	LDA (concepts)	0.58±0.01	0.42±0.01
Similar-4	**Agglomerative**	0.58	**0.38**
	Partitonal	0.55±0.02	0.27±0.03
	LDA (terms)	**0.66±0.01**	0.37±0.01
	LDA (concepts)	0.37±0.02	0.05±0.01
Webkb-4	Agglomerative	0.59	0.32
	Partitonal	0.62±0.01	0.34±0.01
	LDA (terms)	**0.64±0.01**	**0.37±0.02**
	LDA (concepts)	0.39±0.01	0.07±0.01

the topics of documents are general, such as in news documents, it is better to rely on frequency of terms in BOW and use *LDA* for clustering.

Table 3: Time costs in creating a similarity matrix for *Classic-4* based on different measures

Similarity Measure	Time cost in second
BOW+*Cosine*	0.217
BOC+*Cosine*	0.069
SCM	1153.894
SMM	890.512
OOM	768.333
MOM	710.127
M3	1420.665

5.4 Time Complexity Analysis

In this section, we conducted extensive studies to evaluate the efficiency of the proposed semantic similarity measures. All the measures were implemented using Matlab 2014b and tested on a PC with 3.1GHz CPU and 32.0 GB memory running on Windows 7.

From the experiment framework in Fig. 6, we can see that the differences among measures are in computing *document-document* similarity matrix. For a better description of the comparison, we took one dataset, *Classic-4*, as an example to analyze the time costs during matrix creation using different similarity measures.

The wikification of the original documents in *Classic-4* took around 235 seconds via the online *wikify* service. We have to measure the relatedness between any two concepts. The concept relatedness measure via the online *compare* service took almost 9 hours. We store the concept relatedness in a matrix *W* for further use during similarity computation. Given the concepts and their pair-wise relatedness, the time needed to create similarity matrices are calculated and shown in Table 3. We can see that although our new proposed similarity measures have the same theoretical time complexity, the actual time costs vary from each other. *Cosine* similarity based on BOW took less time than our measures. *M3* took more time than the others because of more complex calculation.

6. CONCLUSIONS AND FUTURE WORK

Our experiments on six datasets demonstrated that simply replacing the original documents with Wikipedia concepts would result in poor clustering. To improve the conceptual text similarity, we proposed five semantic measures. The best measure in our experiments, *M3*, is an extension to cosine similarity based on vector space model. Similar to the most concept-based measures, it works well if the concepts mentioned in the documents exist in Wikipedia. Besides, *M3* totally relaxes the orthogonality assumption in conceptual text document similarity.

One possible extension is to focus on word-word relatedness in the BOW model. We would like to propose an approach based on Google n-gram corpus to measure this relatedness.

Another possible extension of this work is to involve the users' feedback in measuring similarities. In [17], they have considered users' intention into document clustering process to make a user-supervised algorithm. Users can easily integrate their point of view into the concept selection, which would be an advantage over term-based *LDA*.

We can see that our proposed measures take more time than normal *Cosine* similarity for two main reasons: (1) the online services *wikify*, for wikification, and *compare*, for concept relatedness measure, impose significant overhead time; (2) complex calculation in the concept mapping procedure. Further improvement, such as performing *wikify* and *compare* locally as opposed to over the web services, can be pursued to reduce the required time.

7. ACKNOWLEDGMENTS

This work was supported by the Natural Sciences and Engineering Research Council of Canada (NSERC) and the Boeing Company.

8. REFERENCES

[1] C. C. Aggarwal and C. Zhai. A survey of text clustering algorithms. In *Mining Text Data*, pages 77–128. Springer, 2012.

[2] D. M. Blei, A. Y. Ng, and M. I. Jordan. Latent Dirichlet allocation. *the Journal of machine Learning research*, 3:993–1022, 2003.

[3] M. Celebi. *Partitional Clustering Algorithms*. Springer, 2015.

[4] E. Gabrilovich and S. Markovitch. Overcoming the brittleness bottleneck using wikipedia: Enhancing text categorization with encyclopedic knowledge. In *American Association for Artificial Intelligence*, volume 6, pages 1301–1306, 2006.

[5] F. Goossen, W. IJntema, F. Frasincar, F. Hogenboom, and U. Kaymak. News personalization using the cf-idf semantic recommender. In *Proceedings of the International Conference on Web Intelligence, Mining and Semantics*, WIMS '11, pages 10:1–10:12, New York, NY, USA, 2011. ACM.

[6] A. Hotho, S. Staab, and G. Stumme. Ontologies improve text document clustering. In *Data Mining, 2003. ICDM 2003. Third IEEE International Conference on*, pages 541–544. IEEE, 2003.

[7] X. Hu, X. Zhang, C. Lu, E. K. Park, and X. Zhou. Exploiting wikipedia as external knowledge for document clustering. In *Proceedings of the 15th ACM SIGKDD International Conference on Knowledge Discovery and Data Mining*, KDD '09, pages 389–396, New York, NY, USA, 2009. ACM.

[8] A. Huang, D. Milne, E. Frank, and I. H. Witten. Clustering documents with active learning using wikipedia. In *Data Mining, 2008. ICDM'08. Eighth IEEE International Conference on*, pages 839–844. IEEE, 2008.

[9] L. Huang, D. Milne, E. Frank, and I. H. Witten. Learning a concept-based document similarity measure. *Journal of the American Society for Information Science and Technology*, 63(8):1593–1608, 2012.

[10] A. Islam and D. Inkpen. Semantic text similarity using corpus-based word similarity and string similarity. *ACM Transactions on Knowledge Discovery from Data (TKDD)*, 2(2):10, 2008.

[11] B. Larsen and C. Aone. Fast and effective text mining using linear-time document clustering. In *Proceedings of the Fifth ACM SIGKDD International Conference on Knowledge Discovery and Data Mining*, KDD '99, pages 16–22. ACM, New York, NY, USA, 1999.

[12] C. Li, B. Kuo, and C. Lin. LDA-based clustering algorithm and its application to an unsupervised feature extraction. *IEEE Transactions on Fuzzy Systems*, 19(1):152–163, Feb. 2011.

[13] P. N. Mendes, M. Jakob, A. García-Silva, and C. Bizer. Dbpedia spotlight: Shedding light on the web of documents. In *Proceedings of the 7th International Conference on Semantic Systems*, I-Semantics '11, pages 1–8. ACM, New York, USA, 2011.

[14] R. Mihalcea, C. Corley, and C. Strapparava. Corpus-based and knowledge-based measures of text semantic similarity. In *Proceedings of the 21st National Conference on Artificial Intelligence - Volume 1*, American Association for Artificial Intelligence, pages 775–780. AAAI Press, 2006.

[15] R. Mihalcea and A. Csomai. Wikify!: linking documents to encyclopedic knowledge. In *Proceedings of the sixteenth ACM conference on Conference on Information and Knowledge Management*, pages 233–242. ACM, 2007.

[16] D. Milne and I. H. Witten. An open-source toolkit for mining wikipedia. *Artificial Intelligence*, 194:222–239, 2013.

[17] S. Nourashrafeddin, E. Milios, and D. V. Arnold. Interactive text document clustering using feature labeling. In *Proceedings of the 2013 ACM Symposium on Document Engineering*, DocEng '13, pages 61–70, New York, NY, USA, 2013. ACM.

[18] S. Nourashrafeddin, E. Milios, and D. V. Arnold. An ensemble approach for text document clustering using wikipedia concepts. In *Proceedings of the 2014 ACM Symposium on Document Engineering*, DocEng '14, pages 107–116, New York, NY, USA, 2014. ACM.

[19] L. Rokach and O. Maimon. Clustering methods. In *Data Mining and Knowledge Discovery Handbook*, pages 321–352. Springer US, 2005.

[20] C. Stokoe, M. Oakes, and J. Tait. Word sense disambiguation in information retrieval revisited. In *Proceedings of the 26th Annual International ACM SIGIR Conference on Research*

and Development in Informaion Retrieval, SIGIR '03, pages 159–166, New York, NY, USA, 2003. ACM.

[21] B. Szalkai. An implementation of the relational k-means algorithm. *arXiv preprint arXiv:1304.6899*, 2013.

[22] G. Tsatsaronis and V. Panagiotopoulou. A generalized vector space model for text retrieval based on semantic relatedness. In *Proceedings of the 12th Conference of the European Chapter of the Association for Computational Linguistics: Student Research Workshop*, EACL '09, pages 70–78, Stroudsburg, PA, USA, 2009. Association for Computational Linguistics.

[23] P. D. Turney. Mining the web for synonyms: PMI-IR versus LSA on TOEFL. In *Proceedings of the 12th European Conference on Machine Learning*, EMCL '01, pages 491–502, London, UK, UK, 2001. Springer-Verlag.

[24] I. Witten and D. Milne. An effective, low-cost measure of semantic relatedness obtained from Wikipedia links. In *Proceeding of AAAI Workshop on Wikipedia and Artificial Intelligence: an Evolving Synergy, AAAI Press, Chicago, USA*, pages 25–30, 2008.

[25] Z. Wu and M. Palmer. Verbs semantics and lexical selection. In *Proceedings of the 32nd annual meeting on Association for Computational Linguistics*, pages 133–138. Association for Computational Linguistics, 1994.

[26] X. Zhang, L. Jing, X. Hu, M. Ng, and X. Zhou. A comparative study of ontology based term similarity measures on pubmed document clustering. In *Advances in Databases: Concepts, Systems and Applications*, pages 115–126. Springer, 2007.

[27] S. Zhong and J. Ghosh. Generative model-based document clustering: a comparative study. *Knowledge and Information Systems*, 8(3):374–384, 2005.

Enhancing the Searchability of Page-Image PDF Documents Using an Aligned Hidden Layer from a Truth Text

Ian A. Knight
School of Computer Science
University of Nottingham
Nottingham, NG8 1BB, UK
ian.knight.1990@gmail.com

David F. Brailsford
School of Computer Science
University of Nottingham
Nottingham, NG8 1BB, UK
dfb@cs.nott.ac.uk

ABSTRACT

The search accuracy achieved in a PDF image-plus-hidden-text (PDF-IT) document depends upon the accuracy of the optical character recognition (OCR) process that produced the searchable hidden text layer. In many cases recognising words in a blurred area of a PDF page image may exceed the capabilities of an OCR engine.

This paper describes a project to replace an inadequate hidden textual layer of a PDF-IT file with a more accurate hidden layer produced from a 'truth text'. The alignment of the truth text with the image is guided by using OCR-provided page-image co-ordinates, for those glyphs that are correctly recognised, as a set of fixed location points between which other truth-text words can be inserted and aligned with blurred glyphs in the image. Results are presented to show the much enhanced searchability of this new file when compared to that of the original file, which had an OCR-produced hidden layer with no truth-text enhancement.

CCS Concepts

•**Applied computing** → *Document analysis; Document searching; Optical character recognition;*

Keywords

PDF, OCR, Tesseract, searchability, truth text

1. INTRODUCTION

In a previous paper [3] we presented the first stages of an effort to provide a computer-assisted framework for tagging key phrases within a variable-quality PDF document collection, followed by automated extraction and assembly of the tagged phrases into standardised summary documents. The corpus of 20,000 documents used for this work was that held by the Cochrane Schizophrenia Group's register of trials. This corpus is overwhelmingly archived as PDF documents.

As a first step in automating the extraction of qualitative and quantitative data it is vital that all PDF documents in the collection be as searchable as possible, so that key words and phrases can be highlighted by the PDF viewer.

PDF supports the rendering of arbitrarily complex text, in any chosen font, with diagrams being drawn using the correct arc, line and spline primitives. Bitmapped material such as photographs (either lossily or losslessly compressed) are handled by the PostScript/PDF **image** operator. PDF files of this quality are nowadays referred to as 'PDF—Formatted Text and Graphics' (PDF-FTG). The key advantage of this format is that text strings can usually be accurately located anywhere within the PDF file.

For the most part, the Cochrane collection contains papers of PDF-FTG quality. However, in the previous paper [3] we reported that fully one-third of the corpus was not in searchable format because PDF allows pages to be rendered simply as (unsearchable) bitmapped page-images (PDF-I).

Since 1994 an extra hybrid format has existed for PDF files, called 'PDF Image plus Hidden Text' (PDF-IT). here an invisible, searchable, text overlay is created for each page image. With careful choice of font, type size and inter-word spacing, in this hidden layer, it is possible to make it be in exact registration with the perceived words in the page image.

PDF-IT has the great virtue that searched-for words are highlighted by illuminating the correct bounding box in the hidden layer but this manifests itself as a highlight in the exactly superposed image layer, thereby creating the illusion of a textually searchable image.

Thus, by using OCR techniques to add a hidden, but searchable, text overlay to the 6,000 PDF-I documents in the Cochrane collection, an enhanced degree of searchability was achieved. However, in many cases poor quality source material (often from scanned-in papers) resulted in material which caused the OCR software enormous problems. It was decided to investigate whether the OCR process might be helped if assisted by a truth text for the papers in question.

1.1 Truth texts

A *truth text* (or *ground truth text*) is essentially a canonically correct version of the textual content of a paper. The characteristic of such a truth text is that it will contain the correct words in the correct order, but it will not reflect any of the typesetting or layout decisions made by the publisher in the final printed version. For example, paragraph breaks may be altered, hyphens may be introduced and text may be set in multiple columns or wrapped around figures. As a consequence, the process of *aligning* such a truth text with the PDF document produced from it is complicated.

1.2 Related work

While there is little work on the actual creation of PDF-IT documents in the manner we describe, there is a large body of work focused on aligning OCR results with a ground truth text for the purposes of training. We now give a description of some recent approaches to the alignment problem.

Several authors [5, 2, 6] describe methods for aligning ground truth with OCR results. These involve computing a transformation function that will map the image used as ground truth onto the OCR results as closely as possible, so that the results may be matched character for character. They presuppose that the ground truth exists in electronic form, generated from the same typesetting code used to produce the document undergoing OCR. We find their approaches to be very useful in terms of attempting to closely couple the words in the OCR results with their corresponding words in the truth text, but in our case the original code used for the typesetting will not be available to us.

Feng [1] and Yalniz [8] both present different methods of aligning ground truth with OCR that do not rely on the existence of a canonically correct electronic document. Instead, both assume their ground truth texts to be in the form of plain text, typically ASCII. Feng constructs a hidden Markov model of the words in the ground truth, using it to predict the ground truth for each of the OCR results, while Yalniz solves the problem recursively by dividing the texts into sections bounded by unique words, and repeatedly subdividing until the sections are small enough to be easily aligned word-for-word. These approaches both have advantages in that they do not presuppose any correspondence between the layout of the ground truth and the layout of the actual document: they assume the ground truth to contain only the correct words in the correct order. However, both approaches require a considerable amount of preprocessing of one or both texts in order to run. We wished to explore the possibility of using a similarly unformatted ground truth text, but without requiring the overhead of constructing a hidden Markov model or similar.

It is worth emphasising again that we are *not* concerned with training the OCR to better recognise words it has difficulty with; instead, we take the possibly flawed OCR output and use the truth text to establish the locations of corresponding word before inserting the corrected words into the document as a hidden layer.

1.3 Structure

The rest of the paper is organised as follows. Sec. 2 describes our method of constructing PDF-IT documents using OCR results from a PDF-I document and a truth text. Sec. 3 describes the performance of our method in terms of the accuracy of the corrected hidden text layer, and Sec. 4 concludes and suggests some avenues for future work.

2. PDF-IT CREATION

In this section we describe our method for constructing PDF-IT documents from pre-existing PDF-I/IT documents. The method is divided into three phases: generation of a first estimate of the hidden text layer using OCR, correction of

the hidden text using the truth text, and inserting the corrected hidden text layer into the PDF. Each of these phases is described below.

2.1 OCR generation of hidden text

In the first phase we run the page images from the original PDF through an OCR engine in order to produce an initial estimate of the pages' contents. This was done even if the provided document was already PDF-IT, with some version of a hidden text layer already present.

The OCR engine we used was Tesseract, an open-source engine owned by Google that provides a very comprehensive C++ API. We made use of Tesseract rather than Adobe's built-in OCR engine for two reasons: firstly, Tesseract is freely available whereas access to Adobe's PDF APIs is expensive; and secondly, Tesseract makes it very easy to access not just the strings it identifies but also the bounding boxes of these strings. This makes the creation of a new hidden text layer at the end of the process much more straightforward. Tesseract's accuracy is broadly comparable to that of Acrobat Capture, so we felt confident in using Tesseract for our preliminary investigations.

2.2 Correction of hidden text

In the second phase, we correct the OCR output obtained previously using the provided truth text. The OCR results are here represented as a vector O of words $O_1, O_2, \ldots, O_n$, while the words obtained from the truth text are similarly represented as a vector T of words $T_1, T_2, \ldots, T_m$. We also constructed a BK-tree (see Sec. 2.2.3) of the words in the truth text, denoted $\text{BK}(T)$, using edit distance as the distance metric.

Our approach consists of stepping through both vectors word by word, attempting to determine which word from the truth text best matches the current word in the OCR results. Word matching consisted of two phases: an attempt to find an *exact* match to the OCR word in the words near to our current position in the truth text; and an attempt to find the best *approximate* match in the entire truth text, if no exact match could be found. The method is summarised in Alg. 1. If an exact match was found, no correction is needed and iteration continues. If no exact match was found, then the best-guesses of ExactMatch and ApproximateMatch were compared, and the string closest to the OCR result was used to correct the OCR.

Algorithm 1 Method for OCR correction

1: $i \leftarrow 1; j \leftarrow 1$
2: **while** $i \leq n$ **do**
3:     $(j, m) \leftarrow \textsc{ExactMatch}(i, j)$
4:     **if** $m \neq 1$ **then**
5:         $j' \leftarrow \textsc{ApproximateMatch}(i, j)$
6:         **if** $d_A(O_i, T_{j'}, T_j) = 1$ **then**
7:             $j \leftarrow j'$
8:         **end if**
9:     **end if**
10:     $O_i \leftarrow T_j$
11:     $i \leftarrow i + 1; j \leftarrow j + 1$
12: **end while**

2.2.1 String distance metrics

When finding a match, two distance metrics were used: *Levenshtein (edit) distance*, d_L, and *Jaccard distance*, d_J.

The edit distance between two strings is the minimum number of character insertions, deletions, and substitutions required to transform one string into another. Jaccard distance [7] is derived from the *Jaccard index*, which is a generic measure of set similarity [4]. The Jaccard index $J(A, B)$ of two sets is the size of the intersection of the two sets divided by the size of their union. This yields a real number between 0 and 1; the Jaccard distance $d_J(A, B)$ is then $1 - J(A, B)$. Jaccard distance may be used as a string distance metric by taking the two sets A and B to be the sets of bigrams from the two strings under consideration.

These two distance metrics were used to compare potential matches from the BK-tree against an OCR result. Matches were ordered first in ascending order of edit distance from the OCR result, with Jaccard distance used to distinguish matches with the same edit distance. We define the sorting function $d_A(s, t_1, t_2)$, which returns 1 if t_1 is considered closer to s than t_2 and 0 if not.

2.2.2 Exact matching

Searching for an exact match was a relatively straightforward procedure, shown in Alg. 2. We compared the current word in the OCR results with the words surrounding it in the truth text, rather than simply comparing with the current word. In this way we could account for slight discrepancies in reading order between the OCR and the truth text. The function returns the index of the truth text word with the shortest metric distance from the OCR result, and a binary value indicating whether the match was exact or not.

Algorithm 2 Exact matching

1: **function** EXACTMATCH(i, j)
2:    $k^* \leftarrow 0$
3:    **for** $k \leftarrow 0, 1, -1, 2, -2$ **do**
4:       **if** $O_i = T_{j+k}$ **then**
5:          **return** $(j + k, 1)$
6:       **else if** $d_A(O_i, T_{j+k}, T_{j+k^*}) = 1$ **then**
7:          $k^* \leftarrow k$
8:       **end if**
9:    **end for**
10:   **return** $(j + k^*, 0)$
11: **end function**

2.2.3 Approximate matching

If no exact match could be found, we searched the entire truth text for the best approximate match to the OCR result using BK(T), following Alg. 3. The truth text string with the shortest metric distance from the OCR result is found, and we then find the index of the occurrence of that word with the smallest difference from our current position in the truth text to return.

A BK-tree is a tree data structure that organises its nodes according to their distance from each other according to some distance metric; in our case, nodes are ordered according to their edit distance from the first word in the truth text. This BK-tree can be used to find all the words in the truth text that are within a given edit distance of a query word in $O(\log n)$ time in the average case.

2.2.4 Special cases

The approach outlined above, while generally accurate, required a few specific modifications to cope with situations

---

Algorithm 3 Approximate matching

1: **function** APPROXIMATEMATCH(i, j)
2:    **for** $k \leftarrow 1, 2, \dots$ **do**
3:       $ms \leftarrow \{m : m \in \mathrm{BK}(T), d_L(O_i, m) \leq k\}$
4:       **if** ms is not empty **then**
5:          sort ms according to d_A
6:          **return** index of ms_0 closest to j
7:       **end if**
8:    **end for**
9: **end function**

---

where the OCR results contained word breaks not present in the truth text. Without special consideration, these additional word breaks would cause the OCR correction to introduce new errors into the document, even if the two halves of the split word were in themselves correct.

The first cause of such word breaks was the hyphenation of long words. This was solved by checking the last character of an OCR result prior to matching; if the last character was a hyphen, the word was combined with the one following it before searching for a correction, and the match was then divided into two fragments again to correct the OCR.

The second cause was the result of irregular letter spacing in the page image, causing the OCR engine to insert additional word breaks. To solve this, an additional step was inserted into the algorithm after the first check for an exact match. If exact matching failed, the OCR result was combined with the word following it, and a second search for an exact match was run using the new word. If a match was found, the first of the OCR results was expanded to contain the entire word, and the second of the results was deleted.

2.3 Insertion of hidden text layer

The final phase was to take the corrected OCR results and use them to construct a new PDF-IT document from the original page images.

Each separate OCR result was used to construct a PDF text object, using the provided bounding box coordinates to position the text on the appropriate page correctly. For each distinct font in the OCR results, a font object was inserted into the PDF document, followed by a series of text streams, each consisting of all the text objects present on a single page. The page objects themselves were then updated to refer to these new objects, and the document's cross-reference table was updated.

3. PERFORMANCE

In this section we demonstrate the effectiveness of the algorithm described in Sec. 2, by presenting the results of applying the OCR correction algorithm to four PDF documents. Truth texts for the documents were created by manually transcribing the documents into plain text files, preserving capitalisation, punctuation, and spelling but omitting text found in the header or footer of the document, such as page numbers.

Performance was measured simply by counting the number of errors present in the OCR results before and after correction, and calculating the percentage change in the number of errors. An *error* was defined as any word appearing in an incorrect place in the OCR results, relative to the original PDF document, or any word that was found to be missing in the results. The error rate was then the number of errors

Table 1: No. of errors in OCR results (all text)

Document	Errors		Change
	raw	corrected	
1	47	49	+4.26%
2	30	24	−20.0%
3	24	14	−41.7%
4	20	25	+25.0%

Table 2: No. of errors in OCR results (body only)

Document	Errors		Change
	raw	corrected	
1	44	15	−65.9%
2	30	23	−23.3%
3	24	13	−45.8%
4	17	9	−47.1%

in the OCR results divided by the total number of words in the results.

3.1 Results

Tables 1 and 2 show the number of errors found in the OCR results of four PDF documents before and after running the correction algorithm.

All four documents contained text that was not properly part of the document itself: page numbers, headers and footers, handwritten annotations, and other publisher artifacts. As noted above, such text was excluded from the prepared truth texts, on the grounds that such text would not be found in a truth text obtained, say, from an author-submitted typescript. This caused problems, because the OCR would generally recognise this extra text well (with the exception of handwriting), while the truth text would attempt to 'correct' what it saw as invalid text.

For completeness' sake, we present both sets of results, with Table 1 showing error count with artifacts included, and Table 2 showing error count with artifacts excluded.

3.2 Discussion

When publisher artifacts were excluded from the error count, all four documents saw a significant reduction in the number of errors in the OCR results. An inspection of the corrected OCR results indicated that the majority of errors that remained were the result of words being incorrectly split into *several* fragments, so that a string appearing as a single word to a human was interpreted as three or more separate words by the OCR. In Sec. 2.2.4 we described a method of identifying where a word had been split into two, but we do not attempt to check further for other breaks. In principle we could extend the solution outlined above to test three-word or even four-word strings, but it would be difficult to determine when to stop trying to combine words and instead to search for an approximate match.

4. CONCLUSIONS

By using a ground truth text containing a canonical version of the words found in the document, we were able to significantly improve the accuracy of the hidden text layer within a PDF-IT document.

Our method successfully matches the reading order of the OCR results to the truth text, but is still prone to being misled. Erroneous word breaks inserted by the OCR engine can cause the algorithm to attempt to 'correct' words that do not actually exist within the document, and such correction will alter the algorithm's perception of its position within the truth text. Despite this, once a well-recognised word is found, we are able to recover the correct position in the text. Our test results show that it is possible to align the truth text to the page image with a high degree of accuracy without a large amount of preprocessing of the truth text.

4.1 Future work

We feel very pleased at the success of this preliminary work but it is clear that some degree of pre-processing, using document recognition techniques, for recognising headers, footers and figures-with-text would certainly pay dividends. Equally there are certainly better OCR engines than Tesseract (the commercial alternatives such as Abbyy Fine Reader and Nuance Omnipage have a strong reputation)

A low-cost possibility to be investigated is whether retaining any Adobe-created OCR layer and comparing its recognition results with those of Tesseract might improve recognition performance, particularly if the bounding boxes of glyphs in the Adobe OCR stream could be extracted with a public domain tool such as PDF Box.

5. ACKNOWLEDGEMENTS

We thank Clive Adams of the Institute for Mental Health, University of Nottingham, for making available to us PDF documents from the Cochrane Schizophrenia Group's collection, around which this work is based.

6. REFERENCES

[1] S. Feng and R. Manmatha. A hierarchical, HMM-based automatic evaluation of OCR accuracy for a digital library of books. In *Proceedings of the 6th ACM/IEEE-CS Joint Conference on Digital Libraries, 2006. JCDL'06.*, pages 109–118. IEEE, 2006.

[2] J. D. Hobby. Matching document images with ground truth. *International Journal on Document Analysis and Recognition*, 1(1):52–61, 1998.

[3] J. Hughes, D. F. Brailsford, S. R. Bagley, and C. E. Adams. Generating summary documents for a variable-quality PDF document collection. In *Proceedings of the 2014 ACM Symposium on Document Engineering*, pages 49–52. ACM, 2014.

[4] P. Jaccard. The distribution of the flora in the alpine zone. *New Phytologist*, 11(2):37–50, 1912.

[5] T. Kanungo and R. M. Haralick. Automatic generation of character groundtruth for scanned documents: a closed-loop approach. In *Proceedings of the 13th International Conference on Pattern Recognition, 1996*, volume 3, pages 669–675. IEEE, 1996.

[6] D.-W. Kim and T. Kanungo. Attributed point matching for automatic groundtruth generation. *International Journal on Document Analysis and Recognition*, 5(1):47–66, 2002.

[7] M. Levandowsky and D. Winter. Distance between sets. *Nature*, 234(5323):34–35, 1971.

[8] I. Z. Yalniz and R. Manmatha. A fast alignment scheme for automatic OCR evaluation of books. In *2011 International Conference on Document Analysis and Recognition (ICDAR)*, pages 754–758. IEEE, 2011.

Design Is Not What You Think It Is

Peter Bil'ak
Typotheque
The Hague, Netherlands
peter@typotheque.com

ABSTRACT

In this talk, Peter Bil'ak will examine the ways that current publishing practices are rooted in the 19th century, and how in order to move forward, we may have to go back to the roots and reconnect with readers. He will also talk about his recent project, *Works That Work* magazine, which set out to rethink publishing paradigms, starting with its financing, distribution and production. Works That Work aims to discuss design outside of the traditional design discourse, and Peter Bil'ak will argue for widening the understanding of the design discipline.

Keywords
Publishing Practices, Publishing Paradigms, Design Disciplines

1. SHORT BIOGRAPHY

Peter Bil'ak was born in Czechoslovakia and lives in the Netherlands. He works in the field of editorial, graphic, and type design, teaches at the Royal Academy of Arts in The Hague. Started Typotheque in 1999, Dot Dot Dot magazine in 2000, Indian Type Foundry in 2009, and *Works That Work* magazine in 2012.

DocEng '16 September 12-16, 2016, Vienna, Austria

© 2016 Copyright held by the owner/author(s).

ACM ISBN 978-1-4503-4438-8/16/09.

DOI: http://dx.doi.org/10.1145/2960811.2967145

Design is Not What You Think it Is

Peter Biľak
Typotheque
The Hague, Netherlands
peter@typotheque.com

ABSTRACT

Keywords

1. SHORT BIOGRAPHY

SEL: a Unified Algorithm
for Entity Linking and Saliency Detection

Salvatore Trani
ISTI–CNR, Pisa, Italy
University of Pisa, Italy
s.trani@isti.cnr.it

Diego Ceccarelli
Bloomberg LP
dceccarelli4@bloomberg.net

Claudio Lucchese
ISTI–CNR, Pisa, Italy
c.lucchese@isti.cnr.it

Salvatore Orlando
Università Ca' Foscari
Venezia, Italy
orlando@unive.it

Raffaele Perego
ISTI–CNR, Pisa, Italy
r.perego@isti.cnr.it

ABSTRACT

The *Entity Linking* task consists in automatically identifying and linking the entities mentioned in a text to their URIs in a given Knowledge Base, e.g., Wikipedia. Entity Linking has a large impact in several text analysis and information retrieval related tasks. This task is very challenging due to natural language ambiguity. However, not all the entities mentioned in a document have the same relevance and utility in understanding the topics being discussed. Thus, the related problem of identifying the most relevant entities present in a document, also known as *Salient Entities*, is attracting increasing interest.

In this paper we propose *SEL*, a novel supervised two-step algorithm comprehensively addressing both entity linking and saliency detection. The first step is based on a classifier aimed at identifying a set of candidate entities that are likely to be mentioned in the document, thus maximizing the precision of the method without hindering its recall. The second step is still based on machine learning, and aims at choosing from the previous set the entities that actually occur in the document. Indeed, we tested two different versions of the second step, one aimed at solving only the entity linking task, and the other that, besides detecting linked entities, also scores them according to their saliency. Experiments conducted on two different datasets show that the proposed algorithm outperforms state-of-the-art competitors, and is able to detect salient entities with high accuracy.

Keywords

Entity Linking; Salient Entities; Machine Learning

1. INTRODUCTION

Lately, much research has been spent to devise effective solutions to Entity Linking (EL). The task, also known as *Wikification*, has been introduced by Mihalcea and Csomai [9], and consists in

DocEng '16, September 12 - 16, 2016, Vienna, Austria

© 2016 Copyright held by the owner/author(s). Publication rights licensed to ACM.
ISBN 978-1-4503-4438-8/16/09. . . $15.00

DOI: http://dx.doi.org/10.1145/2960811.2960819

finding small fragments of text (hereinafter named *spots* or *mentions*) referring to an entity that is listed in a given knowledge base, e.g., Wikipedia. Natural language ambiguity makes this task non trivial. Indeed, the same entity may be mentioned with different text fragments, and the same mention may refer to one of several entities.

EL is strictly correlated with another task, referred to as *document aboutness* problem [11] or *Salient Entities* (SE) discovery problem [6], which goal is labeling the entities mentioned in the document according to a notion of saliency, where the most relevant entities are those that have the highest utility in understanding the topics discussed.

As an example, consider the annotations performed by an EL algorithm that uses Wikipedia on the following text:

> **Maradona** (→Diego_Maradona) played his first **World Cup tournament** (→FIFA_World_Cup) in 1982, when **Argentina** (→Argentina_national_football_team) played **Belgium** (→Belgium_national_football_team) in the opening game of the **1982 Cup** (→1982_FIFA_World_Cup) in **Barcelona** (→Barcelona).

Such an algorithm performs the EL task by first spotting the fragments of text that are likely to refer to some entity, e.g., spots **Maradona** or **Belgium**. Indeed, in this phase multiple candidate entities can be generated for each spot. Then, the algorithm proceeds by trying to link each spot to the correct entity, e.g., links the spot **Maradona** to the corresponding Wikipedia page[1]. Due to the presence of multiple candidates for each spot and to the inherent ambiguity of natural language, the disambiguation phase of the EL process is not trivial, e.g., the mention **Belgium** does not refer to its most common sense, i.e., the country, but rather to its national football team[2]. A final stage of pruning discards annotations that are considered not correct or consistent with the overall interpretation of the document.

As previously stated, Salient Entities (SE) discovery can be combined with EL. The easiest integration is to perform the SE discovery as a subsequent step to EL, by finally choosing the most relevant entities that have high utility in understanding the topics being discussed among the set of entities returned by the EL algorithm. However, we claim this pipeline approach is somehow limiting since the disambiguation could benefit from the saliency signal. In our example, the most relevant entities are probably the ones referred by mentions **Maradona** and **1982 Cup**.

---

[1]https://en.wikipedia.org/wiki/Diego_Maradona

[2]https://en.wikipedia.org/wiki/Belgium_national_football_team

Entity saliency impacts on information extraction from text in a broader sense. Consider for example a semantic clustering approach where linked entities are exploited to provide a high-level summary of each document. In this application scenario the capability of weighting entities on the basis of their saliency is crucial. In addition, the knowledge about the saliency of entities recognized by an EL algorithm in a document should also impact on the evaluation of the effectiveness of the EL algorithm itself. Let us come back to the previous example where the entity **1982 Cup** provides much more information about the document than the entity **Barcelona**. Thus, an EL algorithm that links only the mention **1982 Cup** should be preferred in terms of effectiveness to another algorithm that only links the spot **Barcelona**.

In this paper we propose a novel supervised *Salient Entity Linking (SEL)* algorithm to comprehensively address EL and SE detection. The *SEL* algorithm entails two steps: *Candidate Pruning* and *Saliency Linking*. During the *Candidate Pruning* step, a classifier is used to prune the large set of candidate entities generated by the spotting phase. The aim is to detect a relatively small collection of candidates that encompasses all the entities actually mentioned in the document. Thus the emphasis is on training a classifier able to achieve a good precision without hindering recall. The proposed approach has proved to outperform heuristic methods that prune unlikely candidates on the basis of simple likelihood measures such as *commonness* or *link probability* [9, 10]. The *Saliency Linking* step also exploits machine learning, and, in addition to addressing EL, it is able to predict the saliency of the entities that survived the *Candidate Pruning* step. Thanks to the *Candidate Pruning* step, the candidate set processed during the *Saliency Linking* step is less noisy and smaller in size, which allows to use more complex and powerful graph-based entity correlation features.

The experiments conducted on two different datasets show that *SEL* outperforms state-of-the-art competitors in the EL task. In addition, it is able to detect salient entities with high accuracy. Since both steps of the algorithm are based on machine learning, we also analyzed in depth feature importance, and we took into consideration feature extraction costs. We show that an efficient and effective classifier for the first step can be trained on the basis of a small and easily computable set of features. This is particularly important since the classifier must be applied to a very large set of initial candidates. On the other hand, in the second step we have a reduced number of survived candidates and we benefit from the exploitation of further graph-based features, which are more expensive to compute, but which are proved to be very effective for improving the quality of entity linking and saliency detection.

In summary, the main contributions of this paper are:

- a novel *Salient Entity Linking (SEL)* algorithm, that accurately estimates entity saliency and outperforms state-of-the-art EL techniques by providing a comprehensive solution to the EL and the SE detection problems;
- an evaluation of a wide set of heterogeneous features, including novel features, used to represent entities within the machine learning algorithms adopted;
- a novel dataset of news manually annotated with entities and their saliency, hereinafter publicly available to the research community.

2. RELATED WORK

Entity Linking. Entity Linking algorithms usually work by following a well defined schema, that could be roughly summarized in three steps: *spotting*, *disambiguation* and *pruning*. *Spotting* detects potential mentions in a text and, for each mention, produces a list of *candidate entities*. *Disambiguation* aims at selecting a single entity for each mention produced in the previous step, by trying to maximize some *coherence* measure among the selected entities in the document. *Pruning* detects and removes non-relevant annotations in order to improve the precision of the system. In performing the three steps, EL algorithms rely on three effective signals: *(i)* the probability for a mention to be a link to an entity (*link probability*); *(ii)* the prior probability for a mention to refer to a specific entity (*commonness*); *(iii)* the *coherence* among the entities in a document, e.g., estimated by the Milne-Witten *relatedness* [10]. In addition to annotate mentions to the entities, EL algorithms usually assign to each annotation a *confidence score*, roughly estimating the correctness of the annotation.

Several EL approaches have been proposed following the problem formalization given by Mihalcea and Csomai with *Wikify* [9]. A substantial improvement has been the WikiMiner approach proposed by Milne and Witten [10]. It works by first identifying a set of non-ambiguous mentions and then using this set to disambiguate the ambiguous ones. Ferragina and Scaiella proposed an improved approach called Tagme [5], which tries to find a collective agreement for the best candidates using a voting scheme based on the the Milne-Witten relatedness. Candidate entities with a coherence below a given threshold are discarded, and for each mention the one with the largest commonness is selected. In Spotlight [8], Mendes *et al.* represent each entity with a context vector containing the terms from the paragraphs where the entity is mentioned; they also exploit NLP methods, removing all the spots that are only composed of verbs, adjectives, and prepositions. In Wikifier 2.0 [2] (which is an extension of [13]), Cheng and Roth use a machine learning based hybrid strategy to combine local features, such as commonness and TF-IDF between mentions and Wikipedia pages, with global coherence features based on Wikipedia links and relational inference. This system combines Wikipedia pages, gazetteers, and Wordnet. In AIDA [7], Hoffart *et al.* proposed a weighted mention-entity graph for collective disambiguation. This model combines three features into a graph model: entity popularity, textual similarity (keyphrase-based and syntax-based) as well as coherence between mapping entities. The authors also published a manually annotated dataset for EL, named AIDA-CoNLL 2003. In WAT [12] authors extended Tagme with a new spotting module (using gazetteers, named-entity recognition analysis and a binary classifier for tuning performance), voting-based and graph-based disambiguation approaches as well as a pruning pipeline. Note that neither the source code nor a remote annotation service of WAT is publicly available. One of the main conclusions from their experiments was that while many systems focused on improving disambiguation, the spotter and the pruner are actually responsible for introducing many of the false positives in the EL process. A thorough overview and analysis of the main approaches to EL and their evaluation is presented by Shen *et al.* [15].

Entity Saliency. The problem of understanding the main topics of a document has been the goal of many IR tasks, including latent semantic topics and text summarization. In this work we tackle the related task of finding the most important entities mentioned in a given document. This task has previously been referred to as *document aboutness* [6] or *salient entity discovery* [14] problem.

Gamon *et al.* [6] studied the *aboutness* problem referred to the named entities occurring in Web pages. The approach used is partially inspired by [11], where click-through data are exploited to rank named entities mentioned in queries. The authors estimate the entity saliency for a Web page by exploiting the click-through recorded in a query log. Roughly, a document is considered to be relevant for a given entity when it is returned by a Web search engine and clicked by multiple users in answer to queries mentioning the entity. A number of text-based features are proposed in the paper, most of them applicable only to a Web scenario, e.g., url depth. In such work entities are just pieces of text (and not entities listed in a given knowledge base) and the disambiguation problem is not tackled at all.

When entities in a knowledge base such as Wikipedia are considered, rich contextual information coming from its graph structure can be fruitfully exploited. Given the set of entities occurring in a document, an *entity graph* can be built by projecting the subgraph of the knowledge base graph including all the entities possibly mentioned in the document. Entities can finally be ranked according to some measure of their importance in such a graph.

Dunietz and Gillick [3] proposed a method for classifying salient entities mentioned in news by exploiting graph-based measures. They show that the eigenvector centrality computed on the mentioned entities can slightly improve the performance of a binary classifier aimed at discriminating salient entities with respect to a classifier learned with text-based features only. The same task is addressed in [14], where text-based features are fruitfully complemented with graph-based ones to improve accuracy. The work by Dunietz and Gillick is closely related to ours but, in order to automatically generate the ground truth, they consider as salient entities those mentioned in the abstract of the news. Thus, the authors cannot use features related to the position of the mention for predicting the saliency, and how the graph-based and other features contribute to improve the classification accuracy. We instead exploited a manually assessed dataset that allows us to perform this analysis. Moreover, their paper assumes to know in advance the correct entities mentioned in the document, and addresses only the problem of ranking them by saliency. Instead we addressed comprehensively the EL and SE problems, and studied the importance of different features for identifying the correct entities mentioned as well as their saliency.

3. THE SALIENT ENTITY LINKING ALGORITHM

Let $\mathbb{KB}$ be a knowledge base with a set of entities $\mathbb{E}$. The EL problem is to identify the entities $\mathbb{E}_D \subseteq \mathbb{E}$ mentioned by the *spots* S_D of a given document D. As in state-of-the-art approaches, Wikipedia is used as knowledge base and every Wikipedia article is considered as an entity. Entities that are not in Wikipedia are not linked (i.e., we do not take into account the NIL problem).

In this paper the *saliency* $\sigma(e|D)$ of the entities e mentioned in a document D is also considered. Without loss of generality, we define the domain of function σ as the set $\{0,1,2,3\}$, with the following meaning:

- **3 - Top Relevant**: the entity describes the main topics or the leading characters of a document;

- **2 - Highly Relevant**: these are satellite entities that are not necessary for understanding the document, but they provide important facets;

- **1 - Partially Relevant**: entities that provide background information about the content of the document, but disregarding them would not affect negatively the comprehension of the document;

- **0 - Not Relevant/Not Mentioned**: any other entity in $\mathbb{E}$ that is not relevant or not mentioned in D.

The SE detection problem is to predict the saliency $\sigma(e|D)$ for each $e \in \mathbb{E}$. Note that the EL and SE problems are correlated and

they almost coincide when a binary saliency function returning the relevance of an entity for D is adopted, i.e., $\sigma(e|D) = 1$ if $e \in \mathbb{E}_D$ and 0 otherwise.

The proposed *SEL* algorithm is able to discover $\mathbb{E}_D$, and in addition solves the SE problem, thus predicting $\sigma(e|D)$ for each $e \in \mathbb{E}_D$. The first step of *SEL* performs a *spotting* process, which detects potential entity mentions in the text. The hyperlink information of Wikipedia is exploited for this purpose. If the given document D contains a fragment of text s that is used as anchor text in Wikipedia to link to an entity e, then e is considered a *candidate entity* for the spot s. Since the same anchor text can be used in Wikipedia to reference any of several entities, a spot s might be associated with several candidate entities. The set of candidate entities can be very large, which makes it difficult to select the single correct entity for each spot, i.e., to disambiguate spots. However not all the possible entities are equally probable for a given spot, and candidate entities can be pruned to make the subsequent *disambiguation* step easier.

The first novelty in the proposed *SEL* algorithm is the usage of a machine-learned classifier with a set of easy-to-compute features to prune the candidate entities before disambiguation takes place. The goal of such classifier is to improve the precision of the state-of-the-art unsupervised techniques, without hindering recall: the classifier aims at filtering a small set of candidates without pruning any entity in $\mathbb{E}_D$. To train the classifier we investigated a novel and rich set of features, from which we selected only 8 *light* features.

The second step implements spot disambiguation. We devise two different solutions: the former aimed at solving the EL problem only, and the latter that, besides linking spots to correct entities, also scores them according to their saliency, thus combining the EL and SE discovery tasks. Also this step is based on machine-learning, this time using a regressor which is well suited for both the binary EL task (with a learned threshold value), or the multi-class SE problem.

The second novelty in the *SEL* algorithm is the blending of disambiguation and saliency prediction in a single step. We claim that this blending makes it possible to improve the accuracy of disambiguation for those spots/entities that are likely to be salient. The reason is that an EL task should not link everything, but just the relevant concepts, i.e., the salient ones (thus excluding not relevant concepts, with a saliency score of 0). To learn an effective regressor for disambiguation, we analyzed a feature set wider than in the first step. By focusing on the relatively small number of candidate entities coming from the first step, it is possible to exploit complex and computationally *heavy* features, like those considering the entity relatedness graph.

3.1 Supervised Candidate Pruning

Potential entity mentions in a text are detected by exploiting the $\mathbb{KB}$: all the possible spots occurring in a given document D are matched against all the anchor texts and page titles in Wikipedia, and in case of an exact match (without any normalization on the text), a relationship is created between a spot s and the entities referred by s in Wikipedia.

Due to language ambiguity, the number of entities for each spot can be large. Formally, let $S_D = \{s_1, s_2, \ldots\}$ be the set of spots detected in D and $C_D = \{c_1, c_2, \ldots\}$, $C_D \subseteq \mathbb{E}$, the set of candidate entities, each of which is associated with some spot s_i. Indeed, the output of the spotting phase is a directed bipartite graph $G_D = (S_D, C_D, E_D)$, where E_D are the edges of the graph such that $(s_i, c_j) \in E_D$ if s_i is a text fragment used in Wikipedia for referring to entity $c_j \in \mathbb{E}$.

The goal of *Candidate Pruning* is to devise an effective entity pruning function ϕ: given a set of candidate entities C_D of the bipartite graph G_D identified by the spotting phase, ϕ finally produces a new set $C'_D = \phi(C_D)$, such that $|C'_D|$ is minimized and $|C'_D \cap \mathbb{E}_D|$ is maximized.

State-of-the-art algorithms perform a Heuristic Pruning (HP) of candidate entities C_D, by exploiting two measures, namely *commonness* and *link probability*, that can be precomputed as follows:

- The commonness of a candidate $c_j \in C_D$ for spot $s_i \in S_D$ is defined as the prior probability that an occurrence of an anchor s_i links to c_j. The commonness is a property of the edges of our bipartite graph. Given a spot $s_i \in S_D$, it is possible rank the outgoing edges and remove edges with low commonness.

- The link probability for a spot $s_i \in S_D$ is defined as the number of occurrences of s_i being a link to an entity in $\mathbb{K}B$, divided by its total number of occurrences in $\mathbb{K}B$. Therefore a spot with low link probability is rarely used as a mention to a relevant entity, and can be pruned from graph G_D.

Let τ_c and τ_{lp} be the *minimum commonness* and the *minimum link probability* (heuristic thresholds), it is possible to discard those graph edges with commonness lower than τ_c, and those spots with *link probability* lower than τ_{lp}. Note that when a spot s_i is pruned, also its outgoing edges are removed. After pruning the graph G_D on the basis of τ_c and τ_{lp}, some candidate entities in C_D may result disconnected from any spot, and they can thus be removed as well.

Setting a minimum threshold on commonness and link probability has been proven to be a simple and effective strategy, although heuristic, to limit the number of spots and associated candidate entities, without harming the recall of the EL process. Table 1 reports the performance of such heuristic pruning (HP) method over a well-known dataset (AIDA-CoNLL 2003 [7]) for different values of τ_c and τ_{lp}. The metrics adopted are precision (i.e., ratio of positive entities retained to the whole set of entities retained) and recall (i.e., ratio of positive entities retained to the whole set of positive entities). It is worth noting that commonly adopted thresholds ensure a good recall at the cost of a very low precision. The same table also reports the performance of the proposed solution, which is described below. For $\tau_c = 2\%$ the HP obtains up to 2% of improvement in recall with respect to the proposed method. On the other hand, with this setting the HP obtains a maximum precision of only 0.074, while the supervised solution achieves a precision of 0.367, i.e., 500% of improvement. Further experimental analysis is discussed in Section 4.2. Note that both Wikiminer [10] and Tagme [5] use $\tau_c = 2\%$, with the former using $\tau_{lp} = 6.5\%$ and the latter exploiting a more complex usage of the link probability value. In the following, we refer to the heuristic pruning strategy of Wikiminer as HP_W.

The *Candidate Pruning* method improves on the previous heuristic strategies by using a supervised technique. A binary classifier is learned to distinguish between relevant and irrelevant entities. Note that saliency has not taken into account in this step: a candidate entity c_j is considered relevant *iff* it is mentioned by the given document D. The training set is built from the ground truth on the basis of the bipartite graph $G_D = (S_D, C_D, E_D)$ generated by the spotting phase. A positive label is associated with $c_j \in C_D$ if $c_j \in \mathbb{E}_D$, and a negative label otherwise. Each entity $c_j \in C_D$ is represented with a large set of features extracted from the document, from the bipartite graph G_D and from the knowledge base $\mathscr{K}\mathscr{B}$. These features are deeply discussed in Section 3.3. Eventually, only the candidate entities that are predicted to be relevant by the classifier are saved for the subsequent *Saliency Linking* step.

There are a couple of aspects relative to the ground truth that is worth discussing. First, class imbalance characterizes the train-

Table 1: Spotting performance for different values of τ_c and τ_{lp} (AIDA-CoNLL 2003 dataset).

Commonness	Link-Probability	Precision	Recall
0.005	0.02	0.022	0.907
0.005	0.03	0.025	0.900
0.005	0.04	0.029	0.893
0.005	0.05	0.036	0.893
0.01	0.02	0.032	0.891
0.01	0.03	0.038	0.884
0.01	0.04	0.043	0.877
0.01	0.05	0.052	0.877
0.02	0.02	0.048	0.864
0.02	0.03	0.056	0.856
0.02	0.04	0.063	0.850
0.02	0.05	0.074	0.850
0.04	0.02	0.072	0.839
0.04	0.03	0.082	0.831
0.04	0.04	0.092	0.826
0.04	0.05	0.103	0.826
Proposed *Candidate Pruning*		0.367	0.848

ing dataset, since on average we have that $|\mathbb{E}_D \cap C_D| \ll |C_D|$. Unfortunately a classifier learned from a training set with a strongly skewed class distribution may lead to poor performance. This is because most algorithms minimize the misclassification rate on the training set, hence favoring most frequent class, which in the specific case is the negative one. In order to deal with this issue, a cost model is introduced. Therefore, the classifier incurs a higher penalization when misclassifying an instance in a rare class. Another key property which deserves attention concerns the choice of the feature space used to represent instances. Indeed, we distinguish between *light* and *heavy* features, i.e., either cheap or expensive to compute. We show that a small subset of these light features is able to generate a good classifier for the *Candidate Pruning*. The resulting classifier improves state-of-the-art heuristic techniques in terms of precision without hindering the recall, thus retaining most of the positive entities for the *Saliency Linking* step.

3.2 Supervised Saliency Linking

The *spotting* step in EL algorithms is always followed by a *disambiguation* phase: among the several candidates for a given spot, only one entity can be selected. The proposed *SEL* algorithm distinguish the following two tasks:

i) disambiguating spots also using contextual features, thus addressing the EL problem;

ii) predicting a saliency score for the relevant entities, thus addressing the EL and SE problem at the same time.

Both tasks are solved by learning a predictor of entity saliency. In the former case, an entity is considered relevant or irrelevant, i.e., $\sigma(e|D) \in \{0, 1\}$, while, in the latter, we have several degrees of relevance, i.e., $\sigma(e|D) \in \{0, 1, 2, 3\}$. The training dataset is built from the ground truth by considering only the candidate entities filtered by the *Candidate Pruning* step, and each entity c_j is labeled according to $\sigma(c_j|D)$. Note that all candidate entities c_k not mentioned in the document are labeled with $\sigma(c_k|D) = 0$.

This training dataset has two interesting properties. First, thanks to the *Candidate Pruning* step, the number of irrelevant entities is

Table 2: Light Features for Supervised Candidate Pruning: features are relative to a candidate entity c_j

1. **positions**	first, last, average, and standard deviation of the normalized positions of the spots referring to c_j
2. **first field positions**	document D is subdivided in 4 fields: *the title, the first three sentences, the last three sentences,* and *the middle sentences*; the normalized position of the first spot referring to c_j is computed for each field
3. **average position in sentences**	the average position of spots referring to c_j across the sentences of the document (salient entities are usually mentioned early)
4. **field frequency**	number of spots referring to c_j computed for each field of the document
5. **capitalization**	True *iff* at least one mention of c_j is capitalized
6. **uppercase ratio**	maximum fraction of uppercase letters among the spots referring to c_j
7. **highlighting**	True *iff* at least one mention of c_j is highlighted in bold or italic
8. **average lengths**	average term- and character-based length of spots referring to c_j
9. **idf**	maximum Wikipedia inverse document frequency among the spots referring to c_j
10. **tf-idf**	maximum document spot frequency multiplied by *idf* among the spots referring to c_j
11. **is title**	True *iff* at least one mention of c_j is present in the document title
12. **link probabilities**	maximum and average *link probabilities* of the spots referring to c_j
13. **is name/person**	True *iff* at least one mention of c_j is a common/person name (based on Yago – `http://goo.gl/glfBYN`)
14. **entity frequency**	total number of spots referring to c_j
15. **distinct mentions**	number of distinct mentions referring to c_j
16. **not ambiguity**	True *iff* at least one mention of c_j for which c_j is the only candidate entity
17. **ambiguity**	minimum, maximum and average ambiguity of the spots referring to c_j; spot ambiguity is defined as 1 minus the reciprocal of the number of candidate entities for the spot
18. **commonness**	maximum and average *commonness* of the spots referring to c_j
19. **max commonness × max link probability**	maximum *commonness* multiplied by the maximum *link probability* among the spots referring to c_j
20. **entity degree**	in-degree, out-degree and (undirected) degree of c_j in the Wikipedia citation graph
21. **entity degree × max commonness**	maximum *commonness* among the spots of c_j multiplied by the degree of c_j
22. **document length**	number of characters in D

significantly reduced, and therefore the predictor is able to train on a quite balanced dataset with less noise. Second, by having a smaller number of candidate entities to deal with, it is possible to exploit more complex and powerful features able to better capture entity correlations. Indeed, besides the set of light features used in the *Candidate Pruning* step, an additional set of *heavy* features is added. These are mainly computed on the graphs induced by the Wikipedia hyperlinks, thus modeling the relationships among the candidate entities. It is worth remarking that this expensive feature extraction becomes feasible because the first step is able to strongly prune the original candidate set C_D. This new set of features is discussed in Section 3.3.

We remark that the *Saliency Linking* step implements disambiguation and saliency prediction at the same time. Disambiguation occurs implicitly as an incorrect entity c_k for a spot is predicted to have no saliency, i.e., $\sigma(c_k|D) = 0$. By tackling disambiguation and saliency prediction at the same time *SEL* achieves the goal of being accurate in linking the most relevant entities.

Note that during the *Saliency Linking* step the graph G_D is not considered, except via the features computed. When predicting the saliency of an entity, no information about the predicted saliency of other entities is exploited. Therefore, it is possible to have spots without any predicted relevant entity, and spots with more than one relevant entity. If needed, this can be easily fixed with a postprocessing step not implemented in this work for the following reasons. First, it is much easier and clearer to consider the output of the *Saliency Linking* step as a flat set of entities, thus making it possible to easily adopt standard information retrieval measures, such as precision and recall. Second, it might be interesting in some application scenarios to have more than one annotation per spot, especially when more than one *facet* is relevant.

3.3 Features

Given the candidate entities devised by the spotting phase in document D, the *SEL* algorithm represents with a vector of numerical features each candidate entity $c_j \in C_D$ in the bipartite graph $G_D = (S_D, C_D, E_D)$. Specifically, we distinguish between *light* features (i.e., cheap to be computed) which are generated for all $c_j \in C_D$, and *heavy* features (i.e., computationally expensive) which are computed only for the filtered candidate entities $C'_D = \phi(C_D) \subseteq C_D$, where $|C'_D| \ll |C_D|$.

Light features. Light features, illustrated in Table 2, are mainly derived from *attributes* associated with the mentions in S_D, which are then aggregated to build features for the mentioned entities. Some of them are computed on the basis of the occurrences of spots $s_i \in S_D$ within document D. For example, the positions of spots (1–3), their count (4), some typesetting features (5–7), their length (8). Features 9–10,12,18, rely instead on Wikipedia, but they are precomputed and stored in the dictionary used for spotting. We included features related to spots ambiguity, see 16–17. Finally, we included two novel features, 19 and 21, trying to blend together commonness, link probability and ambiguity signals.

Note that some of the features (2–4) explicitly refer to a semi-structure present in the dataset, with separate fields for different sections of each document. We exploited this semi-structure by distinguishing among spots occurring in the title of the document, in the first/last three sentences, and in the middle sentences. These features are aimed at exploiting information provided by the document structure.

Heavy features. These features are extracted for each candidate entity $c_j \in C'_D = \phi(C_D)$ to model the relationships among c_j and all the other entities in C'_D. To compute these features, specific sub-

Table 3: Heavy features for Supervised Saliency Linking: most features are global and depend on the structure of the graph WG_D, others are specific for an entity

1. **graph size**	number of entities in WG_D
2. **graph diameter**	the diameter of WG_D
3. **node degree**	degree of given entity e in the undirected version of graph WG_D
4. **node average/median in-degree**	average and median node in-degree of WG_D
5. **node average/median out-degree**	average and median node out-degree of WG_D
6. **node average/median in-out-degree**	average and median node degree in the undirected version of graph WG_D
7. **farness**	the sum of the shortest paths lengths between entity e and all the other nodes in WG_D
8. **closeness**	the inverse of farness
9. **eigenvector centrality**	a measure of influence of a node in a network (Erkan and Radev [4])
10. **random walk**	the probability for a random walker to be at node e while visiting WG_D
11. **personalized random walk**	same as random walk, with a preference vector given by the entity frequencies in D
12. **graph cliques**	number of cliques in WG_D
13. **cross-cliques centrality**	a measure of connectivity of a node e in WG_D
14. **TAGME-like voting schema**	for each $e \in V_D$, we propose two normalizations of the TAGME-like voting schema: $$\sum_{e' \in V_D \setminus \{e\}} \frac{Max\_comm(e') \cdot rel(e,e')}{Max\_ambig(e')} \qquad \sum_{e' \in V_D \setminus \{e\}} \frac{Max\_comm(e') \cdot rel(e,e')}{|V_D|}$$ where $rel(e,e')$ is the Milne and Witten relatedness function, whereas $Max\_ambig(e')$ and $Max\_comm(e')$ are defined in Table 2 (sections 16-17). Feature not dependent from WG_D.

graphs of Wikipedia graph are considered. Let $WG_D = (V_D, A_D)$ be one of such subgraphs, where both the set of vertices V_D and the set of arcs A_D can be defined in different ways:

Vertices V_D: the entities, i.e., Wikipedia nodes, identified by C'_D are extended with their neighborhoods in the Wikipedia graph. Two sets of vertices are exploited, denoted by V_D^0 and V_D^1: *i)* V_D^0 is simply equal to C'_D, as identified by our filtering step; *ii)* V_D^1 contains the vertices in V_D^0 extended with the entities associated with the Wikipedia pages that *link to* or are *linked by* entities in V_D^0.

Arcs A_D: three types of directed arcs are investigated: *i)* all the hyperlinks in Wikipedia between entities in V_D, considered as directed unweighted arcs. Therefore, we have two different sets of arcs, $A_D^0 \subset A_D^1$, one for each set of vertex sets $V_D^0 \subset V_D^1$; *ii)* the arcs derived from the Wikipedia hyperlinks, weighted by the Milne and Witten relatedness function [10], by pruning arcs whose relatedness is zero; *iii)* a weighted and undirected clique graph (i.e., each node is connected to each other), where edges are weighted by the Milne and Witten relatedness function. Also in this case, there are two sets of arcs $A_D^0 \subset A_D^1$. Finally, arcs with a weight below the median are discarded in order to preserve only the most important ones.

Heavy features, listed in Table 3, are computed on the 6 graphs resulting by the combination of the two vertex sets on the three edge sets described above. In total, each candidate entity is represented by a vector of 39 *light* features and 99 *heavy* features (16 features WG_D dependent times the 6 graphs, 2 from the TAGME-like scores and 1 the confidence score of the candidate pruning classifier at step 1).

It is worth remarking that the sets of vertices of WG_D (V_D^0 or V_D^1) are small enough to make the computation of these graph features feasible. This is due to the pruning capability of our first pruning step, which greatly reduces the size of the set of candidate entities.

4. EXPERIMENTS

4.1 Datasets

For the evaluation of EL performance we used the Test B part of the AIDA-CoNLL 2003 dataset [7]. This dataset contains a subset of news from Reuters Corpus V1 which were manually linked to Wikipedia entities starting from candidates generated by the spotter of Aida [7]. The CoNLL dataset is composed of 231 documents with an average of 10.94 entities per document, hence resulting in $\approx 2,500$ mention to entities. Note that entities are not annotated with a saliency score. There exist other similar datasets such as the Knowledge Base Population track held by NIST Text Analysis Conference. However, the task is quite different as it requires annotating a given single mention in contrast to linking the full document, and it is released only with paid membership (free for the track participants).

In order to evaluate SE prediction performance, a human-assessed dataset of news was created and made publicly available, by relying on the Wikinews project[3]. Wikinews promotes the idea of participatory journalism, and provides a user-contributed repository of news. We chose this source for two main reasons: first, it is *open domain*, thus allowing us to redistribute the annotated dataset without the copyright constraints that affects similar datasets; second, because the news in Wikinews are already manually linked to entities of Wikipedia, thus making the dataset independent from the specific EL system used to detect entities. Due to some subjectivity in the assignment of a saliency score, each document (and thus also its entities) was annotated by multiple annotators, averaging the saliency scores.

An English dump of Wikinews containing news published from November 2004 to June 2014 was used, and the news that users linked to less than 10 or to more than 25 entities were filtered out. In addition, special news pages (e.g., News Briefs, or Wikinews shorts) were removed, as well as news longer than 2500 characters. The resulting dataset contains 604 news articles, uniform in text length and number of linked entities, each one with *title* and *body* fields.

---
[3]http://en.wikinews.org

90

Table 4: Agreement between groups of Expert (Exp) or Crowdflower (CF) annotators.

Annotators	Docs	Kendall's τ	Fleiss' κ	Kendall's τ binary	Fleiss' κ binary
CF vs CF	329	$0.54_{\pm.03}$	$0.33_{\pm.03}$	$0.68_{\pm.08}$	$0.49_{\pm.10}$
Exp vs Exp	62	$0.67_{\pm.11}$	$0.44_{\pm.14}$	$0.72_{\pm.03}$	$0.66_{\pm.04}$
CF vs Exp	62	$0.40_{\pm.06}$	$0.19_{\pm.03}$	$0.48_{\pm.09}$	$0.40_{\pm.08}$

Crowdflower[4], a crowd-sourcing platform, was then exploited for annotating linked entities with saliency scores. In order to get reliable human annotations, a *golden dataset* was created by asking to 4 expert annotators to provide entity saliency scores in a specific subset of 62 documents. Then, the Crowdflower quality control mechanisms allowed to use the golden dataset produced by the expert annotators to detect and ban malicious annotators. With a reward of 0.35$ per document, 400 documents (including the golden subset) were annotated by at least 3 different Crowdflower annotators in one week. Finally, documents where the annotators exhibited a low agreement were removed, obtaining the final Wikinews dataset, consisting of 365 annotated documents having an average of 12.02 entities per document, hence resulting in $\approx 4,400$ mentions to entities.

To evaluate the quality of the annotations we measured the Crowdflower annotators agreement with Fleiss' κ and Kendall's τ coefficients. The latter was measured by considering the ranked lists obtained by sorting the entities by the saliency label provided by the users. As reported in Table 4, we have $\kappa = 0.33_{\pm.03}$ and $\tau = 0.54_{\pm.03}$ among CrowdFlower users. The Fleiss' κ value suggests a *fair* agreement. This is due to the highly subjectivity of the task: different users may give different rates based on their experience, culture, etc. Our agreement results are however consistent with those reported in similar works [1]. Nevertheless, the Kendall's τ coefficient suggests a *good* ranking agreement. We also investigated agreement by collapsing *Highly Relevant* and *Partially Relevant* thus achieving a *binary* labeling. The agreement on such binary formulation is consistently higher, with $\kappa = 0.68_{\pm.08}$ and $\tau = 0.49_{\pm.10}$. This suggests that users agree in identifying *Top Relevant* entities, and they have slightly less agreement in discriminating between different degrees of relevance. Good agreement values were achieved also when comparing Crowdflower users with expert users.

Finally, the different saliency labels provided by annotators were aggregated in order to have one unique saliency label per entity. The aggregation was achieved by averaging the annotators labels and by rounding the average value when a sharp classification is needed. The Wikinews dataset is publicly available and can be downloaded at the address `http://dexter.isti.cnr.it/`. Comparing with other datasets, we believe the annotations it provide are of high quality since it is not biased by users' queries to a search engine as in [11], and it does not rely on the naïve assumption, as in [3], that entities occurring in news abstract are salient while others are not salient.

Table 5 reports some statistics about the two dataset used in our experiments. Note that only 10% of the entities annotated in the Wikinews dataset are considered as *Top Relevant*. This suggests the importance of being able to detect the most salient entities in a document. We also report some statistics about the results of the Wikipedia-based spotter. The average number of candidate entities generated per document ranges between 500 and 800, corre-

[4] http://www.crowdflower.com

Table 5: Datasets description and spotting results.

	CoNLL	Wikinews
Documents	231	365
avg. $|\mathbb{E}_D|$	10.94	12.02
Top Relevant	—	436 (10%)
Highly Relevant	—	1685 (38%)
Partially Relevant	—	2261 (52%)
avg. $|C_D|$	549.54	790.05
avg. Max Rec $= \frac{|C_D \cap \mathbb{E}_D|}{|\mathbb{E}_D|}$	0.907	0.925

sponding to an average number of per-entity candidates of about 50 and 66 for the CoNLL and Wikinews datasets, respectively. These figures give a rough idea of the complexity of the disambiguation step. Altough the two datasets contain collectively ≈ 600 documents, they also contain a large number of mentions to entities, $\approx 6,900$, which are essential in the creation and evaluation of the model, since the two phases are done on a per-entity basis.

The evaluation of the two steps of the *SEL* algorithms were carried out using *5-fold cross-validation* and averaging the results.

4.2 Candidate Pruning Step

For each document D, a set of candidate entities C_D was generated with a dictionary based spotter, which exploits the Wikipedia anchors' text and article titles. This preliminary step generates an average of 549.54 and 790.05 candidate entities C_D for the CoNLL and Wikinews datasets respectively, as illustrated in Table 5.

To prepare the training set for a classifier used to prune C_D, a *positive* class label was associated to entities in $C_D \cup \mathbb{E}_D$, and a *negative* one to entities in $C_D \setminus \mathbb{E}_D$. It is worth remarking the *highly skewed* class imbalance. Indeed only 2% of $|C_D|$ are positive on CoNLL and 1.5% on Wikinews (see the corresponding sizes of $\mathbb{E}_D$ in Table 5).

An interesting information reported in Table 5 is the maximal recall achievable for the EL task, averaged over the set of documents in the given collection. This is smaller than 100% because a few positive entities in $\mathbb{E}_D$ were not detected by the spotter, that is $\mathscr{E}_D \cap C_D \neq \mathscr{E}_D$. This depends on the human annotation: in these cases annotators were able to recognize an entity in $\mathbb{K}B$ even if its mention in D is different from all the ones used in the $\mathbb{K}B$ and stored in our dictionary.

Table 6 shows the performance of the various pruning methods producing $C'_D = \phi(C_D)$. Note the column $|C'_D|$, which reports the *average* number of entities obtained after the pruning step, and compares its size with the original size $|C_D|$, reported in Table 5. The table also shows the Recall/Precision of the various methods in detecting the positive instances, i.e., the entities of C_D that are in $\mathbb{E}_D$.

Table 6: Recall-oriented spotting performance.

	CoNLL			Wikinews		
	Rec	Prec	$|C'_D|$	Rec	Prec	$|C'_D|$
GBDT-$\mathbb{F}_l$	0.63	0.76	8.9	0.66	0.76	11.6
GBDT$_\omega$-$\mathbb{F}_l$	0.85	0.39	27.1	0.87	0.36	32.7
GBDT$_\omega$-$\mathbb{S}_l$	0.85	0.37	28.2	0.87	0.35	34.1
HP$_W$	0.85	0.07	127.4	0.91	0.06	171.9

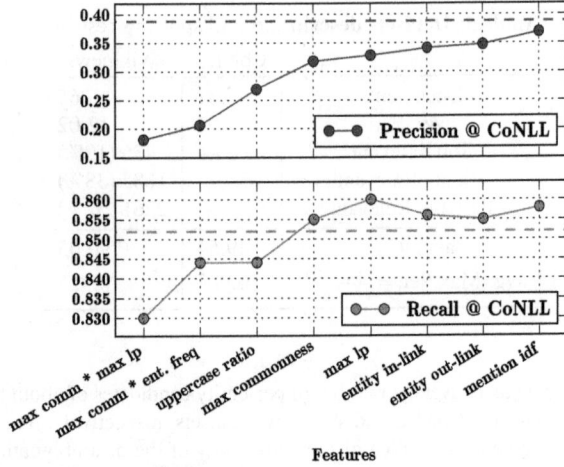

Figure 1: Incremental performance on step 1 using top k features.

Table 7: Entity linking performance.

	CoNLL				Wikinews			
	Rec	Prec	F_1	$P@3$	Rec	Prec	F_1	$P@3$
GBRT-$\mathbb{F}$	0.76	0.71	0.72	0.82	0.76	0.72	0.72	0.88
GBRT$_\omega$-$\mathbb{F}$	0.73	0.74	0.72	0.81	0.77	0.70	0.72	0.85
GBRT-$\mathbb{S}_u$	0.71	0.71	0.69	0.80	0.74	0.71	0.71	0.85
Aida	0.76	0.72	0.73	0.82	0.66	0.73	0.68	0.80
Tagme	0.68	0.59	0.61	0.74	0.77	0.67	0.70	0.85
Wikiminer	0.55	0.43	0.46	0.65	0.78	0.53	0.62	0.87
Wikifier	0.52	0.33	0.36	0.43	0.41	0.34	0.36	0.35
Spotlight	0.48	0.30	0.32	0.46	0.56	0.31	0.38	0.54
1-Step GBRT-$\mathbb{F}_l$	0.69	0.69	0.67	0.81	0.70	0.73	0.69	0.86

In particular, Table 6 compares the heuristic pruning strategy HP$_W$ with the proposed supervised method. Indeed, the *Candidate Pruning* step adopts a state-of-the-art classification algorithm, the *Gradient Boosting Decision Tree* (GBDT) provided by the `scikit-learn` python library for machine learning. GBDT is trained on the light set of features $\mathbb{F}_l$. We denote this classifier by GBDT-$\mathbb{F}_l$.

Unfortunately, due to the severe class imbalance in the training set, the recall of GBDT-$\mathbb{F}_l$ is significantly worse than the baseline HP$_W$. This means that the classifier prunes too many positive entities. As expected, the precision of GBDT-$\mathbb{F}_l$ is better than the one obtained by HP$_W$, but its global performance is not satisfying. It is worth remarking that different settings of HP, not reported here, did not exhibit better performance in terms of precision.

We mitigated the issue of class imbalance by a re-balancing weight strategy, which re-weights the samples in the empirical objective function being optimized by the classifier. The weight given to each sample is inversely proportional to the frequency of its class in the training set. We denote by GBDT$_\omega$-$\mathbb{F}_l$ this new trained classifier, whose performance is very good. Its recall is similar to the one obtained by HP$_W$, but its precision is remarkably higher. By comparing the number of pruned candidate entities (column $|C'_D|$) with the non-pruned ones ($|C_D|$), the superior pruning power of the proposed method over HP$_W$ becomes apparent. Our supervised method is in fact able to prune $\approx 95\%$ of the initial set of candidates C_D, without hindering the recall.

The adopted GBDT implementation provides a standard measure of features' importance according to their contribution in optimizing the decision tree accuracy. We thus performed feature selection by considering the features sorted by importance, and trained a different classifier with the *top-k* features. Figure 1 shows the performance on the CoNLL dataset obtained by varying k up to the best 8 features. We denote this small set of top-8 features by $\mathbb{S}_l$. Note that the most important features are combinations of link probability, commonness, and entity frequency in Wikipedia. The performance of the classifier improves when we add further features. In fact, the performance of our GBDT$_\omega$-$\mathbb{S}_l$ classifier which employs the top-8 features, turned out to be very similar to the one of the classifier that employs the full set $\mathbb{F}_l$ (dashed line). This can also be observed by considering Table 6, where the performance of GBDT$_\omega$-$\mathbb{S}_l$ is reported for both CoNLL and Wikinews.

We conclude that the GBDT$_\omega$-$\mathbb{S}_l$ classifier provides the best performance on average for the two datasets, and that the *light* feature set $\mathbb{F}_l$ provides sufficient quality. Indeed, a smaller set of eight light features $\mathbb{S}_l$ suffices to train an effective classifier GBDT$_\omega$-$\mathbb{S}_l$, which is able to strongly prune the set of candidate entities, thus making feasible the subsequent step which needs to extract expensive graph-based features for each of these candidate entities.

4.3 Saliency Linking Step

In the second step, disambiguation and saliency prediction were performed by training a new model on the filtered set of candidates C'_D. In this case, the full feature set $\mathbb{F}$ was considered, including also an additional feature given by the confidence score of the candidate pruning classifier at step 1. The graph-based features are expensive to compute, but given the reduced number of entities per document, the computation is affordable.

In order to use the same model for both EL and SE tasks, we adopted a state-of-the-art regression algorithm, the *Gradient Boosting Regression Tree* (GBRT), again provided by the `scikit-learn` library, trained on the full set of features $\mathbb{F}$. The resulting model is denoted by GBRT-$\mathbb{F}$. A threshold was learned on the training set by optimizing the F_1 measure, and then used to filter out not relevant entities, i.e., having a score smaller than the learned threshold. The same linear search process was used for learning a filtering threshold on the confidence score for the competitors algorithms simply solving the EL problem.

To prove the benefits of the proposed two-steps algorithm, a regressor model trained on the original set of candidate entities C_D to predict the entity saliency (namely 1-Step GBRT-$\mathbb{F}_l$) was trained. This model exploited the light features $\mathbb{F}_l$ only, due to the high number of candidate entities, for which it was impossible to compute the heavy features.

The accuracy of the EL task was first analyzed by measuring precision, recall and F_1 score on the set of returned entities. The precision was also measured considering only the top-3 entities returned by the model, sorted by the annotation confidence for state-of-the-art algorithms or by the predicted score for our regression models. Note that, given the nature of the EL task, we are only interested in predicting relevant vs. irrelevant entities, resulting in the training of a binary model. Regarding the multi-class Wikinews dataset, all the positive scores were collapsed into a single relevant score. The distribution of positive and negative classes in $C'_D = \phi(C_D)$ became much more balanced after the pruning phase compared to the previous step (with a proportion of 35% / 65% respectively). Table 7 reports the EL performance for the various methods. In particular, state-of-the-art algorithms were compared with the proposed

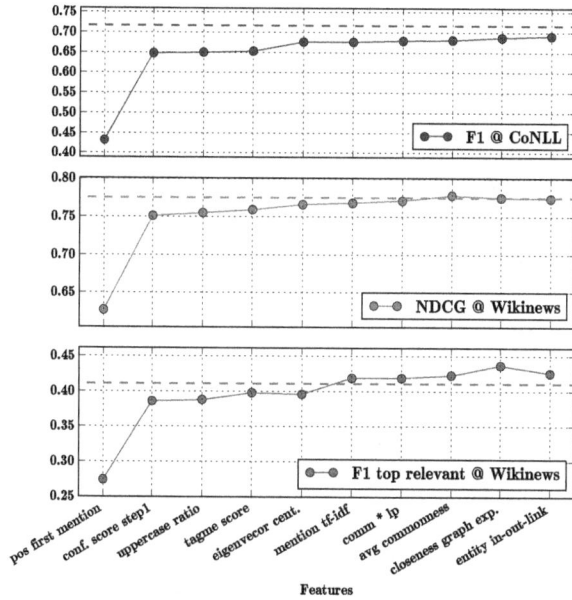

Figure 2: Incremental performance on step 2 using top k features.

supervised method. The publicly available annotation service was used for each competitor algorithm except Wikifier, for which its available source code was used, with the best performing settings reported in the paper by the authors. The first two rows report the performance of the unbalanced model vs. the balanced one: since the dataset is only slightly unbalanced, they perform very similarly.

Also for this study, a subset of the top-10 most important features, denote as $\mathbb{S}_u$, was selected. The model trained using only this subset of features is GBRT-$\mathbb{S}_u$. It performs only slightly worse (-3% on F1 on CoNLL and -1% on Wikinews) than the model that uses all the features. Figure 2 reports the incremental F1 scores obtained by using this subset of features over CoNLL. It is worth noting that the top-2 features of this subset suffice to obtain performance higher then most state-of-the-art solutions. The most important features belong to different *families* of categories. We have some mention-based features (e.g., uppercase ratio or position first mention), some graph related features (e.g., eigenvector and Tagme-like) as well as features coming from the Wikipedia graph (e.g., entity degree) and the confidence score of the *Candidate Pruning* binary classifier.

The performance of the proposed solution were compared against state-of-the-art methods Aida, Spotlight, Tagme, Wikiminer and Wikifier 2.0. The proposed full learned model obtained similar or even better performance when compared to the best performing algorithm on CoNLL (Aida) and Wikinews (Tagme), with an F1 of 0.72 on both the datasets. Indeed on Wikinews *SEL* exhibits +3% improvement on F1 compared to Tagme and +6% compared to Aida, while on CoNLL it performs only slightly worse than Aida (−1%) but it outperforms Tagme (+18%). It is worth noting that CoNLL dataset was created by using the Aida spotter, thus giving Aida an implicit advantage. Another interesting result is that it exhibits well balanced precision and recall values on both the datasets, while state-of-the-art competitors do not show a similar positive behaviour. Indeed, the proposed method shows the best performance on average across the two datasets for every measure adopted when using the full set of features, and it notably provides the best P@3 on average when us-

Table 8: Saliency prediction performance on Wikinews.

	NDCG	Rec^{top}	Prec^{top}	F1^{top}
GBRT-$\mathbb{F}$	0.78	0.42	0.38	0.36
GBRT$_\omega$-$\mathbb{F}$	0.78	0.47	0.42	0.41
GBRT$_\omega$-$\mathbb{S}_u$	0.77	0.51	0.42	0.43
Aida	0.58	0.59	0.10	0.16
Tagme	0.65	0.45	0.13	0.18
Wikiminer	0.64	0.31	0.12	0.16
Wikifier	0.32	0.55	0.05	0.09
Spotlight	0.47	0.33	0.07	0.10
1-Step GBRT-$\mathbb{F}_l$	0.73	0.47	0.30	0.34

ing the feature set $\mathbb{S}_u$ only. Finally, some considerations about the 1-Step algorithm: despite its good performance, the method always performs worse than GBRT-$\mathbb{F}$ and GBRT-$\mathbb{S}_u$. It is worth noting that this single step algorithm provides EL annotations comparable or even better than most state-of-the-art algorithms. This confirms that entity saliency plays an important role as it also boosts entity linking methods. It is apparent that annotation confidence cannot approximate saliency.

Table 8 shows the saliency performance of the trained models. In this case the regressor makes use of all the saliency labels. For this experiment we used only the Wikinews dataset, since CoNLL is not annotated with the saliency. The performance on predicting the saliency was evaluated by using: i) the NDCG considering the entities sorted by saliency, in order to know how good is the function in ranking the entities by saliency, ii) Precision, Recall and F_1, considering only the most important entities, in order to know how good is our learned model in identifying the set of the *Top Relevant* entities (denoted as P^{top}, R^{top} and F_1^{top}). NDCG was measured on the set of entities selected by optimizing F_1 (as above), sorted by saliency/confidence score, whereas F_1^{top} is measured after optimizing a filtering threshold on the training data. It is worth recalling that state-of-the-art algorithms do not provide saliency scores, so we used the confidence scores as an indicator of how related are the entities to the document.

We observe that in this setting, the weighted model performs better than the unweighted one, since the distribution of the positive labels is not uniform. Moreover, the model that makes use of only the subset $\mathbb{S}_u$ of features has similar performance with respect to the model with all the features. As reported, *SEL* significantly outperforms the best performing state-of-the-art algorithm (Tagme) both in terms of NDCG and F_1^{top} with a relative improvement of +18% and +139% respectively.

We conclude that the recall-oriented pruning of the spotting results, along with the additional features extracted in the second step, provide a significant improvement over the 1-Step approach, with a substantial performance gap between the two models.

5. CONCLUSIONS

In this work we proposed a novel supervised Salient Entity Linking (*SEL*) algorithm that comprehensively addresses Entity Linking and Salient Entities detection problems. Besides improving Entity Linking performance with respect to state-of-the-art competitors, *SEL* predicts also the saliency of the linked entities. The algorithm exploits a two-step machine-learned process: first a *Candidate Pruning* step aimed at filtering out irrelevant candidate entities is performed, thus obtaining good precision figures without hindering recall; then, a *Saliency Linking* step effectively chooses the entities that are likely to be actually mentioned in the document and predicts their saliency.

The experiments conducted on two different datasets confirmed that the proposed solution outperforms state-of-the-art competitor algorithms in the Entity Linking task. In particular improvements in terms of F_1 of 6% w.r.t. Aida and 18% w.r.t. Tagme were measured. Moreover, *SEL* significantly outperforms the same competitors in the Salient Entities detection task of up to 18% and 139% in terms of NDCG and F_1^{top}, respectively. The latter analysis has been made possible thanks to the creation of a novel dataset of news manually annotated with entities and their saliency, hereinafter publicly available to the research community.

We believe that our comprehensive Entity Linking and Salient Entities detection approach constitutes a remarkable contribution to the field, since entity saliency detection is an important aspect of the whole document annotation pipeline, and salient entities should be weighted more than non salient ones in the evaluation of the annotation.

Acknowledgments

This work was partially supported by the EC H2020 Program INFRAIA-1-2014-2015 SoBigData: Social Mining & Big Data Ecosystem (654024).

6. REFERENCES

[1] R. Blanco, H. Halpin, D. M. Herzig, P. Mika, J. Pound, H. S. Thompson, and T. Tran Duc. Repeatable and reliable search system evaluation using crowdsourcing. In *ACM SIGIR*, 2011.

[2] X. Cheng and D. Roth. Relational inference for wikification. In *Urbana*, 2013.

[3] J. Dunietz and D. Gillick. A new entity salience task with millions of training examples. In *EACL*, 2014.

[4] G. Erkan and D. R. Radev. Lexrank: Graph-based lexical centrality as salience in text summarization. In *Journal Artificial Intelligence Res. (JAIR)*, 2004.

[5] P. Ferragina and U. Scaiella. Tagme: on-the-fly annotation of short text fragments (by wikipedia entities). In *ACM CIKM*, 2010.

[6] M. Gamon, T. Yano, X. Song, J. Apacible, and P. Pantel. Identifying salient entities in web pages. In *ACM CIKM*, 2013.

[7] J. Hoffart, M. A. Yosef, I. Bordino, H. Fürstenau, M. Pinkal, M. Spaniol, B. Taneva, S. Thater, and G. Weikum. Robust disambiguation of named entities in text. In *ACL EMNLP*, 2011.

[8] P. N. Mendes, M. Jakob, A. García-Silva, and C. Bizer. Dbpedia spotlight: shedding light on the web of documents. In *ACM SEMANTiCS*, 2011.

[9] R. Mihalcea and A. Csomai. Wikify!: linking documents to encyclopedic knowledge. In *ACM CIKM*, 2007.

[10] D. Milne and I. H. Witten. Learning to link with wikipedia. In *ACM CIKM*, 2008.

[11] D. Paranjpe. Learning document aboutness from implicit user feedback and document structure. In *ACM CIKM*, 2009.

[12] F. Piccinno and P. Ferragina. From tagme to wat: a new entity annotator. In *Int. workshop on Entity recognition & disambiguation*, ACM SIGIR, 2014.

[13] L. Ratinov, D. Roth, D. Downey, and M. Anderson. Local and global algorithms for disambiguation to wikipedia. In *ACL HLT*, 2011.

[14] H. Rode, P. Serdyukov, D. Hiemstra, and H. Zaragoza. Entity ranking on graphs: Studies on expert finding. 2007.

[15] W. Shen, J. Wang, and J. Han. Entity linking with a knowledge base: Issues, techniques, and solutions. In *IEEE KDE*, 2015.

Automated Intrinsic Text Classification for Component Content Management Applications in Technical Communication

Jan Oevermann
University of Bremen &
Karlsruhe University of Applied Sciences
76133 Karlsruhe, Germany
jan.oevermann@hs-karlsruhe.de

Wolfgang Ziegler
Karlsruhe University of Applied Sciences
76133 Karlsruhe, Germany
wolfgang.ziegler@hs-karlsruhe.de

ABSTRACT

Classification models are used in component content management to identify content components for retrieval, reuse and distribution. Intrinsic metadata, such as the assigned information class, play an important role in these tasks. With the increasing demand for efficient classification of content components, the sector of technical documentation needs mechanisms that allow for an automation of such tasks. Vector space model based approaches can lead to sufficient results, while maintaining good performance, but they must be adapted to the peculiarities that characterize modular technical documents.

In this paper we will present domain specific differences, as well as characteristics, that are special to the field of technical documentation and derive methods to adapt widespread classification and retrieval techniques for these tasks. We verify our approach with data provided from companies in the sector of manufacturing and mechanical engineering and use it for supervised learning and automated classification.

Keywords

Technical Documentation; Content Management; Vector Space Model; Machine Learning; Text Classification

1. INTRODUCTION

Complex documents, such as technical product documentation required in industrial engineering, are mostly composed of small *content components*[1] that allow for referenced reuse and cost efficient translation [21]. XML-based component content management systems (CCMS) provide a professional environment to create and assemble these components.

CCMS are often enhanced by classification methods in order to identify content components for retrieval and distribution [5]. For example the assignment of information classes is usually done

---

[1]In other literature and commercial applications *content components* are also referred to as *topics*, *modules* or *content modules* [5, 19].

Table 1: Training and test sets

Set	Sector	Units	$\frac{words}{unit}$	Classes
A	mechanical eng.	570	173	11
B	mechanical eng.	278	41	10
C	manufacturing eng.	3947	97	22

manually by technical writers at the time of creation and is based on experience and editorial guidelines. However, for large amounts of content, (e.g. migrating legacy data) this method is extremely time consuming. There are currently no tools or specific methods available for automating this task focusing on characteristics of technical product documentation.

Vector space classification is, in general, an efficient way to do such bulk classifications but is often optimized towards whole documents and not parts thereof. In addition, the method usually does not recognize semantic structures which are widely used in component content management (CCM). Therefore, CCM content is in most cases ideal training data due to its semantic richness, consistent style of writing and the XML-based data format.

In our approach we want to consider these peculiarities of technical documentation and adjust standard vector space classification to utilize them for better accuracy in automated classification tasks.

2. METHODOLOGY

At first we characterize important properties of component content management based on industry best practices and international standards. We then make assumptions about the effects on classification tasks and verify them in a test set-up with three different real-world data sets (about 4,800 manually classified content components). All test data was provided by companies in the sectors of manufacturing and mechanical engineering and is in German.

In preprocessing, text from components was extracted and unnecessary punctuation and XML syntax removed (for use of semantics see section 4.3). The multi-class test set-up was based on a vector space model (VSM), instead of more sophisticated methods (such as *Neural Networks*), for performance reasons. A content component for classification is represented as a vector $\vec{m} = (w_1, w_2, ..., w_n)$ where n is the number of tokens chosen as features of the component. The value w_i represents the *semantic weight* of token i [11]. In supervised learning we built a $n \times c$ token-by-class matrix $M = \{w_{ij}\}$ for a set of distinct classes C. As classifier we use *cosine similarity* [14].

For cross validation we randomly divided the test data into a training set and a validation set (4:1).

3. CHARACTERISTICS OF CCM

The following sections outline characteristics of CCM that are different from other content types and which are relevant for classification tasks based on vector space models.

3.1 Classification models

In the field of technical communication, manuals and document sections contained therein, are constrained in many ways by standards and regulatory rules. One of the most important regulations states predefined content types in the sequence of traditional chapter structures of manuals and of interactive electronic technical documentation [7]. Well known examples are manuals of military and avionic vehicles or of medical devices [6, 18, 20]. For content component management applications, this usually translates into distinct sets of information classes, which then depend on specific business domains. Content components have to be created according to the predefined information classes and are, therefore, instances of one intrinsic information class. Consequences for the use of terminology and other editorial guidelines are outlined in the following sections.

A metadata-driven approach for defining content components is defined as *PI Classification* method in [5]. In this model *intrinsic* metadata is coupled with product components by corresponding product classes (P) and include the required set of information classes (I). Usually, PI classification models are defined as taxonomies and describe an, at least, two dimensional information space. Each content component has to have distinct coordinates in the space of intrinsic product and information classes. Technical writers have to assign content to a unique class and have to follow the corresponding rules for content creation.

In this framework, there are additional *extrinsic* PI classes describing the intended or actual use of components in end-products and final document types (which can usually be coupled to named-entity recognition). In the course of this paper, we focus mainly on the *intrinsic* information classes. The most common starting point for defining information classifications are the distinct sets of descriptive vs. procedural content classes. Descriptive content includes, for example, set-up of machines, process or functional descriptions of hard and software or introductory sections. Procedural content covers all types of task-oriented information like installation, how-to-use instructions, maintenance and repair or disposal of products. In general, procedural content and the corresponding taxonomy of information classes is organized according to the product life cycle. The *intrinsic* information classes used in industrial CCMS applications build up a well-known set of classifications and are a starting point for our approach to automated text classification.

3.2 Standardized patterns

Due to their normative nature, technical documents have to be concise and unambiguous. This is often resembled in editorial guidelines or *style guides* [7], which remind technical writers to abstain from the use of synonyms, ambiguity, direct speech, filler words, sentiments or empty phrases. Instead standardized grammatical patterns are used within content components to increase consistency and reusability across multiple documents. This decreases translation costs when used in combination with translation management systems (TMS) and improves reading comprehension for users. These patterns differ in style, whether they depict instructive or descriptive content. This helps readers to differentiate, for example, between tasks, concepts or *embedded safety messages* [2]. Content components of one information class often contain only one kind or one specific combination of grammatical patterns

and word classes (e.g. only imperative verbs in instructions).

XML-based information models, such as DITA [16], DOCBOOK [15] or PI-MOD [23], reflect this with semantic content components, as for example "descriptive", "task" or "concept".

3.3 Specific terminology

Terminology and overall choice of words used in technical documents is often highly specific to the company that manufactures the product and is strictly controlled within the principles of *terminology work* and enforced by *terminology management system* [8, 9]. Terms for describing tasks and concepts are mostly precise technical expressions that are usually unique to the engineering sector, to which the product belongs (e.g. printing presses or construction machinery).

For better brand recognition among customers, some companies also explicitly mention the full brand/model combination with every occurrence of the product. This leads to very characteristic word distributions in content components that are often unique for one company or even one branch of a company.

3.4 Size of components

The actual size of content components depends on several factors, such as strategic decisions, product complexity or software features of the CCMS. Component properties have been analyzed systematically for various companies and results range from small content fragments with just a few words up to components including several hundreds or thousands of words. For one example corpus in [17], the average component size was about 150 words, whereas the usual size of a document was approximately 12,000 words (German language).

Fragments are usually included within other content components, but can also be manually classified within CCMS. One can find that small size content fragments are used, for example, in more complex reuse scenarios within variant management functionality of CCM applications [19, 22].

The data examined for this paper had average word counts per content component or fragment of respectively 173, 97 and 41 words (cf. Table 1). The size of components is, therefore, significantly smaller than that of typical documents (approx. 1:75). This results in fewer features per unit which can be evaluated by prediction algorithms in comparison to document classification.

3.5 Training and validation data

Companies, which are using component content management in combination with a well defined classification model already have high quality training material at hand that is suitable for supervised learning. Content was classified manually by experts and written in a controlled manner according to editorial guidelines. Standardized information models can also provide further information about semantic properties and functions of parts of the text [4]. However, for some parts, the technical nature of the content has a negative impact on classification performance (e.g. for tables, legends or lists).

Validation data can either be unclassified content components (from sources other than the CCMS) or unstructured and unclassified PDF documents or other file formats used for archiving. This results in potential differences between training and validation data regarding format and structure of the content.

3.6 Quality assurance

Due to high safety standards and legal implications that adhere to technical documentation, a proper quality assurance is mandatory before publishing [7, 10]. Especially in the European Union all necessary technical documentation for machinery is considered

Table 2: Accuracy for different n-grams as tokens

n	Set A [%]	Set B [%]	Set C [%]	Avg. [%]
1	79.26	77.78	67.13	74.72
2	80.49	73.91	76.88	77.09
3	78.75	68.42	76.29	74.49
$\{1,2\}$	82.14	80.43	73.70	78,76
$\{1,2,3\}$	**90.48**	**85.36**	**78.12**	**84.65**

Table 3: Accuracy for different weighting methods

w_{ij}	Set A [%]	Set B [%]	Set C [%]	Avg. [%]
TF-IDF	52.13	56.27	50.45	52.95
TF-IDF-CF	75.79	76.08	63.37	71.75
TF-ICF-CF	**90.45**	**85.36**	**78.12**	**84.65**

as part of the product [1]. The correctness and completeness of published documents is, therefore, crucial for the integrity of the whole product. Because some CCMS rely on classifications of content components for the automated composition of documents, the classification algorithm is a possible vulnerability for product integrity. This entails the need for manual control in cases where the classification algorithm is not confident in its results.

4. IMPLICATIONS

In the following section we derive implications for supervised learning and automated classification for content components from characteristics presented in the previous section and verify them with our test data (cf. Table 1).

4.1 Feature selection

Standardized wording and grammatical patterns decrease the total number of distinct words and word combinations in technical documentation in comparison to other text types (cf. section 3.2 & 3.3). This is generally preferable in text classification because it reduces the usually high dimensionality of the feature space [3]. As content components are also much smaller than documents (cf. section 3.4), the number of features for representing an object for classification is further reduced by a great amount.

However, most content components in technical communication have both distinct single words and recognizable word patterns as important characteristics of their information classes. This means using single terms or n-grams (e.g. bigrams or trigrams) as exclusive features is not optimal. Our results confirm the assumption that a combination of n-grams of different n is in most cases the preferable method for representing content components (cf. Table 2 for $q = 2.5$ and $w_{ij} =$ TF-ICF-CF).

4.2 Token weighting

There are several ways to assign semantic weight to a token with TF-IDF as the best known method [3, 11, 12, 13]. To improve accuracy in document categorization, TF-IDF has been extended to TF-IDF-CF, which considers in-class characteristics of tokens [13]. However, in CCM the reference size of one unit is a content component and not a document. Therefore, document-based weighting is not always suitable for classification tasks.

Due to the nature of our training data, from which we can derive overall *token frequency* tf_i as well as *in-class frequency* tcf_{ij} and *inverse class frequency* icf_{ij}, we adapted TF-IDF-CF to utilize inverse *inverse class frequency* (ICF) to differentiate between classes instead of IDF. For a set of distinct classes C with classes j and tokens i weight w_{ij} is:

$$w_{ij} = \log(1 + tf_i) * \log(1 + \frac{|C|}{tf_i}) * \frac{tf_{ij}}{C_j} \qquad (1)$$

Our results confirm that this method performs best as weighting method on our data compared to other schemes (cf. Table 3 for $q = 2.5$ and $n = \{1,2,3\}$).

4.3 Semantic quantifiers

As shown in section 3.5, semantic information about the text structure of content components is usually available in training data but cannot be directly applied in classification due to the lack of reliable structure elements (as for example in legacy documents). To circumvent this, it is possible to artificially increase the term frequency tf_i with a quantifier q for tokens that have special semantic meaning in one specific class (e.g. function or setup descriptions, action sequences), so that in supervised learning tf_i is extended to:

$$tf_{iq} = tf_i * q \text{ for } q > 0 \qquad (2)$$

Test results show that for q between 2 and 5, classification accuracy can be increased up to 10% ($q = 2.5$). However, quality and choice of semantic structures for quantification heavily influences the benefits of semantic qualifiers. Thus in future work we want to examine methods for compiling comprehensive lists of semantic structures which are relevant for token weighting and their corresponding quantifiers.

4.4 Confidence scoring

For reasons discussed in section 3.6, it must be possible to measure confidence of classification results in regard to content components which could belong to multiple classes. There are several methods for comparing per-class classification scores, such as the *softmax function* or the *standard deviation*, however neither of them suited our need for a reliable quality assurance measure.

$$p = \frac{s_1 - s_2}{s_1 - s_n} \qquad (3)$$

We base our confidence score p on the presence of single outliers (high confidence) or close runner-ups (low confidence). Per-class classification scores s_c for n classes c are sorted from high (1) to low (n). p is then expressed as ratio of first to second and first to last classification choice. After examining confidence scores on our test sets, we can see that only a small fraction ($0 - 3\%$) of content components are incorrectly classified and have high confidence scores ($p > 0.7$).

5. APPLICATIONS

In this section we want to give a short overview of potential applications for an automated classification of content components in technical communication.

Quality management.

Well defined classification models and good classification by technical writers should result in a close to 100% accuracy rate when training and validating with the same data set. This circumstance can be utilized to measure general quality of classification or the overall classification model. In our tests, we observed that classification errors in self-validation can be a strong indicator of wrong manual classification of a content component. Results for our data match our subjective rating with set A (97.21 %) and B (96.39 %) having high quality classification as opposed to Set C (89.03 %) with a more ambiguous classification model.

Data migration.

With the implementation of a CCMS, companies often start using classification models (e.g. PI classification) to take advantage of more advanced features, such as document aggregation or retrieval functions. To migrate existing (structured) content to the system it is also necessary to have legacy content classified, which is a time consuming task. In this case, automated classification of content components, which can utilize newly composed and manually classified content as training data, is desired.

6. RELATED AND FUTURE WORK

Domain-specific classification and their applications for construction project documents were analyzed in [3]. Similarities of this work are the availability of predefined classification frameworks and the focus on automation of the classification task.

Research on utilizing text similarity measures to aid technical writers in reusing content components was presented in [21]. The results could be used to verify if components identified for reuse have matching classes assigned.

The TF-IDF-CF method we base our token weighting on was introduced and tested in [13]. More weighting schemes are discussed and compared in [11] and [12].

In future work we will extend our research further to other data sets and focus on unstructured documents as a source for classification. We examine optimization potentials for semantic quantifiers and confidence scoring. We plan to refine our models to include grammatical patterns with advanced NLP technologies (Part-of-speech tagging).

7. CONCLUSIONS

Component content management has different characteristics and requirements than default document classification but multiple real-world scenarios where automated classification is applicable and necessary. PI classification models provide a suitable framework for these applications.

We identified several areas of improvement and made proposals for adapting existing models for use in technical communication. The improvements include the combination of terms and n-grams as features for classification, a modified token weighting scheme for in-class characteristics, semantic quantifiers to leverage information present in training data and a first approach to reliable confidence scoring on cosine similarity classifier results.

Results of this paper are based on content components from specific engineering disciplines but can also be applied to other sectors (e.g. software documentation). Our adjustments have shown significant improvements over document-oriented classification techniques and are a good foundation for future research.

8. ACKNOWLEDGMENTS

We would like to thank Christoph Lüth (Univ. of Bremen) and Claudia Oberle (Karlsruhe UAS) for insightful discussions, Reilly Lorenz for thorough proofreading and Stephan Steurer for support.

9. REFERENCES

[1] 2006/42/EC. Machinery Directive of the European Parliament and of the Council, 2006.

[2] ANSI Z535.6. American National Standard for Product Safety Information in Product Manuals, Instructions, and Other Collateral Materials, 2006.

[3] C. H. Caldas, L. Soibelman, and J. Han. Automated Classification of Construction Project Documents. *Journal of Computing in Civil Engineering*, 16(4):234–243, 2002.

[4] A. Di Iorio, S. Peroni, F. Poggi, and F. Vitali. A First Approach to the Automatic Recognition of Structural Patterns in XML Documents. In *Proceedings of the 2012 ACM Symposium on Document Engineering*, DocEng '12, pages 85–94, New York, NY, USA, 2012. ACM.

[5] P. Drewer and W. Ziegler. *Technische Dokumentation*. Vogel, Würzburg (DE), 2011.

[6] GHTF/SG1/N70. Label and Instructions for Use for Medical Devices, 2011.

[7] IEC 82079-1. Preparation of Instructions for Use – Structuring, Content and Presentation, 2012.

[8] ISO 26162. Systems to manage terminology, knowledge and content: Design, implementation and maintenance of terminology management systems, 2012.

[9] ISO 704. Terminology work – Principles and methods, 2009.

[10] ISO 9001. Quality management systems – Requirements, 2008.

[11] Y. Ko. A Study of Term Weighting Schemes Using Class Information for Text Classification. In *SIGIR 2012*. ACM, 2012.

[12] M. Lan, C.-L. Tan, H.-B. Low, and S. Sung. A Comprehensive Comparative Study on Term Weighting Schemes for Text Categorization with Support Vector Machines. In *14th International World Wide Web Conference (WWW 2005)*, 2005.

[13] M. Liu and J. Yang. An improvement of TFIDF weighting in text categorization. In *IPCSIT*, volume 47. IACSIT Press, Singapore, 2012.

[14] C. D. Manning and H. Schütze. *Foundations of statistical natural language processing*. MIT Press, Cambridge, 1999.

[15] OASIS. The DocBook Schema, CD 5.0, 2008.

[16] OASIS. DITA Version 1.2 Specification, 2010.

[17] C. Oberle and W. Ziegler. Content Intelligence for Content Management Systems. *tcworld e-magazine*, 2012(12), 2012.

[18] A. T. A. of America. ATA iSpec 2200: Information Standards for Aviation Maintenance, 2014.

[19] A. Rockley, P. Kostur, and S. Manning. *Managing Enterprise Content: A Unified Content Strategy*. New Riders, Berkley, 2003.

[20] S1000D. Issue 4.1: International specification for technical publications using a common source database. http://s1000d.org, 2012.

[21] A. J. Soto, A. Mohammad, A. Albert, A. Islam, E. Milios, M. Doyle, R. Minghim, and M. C. Ferreira de Oliveira. Similarity-Based Support for Text Reuse in Technical Writing. In *Proceedings of the 2015 ACM Symposium on Document Engineering*, DocEng '15, pages 97–106, New York, NY, USA, 2015. ACM.

[22] W. Ziegler. Variantenverwaltung in CMS – Fünf Methoden für die Feinarbeit. *technische kommunikation*, 27(3):40–44, 2005.

[23] W. Ziegler. PI-Mod: An information model for plant construction and mechanical engineering (and others). http://pi-mod.de/index.php?lang=en, 2011.

Centroid Terms as Text Representatives

Mario M. Kubek
Chair of Communication Networks
University of Hagen
Universitätsstr. 27, Hagen, Germany
mario.kubek@fernuni-hagen.de

Herwig Unger
Chair of Communication Networks
University of Hagen
Universitätsstr. 27, Hagen, Germany
herwig.unger@fernuni-hagen.de

ABSTRACT

Algorithms to topically cluster and classify texts rely on information about their semantic distances and similarities. Standard methods based on the bag-of-words model to determine this information return only rough estimations regarding the relatedness of texts. Moreover, they are per se unable to find generalising terms or abstractions describing the textual contents. A new method to determine centroid terms in texts and to evaluate their similarity using those representing terms will be introduced. In first experiments, its results and advantages will be discussed.

Keywords

text processing, centroid term, co-occurrence graph, document similarity

1. INTRODUCTION

After only a few lines of reading, a human reader is able to determine which category of texts and which abstract topic category a given document belongs to. This is a strong demonstration of how well and fast the human brain, especially the human cortex, can process and interpret data. It is able to not only understand the meaning of single words -as representations of real-world entities-but a certain composition of them [1], too.

In order to be able to topically classify unseen content, the brain acts as a knowledge base. It tries to match the terms (words that carry a meaning) in such a document with previously learned terminology and can, in doing so, instantly and unconsciously perform at least a rough classification. At the same time, it gradually and constantly learns about new concepts. Also, it automatically abstracts from topical details and can associate a highly specific document with its more general topics (and its representing terms). As an example, given an article about steering wheels, the more general topics/terms 'car parts' or 'car' could be found.

In many text processing applications, the topical classification and grouping of texts are common tasks. For this purpose, it is necessary to measure the semantic distance or similarity of the documents to be clustered or classified.

The usual approach is to represent the documents by their term vectors -following the -bag-of-words model- which contain the texts' characterising terms and their score (typically, a TF-IDF-based statistic [2] is used) as a measure for their importance. The similarity of two term vectors can be determined e.g. using the cosine similarity measure or by calculating their overlap, e.g. using the Dice coefficient [3].

However, in some cases, these measures do not work correctly (with respect to human judgement), mostly if different people write about the same topic but are using a completely different vocabulary for doing so. The reason for this circumstance can be seen in the isolated view of the words found in documents to be compared without including any relation to the vocabulary of other, context-related documents. Moreover, short texts as often found in posts in online social networks or short (web) search queries with a low number of decriptive terms can therefore often not be correctly classified or disambiguated. Another disadvantage is that these measures cannot find abstractions or generalising terms by just analysing the textual data provided. For this purpose, static lexical databases such as WordNet [4] must be consulted as a reference. Despite their usefulness, these resources are -in contrast to the human brain- not able to learn about new concepts and their relationships.

In order to address these problems, this article presents a new graph-based approach to determine centroid terms of text documents. It is shown that those terms can actually represent text documents in text processing tasks, e.g. to determine their semantic distances. In the next section, the fundamentals of this method are presented. Afterwards, section 3 describes its mathematical and technical details. Section 4 proves the validity of this approach by explaining the results of first experiments. In section 5, the method's working principles and advantages are discussed. Section 6 summarises the article and suggests further application fields of the introduced method.

2. FUNDAMENTALS

For the approach presented herein, co-occurrences and co-occurrence graphs are the basic means to obtain more detailed information about text documents than term frequency vectors etc. could ever offer. The reason for this decision is that co-occurrence graphs are able to accumulate a certain knowledge obtained from a few selected or all documents of a text corpus while (at least to some extent) maintaining the semantic connection of terms found in them. A co-occurrence graph -similarly to the knowledge in the human brain- may be built step by step over a long time taking one document after another into consideration, too.

Two words w_i and w_j are called *co-occurrents*, if they appear together in close proximity in a document D. The most prominent kinds of such co-occurrences are word pairs that appear as immediate neighbours or together in a sentence. A *co-occurrence graph* $G = (W, E)$ may be obtained, if all words of a document or set of documents W are used to build its set of nodes which are then connected by an edge $(w_a, w_b) \in E$ if $w_a \in W$ and $w_b \in W$ are co-occurrents. A weight function $g((w_a, w_b))$ indicates, how significant the respective co-occurrence is in a document. If the significance value is greater than a pre-set threshold, the co-occurrence can be regarded as significant and a semantic relation between the words involved can often be derived from it. Commonly used significance measures are the Dice coefficient [3], the mutual information measure [5], the Poisson collocation measure [6] and the log-likelihood ratio [7].

The use of the immediate neighbourhood of nodes in a co-occurrence graph has been widely considered in literature, e.g. to cluster terms [8] and to determine the global context (vector) of terms in order to evaluate their similarity [9] or to derive paradigmatic relations between them [10]. In the authors' view, indirect neighbourhoods of terms in co-occurrence graphs (nodes that can be reached only using two or more edges from a node of interest) and the respective paths with a length ≥ 2 should be considered as well as indirectly reachable nodes may still be of topical relevance, especially when the co-occurence graph is large. The benefit of using such nodes/terms in co-occurrence graphs has already been shown by the authors for the expansion of web search queries using a spreading activation technique on local and user-defined corpora [11]. The precision of web search results could be noticably improved when taking them into account, too.

The field of application of indirect term neighbourhoods in co-occurrence graphs shall be extended in the next section by introducing an approach to determine centroid terms of text documents that can act as their representatives in further text processing tasks. These centroid terms can be regarded as the texts' topical centers of interest (a notion normally used to describe the part of a picture that attracts the eye and mind) that the authors' thoughts revolve around.

3. FINDING CENTROID TERMS

In physics, complex bodies consisting of several single mass points are usually represented and considered by their so-called center of mass, as seen in Figure 1. The distribution of mass is balanced around this center and the average of the weighted coordinates of the distributed mass defines its coordinates and therefore its position.

For discrete systems, i.e. systems consisting of n single mass points $m_1, m_2, .., m_i$ in a 3D−space at positions $\vec{r}_1, \vec{r}_2, .., \vec{r}_i$, the center of mass $\vec{r}_s$ can be found by

$$\vec{r}_s = \frac{1}{M} \sum_{i=1}^{n} m_i \vec{r}_i, \tag{1}$$

whereby

$$M = \sum_{i=1}^{n} m_i. \tag{2}$$

Usually, this model simplifies calculations with complex bodies in mechanics by representing the whole system by a single mass at the position of the center of mass. Exactly the same problem exists in text processing: a whole text shall be represented or classified by one or a few single, descriptive terms which must be found.

To adapt the situation for text processing, first of all, a *distance* d shall be introduced in a co-occurrence graph G. From literature it is known that two words are semantically close, if $g((w_a, w_b))$

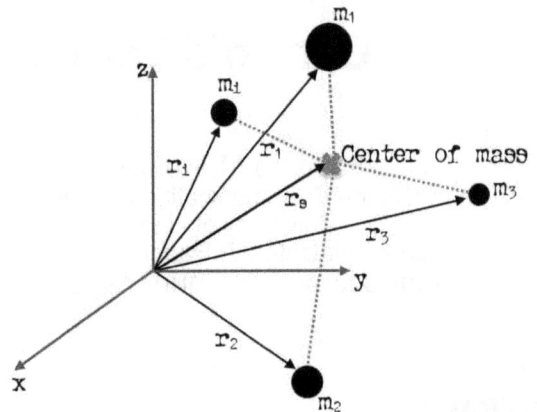

Figure 1: The physical center of mass

is high, i.e. they often appear together in a sentence or in another predefined window of k words. Consequently, a distance $d(w_a, w_b)$ of two words in G can be defined by

$$d(w_a, w_b) = \frac{1}{g((w_a, w_b))}, \tag{3}$$

if w_a and w_b are co-occurrents. In all other cases (assuming that the co-occurrence graph is connected[1]) there is a shortest path $p = (w_1, w_2), (w_2, w_3), .., (w_k, w_k + 1)$ with $w_1 = w_a$, $w_{k+1} = w_b$ and $w_i, w_{i+1} \in E$ for all $i = 1(1)k$ such that

$$d(w_a, w_b) = \sum_{i=1}^{k} d((w_i, w_{i+1})) = MIN, \tag{4}$$

whereby in case of a partially connected co-occurrence graph $d(w_a, w_b) = \infty$ must be set.

Note, that differing from the physical model, there is a distance between any two words but no direction vector, since there is no embedding of the co-occurrence graph in the 2− or 3−dimensional space. Consequently, the impact of a word depends only on its scalar distance.

In continuation of the previous idea, the distance between a given term t and a document D containing N words $w_1, w_2, .., w_N \in D$ that are reachable from t in G can be defined by

$$d(D, t) = \frac{\sum_{i=1}^{N} d(w_i, t)}{N}, \tag{5}$$

i.e. the average sum of the lengths of the shortest paths between t and all words $w_i \in D$ that can be reached from it. Note that - differing from many methods found in literature- it is not assumed that $t \in D$ holds! Also, it might happen in some cases that the minimal distance is not uniquely defined, consequently a text may have more than one centroid term (as long as no other methods decide which one is to use). The centroid terms of documents can now be used to define the centroid-based distance ζ between any two documents D_1 and D_2. Therefore, let t_1 be the term with $d(D_1, t_1) = MIN$, then we call this t_1 the center term or *centroid term* of D_1. If at the same time t_2 is the centroid term of D_2,

$$\zeta(D_1, D_2) = d(t_1, t_2) \tag{6}$$

can be understood as the semantic distance ζ of the two documents

---

[1]This can be achieved by adding a sufficiently high number of documents to it during its building process.

D_1 and D_2. In order to obtain a similarity value instead,

$$\zeta_{sim}(D_1, D_2) = \frac{1}{1 + \zeta(D_1, D_2)} \qquad (7)$$

can be applied.

It is another important property of the described distance calculation that documents regardless of their length as well as single words can be assigned a centroid term by one and the same method in a unique manner. The presented approach relies on the preferably large co-occurrence graph G as its reference. It may be constructed from any text corpus in any language available or directly from the sets of documents whose semantic distance shall be determined. The usage of external resources such as lexical databases or reference corpora is common in text processing: as an example, the so-called difference analysis [9] which measures the deviation of word frequencies in single texts from their frequencies in general usage (a large topically well-balanced reference corpus is needed for this purpose) is an example for it. The larger the deviation is, the more likely it is that a term or keyword of a single text has been found.

In the following section, the quality and properties of the centroid terms and the new centroid-based diatance measure shall be investigated and discussed.

4. FIRST EXPERIMENTS

For all of the examplary experiments (many more have been conducted) discussed herein, linguistic preprocessing has been applied on the documents to be analysed whereby stop words have been removed and only nouns (in their base form), proper nouns and names have been extracted. In order to build the undirected co-occurrence graph G (as the reference for the centroid distance measure), co-occurrences on sentence level have been extracted. Their significance values have been determined using the Dice coefficient [3]. The particularly used sets of documents will be described in the respective subsections[2].

4.1 Centroids of Wikipedia Articles

As the centroid terms are the basic components for the centroid-based distance measure, it is useful to get a first impression of their quality in terms of whether they are actual useful representatives of documents. Table 1 therefore presents the centroid terms of 25 English Wikipedia articles. The corpus used to create the reference co-occurrence graph G consisted of 100 randomly selected articles (including the mentioned 25 ones) from an offline English Wikipedia corpus from http://www.kiwix.org. It can be seen that almost all centroids properly represent their respective articles.

4.2 Comparing similarity measures

In order to evaluate the effectiveness of the new centroid-based distance measure, its results will be presented and compared to those of the cosine similarity measure while the same 100 online news articles from the German newspaper "Süddeutsche Zeitung" from the months September, October and November of 2015 have been selected (25 articles from each of the four topical categories 'car', 'travel', 'finance' and 'sports' have been randomly chosen) for this purpose. As the cosine similarity measure operates on term vectors, the articles' most important terms along with their scores have been determined using the extended PageRank [12] algorithm which has been applied on their own separate (local) co-occurrence graphs (here, another term weighting scheme such as a TF-IDF

[2]Interested researchers can download these sets (1,3 MB) from: http://www.docanalyser.de/cd-corpora.zip

Table 1: Centroids of 25 Wikipedia articles

Title of Wikipedia Article	Centroid Term
Tay-Sachs disease	mutation
Pythagoras	Pythagoras
Canberra	Canberra
Eye (cyclone)	storm
Blade Runner	Ridley Scott
CPU cache	cache miss
Rembrandt	Louvre
Common Unix Printing System	filter
Psychology	psychology
Universe	shape
Mass media	database
Stroke	blood
Mark Twain	tale
Ludwig van Beethoven	violin
Oxyrhynchus	papyrus
Fermi paradox	civilization
Milk	dairy
Health	fitness
Tourette syndrome	tic
Agriculture	crop
Malaria	disease
Fiberglass	fiber
Continent	continent
United States Congress	Senate
Turquoise	turquoise

variant [2] could have been used as well). The cosine similarity measure has then been applied on all pairs of the term vectors. For each article A, a list of the names of the other 99 articles has been generated and arranged in descending order according to their cosine similarity to A. An article's A most similar article can therefore be found at the top of this list.

In order to apply the new centroid distance measure to determine the articles' semantic distance, for each article, its centroid term has been determined with the help of the co-occurrence graph G using formula 5. The pairwise distance between all centroid terms of all articles in G has then been calculated. Additionally, to make the results of the cosine similarity measure and the centroid distance measure comparable, the centroid distance values have been converted into similarity values using formula 7.

The examplary diagram in Figure 2 shows for the reference article ("Abgas-Skandal - Schummel-Motor steckt auch in Audi A4 und A6") its similarity to the 50 most similar articles. The cosine similarity measure was used as the reference measure. Therefore, the most similar article received rank 1 using this measure (blue bars). Although the similarity values of the two measures seem uncorrelated, it is recognisable that especially the articles with a low rank (high similarity) according to the cosine similarity measure are generally regarded as similar by the centroid distance measure, too. In case of Figure 2, the reference article dealt with the car emissions scandal (a heavily dicussed topic in late 2015). The articles at the ranks 3 ("Abgas-Affäre - Volkswagen holt fünf Millionen VWs in die Werkstätten"), 7 ("Diesel von Volkswagen - Was VW-Kunden jetzt wissen müssen") and 12 ("Abgas-Skandal - Was auf VW- und Audi-Kunden zukommt") according to the cosine similarity measure have been considered most similar by the centroid distance measure, all of which were indeed related to the reference article. The strongly related articles at the ranks 1, 4, 6 and 9 have been regarded as similar by the centroid distance measure, too. In many experiments, however, the centroid distance measure considered articles as similar although the cosine similarity measure did not. Here, another implicit yet important advantage of the new

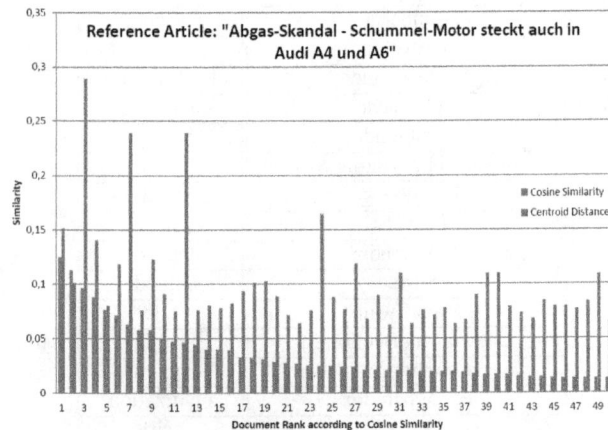

Figure 2: Cosine similarity vs. centroid distance (topic: car emissions scandal)

centroid distance measure becomes obvious: two documents can be regarded as similar although their wording differs (the overlap of their term vectors would be small or even empty and the cosine similarity value would be very low or 0). The article at rank 49 ("Jaguar XF im Fahrbericht - Krallen statt Samtpfoten") is an example for such a case. The centroid distance measure uncovered a topical relationship to the reference article, as both texts are car-related and deal with engine types.

5. DISCUSSION

The bag-of-words model that e.g. the cosine similarity measure solely relies on is used by the centroid-based measure as well, but only to the extend that the entries in the term vectors of documents are used as anchor points in the reference co-occurrence graph G (to 'position' the documents in G) in order to determine their centroid terms. Also, it needs to be pointed out once again that a document's centroid term does not have to occur even once in it. In other words, a centroid term can represent a document, even when it is never mentioned in it.

While the cosine similarity measure considers especially those documents as similar that actually use the same words (their term vectors have a significantly large overlap), the centroid diatance measure can uncover a topical relationship between documents even if their wording differs. Due to their completely different working principles, it might be sensible to combine both approaches in a new measure that factors in the results of both methods. Further experiments in this regard will be conducted.

Additionally, the herein presented experiments have shown another advantage of the centroid distance measure: its language-independence. It relies on the term relations and term distances in the reference co-occurrence graph G that has been naturally created using text documents of any language.

6. CONCLUSION

A new physics-inspired method has been introduced to determine centroid terms of particular text documents which are strongly related to them and yet do not need to occur in them. As text representatives, these terms are useful to determine the semantic distance

and similarity of text documents. Especially, texts with similar topics yet different descriptive terms, may be classified more precisely than with commonly known measures. As the text length's influence does not play a role in doing so, even short texts or (search) queries may be matched with other texts using the same approach. It may therefore be applied in future (decentralised) search engines and text clustering solutions.

7. REFERENCES

[1] J. Hawkins and S. Blakeslee. *On Intelligence*. Times Books, New York, NY, USA, 2004.

[2] R. A. Baeza-Yates and B. Ribeiro-Neto. *Modern Information Retrieval*. Addison-Wesley Longman Publishing Co., Inc., Boston, MA, USA, 1999.

[3] L. R. Dice. Measures of the amount of ecologic association between species. *Ecology*, 26(3):297–302, July 1945.

[4] G. A. Miller. WordNet: A Lexical Database for English. *Commun. ACM*, 38(11):39–41, Nov. 1995.

[5] K. W. Church and P. Hanks. Word association norms, mutual information, and lexicography. *Computational Linguistics*, 16(1):22–29, Mar. 1990.

[6] U. Quasthoff and C. Wolff. The poisson collocations measure and its application. In *Workshop on Computational Approaches to Collocations*, Wien, Austria, 2002.

[7] T. Dunning. Accurate methods for the statistics of surprise and coincidence. *Computational Linguistics*, 19(1):61–74, Mar. 1993.

[8] C. Biemann. Chinese whispers: An efficient graph clustering algorithm and its application to natural language processing problems. In *Proceedings of the First Workshop on Graph Based Methods for Natural Language Processing*, TextGraphs-1, pages 73–80, Association for Computational Linguistics, Stroudsburg, PA, USA, 2006.

[9] G. Heyer, U. Quasthoff, and T. Wittig. *Text Mining: Wissensrohstoff Text – Konzepte, Algorithmen, Ergebnisse*. IT lernen. W3L-Verlag, Herdecke, Germany, 2008.

[10] C. Biemann, S. Bordag, and U. Quasthoff. Automatic acquisition of paradigmatic relations using iterated co-occurrences. In *Proceedings of LREC2004*, Lisboa, Portugal, 2004.

[11] M. Kubek and H. F. Witschel. Searching the web by using the knowledge in local text documents. In *Proceedings of Mallorca Workshop 2010 Autonomous Systems*, pages 75–79. Shaker Verlag, Aachen, Germany, 2010.

[12] M. Kubek and H. Unger. Search word extraction using extended pagerank calculations. In *Autonomous Systems: Developments and Trends*, pages 325–337. Springer Berlin Heidelberg, 2012.

Frequent Multi-Byte Character Subtring Extraction Using a Succinct Data Structure

Phanucheep Chotnithi
SOKENDAI (The Graduate University for
Advanced Studies)
2-1-2 Chiyoda-ku
Tokyo, Japan
phanucheep@nii.ac.jp

Atsuhiro Takasu
National Institute of Informatics
2-1-2 Chiyoda-ku
Tokyo, Japan
takasu@nii.ac.jp

ABSTRACT

Frequent string mining is widely used in text processing to extract text features. Most researchers have focused on text using single-byte characters. Consequently, their applications have problems when applied to text represented with multibyte characters such as Japanese and Chinese text. The main drawback is huge memory usage for treating multibyte character strings. To solve this problem, we use wavelet tree-based compressed suffix arrays instead of the normal suffix array to reduce the memory usage, and a novel technique that utilizes the rank operation to improve runtime efficiency. Our experimental evaluation shows that the proposed method reduces the processing time by 45% compared with a method using only compressed suffix arrays. The proposed method also reduces the memory usage by 75%.

Keywords

frequent string mining, multibyte, wavelet tree, suffix array, longest common prefix

1. INTRODUCTION

Mining frequent strings from text is a common problem in text processing and is widely used in many applications. For example, maximal substrings are used for text classification [9]. Entity resolution also requires representative substrings, which are derived using frequent substring mining to measure the similarity between records. Most text processing research concerns English text, where strings are represented with single-byte characters. However, these methods cannot be applied directly to text in other languages such as Japanese and Chinese, where characters are represented with multiple bytes. To extend the usage of frequent string mining to such documents, we need an efficient frequent string mining technique for multibyte characters.

Multibyte character encoding standards such as UTF-8 and UTF-16 were introduced to deal with those character sets. Mining frequent strings using suffix arrays and longest common prefix (LCP) arrays [4] is a reasonable method to solve this problem. Instead

DocEng '16, September 12-16, 2016, Vienna, Austria
© 2016 ACM. ISBN 978-1-4503-4438-8/16/09. . . $15.00
DOI: http://dx.doi.org/10.1145/2960811.2967161

of using a suffix tree as the base structure to mine frequent substrings, which is the typical method, we propose a simpler and more efficient way to mine frequent substrings with a more appropriate data structure. Using this structure, we developed an algorithm that can cope with multibyte characters more easily. There are still some problems when applying this method to multibyte characters in its present form. First, memory consumption tends to be large. Because multibyte characters require more space than single-byte characters, the memory usage to mine multibyte character strings grows rapidly. The second problem is erroneous results caused by unawareness of multibyte character boundaries; the enumerated frequent substrings may start from and/or end at a byte inside a multibyte character. The multibyte characters are often transformed into byte arrays but the algorithm still processes the arrays as single-byte characters.

To solve these problems, we propose a novel method to extract correct results with low memory usage. We first use a compressed suffix array to reduce the memory usage, and then use a bit array to flag the beginning byte of each multibyte character [11] to obtain the correct mining results. Our experiments show that the proposed method successfully reduces memory usage with a small increase in processing time. To reduce the processing time, we exploit the rank operation provided by the wavelet tree structure of the compressed suffix array to calculate the number of nonfirst bytes of the character in constant time. In this way, we can skip the nonfirst bytes to reduce the processing time.

2. BACKGROUND AND RELATED WORK

2.1 Notation and Problem Definition

Suppose Σ denotes the set of an alphabet and consider a string $S := s_1...s_n$ where $s_i \in \Sigma$. Let $S_{n..m}$ denote the substring of S from position n to m. For strings R and $S \in \Sigma^\star$, $R \preceq S$ denotes that R is a substring of S. We define $lcp(R,S)$ as the *length* of the *longest common prefix* of R and S. For a database DB consisting of a set $\{S_1, S_2, ..., S_k\}$ of strings, Fischer et al. [4] defined the *frequency* of pattern p as the number of strings $S (\in DB)$ such that $p \preceq S$. In this paper, given a string $S (\in \Sigma^\star)$, we define the *frequency* of a pattern $p \in \Sigma^\star$ as

$$freq(p,S) = |\{s \preceq S : s = p\}| \, .$$

For a threshold *minfreq* as the minimum frequency, a pattern $p \in D$ is *frequent* if $freq(p,S) \geq min$ holds. We denote a set of *frequent patterns* in string S as D. For example, let $\Sigma = \{a,b,c,d\}$, S=ababcabdabcd and *min*=2. Then, frequent patterns of string S are $\{a,b,c,ab,abc\}$.

2.2 Frequent String Mining with Suffix and LCP arrays

To mine frequent patterns from a string, [4] proposed an efficient method that makes the frequent string mining more scalable by using suffix and LCP arrays instead of a suffix tree [2]. Given a text T of length n, a *suffix array* [7] for T is an integer array $SA[1,n]$ by $T_{SA[i]..n} \geq T_{SA[i+1]..n}$ for all $1 \leq i \leq n$. In other words, the suffix array describes the lexicographical order of the text's suffixes. The suffix array can be constructed in $O(n)$ [10]. The LCP array $LCP[1, n+1]$ defined by $LCP[i] = lcp(T_{SA[i]..n}, T_{SA[i-1]..n})$ for all $1 \leq i \leq n$ and $LCP[1] = LCP[n+1] = -1$. LCP shows the length of the longest common prefix of the text's suffixes, which are ordered in lexicographical order. It can be computed in $O(n)$ time using the algorithm of Kasai et al. [6]. Together, the suffix array and the LCP array take about 9 times as much space as the input text for the two integer arrays (4 times for each integer array), and the text itself must also be stored.

SA and LCP can be used to calculate frequent strings by looking for intervals (l, r) in D in which $SA[l-1], ..., SA[r]$ appears in at least min strings.

For a string database D, we compute the minimum frequency by constructing the suffix and LCP arrays for the database in advance, then scan all local maxima in LCP that satisfy $minfreq$ as follows. Select p as a prefix and count the number of patterns in D that contain p. These strings contain the substring corresponding to $SA[l-1], ..., SA[r]$. If the frequency of p is greater than or equal to $minfreq$, store p as a frequent string and mark the bit-array flag $freq$ at its position to avoid returning to p more than once. Otherwise, try to extend the interval (l, r) in the direction that has the maximum LCP value ($max(LCP[l-1], LCP[r+1])$) and update the number of strings covered by the new interval (l', r'). Iterate this process until the end of SA and LCP is reached.

2.3 Compressed Suffix Array

Since the SA uses large memory ($4n$ for the integer array where n is the text length), a compressed suffix array is sometimes used to reduce the memory requirement. The wavelet tree [5], which can be used to implement the compressed suffix tree, is the base structure built on the *Burrows–Wheeler transform* (BWT) [1].

2.4 Multibyte Characters

Multibyte encoding can be both fixed and variable length. The most popular multibyte character encodings are versions of *Unicode Transformation Format* or UTF (especially UTF-8, UTF-16 and UTF-32), which are variable length. UTF is also backward compatible with ASCII.

To deal with multibyte characters in an application originally designed for single-byte characters, Wong proposed four approaches [11] to apply BWT and backward search in an FM-Index [3]. Approach A is to define each character as fixed length in m byte-width encoding. Approach B treats every symbol as being one byte long and checks the word boundaries. Approaches C and D have the same idea: to split a given text according to the byte location of each character, then separately apply BWT encoding to each byte. Approach D simply stores a mapping information byte for every g bytes by g is any integer number.

3. PROPOSED METHOD

3.1 Frequent Substring Enumeration Algorithm

We propose a frequent string mining algorithm for multibyte

character strings. We calculate the number of occurrences of pattern p in a string S, denoted by $freq$, using the interval (l, r) in the LCP array.

In the LCP array, $LCP[i]$ is a *local maximum* iff $LCP[i] \geq LCP[i-1]$ and $LCP[i] > LCP[i+1]$ both hold. For example, positions 5, 9, and 12 in Fig. 1 are local maxima. For a string t, let SA and LCP be the corresponding suffix and LCP arrays, respectively. For any local maximum i, let k be the maximum value of $LCP[i+1]$ and $LCP[i-1]$. Let us consider the interval (l, r) of the LCP array that holds $l \leq i \leq r$ for which $LCP[l-1]$ and $LCP[r+1] < k$. Then, the frequency of substring $t_{SA[r]..SA[r]+k-1}$ is given by $r-l+2$, because all the suffixes from $SA[l-1]$ to $SA[r]$ have the substring $t_{SA[r]..SA[r]+k-1}$ as prefix, i.e., the substring appears $r-l+2$ times in the string t.

From this property, we can enumerate frequent substrings in the following way. For each local maximum position i, we extend its range from the local maximum position to the interval (l, r) such that the frequency of its corresponding substring is greater than $minfreq$. For example, let us consider a string t="aababcabcac". According to Fig. 1, the first local maximum of LCP is position 5 and $k = 2$, because $LCP[4] = 2 > LCP[6] = 1$. Then, we extend interval (l, r) to the left and finally we obtain the interval $(4, 5)$. From the property, we find that the frequency of "ab" is 3.

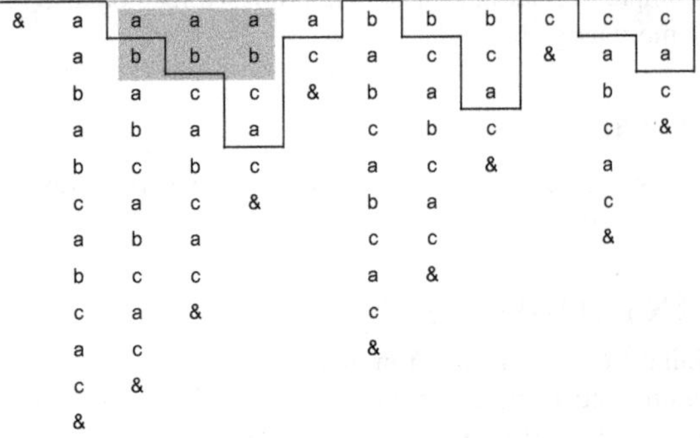

Figure 1: The suffix array for t and LCP array

3.2 MultiByte Character Processing

The main purpose of this research is to extend the usability of this frequent string mining to multibyte character strings. We need to overcome several problems in this task. First, the space usage significantly increases for a multibyte character string of length n, because $9n$ storage is required for SA and LCP. For example, most Japanese (Hiragana, Katakana and Kanji) characters in UTF-8 are represented by 3 bytes. We therefore need $27n$ bytes instead of $9n$ (two integer arrays and the original text) for a single-byte string, where n is the string length. Secondly, incorrect substrings can be enumerated because SA and LCP treat symbols as single bytes and they do not consider character boundaries in multibyte strings. For example, let us consider t="こんにちは"; its UTF-8 code is shown in Fig. 2. If query $minfreq = 3$, substring "0xE3 0x81" will be returned as a frequent string, even though it is not a Japanese string.

We use a compressed data structure for SA and LCP to reduce space usage. In practice, we implement the compressed suffix and LCP arrays by using a wavelet tree that provides *rank/select* oper-

Figure 2: UTF-8 byte array for "こんにちは"

ations in $O(1)$ time [8]. To solve the character boundary problem, we adopt approach B of Wong's methods for BWT and backward search.

After some experiments on frequent substring mining with a compressed suffix array, we found some problems caused by using compressed suffix arrays. Although the space usage is reduced, the runtime is longer. This is because the access time for any element of the more complex compressed data structure is greater than that for the normal suffix array.

A suffix that starts with a nonfirst byte of a character should not be included in the frequent string results. We jump through any nonfirst bytes of characters to eliminate useless processing in the algorithm. The number of positions to skip can be obtained by counting the number of occurrences of nonfirst bytes. The wavelet tree enables counting the occurrences in $O(1)$ time. For example, there is a nonfirst byte "0x81" at position 2 in Fig. 3. A nonfirst byte can be identified by its characteristic ($10xxxxxx$ for UFT-8 and x can be any binary digit). Let $rank(e,i)$ denote the number of elements e in the range $[0,i]$. If we identify the first byte of a substring corresponding to any algorithm iteration as a nonfirst byte ("0x81" for this example), the query function $rank(0x81,16)$ returns the number of occurrences of "0x81" from position 0 to 16 (count through all string length), which is equal to four. Once we know the number of occurrences, we can jump from position 2 to 6 to the next character instantly. Note that all suffices beginning with "0x81" appear consecutively in suffix and LCP arrays. In this way, we can skip every nonfirst byte, which eliminates unnecessary processing and improves the efficiency.

Figure 3: *SA* and *LCP* for "こんにちは"

4. EXPERIMENT AND RESULTS

We applied the proposed method to Thai news articles extracted from www.thairath.co.th/ and to the Wikipedia pages dataset for languages with 3-byte characters, i.e., Japanese, Korean, and Chinese, as shown in Table 1. A program was written in C++ with the SDSL-lite library [1] for the compressed suffix array. The experiment was conducted using an Intel Core i7 2.2 GHz processor with 16 GB of RAM. The purpose of the experiments was to compare the efficiency of frequent substring mining using:

- a standard suffix array, referred to as "Original",

- a compressed suffix array referred to as "W/O Jump", and

[1] https://github.com/simongog/sdsl-lite

- a compressed suffix array with the rank jump technique referred to as "With Jump".

Thai news articles	Wikipedia pages		
	Japanese	Korean	Chinese
1000 MB	1700 MB	1500 MB	2000 MB

Table 1: Dataset

First, we tested the runtime efficiency of the three kinds of indices. Figure 4 shows the processing time for substring mining of the Thai news text with text sizes of 40 MB, 100 MB, 200 MB, 250 MB, and 500 MB. The articles were randomly chosen from the Thai news articles in addition to the full dataset. We defined parameter $minfreq$=200. As shown in the graph, the compressed suffix array ("W/O Jump") requires about 2.5 times more processing time than the uncompressed suffix array ("Original"). This is because of the overhead of processing the compressed suffix array, which makes access to each element slower than that in the standard suffix array. By introducing the rank jump technique ("With Jump"), we can reduce the runtime by 43% compared with the compressed suffix array without jump. However, it is still about 43% slower than using the standard suffix array. Note that we could not evaluate the standard suffix array for the 750 MB and 1000 MB datasets because they were too large to fit in the available memory of the computer we used in the experiment.

For the second test, we evaluated the space usage of the two indices. Figure 5 shows their space usage. The compressed suffix array can reduce the space usage by 75% compared with the standard suffix array structure. The results show that the compressed suffix array approach allows us to mine frequent multibyte character strings from larger datasets.

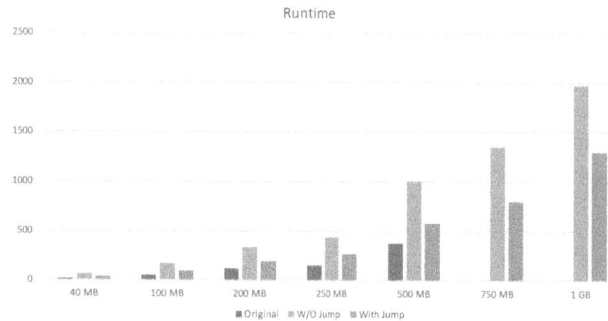

Figure 4: Runtime (s) with respect to the size of Thai text.

In the next experiment, we evaluated the efficiency of the rank jump technique for various languages. We compared the performance of the indices for three languages using the Wikipedia dataset described in Table. 1 using $minfreq$=200. Figures 6 and 7 show the space usage and runtimes for three datasets. Figure 6 shows that the space usage with the compressed suffix array is still impressive. SA (Theory) represents the space used by the normal suffix array by theoretical calculation, because of the limited memory of the machine. We could only compute the large size of these datasets. The jump technique improves the processing efficiency as in the case of Thai articles, but the degree of improvement differs depending on the language. As we can see in Fig. 7, the rank jump technique cannot reduce the runtime for these languages as much

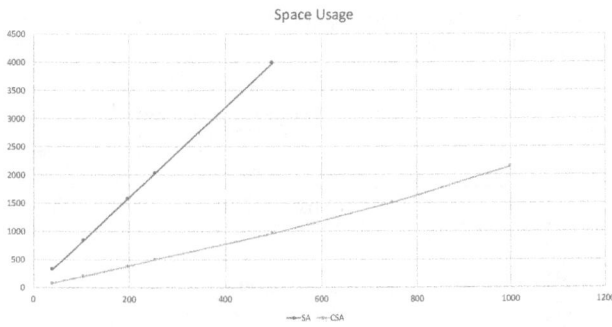

Figure 5: Space usage (MB) of indices with respect to the size of Thai text.

as it does for the Thai dataset. We checked the datasets and found that these datasets contain smaller numbers of multibyte characters, which leads to the limitation of the improvement. The rank jump technique can eliminate the processing of candidate frequent substrings that begin with nonfirst bytes of characters. If the objective text contains more multibyte characters, the rank jump technique can reduce the runtime more. The reduction also depends on the number of bytes used to represent each character.

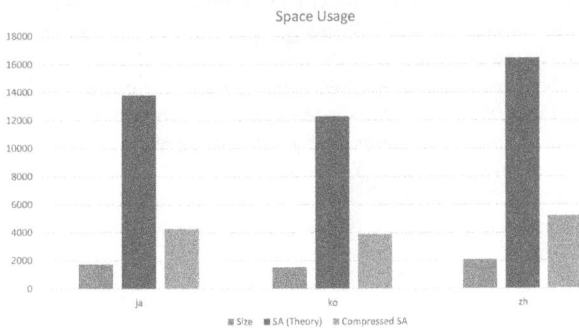

Figure 6: Space usage (MB) for to the datasets in three languages

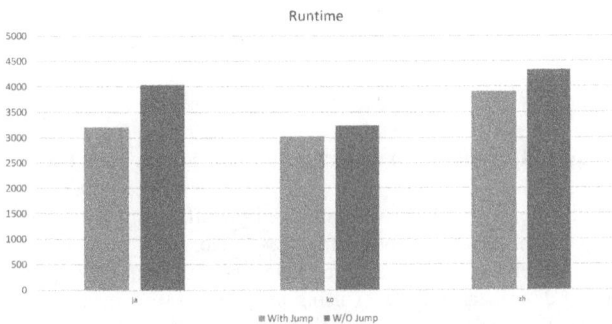

Figure 7: Runtimes (s) for the datasets in three languages

5. CONCLUSIONS

We have proposed a new technique to apply frequent substring mining to multibyte character strings. We introduced compressed

suffix arrays to reduce space usage and preserved runtime efficiency with the rank jump technique. The experimental evaluation shows that the proposed method reduces memory usage significantly. The compressed array causes increased processing time, but the rank jump technique can reduce the deterioration.

However, there are many ways we can improve this research. The rank jump technique is used to eliminate the process that deals with substrings that start with uncompleted characters. We must also consider substrings that end with uncompleted characters individually in the postprocessing. We plan to apply other techniques to deal with this kind of substring to improve the efficacy of our approach.

6. ACKNOWLEDGMENT

This work was supported by a JSPS Grant-in-Aid for Scientific Research (B) (15H02789).

7. REFERENCES

[1] M. Burrows and D. Wheeler. A block-sorting lossless data compression algorithm. In *DIGITAL SRC RESEARCH REPORT*. Citeseer, 1994.

[2] L. De Raedt, M. Jaeger, S. D. Lee, and H. Mannila. A theory of inductive query answering. In *Data Mining, 2002. ICDM 2003. Proceedings. 2002 IEEE International Conference on*, pages 123–130. IEEE, 2002.

[3] P. Ferragina and G. Manzini. Opportunistic data structures with applications. In *Foundations of Computer Science, 2000. Proceedings. 41st Annual Symposium on*, pages 390–398. IEEE, 2000.

[4] J. Fischer, V. Heun, and S. Kramer. Fast frequent string mining using suffix arrays. In *Proceedings of the Fifth IEEE International Conference on Data Mining*, pages 609–612. IEEE, 2005.

[5] R. Grossi, A. Gupta, and J. S. Vitter. High-order entropy-compressed text indexes. In *Proceedings of the fourteenth annual ACM-SIAM symposium on Discrete algorithms*, pages 841–850. Society for Industrial and Applied Mathematics, 2003.

[6] T. Kasai, G. Lee, H. Arimura, S. Arikawa, and K. Park. Linear-time longest-common-prefix computation in suffix arrays and its applications. In *Combinatorial pattern matching*, pages 181–192. Springer, 2001.

[7] U. Manber and G. Myers. Suffix arrays: a new method for on-line string searches. *SIAM Journal on Computing*, 22(5):935–948, 1993.

[8] G. Navarro. Wavelet trees for all. *J. of Discrete Algorithms*, 25:2–20, Mar. 2014.

[9] D. Okanohara and J. Tsujii. Text categorization with all substring features. In *SIAM International Conference on Data Mining*, pages 838–846. SIAM, 2009.

[10] S. J. Puglisi, W. F. Smyth, and A. H. Turpin. A taxonomy of suffix array construction algorithms. *ACM Comput. Surv.*, 39(2), July 2007.

[11] R. K. Wong, F. Shi, and N. Lam. Full-text search on multi-byte encoded documents. In *Proceedings of the 2012 ACM symposium on Document engineering*, pages 227–236. ACM, 2012.

Mobile Summarizer and News Summary Navigator
Two Multilingual News Article Summarization Tools for Mobile Devices

Luciano Cabral[1,2],
Manoel Neto[1], Artur Borges[1]
[1]Federal Institute of Pernambuco
Jaboatão/Caruaru, PE, Brazil
+55 81 98805-4131
{lscabral,mneto,aborges}@gmail.com

Rafael Lins[2,3], Rinaldo Lima[2,3]
Rafael Ferreira[2,3]
[2]U.F.PE., Recife, PE, Brazil
[3]U.F.R.PE., Recife, PE, Brazil
+ 55 81 2126-8430
{rdl,rflm,rjl4}@cin.ufpe.br

Marcelo Riss[4] and
Steven J. Simske[5]
[4]Hewlett Packard, P.Alegre, RS, Brazil
[5]HP Labs. Fort Collins, CO, USA
+55 81 99921-7995
{marcelo.riss,steven.simske}@hp.com

ABSTRACT

Mobile devices such as smart phones and tablets are omnipresent in modern societies. Such devices allow browsing the Internet. This paper briefly describes two tools for news article summarization in mobile devices that attempts to automatically collect and sieve the most important information of news article in WebPages.

CCS Concepts

Information systems → Information systems applications → Mobile information processing systems / → Summarization

Keywords

Mobile applications; Text Summarization; Multilingual Summarization

1. INTRODUCTION

Mobile devices are deeply integrated in the lifestyle of the majority of the population in modern societies. Smart phones and tablets are already responsible for about 15% of Internet traffic, by byte volume, today. This percentage is increasing steadily, and it is foreseen that in the near future it will surpass laptop and desktop web traffic [11]. Web browsing is responsible for a reasonable part of such volume of data transfer. The nature of mobile devices enforces portability, flexibility and a small format/footprint. Being able to extract fundamental information from a web page is thus well-suited to the nature and functionality of mobile devices.

This paper briefly describes two applets, which perform automatic text summarization of web pages of news articles in mobile devices. The first one is called *Mobile Summarizer*, which is an improved version of the original extractive summarizer introduced in [2]. This new version provides a personalized extractive summary, since it allows the user to choose or combine the summarization algorithms available in the application software, which can operate with 100 distinct languages. The second tool is

DocEng '16, September 12 - 16, 2016, Vienna, Austria
Copyright is held by the owner/author(s). Publication rights licensed to ACM.
ACM 978-1-4503-4438-8/16/09 ... $15.00.
DOI: http://dx.doi.org/10.1145/2960811.2967156

the *News Summary Navigator*, which consists of a news browser, with support for the English and Portuguese languages. Its interface automatically switches to the language currently used on the mobile device, providing updated information to the user through a news browser similar to Google News and weather. It has the added feature of displaying a summary of the original news before presenting the whole web page. The remainder of this article details the aforementioned multilingual mobile applications for news article summarization.

2. RELATED MOBILE APPLICATIONS

Currently, there are a few mobile applications targeting text summarization such as: GPLSI [7], the Essential Summarizer [9], the Friendly Reader [10] and the Lessy Summarizer [11]. GPLSI is an implementation of the Compendium summarizer [8], which is a desktop platform. It conveys only 6 different summarization methods that can be applied individually, with support for English and Spanish. The Essential Summarizer is an application that summarizes a text, webpage or a text file with support for English, French and Arabic. The Friendly Reader application was generated from research developed at Linköping University, and provides a summary of a larger text with controls for better interaction on the mobile device. It has support for English and Swedish. The Lessy Summarizer uses the MUSE (Multilingual Sentence Extractor) algorithm [12, 13] which is based on 31 features for text summarization. It can be used for Hebrew and English. There are some other applets for mobile summarization which either support only one language or are too old to run in the current mobile devices.

Focusing on news processing on mobile devices, there is the well-known Google News and Climate [14], which provides a simple categorization, many RSS news feeds and several supported languages. However, there are no summarization features; at most, it shows the first paragraph of the news article to the user. Plexi Digest [15] and FirstWire [16] are similar tools, with two differences: they support only the English language, but provide a short summary of the news. The Zuppit [17] provides summaries instantly of news obtained from +1,000 Hindi and English newspapers and websites, with support only for those two languages.

The MS and NSN tools presented here both provide the possibility of using seven summarization algorithms. MS supports over 100 languages providing an intermediate summary between the news title option and the news website. On the other hand, the weak point of MS is that the statistical generalization for Multilanguage summaries may yield summaries of poorer quality than some specific language summarization system; The current version of the NSN tool provides support for only the English and Portuguese languages.

3. THE MOBILE SUMMARIZER

The MS[1] [1] is a new and efficient tool for text summarization in smart phones and tablets freely available for download at Google Play[1]. In addition to providing a summarization application with easy access and use for mobile devices, it performs summarization of news articles using seven different methods. The MS is able to combine such methods to improve the quality of resulting summaries. Figures 1 and 2 show some screenshots of the application running on a mobile device.

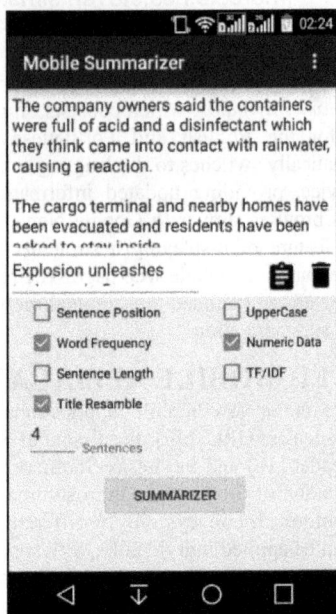

Figure 1. The settings of the MS

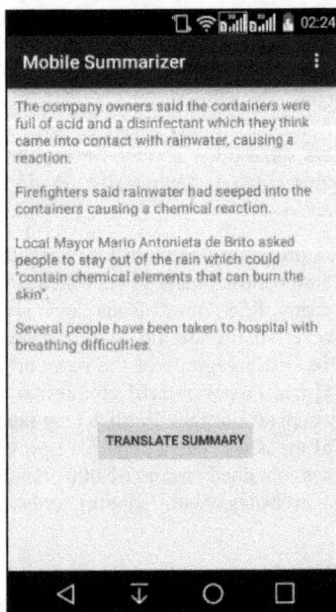

Figure 2. A summary generated by the MS

The MS also provides the means for visualizing the summary in different languages using the Google Translate API [3] (supporting over 100 languages), enabling users to read the main information of the texts in different languages (Figures 3 and 4).

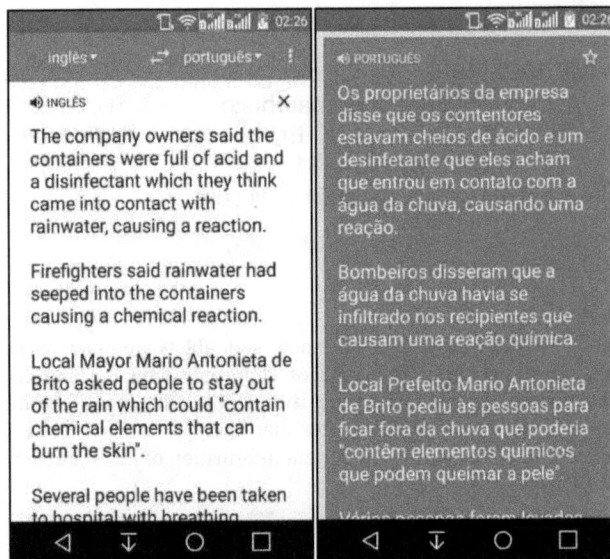

Figure 3. Summary in the original language (English)	**Figure 4. Portuguese version of the text in Fig.3**

Another interesting application scenario for MS is in learning foreign languages, as the user may compare the summaries after translation. To the best of the knowledge of the developers of the MS, there is no similar mobile solution for multilingual automatic summarization which incorporates such summarization algorithms and the possibility of combining their results for even more precise results. Detailed information about the MS, its architecture, algorithms, and analysis of the quality of summaries is provided in reference [1].

4. THE NEWS SUMMARY NAVIGATOR

The News Summary Navigator (NSN) is also freely available at Google Play[2]. It provides to the user the possibility of organizing the news articles into several different categories chosen by the user and saving them for later reading. This makes the NSN a more user-friendly tool than the Google News platform, which originally inspired it. Besides generating summaries of the web pages, as done by the MS, the NSN allows the user to save his favorite news articles for reading in its integrity later on.

The NSM implements the top two of the summarization methods carefully selected according to a comparative performance among several state-of-the-art summarization algorithms proposed in the last five years [1, 2, 4, 5], they are: (i) *Word Frequency* and (ii) *Sentence Position*.

Word Frequency (WF). WF works by counting the number of distinct words in the text to be summarized. In other words, by weighting all, the most relevant words (after eliminating stop words); the sentences are ranked in descending order according to their normalized weighting scores.

---

[1]: https://play.google.com/store/apps/details?id=com.br.mobilesummarizer

[2]: https://play.google.com/store/apps/details?id=com.br.newsnavigation

Sentence Position (SP). This method selects the first and last sentences of the news text. It is based on the simple heuristics derived from the common way that news journalists or authors write their articles: they usually introduce the most important information of the news article in the first sentences and other complementary information at the end (conclusions).

Although the selected summarization methods described above are straightforward, they achieved very competitive performance against other state-of-the-art extractive summarizers using more complex summarization methods and needing more processing time [4]. For instance, WF and SP outperformed Lexical Similarity, Word co-occurrence and all graph based methods, in terms of R1-ROUGE [18] on the CNN corpus [4].

One can expect to have even better results by combining the above methods (linear combination) as shown in [2]. Then, according to the conclusions in [2], assigning the weights α and β in the next formula to 0.7 and 0.3, respectively.

$$NSN_{Summary} = \alpha * \text{WordFreq} + \beta * \text{SentPos}$$

Another simple but efficient heuristic is to select between 10 to 30 percent of the total number of original sentences to compose the final summary. Figures 5 and 6 display the NSN main screenshots. NSN retrieves the preferences of the users, such as the language to be used in the summarization process. In its current version, NSN supports three languages: English, Portuguese, and Spanish. In addition, the NSN takes advantage of the RSS feed technology for retrieving news articles from CNN.com (in English) and G1.com (Portuguese).

For each category provided by the source RSS feed selected by the user, a list of the most recent news in each of the categories chosen by the user are retrieved and displayed as shown in Fig. 6.

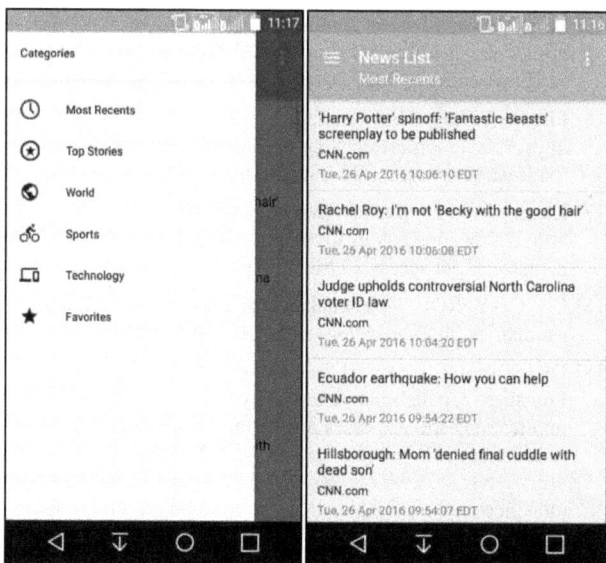

user can go through the entire news article or return to the previous screen. Figure 8 shows a screenshot of the original news article from the CNN.com website. Figure 9 displays the favorite news articles on a certain set of subjects selected by the user. The underlying idea of NSN is to help the users to quickly decide whether if they really want to spend further time on a recently published news article. Thereby, the user has better elements in order to decide which news articles match his interest.

These additional features in NSN can save users time if, before going to read a given news article, as they preview the main points by a generating an extractive summary.

Figure 7. Summary of the previous news

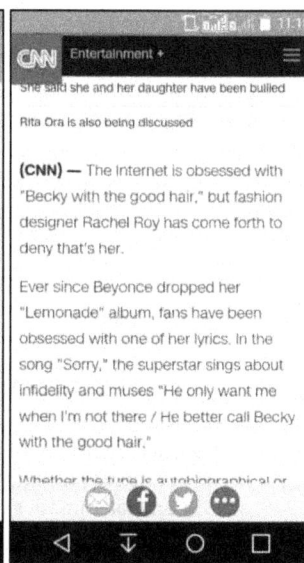

Figure 8. News at the CNN.com website

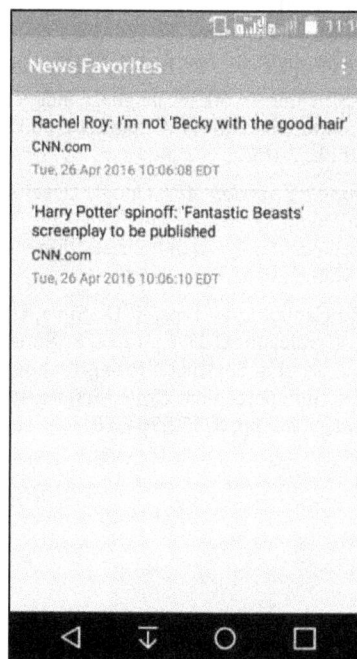

Figure 5. Subject categories in English

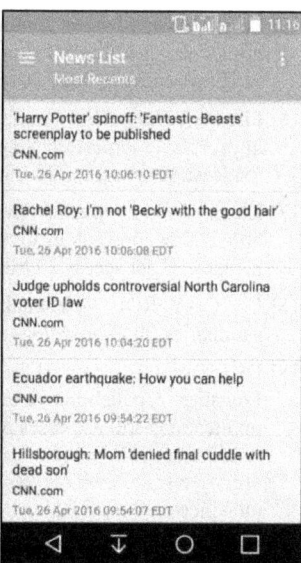

Figure 6. List of the most recent news from CNN.com

Then, by selecting a specific news headline, an extractive summary with the headline, publication date, and the summary of the text body is generated as shown in Figure 7. If desired, the

Figure 9. The favorite news articles selected.

5. CONCLUSIONS AND FURTHER WORK

This paper briefly describes two state of the art tools for automatic text summarization of web pages of news articles in mobile devices, which are freely available for download at Google Play, which will be demonstrated at the 2016 ACM Conference on Document Engineering, held in Vienna, Austria, from 13 to 16, September 2016.

The current versions of the Mobile Summarizer (MS) and the News Summary Navigator (NSN) were developed for Android devices. The MS was made freely available at Google Play on 14 June 2015. Its latest update was made on 23 July 2015. Since its last code update up to 12 July 2016, 437 downloads were made. The NSN was also made freely available at Google Play on 29 December 2015. Its latest code update was made on 24 March 2016 and has up to 12 July 2016 42 downloads so far.

The Mobile Summarizer code is being reworked in the versions for iOS and Windows Phone, and is planned for completion to be made freely available in October 2016. The current improvement under development in the News Summary Navigator is towards the increase of the supported languages, including user interfaces translated into all the supported languages. Support in Spanish is nearly completed, and will be integrated with the news from the CNN Mexico web site. Others improvements planned are: an evaluation of the usability of the system, and an assessment of the degree of user satisfaction with the presented tools.

6. ACKNOWLEDGMENTS

The present research has been partly funded by a R&D project between Hewlett-Packard Brazil R&D and the Federal University of Pernambuco originated from tax exemption (IPI - Law number 8.248, of 1991 and later updates).

The authors are also grateful to PROPESQ-IFPE and CNPq by supporting this research.

7. REFERENCES

[1] Cabral, L., Lima, R., Lins, R., Neto, M., Ferreira, R., Simske, S. and Riss, M. 2015. Automatic Summarization of News Articles for Mobile Devices. 14th *Mexican International Conference on Artificial Intelligence,* 2015, pp. 8-13.

[2] Cabral, L. S. A framework for language independent automatic summarization (in Portuguese). Ph.D. Thesis, PPGEE, UFPE. 2015.

[3] Google, *Google Translate API*, Google Developers, 20 April 2012. Available: https://developers.google.com/translate/?hl=pt-BR. [Last access 11 March 2016].

[4] Ferreira, R., Cabral, L. S., Lins, R. D., Silva, G. F. P., Freitas, F., Cavalcanti, G. D. C., Lima, R. Simske, S. J. and Favaro, L. Assessing Sentence Scoring Techniques for Extractive Text Summarization. *Expert Systems with Applications*, v. 40, pp. 5755-5764, 2013.

[5] Cabral, L. S., Lins, R. D., Mello, R. F., Freitas, F., Ávila, B., Simske, S. J. and Riss, M. A platform for language independent summarization. *ACM symposium on Document engineering (DocEng '14)*, 203-206, 2014.

[6] Lins, R. D., Simske, S. J., Cabral, L. S., Silva, G. F. P., Lima, R. J., Mello, R. F. and Favaro, L. A multi-tool scheme for summarizing textual documents. *11th IADIS International Conference WWW/INTERNET*, 2012.

[7] Jiménez, A. *GPLSI Compendium App*. Available: https://play.google.com/store/apps/details?id=antonio.sumup. [Last access 18 May 2016].

[8] Lloret, E. *Text Summarization based on Human Language Technologies and its Applications*, Universidad de Alicante: PhD. Thesis, 2011.

[9] Mining Essentials. *Essential Summarizer*. Available: https://play.google.com/store/apps/details?id=com.essentialmining.summarizer.android. [Last access 18 May 2016].

[10] Marklund, A. *Friendly Reader*. Available: https://play.google.com/store/apps/details?id=com.friendlyreader. [Last access 18 May 2016].

[11] Mackover, S. *Lessy summarizer*. Available: https://play.google.com/store/apps/details?id=com.friendlyreader. [Last access 18 May 2016].

[12] Litvak, M., Last, M., Friedman, M. and Kisilevich, S. MUSE – A Multilingual Sentence Extractor. In Proceedings of the Computational Linguistics-Applications Conference, Jachranka, Poland, 2011.

[13] Litvak, M., Last, M. and Friedman, M. Multilingual Sentence Extractor. US Patent, US8594998 B2, 26 nov 2013.

[14] Google Inc. *Google News & Weather*. Available: https://play.google.com/store/apps/details?id=com.google.android.apps.genie.geniewidget. [Last access 18 May 2016].

[15] Stremor. *Plexi Digest*. Available: https://play.google.com/store/apps/details?id=com.PlexiDigest. [Last access 19 May 2016].

[16] FirstWire. *FirstWire*. Available: https://play.google.com/store/apps/details?id=com.firstwire.broadcast. [Last access 20 May 2016].

[17] Zuppit Tech. *Zuppit: Live News Summary*. https://play.google.com/store/apps/details?id=com.lockscreen.zuppit. [Last access 20 May 2016].

[18] Lin, C. -Y. ROUGE: A package for automatic evaluation of summaries. In *Proceedings of the ACL-04*, 2004 (pp.74-81).

[19] DHL Trend Research &Cisco Consulting Services. IoE in Logistics. A collaborative report by DHL and Cisco on implications and use cases for the logistics industry. 2015. Available: http://www.dhl.com/content/dam/Local_Images/g0/New_aboutus/innovation/DHLTrendReport_Internet_of_things.pdf. [Last access 25 May 2016].

Rendering Mathematics for the Web using Madoko

Daan Leijen
Microsoft Research
daan@microsoft.com

1. INTRODUCTION

Madoko [6–8] is a novel authoring system for writing complex documents. It is especially well suited for complex academic or industrial documents, like scientific articles, reference manuals, or math-heavy presentations. One particular important aspect of Madoko is to write a document in high-level Markdown [5] with a focus on semantic content. From this document specification we can generate both high-quality PDF output (via LaTeX) but also generate high-quality HTML that can re-scale and re-flow dynamically. Styling is done through standard CSS attributes and can be done orthogonal to the content.

Madoko provides extensive support for mathematics rendering. All math is rendered using LaTeX with full compatability with any LaTeX packages and commands. Rendering to PDF comes this way for free but a high quality rendering of the math in the resulting HTML is more involved. This application note article describes in detail how Madoko deals with the various technical challenges. Moreover we show how other mechanisms, like replacement rules, help with creating mini domain-specific extensions to cleanly express complex math.

Since this article is about the rendering of math to HTML, it is highly recommended to read this article as an HTML page instead of PDF! It can be found at http://tinyurl.com/madokomath.

2. AN OVERVIEW OF MADOKO

Madoko is based on *Markdown* [5] as its input format. The main design goal is to enable light-weight creation of high-quality scholarly and technical documents for the web and print, while maintaining John Gruber's Markdown philosophy of simplicity and focus on plain text readability. Since the Markdown input format is well-structured, this allows Madoko to generate both high quality HTML *and* PDF (through LaTeX and BibTeX). There has been a lot of effort in Madoko to make the LaTeX generation robust and cus-

DocEng '16, September 12-16, 2016, Vienna, Austria
© 2016 ACM. ISBN 978-1-4503-4438-8/16/09...$15.00
DOI: http://dx.doi.org/10.1145/2960811.2967168

tomizable while integrating well with the various academic document- and bibliography styles.

On modern devices like tablets and phones it is generally much more pleasant to read a paper or technical document as HTML instead of PDF since HTML can scale and reflow dynamically. A study by Franze et al. [2] showed that the most desired features when reading papers is being able to change the font size, alter margins, or have a single column layout; all of these are trivial in a web browser. Of course, this article itself was written in Madoko, and the HTML version can be viewed at http://tinyurl.com/madokomath. Others have tried to create re-scalable and re-flowable content from paginated PDF [11], or the other way around, paginating dynamic content [3], but we believe starting from a more high-level structured input format is a better way of approaching this problem.

The move to Markdown makes the the documents *structured*, *readable*, and output *independent*. The final ingredients that Madoko adds are to make the documents *styleable* through standard CSS rules, and *programmable* through transformation rules. These additions also makes it easy to add custom domain specific document elements, like *exercise* or *answer*, that can be transformed, numbered, and styled in a declarative manner.

Finally, the online version at madoko.net integrates seamlessly with Dropbox, GitHub, and OneDrive, making documents available anywhere on any device. Madoko synchronizes automatically and multiple authors can work concurrently on the same document using robust three-way merges on concurrent updates. This means that updates by others are not quite real-time as in other collaborative environments (although they are performed frequently), but anyone can now work off-line and still reliably merge when connecting again. Madoko.net is itself a HTML5 web application and the editor continues to work in the browser even when offline. Of course, you can always use the plain command line version of Madoko locally (`npm install -g madoko`).

3. SCALABLE MATH ON THE WEB

Madoko uses regular LaTeX for describing math formulas since TeX is still the gold standard for rendering and describing mathematics. Any formula can be directly embedded in a Madoko document. For example:

```
A famous formula is $e^{i\pi} + 1 = 0$, but the
following one is also well-known:
~ Equation { #eq-gaussian }
\int_{-\infty}^\infty e^{-a x^2} d x
```

```
   = \sqrt{\frac{\pi}{a}}
~
~>
```

A famous formula is $e^{i\pi} + 1 = 0$, but the following one is also well-known:

$$\int_{-\infty}^{\infty} e^{-ax^2} dx = \sqrt{\frac{\pi}{a}} \qquad (1)$$

Here we use $ to start inline math as in LATEX. For the equation we used a so-called *custom block* of Madoko. The standard prelude of Madoko defines `~ equation` for numbered equations, `~math` for plain display math, and `~mathpre` for pre-formatted math discussed in Section 4. In the example, we also give the equation a name so we can refer to it using links in Markdown where `[#eq-gaussian]` expands to the equation number, e.g. Equation (1).

When creating PDF output, Madoko can simply include the literal formula in the generated LATEX with full compatibility with any LATEX package. Unfortunately, for HTML output the process is more involved as we need to render math seperate from the rest of the HTML. There exist various tools that use JavaScript to interpret LATEX math commands directly and generate a rendering on the client. One of the most well-known libraries to do that is MathJax [1].

This works well for simple mathematics but one of the great advantages of using LATEX for math is that it comes with many many packages to render advanced mathematics, or packages that render math in the style required by a journal. Such packages are generally not supported by tools like MathJax. Even though Madoko has an option to use MathJax for dynamic math rendering, the default mode is to invoke LATEX and render all math at compile time.

In Madoko any LATEX package can be used through a metadata key at the start of the document, for example:

```
Package: [curve]xypic
```

after which we can use the `\xymatrix` command to render category theory diagrams:

```
~ Math
\xymatrix @-0.5em{
U \ar@/_/[ddr]_y \ar@/^/[drr]^x \ar@{.>}[dr]|-{(x,y)} \\
 & X \times Y \ar[d]^q \ar[r]_p & X \ar[d]_f \\
 & Y \ar[r]^g & Z }
~
~>
```

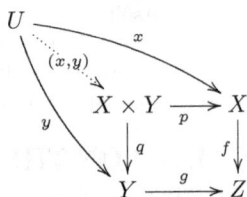

$$
\begin{array}{ccc}
U \\
 & X \times Y \xrightarrow{p} X \\
 & Y \xrightarrow{g} Z
\end{array}
$$

Generating good looking HTML from LATEX rendered formulas is a challenging problem though and we describe here various solutions adopted by Madoko.

Hashing of formulas

When rendering a document, Madoko first collects all math formulas and assigns a unique MD5 hash to each individual formula. This ensures that each formula is only rendered

it follows that
$$e^{i\pi} = -1 + 0i,$$
which yields Euler's identity:
$$e^{i\pi} + 1 = 0.$$

it follows that
$$e^{i\pi} = -1 + 0i,$$
which yields Euler's identity:
$$e^{i\pi} + 1 = 0.$$

Figure 1. Screenshots of different math renderings in the browser: the left image is rendered by Madoko using SVG graphics, while the right image is a rendering by Wikipedia using PNG images (https://en.wikipedia.org/wiki/Euler%27s_identity)

once which is important since many short formulas are usually often repeated. Madoko generates a special LATEX math file that contains 'snippet' entries for each formula. For example, for this document, one of the entries is:

```
%mdk-data-line={138}
\begin{mdInlineSnippet}[f2d2e607c3e99d5c34bc0aad01893a0d]
$e^{i\pi} + 1 = 0$%
\end{mdInlineSnippet}
```

The initial comment is how Madoko maps back LATEX error messages to the correct line in the original Madoko file – this is very important in practice to quickly solve LATEX problems. Next, the `mdInlineSnippet` command ensures that each formula gets rendered on its own page in the resulting DVI file. That DVI file is now passed to another tool to extract the rendering.

Madoko uses the excellent `dvisvgm` converter by Martin Gieseking [4] to convert LATEX generated DVI files to *scalable vector graphics* (SVG) files. The `dvisvgm` converter automatically extracts an SVG file for each page in the DVI file, numbering them sequentially. Since Madoko maintains a mapping between the MD5 hashes and the page numbers, it can then automatically include the correct SVG images in the generated HTML for each formula.

Many tools extract math formulas as PNG images from a rendered PDF or Postscript file. Unfortunately, this is a non-scalable image and looks generally quite fuzzy on a screen especially for inline formulas surround by text. Figure 1 compares the rendering of Euler's identity in Wikipedia, which uses PNG images, versus the rendering in Madoko which uses SVG. The difference is quite stark and the quality of SVG rendering is excellent even compared to PDF – when demoing Madoko, often people are under the impression of viewing PDF while they are actually seeing the HTML rendering of a Madoko document in the browser.

Baseline alignment

There are still various technical hurdles to overcome though. The most tricky one is proper baseline alignment. In particular, an inline formula should align as $\sum_{i=0}^{\infty} e^i$ with the e aligned with the text baseline. Contrast this with $\sum_{i=0}^{\infty} e^i$ for example where the bottom of the extracted image aligns with the baseline. There are often a lot of small inline formulas and not aligned well with the baseline looks very irregular to the eyes.

To achieve proper baseline alignment, we need to have an exact measurement of the *depth* of the formula, i.e. the bottom vertical distance to the baseline. If we know the depth, we can adjust the vertical alignment of the extracted image by lowering it by its depth.

The `mdInlineSnippet` environment does this by first rendering the formula in a TeX *box*. This box can be queried for its rendered height, width, and depth. After figuring out the dimensions the box is rendered to the page. For each formula, we write out the measured dimensions together with its hash (which is an argument to `mdInlineSnippet`) to a separate text file. After the LaTeX run, Madoko reads this dimension file to determine the precise baseline alignment for each formula in the HTML.

The final height of the math image should be determined by the relative font size of the surrounding text used in the HTML. This means that the height and baseline adjustment must be made in font-relative `em` units instead of absolute units. Madoko renders mathematics in a `10pt` font size when taking measurements. For output to HTML we read the measurements from the dimension file (in `pt`) and divide by 10 to get the relative `em` units. We use the CSS `vertical-align` attribute to lower the math image by its measured depth. In practice we also scale the math image by 105% in order to look more natural with most web fonts. For example, our initial example, $\sum_{i=0}^{\infty} e^i$ is positioned in the HTML output as:

```
<svg style="vertical-align:-0.3502em;height:1.2355em"
     viewBox="88.467 53.397 33.929 11.767"
     class="math-inline math-render-svg math">
 <desc>$\sum_{i=0}^{\infty}e^i$</desc>
 <g id="page26">
  <use x="88.667" y="54.364" xlink:href="#g14-80"
   xmlns:xlink="http://www.w3.org/1999/xlink"></use>
  ...
 </g></svg>
```

The `<use>` element puts the glyph `#g14-80` (the Σ) at a specific position. That glyph is defined separately to enable sharing of graphical elements between different formulas.

Sharing glyph paths
Math heavy documents can easily contain thousands of formulas. Madoko already shares representations for equal formulas through hashing but more is needed. For example, in one example math-heavy article [10] the math formulas generate 2242kb of SVG images. It turns out though that many formulas contain similar glyphs, like e, or x. Each of these glyphs is (usually) rendered as a *path* in the SVG image. For example, the formula x is described in SVG as:

```
<defs>
  <path d="M3.328 -3.009C3.387 -3.268 3.616 -4.184 ...
    -0.986 2.879 -1.205 2.989 -1.644L3.328 -3.009Z"
    id="g6-120"></path></defs>
<g><use x="88.667" y="61.836" xlink:href="#g6-120"
    xmlns:xlink="http://www.w3.org/1999/xlink">
    </use></g>
```

Here we see how the image places the path element `#g6-120` at a specific position using an `xlink`. The path element though just traces a specific glyph, in this case the x, independently of its position. As the shapes are independent of the position, we can share all the glyph paths between different formulas. Madoko will collect all equivalent paths in a separate definition block and all formulas reference these shared paths. This can lead to significant space savings in practice – in the example article the space usage went down 79% from 2242kb to 467kb.

More significant space savings can be made by not describ-

$$\int_{-\infty}^{\infty} e^{-ax^2} dx = \sqrt{\frac{\pi}{a}} \quad \text{vs.} \quad \int_{-\infty}^{\infty} e^{-ax^2} dx = \sqrt{\frac{\pi}{a}}$$

Figure 2. A browser screenshot of two math SVG images generated by Madoko. The left image used SVG path elements to trace glyphs, while the right image uses direct font elements.

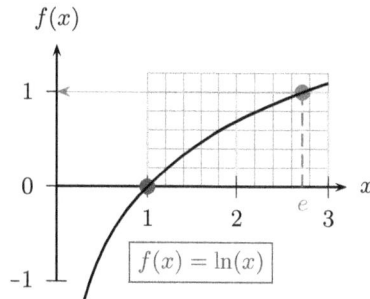

Figure 3. SVG image of a log graph rendered using the `pstricks` and `pst-plot` packages which emit Postscript specials.

ing glyphs with paths at all but using direct font entries and text elements in the SVG description. Unfortunately, font support in SVG is very spotty across browsers and most formulas do not render faithfully when using fonts directly[1]. Figure 2 shows two browser screenshots where one formula is rendered using traces while the other uses font elements.

Rendering of DVI specials
Some LaTeX commands depend on specific output drivers. For example, the advanced TikZ package draws vector graphics using specific PDF primitives which are not directly supported in DVI files. In many cases, we can still extract correct SVG images from the DVI since `dvisvgm` supports many extensions. Ultimately, if that fails Madoko can also generate PNG files from a PDF or Postscript rendering although such image will no longer be scalable. However, currently even large packages like `pstricks` and `TikZ` work with DVI output so in practice this is almost never necessary. Figure 3 shows the SVG output of a log graph using the `pstricks` package which issues Postscript specials.

4. PRE-FORMATTED MATHEMATICS
Mathematics mode in TeX can be surprising in its handling of whitespace and identifiers. In general, whitespace in the text is not relevant and a sequence of letters is *not* seen as a single identifier. Look for example at the following formula:

```
$function sqr( x : int)$
```
$\rightsquigarrow$
$$functionsqr(x : int)$$

We can see that there is no whitespace between `function` and `sqr`, and how they are rendered as a sequence of letters instead of two identifiers; note in particular the whitespace between the `f` and `u` for example.

This behavior may be good for general mathematics, but in many fields, like computer science, this is often cumber-

---
[1]Madoko supports this option though through a metadata flag.

some to program with. To make programming with formulas more direct, Madoko offers a 'pre-formatted math' mode where:

- Whitespace is relevant where every space becomes a small math space (\;),
- An identifier is enclosed in a \mathid command so it gets rendered as *function* (instead of *function*).
- An identifier starting with @ is enclosed in a \mathkw command and rendered as a keyword.
- Digits after an identifier are automatically subscripted where x1 becomes x_1.
- Text that is an argument to \begin, \end, \text*xx*, or \math*xx* commands is kept unchanged.

Using these rules it becomes much easier to use more descriptive names and simple alignment. For example:

```
~ MathPre
@function sqr_\pi( x : int) \{
  @return (x\times x\times\pi);
\}
~
⤳
```

```
function sqr_π( x : int) {
  return (x × x × π);
}
```

Domain specific math
As a final example we look combining existing Madoko features to math. In particular, Madoko extends CSS with a **replace** attribute where one can specify regular expression replacements over the content of a custom block. As an example, we will define a mini domain specific math language for defining natural deduction rules.

First, let's start with some simple replacement rules to make it easier to write type rules. For example, we would like to replace a capital G with Γ, or a plain t with τ. In Madoko we can simply use a CSS style rule with the special **replace** attribute:

```
.mathpre {
  replace: "/\bt\b/\tau{}/g";
  replace: "/\bG\b/\Gamma{}/g";
}
```

Here the \b specifies a word-boundary in the regular expression. The format of each replacer is */regex/replacement/*g, where the **g** flag specifies that the replacer should apply at every match in the content. Another flag is **i** which matches case-insensitive for example. See the reference manual for more information [9].

For natural deductions, we need a more complex regular expression. Let's assume we call our new custom block ~infer, then we can define:

```
infer {
  replace:"/([\s\S]*?)\n *----+ *\[([^\]]*)\] *\n([\s\S]*)/\
           \\infer{\1}{\3}{\textsc{\2}}/m";
  replace:"~Begin MathPre {.infer}&nl;&nl;&source;&nl;\
           ~End MathPre";
}
```

The rule looks somewhat complicated but it is a straightforward regular expression where we first lazily match on any input ([\s\S]*?) until we hit a horizontal line. Once that is matched, we pass the top and bottom part, together with

an optional rule name as arguments to a new LaTeX command that we define ourselves to neatly typeset the inference rule. Combining these replacements (and adding some more), we can now write inference rules in a very natural style in pre-formatted math:

```
~ infer
G      & |- e1 : s | <>
G, x:s & |- e2 : t | eff
------------------------------------[Let]
G |- @let x = e1 @in e2 : t | eff
~
⤳
```

$$\frac{\begin{array}{l}\Gamma \qquad\vdash e_1 : \sigma \,|\, \langle\rangle \\ \Gamma, x:\sigma \;\vdash e_2 : \tau \,|\, \epsilon\end{array}}{\Gamma \vdash \mathsf{let}\, x = e_1 \,\mathsf{in}\, e_2 : \tau \,|\, \epsilon}\; [\text{LET}]$$

Note how close the specification is to how one usually writes such rules in an email or while designing the rules – we can now concisely describe the rules while immediately rendering them nicely.

5. CONCLUSION

Try Madoko at madoko.net. Madoko is still a young project and any feedback is much appreciated. The author would like to thank Martin Gieseking for his help in making **dvisvgm** work well with Madoko.

REFERENCES

[1] Davide Cervone, Volker Sorge, Christian Perfect, and Peter Krautzberger. "MathJax: A Javascript Library for Rendering Mathematics." 2009. https://mathjax.org.

[2] Juliane Franze, Kim Marriott, and Michael Wybrow. "What Academics Want When Reading Digitally." In *DocEng '14*, 199–202. Fort Collins, CO. 2014.

[3] Fabio Giannetti. "Paginate Dynamic and Web Content." In *DocEng '11*, 143–152. Mountain View, California, USA. 2011.

[4] Martin Gieseking. "Dvisvgm: Converting DVI to SVG." 2005. http://dvisvgm.bplaced.net.

[5] John Gruber. "Markdown." 2004. http://daringfireball.net/projects/markdown.

[6] Daan Leijen. "Madoko: A Scholarly Markdown Processor." 2014. http://madoko.codeplex.com.

[7] Daan Leijen. "Madoko: Scholarly Markdown in the Cloud." In *SNAPL'15: The Inaugural Summit on Advances in Programming Languages*. May 2015. http://tinyurl.com/n6k3kht.

[8] Daan Leijen. "Madoko: Scholarly Documents for the Web." In *DocEng 2015, Lausanne, Switzerland*, 129–132. Sep. 2015. doi:10.1145/2682571.2797097. HTML available at: http://tinyurl.com/p4bm62o.

[9] Daan Leijen. "Madoko Reference Manual." http://research.microsoft.com/en-us/um/people/daan/madoko/doc/reference.html.

[10] "Madoko Sample Academic Article." 2015. http://tinyurl.com/madoko-effects.

[11] Simone Marinai. "Reflowing and Annotating Scientific Papers on eBook Readers." In *DocEng '13*, 241–244. Florence, Italy. 2013. doi:10.1145/2494266.2494311.

A PDF Wrapper for Table Processing

Roya Rastan
CSE, Univ. of NSW, Australia
rrastan@cse.unsw.edu.au

Hye-Young Paik
CSE, Univ. of NSW, Australia
hpaik@cse.unsw.edu.au

John Shepherd
CSE, Univ. of NSW, Australia
jas@cse.unsw.edu.au

ABSTRACT

We propose a PDF document wrapper system that is specifically targeted at table processing applications. We (i) review the PDF specifications and identify particular challenges from the table processing point of view, (ii) specify a table-oriented document model containing the required atomic elements for table extraction and understanding applications. Our evaluation showed that the wrapper was able to detect important features such as page columns, bullets and numbering in all measures, recording over 90% accuracy, leading to better table locating and segmenting.

Keywords

Table processing, PDF wrappers, Document model

1. WRAPPING PDF FOR TABLES

We present a PDF wrapper named PDF2TableDoc, whose purpose is to enrich the capability of table processing on PDF documents. Our wrapper helps capture the relevant atomic elements in documents so that it is possible to express every level of description for a table.

For table processing systems, it is common to use an existing text extraction tools, such as XPDF[1] or PDFBOX[2], to obtain the low-level document objects. Then process the output to build a *pre-processor* for further analysis to recognise or extract tables.

There are a few pre-processors in the area, but they tend to ignore some features present in the low-level document objects which could help more effective table processing. The print-oriented nature of PDF leads to serious drawbacks for table processing. For example:

- There is little explicit structural information about the content. This creates difficulties such as table boundary detection [5], distinguishing page columns and table columns [1], multi-line cell detection [2].

---

[1] http://www.foolabs.com/xpdf
[2] http://pdfbox.apache.org/

DocEng'16, September 13–16, 2016, Vienna, Austria.

© 2016 ACM. ISBN 978-1-4503-4438-8/16/09. . . $15.00

DOI: http://dx.doi.org/10.1145/2960811.2967162

- Often the rendering order in a PDF is totally different from the reading order (i.e., its final appearance). Although the lack of standard in rendering order does not affect the PDF document displaying, it heavily impacts the table locating task which relies on relative positions and sequence of text objects in the page [4].
- In many cases formatting and styling could convey information about the logical relationships between the texts. For example, the font style and size for headers are normally different to paragraphs. Bullets are used to show hierarchies. There are aspects in table processing that could benefit from having explicit representation as part of pre-processing.

In PDF2TableDoc, we aim to resolve these issues. For example, we incorporate purposely designed algorithms to detect page columns, logically related text lines, etc. This enhances the performance of the table locating and segmenting tasks. We perform detailed analysis of the styling features to accurately recognise them for future use in the processing pipeline. This improves the accuracy of the functional and structural analysis tasks. The design and implementation of the PDF2TableDoc is underpinned by our own document model suitable for table processing which is introduced in Section 2.1.

2. DESIGN OVERVIEW

This section details the design overview of the wrapper.

2.1 Document Model for Tables

We introduce our document model which becomes the target schema of PDF2TableDoc in terms of extracting *table processing document elements*. To capture the necessary elements to facilitate further table processing, we focus not only on the text content of a PDF document but also on formatting and layout features. Figure 1 shows the hierarchical structure of the elements in our proposed document model. Similar to other tools, *Text Chunks* are the basic elements of the model. To formally define the Text Chunk for our model, we rely on the *Text String* Object introduced in the PDF reference document [3]. We also explicitly represent the features that highly applicable to our table processing pipeline such as font attribute and text styling features.

2.2 Design of the Wrapper

The PDF document content stream lists all of the page objects, such as text, image, and path. Therefore in order to discover the logical components of a PDF document we should analyse and interpret the layouts and attributes of the page objects so as to correctly break or group them into different logical components.

Our design of PDF2TableDoc starts from XPDF which provides the low-level information (characters, words, coordinates, etc.).

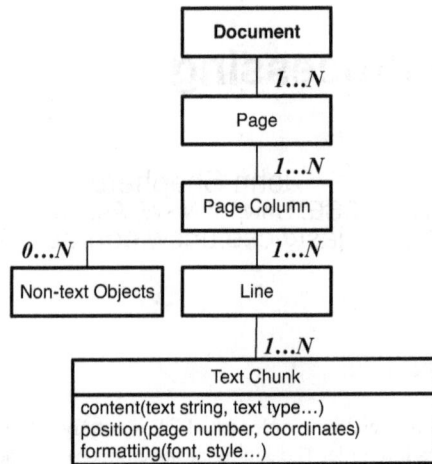

Figure 1: Elements of table-oriented document model

sections between coordinates and the similarity in the font attributes. We consider four positioning of horizontally consequent words in the page to be merged as text chunks as illustrated in Figure 7.

- str_1 is **vertically lower than** str_2 (Fig. 2-a)
- str_1 is **vertically higher than** str_2 (Fig. 2-b)
- str_1 is **entirely contained by** str_2 (Fig. 2-c)
- str_1 **entirely covers** str_2 (Fig. 2-d)

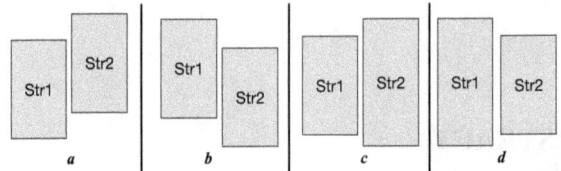

Figure 2: vertical positioning of horizontal consequent words

Since we would like to build our own structure information for table processing, this tool gives enough information as our starting point.

There are two sub modules operating inside `PDF2TableDoc`: `PDFtoXML` and `TableDocWrapper`. The PDF is passed to the `PDFtoXML` module which is implemented using XPDF as the core. XPDF utility reads the document characters along with their state function. `PDFtoXML` then merges characters to detect *Words* and *Text Chunks*. The list of text chunks will be passed to the `TableDocWrapper` module to identify more elements relevant to our document model.

We represent the output of the document converting task in XML format. We chose XML because, if it is utilized correctly, it can be applied to create identical representations of the original documents and also can provide better search-ability and flexibility when analysing documents.

3. IMPLEMENTATION

In this section, we explain the steps undertaken in each sub module of `PDF2TableDoc`. This wrapper is part of our complete table extraction and understanding system named TEXUS [6].

3.1 PDFtoXML

After receiving the document information at individual character level from XPDF, we take the following main steps to present the document at the Text Chunk level.

Step 1: **Word Detection** – We rely on the BBOX information for every character in a PDF file, to form *words*. The algorithm for detecting a word w is in a function called `AddChar()` which receives a Unicode character c, text state, x y coordinates (Top, Left), width and height of c, and the length of c as inputs. First, we actualise the coordinates based on the text state parameters (character space and horizontal spacing) to be able to compare the character coordinates with the *current* w. c is added to w when (i) the character c is in the same direction of the current w, c is horizontally close enough to w and (iii) the distance between w and c is not bigger than a predefined parameter (α). The reason we consider α is that sometimes the horizontal distance between characters is less than a whitespace as noted Ex.1 in Figure 4.

Step 2: **Text Chunk Detection** – The main aim of this step is to merge words represented as text strings based on the inter-

3.2 TableDocWrapper

XPDF reads characters in the raw order and the `PDFtoXML` module merges them to form text chunks, preserving the raw order. However, text sequence error is still a common problem in the existing text extraction tools. This means the extracted text chunks follow a different sequence from its original appearance in PDF documents. In table processing, this type of errors could lead to splitting a single table into several pieces, recognising wrong columns/rows, and omitting cells or missing a whole table.

The main task of `TableDocWrapper` module is to go through the text chunks produced by `PDFtoXML` and analyse/detect the relevant elements of the target document model. It consists of the following sub tasks.

Sub Task 1: Related Text Merging – One of the common features in tables is the existence of *multi-line* where multiple text chunks that appear in different lines form a logical single table cell. We detect these cases before sorting the text chunks based on the coordinates in the page.

We consider each text chunk as a rectangular object represented by its four coordinates attributes and font specifications. Every vertically consequent text chunk which is in the close top distance from the page is compared to see whether there is any horizontal intersection between them or not. Figure 3 shows different scenarios of horizontal intersections between text chunks and how the merged text chunks are actualised. In order to make the merge more accurate, we check if the text chunks share the same font and also the same alignment.

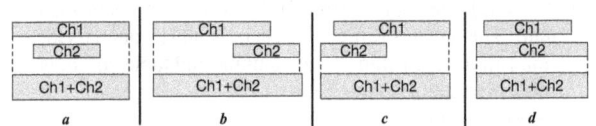

Figure 3: Different interval intersection to merge text chunks

Sub Task 2: Page Column Detection – In this task, we mark page columns. Since the text chunks are created in the raw order, the texts in a page column are supposed to appear sequentially (in reading order). The start of a new page column can be detected by a large decrease (bigger than a predefined threshold α) in the `Top` value in the following text chunks. For all text chunks in the page, we compare the top difference between two consequent text chunks and if the decrease in the distance between them is more than α we add a new column to the page.

Sub Task 3: Line Detection – After detecting the page columns, we mark lines in each column. The main idea of the line formation is to consider the text chunks in the same top distance in each page column belong to the same line. The algorithm for this task takes a page column and a predefined threshold parameter (β) to check the top distance of the text chunks in the page column. Since we have text chunks in raw order and also we have merged some text chunks in `Related Text Merging` (introduced new coordinates for the merged text chunks) we need to sort the text chunks first based on the `Top` and then `Left` attributes. Starting from the first text chunk in the page column if the vertical distance of the following text chunk and the former text chunk is bigger than a threshold, it indicates the start of a new line.

Sub Task 4: Bullet Detection – Most of the current PDF wrappers are unable to detect the detailed formatting of the text elements in the PDF file, such as bullets or numbered text elements. Since these formatting information can convey important hints about hierarchical structure of the content it is useful to properly recognise them in a table processing system [8, 7]. In this task, we examine the text chunks to determine if the first character corresponds to Hexadecimal number belonging to the list of bullets or numbered text patterns.

4. EVALUATION

For the evaluation of `PDF2TableDoc`, we used the well-known corpus in the community which is introduced in the 2013 table competition at ICDAR[3]. It contains 67 PDF documents with 156 tables. The ground-truth is provided for locating and segmenting tasks with the corpus.

We present two scenarios for the evaluation in the following sub-sections.

4.1 PDFtoXML

First, we compare the functionality of our core module `PDFtoXML` with a similar, open system `PDFtoHTML`[4]. `PDFtoHTML` is a utility which is also developed based on XPDF and can be configured to create XML output and list text chunks from PDF documents along with their coordinates.

To compare the performance of the two utilities we run our `TableDocWrapper` module with the outputs from `PDFtoXML`, and also with the outputs from `PDFtoHTML`. In each run, we then feed the output of `TableDocWrapper` to our table extraction system to locate and segment tables. We then compare the locating and segmenting results of each run with the ground-truth.

Here, we are able to compare the performance of `PDFtoXML` and `PDFtoHTML` on their ability to accurately extract the text chunks, as more accurate extraction of text chunks leads to more accurate extraction of the final document model by `TableDocWrapper`.

Table 1 shows the evaluation results. We have compared the performance of two runs by utilising two measures:

- *Completeness* and *Purity*, measured for the whole document set (total number of tables 156). A table is considered as *completely* extracted if it includes all cells in the table region; and a detected table is called *pure* if it does not include any cells which are not in the table region. A correctly detected table is therefore both complete and pure [9].

- *Recall* and *Precision*, measured specifically for the unsuccessful cases and reported in a cell-by-cell comparison with the ground-truth.

---

[3]http://www.tamirhassan.com/dataset
[4]https://sourceforge.net/projects/pdftohtml

Table 1: `PDFtoXML` and `PDFtoHTML` performance comparison

Utility	Per-document average			Whole DocSet #Tables=156	
	Recall	Prec.	F-meas.	Complete	Pure
PDFtoXML	0.9971	0.9729	0.9848	142	148
PDFtoHTML	0.9644	0.9569	0.9606	138	130

Our own detailed study of the results showed that the main improvements obtained by `PDF2XML` is from how the gap analysis between characters is done during the word detection phase. `PDFtoHTML` seems to simply rely on a whitespace character to decide whether to merge characters or not. We check the size of the gap as well as the existence of the whitespace character. If the size is more than a threshold we do not merge characters into one words.

Figure 4 shows some tables that `PDFtoHTML` fails to detect as separate text chunks and merge them as one text chunk because of the small horizontal distance between them (marked by dotted lines).

Figure 4: Examples where `PDF2HTML` failed due to insufficient gap analysis

4.2 TableDocWrapper

In order to evaluate the performance of the TableDocWrapper module, we categorise the documents in the corpus based on the key elements according to the document model (e.g., page columns, bullets, numbering) and then investigate the accuracy of the output at the detected element level. We compare the result with the ground truth documents reviewed and validated by two experts. Table 2 reports on the accuracy of *page column* and *bullet/numbering* detection as well as *related text merge*. The results are calculated per document and then the overall performance is shown by the average on the whole documents. Table 2 shows the results.

The system has 100% accuracy in detecting bullets and numbering in the documents. Particularly, it successfully recognised a bullet point applied on a merged text chunk. Figure 5 shows one example of this.

The system generally performed well in detecting page columns. However in some cases, such as floating tables, the system reports false positive page columns. As shown in Figure 6, the floating

117

Percent	Mean Loss	Fraction of Wealth Lost
75.2	12196	17.4%
11.6	23518	22.5%

Figure 7: Failed to correctly merge related text

Table 2: TableDocWrapper Performance Evaluation

Element Type	Recall	Prec.	F-meas.
Merged text	0.91	0.95	0.93
Bullet and Numbering	1	1	1
Page Column	1	0.92	0.96

Reliability	Test-retest or intra-interviewer reliability (for interviewer-administered PROs only)	Stability of scores over time when no change is expected in the concept of interest
	Internal consistency	• Extent to which items comprising a scale measure the same concept • Intercorrelation of items that contribute to a score

Figure 5: Correct bullet detection for merged text

table on the right caused the system to treat the page as a two-column page.

The majority of the enrolled students in the fall of 2006 attended larger colleges and universities. Specifically, campuses boasting enrollment levels of 10,000 students or more represented only 12 percent of the institutions; however, they enrolled 55 percent of all college students.[14] By comparison, 41 percent of the institutions had enrollment levels of less than 1,000 students, and these institutions enrolled only 4 percent of all college students.	Table 1: Student Enrollment, by Age Group, Fall 2006

Table 1: Student Enrollment, by Age Group, Fall 2006

Age	Enrollment	%
14-17	231,000	1.3
18-19	3,769,000	21.2
20-21	3,648,000	20.5
22-24	3,193,000	18.0

Figure 6: Incorrectly detected page column

For related text merging, the system achieved over 90% performance in all three measures. However, cases with irregular styling and spacing between text chunks result in poor performance. As can be seen in Figure 7, there is a vertical spacing between "Fraction of" and "Wealth Lost" which was slightly larger than the *vertical closeness threshold* and the chunks were not merged.

5. CONCLUSION

In this paper we presented PDF2TableDoc a PDF wrapper designed for table processing applications. We reviewed the specific challenges and issues for wrapping PDF with the focus on table extraction and understanding. We then presented the document model that captures (i) logical groups of objects such as page columns and lines, (ii) more complete text chunk metadata such as styling features (e.g., bullets, numbering) and (iii) merged text chunks for better recognition of table cells. We also presented the implementation of the PDF2TableDoc to produce the model. Our evaluation showed that using the PDFtoXML module resulted in better table locating and segmenting, compared to using PDFtoHTML. The TableDocWrapper module was able to detect important features such as page columns, bullets and numbering in all measures, recording over 90% accuracy.

This PDF wrapping approach underpinned by our model helps focus the task of the pre-processor on producing features that are most useful for table processing.

6. REFERENCES

[1] Jing Fang, Liangcai Gao, Kun Bai, Ruiheng Qiu, Xin Tao, and Zhi Tang. A table detection method for multipage PDF documents via visual seperators and tabular structures. In *Document Analysis and Recognition (ICDAR)*, pages 779–783. IEEE, 2011.

[2] Jing Fang, Prasenjit Mitra, Zhi Tang, and C Lee Giles. Table header detection and classification. In *AAAI*, 2012.

[3] Adobe Systems Incorporated. PDF reference. Technical Report Version 1.7, Novemeber 2006.

[4] Ying Liu, Kun Bai, Prasenjit Mitra, and C Lee Giles. Improving the table boundary detection in pdfs by fixing the sequence error of the sparse lines. In *Document Analysis and Recognition (ICDAR)*, pages 1006–1010. IEEE, 2009.

[5] Ermelinda Oro and Massimo Ruffolo. PDF-TREX: An approach for recognizing and extracting tables from pdf documents. In *Document Analysis and Recognition (ICDAR)*, pages 906–910. IEEE, 2009.

[6] Roya Rastan, Hye-Young Paik, and John Shepherd. Texus: A task-based approach for table extraction and understanding. In *Symposium on Document Engineering*, pages 25–34. ACM, 2015.

[7] Roya Rastan, Hye-Young Paik, John Shepherd, and Armin Haller. Automated table understanding using stub patterns. In *Database Systems for Advanced Applications*, pages 533–548. Springer, 2016.

[8] Sachin Seth and George Nagy. Segmenting tables via indexing of value cells by table headers. In *Document Analysis and Recognition (ICDAR)*, pages 887–891. IEEE, 2013.

[9] Ana Costa E Silva. New metrics for evaluating performance in document analysis tasks application to the table case. In *Document Analysis and Recognition (ICDAR)*, pages 481–485. IEEE, 2007.

Configurable Table Structure Recognition in Untagged PDF documents

Alexey Shigarov
Matrosov Institute for System
Dynamics and Control Theory
of SB RAS
134 Lermontov st.
Irkutsk, Russia
shigarov@icc.ru

Andrey Mikhailov
Matrosov Institute for System
Dynamics and Control Theory
of SB RAS
134 Lermontov st.
Irkutsk, Russia
mikhailov@icc.ru

Andrey Altaev
Matrosov Institute for System
Dynamics and Control Theory
of SB RAS
134 Lermontov st.
Irkutsk, Russia
altaev@icc.ru

ABSTRACT

Today, PDF is one of the most popular document formats in the web. Many PDF documents are not images, but remain untagged. They have no tags for identifying the logical reading order, paragraphs, figures, and tables. One of the challenges with these documents is how to extract tables from them. The paper discusses a new system for table structure recognition in untagged PDF documents. It is formulated as a set of configurable parameters and ad-hoc heuristics for recovering table cells. We consider two different configurations for the system and demonstrate experimental results based on the existing competition dataset for both of them.

CCS Concepts

•**Applied computing** → **Document analysis;** *Document management and text processing;*

Keywords

table extraction, table structure recognition, untagged PDF documents, PDF document analysis, PDF accessibility

1. INTRODUCTION

Today, PDF is one of the most popular document formats in the web as can be measured by Google's "filetype:pdf" search. Many PDF documents are not images, but remain untagged. They have no tags for identifying the logical reading order, paragraphs, figures and tables. Nganji [4] estimates that 95.5% of scientific articles published by four leading publishers are untagged PDF documents. One of the important challenges with these documents is how to extract tables from them.

Table extraction typically consists of two main steps: *table detection*, i. e. recovering the bounding box of a table in a document, and *table structure recognition*, i. e. recovering its rows, columns, and cells. Many of existing methods for extracting tables from unstructured documents traditionally deal with only images or plaintext as source. They are considered in several surveys, including [1,

DocEng '16, September 12-16, 2016, Vienna, Austria
© 2016 ACM. ISBN 978-1-4503-4438-8/16/09. . . $15.00
DOI: http://dx.doi.org/10.1145/2960811.2967152

2]. These methods can be applied to PDF documents through converting PDF to these formats. However, this process leads to the loss of valuable information. Table extraction from PDF directly can provide better results. PDF is a richer representation of documents in comparison with images and plain-text. PDF documents can contain machine-readable text (text chunks with their positions, font characteristics, and order of appearance in a file), as well as vector graphics including table rulings. We expect that these features can allow to extract tables more accurately.

Several methods and tools for PDF table extraction are proposed in two last decades. Some of them are discussed in the surveys [1, 6, 7]. Ramel et al. [11] consider two techniques for detecting and recognizing tables from documents in an exchange format like PDF. The first is based on the analysis of ruling lines. The second is to analyze the arrangement of text components. Hassan et al. [5] expand these ideas for PDF table extraction. In the project TableSeer, Liu et al. [8] propose methods for detecting tables in PDF documents and extracting metadata (headers). They use text arrangement, fonts, whitespace, and keywords (e. g. "Table", "Figure"). Oro et al. [10] present PDF-TREX, a heuristic method where PDF table extraction is realized as building from content elements to tables in bottom-up way.

Yildiz et al. [15] propose a heuristic method for PDF table extraction using the 'pdftohtml'[1] tool for generating its input. Rastan et al. [12] consider a framework for the end-to-end table processing including the task of table structure recognition. They also use the 'pdftohtml' tool to prepare their input. However, this tool occasionally makes mistakes in combining text chunks, which are located too close to each other, thus the input can be corrupted. Nurminen [9] in his thesis describes comprehensive PDF table detection and structure recognition algorithms that have demonstrated high recall and precision on "ICDAR 2013 Table Competition" [4]. Some of them are implemented in Tabula[2] system.

In contrast to the existing methods, we suggest a configurable system that is formulated as a set of customizable parameters and ad-hoc heuristics for recovering table cells from text chunks and rulings. We exploit features of table presentations in untagged PDF documents. Most of them such as horizontal and vertical distances, fonts, and rulings are well known and used in the existing methods. Additionally, we propose to exploit the feature of appearance of text printing instruction in PDF files.

Usually, when a table printed in a PDF document originally was an object (e.g. a table in a Word-document) then 1) one printing instruction forms a part or a whole of textual content of only one

---

[1]http://pdftohtml.sourceforge.net
[2]http://tabula.technology

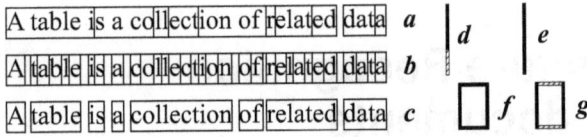

Figure 1: Preprocessing of text chunks (*a–c*) and rulings (*d–g*).

physical cell; 2) printing instructions forming a text inside each physical cell appear in the PDF file in the order that coincides with the human reading order of this text. We notice that it is true for many PDF generators. This feature can be especially useful in case of multi-row cells in table heads without rulings.

We also consider two configurations for the system and demonstrate experimental results based on the existing competition dataset, "ICDAR 2013 Table Competition", for both of them.

2. TABLE STRUCTURE RECOGNITION

We present the process of table structure recognition as three consecutive steps:

1. *preprocessing*: generating and preparing text chunks and rulings from a source document;

2. *text block recovering*: combining text chunks into text blocks;

3. *cell recovering*: dividing table space into rows, columns, and cells via text blocks.

2.1 Preprocessing

We operate two kind of objects: *text chunks* and *rulings*. A *text chunk* is defined as $c = (b, f, o, w)$, where

- $b = (x_l, y_t, x_r, y_b)$ — bonding box with four coordinates: $x_l = x_l(c)$ — left, $y_t = y_t(c)$ — top, $x_r = x_r(c)$ — right, and $y_b = y_b(c)$ — bottom, $x_l, y_t, x_r, y_b \in \mathbb{R}$, the x-coordinate increases from left to right, and y-coordinate increases from top to bottom;

- $f = (f_f, f_s, f_b, f_i)$ — font with the attributes: $f_f = f_f(c)$ — family (string value), $f_s = f_s(c)$ — size in points, $f_b = f_b(c)$: $f_b \in \{\text{true, false}\}$ — bold or not, $f_i = f_i(c)$: $f_i \in \{\text{true, false}\}$ — italic or not;

- $o = o(c) : o \in \mathbb{N}$ — index number in the order of the appearance of text chunks in the source PDF file.

- $w = w(c) : w \in \mathbb{R}$ — space width.

Initially each text chunk corresponds to one instruction of text printing. The same text can be presented in PDF by different printing instructions, depending on the used PDF generator, as shown in Fig. 1, *a–c*. At first, we split all text chunks (Fig. 1, *a*) into one-character chunks (Fig. 1, *b*) and merge them into word chunks with removing space characters and reindexing the order of their appearance (Fig. 1, *c*).

On this stage our system enables applying two ad-hoc heuristics for eliminating some kinds of "insular" text chunks from the further processing:

- H_1, *eliminating itemization text chunks*: if a text chunk contains only one character marking itemized lists (e.g. bullet, square), then it is excluded;

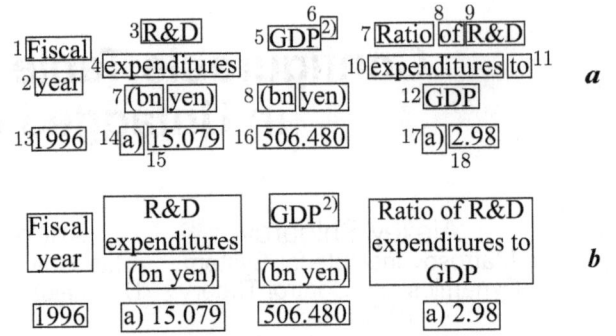

Figure 2: Text chunks and the order of their appearance (*a*), and text blocks constructed from them (*b*).

- H_2, *eliminating padding text chunks*: if a text chunk consists only of a series of padding characters (e.g. series of dots), then it is excluded.

Often, the two kinds of text chunks are visually detached from the rest of text chunks by long spaces. This lead to improperly recovered columns. Thus, eliminating them, we try to prevent some errors.

A *ruling* is defined as a bonding box with four coordinates: $r = (x_l, x_r, y_t, y_b)$. Visual rulings can be originally presented by printing instructions for lines and rectangles. We merge all segments of one visual line (Fig. 1, *d*) into one ruling (Fig. 1, *e*). We also split each rectangle (Fig. 1, *f*) into four rulings corresponding to its boundaries (Fig. 1, *g*).

2.2 Text Block Recovering

We define a *text block* as a set of chunks. On this step all text chunks are combined into blocks (Fig. 2). One chunk can be included only in one text block.

Text chunks are handled in pairs. We make a decision for each pair of chunks: to combine them or not. Two text chunks can be combined into one block when they satisfy the following conditions, in case of horizontal combining:

- P_1, *word spacing*: the horizontal distance between the chunks is less than a configurable threshold;

- P_2, *vertical projections*: there is a configurable intersection of their vertical projections;

or in case of vertical combining:

- P_3, *line spacing*: the vertical distance between the chunks is less than a configurable threshold;

- P_4, *horizontal projections*: there is a configurable intersection of their horizontal projections.

Moreover, a configuration can specify that two combining chunks c_1 and c_2 have to satisfy some or all of the ad-hoc heuristics listed below:

- H_3, *adjacency in the order of the appearance*: they are adjacent in the order of their appearance in the source PDF file, $o(c_1) = o(c_2) + 1$;

- H_4, *no rulings in text blocks*: there are no rulings in the rectangle between the chunks defined as

$$b(c_1, c_2) = \big(x_l(c_1, c_2), y_t(c_1, c_2), x_r(c_1, c_2), y_b(c_1, c_2)\big),$$

where

120

- $x_l(c_1, c_2) = \min\left(x_l(c_1), x_l(c_2)\right)$,
- $y_t(c_1, c_2) = \min\left(y_t(c_1), y_t(c_2)\right)$,
- $x_r(c_1, c_2) = \max\left(x_r(c_1), x_r(c_2)\right)$,
- $y_b(c_1, c_2) = \max\left(y_b(c_1), y_b(c_2)\right)$;

- H_5, *identical font family*: $f_f(c_1) = f_f(c_2)$;

- H_6, *identical font size*: $f_s(c_1) = f_s(c_2)$;

- H_7, *identical font bold attribute*: $f_b(c_1) = f_b(c_2)$;

- H_8, *identical font italic attribute*: $f_i(c_1) = f_i(c_2)$.

We suppose that each text block is a textual content of one cell, and each non-empty cell contains only one block. Thus, we try to recover non-empty cells without their arrangement in rows and columns.

2.3 Cell Recovering

In this step we construct rows and columns that constitute an arrangement of cells. The system provides two algorithms for slicing a table space into rows and columns. A configuration can use one of them.

The first (A_1) is based on the whitespace analysis. We use the algorithm [14] to recover horizontal and vertical gaps between text blocks. Each whitespace gap corresponds to a ruling. Thus, we try to recover all rulings, which separate cells in a table.

The second (A_2) is the analysis of connected text blocks. To generate columns, we first exclude each multi-column text block located in more than one column. We decide that a text block is multi-column when its horizontal projection intersects with the projections of two or more text blocks located in the same line. Each column is considered as an intersection of horizontal projections of one-column text blocks. Similarly, rows are constructed from vertical projections of one-row text blocks.

In this step we also recover empty cells. Some of them can be erroneous, i.e. they absent in the source table. The system provides the ad-hoc heuristic to dispose of erroneous empty cells:

- H_9, *cell singleton*: if a column contains only one non-empty cell then the column is merged with the nearest column to the left.

3. TWO CONFIGURATIONS

In the paper, we consider two configurations for our system. The main difference between them consists in estimation of word (P_1) and line (P_3) spacing, as well as used algorithm for cell construction.

The first C_1-configuration is the following settings:

- P_1, word spacing: $s_w = w * k_w$ where w is a space width of the left chunk, and k_w: $k_w \in \mathbb{R}$, $k_w > 0$ is a width factor;

- P_2, vertical projections: $y_t(c_1) \leq y_t(c_2) \leq y_b(c_1)$ or $y_t(c_1) \leq y_b(c_2) \leq y_b(c_1)$.

- P_3, line spacing: $s_l = h * k_h$, where h is a height of the upper chunk, and k_h: $k_h > 0$ is a height factor;

- P_4, horizontal projections: $x_l(c_1) \leq x_l(c_2) \leq x_r(c_2)$ or $x_l(c_1) \leq x_r(c_2) \leq x_r(c_2)$.

- Cell constructing: A_1-algorithm (whitespace analysis).

- Ad-hoc heuristics: H_1, H_3–H_9;

- Default values: $k_w = 1$ and $k_h = 1$.

The second C_2-configuration consists of the following settings:

- P_1, word spacing:

$$s_w = \begin{cases} w, & \text{if } w_{min} < |d| \leq w_{max} \\ w_{min}, & \text{if } |d| \leq w_{min} \\ w * k_w, & \text{otherwise}; \end{cases}$$

where w is a space width of the left chunk, k_w: $0 < k < 1$ is a width factor, d is the horizontal distance between the chunks, w_{min}: $t_1 \in \mathbb{R}$, $w_{min} > 0$ is a threshold (the minimum width of a space), w_{max}: $w_{max} \in \mathbb{R}$, $w_{max} > w_{min}$ is a threshold (the maximum width of the space);

- P_2, vertical projections: $y_b(c_1) = y_b(c_2)$;

- P_3, line spacing: $s_l = t_2$: $t_2 \in \mathbb{R}$, $t_2 > 0$ is a threshold;

- P_4, horizontal projections: $x_l(c_1) \leq x_l(c_2) \leq x_r(c_2)$ or $x_l(c_1) \leq x_r(c_2) \leq x_r(c_2)$;

- Cell constructing: A_2-algorithm (connected text block analysis);

- Ad-hoc heuristics: H_1–H_8;

- Default values: $k_w = 0.5$, $w_{min} = 4$, and $w_{max} = 56$.

4. EXPERIMENTAL EVALUATION

To evaluate both configurations we use the methodology for algorithms for table understanding in PDF documents proposed in the paper [3]. We also use the existing competition dataset[3], "ICDAR 2013 Table Competition" [4]. It contains 156 tables in 67 PDF documents collected from EU and US government websites.

The evaluated prototype of our system uses the iText[4] library for PDF interpretation to extract PDF objects from source documents and to generate the text chunks and rulings. In the evaluation, the parameters for both configurations have been set up by default values without searching for their optimal values. The experimental results are shown in Table 1. The highest F-score reaches more than 0.93.

Note that the evaluation was performed automatically using Nurminen's Python scripts[5] for comparing ground-truth and result files that implement this methodology with slight modifications. Therefore our results shown in Table 1 should not be matched directly with others demonstrated on "ICDAR 2013 Table Competition". Nevertheless, we can declare that the experimental results show the high performance of our system on the recognized dataset of PDF tables.

Table 1: Experimental results

Configuration	C_1	C_2
recall	0.9121	0.9233
precision	0.9180	0.9499
F-score	0.9150	0.9364

Moreover, we can improve F-score via setting optimal values for the configuration parameters. In both configurations, the numeric thresholds and factors can be set as the result of searching for maximum of F-score on a target dataset. For example, we have searched

---

[3]http://www.tamirhassan.com/dataset.html
[4]https://sourceforge.net/projects/itext
[5]http://tamirhassan.com/competition/dataset-tools.html

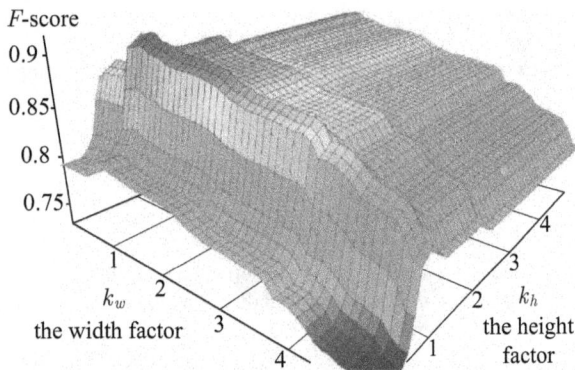

Figure 3: Searching for factor values to maximize F-score in C_1-configuration.

for the maximum of F-score as the function of two variables (the width and height factors) in the C_1-configuration on the competition dataset "ICDAR 2013 Table Competition" (Fig. 3). We have evaluated 2500 tests, where both k_w and k_h have increased from 0 to 5 with the step 0.1. The F-score have reached the maximum (0.9189) when the width factor k_w is 0.9 and the height factor is 1.0.

5. CONCLUSION AND FURTHER WORK

Unlike the existing solutions, our system enables the advanced configuration options which allow to adapt it to different sources. We have formulated a set of valuable ad-hoc heuristics that can be enhanced in the future. It is important to note, that it was for the first time, that we have examined the possibility of applying the order of the appearance of text chunks in PDF files for table structure recognition.

The main applications of our system are in the field of data accessibility, information extraction, and unstructured data integration. Particularly, we develop an experimental web-application[6] for PDF table extraction based on the prototype of our system. In the current state, this tool enables only manual table selection in a page of a PDF document and automatic table structure recognition. As the result of this process, an extracted table is accessible in the editable format, HTML or spreadsheet, that can be used as input in our rule-based spreadsheet data canonicalization system[7] for further transforming data from arbitrary tables to relational ones [13].

The further work is in progress on expanding the set of ad-hoc heuristics. We believe the involvement of the additional features such as text alignment, superscript, and subscript will allow to improve our system. We also expect an advancement in the preprocessing step for excluding "messy" rulings, which originate from underlined or striked text. In the future, our system also can be extended for supporting automatic PDF table detection.

6. ACKNOWLEDGMENTS

We thank Tamir Hassan for the detailed discussion and explanation of the methodology for evaluating algorithms for table understanding in PDF documents [3] in the part of table structure recognition. We also thank Anssi Nurminen for providing his Python scripts, which have allowed us to automate the evaluation process.

This work was financially supported by the Russian Foundation for Basic Research (grants 15-37-20042, 14-07-00166) and Council for Grants of the President of Russian Federation (grant NSh-8081.2016.9). Our web-application for PDF table extraction is performed on resources of the Shared Equipment Center of Integrated Information and Computing Network for Irkutsk Research and Educational Complex[8].

7. REFERENCES

[1] B. Coüasnon and A. Lemaitre. *Handbook of Document Image Processing and Recognition*, chapter Recognition of Tables and Forms, pages 647–677. Springer London, 2014.

[2] A. C. e Silva, A. M. Jorge, and L. Torgo. Design of an end-to-end method to extract information from tables. *International Journal of Document Analysis and Recognition (IJDAR)*, 8(2):144–171, 2006.

[3] M. Göbel, T. Hassan, E. Oro, and G. Orsi. A methodology for evaluating algorithms for table understanding in PDF documents. In *Proc. of the 2012 ACM Symposium on Document Engineering*, pages 45–48, New York, NY, USA, 2012.

[4] M. Göbel, T. Hassan, E. Oro, and G. Orsi. ICDAR 2013 table competition. In *Proc. of the 12th Int. Conf. on Document Analysis and Recognition*, pages 1449–1453, 2013.

[5] T. Hassan and R. Baumgartner. Table recognition and understanding from PDF files. In *Proc. of the 9th Int. Conf. on Document Analysis and Recognition - Volume 02*, pages 1143–1147, Washington, DC, USA, 2007. IEEE Comp. Soc.

[6] J. Hu and Y. Liu. *Analysis of Documents Born Digital*, pages 775–804. Springer London, London, 2014.

[7] S. Khusro, A. Latif, and I. Ullah. On methods and tools of table detection, extraction and annotation in PDF documents. *J. Inf. Sci.*, 41(1):41–57, Feb. 2015.

[8] Y. Liu, K. Bai, P. Mitra, and C. L. Giles. TableSeer: Automatic table metadata extraction and searching in digital libraries. In *Proc. of the 7th ACM/IEEE Joint Conf. on Digital Libraries*, pages 91–100, 2007.

[9] A. Nurminen. Algorithmic extraction of data in tables in PDF documents. Master's thesis, Tampere University of Technology, Tampere, Finland, 2013.

[10] E. Oro and M. Ruffolo. PDF-TREX: An approach for recognizing and extracting tables from PDF documents. In *Proc. of the 10th Int. Conf. on Document Analysis and Recognition*, pages 906–910, 2009.

[11] J. Y. Ramel, M. Crucianu, N. Vincent, and C. Faure. Detection, extraction and representation of tables. In *Proc. of the 7th Int. Conf. on Document Analysis and Recognition*, pages 374–378 vol.1, 2003.

[12] R. Rastan, H.-Y. Paik, and J. Shepherd. Texus: A task-based approach for table extraction and understanding. In *Proc. of the 2015 ACM Symposium on Document Engineering*, pages 25–34, 2015.

[13] A. Shigarov. Table understanding using a rule engine. *Expert Systems with Applications*, 42(2):929–937, 2015.

[14] A. Shigarov and R. Fedorov. Simple algorithm page layout analysis. *Pattern Recognition and Image Analysis*, 21(2):324–327, 2011.

[15] B. Yildiz, K. Kaiser, and S. Miksch. pdf2table: A method to extract table information from PDF files. In *Proc. of the 2nd Indian Int. Conf. on Artificial Intelligence, Pune, India*, pages 1773–1785, 2005.

---

[6]available at http://cells.icc.ru/pdfte
[7]available at http://cells.icc.ru/ssdc

[8]http://net.isc.irk.ru

Extending Data Models by Declaratively Specifying Contextual Knowledge

Tobias Gradl
Media Informatics Group
University of Bamberg
96047 Bamberg, Germany
tobias.gradl@uni-bamberg.de

Andreas Henrich
Media Informatics Group
University of Bamberg
96047 Bamberg, Germany
andreas.henrich@uni-bamberg.de

ABSTRACT

The research data landscape of the arts and humanities is characterized by a high degree of heterogeneity. To improve interoperability, recent initiatives and research infrastructures are encouraging the use of standards and best practices. However, custom data models are often considered necessary to exactly reflect the requirements of a particular collection or research project.

To address the needs of scholars in the arts and humanities for a composition of research data irrespective of the degree of structuredness and standardization, we propose a concept on the basis of formal languages, which facilitates declarative data modeling by respective domain experts. By identifying and defining grammatical patterns and deriving transformation functions, the structure of data is generated or extended in accordance with the particular context and needs of the domain.

Keywords

Digital humanities; descriptive data modeling; language applications; DARIAH

1. INTRODUCTION

Digital collections of the arts and humanities—like the traditional forms of museums, archives or libraries—provide access to various types of research objects. As either originally digital or digitalized resources, they can be preserved and—if tolerant licenses are chosen and technical infrastructure is available—provided to a greater and potentially distributed public. If digital objects are encapsulated or referenced by metadata, the application of quantitative methods to support qualitative research is further facilitated. Despite the ongoing trend towards the development of standards and best practices for the digitization and description of research data within the arts and humanities, recent studies indicate a hesitant or practically non-existent adaption of standards–other than that of simple Dublin Core (DC) [6, 7]. As a result of the instantiated research infrastructures such as Europeana, DARIAH or CLARIN, standards might increasingly be favored over the definition of custom data models. However, the use and publication

DocEng '16, September 12 - 16, 2016, Vienna, Austria
© 2016 Copyright held by the owner/author(s). Publication rights licensed to ACM.
ISBN 978-1-4503-4438-8/16/09. . . $15.00
DOI: http://dx.doi.org/10.1145/2960811.2967147

of data conforming to custom or legacy data models can be expected to persist as (1) the funding required to restructure data in the collections might not be available, (2) information might expected to be lost when transforming existing data or (3)—even for new digitization projects—a standard that exactly matches the demands might not exist and the collection choses a custom design.

In this paper we present an approach that allows experts within the digital humanities to declaratively model original data—irrespective of the degree of structuredness and standardization. The novelty of our approach consists in the language theoretical foundation of this modeling task, which results in data description facilities that are (1) expressive enough to incorporate the complex models required for scholarly research and (2) reduce technical overhead—allowing domain experts to focus on the semantic aspects of data modeling.

This paper is structured as follows: In section 2 we will introduce two examples that illustrate the types of data our approach is focused on. Section 3 will present a formal foundation of data models into which *labeling functions*—the central element of our approach—are incorporated. After detailing the composition of such functions and providing an overview over the behavior of the implemented framework, we conclude this paper with section 4 and a brief reflection of a research-oriented application that has been implemented on the basis of our framework.

2. CONTEXT

Ultimately, our goal is to provide capabilities for domain experts of the arts and humanities to describe data within its context. By explicating their contextual knowledge, they are enabled to extend and enrich original data. Due to the diversity of the domain, its research questions and data, we developed a concept that abstracts semantic aspects of data modeling from technical problems [1]. The main intention is to allow experts within a specific discipline or collection to focus on those aspects of data processing, which require their domain expertise. Technical problems of data access, decoding, processing or integration are solved in a generic, reusable fashion.

Structured data. As an example of data that is often provided by digital collections, consider the excerpt of a simple DC metadata record taken from the PANGAEA (Data Publisher for Earth & Environmental Science)[1] database. With respect to *atomicity*, the structural decomposition of each element seems obvious and would enhance the structure of the document. Although metadata facilitates access to information, the described digital resource might be particularly relevant for answering research questions. Our concept

---

[1] https://pangaea.de/

is intended to be applicable for modeling structural elements within unstructured text—allowing the domain-driven enrichment of such data.

```
<oai_dc:dc>
  <dc:creator>Grobe, Hannes</dc:creator>
  <dc:date>1996-02-29</dc:date>
  <dc:format>text/tab-separated-values, 1148 data points<
      /dc:format>
  <dc:language>en</dc:language>
  <dc:coverage>LATITUDE: 68.556667 * LONGITUDE:
      -21.210000 * DATE/TIME START: 1994-09-19T14:56:00
      * DATE/TIME END: 1994-09-19T14:56:00 * MINIMUM
      DEPTH, sediment/rock: 0.0 m * MAXIMUM DEPTH,
      sediment/rock: 11.5 m</dc:coverage>
  <dc:subject>ARK-X/2; AWI_Paleo; Denmark Strait; Gravity
      corer (Kiel type); Ice rafted debris; IRD-
      Counting (Grobe, 1987); Paleoenvironmental
      Reconstructions from Marine Sediments @ AWI;
      Polarstern; PS2646-5; PS31; PS31/162</dc:subject>
</oai_dc:dc>
```

Listing 1: Pangaea DC example

Unstructured data. Listing 2 shows the first few lines of the wikipedia article on Gustave le Bon. The document is composed of a mixture of structured and unstructured elements as the document itself conforms to the Extensible Markup Language (XML) and the MediaWiki export schema and the content of the *text* element conforms to Wiki markup. As such, the unstructured text of the article is complemented with structural components such as headings and links.

```
<page xmlns="http://www.medi...export-0.9/">
  <title>Gustave Le Bon</title>
  <ns>0</ns>
  <id>104619</id>
  <revision>
    <id>135522322</id>
    <parentid>135491542</parentid>
    <timestamp>2014-11-04T17:40:26Z</timestamp>
    <contributor>
      <ip>146.52.78.48</ip>
    </contributor>
    <comment>/* Der Rassebegriff bei Le Bon */</comment>
    <text xml:space="preserve">[[Datei:Gustave Le Bon.jpg
        |thumb|Gustave Le Bon im [[fin de siècle]]]] '''
        Gustave Le Bon''' (* [[7. Mai]] [[1841]] in [[
        Nogent-le-Rotrou]]; âĂă [[15. Dezember]]
        [[1931]] in [[Paris]]) gilt als Begründer der [[
        Massenpsychologie]]. Seine Wirkung auf die
        Nachwelt, wissenschaftlich auf [[Sigmund Freud]]
        und [[Max Weber]], politisch insbesondere auf
        den [[Nationalsozialismus]] und seine   ...
```

Listing 2: Wikipedia example

3. DATA MODELING

3.1 Perspectives on data

Based on the foundation in [8] and [3], semi-structured data models can be interpreted in terms of finite structures $\langle N, T, R, P \rangle$—regular-tree grammars with the finite sets of nonterminals (N) and terminals (T), the root symbol ($R \in N$) and the set of production rules (P). This definition allows the production of a semi-structured document according to its e.g. XML or JavaScript Object Notation (JSON) schema formulated constraints. As such, we consider the

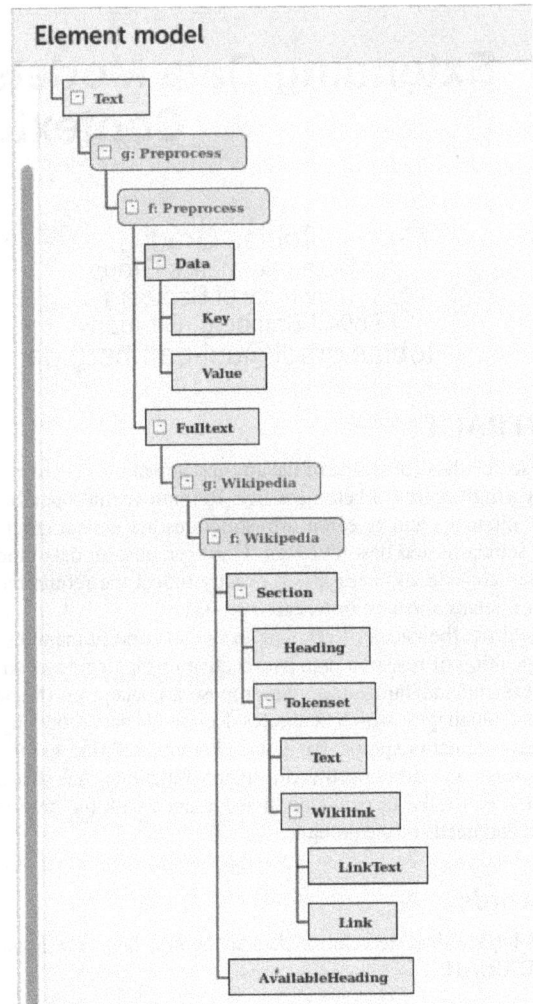

Figure 1: Modeled tree of the wikipedia example

interpretation of a schema as $\langle N, T, R, P \rangle$ the *parsing-oriented perspective* on semi-structured data. The definition allows the specification of production rules of the form $n \rightarrow te_c$, where $n \in N, t \in T$ and $e_c \subset N$ reflects the content model that is defined over the set of non-terminals.

With regard to the introduced examples, this definition allows the production of terminal symbols of the XML documents from nonterminals and hence the formal definition of an XML schema. Although a strictly parsing-oriented perspective is necessary for the syntactically correct interpretation of data, the presented definition does not allow the extension of document structure based on the content of the elements.

To allow the representation of substructures or alternative elements within the formal definition of a schema, we extend the parsing-oriented view to a 6-tuple $S = \langle N, T, R, P, L, F \rangle$, where N, T, R and P form components of the original definition. The components of L and F provide the extension of the schema, where:

- L forms a set of labels and
- F is a set of labeling functions $x \rightarrow le_l$, where:
  - $x \in (N \cup L)$,
  - $l \subseteq L$ and
  - $e_l := \{I, op\}$ defining a function over a set of input values $I \subseteq N$ and an operation of the arity $|I|$.

Figure 1 shows the editor component of the modeling interface of our framework[2]. In this editor, the blue nodes represent the nonterminals. The yellow nodes are labeling functions, which are formed of a grammatical and a transformation component. The purple nodes finally represent produced labels. Through the hierarchy, parenting nodes of labeling functions also define the set of input values.

3.2 Labeling functions

Within the framework, labeling functions are composed of the two constructs *grammars* and *functions*, which represent two distinguishable modeling tasks. Whereas grammars are used to define the grammatical constraints that generate a language—i.e. the Domain Specific Language (DSL) that an element conforms to—functions build on resulting syntax trees to transform data into subsequent labels.

The example in figure 1 shows an intermediary result of modeling the presented Wikipedia example: the *grammar* g: Preprocess for the separation of encapsulated structured information from unstructured text is inserted below the Text element. The *transformation function* f: Preprocess applies commands to produce key/value pairs of structured data and the remaining article (Fulltext). An additional grammar g: Wikipedia then decomposes Wiki markup from encapsulated textual content. The transformation function f: Wikipedia is then applied on the produced parse tree and generates the element hierarchy modeled under Section.

Description grammars

The specification of data with respect to syntactical and semantic constraints is accomplished by means of an individual, element-specific DSL [5].

```
page       : container+;
container  : (block | preface) block*;
preface    : content;
block      : h1block | ... | h6block;

h1block    : h1  (h2block | ... | h6block | content)*;
...
h6block    : h6  (content)*;

h1         : H1_OPEN title EQ;
...
h6         : H6_OPEN title H6_CLOSE;

content    : (tokenset | categoryContainer)+;
title      : tokenset+;
tokenset   : text
           | link;
...
text       : TEXT | EXCL | EQ;

intLink     : intLinkOpen intLinkCont INT_LINK_CLOSE;
intLinkCont : intLinkComp? linkValue;
intLinkComp : intLinkRes INT_LINK_SEP
              (linkContent INT_LINK_SEP)*;
intLinkRes  : linkContent;
...
```

Listing 3: Wikipedia grammar

Listing 3 shows an excerpt of the *parser grammar* for g: Wikipedia. The complete *parser grammar* has 74 lines (including comments etc.) and defines rules (e.g. page, h1block, text) for the syntactic analysis of a provided input. It is complemented

---

[2]http://schereg.de.dariah.eu

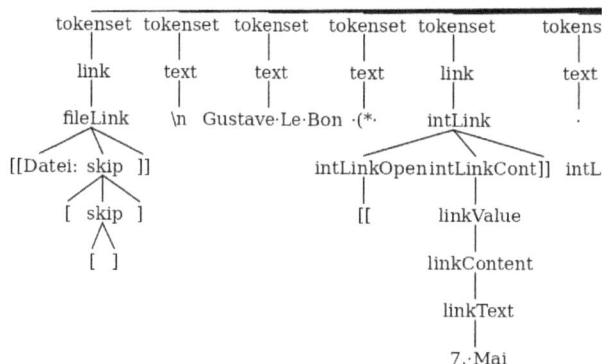

Figure 2: Parse tree of the wikipedia sample

by a *lexer grammar* of 109 lines, which specifies the rules (e.g. TEXT, EQ, H1_OPEN) for a preliminary lexical analysis—i.e. the tokenization of input. Please consider the lexer rule h1: it defines that the title of a level 1 heading is embraced by the lexer rule H1_OPEN (defined as '\n=') and EQ ('=')—the latter being also used in parser rules other than h1 such as text in the presented excerpt.

Applying the grammars at the modeled element results in the generation of Java code and classes that represent a lexer, a parser, tree traversal helpers and auxiliary classes per defined rule. Upon requiring the grammar during the runtime of our developed system, these classes are dynamically loaded and hence—without any intervention by a programmer—the declarative definition of data in terms of DSLs results in the execution of native Java code that processes the defined data. As an end-result of the descriptive phase, a parse-tree is generated and reflects input data with respect to the specified grammar. Figure 2 shows the resulting parse tree of the first tokens of the textual content in listing 2.

Transformation functions

Comparable to its native context in compiler engineering, a parse tree reflects only an intermediate representation for the derivation of an enriched document and does not conclude our data enrichment process. Transformation functions form a subsequent step and are applied to parse trees. Listing 4 reflects the transformation function in f: Wikipedia. Opposed to the grammar, this function is not generic, but influenced by a specific application context in which only biographical sections are considered relevant. Whereas the first statement assigns any preface of an article to appropriate labels, the second statement contains a (simplified) filtering statement that is only satisfied, if the heading of a top-level (h2 in Wikipedia) heading contains the word 'life'.

Multiple transformation languages have been designed and standardized such as Query/View/Transformation (QVT), which is defined by the Object Management Group (OMG) [4]. Due to the complexity of such languages, we chose to define a simple transformation language that allows the specification of value and object assignments and command execution. To this point, the constraints of that language have not limited the use of the framework. However, as indicated in figure 3, the transformation language is merely

125

```
Section = @page.container.preface {
  Tokenset = @content.tokenset {
    Text = @[text , extLink.extLinkCont.linkValue ];
    Wikilink = @intLink {
      LinkText = @linkValue;
      Link = @intLinkRes;
    };
  };
};
Section = @page.container.block.h2block[CORE::CONTAINS(
    @h2.title , "true", "life")] {
  Heading = @h2.title;
  Tokenset = @content.tokenset {
    Text = @text;
    Wikilink = @link {
      LinkText = @linkValue;
      Link = @intLinkRes;
    };
  };
};
AvailableHeading = @page.container.block.h2block.h2.title
  ;
```

Listing 4: Wikipedia function

another DSL and a set of user-selectable transformation languages
could be integrated per request.

3.3 Rule processing overview

Figure 3 shows the overall concept of the transformation rule
framework, which forms a combination of the application of DSLs
for the description of data and a transformation language for the
formulation of transformation rules. The building blocks within
the framework are summarized in two interpreters, one for the
validation and processing of input against a DSL and one for the
validation and processing of a transformation function against the
transformation language. Both are conceptualized as autonomous
language application components—each accomplishing the tasks
of processing input, constructing intermediate representations and
traversing and rewriting these according to the needs of the concluding back end (*semantic analysis* or *optimization*). These *needs*
are the named nodes and subtrees of parsed input and are known as
soon as the transformation function has been parsed and analyzed.

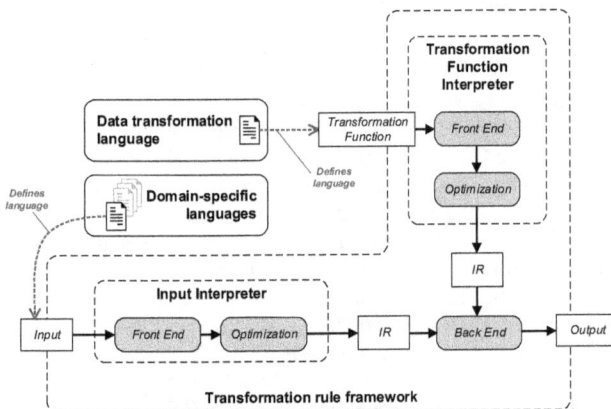

Figure 3: Transformation rule framework

At runtime of the rule framework, transformation functions are
assumed to be reused for multiple instances of a defined element
model. As such, only the content of individual documents needs to

be interpreted, whereas the executable representation of the transformation function is cached in its intermediary state.

4. CONCLUSION

Although the example here touches all introduced topics, the results present only an intermediary step towards data that has been
specifically modeled for a domain and research question. As subsequent steps, we have e.g. implemented functionality as usable
commands for transformation functions to detect named entities by
analyzing internal Wiki links or execute state-of-the-art methods of
natural language processing (NLP)—to which the named entities
that were identified by analyzing internal Wiki links can then be
provided as known entities. With the help of the modeling framework we were able to compile an integrated data source for the
prototypical implementation of a biographical analysis tool, which
has been motivated by a feasibility study at the Leibniz Institute of
European History in Mainz, Germany [2]. Despite the functional
extensions to support NLP or Wiki link analysis functionality, no
code was required to be written in order to access, process and
transform data. These aspects have been solved by modeling data
(along with the application context) in a declarative fashion, which
not only resulted in a quicker prototypical implementation of the
tool, but improved transparency and iterative adaptability for the
domain experts.

5. REFERENCES

[1] T. Gradl and A. Henrich. A novel approach for a reusable
    federation of research data within the arts and humanities. In
    Digital Humanities 2014 - Book of Abstracts, pages 382–384,
    Lausanne, Switzerland, 2014.

[2] T. Gradl and A. Henrich. Nutzung und kombination von daten
    aus strukturierten und unstrukturierten quellen zur
    identifikation transnationaler lebensläufe. In E. Burr, editor,
    DHd 2016, pages 135–138. nisaba Verlag, 2016.

[3] M. Murata, D. Lee, M. Mani, and K. Kawaguchi. Taxonomy
    of xml schema languages using formal language theory. *ACM
    Transactions on Internet Technology*, 5(4):660–704, 2005.

[4] OMG. Meta object facility (mof) 2.0
    query/view/transformation specification, 2015.

[5] T. Parr and K. Fisher. Ll(*): The foundation of the antlr parser
    generator. In *Proceedings of the 32Nd ACM SIGPLAN
    Conference on Programming Language Design and
    Implementation*, PLDI '11, pages 425–436, New York, NY,
    USA, 2011. ACM.

[6] M. Polfreman. Commonly-used metadata formats in the arts
    and humanities, 2005.

[7] P. Vierkant. Leuchttürme der deutschen
    repositorienlandschaft, 2013.

[8] Z. Zhang, P. Shi, H. Che, and J. Gu. An algebraic framework
    for schema matching. *Informatica*, 19(3):421–446, 2008.

Using Convolutional Neural Networks for Content Extraction from Online Flyers

Alessandro Calefati, Ignazio Gallo, Alessandro Zamberletti, Lucia Noce
Universita' degli Studi dell'Insubria
Varese, Italy
http://artelab.dicom.uninsubria.it/

ABSTRACT

The rise of online shopping has hurt physical retailers, which struggle to persuade customers to buy products in physical stores rather than online. Marketing flyers are a great mean to increase the visibility of physical retailers, but the unstructured offers appearing in those documents cannot be easily compared with similar online deals, making it hard for a customer to understand whether it is more convenient to order a product online or to buy it from the physical shop. In this work we tackle this problem, introducing a content extraction algorithm that automatically extracts structured data from flyers. Unlike competing approaches that mainly focus on textual content or simply analyze font type, color and text positioning, we propose a new approach that uses Convolutional Neural Networks to classify words extracted from flyers typically used in marketing materials to attract the attention of readers towards specific deals. We obtained good results and a high language and genre independence.

CCS Concepts

•Computing methodologies → Machine learning; *Machine learning approaches; Machine learning algorithms;*

Keywords

Content Extraction; Portable Document Format; Convolutional Neural Network; Marketing Flyers.

1. INTRODUCTION

Although e-commerce has been increasing in popularity in recent years, unstructured documents such as marketing flyers and advertising emails are still effective ways to promote products and special offers. In this study we propose a novel content extraction algorithm to automatically extract entities of interest from marketing flyers containing commercial product offers.

Most of the deals appearing within commercial flyers refer to physical retailers, and the data that can be gathered from those marketing documents is particularly appealing to online price comparison shopping engines to fill the existing gap between online and

DocEng2016 September 13–16, 2016, Vienna, Austria

© 2016 ACM. ISBN 978-1-4503-4438-8/16/09. . . $15.00

DOI: http://dx.doi.org/10.1145/2960811.2967148

physical shopping. In fact, a searchable collection containing both physical deals extracted from marketing flyers and offers gathered from online listings would allow customers to determine whether it is more convenient to order a product online and wait for order preparation, shipping and delivery, or to physically drive to the retailer location and buy it straight from the shelf. This represents a great opportunity for physical retailers to compete against online marketplaces.

The PDF standard is increasingly being used by physical retailers to create marketing materials that maintain the same visual characteristics on every different device. This is particularly important, as commercial flyers typically contain many graphic elements specifically designed to let customers quickly understand the positions of relevant offers within the pages or to attract their attention towards particular deals or sections. Recent works have shown that, when dealing with not much structured documents containing lots of graphic elements, textual features are not discriminative enough to accurately identify all the entities of interest. In fact, visual characteristics are typically used to highlight and categorize paragraphs of text, and therefore represent a large amount of information that can and should be used to more accurately distinguish entities of interest having low discriminative textual contents.

Casting the problem to PDF documents, existing studies transform the processed PDF content streams into raw text, wasting the visual formatting information contained within the documents, such as font type, size, color and text positioning. If we delve even deeper into the world of PDF documents and we focus on PDF marketing flyers, it has been proved that combining textual information with additional features describing the visual characteristics of the deals in the processed documents increases classification performances.

The goal of this study is to underline the important role that visual features have in distinguishing different entities of interest within highly unstructured but visually rich documents, considering images that contain them. Unlike other works in literature, we propose novel and simpler approach that uses images of words retrieved directly from flyers avoiding visual distortions that may arise when converting PDF to other formats such as HTML.

Although in this study we focus exclusively on marketing materials, the proposed approach is not handcrafted for that specific domain; as such, it can be used in a wide variety of contexts in which the visual characteristics of the processed documents are discriminative for the entities that need to be identified.

2. RELATED WORKS

In the following paragraphs we introduce some works similar to our paper.

Our study is analogue to the method proposed by Gallo *et*

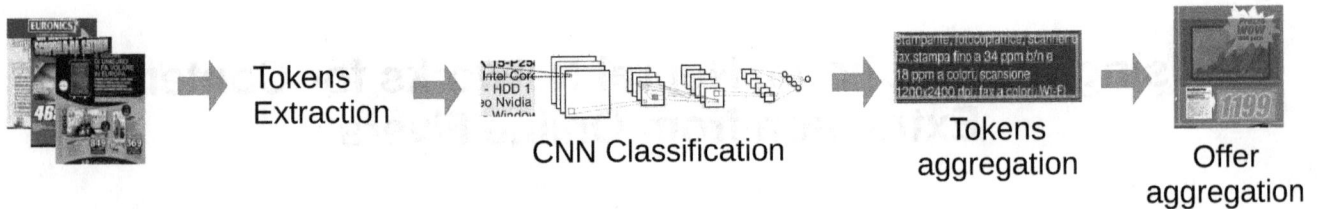

Figure 2: Pipeline of the proposed method.

Figure 1: The conversion of a PDF file (a) to an HTML format (b) may generate formatting alterations that substantially change the visual characteristics of the original document. Conversion tool: PDF2HTML [1].

al. [4], the substancial difference involves the first phase: instead of extracting and analyzing textual and visual features from PDF, the novel approach that we are discussing, uses Convolutional Neural Networks, which actually represent the state-of-the-art in image classification.

The same task has been approached by Apostolova *et al.* [1] that proposed a method to retrieve information from PDF or HTML document using some textual and visual features. Our goal is the same of the one discussed in the paper, but we used different approach, not extracting information from files but using raw images gathered from PDF. As regards to the use of CNNs, Simard *et al.* [7] proposes a set of concrete best practices that document analysis researchers can use to get good results with this kind of neural networks. The paper suggests to enlarge dataset, adding some kind of distorted data beyond the available ones, and supplies a novel architecture of CNN that fits better to solve many problems usually encountered in document analysis. As described in this study, we expanded our dataset extracting a token five times rather than only one time before the CNN training.

Another paper which aims to enhance CNN's performance is the one proposed by Chellapilla *et al.* [2] that studied different strategies to speed up the use of CNNs. Discussed approaches are: unrolling the convolution, using of basic linear algebra subroutines and using the graphic processing unit (GPU) instead of CPU for calculation. These three methods are then compared to determine which one has greater impact on CNNs' performance, showing that using GPU the execution time is 4x faster. For our experiments we used computer equipped with two high performance video cards. So CNN calculus has been done on GPU breaking down training time at about 3 hours.

3. PROPOSED METHOD

The processing pipeline of the proposed approach is presented in this section: (i) single tokens are extracted from the processed mar-

keting flyer; (ii) each token gathered is classified using a properly trained CNN classifier from AlexNet architecture [6]; (iii) neighbouring words having same classification result are merged into semantically correlated paragraphs; (iv) paragraphs representing correlated product titles, descriptions and prices are further merged together to identify the deals contained within the processed flyer. The whole pipeline is summarized in Fig. 2 and described in detail in the remainder of this section.

3.1 Token Classification and Aggregation

Token classification is carried out using CNN classifier trained to produce output of the following classes {*title*, *description*, *price*, *not-class*}. Before training the model, we extract tokens from the PDF flyer using PDFTextStripper, which is a java class of the PDFBox library. It extracts each word from the page with also additional informations like coordinates, useful to get the rectangle sourrounding the token drawn on the page. For our experiment, we used PDF files with readable text inside. Working with images saved as PDF, the proposed approach would not work, because PDFTextStripper would not extract any token. In this case the use of OCR algorithms could help to solve the problem. During training stage, for each token extracted from the ground-truth, we do a squarify operation, since almost tokens have rectangular shape. To transform a rectangle into a square, first, we calculate the difference between the longest and the shortest side, then we divide it by 2 and finally we stretch the shortest side adding the half of the difference between the width and the height of the token's rectangle. Then we magnify the extraction square five times and all page crops obtained are used to train the model. Algorithm involved is shown in Fig. 3. Magnification factor used to expand bounding boxes is not fixed, it is dependent on the ratio between the height of the entire page and the height of the token. The aim was to enlarge smaller squares more than bigger ones looking for other elements useful for the classification with CNN. An example of extracted token is shown in Fig. 4. Steps described above have been repeated in the classification phase. The membership of a token to a class is determined by number of votes received from the CNN. As proposed by [7], with this approach we got a dataset five times bigger than extracting single image for token.

Tokens extracted from the processed flyers are classified as belonging to one of the entities of interest listed in Table 2. The classification task is carried out using a CNN classifier from Caffe [5]. CNN classifiers have high accuracy when trained using a large amount of images, but they need a lot of training time and powerful hardware.

Once every token in the page has been assigned to a class of interest, they need to be aggregated to form products titles, descriptions and prices. This aggregation task is carried out using an ad-hoc clustering algorithm that takes into account the class and the distance from the surrounding elements of a token within the processed flyer.

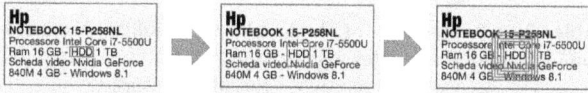

Figure 3: Pipeline of the extraction phase.

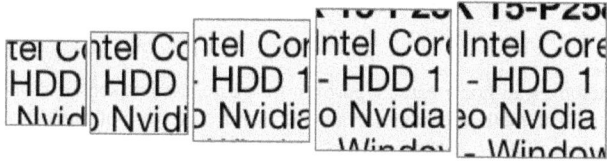

Figure 4: Example of squarified tokens then classified by CNN.

At its first iteration, the algorithm selects the bounding box of a random seed token classified as belonging to either Title, Price or Description class, and tries to join that bounding box with all the other neighbouring bounding boxes of tokens classified as belonging to the same class c that are located at a distance $d < \varepsilon$. This newly formed bounding box is then added to the page in place of all the joined bounding boxes. At each iteration a new seed token, that has not been previously selected, is chosen. The algorithm stops when all the tokens have been aggregated.

The result of this merging phase is a set of bounding boxes that represent titles, descriptions and prices of all the offers available on the flyer (see Fig. 5).

3.2 Offer Aggregation

The offers extraction process from each flyer is the last step of the presented method. This is not a trivial task as it cannot be carried out simply by considering the minimum distance between the various elements that form an offer. In fact, there are many cases in which one or more of the bounding boxes for the 3 relevant elements that make up an offer (Price, Title and Description) are visually closer to the bounding boxes of elements from another offer. In such cases, clustering exclusively on the basis of the distance between different bounding boxes does not lead to optimal results.

A better approach consists in clustering the bounding boxes in such way that the coverage provided by the final clusters over the processed page is maximized. This approach is motivated by the fact that marketing documents do not usually have many void areas, because retailers typically try to lower printing costs by adding as many offers as they can within each page to reduce the total size of the final flyer. As such, each offer within a page is usually localized in a particular area, and its bounding box has a minimal overlap with the other offers.

The textual information associated with an offer O is a triple (T, D, P) composed of a Title T, a Description D and a Price P. In this work, product images are not taken into account because finding the correct association between an image and its respective textual description requires a specific study, which is out of the focus of this work.

As previously stated, our offer aggregation algorithm tries to minimize the intersection area between all the bounding boxes for the offers in the processed page. The algorithm starts by selecting the bounding box of a random Price P_i and merges it with its closest Description D_i and Title T_i bounding boxes to form an offer hypothesis O_i. The same process is repeated for all the remaining Prices in the page to form a finite set of hypotheses $H_{P_i} = \{O_0, \ldots, O_n\}$.

Figure 5: Examples of flyers manually tagged by experts. The relevant entities listed in Table 2 are highlighted as coloured rectangles (Title, Description and Price).

The sum $S_{H_{P_i}}$ of the intersection areas between the bounding boxes for the offers in H_{P_i} is then calculated as follows:

$$S_{H_{P_i}} = \sum_{j \neq k} O_j \cap O_k, \; j, k \in \{0, \ldots, n\} \quad (1)$$

This whole process is repeated multiple times, each time changing the starting seed Price, until all the Prices in the flyer have been selected as initial seeds. The set of offer hypotheses having minimum intra-intersection area is then selected as the best one.

4. EXPERIMENTS

In the remainder of this section we present the experimental results obtained testing the proposed method on marketing flyers randomly collected from different retailers. Throughout our experimental activity we evaluate quantitatively the accuracy of the method both at identifying and classifying entities of interest within the processed flyers and at aggregating the detected entities into offers.

4.1 Dataset

In order to evaluate the proposed approach, a total number of 797 product offers have been gathered from 103 marketing flyers produced by 2 different retailers. The collected documents come from electronic domains and present different design styles. On the ArteLab website, is available a zip file containing a subset of the entire dataset. To get the whole dataset please contact the authors of this paper.

Each flyer has been manually labelled by a team of 4 experts using a specially designed GUI. As shown in Fig. 5, the experts were instructed to provide both the coordinates of all the product Titles, Descriptions and Prices in the pages, and the associations between those bounding boxes and the different offers within the pages. The information gathered from the different experts has been averaged to obtain the final ground-truth data used to evaluate the proposed method.

4.2 Evaluation Metrics

We evaluate the accuracy of the method both at classifying/aggregating individual tokens and at aggregating the merged tokens into product offers.

Since our ground-truth data is composed of labelled bounding boxes manually drawn by experts over the different flyers, we measure the accuracy of the proposed approach by evaluating the intersection-over-union (IoU) [3] score between the bounding boxes detected by the proposed approach and the respective ground-truth information.

Each entity is evaluated independently from the others. Given a page with its ground-truth data for one of the entities from Table 1, and the aggregated predictions provided by the model for the same entity class; the evaluation process for the token classification and aggregation phases is carried out as follows: we compare the IoU score between each ground-truth bounding box and the predictions provided by the model; if one of the predicted bounding boxes achieves an IoU score greater than 0.5 with the ground-truth bounding box, the prediction is considered correct. For every ground-truth bounding box at most one predicted bounding box might be considered correct. Given the number of correct predictions, we compute the classic Precision, Recall and F-measure values.

Given a page with its ground-truth offer data, and the offer hypotheses generated as in Sec. 3.2, the evaluation process for the offer aggregation phase is carried out as follows: we compare the IoU score between each component of a ground-truth offer (Title, Description and Price) and the bounding boxes for the same component in the offer hypotheses; if every predicted component for a given offer hypothesis has an IoU that is greater than 0.5 with its respective ground-truth offer component, then the predicted offer is considered correct. For every ground-truth offer at most one hypothesis might be considered correct.

4.3 Results

Tokens used to train the CNN were 188973 and the number of tokens used to test the model was 49887 which represents about 20% of the entire dataset. For each token, we compute the classification in the following way: first we get the page crop, which usually has a rectangular shape, then we do a squarify operation and resize images into new ones of 256x256 pixels to match the requested input of the AlexNet model. After all these steps we invoke the CNN to get the response according to our classes.

The first experiment aims at measuring the goodness of the proposed CNN classifier. As listed in Table 1, tokens may belong to one of four possible classes: Title, Description, Price and Other.

With the last experiment we evaluate the phases described in Sec. 3.1 and 3.2: the aggregation of tokens, and the subsequent aggregation of merged tokens into product offers. We measure Precision, Recall and F-measure values achieved on test set, while varying the token aggregation threshold ε from $0.1 \cdot \text{token\_height}$ to $10 \cdot \text{token\_height}$. We report the best obtained results in Table 2; they have been obtained setting $\varepsilon = (2 \cdot \text{token\_height})$.

Even though the previous token classification/aggregation phase has not high accuracy values, in the last step we obtain good results because offer aggregation tends to group data into higher level of granularity.

Table 1: Confusion matrix for the CNN classifier.

	Title	Descr.	Price	Other
Title	85.31%	44.26%	1.87%	6.89%
Descr.	0.88%	37.81%	0.94%	1.81%
Price	0.11%	1.93%	73.54%	4.07%
Other	13.70%	16.00%	23.65%	87.24%

5. CONCLUSION

An ad-hoc method for the automatic extraction of structured product offers from marketing flyers has been proposed. The presented approach relies on CNN classification for the first step and

Table 2: Evaluation of both phases: token classification/aggregation and offer aggregation

	Precision	Recall	F-measure
Title	0.417	0.838	0.557
Description	0.495	0.807	0.614
Price	0.799	0.443	0.570
Aggr. offers	0.925	0.541	0.683

then uses ad-hoc created algorithm for aggregating tokens and offers. The method has been evaluated over a collection of randomly collected flyers, achieving satisfying results while also maintaining an excellent language and genre independence due to the limited use of classical textual features.

6. REFERENCES

[1] E. Apostolova and N. Tomuro. Combining visual and textual features for information extraction from online flyers. In *EMNLP*, pages 1924–1929, 2014.

[2] K. Chellapilla, S. Puri, and P. Simard. High performance convolutional neural networks for document processing. In *10th Int. Workshop on Frontiers in Handwriting Recognition*. Suvisoft, 2006.

[3] M. Everingham, L. Van Gool, C. K. I. Williams, J. Winn, and A. Zisserman. The pascal visual object classes challenge. *Computer Vision*, 88(2):303–338, 2010.

[4] I. Gallo, A. Zamberletti, and L. Noce. Content extraction from marketing flyers. In *Computer Analysis of Images and Patterns*, pages 325–336. Springer, 2015.

[5] Y. Jia, E. Shelhamer, J. Donahue, S. Karayev, J. Long, R. Girshick, S. Guadarrama, and T. Darrell. Caffe: Convolutional architecture for fast feature embedding. In *Proceedings of the ACM International Conference on Multimedia*, pages 675–678. ACM, 2014.

[6] A. Krizhevsky, I. Sutskever, and G. E. Hinton. Imagenet classification with deep convolutional neural networks. In *Advances in neural information processing systems*, pages 1097–1105, 2012.

[7] P. Y. Simard, D. Steinkraus, and J. C. Platt. Best practices for convolutional neural networks applied to visual document analysis. In *ICDAR*, volume 3, pages 958–962, 2003.

Combining Taxonomies using Word2vec

Tobias Swoboda, Matthias Hemmje
University of Hagen
Faculty for Mathematics and Computer Science
Universitätsstraße 47, 58085 Hagen, Germany
Tobias.Swoboda@fernuni-hagen.de,
Matthias.Hemmje@fernuni-hagen.de

Mihai Dascalu, Stefan Trausan-Matu
University Politehnica of Bucharest
Computer Science Department
313 Splaiul Independentei, Sector 6, Bucharest, Romania
mihai.dascalu@cs.pub.ro,
stefan.trausan@cs.pub.ro

ABSTRACT

Taxonomies have gained a broad usage in a variety of fields due to their extensibility, as well as their use for classification and knowledge organization. Of particular interest is the digital document management domain in which their hierarchical structure can be effectively employed in order to organize documents into content-specific categories. Common or standard taxonomies (e.g., the ACM Computing Classification System) contain concepts that are too general for conceptualizing specific knowledge domains. In this paper we introduce a novel automated approach that combines sub-trees from general taxonomies with specialized seed taxonomies by using specific Natural Language Processing techniques. We provide an extensible and generalizable model for combining taxonomies in the practical context of two very large European research projects. Because the manual combination of taxonomies by domain experts is a highly time consuming task, our model measures the semantic relatedness between concept labels in CBOW or skip-gram Word2vec vector spaces. A preliminary quantitative evaluation of the resulting taxonomies is performed after applying a greedy algorithm with incremental thresholds used for matching and combining topic labels.

Keywords

Word2Vec, taxonomy integration, ontology alignment, automated semantic integration

1. INTRODUCTION AND MOTIVATION

According to Berners-Lee et al. [1], ontologies are the foundation of the semantic web by conceptualizing different domains and by formally defining the relations among terms. In addition, *"the most typical kind of ontology for the Web has a taxonomy and a set of inference rules."* - Berners-Lee et al. [1]. Lexical taxonomies discriminate concepts (categories or classes), which can have multiple sub-classes (through the hypernym/hyponym relationships), further defining and refining these concepts. This generates a directed acyclic graph (DAG) as underlying representation of our taxonomy. The nodes of the DAG may be abstract and are machine-readable representations of the concept. The readability of concepts is increased by their linkage to labels

DocEng '16, September 12-16, 2016, Vienna, Austria
© 2016 ACM. ISBN 978-1-4503-4438-8/16/09...$15.00
DOI: http://dx.doi.org/10.1145/2960811.2967151

that can be expressed in natural language. After building a coherent, taxonomical representation for a knowledge domain, the aim shifts towards retrieving relevant documents from an information system. Two major approaches emerge: querying and browsing [4]. Both benefit from the usage of taxonomies. Querying can be enhanced by *Named Entity Recognition* (NER), the process of finding text tokens that can be identified as named representations or labels of certain concepts within the taxonomy [7], p 761 ff. Providing content-based categories where each category is based on a concept from the taxonomy enables browsing. This provides a hierarchy of categories and sub-categories to browse for content.

Now the research question arises: How can we effectively build new taxonomies to facilitate automated document classification and retrieval by combining existing taxonomies with specific seed concepts? To start with, a rather prominent taxonomy, commonly used for organizing scientific papers in the knowledge domain of computer science, is the 2012 ACM Computing Classification System (CCS) [6]. Taxonomies organizing large text corpora like the entire set of ACM publications are faced with the problem of creating meaningful relations between the underlying concept hierarchies and of supporting automated text categorization (TC) [12]. In the remainder of this paper, the terms concept and category are used synonymously.

Our aim consists of reusing knowledge from widely adopted standard taxonomies, combining them and facilitating automated document categorization while managing novel or specific knowledge domains or document collections. Our research is conducted in the context of two very large European H2020 research projects – RAGE [15] and EDISON [8] –, but our method and the obtained results are directly applicable to any knowledge domain. Both projects are using digital libraries providing access to knowledge resources, generated by and relevant for these projects. Taxonomies are used to organize and automatically categorize the documents specific to the scope of each project. We were faced with a major drawback of existing and established taxonomies that were either too broad or too extensive, while providing little insights in terms of effectively classifying documents. Large and general taxonomies would have been inappropriate to use within the projects' digital libraries because the majority of collections would have been either over-populated or empty, thus defeating the purpose of equitable content-based categories as presented in Figure 1.

This paper outlines our approach to reuse parts of well-accepted standard taxonomies in order to create domain specific taxonomies. As a specific example, we have opted to focus on the RAGE taxonomy because a small and specific seed taxonomy has already been specifically created for the RAGE project.

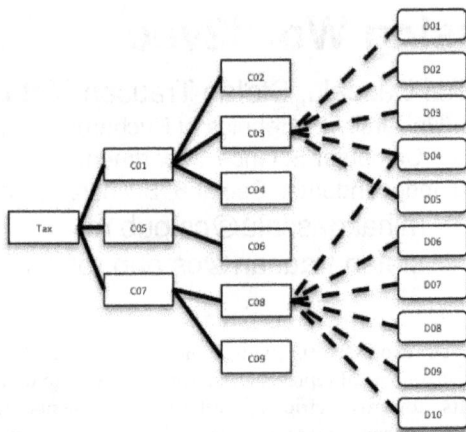

Figure 1. Illustration of an unsuitable taxonomy

In terms of structure, section two presents an evaluation of existing approaches, followed by the presentation of our model and of our generalizable combination algorithm. In contrast to other existing approaches, our method relies on measuring the semantic relatedness between vector representations of taxonomy labels in continuous bag of words (CBOW) or skip-gram Word2vec models [10]. Afterwards, preliminary results are presented, followed by discussion and conclusions.

2. STATE OF THE ART
2.1 Approaches to combine taxonomies

When generating taxonomies from scratch, there are two fundamental strategies: a) manual taxonomy construction and b) automated machine learning and the use of specific natural language processing tools. The manual approach is a cumbersome labor-driven process performed by domain experts or taxonomy engineers. On the upside, the generated taxonomy is subjectively representative for the people who generated it. The United States National Information Standards Organization (NISO) suggests two fundamental strategies when manually generating taxonomies [11]. *Top-down*: A committee of experts selects the broadest terms of a knowledge domain and connects narrower terms with these until a desired level of specificity is reached. *Bottom-up*: A committee of experts starts with a set of terms related to the knowledge domain and aggregates them from narrow terms to more general terms. In a nutshell, although the resulted taxonomy represents a coherent shared view of the domain, the manual generation of taxonomies is a highly time-consuming undertaking. One requires groups of experts to collaborate and agree on a common representation of knowledge.

The alternative approach of automated taxonomy construction requires sample texts and a set of keywords for machine learning algorithms to learn from. For example, Gollub et al. [5] propose the dynamic taxonomy generation based on search terms used during querying. Their approach dynamically updates the utilized taxonomy based on search terms and the amount of documents associated with a given concept.

The main challenge arises: provide suitable texts and adequate keywords. Depending on the knowledge domain and algorithm, the lack of available documents and keywords can lead to results with a limited beneficial impact [9]. However, none of the available automated techniques is applicable for our needs because neither the document set in question, nor a set of search terms are previously available. The remaining challenge lies in combining the small seed taxonomies with sub-trees of the

commonly accepted big taxonomy, without having a set of documents or search terms as reference.

From a broader perspective, the combination of two taxonomies and, in general, ontologies, is an extremely difficult process called ontology matching or alignment [13]. This process involves the modification of the content and structure of both ontologies. Our approach considers a simpler case, in which only one ontology is modified and the changes represent only additions of concepts. Moreover, we work only with the taxonomic backbone of ontologies. However, based on the proposed method and our findings presented in detail in the following sections, we consider that our approach may be extended for ontology mapping.

2.2 Word2vec

Multiple semantic models used to evaluate the relatedness between concepts and/or documents have been proposed in time, ranging from traditional vector spaces (e.g., Latent Semantic Analysis, LSA) [10], probabilistic models (most notable, Latent Dirichlet Allocation, LDA) [2], or the newly introduced Word2vec model based on neural networks [10]. Although all semantic models enable the assessment of similarity between concepts, we opted to rely on Word2vec, as its reported accuracy on the sentence completion task in the Microsoft challenge was highest of all models (58.9% accuracy for determining the correct/appropriate word to be introduced within a sentence) [10]. This emphasizes the fact that Word2vec is one of the most suitable automated models for building coherent representations and for creating context-driven word associations, central elements within our task of combining taxonomies in a coherent overall representation suitable for the domain.

Word2vec uses neural networks to generate high dimensional vector representations for each word or document. Neural networks usually require labeled input-output pairs to learn, but these associations cannot be provided by a flat text. In order to address this limitation, two alternatives have been introduced [10]. First, *CBOW* (continuous bag of words) predicts a word given its context. Therefore, the words before and after every instance of a word are used as input in a training sample expecting this word as output. The second alternative, *skip-gram* works the other way around: it takes single words as input samples, while the surrounding words are the expected output. Cosine similarity can then be used to assess the degree of similarity between words.

Interesting linguistic properties in the arithmetic manipulation of the resulting vectors have been previously shown [10]. Relationships between word vectors are encoded by their offset in the generated high dimensional space. This way, for example, gender is a certain offset that can be applied to the vector representation of "*boy*" in order to get a vector very close to the vector representation of "*girl*". We used these geometric regularities induced by high cosine similarities to compute the relevance of concepts in other taxonomies.

3. METHOD
3.1 Corpus

The 2012 ACM Computing Classification System's (CCS) [6] wide acceptance is largely a result of its critical review and subsequent revision process. In the RAGE project, an initial small seed-taxonomy has already been developed. This taxonomy is highly specific in its field, but not widely accepted outside the RAGE project. The subsequently described model explains our approach to combine parts of widely accepted taxonomies with our own highly specific seed taxonomy.

3.2 Model

Our model is based on the representation of taxonomies $T = \{C, E, L\}$ as directed acyclic graphs (DAGs). These DAGs consist of nodes - concepts (C) and directed hypernym/hyponym relationships $E \subset C \times C$ between the concepts. L is the set of labels for the given concepts.

As a starting point, we consider two given taxonomies: a general one $TG = \{CG, EG, LG\}$, and a specific or seed taxonomy: $TS = \{CS, ES, LS\}$. The resulting new taxonomy is denoted as $TN = \{CN, EN, LN\}$. Because everything in the seed taxonomy is deemed relevant, the resulting new taxonomy is initialized as $CN = CS$, $EN = ES$ and $LN = LS$. Two possible cases for the general concepts $c \in CG$ and e (the connecting edge between both DAGs) have been identified:

- *Case 1*: c is an inner node of TG that is semantically relevant, yet still unutilized in TS. In this case c and all its descendants $CU \subset CG$ along with their Labels $LU \subset LG$ and inner edges $EU \subset EG$ are integrated into TS resulting in $TN = \{CN \cup CU, EN \cup EU \cup \{e\}, LN \cup LU\}$.

- *Case 2*: c is a leaf of TG that is semantically relevant, yet still unutilized in TS. In this case, c along with its labels $LU \subset LG$ are integrated into TN resulting in $TN = \{CN \cup \{c\}, EN \cup \{e\}, LS \cup LU\}$.

In both cases, the edge e integrates the suitable subgraph with TS at its most appropriate place. This approach is illustrated in Figure 2 in which CG7, an inner node, is linked with the root of TS_v while CG2, a leaf, is linked with CS4.

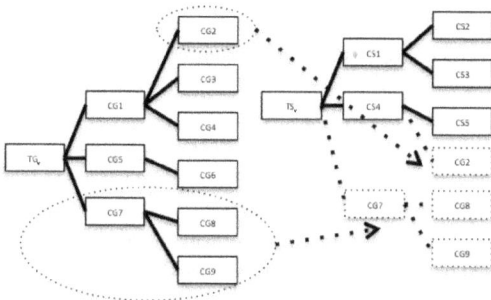

Figure 2. Taxonomy combination

In order to perform the taxonomy integration, the system must determine for every given concept $c \in CG$ if each concept and all its sub-concepts are relevant for the knowledge domain of TS. In case the concept is relevant, the system must also determine which is the best concept from CS to link it to. This evaluation can be alternatively performed manually, but this would have been a cumbersome task as the ACM 2012 CCS has 2299 concepts.

3.3 DFS-based Algorithm

Our approach is essentially a modified depth first search (DFS) through TG [3]. Whenever a concept $c \in CG$ is determined to be relevant for TS, it and all its descending concepts are linked to the most relevant concept $c_s \in CS$. The relevance values of the descendant nodes of c are not computed because they have already been added to TS. We used Word2vec to compute whether a concept $c \in CG$ is relevant for TS and what are the concepts $c_s \in CS$ to which it is linked. Therefore, vector representations for every concept in all taxonomies were generated. Stop words (i.e., natural language words with limited meaning, such as "the", "and", "a", etc.) and punctuation characters of the labels were removed. Afterwards, Word2vec vector representations of every word in the labels for one category

were aggregated in order to compute the concept representation in the high dimensional space as the geometric mean of all word vectors. A concept $c \in CG$ was deemed relevant for TS if its cosine similarity to any $c_s \in CS$ is between configurable upper and lower thresholds. This essentially generates relevance radii around c. A concept $c_s \in CS$ with a cosine similarity value outside these margins would not render c relevant because c is either too similar or too different from these concepts.

After generating a list of concepts $c_s \in CS$ within the threshold, our algorithm uses a Greedy approach [3] to attach c to the concept c_s that has the highest cosine similarity. We additionally implemented a limitation of how many descendant concepts c could have to be relevant. This limited the size of the reusable parts of TG. Without such a restriction in place, the system could for example attach the root of TG to TN and finish after one step. The resulting taxonomy would be too general for the knowledge domain of TN and essentially defeat the purpose of our approach. The next section describes the implementation of this method.

3.4 Word2vec based implementation

The RAGE seed taxonomy models the knowledge domain of applied gaming, it is denoted CS in accordance to the algorithm and contains 46 concepts, out of which the top level categories reflect: *assessment, decision-making and socio-emotional behavior, embodiment and physical interaction, emotion detection, evaluation, game balancing and personalized learning, interaction data and exchange and storage, interactive storytelling, natural language* and *social gamification*.

Before running our algorithm for combining the RAGE seed taxonomy with the ACM taxonomy, we generated vector representations of vocabularies that were then loaded in our software. Word2vec was used with both CBOW and the continuous skip-gram approaches to generate 200 dimensional word vectors. The following training sets were used: A dump of Google news articles, retrieved January 18, 2016 from http://mattmahoney.net/dc/text8.zip and the first billion characters of Wikipedia dump, retrieved January 23, 2016 from http://mattmahoney.net/dc/enwik9.zip. Our approach compares the similarities between category labels; therefore, it does not require sample documents that were already assigned to specific categories. Depending on the training set, our system was able to generate vector representations for a different number of categories. When using word vectors learned from Google news, our system was able to generate vector representations for 2230 concepts from 2299 concepts of CG. After using the first billion characters of Wikipedia as training set, the system was able to generate vector representations for 2266 from the 2299 concepts. The difference is due to the fact that the remaining ACM concepts have labels that have no vector representations, as the underlying words from the labels were not part of the training set vocabulary. Overall, word vectors based on the skip-gram approach yielded higher cosine similarity values. The same is true for the Wikipedia training set over the Google news training set. There were some particular cases. For example, the ACM taxonomy contains 50 concepts with labels containing the term "*analysis*" that all had a high cosine similarity with the RAGE concept "*Assessment dashboard and analysis*".

4. PRELIMINARY RESULTS

We ran multiple experiments with different configurations. As previously described, we used four different vector representations for the vocabulary of the English language. With each of these, the lower cosine similarity threshold was increased in 0.05 intervals. The upper threshold was set to the maximum possible value: 1. As the seed taxonomy had 46 concepts, a threshold of 20 maximum descendants seemed a reasonable size for the sub-trees to be transferred to the new taxonomy.

Multiple properties for the new taxonomy *TN* were measured consisting of: the number of concepts, of leafs and of connections in the taxonomy. For the latter, the amount of connections indicates for how many concepts $c_g \in CG$ of the ACM taxonomy, concepts within the thresholds could be identified within the seed taxonomy $c_s \in CS$. All experiments show, that the amount of connections decreases with an increasing lower threshold while maintaining a high amount of concepts and leafs until a certain point. This is due to the usage of entire sub-taxonomies when a common inner concept is deemed relevant. For threshold values higher than this point, which differs based on algorithm and training set, concepts and leafs begin to decrease. Obviously, the more connections are found, the more concepts from the general taxonomy have a chance to be relevant within the newly generated taxonomy. Depending on the used training set and algorithm, the most adequate taxonomies were generated by imposing a minimum threshold of .6 to .7. These taxonomies contained concepts like *acceptance testing*, *interactive simulation*, *graphics input devices* and *network games*, while remaining small without essentially transferring most of the concepts from the ACM taxonomy to the RAGE seed taxonomy. However, some distant concepts for serious/applied gaming were considered (e.g., *distributed memory*) due to the multiple meanings and senses that concepts like "memory" can have (working memory linked to learner comprehension versus computer memory).

5. DISCUSSION AND CONCLUSIONS

Our approach extends a seed taxonomy by selecting the most semantically related concepts of a general taxonomy and adding them into the seed taxonomy. Because only the seed taxonomy is modified by the addition of new concepts, our task is simpler than that of ontology alignment [13]. However, the underlying concept of projecting concepts as vectors into high dimensional spaces in order to derive their similarities can alternatively be used for a variety of applications like the automated alignment of ontologies and semantic integration. We must also present some limitations induced by the fact that all information about concepts is derived from their labels. By relying only on these few words in order to map a concept into the high dimensional space, we were faced with problems in terms of synonyms and homonyms. Hypernyms and hyponyms are automatically addressed by considering the hierarchical structure of the taxonomy during its generation. In addition, we must highlight another intrinsic limitation as many ACM concepts contain the terms *analysis*, *assessment* or *evaluation* in their labels. Most of them were matched to the RAGE concept *assessment* or *assessment dashboard and analysis*. Overall, the similarities between vocabulary labels induced a higher degree of relatedness and many of the concept associations made sense while relating to human expertise. However, there were some associations that need to be manually cleaned.

Our approach is, to the best of our knowledge, unique as it only relies on the concept labels without requiring query terms, sample documents or domain expert information. A disadvantage of our approach lies in the fact that the available information is limited to the labels of the available concepts. This means that potentially inadequate concepts, with similar labels, can be selected. Therefore, these automatically generated taxonomies are best used to speed up the manual taxonomy generation, by providing potential candidates to domain experts.

In future works, the document corpora for the RAGE and EDISON projects will be curated and automated text categorization will be applied on all documents. Expert interviews will be conducted to evaluate and manually refine the generated taxonomies and provide in-depth validations and an effectiveness assessment. In terms of comparisons, alternative semantic word-vector models will be employed within the proposed approach.

6. ACKNOWLEDGMENTS

This work was partially funded by the EC H2020 RAGE (Realising and Applied Gaming Eco-System) No. 644187 and the EC H2020 EDISON No. 675419 projects.

7. REFERENCES

[1] Berners-Lee, T., Hendler, J., Lassila, O. 2001. The semantic web. *Scientific American Magazine*: pp. 35-44, May 2001

[2] Blei, D. M., Ng, A. Y., Jordan, M. I. Latent Dirichlet Allocation, *Journal of Machine Learning Research 3, pp. 993-1022, 2003*

[3] Cormen, Th. C., Leiserson, C. E., Rivest, R., Stein, C. 2001. *Introduction to Algorithms*. Second Edition, MIT Press, Massachusetts, USA, 2001

[4] Cox, K. 1992. Information Retrieval by Browsing. *Proceedings of The 5th International Conference on New Information Technology*, Hong Kong, 1992

[5] Gollub, T., Volkse, M., Hagen, M., Stein, B. 2014. Dynamic taxonomy composition via keyqueries. *IEEE/ACM Joint Conference on Digital Libraries (JCDL)*, pp. 39-48, London

[6] The 2012 ACM Computing Classification System, Retrieves December 28, 2015 from Association for Computing Machinery, Inc., New York, NY

[7] Jurafsky, D., Martin, J. H. 2009. *Speech and language processing. An introduction to natural language processing, computational linguistics and speech recognition.* 2nd edition, Upper Saddle River, N.J., London: Pearson Prentice Hall

[8] Konijn, J. 2015. Education for Data Intensive Science to Open New science frontiers (EDISON) – Project proposal

[9] Liu, X., Song, Y., Liu, S., Wang, H. 2012. Automatic Taxonomy Construction from Keywords, *ACM SIGKDD conference*, August 12-16, Beijing, China

[10] Mikolov, T., Chen, K., Corrado, G., Dean, J. 2013. Efficient Estimation of Word Representation in Vector Space. *Proceedings of Workshop at ICLR*. Retrieved December 29, 2015 from http://arxiv.org/pdf/1301.3781.pdf

[11] National Information Standards Organization (NISO) 2005. *Guidelines for the Construction, Format, and Management of Monolingual Controlled Vocabularies.*

[12] Sebastiani, F. 2002. Machine Learning in Automated Text Categorization. *ACM Computing Surveys* vol. 34, pp. 1-47

[13] Shvaiko, P., Euzenat, J. 2013. Ontology Matching: State of the Art and Future Challenges. *IEEE Transactions on Knowledge and Data Engineering*, vol. 25, no. 1, pp.158-176

[14] Stein, B., Gollub, T., Hoppe, D. 2011, Beyond Precision @ 10: Clustering the Long Tail of Web Search Results, *20th ACM International Conference on in Information and Knowledge Management*, Glasgow, UK, pp. 2141-2144

[15] Westera, W. 2014, *Realising an Applied Gaming Ecosystem (RAGE) - Annex 1 to the Grant Agreement (Description of the Action) Part B*

Important Word Organization for Support of Browsing Scholarly Papers Using Author Keywords

Junki Tanijiri
Okayama University
Okayama, Japan
tanijiri@de.cs.okayama-u.ac.jp

Manabu Ohta
Okayama University
Okayama, Japan
ohta@de.cs.okayama-u.ac.jp

Atsuhiro Takasu
National Institute of Informatics
Tokyo, Japan
takasu@nii.ac.jp

Jun Adachi
National Institute of Informatics
Tokyo, Japan
adachi@nii.ac.jp

ABSTRACT

When new researchers read scholarly papers, they often encounter unfamiliar technical terms, which may require considerable time to investigate. We have been developing a user interface to support the browsing of scholarly papers, which can provide useful links to information about such technical terms. The interface displays "important terms" extracted from a paper on top of the image of the paper. In this study, we organize the important terms extracted from papers by using author keywords. We first identify the important terms and then associate them with author keywords by using a method based on the word2vec model. Experiments showed that our method improved the classification accuracy of important terms compared with a simple baseline method. It associated each author keyword with about 2.5 relevant important terms.

Keywords

scholarly paper, author keyword, browsing interface, browsing support, word2vec, TF-IDF

1. INTRODUCTION

Digital libraries and e-book reading devices such as iPad and Kindle are now common, following the transition to digital documents throughout our society. We have therefore been developing a user interface that supports screen-based browsing of scholarly papers, particularly by new researchers. Some browsing-support systems have already been developed. For example, Matsuo et al.[2] have developed a browsing-support system that learns a user's interests and highlights keywords based on the user's browsing history. They focus on detecting users' interests by monitoring user access to the Web, whereas our interface aims to support new researchers by enabling them to read scholarly papers more easily. In this paper, we propose organizing the "important terms" extracted from scholarly papers by using "author keywords" to enhance the

DocEng '16, September 12-16, 2016, Vienna, Austria

© 2016 ACM. ISBN 978-1-4503-4438-8/16/09...$15.00

DOI: http://dx.doi.org/10.1145/2960811.2967163

interface. A number of important terms that involve technical concepts will usually appear in a scholarly paper. The paper will often also contain author keywords, supplied by the authors to highlight the contents of the paper properly. The aim of the author keywords is to aid searching by readers who are interested in related studies. They will usually refer to research topics, characteristic terms, or specific terms[7]. We can therefore expect author keywords to be closely related to the authors' various intentions. If we can associate author keywords and important terms properly, we will be providing readers with important terms that reflect the authors' intentions.

This paper is structured as follows. In Section 2, we describe the interface for supporting the browsing of scholarly papers, as implemented for use in tablet terminals by our research group[1]. We then propose a method for important-term organization by classification and by association with author keywords, in Section 3. In Section 4, we report on the experiments performed to evaluate our proposed method. We conclude the paper in Section 5.

2. INTERFACE TO SUPPORT THE BROWSING OF SCHOLARLY PAPERS

2.1 Outline

Our interface first extracts text from the portable document format (PDF) version of a paper and analyzes it morphologically. We use the NSLinguisticTagger[1] class for the morphological analysis. Next, the interface calculates the degree of importance for nouns and unknown words extracted from the text by using the term frequency–inverse document frequency (TF-IDF) measure[6]. The paper image and 30 important terms from the paper are then displayed via the interface. When the user selects one of the terms, the relevant analytical results and related information extracted from the Web are displayed.

2.2 Operational Methods and Functions

In using our interface, a user can browse the image of a paper on the screen of the interface, turn pages by swiping right and left, and scale the images by pinch-in and pinch-out.

There are two buttons at the top left of the screen (see Figure 1). If a user taps "Select Text" and specifies the top left and bottom right of any term, the interface displays the Wikipedia[2] article sum-

---

[1] https://developer.apple.com/reference/foundation/nslinguistictagger
[2] http://en.wikipedia.org/wiki/

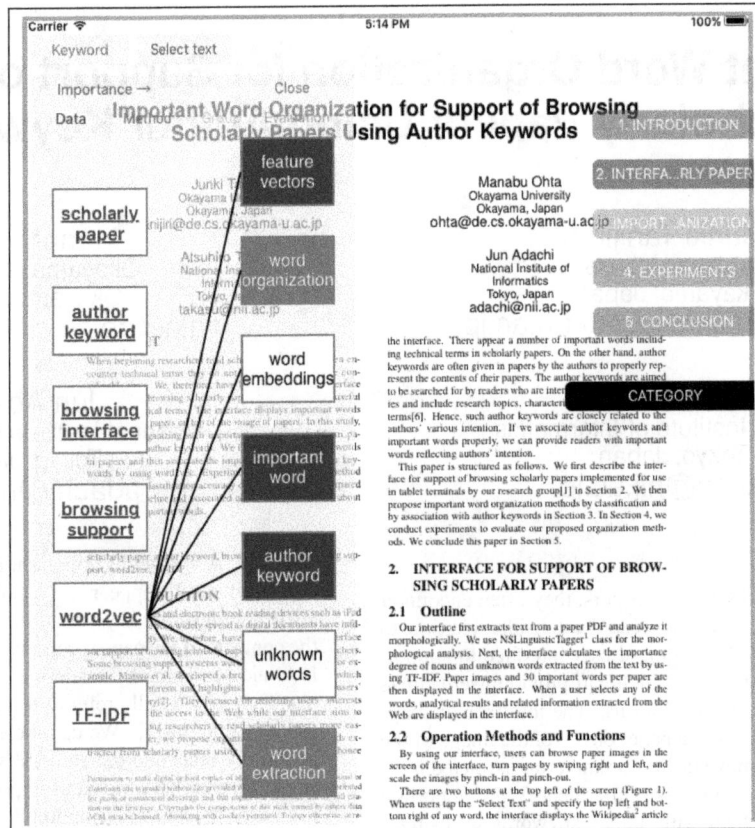

Figure 1: A browsing-support system image.

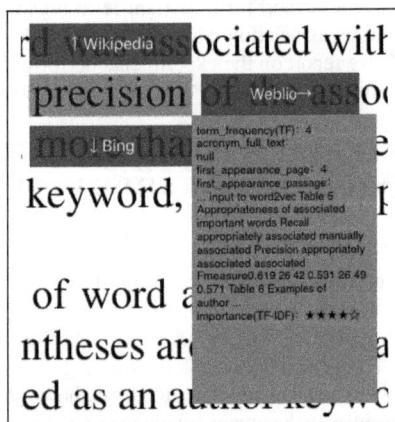

Figure 2: Analytical results for "precision".

mary, the snippets extracted from Weblio[3], and the top three search results from Bing[4], together with links to them. It also displays the frequency and analytical results for the term, as shown in Figure 2. If a user taps "Keyword" (see Figure 1), then 30 important terms are displayed as tag clouds superimposed over the image on the screen.

[3]http://ejje.weblio.jp/
[4]http://www.bing.com/

3. IMPORTANT TERM ORGANIZATION

3.1 Important Term Extraction

We extract nouns and unknown terms that comprise one or two words by morphological analysis, because many of the important terms in papers are nouns and compound nouns. We calculate their importance via the widely used TF-IDF measure. Equation (1) calculates the TF-IDF values of term t_i.

$$tfidf_i = tf_i * \log(\frac{num}{df_i}), \qquad (1)$$

where tf_i is the occurrence frequency of term t_i in the paper, num (= 16,831,499) is the total number of papers stored in CiNii[5], and df_i is the number of search results for t_i in CiNii. From the terms for which $tf > 2$ and $df < 5,000$, we select the 30 terms ranked highest by TF-IDF value as the important terms.

3.2 Important Term Classification

3.2.1 Category

The interface classifies the extracted important terms for browsing support. We define the following five categories for this purpose.

- Data: terms related to experimental data.

- Method: terms related to methods.

- Group: team names and forums, etc.

[5]Scholarly and Academic Information Navigator, http://ci.nii.ac.jp/

Table 1: Adequacy of important terms

Task	Adequacy (appropriate/extracted)
PatentMT	0.767 (23/30)
INTENT	0.667 (20/30)
SpokenDoc	0.700 (21/30)
Total	0.711 (64/90)

Table 3: # of associated important terms per paper

n	# of associated important terms
10	1.818 (60/33)
50	7.303 (241/33)
100	13.182 (435/33)
200	19.909 (657/33)

Table 2: Classification results

Method	Size	Accuracy
Logistic regression	80	0.239
	160	0.565
	240	0.633
	320	0.570
Baseline	-	0.433

Table 4: Statistics on author keywords

# of author keywords per paper	3.636
Wikipedia articles[*]	0.183
# of important terms per author keyword[**]	4.692

[*] The proportion of author keywords whose articles were found in Wikipedia.
[**] $n = 100$

- Evaluation: terms related to evaluation experiments.

- Other: terms that do not fit into the other four categories.

These categories are considered to be useful for reading empirical papers such as those in NTCIR[4]. Users can focus on any of these categories to match their interest best. Classification using other categories might be better suited to other genres of papers.

3.2.2 Classification Method

We use word2vec[3] to generate feature vectors for important terms and to classify them. Mikolov et al.[3] proposed using word2vec to produce word embeddings. In this study, we first obtain the feature vectors of the important terms by processing the full text of papers via word2vec. We then classify the important terms into the five categories listed in Section 3.2.1 by logistic regression. For this, we use the library functions of scikit-learn[5].

3.3 Association of Important Terms and Author Keywords

We make an association between the important terms and the author keywords by calculating the similarity between their word vectors, as generated by word2vec. However, word2vec cannot generate proper feature vectors for author keywords if they do not appear in the body of the paper. Therefore, we augment the text of the paper with text from any Wikipedia articles about the author keywords before using word2vec.

We select the top n terms that are the most similar to each author keyword and associate important terms with the author keyword if the important terms include any of these top n terms. In the experiments in Section 4.3, we vary the value of n from 10 to 200. Figure 1 shows a screen shot of the interface displaying author keywords (left) and important terms (right), where seven important terms are associated with an author keyword. If users tap another author keyword, the important terms associated with it will be displayed.

4. EXPERIMENTS

4.1 Evaluation of Important-Term Extraction

We first evaluated the adequacy of important terms. We selected a paper from each of three tasks of NTCIR-9[4]; namely, PatentMT, INTENT, and SpokenDoc. We then evaluated the appropriateness of the important terms extracted from these papers, based on two criteria:

1. appropriate as terms,

2. not common terms but used in one or more specialized fields.

The first author of this paper judged the appropriateness of the important terms and calculated its "adequacy" as the proportion of appropriate terms among all the important terms (see Table 1).

The table shows that more than 70% of the extracted important terms are appropriate. Most of the inappropriate terms are those that are included in a compound term comprising three or more words such as "patent parallel (corpus)". Therefore, it is necessary to extract such compounds.

4.2 Evaluation of Important-Term Classification

Next, we evaluated the accuracy of the classification method explained in Section 3.2. We classified the same 90 important terms as used in the experiment of Table 1. The first author of this paper determined the "correct" category of the important terms to establish a ground-truth classification. We processed 81 papers selected from NTCIR-9 via word2vec to generate the feature vectors of the 90 important terms. We adopted leave-one-out cross-validation to calculate the classification accuracy.

Table 2 shows the classification results for the 90 important terms, where the baseline signifies the result that all the important terms were classified into the largest category among the five, which was "Method", and the size signifies the number of dimensions for the important term vectors generated by word2vec.

As seen in Table 2, our proposed method showed an accuracy of 0.633 when the dimensionality was 240, which was well above the baseline accuracy of 0.433.

4.3 Evaluation of Term Association

Next, we evaluated our term-association method. Thirty-three papers selected from the same three tasks of NTCIR-9 (see Section 4.1) were processed via word2vec.

Table 3 shows the number of associated important terms found when varying the value of parameter $n (= 10, 50, 100, 200)$, as described in Section 3.3. From these results, 19.909 important terms per paper were associated with one or more author keywords when $n = 200$, whereas only 1.818 important terms were associated when $n = 10$. Other statistics are summarized in Table 4. As seen from this table, many of the author keywords were not explained in Wikipedia. Another result is that 4.692 important terms were associated with an author keyword, on average. However, some

Table 5: Appropriateness of associated important terms

Recall (appropriately associated/manually associated)	Precision (appropriately associated/associated)	F-measure
0.619 (26/42)	0.531 (26/49)	0.571

Table 6: Examples of author keywords and their associated important terms

Author keyword (Task)	Associated important term	Not an associated important term
query intent (INTENT)	subtopic mining, related query, original query, (subtopic string), (subtopic list), document ranking	query reformulation
TF-IDF value (Spoken&Doc)	(web search)	similarity score
statistical machine translation (PatentMT)	EBMT system, SMT system, (MERT), (dataset), Computational Linguistic	patent translation, patent data

author keywords were associated with up to 10 important terms, while some had no associations. The number of associated important terms varied, depending on the author keywords.

Finally, we evaluated the appropriateness of the association of author keywords and important terms. For this evaluation, we used the same three papers as shown in Table 1 and set the parameter $n = 100$. The first author of this paper prepared a ground-truth association by reading the papers used in this experiment. We evaluated the appropriateness by calculating the recall and precision of important terms associated with each author keyword as

$$\text{recall} = \frac{\text{\# of appropriately associated important terms}}{\text{\# of manually associated important terms}}, \quad (2)$$

$$\text{precision} = \frac{\text{\# of appropriately associated important terms}}{\text{\# of associated important terms}}. \quad (3)$$

Table 5 shows the appropriateness of the associated important terms. Because an author keyword was associated with 4.692 important terms on average and the precision of the association was 0.531, as shown in Tables 4 and 5, more than half of the associated terms, about 2.5 terms per author keyword, were appropriate, whereas about 2.2 terms were not.

Table 6 shows some examples of term association, where those "associated important terms" in parentheses were judged to be inappropriate. For example, "query intent" was listed as an author keyword in many papers involving the INTENT task. Our proposed method could associate many important terms with "query intent", as shown in Table 6. For example, "subtopic mining" and "document ranking" are the names of subtasks of INTENT, and the association of these is therefore appropriate. On the other hand, the author keyword "TF-IDF value" was associated with only one (inappropriate) important term. In addition, we could not find its association with an appropriate important term such as "similarity score". The proposed method could associate author keyword "statistical machine translation" with appropriate important terms such as "EBMT system". However, the appropriateness of some of associated important terms such as "dataset" was not clear.

5. CONCLUSION

We have proposed a method for important-term organization by using classification and author keywords to support the browsing of scholarly papers. We evaluated the adequacy of important terms extracted from papers, the classification accuracy of the important terms, and the appropriateness of the association found between important terms and author keywords. The experiments showed that our method improved the classification accuracy considerably compared with a simple baseline. It associated an author keyword

with about 2.5 relevant important terms and with about 2.2 irrelevant important terms.

We plan to improve the accuracy of both important-term extraction and classification, and to reexamine the appropriate association of important terms with their related author keywords. In future work, we aim to perform a user study involving actual users of our browsing-support interface.

6. ACKNOWLEDGMENTS

This work was supported by a JSPS Grant-in-Aid for Scientific Research (B) (15H02789), a JSPS Grant-in-Aid for Scientific Research (C) (25330384), and the Collaborative Research Program of the National Institute of Informatics.

7. REFERENCES

[1] A. Maeno, M. Ohta, and A. Takasu. Use of Acronyms for Interface for Support of Browsing Scholarly Papers. *IPSJ SIG Technical Report*, 2014-DBS-160(16):1–8, 2014 (in Japanese).

[2] Y. Matsuo, H. Fukuta, and M. Ishizuka. Browsing Support by Hilighting Keywords based on a User's Browsing History. In *2002 IEEE International Conference on Systems, Man and Cybernetics*, 2002.

[3] T. Mikolov, I. Sutskever, K. Chen, G. Corrado, and J. Dean. Distributed Representations of Words and Phrases and their Compositionality. In *Advances in Neural Information Processing Systems*, pages 3111–3119, 2013.

[4] N. I. of Informatics. NTCIR (NIINACSIS Test Collection for IR Systems) Project [online]. Available from: <http://research.nii.ac.jp/ntcir/>.

[5] F. Pedregosa, G. Varoquaux, A. Gramfort, V. Michel, B. Thirion, and et al. Scikit-learn: Machine learning in Python. *The Journal of Machine Learning Research*, 12:2825–2830, 2011.

[6] G. Salton, E. A. Fox, and H. Wu. Extended Boolean Information Retrieval. *Communications of the ACM*, 26(11):1022–1036, 1983.

[7] K. Uchiyama. A Study for Identifying Domain-specific Introductory Terms in Research Papers. In *9th International Conference on Terminology and Artificial Intelligence*, pages 146–149, 2011.

Selecting Features with Class Based and Importance Weighted Document Frequency in Text Classification

Baoli Li
College of Information Science and Engineering
Henan University of Technology
100 Lotus Street, High & New Industrial Development Zone
Zhengzhou, Henan, P.R. China
csblli@gmail.com

ABSTRACT

Document Frequency (DF), which counts how many documents a feature appears in, is reported by Yang and Pedersen [1] to be quite effective for feature selection in text classification. Features with the same DF value are likely to have different appearance distribution over categories, and demonstrate quite different discriminative powers for classification. However, the original DF metric is class independent and does not consider features' distribution over classes. On the other hand, different features play different roles in delivering the content of a document. The chosen features are expected to be the important ones, which carry the main information of a document collection. However, the traditional DF metric considers features equally important. To overcome simultaneously the above two problems of the original document frequency metric, we propose a class based and importance weighted document frequency measure. Preliminary experiments on two text classification datasets do validate the effectiveness of the proposed metric.

Keywords

Feature Selection; Document Frequency; Text Classification; Text Categorization; Feature Filtering.

1. INTRODUCTION

To process a large document collection, text classification is usually a necessary step to assign one or more pre-defined categories to each document. In general, we may have at least thousands of candidate features in a text classification problem, and, at the same time, these features are not equally effective in text classification. Therefore, feature selection, which aims at finding the most effective feature subset, is usually a must step [2]. It can not only reduce the time and space costs but also boost the system's performance. Different feature selection measures, such as document frequency, information gain, chi-square, bi-normal separation, odds ratio, mutual information, etc., have been put forward for ranking features in the past years [3]. Document Frequency (DF), among these measures, counts how many documents a feature appears in, and has been reported as a simple yet quite effective measure in solving different text classification problems [1].

DocEng '16, September 12-16, 2016, Vienna, Austria
© 2016 ACM. ISBN 978-1-4503-4438-8/16/09…$15.00
DOI: http://dx.doi.org/10.1145/2960811.2967164

As pointed in [4], the original DF metric does not care about class information. It cares only about whether a feature appears in a document. Thus derived DF values cannot differentiate two features having the same DF value. Those features, which distribute evenly over different categories, may have less discriminative power than those features with biased distribution. On the other hand, features in a document may have different importance in delivering the document's content, but the traditional DF regards features equally [5]. We do expect in the feature selection step to filter out those unimportant features, which are usually considered as noise.

To overcome both the above two weaknesses of the original document frequency measure at the same time, we propose a class based and importance weighted document frequency measure to revise the original DF to some extent. Basically, for each feature, we count its document frequencies in each category and then choose the maximal class document frequency for ranking. To give important features more weights, we add a value between 0 and 1 rather than always 1 when we find a feature appears in a document. The real value indicates how important the feature is in that document. Experiments on two publicly available datasets show that the proposed class based and importance weighted document frequency metric (CBIWDF) performs consistently better than the traditional DF, and achieves at least as good results as Chi-Square and information gain, which are two popular state-of-the-art feature selection measures.

The rest of this short paper is organized as following: section 2 summaries related work; section 3 presents the proposed class based and importance weighted document frequency (CBIWDF) measure; section 4 gives experimental results on two text classification problems and analyzes the results; finally, section 5 concludes the paper with some possible investigation in the future.

2. RELATED WORK

Feature Selection has been widely investigated in machine learning community in recent decades. The successful application includes but is not limited to: gene microarray analysis, combinatorial chemistry, image classification, face recognition, text clustering, spam detection, and text classification. The advent of big data era demands more for feature selection. Literature [6-9] presents excellent review about feature selection in dealing with different problems.

We normally have two alternative feature selection strategies: choosing a subset from a candidate set or deriving a new compact set from all candidate features. In this research, we concentrate on the first strategy, which is further split into two categories: wrapper and filter. Wrapper methods expect to obtain the ideal feature set by evaluating the performance of each candidate subset, where filter methods rank features independently. Filter methods are more popular than wrapper ones, because of their lower computation cost. Forman [3] and Yang and Pedersen [1] empirically compare different feature filtering methods for text classification, including document frequency, information gain, chi-square, bi-normal separation, odds ratio, mutual information, power, and so on. Yang and Pedersen [1] conclude that the DF metric can perform as excellent as chi-square and information gain metrics. In this study, we concentrate on how to further improve Document Frequency (DF) metric.

In [4], we take class based document frequency as measure for ranking features, while an importance weighted document frequency strategy is reported in [5]. In this research, we explore how to solve the two problems of the traditional DF metric simultaneously: neglecting the difference of features' distribution over categories and counting each feature equally. We thus propose a class based and importance weighted document frequency feature selection metric.

3. CLASS BASED AND IMPORTANCE WEIGHTED DOCUMENT FREQUENCY

As pointed out in section 1, the original document frequency metric has two problems: one is ignoring the class distribution of a feature over different categories, and the other is regarding each feature equally. Obviously, features with imbalanced class distribution may have more discriminative capacity than those with balanced distribution, and the chosen features are expected to carry the main content of documents. We, thus, propose a class based and importance weighted document frequency measure to overcome the two weaknesses of the original DF metric. For a feature, we accumulate its importance value for each document it appears over different categories and then choose the maximal importance weighted class document frequency for ranking.

To evaluate the discriminative capacity of a feature t for class CLS_i, we need to count the following numbers:

A_i: how many documents of class CLS_i contain feature t;

B_i: how many documents with feature t do not belong to class CLS_i;

C_i: how many documents of class CLS_i do not contain feature t;

D_i: how many documents without feature t do not belong to class CLS_i.

Suppose that we totally have M categories in a classification problem. Then, the traditional document frequency (DF) measure can be calculated as follows:

$$DF = \sum_{i=1}^{M} A_i \qquad (1)$$

, and the popular Chi-Square feature selection metric can be computed as follows:

$$Chi\text{-}Square = \sum_{i=1}^{M} CHI_i \qquad (2)$$
$$= \sum_{i=1}^{M} \frac{(A_i + B_i + C_i + D_i) \times (A_i \times D_i - C_i \times B_i)}{(A_i + C_i) \times (B_i + D_i) \times (A_i + B_i) \times (C_i + D_i)}$$

A simple class based document frequency metric (CBDF), which is proposed in [4], use the following formula:

$$CBDF = \underset{i=1}{\overset{M}{MAX}} A_i \qquad (3)$$

, which chooses the maximal class document frequency of a feature for ranking.

If there are totally $D(CLS_i)$ documents of class CLS_i in the training data set, A_i can also be calculated as follows:

$$A_i = \sum_{j=1}^{D(CLS_i)} f(t, d_j) \qquad (4)$$

, where $f(t, d_j)$ is defined as follows:

$$f(t, d_j) = \begin{cases} 1, & t \text{ is in } d_j \\ 0, & \text{no } t \text{ in } d_j \end{cases} \qquad (5)$$

In formulas (4) and (5), $f(t, d_j)$ cares only about whether feature t appears in d_j, but fails to consider how important t is in d_j. Important features are expected to have more discriminative power than others. We then replace $f(t, d_j)$ with the following formula:

$$f(t, d_j) = \frac{TFIDF_t}{\sum_{f \in d_j} TFIDF_f} \qquad (6)$$

, where $TFIDF_t$ is the $TFIDF$ value of feature t in document d_j. Formula (6) gives the relative importance of feature t in document d_j.

By combining formulas (1), (4), and (6), we obtain a variant of importance weighted document frequency (IWDF) as reported in [5].

$$IWDF = \sum_{i=1}^{M} \left(\sum_{j=1}^{D(CLS_j)} \left(\frac{TFIDF_t}{\sum_{f \in d_j} TFIDF_f} \right) \right) \qquad (7)$$

From formulas (3), (4), and (6), we derive the class based and importance weighted document frequency metric as follows:

$$CBIWDF = \underset{i=1}{\overset{M}{MAX}} \left(\sum_{j=1}^{D(CLS_j)} \left(\frac{TFIDF_t}{\sum_{f \in d_j} TFIDF_f} \right) \right) \qquad (8)$$

4. EXPERIMENTS AND DISCUSSION

In order to evaluate the proposed CBIWDF metric, we conduct extensive experiments on two text classification problems.

4.1 Datasets

The following two datasets are used in our experiment:

20 Newsgroups: it is a balanced dataset, which has 20 different newsgroups, each corresponding to a specific topic [10]. We use the "bydate" version of this dataset, as it has a standard training and test split. The training set has 11,293 samples and the test set 7,528 samples.

Sector: it is an imbalanced dataset, which has 105 categories, 6,412 training samples, and 3,207 test samples. In the training dataset, the largest categories have 80 samples, while the smallest category has only 10 samples. Most categories have around 40-80 samples. This dataset was first used by McCallum and Nigam in their paper [11]. We used a version of this dataset from the LIBSVM data collection, which has removed stop and rare words (DF=1).

4.2 Experimental Settings

According to the vector space model (VSM), we represent a document as a space vector, whose coordinates correspond to the words in the collection. The weight of a feature, i.e. its TFIDF value, is computed as follows:

$$TFIDF_t = \frac{(1 + \log(TF_{t,d}))\log(\frac{|D|}{DF_t})}{\sqrt{\sum_t((1 + \log(TF_{t,d}))\log(\frac{|D|}{DF_t}))^2}} \quad (9)$$

, which is the standard feature weighting schema "ltc" in Manning and Schutze [11]. D is the document collection, where TF and DF are the frequency of feature t in document d and its document frequency in the collection D respectively. We experiment with four widely used algorithms: Centroid, Multinomial Naive Bayes[11], Linear (Liblinear [13]) and SVM (Libsvm [14]).

We compare the performance of different classification algorithms with the original DF, Chi-Square, information gain, CBDF, IWDF, and CBIWDF feature selection metrics. The original DF, Information Gain, and Chi-Square are used as baselines. We explore how to revise the original DF to get a better metric, and the Information Gain and Chi-Square metrics have been reported to perform well on many different problems and can be taken as state-of-the-art feature selection metrics.

We use Micro-averaging F1 and Macro-averaging F1 as evaluation metrics.

4.3 Results and Discussion

In our experiments, Liblinear achieves the highest scores among the four experimented text classification algorithms. Due to the limited space, we thus only report the results of this algorithm here. For each dataset, we experiment with top N features, where N varies from 500 to 10,000 with interval of 500.

Figure 1 and figure 2 show the averaging Micro-F1 and Macro-F1 results of the DF, CBDF, IWDF, CBIWDF, information gain, and Chi-square as feature selection metrics on two datasets respectively.

On the 20 newsgroups dataset, CBDF, IWDF and CBIWDF constantly perform much better than the original DF. The difference is evident when using fewer features, but tends to be narrower when using more features. DF looks approximately good as others when we use more than 9,000 features (the total number of candidate features is 73,712), although all of them (CBDF, IWDF, and CBIWDF) do beat the original DF.

CBIWDF, which aims at solving the two problems of the original DF, does exhibit advantages over both CBDF and IWDF, as verifies that considering more factors do result in much better performance. On this dataset, CBDF achieves better result than IWDF. The problem of features' imbalanced distribution over categories is much serious in this dataset.

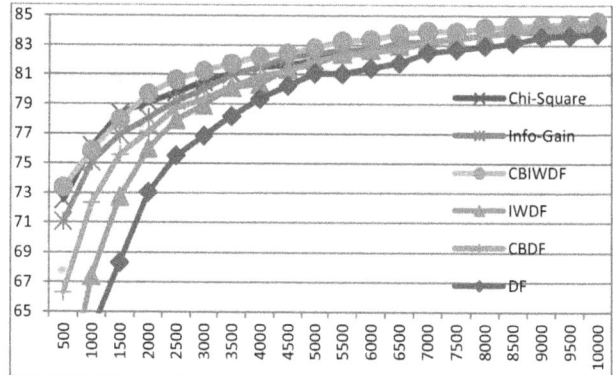

(a)   Micro-Averaging F1 Scores

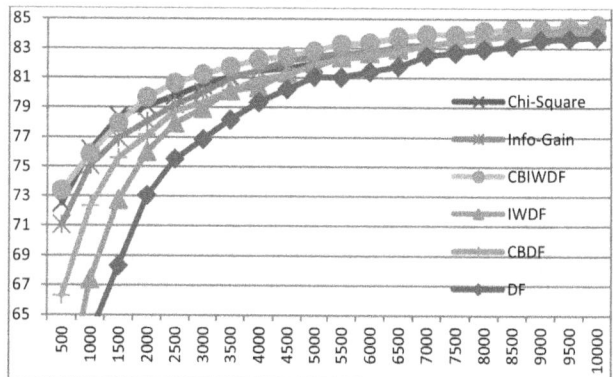

(b)   Macro-Averaging F1 Scores

Figure 1. Performance of different feature selection methods on the 20 newsgroup dataset.

CBIWDF performs a little better than both information gain and Chi-square on this dataset, where chi-square obtains a little better result than information gain metric.

Figure 2 shows the results on the sector dataset. There are totally 48,988 candidate features in this dataset. When using less than 1,000 features, information gain metric obtains the best results, chi-square performs the worst, and the original DF does beat chi-square. Similarly as on the 20 newsgroups dataset, all the three variants of DF (CBDF, IWDF, and CBIWDF) demonstrate strong advantages over DF. When using more than 1,000 features, CBIWDF metric shows big advantages over all other metrics. When using less than 3,500 features, the preference order is as follows: IWDF > Info-Gain > CBDF > DF > Chi-square, where when using more than 3,500 features, this order is changed to be: IWDF > Chi-square > CBDF > Info-Gain > DF. Comparatively speaking, Information Gain, CBIWDF, IWDF, and CBDF metrics perform stably. On this dataset, IWDF achieves better result than CBDF, which means that features' importance plays key role in differentiating different features.

Chi-Square, one of popular feature selection metrics, obtains the poorest results when using less than 3,500 features. We attribute it to the fewer samples for each categories in this dataset, which make the class based Chi-Square metric less accurate and stable.

Overall, CBIWDF achieves at least as good results as information gain and Chi-Square do across all the two datasets. Compared to Chi-Square and information gain, the calculation and implementation of CBIWDF is much straightforward and trivial.

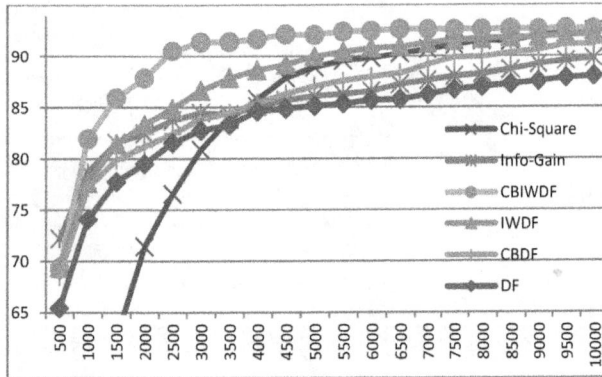

(a) Micro-Averaging F1 Scores

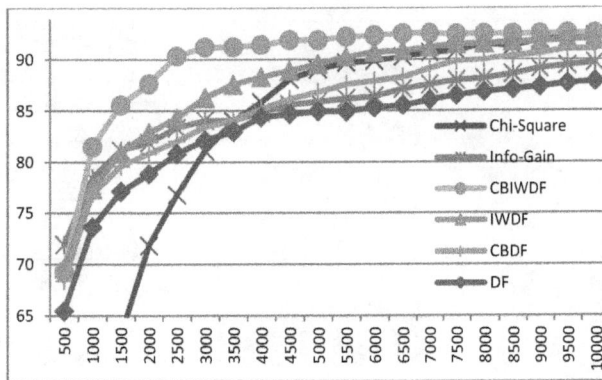

(b) Macro-Averaging F1 Scores

Figure 2. Performance of different feature selection methods on the sector dataset.

5. CONCLUSIONS AND FUTURE WORK

As an unsupervised and class independent metric, Document Frequency, is reported as a simple yet quite effective feature selection measure in text categorization. However, the original DF measure has two problems: one is ignoring the class distribution of a feature over different categories, and the other is regarding each feature equally. Targeting at solving these two problems simultaneously, we propose a class based and importance weighted document frequency measure for selecting features in text classification. Experiments on two publicly available datasets demonstrate that: 1) the proposed CBIWDF metric does perform better than the traditional DF metric, and two previously revised metrics, CBDF and IWDF; 2) CBIWDF can achieve at least as good results as Chi-Square and information gain, which are two popular state-of-the-art feature selection metrics.

In the future, we plan to experiment with more datasets and apply the proposed feature selection metrics into other text mining applications, e.g. text clustering, sentiment analysis, and so on. We also consider revising other existing feature selection metrics with similar strategies.

6. ACKNOWLEDGMENTS

This work was supported by the High-level Talent Foundation of Henan University of Technology (No. 2012BS027), and the Henan Provincial Research Program on Fundamental and Cutting-Edge Technologies (No. 112300410007).

7. REFERENCES

[1] Yang Y. and Pedersen J. O.1997. A comparative study on feature selection in text categorization. In *Proceedings of Fourteenth International Conference on Machine Learning.* 412-420.

[2] Forman, G. 2003. An extensive empirical study of feature selection metrics for text classification. *J. Mach. Learn. Res.* 3 (Mar. 2003), 1289-1305.

[3] Forman, G. 2007. Feature Selection for Text Classification. Technical Report (No. HPL-2007-16R1), HP Laboratories Palo Alto.

[4] Li B., Yan Q., and Han L. 2016. Using Class Based Document Frequency to Select Features in Text Classification. In Proceedings of the First National Conference on Big Data Technology and Applications (BDTA-2015): 200-210.

[5] Li B., Yan Q., Xu Z., and Wang G. 2015. Weighted Document Frequency for Feature Selection in Text Classification. In Proceedings of 2015 International Conference on Asian Language Processing: 132-135.

[6] Guyon, I., & Elisseeff, A. 2003. An introduction to variable and feature selection. *J. Mach. Learn. Res.* 3 (Mar. 2003), 1157-1182.

[7] Chandrashekar, G., & Sahin, F. 2014. A survey on feature selection methods. *Computers & Electrical Engineering*, 40(1), 16-28.

[8] Tang, J., Alelyani, S., & Liu, H. 2014. Feature selection for classification: A review. *Data Classification: Algorithms and Applications*. Editor: Charu Aggarwal, CRC Press In Chapman & Hall/CRC Data Mining and Knowledge Discovery Series.

[9] Lazar, C., Taminau, J., Meganck, S., Steenhoff, D., Coletta, A., Molter, C., & Nowe, A. 2012. A survey on filter techniques for feature selection in gene expression microarray analysis. *IEEE/ACM Transactions on Computational Biology and Bioinformatics* (TCBB), 9(4), 1106-1119.

[10] Lang, K.1995. Newsweeder: learning to filter netnews. In *Proceedings of the Twelfth International Conference on Machine Learning*, 331-339.

[11] McCallum A. and Nigam K. 1998. A Comparison of Event Models for Naive Bayes Text Classification. In *Proceedings of the AAAI-98 Workshop on Learning for Text Categorization.*

[12] Manning C. D. and Schutze H. 1999. *Foundations of Statistical Natural Language Processing.* MIT Press, Cambridge, MA.

[13] Fan R.-E., Chang K.-W., Hsieh C.-J., Wang X.-R., and Lin C.-J.2008. LIBLINEAR: A library for large linear classification. *J. Mach. Learn. Res.*9(2008), 1871-1874.

[14] Chang C.-C. and Lin C.-J.. 2011. LIBSVM: a library for support vector machines. *ACM Transactions on Intelligent Systems and Technology*, 2:27:1--27:27.

Bayesian mixture models on connected components for Newspaper article segmentation

Giorgos Sfikas   Georgios Louloudis   Nikolaos Stamatopoulos

Basilis Gatos

Institute of Informatics and Telecommunications
NCSR "Demokritos"
Athens, Greece
{sfikas, louloud, nstam, bgat}@iit.demokritos.gr

ABSTRACT

In this paper we propose a new method for automated segmentation of scanned newspaper pages into articles. Article regions are produced as a result of merging sub-article level content and title regions. We use a Bayesian Gaussian mixture model to model page Connected Component information and cluster input into sub-article components. The Bayesian model is conditioned on a prior distribution over region features, aiding classification into titles and content. Using a Dirichlet prior we are able to automatically estimate correctly the number of title and article regions. The method is tested on a dataset of digitized historical newspapers, where visual experimental results are very promising.

1. INTRODUCTION

Digitization of machine-printed and handwritten documents of various kinds has led to a subsequent demand for tools to handle more effectively the digitized content. Automatic document understanding techniques have been employed to ease access to scholar, students, or casual users alike. Page layout analysis, optical character recognition and keyword spotting [10] are techniques that are widely used today, and attract considerable interest from the part of end-users as well as researchers.

Newspapers are a special class of documents, from the point of view of their layout as well as their content structure. Content is organized into a set of articles, presented typically in a small number of columns. Article tracking, or otherwise called article identification or article segmentation [7], is the process of segmenting a scanned input page into a set of semantically-coherent regions that would correspond to the area covered by each newspaper article in the scanned image. Article tracking typically is built on top of a page segmentation step that clusters the page into sub-article areas containing article body text, titles, supertitles, or other content.

Newspaper segmentation can be considered as a special form of generic document or page segmentation. Segmenting newspaper pages can be aided if the used algorithm encodes succes-

fully the prior knowledge that newspaper layout is in practice constrained. For example, newspapers present their material as a series of semantically-coherent articles, which are usually presented in a number of columns. On the other hand, newspapers can be also more difficult to segment than the average document, due to factors that may hinder the performance of generic algorithms. A typical factor that may hinder performance is the usually close contact of regions in newspapers [7].

In this work we present a novel algorithm for segmentation of a newspaper image into articles. Our algorithm identifies articles after performing newspaper segmentation at a lower-level, where the page is clustered into sub-article components. We experiment with using a Fully Bayesian Gaussian mixture model (FBGMM) [5] as a classifier in the current context of newspaper image data. Connected component analysis provides input to the FBGMM, used here to cluster connected components into region types and title groups. We take advantage of the fully probabilistic structure of the used mixture model to include parameter priors and detect numbers of components automatically. Tests on a number of digitized historical newspapers show promising results.

The remainder of this article is organized as follows. In section 2 we provide the reader with a brief overview of related work in newspaper segmentation. We briefly present the Bayesian model we use as a classifier in section 3. In section 4 we present the proposed algorithm in detail. In section 5 we present the dataset of newspaper pages we used for experiments, and present experiment visual results. Finally, we conclude the paper and discuss future work in section 6.

2. RELATED WORK

Works in newspaper article segmentation in general aim first to segment the input page into sub-article layout components, before merging these into output articles. Sub-article components can be tagged with regard to the content of the region they refer to. Possible choices are mainly tagging a region as text-containing or image-containing, though other considerations are also possible. Such a consideration would be using a separate class for titles and another one for article body text, or to an even finer class taxonomy. In [8] for example, a total of 12 different classes to tag text regions are possible.

A considerable number of works propose methods to segment the newspaper page into sub-article layout components, without proceeding to use these as a base step to identify articles. We shall briefly refer to a number of such works here. In [19] a neural network is used to classify a newspaper image into image and text

Publication rights licensed to ACM. ACM acknowledges that this contribution was authored or co-authored by an employee, contractor or affiliate of a national government. As such, the Government retains a nonexclusive, royalty-free right to publish or reproduce this article, or to allow others to do so, for Government purposes only.

DocEng '16, September 12 - 16, 2016, Vienna, Austria

ACM ISBN 978-1-4503-4438-8/16/09... $15.00

DOI: http://dx.doi.org/10.1145/2960811.2967165

regions. The neural network is trained on high-probability output data of a preliminary segmentation step. In [1], a neural network is trained to identify text and non-text regions, using a manually created training set and a variety of hand-crafted features. In newspaper segmentation competitions [6] and [2], the competitor systems were required to cluster the image into sub-article components. In [13], the winning system of the competition [6], regions are clustered by merging together connected components, after estimating region boundary positions.

Segmentation into articles, or otherwise referred to as article tracking or article identification, has been addressed in [7]. In this work, a rule-based method is used to group text, images and titles into articles. Sub-article components are produced in the first stage of the method. First vertical/horizontal line extraction is performed, followed by image/drawing region identification and text/title extraction. A DFT-based algorithm is used to identify image areas, and RLSA with adaptive parameters is used to identify text areas. Regions are grouped into articles with a rule-based decision stage that includes over 40 empirical rules. Subsequent works [8, 15, 16, 14] are closely related to this base model for article tracking. Recent works in article tracking [11, 18] also use sets of hand-crafted rules to segment pages into articles.

Extraction of horizontal and vertical lines is recognized as an important step for the success of the whole algorithm in a multitude of works [7, 12, 17]. This is due to the fact that lines, either made up of foreground pixels or by background pixels (i.e. virtual separating lines), are typically used to demarcate region and article areas. In [12], the problem of line extraction for degraded documents in particular is studied. In [13] and [17], lines are extracted before merging connected components into regions. In the current work, we also use line separator detection as a step in our processing pipeline, and also use connected components as a base entity that is merged into sub-article regions and articles.

More complex models have been proposed to encode the newspaper hierarchy of articles and regions. A Conditional Random Field is used in [18] to model the newspaper page structure into coherent regions. In [3] a learning-based method, using a fixed-point model, has been proposed to identify articles. In the current work, we have experimented incorporating a Fully Bayesian Gaussian Mixture Model (FBGMM) [5] as a classifier for an article tracking pipeline. FBGMM has the advantage of being able to automatically estimate the number of classes of the data to be modeled, in contrast to the typical paradigm where the user has to specify the number of classes beforehand. In the context of newspaper segmentation, we use FBGMM to handle parameter prior knowledge and model region features, where the number of regions is a priori unknown.

3. BAYESIAN MODEL

We have used a Fully Bayesian Gaussian Mixture Model as a CC classifier, as part of the proposed segmentation pipeline. The Bayesian model is presented in detail and solved [1] in [5, ch. 10]. Input X is assumed to be a set of N real-valued vectors of dimension d, $X = [x^1, \cdots, x^N]$. These are modeled as being generated by a set of (maximum) K classes. For each class j, a one-zero vector z^n keeps track of the class responsible for generating the datum. Responsibility vectors z^n follow a multinomial distribution, $z^n \sim Mult(w)$ where w is a K-sized vector that encodes *a priori* responsibilities. All vectors are grouped in $N \times d$ matrix Z. Class emissions are modelled as Gaussians of class-specific mean μ_j and covariance Σ_j, with $x_j^n \sim N(\mu_j, \Sigma_j)$, $\mu = [\mu_1, \cdots, \mu_K]$, $\Sigma = [\Sigma_1, \cdots, \Sigma_K]$. Model

---

[1] An implementation can be found at http://www.cs.uoi.gr/~sfikas

parameters μ, Σ, Z are assumed to follow prior distributions that are conjugate to the Gaussian and Multinomial distributions (these are respectively Gaussian/Wishart and Dirichlet priors); this enables us to solve the otherwise intractable model with approximate inference [5, ch. 10]. Solution of the model returns posteriors given observations, over model parameters. For the current problem, we are specifically interested in the posterior for Z, i.e. $p(Z|X)$. Input data are clustered according to the class that maximizes their responsibility in the posterior for Z.

As part of the proposed algorithm, we use the FBGMM for clustering in two different parts of the pipeline. We cluster CCs into text, content, and non-text/non-content elements. We exploit the Bayesian formulation of the FBGMM to specify a prior mean for each component. Prior means are specified in terms of a base mean $\hat{\mu}$, with priors given as $[.25\mu, 4\mu, 20\mu]$.

In the second use of the FBGMM, the Dirichlet prior hyperparameter is set to a small value $\alpha = 10^{-6}$ and maximum $K = 50$ to enable the model to automatically estimate the true number of clusters. The clusters in this case correspond to title regions.

4. SEGMENTATION MODEL

The proposed algorithm for newspaper segmentation is made up of two main stages. In the first stage regions containing text, titles or other content are detected. These sub-article regions are merged in the second stage of the algorithm to create article-level regions.

We first run Connected Component Analysis on a binarization of the input page image [9]. Connected Components (CCs) are used throughout the algorithm as the element of base that is used to form regions of all levels. Convex regions of CCs with a major axis dominant over their minor axis are marked as separators. The CCs minus separators and CCs that are too small (compared to the average CCs) are clustered with FBGMM as described in the previous section (section 3). We have used 3 features for each CC. These are CC width, CC height and CC thickness. CC thickness is computed as the maximum value of each CC's distance transform. The resulting clustering is smoothed by a max-voting step.

Regions, title or content, are split when overlap with a separator is detected. Content CCs are then dilated in an RLSA-like step in both dimensions. We exclude title and separator pixels from the resulting dilation, and CCA is run to form content regions.

Article tracking is performed on the basis of the previous segmentation step of the image into title and content regions. Title regions are first grouped into title groups. Title regions are dilated in the vertical direction and CCA is performed on the image, excluding all pixels marked as non-title. The resulting CCs form our title groups. Afterwards content regions are assigned each to a single title group. We assign each content region to the nearest title group that is found above the region. Groups of title groups and assigned content regions form the required article segments.

5. DATASET AND EXPERIMENTS

In order to test our article tracking system, we used samples from a collection of digitized historical editions of the regional greek newspaper "*Tharros*". *Tharros* started being published as far back as 1899, and is still today in circulation in Greece. In this paper we show results of our method for 5 pages of *Tharros*, coming from editions published in different dates. While the test set is admittedly small, we feel that these pages are representative, to an extent, of most of the core variations in layout of the newspaper throughout its years of publication. We used pages with publication dates: February 9, 1901; February 18, 1917; June 4, 1948; March 1, 1975; June 23, 1989. Results of application of our method on

144

Algorithm 1 Proposed newspaper segmentation algorithm
___

Segmentation into sub-article components
Connected Component Analysis
   Compute CC features
   Detect separator components
Cluster CCs into content, title, other components
   Use FBGMM with appropriate priors
   Smooth clustering with max voting
Detect title regions
   Estimate number of regions with FBGMM
   Cluster into title regions with FBGMM
Post-processing
   Split regions when overlap with separators
Article tracking
Merge neighbouring titles into title groups
Assign content regions to a unique title group
Merge titles and content into articles
___

these images can be examined in fig. 1. Intermediate stages and the segmentation end result are shown. Comparison of the article tracking result with the input images suggests that our method in general identifies the number and position of articles correctly.

6. CONCLUSION AND FUTURE WORK

In this paper we have presented a novel system for newspaper segmentation into article and sub-article components. We used a Bayesian GMM, solved with Variation inference, to cluster the page more accurately.

In this work we have presented qualitative/visual results. Due to lack of annotated ground truth, we have not presented numerical results. Numerical methods for evaluation of region and article tracking have been considered elsewhere [7, 3, 4]. We envisage presenting numerical evaluation figures for our method, with tests on a dataset of larger scale in the future.

Samples from a single newspaper were used in the current work. While our algorithm is in principal not dependent to the specific layout of the *Tharros* newspaper, and throught the years there is considerable variance in the paper layout, we would like to test the method on other/different editions. Discriminating into more sub-classes of content, and providing an estimate of reading order is also left as future work.

Finally, we envisage working on a unified model for newspaper document understanding, where layout analysis in multiple levels and optical recognition would work jointly, and not as independent tasks.

7. REFERENCES

[1] T. Andersen and W. Zhang. Features for neural net based region identification of newspaper documents. In *Proceedings of the International Conference on Document Analysis and Recognition (ICDAR)*, pages 403–407, 2003.

[2] A. Antonacopoulos, C. Clausner, C. Papadopoulos, and S. Pletschacher. ICDAR 2013 competition on historical newspaper layout analysis (HNLA 2013). In *Proceedings of the International Conference on Document Analysis and Recognition (ICDAR)*, pages 1454–1458, 2013.

[3] A. Bansal, S. Chaudhury, S. D. Roy, and J. Srivastava. Newspaper article extraction using hierarchical fixed point model. In *Proceedings of the IAPR International Workshop on Document Analysis Systems (DAS)*, pages 257–261, 2014.

[4] R. Beretta and L. Laura. Performance evaluation of algorithms for newspaper article identification. In *Proceedings of the International Conference on Document Analysis and Recognition (ICDAR)*, pages 394–398, 2011.

[5] C. M. Bishop. *Pattern Recognition and Machine Learning.* Springer, 2006.

[6] B. Gatos, S. Mantzaris, and A. Antonacopoulos. First international newspaper segmentation contest. In *Proceedings of the International Conference on Document Analysis and Recognition (ICDAR)*, pages 1190–1194, 2001.

[7] B. Gatos, S. Mantzaris, K. Chandrinos, A. Tsigris, and S. J. Perantonis. Integrated algorithms for newspaper page decomposition and article tracking. In *Proceedings of the International Conference on Document Analysis and Recognition (ICDAR)*, pages 559–562, 1999.

[8] B. Gatos, S. Mantzaris, S. Perantonis, and A. Tsigris. Automatic page analysis for the creation of a digital library from newspaper archives. *International Journal on Digital Libraries*, 3(1):77–84, 2000.

[9] B. Gatos, I. Pratikakis, and S. J. Perantonis. Adaptive degraded document image binarization. *Pattern recognition*, 39(3):317–327, 2006.

[10] A. P. Giotis, G. Sfikas, B. Gatos, and C. Nikou. A survey of document image word spotting techniques. *Submitted to Pattern Recognition*, 2016.

[11] A. Jain, V. Sahasranaman, S. Saxena, and K. Chaudhury. Segmenting printed media pages into articles, Oct. 16 2012. US Patent 8,290,268.

[12] A. Lemaitre, J. Camillerapp, and B. Couasnon. Approche perceptive pour la reconnaissance de filets bruités, application à la structuration de pages de journaux. In *Colloque International Francophone sur l'Ecrit et le Document*, pages 61–66. Groupe de Recherche en Communication Ecrite, 2008.

[13] F. Liu, Y. Luo, M. Yoshikawa, and D. Hu. A new component based algorithm for newspaper layout analysis. In *Proceedings of the International Conference on Document Analysis and Recognition (ICDAR)*, pages 1176–1180, 2001.

[14] S. Mantzaris, B. Gatos, and N. Gouraros. Creating a digital library from newspaper archives. In *SDIUT*, page 285, 2001.

[15] S. Mantzaris, B. Gatos, N. Gouraros, and S. Perantonis. Linking article parts for the creation of newspaper digital library. In *RIAO*, pages 997–1005, 2000.

[16] S. Mantzaris, B. Gatos, N. Gouraros, and P. Tzavelis. Integrated search tools for newspaper digital libraries. In *Proceedings of the 23rd annual international ACM SIGIR conference on Research and development in information retrieval*, page 389, 2000.

[17] P. E. Mitchell and H. Yan. Newspaper layout analysis incorporating connected component separation. *Image and Vision Computing*, 22(4):307–317, 2004.

[18] T. Palfray, D. Hebert, S. Nicolas, P. Tranouez, and T. Paquet. Logical segmentation for article extraction in digitized old newspapers. In *Proceedings of the ACM symposium on Document engineering (DocEng)*, pages 129–132, 2012.

[19] P. S. Williams and M. D. Alder. Generic texture analysis applied to newspaper segmentation. In *IEEE International Conference on Neural Networks*, volume 3, pages 1664–1669, 1996.

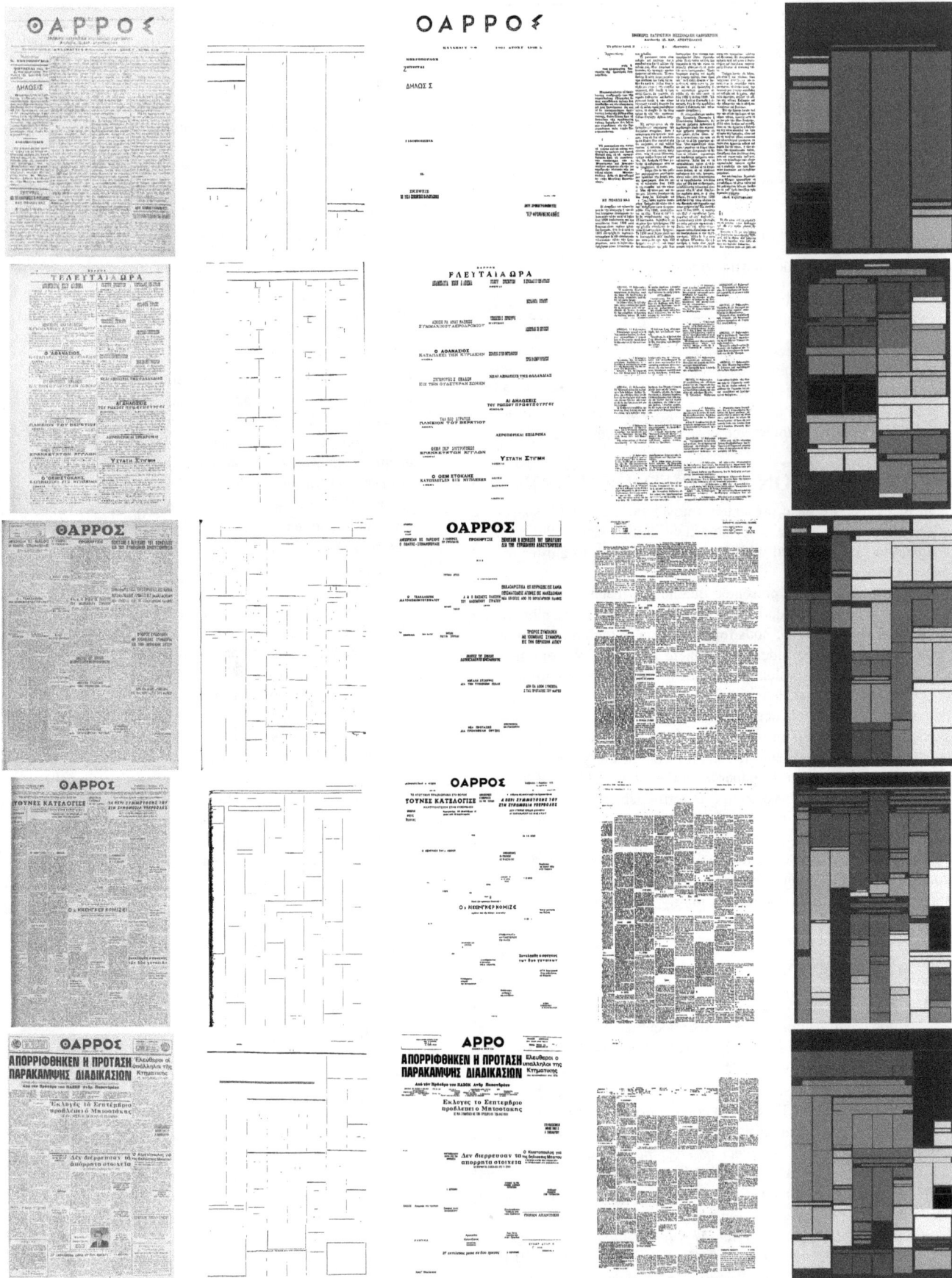

Figure 1: Sample of newspaper pages we used to test the proposed method and corresponding results using our method. All samples are historical editions of the greek newspaper "Tharros". From top to bottom, years of publication for the depicted pages are: 1901, 1917, 1948, 1975, 1989. From left to right, we show: the original image; detected separating lines; titles only; content only; segmentation into articles. Regions under the same article are painted with the same colour.

Generation of Search-able PDF of the Chemical Equations segmented from Document Images*

Prerana Jana
IIEST-Shibpur
India
prerana.jana@gmail.com

Anubhab Majumdar
IIEST-Shibpur
India
anubhabmajumdar93
@gmail.com

Sekhar Mandal
IIEST-Shibpur
India
sekhar@cs.iiests.ac.in

Bhabatosh Chanda
ISI-Kolkata
India
chanda@isical.ac.in

ABSTRACT

PDF format of scanned document images is not searchable. OCR tries to remedy this adversity by converting document images into editable and searchable data, but it has its own limitations in presence of equations - both mathematical and chemical. OCR system for mathematical equation is already a major research area and has provided successful result. However, chemical equation segmentation has been a less ventured road. In this paper, we present a novel method for automated generation of searchable PDF format of segmented chemical equations from scanned document images by performing chemical symbol recognition and auto-correction of OCR output. We use existing OCR system, pattern recognition technique, contextual data analysis and a standard LaTeX package to generate the chemical equation in searchable PDF format. The effectiveness of the proposed method is verified through exhaustive testing on 234 document images.

Keywords

Chemical equations, mathematical symbols, morphological operation.

1. INTRODUCTION

Text keywords are used for retrieving documents from WWW using search engines like Google. A large number of documents are being digitized today for the purpose of archival, transmission and browsing. The existing OCR systems show high accuracy in interpreting text portions, but

*(Produces the permission block, and copyright information). For use with SIG-ALTERNATE.CLS. Supported by ACM.

DocEng '16, September 12-16, 2016, Vienna, Austria

© 2016 ACM. ISBN 978-1-4503-4438-8/16/09. . . $15.00

DOI: http://dx.doi.org/10.1145/2960811.2960822

fail to process other components like graphics, half-tones, chemical and mathematical equations properly. A few studies [19], [20], [21] are directed toward math-symbol or math equation recognition assuming that the math-zones are already marked. A number of work has been done over the past decade to detect and extract the mathematical equations present in heterogeneous document images.

Fateman et al. [4] proposed a scheme which utilised character size, font information etc. to identify the connected components. Two bags, namely *text* and *math* are defined. The *text* bag is used to keep all letters and numbers; whereas the *math* bag collects punctuation, special symbols, Roman digits, italic letters, lines and dots. Objects in the *math* bag are then grouped together according to their spatial proximity. Grouping of items in text bag is redefined next followed by review and correction to move isolated items to their proper destinations. Math component segmentation is done in [5] through physical and logical segmentation using spatial characteristics of the math zone as well as identifying some math-symbols. The document is then segmented to characters, words, lines and blocks by physical segmentation. The logical segmentation process that follows consists of two steps; first the displayed math is detected by identifying their usual center position and in the next step in-line maths is detected by identifying special symbols.

Kacem et al. [6] extracted the equations using fuzzy logic by detecting mathematical operators like '+', '-', etc. Their method was tested on a dataset consisting of 300 expressions and the success rate is about 93%. As some of the operators like '+', '-', '(' and ')' do appear in chemical equations as well, it leads to the miss-classification of chemical equations as mathematical equations reducing the success rate. A similar method has been proposed in [7] to segment the mathematical expression in printed documents. The statistical approach taken by Garain [9] on the corpus of 400 pages to differentiate normal text lines and lines containing equations/expressions is on the basis of their white spacings which are usually larger in math-equation than the normal text. However, the chemical equations in the documents bear the same property. Jin et al. [11] proposed a similar method to extract displayed formulas using Parzen classifier.

Drake and Baird [12] came up with a graphical approach; similarly Guo et al. [13] developed a Gaussian mixture model to describe spatial relationships between sub-components of a math expression. Another method to check text style (regular, italic, bold) at the character level has been proposed in [10]. Garain [8] proposed a method to segment the displayed and embedded mathematical formulas from the documents using a bunch of features. The method is tested on a dataset of 200 images containing 1163 embedded and 1039 displayed expressions and the success rate is 88.3% and 97.2% respectively for embedded and displayed expressions. A method proposed by Chu and Liu [14] used features based on centroid fluctuation information on non-homogeneous regions to detect displayed and embedded formulas.

In a nutshell, in all the above methods emphasis is given only in mathematical equation. In eventual segmentation or classification, the chemical equations would automatically be included as a part of mathematical (or other) equations thereby reducing the success rate of the segmentation and effectiveness of the subsequent classification, if any.

There are some methods that are used to reconstruct chemical formula from scanned image. They have used chemical datasets. Algorri et al. [23, 24] proposed a system that reconstructs chemical molecules from scanned document. They have used connected component analysis and their own vectorisation algorithm for character recognition. Connected components that are not recognised by the OCR engine, are used to produce a graph of vectors. A rule based approach reconstructs the formula from the vector graph and the character information. ChemReader [25] starts with connected component. Alphanumerics are recognised using the GOCR open source OCR tool. Graphical components are identified using Hough transforms, corner detection and other bespoke algorithms.

Jana et al. [27] proposed a fully automated segmentation and detection technique of chemical equations present in heterogeneous document images. This paper is an extension of their work with some improvements to the original method. We propose a novel automated approach to auto-correct the extracted chemical equations and convert the same into an editable LaTeX file.

The paper is organized as follows – Detection and segmentation of chemical equations, auto-correction of the extracted chemical equations and its conversion to PDF form is presented in section 2. Section 3 presents experimental results. We conclude the paper in section 4.

2. PROPOSED WORK

The proposed method consists of three distinct steps and they are as follows: (i) Extraction of displayed chemical equations; (ii) Refining OCR output; and (iii) Converting the extracted chemical equations into search-able PDF format.

2.1 Extraction of displayed chemical equations

For this portion of the work, we have largely followed the method proposed in [27] with few improvements.

A skew free heterogeneous binary image is the input to the proposed algorithm.

Steps involved for identification of displayed chemical equations are - (i) Text line segmentation; (ii) Word blob formation; (iii) Operator identification; (iv) Displayed equation (DE) zone segmentation; and (v) Classification of extracted DE zone(s);

The details of the aforementioned steps are described in the following subsections.

2.1.1 *Text line segmentation*

To detect DE zones, text lines have to be segmented first from which the operators are identified to determine whether a text line is a displayed equation or not. We have taken the horizontal projection profile of the document page to segment the text line.

2.1.2 *Word blob formation*

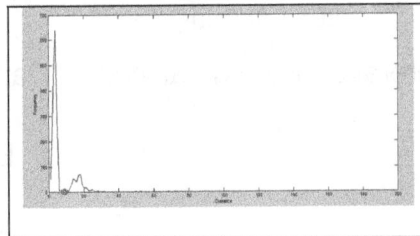

Figure 1: Distance histogram.

This is done by coalescing the characters in a word using morphological closing operation. Such character coalescing process depends on the accuracy in detecting the normal character gap and the gap between the consecutive connected components in that text line. A histogram with the distribution of distance between two consecutive characters in the document is plotted.

The distance histogram is a multi-modal histogram. The first peak corresponds to the character gaps. A distance histogram is shown in Fig. 1.

Our intention is to find out character gaps in running texts of a document page so that we can combine the consecutive characters into a single blob. Hence, we consider the upper boundary (l) of the first hump as the length of structuring element. Morphological close operation with a line structuring element of length (l) is carried out to form the word blobs.

2.1.3 *Operator detection*

In a mathematical or chemical equation, one or more operators are present. These operators signal us the presence of displayed equations in a document. We have considered the set of *operators* $(+, -, \rightarrow, \leftarrow, \leftrightarrow, \rightharpoonup, \leftharpoonup)$ which are commonly used both in chemical equations as well as mathematical equations to fulfil our aim to identify displayed zones containing chemical or other equations.

After blob formation, small component like dots of i *and* j are eliminated on the basis of area. The region (R_c) corresponding to each blob is cropped using its bounding box information from the original image and the number of connected component(s) present in R_c is counted. If the number of components is more than 1, then that blob is not an operator and is removed from the blob image.

The remaining components in the blob image are operators along with some alphanumerics like a, A, (, etc. The logical AND operation is performed between the blob image and the original image. The Euler number of the operators that we have considered is 1 and based on this feature some of the alphanumerics are discarded and the resultant image is denoted by I_s

Our next task is identify operator from I_s and for this, we have used a neural network with the following feature set.

- Aspect ratio: (f_a) of each component

- Density:

$$f_d = \frac{\#pixels_o}{\#pixels_b},$$

where $\#pixels_o$ denotes the number of object pixels and $\#pixels_b$ denotes area of the bounding box.

- The horizontal and vertical projection profiles of each component is obtained.
  (i)Spike for horizontal projection profile

$$f_{sh} = \frac{\#pixels_{on}}{w}$$

where $\#pixels_{on}$ denotes the number of on-pixels at the middle of the projection profile and w denotes the width of the profile.
(ii) Spike for vertical projection profile

$$f_{sv} = \frac{\#pixels_{on}}{h}$$

where $\#pixels_{on}$ denotes the number of on-pixels at the middle of the projection profile and h denotes the height of the profile.

- Ratio of

$$f_{dr} = \frac{\#pixels_{on}}{\#pixels_{off}},$$

where $\#pixels_{on}$ denotes the number of object pixels and $\#pixels_{off}$ denotes the number of background pixels along the diagonal of each component. The ratio is determined for both the right(rd) and left(ld) diagonals.

- A binary variable (f_{open}): $f_{open} \in \{1, 0\}$.
  The value of f_{open} is obtained using morphological opening operation with a line like structuring element (SE) of length $\frac{w}{2}$, where w is the width of the component. If the output of the opening operation has a single component, f_{open} is set to 1, else f_{open} is 0.

- Number of end points (f_{ep}): f_{ep} is number of end points of a connected component. This is determined using thinning operation. After thinning each connected component in I_s, if a pixel has a single 8-connected neighbor, then that pixel represents an end point.

Now, $[f_a, f_d, f_{sh}, f_{sv}, f_{dr}^{rd}, f_{dr}^{ld}, f_{open}, f_{ep}]$ is the feature vector for classification of operators from I_s.
We classify all single components in I_s into following 4 classes:

1. Arrows ($\rightarrow, \leftarrow, \leftrightarrow, \rightharpoonup, \leftharpoonup$)

2. Minus (-)

3. Plus (+)

4. Others (, (,), etc)

The classification is done using a two-layer feed-forward network with 100 nodes in the hidden layer and sigmoid hidden and softmax output neurons. The network is trained with scaled conjugate gradient back propagation.
We have taken a set of 7046 samples from our image dataset. This set consists of aforesaid operators and other symbol/character. Out of these 7046 images - 1000 plus,

Table 1: Results of classifier for identification of *operators*

	1	2	3	4
1	319	0	0	2
2	0	120	0	0
3	0	0	2267	3
4	0	0	0	335

1000 minus, 1000 arrows and 1000 other single characters are taken for the training set.

The remaining 3046 samples are used for testing the classifier. The accuracy of the network is depicted by the confusion matrix of the test dataset in Table 1. The reason for high number of '+' sign in the dataset is because it is the most frequently encountered *operator* as compared to the other operators or single characters.

We also need to identify the direction of the arrowhead for its correct representation. The direction of arrowhead is identified by measuring the height of the arrow elements near its two ends.

To detect '=' or '⇌' one extra step is required. For each '-' and '→', a rectangular window of size $l \times l/2$ is placed below the symbol to check if there is '-' and '⇌' respectively within the window; if present, they are considered to form either '=' or '⇌' sign. l be the length of the symbol. The upper boundary of the window coincides with the lower boundary of the bounding box of each aforesaid symbol.

2.1.4   DE zone exraction

Initially, all the text lines consisting of at least one *operator* are considered candidate displayed equations (CDE). The *operators* are separated from CDE. The upper boundary (u_v) of the second hump of distance histogram (Fig. 1) is obtained which represents the word gaps in the text line. For each CDE zone morphological closing operation with a line structure element of length u_v is carried out. If the distance between two neighbouring components is less than u_v, it means they belong to a same word and are merged by closing operation.

For each CDE we count the number of *operators* and other corresponding components in the output of closing operation. If the number of components $\leq 2\times$ number of *operators*, then the CDE is considered displayed equation; otherwise some embedded formulae/equations may exist in the line.

2.2   Classification of extracted DE zone

The extracted DE zones can be either chemical or other (ex:- mathematical) equations. Now, each displayed equation is an input to the inbuilt OCR of MATLAB R2014a. The OCR returns each DE zone as a text string. We made a dictionary out of all the elements in the periodic table. An important observation is that an element always starts with a capital letter. Using this property, an element can be expressed by a regular expression [A-Z][a-z]*. It means an element's symbol starts with an upper case letter and may or may not have one or more lower case letters (for example H, He, Uut etc). We have designed a parser to extract the sub-string matching the regular expression mentioned above with the following grammar:

$$start \rightarrow capital.follow$$
$$follow \rightarrow small.follow| \in$$
$$capital \rightarrow A|B| \ldots |X|Y|Z$$
$$small \rightarrow a|b| \ldots |x|y|z$$

Each of the substring returned by the parser is matched against the aforesaid dictionary and if it is a positive match then that substring is considered as a symbol of the chemical element. Let us consider, the number of substrings extracted from the OCR output by the parser is n and the number of positive matches the aforementioned dictionary is m. If m:n ratio is more than a threshold value β then this DE is considered a Chemical Equation. This threshold (β) is set to 0.7 experimentally by running the proposed algorithm on dataset containing 1390 displayed equations. The reason for the ratio not being 1 are: (i) Limitations of OCR, and (ii) Touching and broken characters.

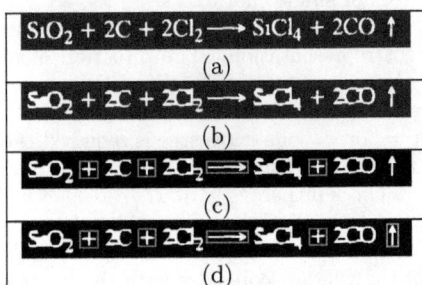

Figure 2: Up and down arrow detection (a) A chemical equation; (b) Image after blob formation ; (c) Operators are marked in red; (d) Detected arrow in blue.

The $\uparrow$ and $\downarrow$ are frequently used in chemical equation to represent the state of compounds and are thus important to detect. For each identified chemical equation, blob formation is done as discussed in Sec. 2.1.2. After blob formation, we apply component analysis method. Then operators are marked (Fig. 2(c)) in the blob image, as they are already identified. For each component in blob image (which is not an operator), we check its immediate left component (C_l) and right component (C_r). If none of C_l or C_r is an *operator*, the the component under consideration is an up arrow or a down arrow. Fig. 2(d) shows the detected up arrow in blue. The identification of the arrowhead is done in the same way as discussed in *operator* detection.

An example of chemical equation segmentation from a sample document image is given in Fig. 3. Fig. 3(c) shows the output in PDF without any correction.

2.3 Refinement of OCR output

Due to the limitations of OCR, the output of OCR is not fully correct in the paradigm of chemical equation/formula. Out of 3406 chemical compounds in our dataset, the accuracy of OCR conversion is only 43.13%. Hence, refinement of the recognized chemical formula in the equations is an absolute necessity.

The output of closing operation is taken as input here. Each connected component i.e. character within a word blob is an input to the the OCR and the corresponding output is stored in a cell and these cells form a string ($S_{chemical}$) for each word blob. For each superscript and subscript, '^' and '_' are inserted before them respectively in $S_{chemical}$.

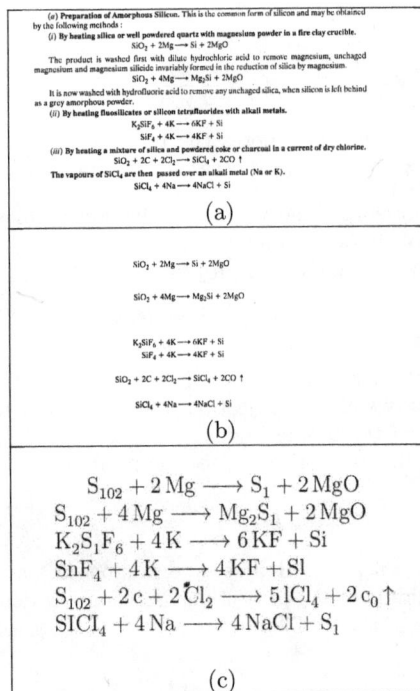

Figure 3: Experimental result; (a) Input image; (b) Segmented Chemical equation; (c) OCR output in PDF format.

First, an error table is created based on the observation of OCR outputs of 280 chemical equations consisting of 1022 compounds (Table 2). Table 2 consists of two columns; first column is actual input to the OCR and the second column contains all erroneous OCR outputs. Next, this table is stored into a hash map H where each key is the erroneous OCR output and its value is the possible input set. Table 3 shows this hash map where the first column is the key and the second column contains its corresponding values. For example, if '8' is an erroneous OCR output for inputs 'g', '3' and 'a' (Table 2) then, in the hash map H (Table 3) , the key is '8' and its corresponding value is [g, 3, a] .

Each chemical compound in any equation (Fig. 4) has the following format - [Coefficient]$^{[0,1]}$[Formula Unit][State]$^{[0,1]}$.

Table 2: Part of the Error list

correct input	corresponding erroneous OCR outputs
g	8 3 S
O	0
3	8 'E s w
a	3. 21 8 El 8.
l	1 I
s	S
n	ll 1'1 Il 11 X1 Il
q	Cl Q
H	1-l 1-1 l-l l-1
2	7 4 Z z
I	l
u	11 U ll ll 11
i	1 I

Table 3: Part of the Error Hash Map

Erroneous OCR Output	Possible Input Set
8	g 3 a
3	g
S	g s
0	O
'E	3
s	3
w	3
3.	a
21	a
El	a
8.	a
1	l i
I	l i
l1	n u
1'1	n
I1	n
11	n u
X1	n
Il	n
Cl	q

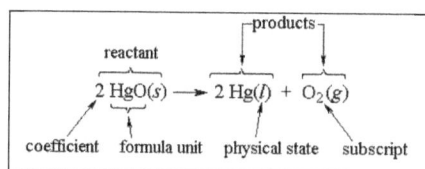

Figure 4: Different components of a chemical equation.

This represents that each chemical compound in an equation may or may not start with a numeric Coefficient, must be followed by a *Formula Unit* and may or may not end with a *State* representation. Hence, refinement or auto correction of the OCR output corresponding to each word blob includes the following steps - (i) Coefficient extraction; (ii) State separation; (iii)Auto correction of the formula unit; and (iv) Auto correction of the entire equation using Context Table.

2.3.1 Coefficient Extraction

Numeric coefficient denotes the number of molecules/atoms taking part in the reaction. Coefficient extraction is done by matching its regular expression $[2-9]^+[0-9]^*$ at the beginning of $S_{chemical}$ as it has numerical values. In the regular expression, $+$ indicates number of occurrence must be 1 or greater and $*$ indicates the occurrence is 0 times or greater. 0 and 1 are excluded from the first digit as number of molecules or atoms cannot be 0 and if the number is 1, the numeric coefficient is not mentioned by default. Matched coefficients are stored in S_{coeff}.

2.3.2 State separation

The four physical states of a chemical compound - solid, gaseous, liquid, and aqueous are denoted by '(s)', '(g)', '(l)', and '(aq)', respectively. To detect the physical state of the compound, regular expression $[(|[A-Za-z0-9]^+|)]$ is used and

the checking starts from the end of $S_{chemical}$. The matched substring, S is extracted from $S_{chemical}$ and Algorithm 1 is run. As mentioned earlier, OCR output for each character is stored in a cell of S. In this algorithm, S (after removing first and last character - opening and closing brackets) and H are taken as inputs and all possible *Combinations* of OCR output is produced by *GetAllCombinations* (See Fig. 5). For each cell element in S, corresponding values from hash map, H is assigned to a set, *InputSet* (See Line 3 in Algorithm 1). This set contains all possible inputs to the OCR system. Now, the key itself is added with its corresponding values in the hash table to make the *InputSet* if the length of key is 1. For example, '8' is added to the *InputSet* as its length is 1 (Fig. 5). On the contrary, in the second *InputSet*, 'Cl' is not included as its length is 2 (Fig. 5).

Each cell element of S gives one *InputSet*. Now, cartesian product of all the *InputSet* is taken to give us all possible *Combinations* and only one of the combinations is correct under proper chemical context. These *Combinations* are compared with 's', 'g', 'l' and 'aq'. If no match is found, the substring extracted from $S_{chemical}$ is concluded as a radical (Fig. 6, the compound contains a radical having the same regular expression mentioned earlier) , not a state; else, we separate the state from the compound and store it in S_{state} (after adding '(' and ')' at the start and end of S).

Algorithm 1 Attempts to find out all possible combinations of the initial error corrected OCR converted texts

1: **procedure** GETALLCOMBINATIONS(S,H)
2:     For each element in S, corresponding values from H is assigned to a set, InputSet
3:     If the InputSet is null, this indicates that the OCR output is not in the Hash map
4:     Since each element is OCR output of one letter, its ideal text length should be 1. Anything more than that indicates error
5:     Cartesian product of all letters in InputSet is taken and stored into an 2D array, Combinations
6: **end procedure**

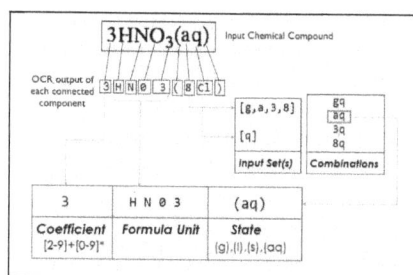

Figure 5: Extracting the formula unit, numeric coefficient and physical state from a chemical compound.

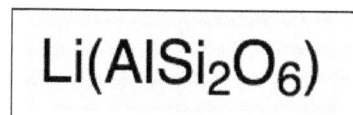

Figure 6: Example of chemical compound having a radical in the end.

151

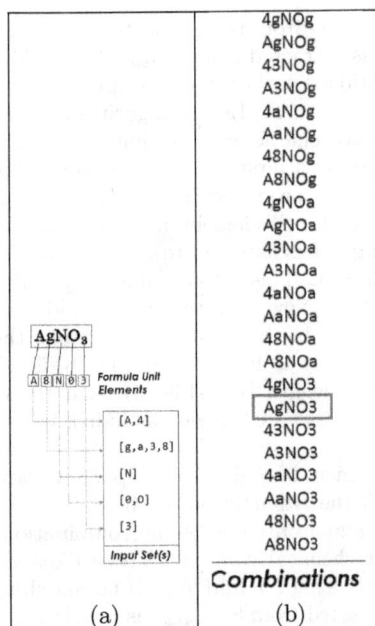

Figure 7: Example of auto correction of a formula unit.

2.3.3 Refinement of the formula unit

After extracting coefficient and state, only the formula unit is left in $S_{chemical}$. The algorithm for auto correction of each formula unit is done in two steps using Algorithm 1 and Algorithm 2. First, Algorithm 1 is performed on the formula unit to get all possible combinations. Next, the output of Algorithm 1(*Combinations*) is taken as the input of Algorithm 2. This algorithm is used to match the *Combinations* against a nearly exhaustive list of all molecules, chemical compounds, radicals and atoms namely *ChemList* collected from Wikipedia. [1].

Three cases may arise as follows–
(i) Exactly one match –
Fig. 7(b) shows the output of Algorithm 1. This is matched against *ChemList* using Algorithm 2 and algorithm finds one exact match as indicated by the red rectangle. This match is considered as the *Corrected* formula unit.

(ii) No match –
Longest common substring(s) (LCS) between *Combinations* and *ChemList* is computed and the formula unit in *Chemlist* having the longest common substring with *Combinations* is considered as *SubMatch*. There can be multiple such *SubMatch*. If there is only one, then the corresponding formula unit in *ChemList* is considered as the *Corrected* formula unit; else the *SubMatch*es having the same length as that of the *Combinations* are considered as *PossibleFormulaUnits*. Fig. 8 (a) is a sample chemical compound. The OCR converted string is 'N 21 B l'. Algorithm 1 returns 'NaBl' and 'NaBl' as the two combinations. None of them match with any chemical compound in *ChemList*. Hence, LCS is computed between these two possible combinations and *ChemList*. Six compounds with LCS length 3 is found as shown in Fig. 8(b). Since the number of *SubMatch*es is six, the *SubMatch* having the closest length as that of

[1]http://en.wikipedia.org/wiki/Dictionary_of_chemical_formulas

Combination (i.e. 4) is considered as *PossibleFormulaUnit*. In this case, it is 'NaBr'.

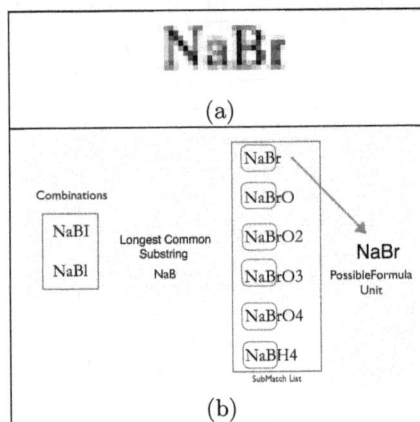

Figure 8: (a) Sample Chemical Compound; (b) LCS Match.

(iii) More than one exact match –
In Fig. 9, 'u' of 'Cu' in left hand side of the equation is '11' as the output of OCR. Among all possible combinations returned by Algorithm 1, 'Cu' and 'Cn' both match with *ChemList*. Hence, more than one exact match are found and both are considered as *PossibleFormulaUnit*.

The above steps are precisely mentioned in Algorithm 2. This algorithm returns *Corrected* and *PossibleFormulaUnit*s upon which context analysis is done and is discussed in the next section.

Algorithm 2 Find Match between ChemList and Combinations derived from Algorithm 1

1: **procedure** FINDMATCH(*ChemList,Combinations*)
2:　　Each combination is looked up against ChemList to find a match. Depending on the type of match, different steps are taken
3:　　If it's an exact match, that combination is considered as Corrected compound
4:　　If it's not an exact match, longest common substring of that combination and ChemList is taken. If there are multiple longest common substrings, all of them are considered for next steps
5:　　**if** The longest common substring is a match with ChemList
6:　**then**
7:　　　　This is considered as Corrected compound
8:　　**else**
9:　　　　The longest common substring(s) is(are) stored as PossibleFormulaUnit(s)
10:　　**end if**
11: **end procedure**

2.3.4 Auto correction of the entire equation using Context Table

Here, we have *Corrected* and *PossibleFormulaUnit*(s) and try to find out the *FinalEquation* in the context of the equation itself. If a chemical equation does not have any *PossibleFormulaUnit*, context analysis is not required. The process exits after performing Line 2 of Algorithm 3.

Algorithm 3 takes all *Corrected* and *PossibleFormulaUnit*s and returns the *FinalEquation* by forming the Context Table. As the universe is a closed

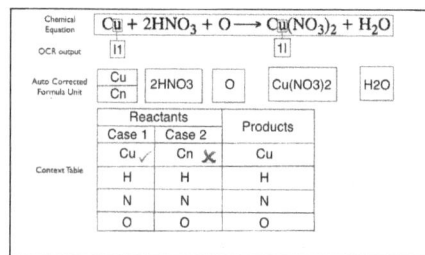

Figure 9: Formation of context table.

system, all chemical equations have the same periodic elements in the left hand side, called *Reactants* as that in the right hand side, called *Products*. All the periodic elements follow the regular expression [A-Z][a-z]*. So, for each *PossibleFormulaUnit*, the set of periodic elements in the *Reactants*, P_R and in the *Products*, P_P are computed and stored in the *ContextTable*. When the set difference of P_R and P_P in the table is empty, that *PossibleFormulaUnit* is considered as *Corrected* (Fig. 9 Case 1). In the Case 1 of P_P, the empty set condition satisfies. Hence, 'Cu' will be the *Corrected* formula unit, not 'Cn'. But if the above condition comes true for multiple possibilities, we cannot decide which of the possible formula units are actually in the original equation. This is considered an *ERROR* case. Finally, S_{coeff} and S_{state} (if any) are added with their corresponding *Corrected* formula unit after the context analysis and this results in *FinalCompound*s for each equation.

Now according to the stoichiometry of the chemical reaction, pre-recognised operators along with *FinalCompound*s are concatenated together. This gives us the final auto-corrected chemical equation.

Algorithm 3 Auto-Correction of the entire equation using chemical context table

---

1: **procedure** GETFINALEQN(*PossibleFormulaUnit,Corrected*)
2:   All PossibleFormulaUnits and Corrected compounds from Algorithm 2 are taken as input and all corrected compounds are directly placed in the equation
3:   Now for every PossibleFormulaUnits in the Reactants side, set of periodic elements are computed (Pr)
4:   Similarly for every PossibleFormulaUnits in the Products side, set of periodic elements are computed (Pp)
5:   If Pr and Pp are complete match, then that PossibleFormulaUnit is taken as Corrected and placed into the final equation
6:   Now finally with every corrected compound corresponding coefficient and state is added before and appended respectively
7:   If there are multiple Corrected compounds for one PossibleFormulaUnit then this algorithm fails and shows all possible corrected final equations
8: **end procedure**

2.4   Generation of chemical equation in searchable PDF format

The final auto-corrected chemical equation is then converted to LaTeX using the format specified by *mhchem* [2] package which provides commands for typesetting chemi-

---

[2]ftp://www.ctan.org/tex-archive/macros/latex/contrib/mhchem/mhchem.pdf

cal molecular formulae and equations. This produces the searchable PDF format.

Documents like research papers or patents often have an abundance of chemical equations. To search for any particular reaction or compound would involve ploughing through the entire document manually. The proposed system can significantly and efficently reduce this effort. By providing the scanned document as input, the output would be a searchable list of all chemical equations present in the entire document. Users can search the PDF by case insensitive linear string queries as shown in Fig. 10. Each chemical element or compound present in the PDF can be searched with complete or partial search string. For example, to identify all chemical compounds containg zinc, user just have to search the generated PDF with "zn"; or to identify all chemical equations involving water, user have to search with "h2o".

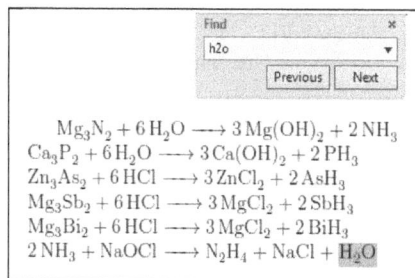

Figure 10: Searchability of generated PDF

3.   EXPERIMENTAL RESULT

We have implemented our algorithm in MATLAB 8.3.0.532 (R2014a) in a PC (Intel(R) Core(TM) i5-3337U CPU @ 1.80GHz running Windows 8). The proposed method has been tested on a dataset consisting of 234 document images. Out of 234 pages 50 are taken from ICDAR 2013 Mathzone segmentation datasets and other document pages are scanned from different Mathematics and Chemistry books. The summary of the experimental results is shown in Table 4. Out of 3406 chemical formula in the test dataset, 114 formula were partially corrected and 52 formula could not be corrected at all. The overall accuracy of complete refinement is 95.12%. This is measured by (#Completely Corrected formula / #Total number of formula). Due to the longest common substring match and then performing context analysis of the entire equation, there is a very small window of zero correction. Zero correction is the case when there have been no correction to the OCR output by the auto-correction algorithm. For example, OCR output of 'Mg'- I^I3 could not be corrected by our auto-correction algorithm as this erroneous conversion was not in the error hash map.

With our dataset, zero correction rate is 0.01% (It is computed as #Zero Correction Compound / #Total Compounds).These results are quite encouraging.

Consider the sample image (Fig. 3(a)) and its corresponding segmented displayed chemical equations are shown in Fig. 3(b). Fig. 3(c) shows the direct OCR output where 'i' has been wrongly identified as 'l', 'I' and '1' (for Si in all the lines of Fig. 3(c)). Similarly 'O' results in '0' (line 1,2,3). 'S' sometimes is detected as '5' (line 5). Our auto correction algorithm remedies these issues. Fig. 11 demonstrates the

153

Table 4: Summary of Experimental Results

#Total Images	234
#Total DEs	1390
Operator recognition	99.8%
DE segmentation accuracy	98.63%
Chemical DE Classification Accuracy	98.83%
#Total Chemical Operands	3406
Complete refinement accuracy	95.12%
Zero Auto correction rate	0.01%

effect of our auto correction algorithm. This algorithm is targeted towards chemical equation with linear representation. Organic bonds cannot be detected in this system.

Some sample experimental results are shown in Fig. **??**, Fig. **??**, Fig. 14 and Fig. **??**. More results are shown in https://sites.google.com/site/chemeqndb/home.

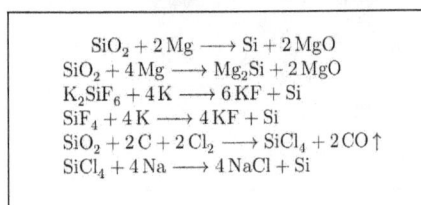

Figure 11: Auto corrected output of Fig. 3(c).

Next, we try to analyse the sources of some of the errors and shortcomings of our algorithm which have negative effect on the performance figures for auto correction.

Case 1 : Chemical equations sometimes contain some texts such as 'and', 'or' etc between two chemical compounds (See Fig. 12(a)). Sometimes two chemical equations are conjuncted by these words in the same line. If these words are not in chemical context and OCR does not convert them correctly, our autocorrection algorithm cannot match them against *ChemList*, hence the error occurs. But OCR conversion has a high accuracy rate for such type of texts. Therefore, this is not a severe error.

Case 2 : When the chemical compound is written in formats such as $(Na_2SiO_3)_n$ (Fig. 12(a)), only Na_2SiO_3 is detected based on *ChemList* and LCS matching. This is considered as a partial autocorrection case.

Case 3 : Some equations have conditions (pressure, temperature) written over the arrows (See Fig. 12(b)). In this work, we only concentrated on chemical compounds in the equation. This does not effect the autocorrection accuracy rate as most of the time they get segmented in separate text lines; else we ignore the over arrow conditions beforehand.

Case 4 : Fractions in the numeric coefficients (Fig. 12(c)) are not dealt with in our autocorrection algorithm as they are not very common in chemical equations.

Case 5 : Here, in the equation shown in Fig. 13. both the 'g's in reactant and product side have been converted to 'S' by the OCR which results in multiple auto-corrected formula units on both side. At this point, we reach Step 17 of Algorithm 3 where context table formation cannot conclude which one is the final corrected compound. However, normally the probability of occurrence of such situation is extremely rare, so no further steps are taken to rectify this.

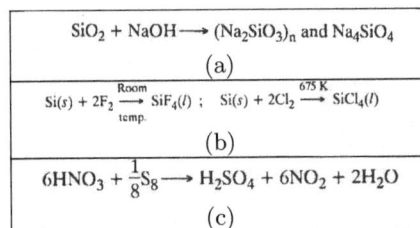

Figure 12: Sample error cases (a) presence of non-chemical words in segmented chemical equation; (b) presence of over arrow conditions; (c) fractional coefficient.

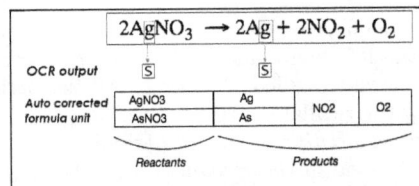

Figure 13: Error case of multiple *Corrected* compounds

4. CONCLUSIONS

We have presented an automated chemical equation segmentation and chemical context based auto correction system that is able to provide the exact searchable format of linear chemical equations in any document image. The experimental results demonstrate the efficiency of our proposed method. One of the drawbacks of our system is the time complexity as the search space in the *ChemList* is quite big and is growing over time due to discovery of new compounds. The search method can be improved and made more efficient. Since our proposed method is novel, we have not concentrated on making the system time efficient yet but more on the accuracy of the auto correction. This work leads to several research avenues. Chemical context horizon can be widened. Auto correction on non-linear or bond structure representations of chemical equations could be ventured in.

5. REFERENCES

[1] D. Blostein and A. Grabavec. *"Recognition of Mathematical Notation", Handbook of Character Recognition and document Image Analysis*, 557–582, 1997.

[2] K-F. Chan and D-Y. Yeung. *"Mathematical Expression Recognition: A Survey". IJDAR, Vol. 3, no, 1*, 3–15, 2000.

[3] U. Garain and B. B. Chaudhuri. *On OCR of Printed mathematical Expressions. "Digital Document Processing",Ed. B. B. Chaudhuri, Advances in pattern Recognition*, 235–259 , 2007.

[4] R. Fateman, T. Tokuyasu, B. Berman, and N. Mitchell. *"Optical character recognition and parsing of typeset mathematics", Visual Commun. And Image Representation, Vol 7, no 1*, 2–15, 1996.

[5] J. Y. Toumit, S. Garcia-Saliccetti, and H. Emptoz. *"A hierarchical and recursive model of mathematical expressions for automatic reading of mathematical documents"*. In Proc. of ICDAR, 116–122, 1999.

[6] A. Kacem, A. Beliad and M. Ben Ahmed. *"Automated Extraction of printed mathematical formulas using fuzzy*

logic and propagation of context", *IJDAR, vol.4 no. 2*, 97–108, 2001.

[7] M. Suzuki, F. Tamari, R. Fukuda, S. Uchida and T. Kanahori. *"INFTY - An Integrated OCR system for Mathematical Documents", Proc. of ACM Symposium on Document Engineering*, 95–104, 2003.

[8] Utpal Garain. *" Identification of Mathematical Expressions in Document Images", Proc. of ICDAR*, 1340–1344, 2009.

[9] Utpal Garain. *"Recognition of Printed Handwritten Mathematical Expressions", Ph.D Thesis, ISI, Kolkata, India*, 2005.

[10] B. B. Chaudhuri and U. Garain. *"Extraction of type atyle based meta-information from Imaged documents", IJDAR, vol. 3 no. 3*, 138–149, 2001.

[11] J. Jin, X. Han and Q. Wang. *"Mathematical formulas extraction", Proc. of ICDAR*, 1138–1141, 2003.

[12] D. M. Drake and H. S. Baird. *"Distinguishing mathematical notation from english text using computational geometry", Proc. of ICDAR*, 1270–1274, 2005.

[13] Y.-S. Guo, L. Huang and C.-P. Liu. *"A new approach for understanding of structure of printed mathematical expressions", Proc. of ICMLC*, 2633–2638, 2007.

[14] We-Te Chu and Fan liu. *"Mathematical formula detection from heterogeneous document Images", Proc. of CTAAI*, 140–146, 2013.

[15] S. P. Chowdhury, S. Mandal, A. K. Das, and B. Chanda. *"Segmentation of Text and Graphics from Document Images"*, in *Proc. of ICDAR*, 619–623, 2007.

[16] S. Mandal, S. P. Chowdhury, A. K. Das, and B. Chanda, *A simple and effective table detection system from Document Images*, IJDAR, Vol. 8(2), 172âĂŞ182, 2006.

[17] S. P. Chowdhury, S. Mandal, A. K. Das, and B. Chanda, *Segmentation of Text and Graphics from Document Images*, In Proc. of ICDAR, pp. 619âĂŞ623,2007.

[18] R. C. Gonzalez and R. Wood, *Digital Image Processing*, Addision-Wesley, 1992.

[19] D. Blostein and A. Grabavec, *Recognition of Mathematical Notation*, Handbook of Character Recognition and document Image Analysis, 577–582, 1997.

[20] K-F. Chan and D-Y. Yeung, *Mathematical Expression Recognition: A Survey*, IJDAR, Vol. 3, no: 1, 3âĂŞ15, 2000.

[21] U. Garain and B. B. Chaudhuri *An OCR of Printed mathematical Expressions, Digital Document Processing*, Ed: B. B. Chaudhuri, Advances in pattern Recognition, 235âĂŞ259 , 2007.

[22] A. Fujiyoshi, M. Suzuki, S. Uchid, *Grammatical Verification for Mathematical Formula Recognition Based on Context-Free Tree Grammar*, Mathematics in Computer Science, 279–298, 2010.

[23] M. E. Algorri, M. Zimmermann, C. M. Friedrich, S. Akle, and M. Hofmann-Apitius, *Reconstruction of chemical molecules from images*, In Proc. 29th Annual International IEEE Conference on Engineering in Medicine and Biology Society, 4609–4612, 2007.

[24] M. E. Algorri, M. Zimmermann, and M. Hofmann-Apitius, *Automatic recognition of chemical images*, In pro. Eighth Mexican International Conference on Current Trends in Computer Science, 41–46, 2007.

[25] J. Park, G. R. Rosania, K. A. Shedden, M. Nguyen, N. Lyu, and K. Saitou, *Automated extraction of chemical structure information from digital raster images*, Chemistry Central journal, vol. 3(1), 2009.

[26] A. K. Jain, J, Mao, K. M. Mohiuddin *Artificial Neural Network: A Tutorial*, Computer (Volume:29 , Issue: 3), Mar 1996.

[27] P. Jana and A. Majumdar *"Automated Segmentation and Classification of Chemical and other Equations from Document Images", 8th International Conference on Advances in Pattern Recognition*, 127-129, 2015.

(a) Input Image

7.30. CARBON-NITROGEN COMPOUNDS*

An important compound containing carbon as well as nitrogen is calcium cyanamide, $CaCN_2$. It is obtained by heating CaC_2 with nitrogen at 1373 K.

$$CaC_2(s) + N_2(g) \longrightarrow CaNCN_{(s)} + C_{(s)}$$

Mixture of CaNCN and C is used as a fertilizer under the name **nitrolim**. It is also used to manufacture **melamine plastics**. Calcium cyanamide is the starting material for the manufacture of sodium cyanide which is obtained by fusing calcium cyanamide with C and Na_2CO_3.

$$CaCN_2 + C + Na_2CO_3 \longrightarrow CaCO_3 + 2NaCN$$

Sodium cyanide is used for the extraction of silver and gold from their ores. On treatment with strong acids, sodium cyanide liberates HCN which is a colourless gas and behaves as a weak acid in aqueous solution (pKa = 9.0).

On a large scale HCN is obtained by heating ammonia with methane at a high temperature.

$$CH_{4(g)} + NH_{3(g)} \xrightarrow[1500\,K]{Pt.\,Catalyst} HCN_{(g)} + 3H_2(g)$$

Cyanides and HCN are extremely poisonous and their ingestion or inhalation may prove fatal. HCN is used in the manufacture of methyl methacrylate polymers and adiponitrile, which is an intermediate for nylon.

Two other compounds containing carbon and nitrogen are cyanogen, $(CN)_2$ and cyanamide, H_2NCN. Cyanogen has superficial resemblance to halogens (X_2) and is referred to as a **pseudohalogen**. Cyanogen can be obtained by the oxidation of HCN by O_2 using a silver catalyst or by the oxidation of CN^- by Cu^{2+}

$$4HCN + O_2 \xrightarrow{Ag} 2(CN)_2 + 2H_2O$$

$$4CN^- + 2Cu^{2+} \longrightarrow 2Cu(CN) + (CN)_2$$

Cyanogen is a poisonous gas like HCN. It has linear structure and disproportionates in basic solution to cyanide and cyanate ions.

$$(CN)_2 + 2OH^- \longrightarrow CN^- + OCN^- + H_2O$$

Ca NCN on treatment with water gives cyanamide which is a solid having m.p. 318 K.

$$CaNCN + H_2O \longrightarrow CaO + H_2NCN$$

7.31. SILICON

It is the second member of group 14. Silicon appears just below carbon in the periodic table. Its atomic number is 14 and therefore, it has the electronic configuration $1s^2 2s^2 2p^6 3s^2 3p^2$. Silicon is expected to give characteristics similar to that of carbon since the two have similar electronic configuration $(ns^2 np^2)$. This is true in certain cases. For example, silicon forms compounds such as SiH_4 and $SiCl_4$ which are covalent compounds and have tetrahedral geometry just like CH_4 and CCl_4. However, carbon and silicon differ in most of their characteristics. For example,

(i) CO_2 is a gas while SiO_2 is a solid.

(ii) Melting point of carbon (3773K) is much higher than that of silicon (1700 K).

(iii) CCl_4 is not hydrolysed by water while $SiCl_4$ is hydrolysed.

*For Entrance Examinations.

(b) Segmented Displayed Chemical Equations

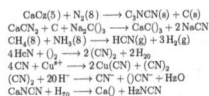

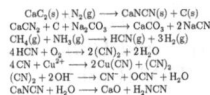

$$CaC_2(s) + N_2(g) \longrightarrow CaNCN(s) + C(s)$$
$$CaCN_2 + C + Na_2CO_3 \longrightarrow CaCO_3 + 2NaCN$$
$$CH_{4(g)} + NH_{3(g)} \longrightarrow HCN(g) + 3H_2(g)$$
$$4HCN + O_2 \longrightarrow 2(CN)_2 + 2H_2O$$
$$4CN^- + 2Cu^{2+} \longrightarrow 2Cu(CN) + (CN)_2$$
$$(CN)_2 + 2OH^- \longrightarrow CN^- + OCN^- + H_2O$$
$$CaNCN + H_2O \longrightarrow CaO + H_2NCN$$

(c) Direct OCR output

$$CaC_2(5) + N_p(8) \longrightarrow C_pNCN(s) + C(s)$$
$$CaCN_2 + C + Na_2CO_3 \longrightarrow CaCO_3 + 2NaCN$$
$$CH_4(8) + NH_3(8) \longrightarrow HCN(g) + 3H_2(g)$$
$$4HeN + ()_2 \longrightarrow 2(CN)_2 + 2H_{2o}$$
$$4CN + Cu^{++} \longrightarrow 2Cu(CN) + (CN)_2$$
$$(CN)_2 + 20H^- \longrightarrow CN^- + ()CN^- + H2O$$
$$CaNCN + H_{7o} \longrightarrow Ca() + H2NCN$$

(d) Auto-corrected OCR output

$$CaC_2(s) + N_2(g) \longrightarrow CaNCN(s) + C(s)$$
$$CaCN_2 + C + Na_2CO_3 \longrightarrow CaCO_3 + 2NaCN$$
$$CH_{4(g)} + NH_3(g) \longrightarrow HCN(g) + 3H_2(g)$$
$$4HCN + O_2 \longrightarrow 2(CN)_2 + 2H_2O$$
$$4CN + Cu^{2+} \longrightarrow 2Cu(CN) + (CN)_2$$
$$(CN)_2 + 2OH^- \longrightarrow CN^- + OCN^- + H_2O$$
$$CaNCN + H_2O \longrightarrow CaO + H_2NCN$$

Figure 14: Experimental result

A Multimodal Crowdsourcing Framework for Transcribing Historical Handwritten Documents

Emilio Granell
Pattern Recognition and Human Language
Technology Research Center
Universitat Politècnica de València
Camino Vera s/n, 46022, Valencia, Spain
egranell@dsic.upv.es

Carlos-D. Martínez-Hinarejos
Pattern Recognition and Human Language
Technology Research Center
Universitat Politècnica de València
Camino Vera s/n, 46022, Valencia, Spain
cmartine@dsic.upv.es

ABSTRACT

Transcription of handwritten historical documents is one of the main topics in document analysis systems, due to cultural reasons. State-of-the-art handwritten text recognition systems allow to speed up the transcription task. Currently, this automatic transcription is far from perfect, and human expert revision is required in order to obtain the actual transcription. In this context, crowdsourcing emerged as a powerful tool for massive transcription at a relatively low cost, since the supervision effort of professional transcribers may be dramatically reduced. However, current transcription crowdsourcing platforms are mainly limited to the use of non-mobile devices, since the use of keyboards in mobile devices is not friendly enough for most users. This work presents the alternative of using speech dictation of handwritten text lines as transcription source in a crowdsourcing platform. The experiments explore how an initial handwritten text recognition hypothesis can be improved by using the contribution of speech recognition from several speakers, providing as a final result a better hypothesis to be amended by a professional transcriber with less effort.

Keywords

Historical handwritten transcription; crowdsourcing framework; speech recognition; multimodal combination

1. INTRODUCTION

Transcription of handwritten documents is a main topic in the document analysis area. Transcription is applied to obtain an easy digital access to the contents of handwritten documents, since simple image digitisation only provides, in most cases, search by image and not by linguistic contents (keywords, expressions, syntactic or semantic categories, ...). Transcription is even more important in historical documents, since most of these documents are unique and the preservation of their contents is crucial for cultural and historical reasons. Interest on historical document transcription is reflected in the development of international projects such as IMPACT[1] and tranScriptorium[2].

Usually, transcriptions are done by specialists (called paleographers) by typing the contents of the manuscripts. In the last decade, development of handwritten text recognition (HTR) [12] tools provided paleographers with an initial transcription that they can amend, obtaining a higher productivity in the transcription task.

However, the rise of crowdsourcing platforms [4], where many volunteers could contribute to a given task at a very small or even null cost, made the transcription of historical texts widespread. Apart from popular platforms such as Mechanical Turk[3] or CrowdFlower[4], several platforms (specific for historical texts) that benefit from this approach have been developed in the last years (such as AnnoTate[5], Transcribe Bentham[6], or Transkribus[7]). However, final supervision of paleographers is required most times in order to obtain accurate enough transcriptions, since historical texts present difficulties such as degraded image quality, ancient vocabulary, or strange calligraphy that make difficult to obtain high quality transcriptions for non-expert transcribers.

In crowdsourcing platforms users generally employ keyboard input to provide transcription. This limits the use of crowdsourcing platforms to desktop or laptop computers, losing the potential transcription capability that could be provided by the use of mobile devices (tablets and smartphones), where keyboard input is not ergonomic enough to make its intensive use attractive. As an alternative to that, volunteers could employ voice as input for transcription. This modality is available in nearly all mobile devices, and would allow to obtain a larger number of volunteers. However, voice presents an ambiguity that typed input lacks of, since automatic speech recognition (ASR) [13] systems are far from perfect, although their performance has incremented substantially over recent years [8].

In any case, since paleographers must finally supervise the transcription, the use of voice input could provide a new more accurate transcription (taking as starting point an HTR transcription) that can reduce substantially the supervision effort of final transcribers. Moreover, it is foreseeable that the more volunteers provide their voice transcription, the more accurate the transcription would be. Thus, since the use of mobile devices is widespread, final performance of the system could be near to that of a typed-input system.

DocEng '16, September 12-16, 2016, Vienna, Austria
© 2016 ACM. ISBN 978-1-4503-4438-8/16/09. . . $15.00
DOI: http://dx.doi.org/10.1145/2960811.2960815

---

[1] http://www.impact-project.eu/
[2] http://transcriptorium.eu/
[3] https://www.mturk.com/
[4] https://www.crowdflower.com/
[5] https://anno.tate.org.uk/
[6] http://blogs.ucl.ac.uk/transcribe-bentham/
[7] https://transkribus.eu/Transkribus/

This work studies how to employ multimodal recognition (combining HTR and ASR) in a crowdsourcing platform where volunteer speakers dictate the transcription of a historical handwritten text image. The framework is based on techniques of language model interpolation [2] and Confusion Network combination [19], that allow the fusion of multimodal outputs in a single transcription hypothesis. Previous results [6] showed that the use of multimodal combination provides significant improvement in the hypothesis to be corrected, and our initial motivation is to check if the addition of new contributions could improve even more the hypothesis finally offered to the paleographer.

Our study applies a new framework for a crowdsourcing platform where multimodality is used. The influence of the order of the volunteers is examined, in order to check its robustness against different sequences of contributors. Apart from that, the framework includes a reliability verification module; thus, different configurations for this module are analysed. Finally, the robustness of the proposed platform against lost contributions (e.g., when volunteers avoid their contribution for a text line because of its difficulty) is tested. The final evaluation will provide clues on the feasibility of using this type of platforms for handwritten historical text transcription.

The paper is structured as follows: Section 2 presents the details on the proposed crowdsourcing framework, Section 3 describes the experimental conditions, Section 4 shows the results, Section 5 summarises the conclusions and future work lines.

2. CROWDSOURCING FRAMEWORK

The HTR and ASR problems can be formulated in a very similar way that allows its integration into a multimodal system. The unimodal formulation is: given a handwritten text image or a speech signal encoded into the feature vector sequence $x = (x_1, x_2, \ldots, x_{|x|})$, finding the most likely word sequence $\hat{w} = (w_1, w_2, \ldots, w_{|w|})$, that is:

$$
\begin{aligned}
\hat{w} &= \arg\max_{w \in W} \Pr(w \mid x) \\
&= \arg\max_{w \in W} \frac{\Pr(x \mid w) \Pr(w)}{\Pr(x)} \\
&= \arg\max_{w \in W} \Pr(x \mid w) \Pr(w)
\end{aligned}
\tag{1}
$$

where W denotes the set of all permissible sentences, $\Pr(x)$ is the probability of observing x, $\Pr(w)$ is the probability of w (approximated by the language model, LM), and $\Pr(x \mid w)$ is the probability of observing x by assuming that w is the underlying word sequence for x (evaluated by the optical or acoustic model, for HTR and ASR respectively).

The main objective of this crowdsourcing framework is to reduce the transcription errors in $\hat{w}$ before giving it to a paleographer for obtaining the actual transcription. This framework is based on two ideas: using the current system output to improve the language model for the next decoding process [1], and combining decoding outputs in order to obtain an output with lower error rate [6].

Unlike previous works where the source of speech was just one speaker (assumed to be the same paleographer), in this new proposal the source of speech is a set of collaborators. Given the nature of the historical manuscripts, the collaborators may hesitate on the pronunciation of some old words or even avoid reading them. In order to deal with this problem, the presented framework includes a speech reliability verification module, which prevents the use of speech utterances that can worsen the final output.

Moreover, the dependence on the task in this framework is due to the HTR and ASR modules, i.e., this framework is generalisable by using the corresponding lexicon, language, optical and acoustic models, meaning that this crowdsourcing framework can be used to transcribe any manuscript (even multiwriter manuscripts) in any language.

Figure 1 presents the working diagram of this multimodal crowdsourcing system. The operation is as follows:

1. The initial system output is given by the HTR decoding module.

2. The crowdsourcing loop starts in the LM interpolation module, where the previous system output is interpolated with the original LM for obtaining an improved LM for the next ASR decoding.

3. The collaborator speech is decoded in the ASR module using the improved LM, and the reliability of the obtained ASR output is verified and filtered, i.e., only the decoding output of those utterances which reach a determined reliability threshold are accessible at the output of the reliability verification module.

4. The system output is updated by combining the previous system output with the current and verified ASR output in the multimodal combination module.

5. If the speech of a new collaborator is available, the steps of the crowdsourcing loop (steps 2, 3, and 4) are repeated with these new audio samples.

The following subsections describe in detail the different modules of the framework.

2.1 Language Model Interpolation

The decoding outputs obtained from handwriting and speech recognisers can be formatted as Word Graph (WG) lattices, and as Confusion Networks (CN). In Figure 2 an example of WG and its corresponding CN is presented.

A WG is a directed, acyclic and weighted graph with an initial node q_I and a final node q_F. The nodes correspond to discrete time points for ASR and horizontal space for HTR. A link l is defined as any edge between a starting node $s(l)$ and an ending node $e(l)$, and it represents a hypothesis word $w(l)$ with a likelihood $f(l)$.

The language interpolation module builds a statistical LM conditioned on x that can be used to calculate the posterior probabilities of Equation (1). This adapted LM can be obtained as follows [1]:

1. The decoding outputs are obtained from the decoding process as WG.

2. The posterior probabilities for each WG node $\Pr(q \mid x)$ and WG link $\Pr(l \mid x)$ are computed. These probabilities are based on the forward $\alpha(q)$ and backward $\beta(q)$ probabilities of the nodes [18].

3. The posterior probability for a specific link l can be computed as the sum of the posterior probabilities of all hypotheses containing it. Therefore, the counts for a word sequence $x_{i-n+1}^i = (w_{i-n+1}, \ldots, w_i)$ can be estimated as:

$$
C^*(w_{i-n+1}^i \mid x) = \sum_{l_1^n \in N(w_{i-n+1}^i)} \frac{\prod_k \Pr(l_k \mid x)}{\prod_k \Pr(s(l_k) \mid x)}
\tag{2}
$$

where $N(w_{i-n+1}^i)$ are all the sequences of concatenated links generating w_{i-n+1}^i.

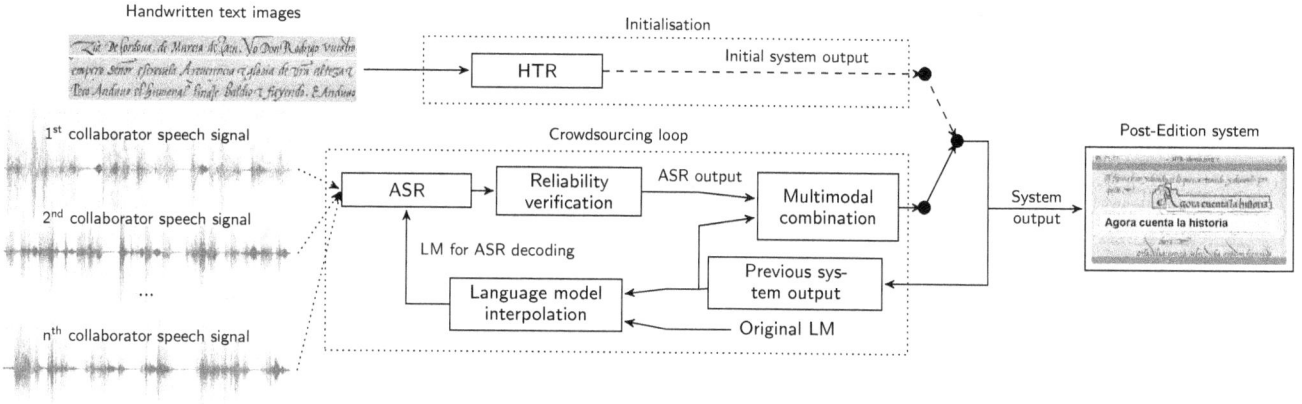

Figure 1: Multimodal crowdsourcing transcription framework.

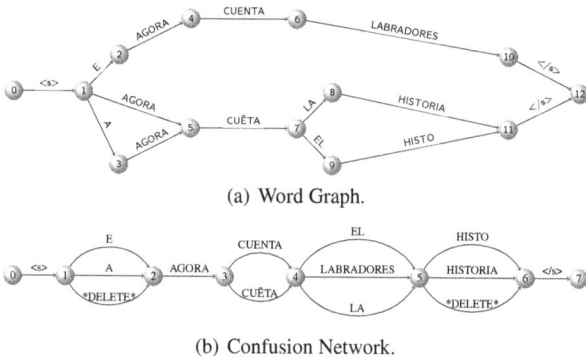

(a) Word Graph.

(b) Confusion Network.

Figure 2: Word Graph and Confusion Network.

4. The word posterior probabilities associated to the current input x can be calculated after applying: a suitable discount method (for back-off estimation), a smoothing method -to avoid the Out Of Vocabulary (OOV) problem-, and a proper normalisation:

$$\Pr^x(w) = \prod_i \frac{C^*(w_{i-n+1}^i \mid x)}{C^*(w_{i-n+1}^{i-1} \mid x)} \qquad (3)$$

5. The new conditioned LM $\Pr^x(w)$ is linearly interpolated with the original LM $\Pr(w)$ by using a weight factor λ:

$$\Pr_\lambda^x(w) = \lambda \Pr^x(w) + (1-\lambda)\Pr(w) \qquad (4)$$

The weight factor λ permits balancing the relative reliability in the LM interpolation between the LM estimated from the previous system output and the original LM.

2.2 Multimodal Combination

The multimodal combination of the ASR decoding output with the previous system output can be performed by means of CN combination methods.

A CN is a weighted directed graph, in which each hypothesis goes through all the nodes. The words and their probabilities are also stored in the edges. A subnetwork (SN) is the set of all edges between two consecutive nodes. The total probability of the words contained in a SN sum up to 1.

The bimodal CN combination method [6, 7] used in the framework works as follows, starting from the system and the speech decoding outputs formatted in CN:

1. A search for anchor SN is performed in order to align the SN of both CN. The algorithm searches coincidences in unigrams, bigrams and skip-bigrams in both directions (from left to right and vice versa) simultaneously, taking only as anchor SN those where both searches coincide according to a gram matching value of the words in the involved SN. The gram matching between words of two subnetworks (SN_A and SN_B) is assessed by using the quadratic mean of the Character Error Rate (CER) and the Phoneme Error Rate (PER) between those words.

$$E(w_A, w_B) = \sqrt{\frac{\mathrm{CER}(w_A, w_B)^2 + \mathrm{PER}(w_A, w_B)^2}{2}} \qquad (5)$$

where w_A and w_B represent the words of the SN_A and SN_B, respectively. CER and PER are the Levensthein distance between the words of both SN, CER at character level, and PER at phoneme level by using the phonetic transcriptions of the recognised words, and E represents the gram matching error.

2. The new CN is composed on the basis of the Bayes theorem and assuming a strong independence between both CN. The editing actions used are: combination, insertion, and deletion of subnetworks:

Combination Given two subnetworks, SN_A and SN_B, the word posterior probabilities of the combined subnetwork SN_C are obtained applying a normalisation on the logarithmic interpolation of the smoothed word posterior probabilities of both SN (SN_A and SN_B) by using a weight factor α:

$$\Pr(w \mid SN_C) = \Pr_s(w \mid SN_A)^\alpha \Pr_s(w \mid SN_B)^{1-\alpha} \qquad (6)$$

where the smoothing of the word posterior probability $\Pr_s(w \mid SN)$ is based on Laplacian smoothing. How-

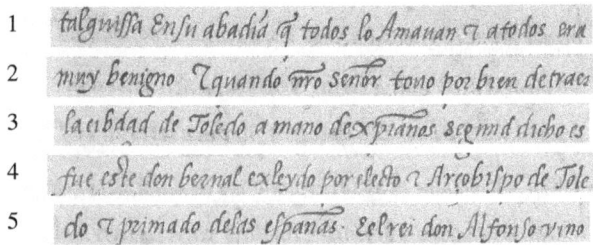

Figure 3: The 5 first lines of the page 515 of *Rodrigo*.

ever, since we are working with probabilities, $\Pr_s(w \mid SN)$ is calculated according to Equation (7):

$$\Pr_s(w \mid SN) = \frac{\Pr(w \mid SN) + \Theta}{1 + n\Theta} \qquad (7)$$

where Θ is a defined granularity that represents the minimum probability for a word and n is the number of different words in the final SN (SN_C).

Insertion and deletion The same process is performed in both actions: the SN to insert or to delete is combined with a SN with an only *DELETE* arc with probability 1.0.

The weight factor α permits balancing the relative reliability in the multimodal combination between the verified ASR decoding output and the previous system output.

2.3 Reliability Verification

Given the conventional formulation of the HTR and ASR problems, the posterior probability $\Pr(w \mid x)$ is a good confidence measure for the recognition reliability. However, recognition scores are inadequate to assess the recognition confidence because most recognition systems ignore the term $\Pr(x)$, as seeing in Equation (1). Nevertheless, when the recognition scores of a fairly large n-best list are re-normalised to sum up to 1, the obtained posterior probability $\Pr(w \mid x)$ can serve as a good confidence measure since it represents a quantitative measure of the match between x and w [15, 18].

Therefore, the re-normalised 1-best posterior probability $\Pr_n(w_1 \mid x)$ is used in the reliability verification module as the confidence measure:

$$\Pr_n(w_1 \mid x) = \frac{\Pr(w_1 \mid x)}{\sum_{w \in W} \Pr(w \mid x)} \qquad (8)$$

where W denotes the set of all permissible sentences in the evaluated decoding output.

3. EXPERIMENTAL CONDITIONS

3.1 Data Sets

The *Rodrigo* corpus [16] was the data set employed in the experiments. It was obtained from the digitisation of the book "Historia de España del arçobispo Don Rodrigo", written in ancient Spanish in 1545. It is a single writer book where most pages consist of a single block of well separated lines of calligraphical text. It is composed of 853 pages that were automatically divided into lines (see example in Figure 3), giving a total number of 20,356 lines. The vocabulary size is of about 11,000 words.

This corpus presents several difficulties, such as, the following examples, that are present in the first 5 lines of the page 515 (Figure 3):

- Text images containing abbreviations (e.g., *nrõ* in the second line) that must be pronounced as the whole word (*nuestro* ['nwes tro]).

- Archaic words (e.g., *Amauan*, *touo*, and *cibdad* in the first, second, and third lines, respectively) that are not used or have a different spelling in modern Spanish (*Amaban*, *tuvo*, and *ciudad*).

- Words written in multiple forms (e.g., *xpiãnos* -in the third line- and *christianos*, or numbers as *5* and *V*) but that are pronounced in the same way ([kris 'tja nos], ['θiŋ ko]).

- Hyphenated words (e.g., *Toledo* in the fourth and fifth lines, where a part of the word *-Tole-* is at the end of a line and the second part *-do-* is at the beginning of the following line).

The partition used was the same used in [6, 7]. For training the optical models, a standard partition with a total number of 5000 lines (about 205 pages) was used. Test data for HTR was composed of two pages that were not included in the training part (pages 515 and 579) and that were representative of the average error of the standard test set (of about 5000 lines). These two pages contain 50 lines and 514 words.

For the training of the ASR acoustic models we used a partition of the Spanish phonetic corpus Albayzin [11]. This corpus consists of a set of three sub-corpus recorded by 304 speakers using a sampling rate of 16 kHz and a 16 bit quantisation. The training partition used in this work includes a set of 4800 phonetically balanced utterances, specifically, 200 utterances read by four speakers and 25 utterances read by 160 speakers, with a total length of about 4 hours. For the multimodal crowdsourcing test we obtained the collaboration of 7 different native Spanish speakers who read the 50 handwritten test lines (those of pages 515 and 579), giving a total set of 350 utterances (about 15 minutes) acquired at 16 KHz and 16 bits. The seven collaborators (one woman and six men) were between 25 and 55 years old, they had higher education, and they were familiar with recognition of historical manuscripts. However, they had no special knowledge regarding old Spanish pronunciation.

3.2 Features

3.2.1 HTR features

Handwritten text features are computed in several steps. First, a bright normalisation is performed. After that, a median filter of size 3×3 pixels is applied to the whole image. Next, slant correction is performed by using the maximum variance method and a threshold of 92%. Then, a size normalisation is performed and the final image is scaled to a height of 40 pixels. Finally, features are extracted by using the method described in [5]. Final feature vectors are of 60 dimensions.

3.2.2 ASR features

Mel-Frequency Cepstral Coefficients (MFCC) are extracted from the audio files. The Fourier transform is calculated every 10 ms over a window of 25 ms of a pre-emphasised signal. Next, 23 equidistant Mel scale triangular filters are applied and the filters outputs are logarithmised. Finally, to obtain the MFCC, a discrete cosine transformation is applied. We used the first 12 MFCC and log frame energy with first and second order derivatives as ASR features, resulting in a 39 dimensional vector.

Table 1: Baseline Results.

Modality	WER
HTR	$39.3\% \pm 4.1$
ASR	$62.9\% \pm 2.2$

3.3 Models

Optical and acoustic models were trained by using HTK [20]. On the one hand, symbols on the optical model are modelled by a continuous density gaussian mixture left-to-right of 106 HMM with 6 states and 32 gaussians per state, while on the other hand, phonemes on the acoustic model are modelled as a left-to-right gaussian mixture of 25 HMM (23 monophones, short silence, and long silence) with 3 states and 64 gaussians per state.

The lexicon models for both systems are in HTK lexicon format, where each word is modelled as a concatenation of symbols for HTR or phonemes for ASR.

The baseline LM was estimated as a 2-gram with Kneser-Ney back-off smoothing [9] directly from the transcriptions of the pages included on the HTR training set (about 205 pages). This LM with respect to the test set presents a 6.2% of OOV words and a perplexity of 298.4.

3.4 Evaluation Metrics

The quality of the transcription is given by the well known word error rate (WER), which is a good estimation of the user post-edition effort. It is defined as the minimum number of words to be substituted, deleted or inserted to convert the hypothesis into the reference, divided by the total number of reference words. Moreover, confidence intervals of 95% were calculated by using the bootstrapping method with 10,000 repetitions [3].

The speech decoding reliability R is verified by using the re-normalised 1-best posterior probability -Equation (8)-, which is a good estimation of the decoding confidence.

3.5 Experimental Setup

Both the HTR and the ASR systems were implemented by using the iATROS recogniser [10]. All processes on language models (inference, interpolation, ...), the decoding output evaluation, and the transformation from WG to CN were done by using the SRILM toolkit [17].

4. EXPERIMENTAL RESULTS

To check the performance of our multimodal crowdsourcing framework, we have experimented with the 50 text line images of the Rodrigo corpus, and the 350 speech utterances recorded from 7 different collaborators described in Subsection 3.1. We started obtaining the baseline values for both modalities. Next, we selected the speaker that best represented the average error rate of the speech set for adjusting the values of the LM interpolation factor λ and the CN combination factor α. Finally, with the other 6 speakers we tested the effects of the speakers ordering, the ASR reliability verification, and the absence of speech utterances.

4.1 Baseline and Framework Adjustment

The baseline values were obtained by using the original LM in the decoding process of both modalities. As can be observed in Table 1, the HTR and ASR WER values are quite high due to the difficulty of the corpus.

The values of the α and λ parameters must be adjusted in order to obtain the best results. We tested the multimodal crowdsour-

Table 2: Framework Adjustment Reliability Results.

α	λ	$\langle R \rangle$	$\langle R_w \rangle$
0.4	0.4	53.3%	45.8%
	0.5	51.7%	44.1%
	0.6	50.3%	42.7%
0.5	0.4	45.5%	38.4%
	0.5	44.8%	37.7%
	0.6	43.4%	36.3%
0.6	0.4	**62.4%**	**54.5%**
	0.5	61.3%	53.4%
	0.6	61.1%	53.3%

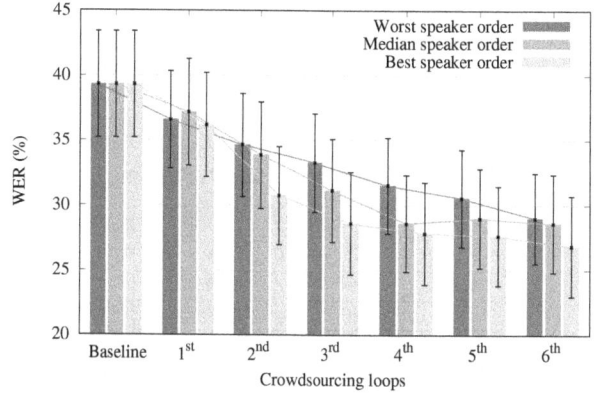

Figure 4: Results of the speaker ordering experiments. Best, worst and the median of 11 different random orders.

Table 3: Ordering Experiments Final Results.

Order	WER
Worst	$29.0\% \pm 3.5$
Median	$28.6\% \pm 3.8$
Best	$26.9\% \pm 3.9$

cing framework adjusting the α and λ parameters with the values $\{0.4, 0.5, 0.6\}$, by using only the speech of the selected speaker. We measured the average reliability $\langle R \rangle$ of the speech decoding output, and the same average reliability but weighted by the number of words contained in the 1-best $\langle R_w \rangle$. Table 2 presents the obtained results for the adjustment. Both measures, $\langle R \rangle$ and $\langle R_w \rangle$, present the same tendency. The system presents the highest reliability when the multimodal combination is a bit balanced to the speech output ($\alpha = 0.6$), and the LM interpolation to the original LM ($\lambda = 0.4$).

4.2 Speaker Ordering

The 6 speakers not used in the framework adjustment were randomly sorted 11 times giving 11 different order lists. Figure 4 shows the evolution in the system output, from the initial HTR baseline until the process of the speech of the last collaborator, for the lists that obtained the worst, the median and the best final results (see Table 3).

Regarding the ordering of speakers, the obtained results show as in the best case, only two speakers are needed to obtain significant improvements ($30.7\% \pm 3.8$). Meanwhile, in the worst case at least

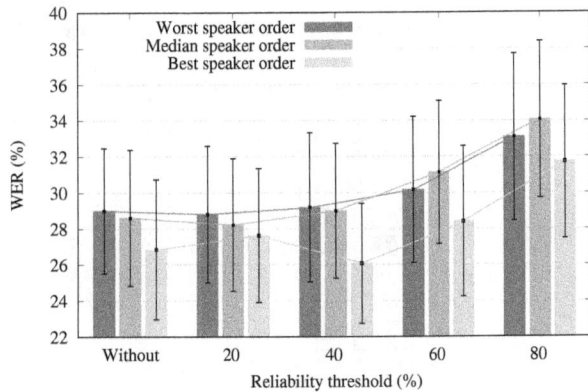

Figure 5: Results of the reliability verification experiments on the best, the worst and the median speaker orders.

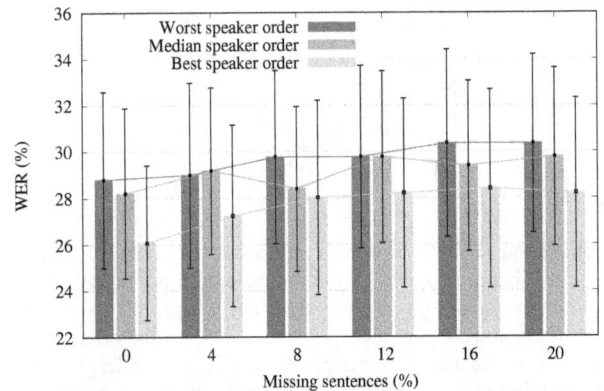

Figure 6: Results of the speech missing experiments on the best, the worst and the median speaker orders.

Table 4: Reliability Experiments Results.

Order	Threshold	WER
Worst	20%	28.8% ± 3.8
Median	20%	28.2% ± 3.7
Best	40%	26.1% ± 3.3

four speakers are needed (31.5% ± 3.6). As can be seen in the final results from Table 3, the presented framework reached, in the worst order, a relative statistically significant improvement higher than 26% when compared with the HTR baseline (39.3% ± 4.1).

4.3 ASR Reliability Verification

In the presented framework, if the dictation were made only by expert speakers in historical manuscripts with good pronunciation of ancient words, the output error could be reduced significantly with the collaboration of less people. However, the aim of this framework is to distribute the effort among a larger group of non-experts. Therefore, in order to ensure that the speech of the collaborator enriches the final system output it is necessary to set a minimum reliability threshold.

Figure 5 presents the obtained results when varying the reliability threshold on 3 of the 11 lists (which presented the worst, the median, and the best final results). As can be seen, in all cases there exist a threshold where the rejection of several speech utterances improves the final results.

In Table 4 the summary of the best obtained results is shown. Although these improvements are not statistically significant when compared with the results obtained without reliability verification (see Table 3), it highlights the importance of verifying the reliability of the speech recognition for obtaining the best results in a crowdsourcing framework as the one presented in this paper.

Moreover, we observed that the corrections were made in most cases at the beginning and/or at the end of the sentences. This is due to the fact that this selection permits a better refinement of the language model, making it more reliable for the parts of the lines where its estimation is more complicated in the initial training.

4.4 Absence of speech utterances

In the last experiment we tested the strength of this crowdsourcing framework against the absence of speech utterances. The absence of speech utterances can appear because some collaborators did not read part of the sentences, or because some speech samples got lost in the communication process.

For each of the 6 speakers used for the test experiments, a 20% of their speech samples were randomly selected as missing utterances. Then, we tested the performance of this crowdsourcing framework against the lost of speech samples from 2% to 20% in an incremental way, i.e., the missing sentences set of the 4% contains the missing sentences of the previous 2% and so on.

As can be seen in Figure 6, the performance of the presented framework decays when some speech utterances are missing. Nevertheless, even losing the 20% of the speech utterances of each speaker, in the worst order the obtained final result still achieved a statistically significant value of 30.4% ± 3.8, that represents a relative improvement of 22.6% over the HTR baseline.

5. CONCLUSIONS AND FUTURE WORK

In this paper we have presented a multimodal crowdsourcing framework for the transcription of historical handwritten documents. This framework is based on the iterative refinement of the language model, and on the combination of decoding outputs. The experiments showed that in this framework the number of collaborators is more important than the order in which their speech is processed. Moreover, the speech reliability verification permits to achieve better results. Apart from that, the framework is robust against the absence of speech utterances, which makes it feasible even for volunteers with low involvement in the task.

The improvements over the HTR baseline achieved by the crowdsourcing framework presented in this paper are remarkable. Some preliminar experiments in an assisted transcription tool [14] showed that the obtained results provide a significant reduction of the paleographer transcription effort with respect to using the HTR baseline recognition.

In view of these results, we believe that there is still room for improvement. We propose for future studies the use of more robust methods of optical and acoustic modelling. Moreover, the use of sentences in the handwritten text corpus instead of lines could make multimodality more natural for the speakers.

Finally, we are planning to test this crowdsourcing framework publicly, where we expect to obtain the collaboration of a huge amount of speakers. Moreover, this framework is open to be tested with other datasets or integrated in the crowdsourcing platforms mentioned in Section 1.

6. ACKNOWLEDGMENTS

Work partially supported by projects SmartWays - RTC-2014-1466-4 (MINECO) and CoMUN-HaT - TIN2015-70924-C2-1-R (MINECO/FEDER).

7. REFERENCES

[1] V. Alabau, V. Romero, A. L. Lagarda, and C. D. Martínez-Hinarejos. A Multimodal Approach to Dictation of Handwritten Historical Documents. In *Proc. 12th Interspeech*, pages 2245–2248, 2011.

[2] J. R. Bellegarda. Statistical language model adaptation: review and perspectives. *Speech Communication*, 42(1):93 – 108, 2004.

[3] M. Bisani and H. Ney. Bootstrap estimates for confidence intervals in ASR performance evaluation. In *Proc. ICASSP*, volume 1, pages 409–412, 2004.

[4] A. Doan, R. Ramakrishnan, and A. Y. Halevy. Crowdsourcing systems on the world-wide web. *Commun. ACM*, 54(4):86–96, Apr. 2011.

[5] P. Dreuw, S. Jonas, and H. Ney. White-space models for offline Arabic handwriting recognition. In *Proc. 19th ICPR*, pages 1–4, 2008.

[6] E. Granell and C. D. Martínez-Hinarejos. Combining Handwriting and Speech Recognition for Transcribing Historical Handwritten Documents. In *Proc. 13th ICDAR*, pages 126–130, 2015.

[7] E. Granell and C. D. Martínez-Hinarejos. Multimodal Output Combination for Transcribing Historical Handwritten Documents. In *Proc. 16th CAIP*, pages 246–260, 2015.

[8] G. Hinton, L. Deng, D. Yu, G. Dahl, A. Mohamed, N. Jaitly, A. Senior, V. Vanhoucke, P. Nguyen, T. Sainath, and B. Kingsbury. Deep neural networks for acoustic modeling in speech recognition: The shared views of four research groups. *Signal Processing Magazine, IEEE*, 29(6):82–97, Nov 2012.

[9] R. Kneser and H. Ney. Improved backing-off for m-gram language modeling. In *Proc. ICASSP*, volume 1, pages 181–184, 1995.

[10] M. Luján-Mares, V. Tamarit, V. Alabau, C. D. Martínez-Hinarejos, M. Pastor, A. Sanchis, and A. H. Toselli. iATROS: A speech and handwritting recognition system. In *V Jornadas en Tecnologías del Habla*, pages 75–78, 2008.

[11] A. Moreno, D. Poch, A. Bonafonte, E. Lleida, J. Llisterri, J. B. Mariño, and C. Nadeu. Albayzin speech database: design of the phonetic corpus. In *Proc. EuroSpeech*, pages 175–178, 1993.

[12] R. Plamondon and S. N. Srihari. On-Line and Off-Line Handwriting Recognition: A Comprehensive Survey. *IEEE Transactions on Pattern Analysis and Machine Intelligence*, 22(1):63–84, January 2000.

[13] L. Rabiner and B.-H. Juang. *Fundamentals of Speech Recognition*. Prentice Hall, 1993.

[14] V. Romero, A. H. Toselli, and E. Vidal. *Multimodal Interactive Handwritten Text Transcription*. Series in Machine Perception and Artificial Intelligence (MPAI). World Scientific Publishing, 2012.

[15] B. Rueber. Obtaining confidence measures from sentence probabilities. In *Proc. Eurospeech*, pages 739–742, 1997.

[16] N. Serrano, F. Castro, and A. Juan. The RODRIGO Database. In *Proc. 7th LREC*, pages 2709–2712, 2010.

[17] A. Stolcke. SRILM-an extensible language modeling toolkit. In *Proc. 3rd Interspeech*, pages 901–904, 2002.

[18] F. Wessel, R. Schlüter, K. Macherey, and H. Ney. Confidence measures for large vocabulary continuous speech recognition. *IEEE Trans. Speech and Audio Processing*, 9(3):288–298, 2001.

[19] J. Xue and Y. Zhao. Improved confusion network algorithm and shortest path search from word lattice. In *Proc. of Int. Conf. in Acoustics, Speech and Signal Processing*, volume 1, pages 853–856, 2005.

[20] S. Young, G. Evermann, M. Gales, T. Hain, D. Kershaw, X. Liu, G. Moore, J. Odell, D. Ollason, D. Povey, et al. The HTK book. *Cambridge university engineering department*, 2006.

Embedded Textual Content for Document Image Classification with Convolutional Neural Networks

Lucia Noce, Ignazio Gallo, Alessandro Zamberletti and Alessandro Calefati
University of Insubria
Varese, Italy
lucia.noce@uninsubria.it

ABSTRACT

In this paper we introduce a novel document image classification method based on combined visual and textual information. The proposed algorithm's pipeline is inspired to the ones of other recent state-of-the-art methods which perform document image classification using Convolutional Neural Networks. The main addition of our work is the introduction of a preprocessing step embedding additional textual information into the processed document images. To do so we combine Optical Character Recognition and Natural Language Processing algorithms to extract and manipulate relevant text concepts from document images. Such textual information is then visually embedded within each document image to improve the classification results of a Convolutional Neural Network. Our experiments prove that the overall document classification accuracy of a Convolutional Neural Network trained using these text-augmented document images is considerably higher than the one achieved by a similar model trained solely on classic document images, especially when different classes of documents share similar visual characteristics.

Keywords

Document Image Classification; Convolutional Neural Network; Natural Language Processing

1. INTRODUCTION

Document image classification and retrieval is an important task in document processing as it is a key element in a wide range of contexts, such as: automated archiving of documents, Digital Library constructions and other general purpose document image analysis applications [4].

Nowadays a large number of documents are produced, processed, transferred and stored as digital images everyday: forms, letters, printed articles and advertisement are only few examples of them. While documents belonging to different macro-areas (*e.g.* financial, advertisement, *etc.*) tipically show substantially different visual layouts from one another and thus can be accurately classified just by comparing their visual characteristics; the same does not hold true for documents belonging to the same macro-area but different sub-areas (*e.g.* house ads, shop ads, *etc.*).

Given this situation, when the task is to perform a highly specific document classification among different document categories which are are both visually and semantically very similar, a combined content and visual analysis is mandatory to achieve satisfying fine-grained classification results. To this end, in this manuscript we propose a novel system to perform fine-grained document image classification exploiting both the content and the visual characteristics of the processed documents.

There are plenty of methods in literature that perform document classification relying exclusively on textual content extracted from the processed documents. While those algorithms can be effective for simple and well-made artificial documents, they have many limitations: (i) they ignore important visual document features (*e.g.* tables, images and diagrams) that may play an important role in the final document classification predictions, (ii) they are limited to printed documents due to Optical Character Recognition (OCR) limits, and (iii) they cannot be used to classify documents that do not contain any textual information or contain machine-unreadable text.

Accordingly, image analysis is complementary to content-based document classification for many classes of documents, and several techniques in literature successfully rely on structural and visual aspects to perform coarse-grained document classification [8].

For documents that present the same fixed structure, such as forms, template matching is adopted [25, 24]: for each class, a template is manually chosen and during the classification phase the input document is matched with one or more class-representative template. Various layout-based features are also adopted, and many works show their effectiveness for the document classification task [6, 1]. Following state-of-the-art results obtained in the Computer Vision research field, many recent works [8, 18] also perform document image classification using Deep Convolutional Neural Networks (CNN), obtaining outstanding results [8]. Starting from these state-of-the-art results and considering the previously described fine-grained document classification problem, we propose a novel method that combines textual and visual features using CNN.

More in details, our proposal consists of embedding content information extracted from text within document images, with the aim of adding elements which help the system in distinguish different classes that appear visually indistinguishable.

Our model was evaluated on two different dataset, and between different numbers and gender of document categories; the results from our experimental phase show that the proposed methodology achieves competitive results when compared to recent related

DocEng '16, September 12-16, 2016, Vienna, Austria
© 2016 ACM. ISBN 978-1-4503-4438-8/16/09. . . $15.00
DOI: http://dx.doi.org/10.1145/2960811.2960814

Figure 1: Documents belonging to three different representative classes are shown. In the first line examples of the class "Family Status" are shown, in the second line documents that belong to the class "Marriage Certificate" are reported, while in the third line documents were extracted from the "Residence Certificate" class. It's almost impossible to distinguish between the 3 classes only relying on the visual style of the documents.

works, and is able to effectively perform fine-grained document image classification.

2. RELATED WORKS

Existing approaches for document image classification and retrieval differ from each other based both on the type of extracted information (textual or visual) and/or the type of image analysis that is performed over the processed documents (global or local). Different supervised and unsupervised models have been proposed in literature throughout the last decade [4]: Random Forest based [10], Decision Tree and Self-organizing Map based [27], K-Nearest Neighbor based [3], Hidden Markov Model based [6], and Graph matching based [21] to name a few.

Features extracted from document images can either be visual, textual, or a combination of those two. The percentage of text and non-text elements in a content region of the image, font sizes, column structures, document structure, bag-of-words, and statistics of features are only few examples of extracted combined textual and visual characteristics adopted by some of the previously cited works for solving the task of document image classification [26, 10, 4].

In literature, visual-based local document image analysis was investigated and adopted for document images classification [9, 25]. Region-based algorithms reach interesting results when applied to structured model, such as letters or forms. Classifying a document based on its whole visual content is also possible [27]. However, all of these cited visual feature based approaches have limitations, such as the manual definition of document templates or specific geometric configurations of fixed features related to different document layouts.

Content-based document classification has also been extensively studied in literature. Content-based analysis of documents is typically performed relying on text extracted using OCR methods, although text allows retrieving information about document content,

visual layout plays an equal important role and it's used to detect some image region where applies OCR in order to have a more accurate extraction of content elements [2]. Nonetheless, OCR is prone to errors and is not always applicable to all kind of documents *e.g.* handwriting text is still difficult to read and those document images must have high resolution.

The recent success of Convolutional Neural Networks (CNN) in Computer Vision research areas [22, 32, 29] inspired novel applications of those algorithms to other domains such as document image analysis, text categorization and text understanding. A recent work by Kang *et al.* [18] shows that CNN are able to learn the entire supervised document image classification process, from feature extraction to final classification. Authors propose the use of a CNN for document image classification: a CNN is trained to recognize the class of given subsampled and pixel value normalized document images. Authors test their model on several challenging datasets, showing that such approach outperforms all previously explored methodologies.

Following the same intuition, Harley *et al.* [8] achieve outstanding results, setting new state-of-the-art results for image document image classification and retrieval.

An extensive evaluation of their CNN model is reported, determining that features extracted from deep CNN exceed the performance of all alternative visual and textual features both on document image classification and retrieval by a large margin. They also investigate about transfer learning, asserting that features learnt using CNN trained on object recognition are also effective in describing documents. Moreover, authors present several experiments varying between a single holistic CNN and ensembles of region-based CNN, exploring different initialization strategies. The performances of the evaluated models are evaluated on 2 different subsets of the IIT CDIP Test Collection [20], the smallest one [11] coincide with the one used by Kang *et al.* [18], while the largest one is composed by a significantly larger set of documents [8]. Evalu-

166

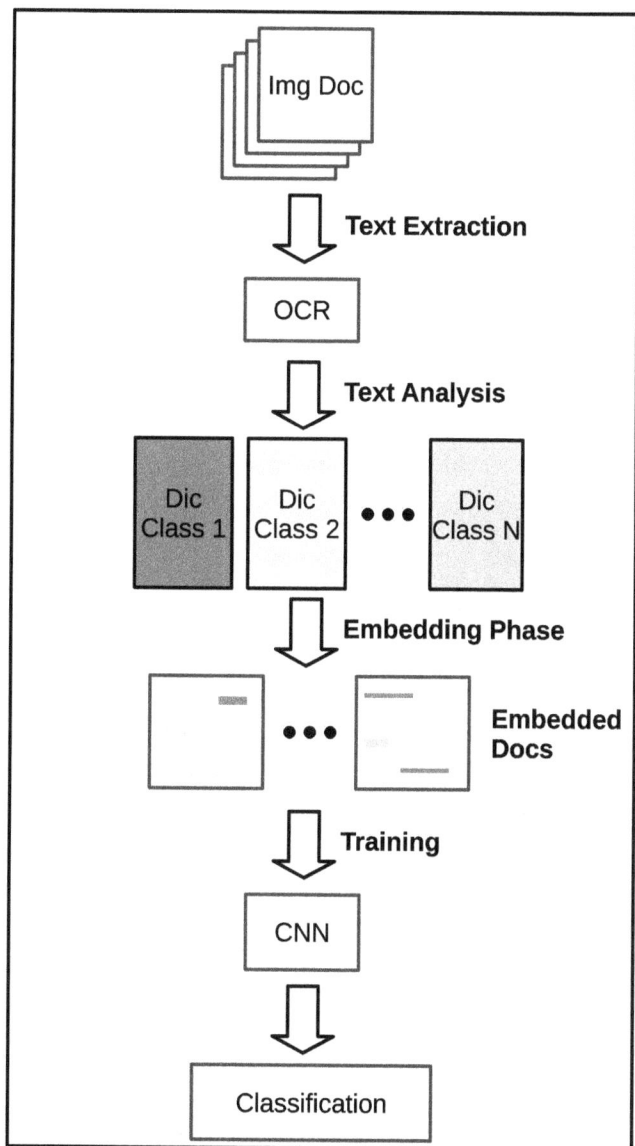

Figure 2: The building phase algorithm's pipeline.

Johnson *et al.* [13] studies CNN for text categorization exploiting word order to lead to more accurate predictions.

Our work exploits CNN in the same manner as in the approaches proposed by Harley *et al.* [8] and Kang *et al.* [18], our aim is to combine both content-based and image analysis, and to do so we embed content information extracted from text into subsampled document images and feed those visually enriched documents to a properly trained CNN model. A comparison between most of the previously cited approaches is provided and demonstrate that our model can easily reach comparable results. We also compare our results applying CNN only to text extracted from document images following the same approach of Kim *et al.* [16]. Results show that even though content-based approach leads to accurate results, our proposal that uses both images and text information performs even better. This demonstrates that the combination of the two different genre of features (visual and content) allows Machine Learning models to reach higher accuracy values in difficult document image classification tasks especially in the case of high visual similarity between different classes of documents.

3. PROPOSED METHOD

The main idea behind this work comes out after considering that in document image classification, intra-class similarity represents an issue that can be solved adding textual information extracted from the processed document images.

Figure 1 shows some representative examples of intra-class similarity, if in our method, we just focused on visual features, it would have been impossible to distinguish between the two classes of documents shown. However, by underlining significant textual information, fine-grained document classification become easier.

With the currently available computational resources, the adoption of CNN only allows the use of small sized document images. Although the original document layouts are distinguishable even sub-sampled document images, text becomes unreadable. Our challenge consists of adding content information in a visual manner, to let the CNN model to exploit such information when performing the classification task to reach higher classification accuracies for documents having high intra-class similarity.

The pipeline of the building phase of proposed approach is shown in Figure 2, its three main phases can be summarized as follows:

- **Text extraction and analysis**: OCR is employed to extract textual information from original sized document images. Texts are analyzed and for each class a dictionary is built.

- **Embedding phase**: exploiting word position coordinates and dictionaries, relevant words are emphasized within each sub-sampled document image.

- **Training phase**: a CNN is trained using sub-sampled document images from the previous phase.

3.1 Text extraction and analysis

Textual information is extracted from each document image through OCR. We employ Tesseract OCR [28], a widely used open-source OCR engine[1].

Optical Character Recognition is a difficult task for noisy or low resolution documents [14], and thus to discard reading errors we preprocess all the automatically extracted text using Natural Language dictionaries (more details about the used Natural Languages will be given in Section 4) and stop-word lists.

ation against all the different CNN configuration and diverse bag-of-words approaches are reported.

CNN are also employed in text categorization and text understanding fields. The text obtained by applying OCR to a document image can be viewed as a document itself. In this manner, document image classification can be reconducted to a sentence-level classification task.

Several interesting works that use CNN for Natural language processing have been recently published. Kim *et al.* [16] propose a simple CNN with one Convolutional Layer and prove that it performs well when applied to a wide range of difficult text classification tasks such as sentiment analysis and question classification. CNN are not the only Deep Model that proved to be effective for document classification tasks; Zhang *et al.* [31] use other Deep Learning algorithms for several text understanding tasks using Temporal Convolutional Networks [19] (ConvNets), working with both English and Chinese languages. An other recent work by

---

[1] https://github.com/tesseract-ocr

Figure 3: Key-words of three classes are underlined within images. It is easier to distinguish between the three classes "Family Status", "Marriage Certificate" and "Residence Certificate". The colors red, green and blue emphasize the content information in images, making it available for the training and classification phases.

To emphasize class relevant textual content within each document image, for each class, a dictionary containing representative words is generated. This is done by collecting all the words extracted by the OCR engine, for all the images belonging to a specific class. To build the final dictionary, we adopt the weighting formula of Peñas et al. [23].

The relevance formula, associates a weight to each word comparing it to other classes' words, the more the higher the value the higher is the relevance of the word for the specific class. In detail, the relevance of a term t_i is computed as follows:

$$Relevance(t_i, sc, gc) = 1 - \frac{1}{\log_2\left(2 + \frac{F_{t_i,sc} \cdot D_{t_i,sc}}{F_{t_i,gt}}\right)} \quad (1)$$

where: (i) sc is the *specific corpus*, it corresponds to the subset of words, extracted from the starting set of words extracted from images of the specified class (ii) gc is the *generic corpus*, it is composed by the whole set of words, extracted from all the classes , (iii) $F_{t_i,sc}$ is the relative frequency of the term t_i in the specific corpus sc, (iv) $F_{t,gc}$ is the relative frequency of the same term t_i in the generic corpus gc and (v) $D_{t,sc}$ is the relative number of documents of sc in which the term t_i appears.

Once we have the relevance value associated to each word of each dictionary, we prune the set of word at the fixed threshold $r = 0.8$ where r has been empirically determined.

Following all the previously described steps, we obtain a set of dictionaries that represent classes' key-words that are used to underline text within images in the next step.

3.2 Embedding phase

Starting from the dictionaries of relevant words per classes, the aim of this phase is to embed textual information obtained from OCR within document images. We perform this to let relevant key-words information become recognizable even at low resolutions where the text is unreadable.

We create a specific visual color feature for each class key-word

contained in the processed image and in at least one of the dictionaries built in Sec. 3.1. The added visual feature consists of a rectangle of the class color drawn across each class key-word found in the document image.

More in details, given an image, Tesseract OCR is performed. The OCR engine output is composed both of the sequence of recognized words and their positions within the image. Once the words are extracted, for each word the system checks whether it belongs to one or more of class key-word dictionaries.

If the word belongs to only one dictionary, a rectangle of the associated class color is drawn across it using the obtained position coordinates, otherwise if it belongs to more than one dictionary the rectangle is divided by the number of corresponding dictionaries and each part is colored using the associated class colors.

In Figure 3 the same documents shown in Figure 1 are shown after the embedding phase. Rectangles of respective classes' colors are drawn; it can be easily noted that, for documents that belong to the same class, the associated class color is the mostly used: in the first line the red color is the most utilized, in the second is the green, while in the third the majority of the key-words' rectangles are blue. Experiments reported in Section 4 show the effectiveness of the embedding phase for these specific three classes of documents.

During CNN training, document images are sub-sampled to fixed dimension therefore text becomes unreadable; however, the marked key-word rectangles remain visible and allow the model to infer textual content. Not only classes information are added but key-words' positions are underlined, giving the model extra characteristics that are exploited during the classification phase.

3.3 Training phase

A deep Convolutional Neural Network is employed as classification model. Our proposal consists of using the images from the previous steps, where textual content information are transformed into visual features and stored in document images, to train the network.

A common practice with CNN is to exploit transfer learning [30].

168

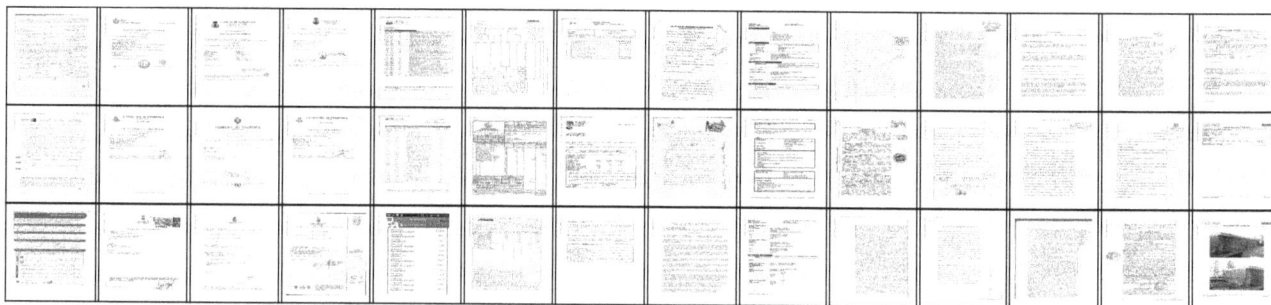

Figure 4: The Loan dataset: for every column, three representative documents of a specif class are displayed. From left to right classes are reported in the following order: "Loan Request", "Family Status", "Marriage Certificate", "Residence Certificate", "Account Balance", "Payroll", "Pension Payslip", "Lease", "Company Registration", "Previous Contract", "Preliminary Purchase", "Loan Contract" ,"Preliminary Report" and "Expertise". It can be noted that documents belonging to different classes present similar visual style.

This technique consist of pre-training a network on a large dataset, and then exploit it either as a fixed feature extractor or as a fine-tuning for the adopted CNN. In the first scenario, given a CNN a training phase on a different dataset is performed, after that the last fully-connected layer is removed and the remaining Convolutional Network is treated as a fixed feature extractor for the new dataset. On the other hand, the second strategy consists of fine-tune the weights of the pre-trained network by continuing the back-propagation.

A popular pre-training dataset is ImageNet. ImageNet dataset [5] is composed of over 15 million labeled high-resolution images in over 22000 categories, a subset of 1.2 million of images divided in 1000 categories is used in ILSVRC ImageNet challenges as training set, networks trained with such a training set are often used for transfer learning methodology.

Supported by the state-of-the-art results obtained by Harley *et al.* [8], we also implement transfer learning using ImageNet dataset and the CNN model of Krizhevsky *et al.* [17]. Implementation details are given is Section 4.2. Multiple experiments demonstrating the effectiveness of our method are reported in the next Section of this manuscript.

4. EXPERIMENTS

Several experiments were conducted in order to evaluate our proposal. As discussed in previous Sections, we aim to add textual content information to document images, to allow the CNN model to better distinguish between classes that have hight intra-class visual similarity.

We compare our results against state-of-the-art outcomes in the document image classification field, and provide a comparison between a CNN that performs classification using the proposed textual content embedded document images and a CNN that uses exclusively textual information, showing that our methodology is significantly more effective.

4.1 Datasets

We test our approach on two datasets, and to better emphasize the effectiveness of our proposal in solving intra-class similarity issue, we use some representative subsets of the same document image collections.

The first dataset, the so-called *Loan* dataset, has been provided by an Italian loan comparison website company. Through their platforms, this company provides a service which let customers quickly compare the best rates and terms of available loans. To

supply the best obtainable loan, website owners need to collect all the necessary documents in a digital format.

We collect a set of 14 different classes that present similar visual styles, this means that a document belonging to a class is often indistinguishable using just visual style features. Documents are used to provide loan offers to customers. A total of 16250 document images are collected and divided into training, evaluation and testing sets following similar proportions as in the ImageNet dataset: 80% training, 10% evaluation and 10% testing. Examples of image documents extracted from the different classes are reported in Figure 4.

Among all the 14 collected classes we select 2 subsets of 3 classes each that have very similar visual layouts and because of that are difficult to classify correctly. Visually similar subset are used to better underline the effectiveness of our proposal.

The first subset is composed by the following classes: "Family Status", "Marriage Certificate" and "Residence Certificate", previously introduced in Figure 1 and 3; we name it *Certificates subset*. The second subset is called *Contracts subset* and it contains the following document classes: "Preliminary Purchase", "Loan Contract" and "Preliminary Report".

In order to compare our approach to existing approaches, we test our method on the same dataset used by Harley *et al.* [8] and Kang *et al.* [18], we refer to it as *Tobacco* dataset. The *Tobacco* dataset is composed of 3482 images divided in the following 10 classes: Advertisement, Email, Form, Letter, Memo, News, Note, Report, Resume, Scientific.

The split of Tobacco dataset is the same used in related works [8, 18, 20]: 800 images are used for training, 200 for validations, and the remainder for testing.

4.2 Implementation details

The CNN is implemented using Caffe[12], and is based on the work of Krizhevsky *et al.* [17]. The network is composed of 5 Convolutional Layers, some of which are followed by Max-pooling Layers, three Fully-connected Layers with a final Softmax, all the details are reported in the reference paper [17].

The full architecture can be written as $227 \times 227 - 11 \times 11 \times 96 - 5 \times 5 \times 256 - 3 \times 3 \times 384 - 3 \times 3 \times 384 - 3 \times 3 \times 256 - 4096 - 4096 - N$. Where N is the number of categories and varying in respect with the utilized dataset. The input images size is 227×227, we down-sampled all the images to a fixed resolution of 256×256, in order to have a constant input dimensionality. The Caffe implementation of the adopted CNN randomly crops images from

(a) Visual Features

(b) Textual and Visual Features

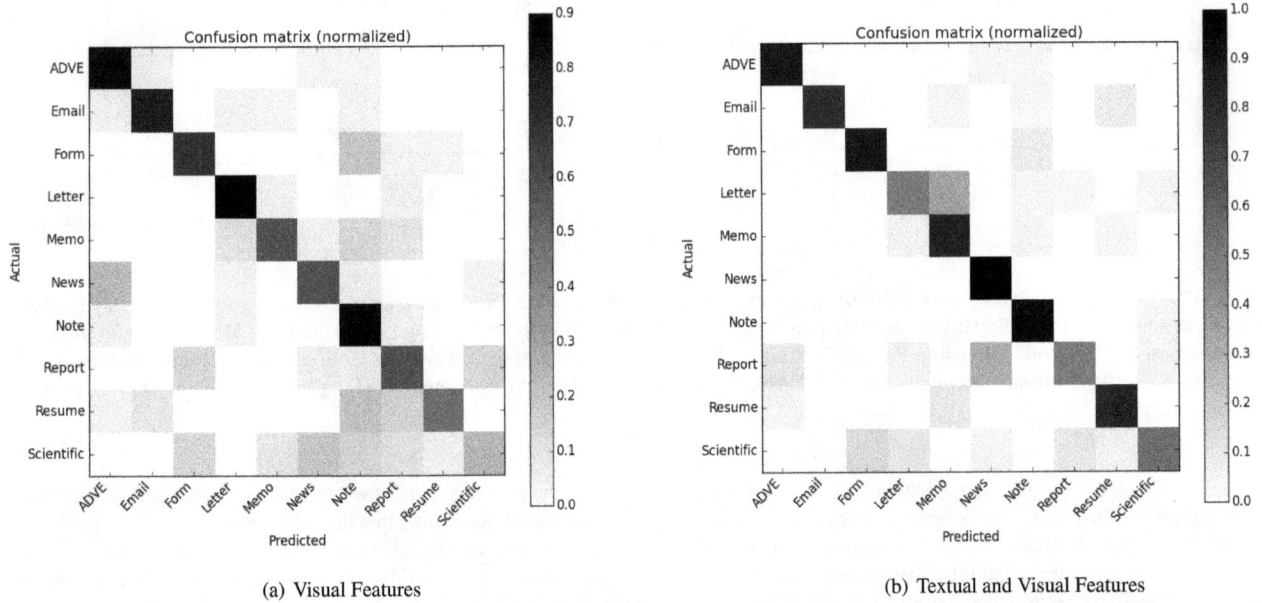

Figure 5: Confusion matrices reporting the results achieved on the Tobacco dataset. Results have been calculated testing the model trained using original images (a) and using images that contained textual information (b).

Table 1: Results achieved by the proposed method are reported, the CNN was trained using original images and with elaborated images. More accurate results are obtained training the network with images in where textual information are embedded.

Dataset	Overall Accuracy
Tobacco V	74.2%
Tobacco V & T	79.8%
Loan V	74.73%
Loan V & T	87.85%
Loan Certificates subset V	60%
Loan Certificates subset V & T	90%
Loan Contracts subset V	62.31%
Loan Contracts subset V & T	88.33%

Table 2: The same experiments performed exploiting visual features are performed using only textual features. Results shows that text is a relevant feature for the selected classes and can not be ignored to better perform the classification task, but at the same time a combinations of textual and visual feature is more effective.

Dataset	Text CNN	Proposed
Loan	69.89%	87.85%
Loan Certificates subset	87.15%	90%
Loan Contracts subset	86.31%	88.33%

256×256 to 227×227, this technique is usually employed because it helps data augmentation and reduces overfitting.

4.3 Results

Experiments are performed to compare different results achieved while training the CNN model with original images and images containing textual information created through the embedding phase (Section 3.2).

Overall accuracies achieved by the proposed model are reported in Table 1. The adopted CNN was trained using the two different types of images. Results demonstrate that when the CNN is trained on the embedded images it reaches higher accuracies, passing from 74.2% to 79.8% on the Tobacco dataset and reaching 87.85% from 74.73% on the Loan dataset. Figure 5 shows the two confusion matrices computed for the Tobacco dataset respectively before and after the embedding phase; matrices underline that information deriving by text is helpful for the classification task and show the achieved improvement.

Table 3: Comparison against models that use only visual features or only textual features are reported, our proposal overcomes or reaches almost the same results achieved by other methods.

Model	Overall Accuracy
Proposed V & T	79.8%
text-CNN Kim [16]	68.92 %
CNN Harley et al. [8]	79.9 %
CNN Kang et al. [18]	65.35%

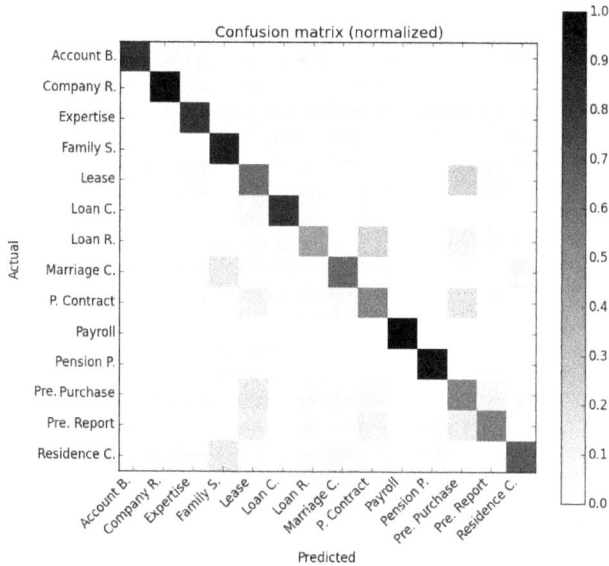

(a) LOAN - Visual Features

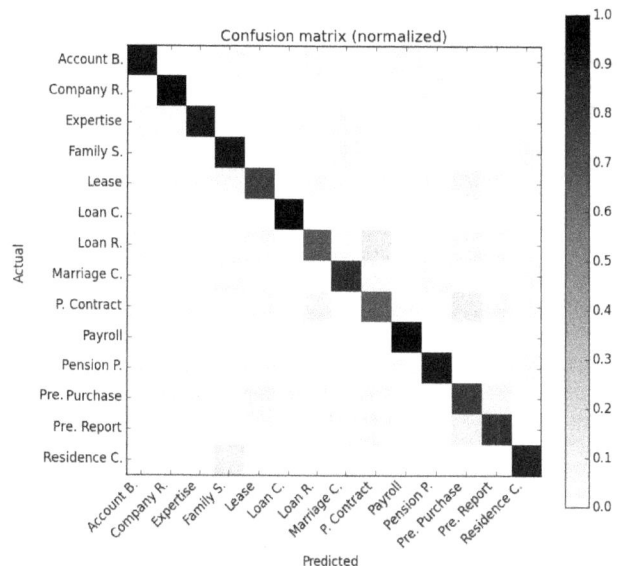

(b) LOAN - Textual & Visual Features

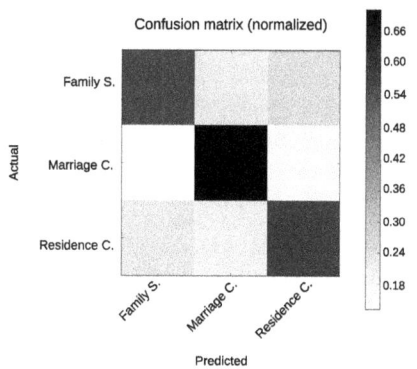

(c) CERTIFICATES - Visual Features

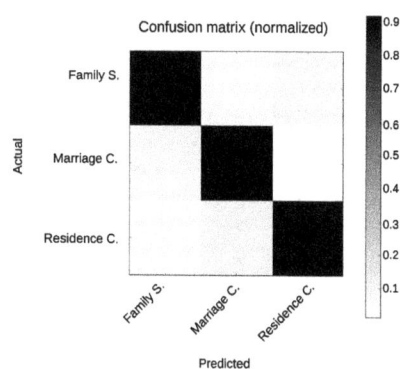

(d) CERTIFICATES - Textual & Visual Features

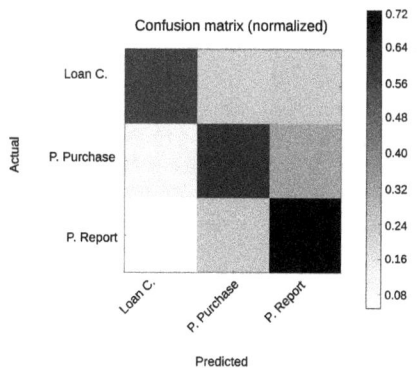

(e) CONTRACTS - Visual Features

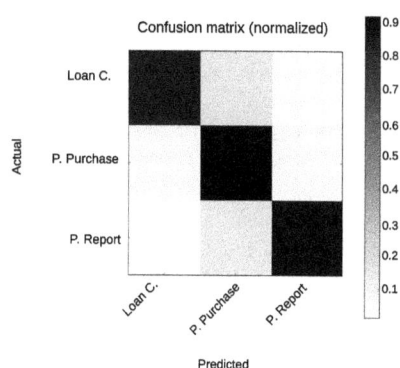

(f) CONTRACTS - Textual & Visual Features

Figure 6: Confusion matrices reporting results achieved on the whole Loan dataset (a), (b) and on the two subsets Certificates (c), (d) and Contracts (e), (f) are displayed. Matrices on the left side report the outcomes of the test phase, training the model using original images, while on the right side, the model was trained using images that contains underlined textual information. Matrices summary the improvement achieved by using the elaborated images in the training phase.

Experiments conducted on the two subsets of the Loan dataset show a high grow in terms of accuracy, the values increase by 30% passing from original images to textual embedded document images for the Certificates subset, and by 26% for the Contracts subsets.

Confusion matrices of the testing phase for both the Loan and the two subsets are provided. Figure 6 displays the confusion matrices related to the Loan dataset and its two subsets, all the three matrices reflect the overall accuracy values obtained, demonstrating the effectiveness of the propose methodology.

Moreover Table 3, reports a comparison carried on the Tobacco dataset among our proposal and related works that deals with only visual features[8, 18] or only textual features [16], which will be better analyzed in Section 4.4.

Although the proposed method does not overcome state-of-the-art results, it reaches comparable outcomes and demonstrates that combining visual and textual feature is an interesting approach to follow.

4.4 CNN applied to text

In this work, we aim to classify images adding textual information to them. Our goal is to demonstrate that a combination of textual and visual features is necessary for better understanding the document image content. To this end, we evaluate the classification of images using just the extracted text.

CNN proved effective in different Natural Language Processing tasks [15, 7]. A recent work proposed by Yoon Kim [16] implements a simple CNN, with one Convolutional Layer and achieves good classification performance across a range of text classification tasks.

We use the model proposed by Kim *et al.* [16] to classify text extracted from document images. For each document, text is divided into sentences, each sentence represents a document that has to be classified into one of the available classes. Results are shown in Table 2 and demonstrate that although the text-CNN reaches interesting results achieving 70% of accuracy on the whole Loan dataset, the exploitation of both visual and textual feature is more effective.

5. CONCLUSIONS

A new method that exploits both textual and visual features for document image classification has been proposed. By adopting Convolutional Neural Networks, we demonstrate that embedding textual information into document images leads to more accurate results for the document image classification task. Our method is able to take advantage of the extra textual key-word information provided by colored rectangles to reach more satisfying document image classification accuracies, especially for document classes having similar visual styles.

Future extensions of our work may rely on testing different embedding methods that permit to apply this approach on classification tasks that involve a consistent number of classes.

6. ACKNOWLEDGMENTS

We gratefully acknowledge the support of NVIDIA Corporation with the donation of the GeForce GTX 980 GPU used for this research.

7. REFERENCES

[1] E. Appiani, F. Cesarini, A. M. Colla, M. Diligenti, M. Gori, S. Marinai, and G. Soda. Automatic document classification and indexing in high-volume applications. *International Journal on Document Analysis and Recognition (IJDAR)*, 2001.

[2] S. Argamon, O. Frieder, D. A. Grossman, and D. D. Lewis. Content-based document image retrieval in complex document collections. In *Document Recognition and Retrieval (DRR)*, 2007.

[3] S. Baldi, S. Marinai, and G. Soda. Using tree-grammars for training set expansion in page classification. In *International Conference on Document Analysis and Recognition (ICDAR)*, 2003.

[4] N. Chen and D. Blostein. A survey of document image classification: Problem statement, classifier architecture and performance evaluation. *International Journal on Document Analysis and Recognition (IJDAR)*, 2007.

[5] J. Deng, W. Dong, R. Socher, L.-J. Li, K. Li, and L. Fei-Fei. ImageNet: A Large-Scale Hierarchical Image Database. In *The IEEE Conferenbasedce on Computer Vision and Pattern Recognition (CVPR)*, 2009.

[6] M. Diligenti, P. Frasconi, and M. Gori. Hidden tree markov models for document image classification. *IEEE Transactions on Pattern Analysis and Machine Intelligence (TPAMI)*, 2003.

[7] C. dos Santos and M. Gatti. Deep convolutional neural networks for sentiment analysis of short texts. In *International Conference on Computational Linguistics (COLING)*, 2014.

[8] A. W. Harley, A. Ufkes, and K. G. Derpanis. Evaluation of deep convolutional nets for document image classification and retrieval. In *International Conference on Document Analysis and Recognition (ICDAR)*, 2015.

[9] J. Hu, R. Kashi, and G. Wilfong. Comparison and Classification of Documents Based on Layout Similarity. *Information Retrieval*, 2000.

[10] Jayant Kumar and David Doermann. Unsupervised Classification of Structurally Similar Document Images. In *Intl. Conf. on Document Analysis and Recognition (ICDAR 13)*, 2013.

[11] Jayant Kumar, Peng Ye, and David Doermann. Structural Similarity for Document Image Classification and Retrieval. *Pattern Recognition Letters*, 2013.

[12] Y. Jia, E. Shelhamer, J. Donahue, S. Karayev, J. Long, R. Girshick, S. Guadarrama, and T. Darrell. Caffe: Convolutional architecture for fast feature embedding. In *ACM International Conference on Multimedia (ACMMM)*, 2014.

[13] R. Johnson and T. Zhang. Effective use of word order for text categorization with convolutional neural networks. *Computing Research Repository (CoRR)*, 2014.

[14] A. Kae, G. B. Huang, C. Doersch, and E. G. Learned-Miller. Improving state-of-the-art OCR through high-precision document-specific modeling. In *The IEEE Conferenbasedce on Computer Vision and Pattern Recognition (CVPR)*, 2010.

[15] N. Kalchbrenner, E. Grefenstette, and P. Blunsom. A convolutional neural network for modelling sentences. *Computing Research Repository (CoRR)*, 2014.

[16] Y. Kim. Convolutional neural networks for sentence classification. *Computing Research Repository (CoRR)*, 2014.

[17] A. Krizhevsky, I. Sutskever, and G. E. Hinton. Imagenet classification with deep convolutional neural networks. In

Advances in Neural Information Processing Systems (NIPS), 2012.

[18] Le Kang, Jayant Kumar, Peng Ye, Yi Li, and David Doermann. Convolutional Neural Networks for Document Image Classification. In *International Conference on Pattern Recognition (ICPR)*, 2014.

[19] Y. Lecun, L. Bottou, Y. Bengio, and P. Haffner. Gradient-based learning applied to document recognition. In *IEEE*, 1998.

[20] D. Lewis, G. Agam, S. Argamon, O. Frieder, D. Grossman, and J. Heard. Building a test collection for complex document information processing. In *ACM Conference on Research and Development in Information Retrieval (SIGIR)*, 2006.

[21] J. Liang, D. S. Doermann, M. Y. Ma, and J. K. Guo. Page classification through logical labelling. In *International Conference on Pattern Recognition (ICPR)*, 2002.

[22] M. Liang and X. Hu. Recurrent convolutional neural network for object recognition. In *The IEEE Conferenbasedce on Computer Vision and Pattern Recognition (CVPR)*, 2015.

[23] A. Penas, F. Verdejo, and J. Gonzalo. Corpus-based terminology extraction applied to information access. In *Corpus Linguistics*, 2001.

[24] H. Peng, F. Long, Z. Chi, and W.-C. Siu. Document image template matching based on component block list. *Pattern Recognition Letters*, 2001.

[25] P. Sarkar. Learning image anchor templates for document classification and data extraction. In *International Conference on Pattern Recognition (ICPR)*, 2010.

[26] C. Shin and D. S. Doermann. Document image retrieval based on layout structural similarity. In *International Conference on Image Processing, Computer Vision, and Pattern Recognition (IPCV)*, 2006.

[27] C. Shin, D. S. Doermann, and A. Rosenfeld. Classification of document pages using structure-based features. *International Journal on Document Analysis and Recognition (IJDAR)*, 2001.

[28] R. Smith. An overview of the tesseract OCR engine. In *International Conference on Document Analysis and Recognition (ICDAR)*, 2007.

[29] R. Wu, B. Wang, W. Wang, and Y. Yu. Harvesting discriminative meta objects with deep CNN features for scene classification. *Computing Research Repository (CoRR)*, 2015.

[30] J. Yosinski, J. Clune, Y. Bengio, and H. Lipson. How transferable are features in deep neural networks? *Computing Research Repository (CoRR)*, 2014.

[31] X. Zhang and Y. LeCun. Text understanding from scratch. *Computing Research Repository (CoRR)*, 2015.

[32] Y. Zhang, K. Sohn, R. Villegas, G. Pan, and H. Lee. Improving object detection with deep convolutional networks via bayesian optimization and structured prediction. *Computing Research Repository (CoRR)*, 2015.

A Lightweight and Efficient Mechanism for Fixing the Synchronization of Misaligned Subtitle Documents

Rodrigo Laiola Guimarães
IBM Research
Rua Tutóia 1157
04007900 São Paulo, Brazil
+55 11 2132 2283
rlaiola@br.ibm.com

Priscilla Avegliano
IBM Research
Rua Tutóia 1157
04007900 São Paulo, Brazil
+55 11 2132 5790
pba@br.ibm.com

Lucas C. Villa Real
IBM Research
Rua Tutóia 1157
04007900 São Paulo, Brazil
+55 11 2132 4548
lucasvr@br.ibm.com

ABSTRACT

Online subtitle databases allow users to easily find subtitle documents in multiple languages for thousands of films and TV series episodes. However, getting the subtitle document that gives satisfactory synchronization on the first attempt is like *hitting the jackpot*. The truth is that this process often involves a lot of trial-and-error because multiple versions of subtitle documents have distinct synchronization references, given that they are targeted at variations of the same audiovisual content. Building on our previous efforts to address this problem, in this paper we formalize and validate a two-phase subtitle synchronization framework. The benefit over current approaches lays in the usage of audio fingerprint annotations generated from the base audio signal as second-level synchronization anchors. This way, we allow the media player to dynamically fix during playback the most common cases of subtitle synchronization misalignment that compromise users' watching experience. Results from our evaluation process indicate that our framework has minimal impact on existing subtitle documents and formats as well as on the playback performance.

CCS Concepts

• **Information systems → Multimedia information systems, Speech / audio search • Applied computing → Document management and text processing, Document metadata, Document preparation, Annotation, Format and notation, Multi / mixed media creation.**

Keywords

Subtitles; Audio fingerprinting; Synchronization; SRT.

1. INTRODUCTION

Downloading a subtitle document from the Internet and playing it alongside audiovisual content (*e.g.*, a movie or a TV series episode) is not rocket science; but it sure can feel that way sometimes. Considering a user already has the media file on his or her local device and that s/he has identified multiple versions of potential subtitle documents on an online repository, s/he still has

to figure out which of such files gives satisfactory synchronization. The problem is that even with the efforts of online communities to review and correct user-contributed subtitle documents as well as media players that try to download suitable subtitle documents automatically, the user may still run endless times into versions that do not sync up perfectly with the base audiovisual content. The underlying problem is that even if the synchronization is off for just a couple of seconds, misaligned subtitle entries will most probably be a constant annoyance.

Take Figure 1 as an example. Here, we illustrate the playback of 2 subtitle documents with the corresponding audiovisual content (track in light blue with dot pattern). Figure 1.a represents the ideal scenario where subtitle entries (in yellow with line pattern) are perfectly synchronized with the base content. On the other hand, in Figure 1.b the timing of all subtitle entries (in orange with line pattern) are shifted ∂t seconds. Note that this latter

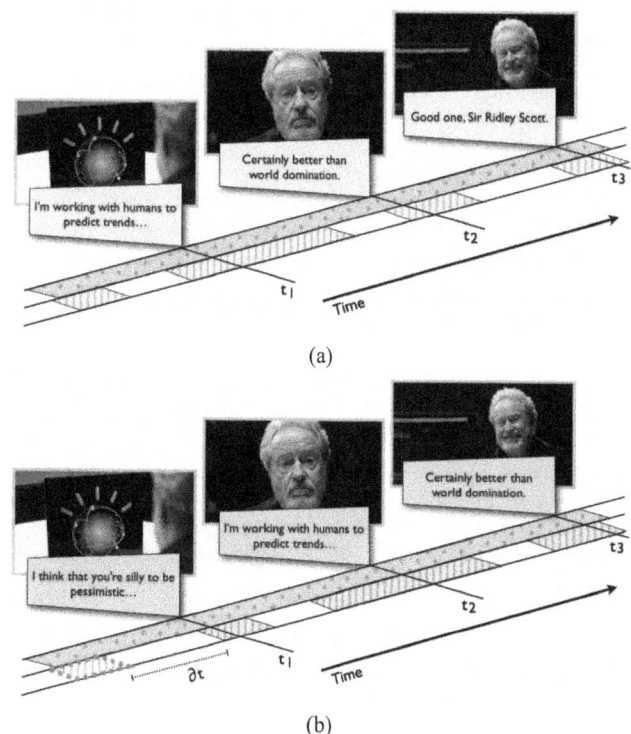

(a)

(b)

Figure 1. Playback of audiovisual content together with subtitle documents using a local media player: a) subtitle entries with perfect timing and b) shifted ∂t seconds. Screenshots extracted from "Ridley Scott + IBM Watson: A Conversation". Available at https://youtu.be/KDtxQRH8aI4.

subtitle document may have been created using a variation of the original audiovisual content (*e.g.*, a version including advertisements in the beginning). The point is that, although this second document is a potential match, even minor synchronization misalignments might compromise the entire experience. In this context, we consider the scenario in which once a candidate subtitle document has been identified – not necessarily only the one synchronized *to the letter* – the viewer can obtain satisfactory synchronization. Our ultimate goal is to provide the media player the ability to dynamically adjust the presentation of the subtitle document in Figure 1.b, so that the experience from the viewer's perspective looks just like the one in Figure 1.a. By supporting this functionality we expect to minimize the burden on the viewer before the *fun* starts (after all, this is what really matters).

In previous work, we performed a qualitative analysis of several subtitle documents for a popular movie and TV series episode in order to understand the problem domain [20]. This process allowed us to identify some common types of synchronization problems users[1] face when playing audiovisual content together with subtitle documents downloaded from the Internet. To address these issues (*i.e.*, constant and varying temporal offsets) we proposed a two-phase subtitle synchronization mechanism to 1) enrich subtitle documents with audio fingerprint[2] annotations generated from the base audio signal, that later can serve as second-level synchronization anchors for the media player to 2) adjust misaligned subtitle entries during playback.

In this work, we reflect on our previous findings and look at the subtitle misalignment problem from a document engineering perspective. As our first contribution, we formalize a lightweight method that annotates subtitle documents with representative audio fingerprints. We show that the impact of such method to enrich existing subtitle documents and formats is relatively small. As our second contribution, we propose an algorithm that dynamically adjusts the synchronization of misaligned subtitle entries during playback. Experiments with a proof of concept application that realizes the proposed framework indicate that our solution does an efficient use of computational resources.

In particular, the requirements and constraints that motivated our design choices include:

i. *Minimize user effort:* to be practical, the proposed framework must fix the synchronization of misalignment subtitle documents with minimal user input. That seems to make good sense, specially if users spend much more time than necessary in a process that can be automatized;

ii. *Ensure copyright compliance:* the proposed framework should retain the base video integrity, either in terms of editing, removing or adding third-party material to the base audiovisual content, as well as avoid infringing the copyrights in the reuse and reproduction of unauthorized portions of the audio stream;

iii. *Be backward compatible:* a video player that does not implement the proposed framework should process a new version of the subtitle document containing second-level synchronization anchors in the same way as an older version of such document that does not include audio fingerprint annotations. Similarly, new video players should be capable of processing subtitle documents without synchronization anchors;

iv. *Minimize the impact on subtitle documents and formats:* the effect of inserting synchronization anchors based on audio fingerprints should be minimized not only in terms of extending the specification of existing subtitle formats and storage costs, but also in regards with the playback performance; and

v. *Handle different types of subtitle misalignment problems:* the methods to annotate and fix the presentation of subtitle documents enriched with audio fingerprint annotations should be general enough to address the different types of synchronization problems identified in our initial findings.

This paper is organized as follows. In Section 2 we contextualize and motivate our work. Next, in Section 3 we introduce a general framework that addresses the most typical cases of subtitle synchronization misalignment. In brief, the proposed approach consists of 2 steps. Firstly, the enrichment of exiting subtitle documents with representative audio fingerprint annotations generated from the based audio signal; and subsequently, the resynchronization of misaligned subtitle entries during the playback of a variation of the original audiovisual content. Then, Section 4 reports on the design and implementation of a proof of concept that realizes our contributions, whereas Section 5 presents its evaluation process. Finally, Section 6 reviews our contribution in the light of related work and Section 7 is dedicated to concluding remarks and future work.

2. BACKGROUND

The lifecycle of subtitles can be analyzed from different perspectives. In professional post-production, extensive support is typically available for professionals to create and synchronize subtitle entries along with the base audiovisual content. The result from this process can be either *burned-in* in the base content or encapsulated with other data streams (including subtitle documents in other languages) in a container format[3] and distributed on DVDs[4], Blu-Rays, broadcast television, or on-demand video services. Given that all data is wrapped (and distributed) in a single and self-contained unit, synchronization problems[5] like the ones discussed in this paper are not expected during playback.

Non-professionals can also create subtitle documents, although this task can be timing consuming. Sharing the resulting subtitle documents on the Web is particularly common for popular movies and TV series episodes shared online. As these subtitle documents

---

[1] The terms 'user' and 'viewer' will be used interchangeably in this paper to describe regular people who operate computer software with minimal technical expertise or previous training.

[2] An audio fingerprint is a compact content-based signature that summarizes an audio sample with a predefined length. Especially, it does NOT represent the audio signal at a specific point in time.

[3] Wrapper format whose specification describes how different media types and metadata coexist in a computer file.

[4] Some technologies, if unknown, could easily be identified via an online search; therefore they will not be Web-referenced.

[5] Videos with high resolutions may still not play smoothly on devices with limited computational resources, which may result in a slight synchronization misalignment not only of subtitle entries but also between the audio and video streams.

are often distributed separately from the reference audiovisual content, recipients may face difficulties in finding the version that offers satisfactory synchronization (vide Figure 1). It is important to mention that the existence of multiple versions of subtitle documents may reflect the various editions of the original audiovisual content that may or not include an opening intro, scenes from previous or next episodes, advertisements, and so on. As we will show in the following sections, it is exactly in this scenario that we propose a lightweight and efficient mechanism for fixing automatically the synchronization of misaligned subtitles documents.

2.1 Subtitle Formats on the Web

Bulterman et al. [3] presents an extensive analysis of several subtitle formats, which according to them fall under 2 main categories: embedded and external text formats. Embedded text formats are tightly integrated with the host language. One example of said format is SmilText, which contains intra-block formatting and timing control, with the layout and general rendering control defined in the Synchronized Multimedia Integration Language (SMIL) [4].

External subtitle formats, on the other hand, encapsulate information on synchronization and text styling in an external file or document. Once in the possession of such document, the media player parses its contents and renders the text entries on the screen according to the timestamps and durations specified for each entry. Below, we present some external subtitle formats that are prominent on the Web.

WebVTT[6] (*Web Video Text Tracks Format*) is a technology introduced in HTML5 that can be used to display timed text tracks with the HTML5 `<track>` element alongside `<video>` elements. The file is text-based and contains essentially (i) a header, (ii) a sequence of subtitle entries, and (iii) empty lines. Subtitle entries have a numerical identification, starting and ending times, and a textual payload. This format also admits text-formatting settings such as text direction (*e.g.*, left to right or the other way round), rendering position, text size and alignment, and bold/italic/underlined tags, to name a few. WebVTT also supports comments by starting a line with the string "NOTE". Said lines are not rendered on the screen.

```
01. ...
02. 19
03. 00:01:22,782 --> 00:01:27,221
04. RIDLEY SCOTT: I think that you're silly to be
05. pessimistic...
06.
07. 20
08. 00:01:29,467 --> 00:01:34,172
09. WATSON: I'm working with humans to predict trends...
10.
11. 21
12. 00:01:35,524 --> 00:01:37,248
13. RIDLEY SCOTT: Certainly better than world
14. domination.
15.
16. 22
17. 00:01:37,688 --> 00:01:39,053
18. WATSON: Good one, Sir Ridley Scott.
19. ...
```

Figure 2. Typical SRT document shared online. Each subtitle entry includes a sequence number (in black), the time the text should appear and disappear (in red, left and right side of the '-->' token, respectively), and the textual content (in blue).

SubStation Alpha[7] (SSA) is a popular file format used in conjunction with the Matroska MKV container to store subtitle data along with video streams. The structure of an SSA document is similar to an INI file: sections are declared with `[brackets]`, lines starting with a semicolon (`;`) are treated as comments, and pairs of `key:values` are used to define subtitle metadata and attributes. Attributes include formatting and styling, scaling, rotation, and font names, among others. Actual subtitle entries are described in an `[Events]` section that includes not only the textual payload but also the position of the text, timestamps, and effects. The format is rich in the sense that it enables the creation of complex presentations, although the resulting subtitle document file may not be adequate to be manually edited in a text editor due to its size and relative complexity.

The most popular of the external text-based file formats in use today is, by far, the SRT (*SubRip Text*). SRT is widely supported by both a variety of players and subtitle creation programs. Essentially, a SRT document contains the textual entries to be displayed and the moment of that presentation. There is no support for comments. Some media players recognize text-formatting (bold, italic, underline, and font color) commands entered with HTML tags. As illustrated in Figure 2, SRT is comprised of three main elements: a sequence number (lines 02, 07, 11 and 16), the time in which the subtitle must appear and disappear on the screen (lines 03, 08, 12 and 17), and the subtitle text itself across one or more lines (lines 04-05, 09, 13-14 and 18).

2.2 Preliminary Findings

To identify common synchronization misalignment problems, in previous work [20] we analyzed multiple versions of SRT documents related to a highly rated movie and TV series episode – according to the Internet Movie Database (IMDb). All documents were obtained programmatically using the open API (*Application Program Interface*) available on OpenSubTitles.org. The rationale to analyze subtitle documents related to 2 different productions was that in essence movies have a different structure when compared to TV series. For instance, a TV series episode may start with an opening intro or scenes from the previous episode, and finish with a preview of the next episode.

For the referred movie, we obtained 193 SRT documents distributed across 33 different languages (English, Brazilian Portuguese, and Spanish were among the most frequents). In general, these subtitle documents included advertisements and credits information as actual subtitle entries. Interestingly, we noticed that in several opportunities the very same subtitle document had different file names and different creators listed in the credits. This suggests that ownership infringement is a recurrent problem in subtitle sharing communities on the Internet.

In our analysis for the episode of a popular TV series, we collected 170 SRT documents in 38 different languages. In contrast to the ones for the movie, the presence and absence of prologues and epilogues was often observed and caused a relatively large standard deviation at the presentation time of the first subtitle entry (~45 seconds for an average of 88 seconds in the case of the subtitle documents for Brazilian Portuguese).

In our analysis, we also found that some SRT documents are extracted directly from DVDs and Blu-Rays, whereas others are created using audiovisual content recorded from broadcast TV. More importantly, we noticed that the main synchronization

---

[6] https://www.w3.org/TR/webvtt1/

[7] https://www.matroska.org/technical/specs/subtitles/ssa.html

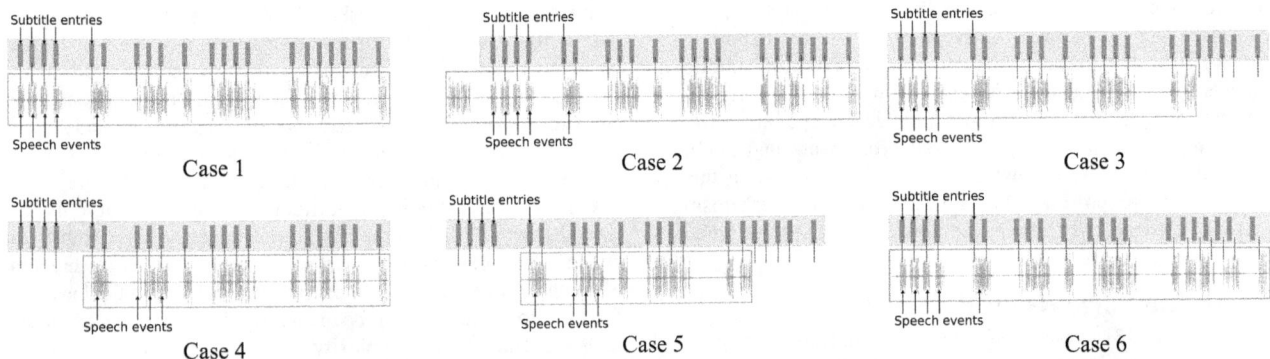

Figure 3. Alignment scenarios when playing audiovisual content together with subtitle documents downloaded from the Internet.

problem between different subtitle documents is a *constant temporal offset* that shifts equally the presentation of equivalent subtitle entries (as illustrated in Figure 1). This is the case, for instance, if one SRT document is generated using an audiovisual content that has a prologue; whereas another document is created using a version of the same audiovisual content that does not include such part.

To a lesser extent, we also observed that some subtitle documents have a *varying temporal offset*. In this case, even when different documents have the first subtitle entry temporally aligned, the next entries increasingly get out of sync with each other. In other words, it is like if the ∂t in Figure 1.b started equals zero but increased over time. The causes of this problem suggest that varying temporal offsets are related to different encoding offsets (*e.g.*, frame rate) used in the corresponding base contents.

Analyzing the collected data, we grouped the synchronization misalignment problems between audiovisual content and subtitle documents in 6 canonical cases[8], as illustrated in Figure 3:

- *Case 1 - Perfectly synchronized:* the audiovisual content and the subtitle document are in sync, or in other words, the offset ∂t is equal to zero;

- *Case 2 - Audiovisual content includes an initial part:* such part did not exist in the version used to generate the subtitle document. In this case, during playback all subtitle entries should be shifted an offset ∂t greater than zero;

- *Case 3 - Audiovisual content trimmed in the end:* the offset ∂t is equal to zero, but the subtitle document has entries that do not have counterparts on the audiovisual content (these are never exhibited during playback by the way);

- *Case 4 - Audiovisual content trimmed in the beginning:* the initial subtitle entries in the document are not presented; hence, the value of the offset ∂t is negative;

- *Case 5 - Audiovisual content trimmed on both ends:* only a subset of the entries in the subtitle document should be presented. As the initial entries would be discarded, the offset ∂t should have a negative value;

- *Case 6 - Audiovisual content with different pace:* this is a peculiar situation, possibly generated when the media file

---

[8] Naturally, a combination of these canonical cases may apply in some scenarios.

was encoded in another format. The subtitle entries start with a given ∂t, but as time passes by, this value increases/decreases.

3. GENERAL FRAMEWORK

The study presented in the previous section reinforces the argument that finding a subtitle document that offers users satisfactory synchronization is a very challenging task. The several synchronization misalignment variations identified also support our premise that a mechanism to automate the synchronization of subtitle documents during playback is indeed relevant and necessary. Therefore, to address this research problem we propose a method that (1) enriches subtitle documents with representative audio fingerprint annotations extracted from the base audio signal during the authoring process and (2) adjusts misaligned subtitle entries based on the comparison of audio fingerprints during playback.

3.1 Enriching Subtitle Documents

The first step of our framework consists in automatically annotating subtitle documents with representative audio fingerprints, as illustrated in Figure 4.a. To do that, the authoring software first extracts the audio signal from the base audiovisual content. Then, it processes the extracted audio signal and generates a number of audio fingerprints that are later encapsulated, preferably as metadata, in the subtitle document. As we will see ahead, such audio fingerprint annotations also include the corresponding offset within the base audiovisual content, so this information can be used during playback as second-level synchronization anchors to fix the presentation of misaligned subtitle entries.

To encompass all the 6 cases listed in Section 2.2, we make use of 3 synchronization anchors. The rationale behind this design choice is the following. In fact, 2 synchronization anchors would be enough to handle all the problems. However, as the audiovisual content may have been trimmed in the beginning or in the end, we propose the insertion of a fallback anchor. As a guideline, the authoring software should extract three audio fingerprints preferably near the beginning, near the middle, and close to the end of the audio signal and then insert such fingerprints with the corresponding offsets as annotations in the subtitle document. It is worth mentioning that audio fingerprint annotations do not necessarily need to be associated with an actual speech event.

3.2 Adjusting Misaligned Subtitle Entries

The second step of our framework takes place during the playback of an enriched subtitle document along with an audiovisual

(a)

(b)

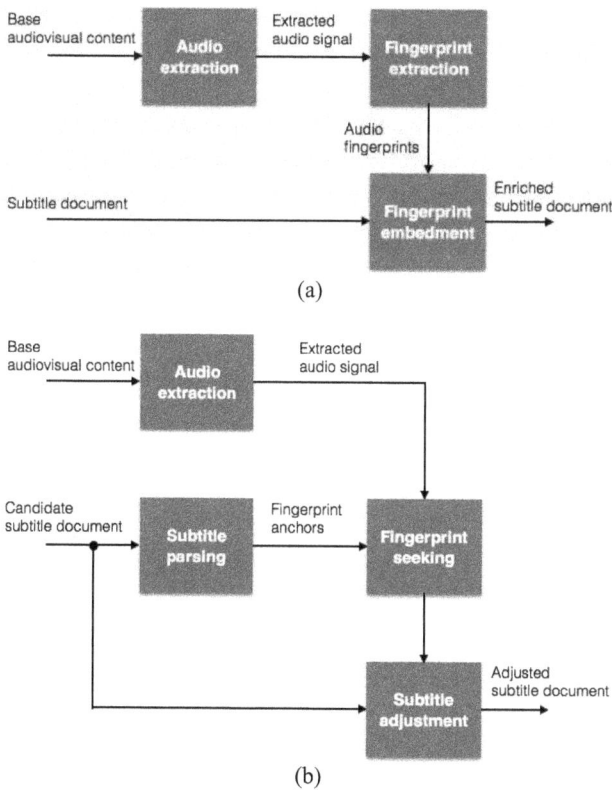

Figure 4. General framework in two steps: (a) enrichment of subtitle document with representative audio fingerprint annotations and (b) dynamic adjustment of subtitle entries based on fingerprints comparison.

content (see Figure 4.b). The process begins with the media player opening the base audiovisual content and extracting the audio signal. Complementary, the media player parses the subtitle

---

Algorithm 1 Fingerprint seeking algorithm

```
01. function seek(fingerprints, timestamps, audio):
02.    match = [NO_MATCH, NO_MATCH, NO_MATCH]
03.    for i = 1 to 3:
04.       nsecs = DEFAULT_FP_DURATION /* in secs */
05.       seek_offset = timestamps[i]
06.       for attempt = 1 to 2:
07.          test = captureFP(audio, seek_offset, nsecs)
08.          if test.matches(fingerprints[i]):
09.             delta = test.matchOffset()
10.             if delta != 0: /* propagate delta */
11.                for j=i+1 to 3: timestamps[j] += delta
12.             match[i] = attempt==1? MATCH : LOCAL_MATCH
13.             break
14.          else:
15.             nsecs = LOCAL_SEARCH_INTERVAL /* in secs */
16.             seek_offset = MAX(seek_offset - nsecs/2, 0)
17.    return match
```

Algorithm 2 Subtitle adjustment algorithm

```
01. /* actions variable corresponds to Table 1 */
02. function adjust(matches, actions):
03.    for i=1 to rows(actions):
04.       if matches[1] == actions[i].FirstAnchor and
05.          matches[2] == actions[i].MiddleAnchor and
06.          matches[3] == actions[i].LastAnchor:
07.          Process action at actions[i].Action
08.          return
```

document, from where subtitle entries and audio fingerprint annotations are read. Then, our algorithm, as illustrated in the simplified pseudocode procedure of Algorithm 1, seeks the synchronization anchors (denoted as the *fingerprints* array of length 3 and its associated *timestamps* array indicating where the fingerprints start) in the extracted audio signal (denoted as the *audio* array with the decoded signal). This algorithm returns an array containing three possible values for each fingerprint comparison: NO_MATCH, MATCH, or LOCAL_MATCH.

First, our algorithm seeks to the exact offset described by each synchronization anchor and generate an audio fingerprint from the audio signal (line 07); if there is a match in the first attempt (line 08), the given synchronization anchor is indeed aligned (delta variable is set to zero in line 09). Algorithm 1 then updates match[i] with MATCH (line 12) and proceeds to the next anchor. In case the audio fingerprint annotation does not match the calculated fingerprint at the expected offset, our method increases the size of the search window (lines 15-16) and performs a new search (attempt variable equals 2). This new search consists in generating all audio fingerprints in a predetermined timeframe around the given offset and comparing each one of them with the referred audio fingerprint (local search). If the algorithm successfully finds a match, it updates match[i] with LOCAL_MATCH (line 12) and proceeds to the next anchor. Otherwise, match[i] keeps the initial value (NO_MATCH).

The candidate subtitle document is perfectly synchronized with the base audiovisual content only when the media player directly finds matches for all synchronization anchors in the first attempt. In case the media player performs a local search to find a match (attempt variable equals 2), the difference between the offset specified in the synchronization anchor and the one calculated from the audio signal is taken into account in the verification of the coming anchors (lines 09-11 in Algorithm 1). Therefore, even if the first synchronization anchor is found through a local search, the next anchors can still match perfectly if such difference of offsets is considered in the calculations ahead.

In most cases, the adjustment action consists in propagating a constant temporal offset (or delta) to all the subtitle entries specified in the subtitle document. However, when the media player finds two synchronization anchors via local searches, it is the case in which the subtitle document and the base audiovisual content have different presentation paces (varying temporal offset). In this scenario, the player could interpolate the difference between the offsets specified and calculated so that such differences are distributed accordingly to all the subtitle entries before, in between and after the synchronization anchors. Table 1 summarizes a naïve algorithmic procedure (Algorithm 2) and adjustment actions for all the 6 cases presented in Section 2.2.

4. IMPLEMENTATION

We prototyped a proof of concept to investigate both the impact of inserting audio fingerprint annotations into preexisting subtitle documents and the performance implications associated with dynamic adjustment of misaligned subtitle entries during playback. For that we used the well-known VLC media player and Chromaprint[9], a client-side open source library written in C implementing a custom algorithm for extracting audio fingerprints from raw uncompressed audio data sources.

---

[9] http://acoustid.org/chromaprint

Table 1. Adjustment actions in different scenarios.

First anchor	Middle anchor	Last anchor	Case	Action
Match	-	Match	Case 1	None
Match	-	Local match	Case 6	Interpolation
Match	Match	-	Case 3	None
Match	Local match	-	Case 6	Interpolation
Local match	-	Match	Case 2	Offset propagation
Local match	-	Local match	Case 6	Interpolation
Local match	Match	-	Case 5	Offset propagation
Local match	Local match	-	Case 6	Interpolation
-	Local match	Match	Case 4	Offset propagation
-	Local match	Local match	Case 6	Interpolation
-	Local match	-	Case 5	Offset propagation
-	-	Local match	Case 5	Offset propagation
-	-	-	-	None

Note: the symbol '-' applies either when a synchronization anchor is not found or when there is no need to use it.

The Chromaprint library works with *spectrograms*, which are visual representations of the spectrum of frequencies in a sound as these vary with time. Spectrograms can be calculated from splitting the original audio into many overlapping frames and then applying a Fast-Fourier transform (FFT) on them. In particular, Chromaprint converts the input audio to the sampling rate of 11025Hz and using a FFT window size of 4096 (0.371s) with 2/3 overlap. It further processes the information by using a Short-time Fourier transform and by converting frequencies into musical notes. The result, which has 12 bins (one for each semitone of a chromatic scale), is known as *chroma features* [1]. It is worth mentioning that this representation of the audio is not radically affected by differences between codecs, and more importantly, it can be used to measure the similarity with other representations (*e.g.*, by calculating bit error rates). By moving a prefixed sliding window over the spectrogram representation of the audio from the left to the right, one pixel at a time, we can generate several sub-images of that spectrogram. On each of the sub-images, Chromaprint applies a pre-defined set of 16 filters that capture intensity differences across musical notes and time (encoded into 2 bits for each filter using the Gray code). Following the same process for each and every single sub-image, Chromaprint obtains the full audio fingerprint.

Chromaprint needs about 3 seconds of audio samples to fill the library's internal buffers; consequently, a larger number of samples are needed to generate enough sub-images. In our prototype, we chose to capture 30 seconds of audio (herein defined as N), which is sufficient to represent unique sequences of audio events in a movie or TV series episode. To compute the correlation between the captured and the reference fingerprints, we check how many bit differences there are between the two. A

moving window accounts for temporal misalignment. As output, we have the fingerprint offset from where the two fingerprints match the best and how similar they are (*i.e.*, a correlation "score"). If the score obtained is greater than a given threshold, we assume that the compared fingerprints match.

To deal with situations in which things like prologues and epilogues are included or removed, we capture audio fingerprints using a different time length every time the player does not find a direct match, and therefore a broader local search is needed. For local searches, we pick the standard deviation D presented in Section 2.2 and make our sample size $D+N+D$.

In our prototype we chose to support the popular SRT subtitle format, as shown in Figure 5. In order to keep backwards compatibility with media players that do not include support for audio fingerprint annotations, we decided to encapsulate synchronization anchors as subtitle entries with zero duration (note the starting and ending times in line 8). The keyword @fingerprint@ (line 09) indicates the presence of the audio signature introduced by our annotation technique. Note that such information is stored in the same area that SRT reserves for the text that must be exhibited on the screen.

5. EVALUATION

We conducted two studies to validate the core contribution of our work. In the first, we analyzed the impact of inserting audio fingerprint annotations into subtitle documents; whereas in the second, we estimated the computational resources demanded to generate audio fingerprints and to run the correlation routines that detect matches between the reference and captured audio samples.

The impact on the document size is measured by the amount of text introduced with the insertion of the audio fingerprint annotation in the SRT file. An audio fingerprint is nothing more than an array of integers – and that is the representation we use in our software when we compute the correlation between two audio signatures. When it comes to storing that information on the subtitle document, however, that representation is not the most adequate; it is both meaningless to users who inspect the subtitle document as well as potentially long in number of characters (spanning several lines in the document). For such reasons, we encode the audio fingerprint as a Base64 string in the document.

```
01. ...
02. 19
03. 00:01:22,782 --> 00:01:27,221
04. RIDLEY SCOTT: I think that you're silly to be
05. pessimistic...
06.
07. 20
08. 00:01:28,000 --> 00:01:28,000
09. @fingerprint@ AQAAjFEiSYmSJJGkAOKP7_hx4...
10.
11. 21
12. 00:01:29,467 --> 00:01:34,172
13. WATSON: I'm working with humans to predict trends...
14.
15. 22
16. 00:01:35,524 --> 00:01:37,248
17. RIDLEY SCOTT: Certainly better than world
18. domination.
19.
20. 23
21. 00:01:37,688 --> 00:01:39,053
22. WATSON: Good one, Sir Ridley Scott.
23. ...
```

Figure 5. SRT document including an audio fingerprint annotation, where keyword @fingerprint@ is followed by a Base64 string representation of such audio signal's signature.

The length of the Base64 string varies according to the value of the elements of the original array. As noticed in the process of annotating 10 movies, the average size of one encoded audio fingerprint was 247±4 ASCII characters. Therefore, when we consider all 3 fingerprints captured along with the text that describes their zero-duration timestamps and sequence numbers, the average overhead added to each document is around 890 characters (or bytes). To put in perspective, in a regular movie with about 1000 subtitle entries, these annotations would represent just about 1% of the file size.

Next, we analyzed the amount of computational resources demanded by our method. We chose a high-definition movie featuring a H.264 video stream with 1920x800 resolution and an AAC (LC) audio stream, and then observed CPU and memory usage during a timespan of 120 seconds through a series of 10 runs. On the hardware side, the tests were performed on a dual-core Intel i7-3520M running at 2.9GHz and with 6GB of main memory. The software stack included our prototype (linked to Chromaprint version 1.3.1 and to VLC media player library version 2.2.1) and an operating system based on Linux 4.5. In order to optimize cache performance, CPU affinity was configured so that our prototype was bounded to the same processing unit during its execution.

The percentage of CPU demanded to decode the video stream (plotted with red filled squares in Figure 6) varies between 15% and 48% for the short segment of the movie selected. This variation reflects the complexity of the scenes; the smaller the differences between a frame X and a frame X+1 the lesser computing resources are used. Decoding the audio stream is a much cheaper task, as the line with hollow circles shows (in blue). In the moments filled with rich sounds, CPU usage goes up to 6%. In a second moment, when music becomes less complex, audio decoding demands drops to about 3% of processing power. Standard deviation was not statistically significant, and therefore it is not plotted in the figure.

In the lower part of Figure 6, the line with filled circles (in purple) shows the percentage of CPU required to process the audio fingerprints. The fingerprinting process begins with the aggregation of audio packets into a buffer. The cost of that task is very low and remains at 1-2% at all times. Once enough data has been aggregated, Chromaprint computes the fingerprint of that buffer and the result is compared with the reference fingerprint (stored in the annotated SRT document). This process produces the peaks at 18 seconds (with 18% of CPU consumption) and at 108 seconds (with 35% of CPU consumption) and lasts no more than 125 milliseconds in our setup.

The difference between the two purple peaks is that in the first we look for a perfect match between the reference and the computed fingerprints. In other words, both audio fingerprints have the same number of elements and represent the same amount of time. The second peak shows the CPU demanded in a local search. In this case, the aggregated buffer includes 45 extra seconds of sampling before and after the reference timestamp of the fingerprint. Because of this larger buffer size, the fingerprint comparison demands the use of a sliding window and, as a consequence, the processing power needed exceeds that of the former case.

Nevertheless, we note that this is a one-time task that can be performed before the media file starts to be reproduced to the user. Also, we note that media parsing for fingerprinting computation purposes does not need to follow the presentation timestamps (PTS). Consequently, users need to wait for no more

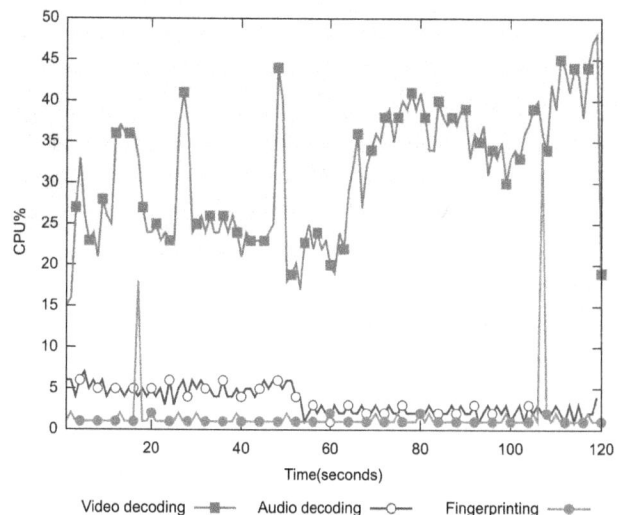

Figure 6. Processing power demands to process audio fingerprints and to decode video and audio streams.

than a few hundred milliseconds before the subtitle document is processed and adjusted (if it really needs be).

The impact on memory consumption (not shown in the figure) is also relatively small, as all it takes is a few seconds of audio samples in memory to buffer and capture the audio fingerprint. When computing a local search (which demands more memory than a perfect match), the amount of memory used by our software is of no more than 4MB. In comparison, the audio software decoding process has a baseline of 43MB. At its peak, memory overhead relative to the baseline stayed at 8,5%. Such a small footprint enables the use of our technique even in embedded devices with limited amount of memory. In such a scenario, we note that memory requirements can be further reduced by tuning the local search window to smaller values.

6. RELATED WORK

Subtitles play an important role in making audiovisual content accessible to everyone. For instance, it is often the case in which subtitles are necessary to watch a movie or TV show in a noisy environment (*e.g.*, in an airplane) or when one is not familiar with the language or accent in the audio streams. The truth is that the benefits of subtitling go beyond speech information and description of representative events in the audiovisual content. In the literature, extant research has investigated the impact of subtitles in terms of accessibility [11], cognitive load [14][15], comprehension of foreign languages [17][18] and vocabulary learning [13], to name a few. In the remaining of this section, we review some representative efforts in the context of our work.

Hong et al. [11] propose a dynamic captioning[10] approach, which explores a set of technologies including face detection and recognition, visual saliency analysis and text-speech alignment. They investigate whether subtitles placed at suitable positions help hearing-impaired people recognize speaking characters and perceive the moods that are conveyed by the variation of volume. Complementary, Wang et al. [21] propose a method to enrich the visualization of videos with visual representation of non-verbal

---

[10] Although the terms 'captions' and 'subtitles' do have different meanings in some countries, such distinction is not relevant in the context of this paper.

sounds. Their approach automatically transforms non-verbal video sounds into animated words, and positions these near the sound source objects in the video. The dynamics of the animation is based on the intensification and attenuation of the sound volume, whereas the animation positioning is computed using a 3D video cost field of the input video depending on the position of the sound source object. Yet in another effort, Brown et al. [2] use eye-tracking data to investigate the effect of dynamic subtitles in the viewing experience of subjects with hearing loss. Finally, Hughes et al. [12] propose the use of responsive Web design practices to rendering subtitles alongside video content. The proposed approach interpolates individual word timings based on each word's position in the subtitle entry and the start and end time of the entry. The authors also consider the use of phonetic models and semantic markup to dynamically re-block subtitles as a response to user interaction. Responsive subtitles are then formatted and displayed appropriately for different devices while respecting the requirements and preferences of the viewer. Our work is related to these efforts, but instead we focus on a different core technology and application domain.

Liu and Wang [16] propose a stroke-like edge detection method based on contours to extract captions that are hard-coded in videos. Instead of regarding each video frame as an independent image, the authors demonstrate that the use of inter-frame information can improve the accuracy of caption localization and segmentation. Our work differs not only in the use of technology, but also in the underlying research problem, that in our case is automatically fixing the synchronization of subtitles entries encoded in an independent subtitle document; so that viewers can still obtain a satisfactory watching experience.

Fererico and Furini [8] propose a caption alignment mechanism that exploits common off-the-shelf automatic speech recognition (ASR) applications to produce time-coded transcripts. Their approach does not require human transcriptions or special dedicated software. They introduce a unique audio markup into the audio stream before passing it to an ASR application. By knowing the temporal locations of the inserted audio markups, the mechanism can automatically transform the plain transcript produced by the ASR application into a time-coded transcript. Similarly, the video-sharing service YouTube™ uses ASR technology to automatically generate, synchronize and translate captions for videos users upload. In a typical (automated) subtitling process, the original speech is first translated fully into the target language and then the target translation is compressed to optimize the length requirements. One of the techniques employed in the text compression phase is to replace a target language word in the original translation with a shorter synonym of it, thus reducing the character length of the subtitle [9]. Although our work shares the same goal for having subtitles aligned with audiovisual content, we address a different research challenge that is adjusting the synchronization of potential subtitle documents with displaced timestamps.

Tiedemann [19] addresses the particular problem of synchronizing movie subtitles to improve alignment quality when building a parallel corpus out of translated subtitles. In the proposed approach, anchor points are identified based on cognate filters, which use string similarity measures and some heuristics for selecting synchronization. Complementary, the author proposes a dictionary-based approach using automatic word alignment and shows an improvement in alignment quality even for related languages compared to the cognate-based approach. In the context of our work, one could perhaps use a similar approach to adjust

the temporal offset of misaligned subtitles. But for that, it would be necessary to know the reference subtitle document that perfectly synchronizes with the base audiovisual content at playback time; what takes us back to *ground zero*.

From a more document engineering perspective, Concolato et al. [6] discuss the synchronized playback of live video and subtitle content using HTTP (*Hypertext Transfer Protocol*) streaming technologies such as MPEG Dynamic Adaptive Streaming over HTTP (DASH). Furthermore, Guimarães et al. [10] describe a set of temporal transformations for multimedia documents that allow users to create and share personalized timed-text comments on third party videos; whereas Fagá Jr. et al. [7] present a vocabulary proposal for third-party applications that allow users to add more generic multimedia annotations to user-generated video content. Most closely related to our work, Bulterman et al. [3] survey many open and proprietary formats for encoding subtitles. Based on a careful analysis, the authors describe a timed-text format that balances the need for style formatting with the requirement for more structured representation that can be easily parsed and scheduled at runtime. Our work builds on these previous findings; however, we go a step further by proposing a framework capable of adjusting the synchronization of tens (or even hundreds) of subtitle documents with displaced timestamps.

Regarding applications, some popular media players offer users a mean to download SRT documents automatically once the base audiovisual content is loaded. For instance, VLC can use an extension called VLSub[11] to search online for the corresponding subtitle document using two different approaches. In the first, the extension uses the media file name to query a remote subtitle database. If there is a match, the corresponding subtitle document is automatically downloaded and presented alongside the audiovisual content. In the second approach, VLSub computes a hash (checksum) of the media file and uses the resulting hash to query the remote subtitle database. Again, if there is a match, the player automatically downloads and displays the corresponding subtitle document. In both cases, the synchronization of subtitle entries might still appear misplaced during playback because: (1) multiple versions of subtitle documents may have the same file name; (2) the based audiovisual content no longer has its original file name due to name mangling or to renaming; or (3) changes to the original encoding settings, such as exporting an original file in H.264 format to a QuickTime .MOV format, will alter the hash of the base media file.

In addition, some media players also allow users to delay or speed up the presentation of subtitle entries during playback, so that users can try to fix synchronization misalignment interactively. Unfortunately, this workaround might require a lot of iterations and yet does not solve the problem once and for all. In this work, we envision a less intrusive mechanism for fixing subtitle synchronization problems without the viewer being even aware that such issues exist. As we demonstrated in the previous sections, this becomes possible through the extraction of audio fingerprints, which is not likely to change drastically when the original audio signal is re-encoded with different settings. Thus, we allow compliant media players to automatically fix the subtitle misalignment problem by considering the audio fingerprint annotations as second-level synchronization anchors. Once such audio fingerprints are identified in a subtitle document, the player

---

[11] https://github.com/exebetche/vlsub

can then calculate and adjust the temporal offset of all the subtitles entries accordingly.

7. DISCUSSION AND FINAL REMARKS

In this paper we formalized and evaluated a two-phase subtitle synchronization framework that uses audio fingerprint annotations extracted from the base audio signal as second-level synchronization anchors. This approach allows compliant media players to automatically fix (requirement i) common cases of subtitle synchronization misalignment (requirement v) that compromise users' watching experience during playback. Our experiments also show that the overhead introduced by our framework is minimum in terms of document length (*i.e.*, a few extra bytes for the audio fingerprint annotations) and of CPU time/cycles required to process fingerprints (requirement iv).

Because the duration of audio fingerprint annotations is equal to zero, media players that do not implement the proposed alignment mechanism simply do not show those subtitle entries on the screen during playback. This way, we assure that the enriched subtitle documents remains backward compliant and renders the same on the screen as non-annotated subtitle documents (requirement iii).

As we have discussed in the introduction of this paper, we took special care to ensure that the fingerprint representation stored in the subtitle document is non-invertible to the original waveform as a way to protect against the creation of derivative work – in this case, of the original audio signal (requirement ii). We note, however, that the definition of what can be considered an extension of the original work may not even be a concern depending on the license under which the original work is published. That is often the case with the Creative Commons license, popular among artists and independent producers. On the other hand, an in-depth discussion on the legal issues involved in the process of enriching subtitles of commercial movies or of movies that do not feature support for certain languages deserves a separate paper on its own.

One can still argue that while a few years ago the automatic production of a video transcript was very hard to achieve, currently, thanks to the advances in speech technologies, generic off-the-shelf automatic speech recognition (ASR) applications produce reasonable textual versions starting from audio streams. Moreover, this process could perhaps be further improved by considering cognitive computing technology (like IBM Watson in Figure 1) and historic data from featured characters. Not to mention that automatic generation of subtitle entries by services like YouTube and by the reach of Netflix and Amazon Prime, may lead to questions about the relevancy of a technique to synchronize offline media. However, estimates are that in the next 5 years video traffic, *including* peer-to-peer, will be responsible for 80% of all consumer Internet traffic [5]. And combined with the facts that online databases of subtitle documents on the Internet keep growing on a daily basis and that not all movies ever produced are in the catalogs of the aforementioned services, our work is yet relevant and timely.

As future work, we intend to deepen the investigation on the causes of the discrepancies between subtitle documents and on streaming delivery support, which would likely preclude the need for downloading the entire video. These aspects will surely require new enhancements and extensions to our current framework. Moreover, we would like to conduct an experiment to measure the sensitivity of users to the lack of subtitles synchronization and another to assess our method on platforms with limited resources such as small set-tops, tablets etc. This

information could be useful for the calculation of the optimized position of anchor points in subtitle documents. We also understand that subtitle formats other than the SRT could also benefit from our work. Thus, a natural sequence to this study would be to conduct a more extensive analysis on a larger corpus of movies and of file formats.

8. REFERENCES

[1] Bartsch, M. A. and Wakefield, G. H. 2005. Audio thumbnailing of popular music using chroma-based representations. *IEEE Transactions on Multimedia*. 7, 1 (Feb. 2005), 96-104. DOI=http://dx.doi.org/10.1109/TMM.2004.840597

[2] Brown, A., Jones, R., Crabb, M., Sandford, J., Brooks, M., Armstrong, M., and Jay, C. 2015. Dynamic Subtitles: The User Experience. In *Proceedings of the ACM International Conference on Interactive Experiences for TV and Online Video* (TVX '15). ACM, New York, NY, USA, 103-112. DOI=http://dx.doi.org/10.1145/2745197.2745204

[3] Bulterman, D. C. A., Jansen, J, Cesar, P., and Cruz-Lara, S. 2007. An efficient, streamable text format for multimedia captions and subtitles. In *Proceedings of the 2007 ACM symposium on Document engineering* (DocEng '07). ACM, New York, NY, USA, 101-110. DOI=http://dx.doi.org/10.1145/1284420.1284451

[4] Bulterman, D. C. A. and Rutledge, L. W. 2008. *SMIL3.0 – Flexible Multimedia for Web, Mobile Devices and DAISY Talking Books*. (2nd ed.). Springer Publishing Company, Incorporated. ISBN: 978-3-540-78546-0

[5] Cisco. 2015. Cisco Visual Networking Index: Forecast and Methodology, 2014-2019. *White paper*. Available at http://www.cisco.com/c/en/us/solutions/collateral/service-provider/ip-ngn-ip-next-generation-network/white_paper_c11-481360.pdf

[6] Concolato, C. and Le Feuvre, J. 2013. Live HTTP streaming of video and subtitles within a browser. In *Proceedings of the 4th ACM Multimedia Systems Conference* (MMSys '13). ACM, New York, NY, USA, 146-150. DOI=http://dx.doi.org/10.1145/2483977.2483997

[7] Fagá Jr., R., Motti, V. G., Cattelan, R. G., Teixeira, C. A. C., and Pimentel, M. G. C. 2010. A social approach to authoring media annotations. In *Proceedings of the 10th ACM symposium on Document engineering* (DocEng '10). ACM, New York, NY, USA, 17-26. DOI=http://dx.doi.org/10.1145/1860559.1860566

[8] Federico, M. and Furini, M. 2014. An automatic caption alignment mechanism for off-the-shelf speech recognition technologies. *Multimedia Tools Appl*. 72, 1 (Sep. 2014), 21-40. DOI=http://dx.doi.org/10.1007/s11042-012-1318-3

[9] Glickman, O., Dagan, I., Keller, M., Bengio, S., and Daelemans, W. 2006. Investigating lexical substitution scoring for subtitle generation. In *Proceedings of the Tenth Conference on Computational Natural Language Learning* (CoNLL-X '06). Association for Computational Linguistics, Stroudsburg, PA, USA, 45-52.

[10] Guimarães, R. L., Cesar, P., and Bulterman, D. C. A. 2010. Creating and sharing personalized time-based annotations of videos on the web. In *Proceedings of the 10th ACM symposium on Document engineering* (DocEng '10). ACM,

New York, NY, USA, 27-36.
DOI=http://dx.doi.org/10.1145/1860559.1860567

[11] Hong, R., Wang, M. Yuan, X., Xu, M. Jiang, J., Yan, S., and Chua, T. 2011. Video accessibility enhancement for hearing-impaired users. *ACM Trans. Multimedia Comput. Commun. Appl.* 7S, 1, Article 24 (Nov. 2011), 19 pages.
DOI=http://dx.doi.org/10.1145/2037676.2037681

[12] Hughes, C. J., Armstrong, M., Jones, R., and Crabb, M. 2015. Responsive design for personalised subtitles. In *Proceedings of the 12th Web for All Conference* (W4A '15). ACM, New York, NY, USA, Article 8, 4 pages.
DOI=http://dx.doi.org/10.1145/2745555.2746650

[13] Kovacs, G. and Miller, R. C. 2014. Smart subtitles for vocabulary learning. In *Proceedings of the SIGCHI Conference on Human Factors in Computing Systems* (CHI '14). ACM, New York, NY, USA, 853-862.
DOI=http://dx.doi.org/10.1145/2556288.2557256

[14] Kruger, J. L., Hefer, E., and Matthew, G. 2013. Measuring the impact of subtitles on cognitive load: eye tracking and dynamic audiovisual texts. In *Proceedings of the 2013 Conference on Eye Tracking South Africa* (ETSA '13). ACM, New York, NY, USA, 62-66.
DOI=http://dx.doi.org/10.1145/2509315.2509331

[15] Kushalnagar, R. S., Lasecki, W. S., and Bigham, J. P. 2013. Captions versus transcripts for online video content. In *Proceedings of the 10th International Cross-Disciplinary Conference on Web Accessibility* (W4A '13). ACM, New York, NY, USA, Article 32, 4 pages.
DOI=http://dx.doi.org/10.1145/2461121.2461142

[16] Liu, X. and Wang, W. Robustly extracting captions in videos based on stroke-like edges and spatio-temporal analysis.

IEEE Transactions on Multimedia. 14, 2 (Apr. 2012), 482–489. DOI=http://dx.doi.org/10.1109/TMM.2011.2177646

[17] Rooney, K. 2014. The Impact of Keyword Caption Ratio on Foreign Language Listening Comprehension. *International Journal of Computer-Assisted Language Learning and Teaching.* 4, 2 (Apr. 2014), 11-28.
DOI=http://dx.doi.org/10.4018/ijcallt.2014040102

[18] Shimogori, N., Ikeda, T. and Tsuboi, S. 2010. Automatically generated captions: will they help non-native speakers communicate in english?. In *Proceedings of the 3rd international conference on Intercultural collaboration* (ICIC '10). ACM, New York, NY, USA, 79-86.
DOI=http://dx.doi.org/10.1145/1841853.1841865

[19] Tiedemann, J. 2008. Synchronizing translated movie subtitles. In *Proceedings of the 6th International Conference on Language Resources and Evaluation* (LREC '08), 5 pages.

[20] Villa Real, L. C., Guimarães, R. L., and Avegliano, P. 2015. Dynamic Adjustment of Subtitles Using Audio Fingerprints. In *Proceedings of the 23rd ACM international conference on Multimedia* (MM '15). ACM, New York, NY, USA, 975-978. DOI=http://dx.doi.org/10.1145/2733373.2806378

[21] Wang, F., Nagano, H., Kashino, K., and Igarashi, T. 2015. Visualizing video sounds with sound word animation. In *Proceedings of the IEEE International Conference on Multimedia and Expo* (ICME '15). 1-6.
DOI=http://dx.doi.org/10.1109/ICME.2015.7177422

DocuGram: Turning Screen Recordings into Documents

Laurent Denoue
FXPAL
3174 Porter Drive
Palo Alto, California 94304 USA
denoue@fxpal.com

Scott Carter
FXPAL
3174 Porter Drive
Palo Alto, California 94304 USA
carter@fxpal.com

Matthew Cooper
FXPAL
3174 Porter Drive
Palo Alto, California 94304 USA
cooper@fxpal.com

ABSTRACT

In this paper we describe DocuGram, a novel tool to capture and share documents originating from any application. As users scroll through pages of their document inside the native application (Word, Google Docs, web browser), the system captures and analyses in real-time the rendered video frames and reconstitutes the original document pages into an easy to view HTML-based representation. In addition to detecting and regenerating the document pages, a DocuGram also includes the interactions users had over them, e.g. mouse motions and voice comments. A DocuGram allows users to flexibly share enhanced documents across applications.

Keywords

Document capture; image processing; video processing; interactive documents.

1. INTRODUCTION

We have numerous available choices to edit and view documents, ranging from native applications such as Word and PowerPoint, to online editing tools like Google Docs and Microsoft Office 365. We also have many ways to share these documents, such as by attaching them in email, embedding them in web pages, or simply sending a link of their online location.

But individual source applications often require users to devise custom means to share that document. One could simply attach a Word document by email, hoping the recipients will have Word installed; or one might export the document as a PDF; or generate a sharable link to the document.

While already complex for our own documents, capturing and sharing is even harder for content we don't author, such as pages from a scanned book hosted on Google Books or a slide deck shown during web conferences. Even the seemingly mundane task of sharing the URL of an online article could cause problems to the recipient (e.g. a pay-wall from the Wall Street Journal).

Furthermore, sharing a document often means leaving out comments and interactions we have over the document. Without

DocEng '16, September 12-16, 2016, Vienna, Austria
© 2016 ACM. ISBN 978-1-4503-4438-8/16/09 $15.00
DOI: http://dx.doi.org/10.1145/2960811.2967154

options, people often need to decontextualize their comments, e.g. in the accompanying email message.

Or export the document into a PDF editor, highlight, and then hope the recipient will also have a PDF reader that understands and renders annotations.

One last resort is for users to record their screen. Although videos can be indexed (see [1] for examples), recipients would typically be shown a video player, making it hard to page through and otherwise read the "document".

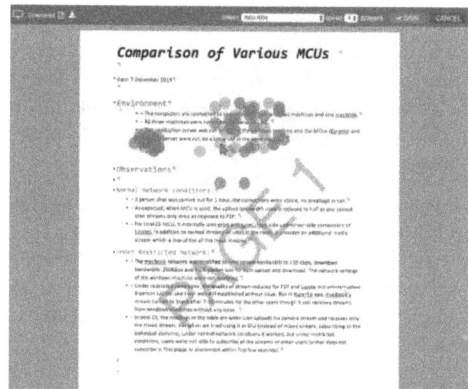

Figure 1. A sample DocuGram is a document reconstituted from a screen recording of any application showing the original document; mouse actions and pages are preserved

With DocuGram, we aim at reconstituting the original document from a screen-recording of that document captured by the user. Using image analysis techniques, the system processes the screen recording to produce a copy of the original document that is immediately available online as a Web page, viewable on any device with a basic web browser. This web-based viewer shows each page as an image, including any interaction and voice comments that the author added while recording, see Figure 1.

We describe below how the system analyses in real-time the video frames captured upon a user's request and turns them into viewable document pages, along with users' interactions over the document while recording[1].

2. INTERACTION DESIGN

To create a DocuGram, users pick one window on their desktop that displays the document to capture, e.g. the Word window showing a DOC file, and click "Start".

---

[1] A video is available at https://youtu.be/phS0TrwZ4Tg

They then interact freely with the document inside the application window (e.g. Word), scrolling up and down through pages they wish to capture and share. During the recording, they have full access to all functions provided by the application, such as selecting text passages and moving their pointer over areas of the document.

Because DocuGram records the screen as a video, users can also talk at the same time, e.g. to describe a figure that needs to be modified or express a feeling about a particular passage in the document. When they are done recording, users simply click the "Stop" recording button.

The system is able to recognize the two major kinds of document viewing metaphors: scrolling and pagination. All word processors or PDF viewers typically implement scrolling, while pagination is used for showing slide decks, e.g. PowerPoint. Page detection is a core problem in document image analysis [5], and has also been studied using video cameras [6]. The screen-based context here is distinct and provides opportunities to accelerate our visual analysis.

Using the same system, users can also pick a browser window showing a video of a lecture, in which the speaker is showing slides. At the end of the session, the user will have a reconstituted copy of the slides that were shown during the video lecture.

During users' interactions, the system analyses every captured frame of the window and turns them into a final DocuGram: a copy of the original document. In order to generate this copy, the system applies these important steps: Region of Interest (ROI) detection, image stitching, and interaction lifting.

All these image-processing algorithms run in real-time inside the user's web browser in JavaScript. The video frames are captured using the media devices API available to modern web apps, allowing us to capture either the full desktop or individual windows. The rest of this paper describes the algorithms required to generate a DocuGram.

3. SYSTEM DESCRIPTION
3.1 Video pre-processing
After the user has stopped recording her window, the system plays the recorded video into a VIDEO element, draws its frames at 30 frames per second into a CANVAS element and only keeps different frames using a simple image difference function comparing corresponding gray scale pixels with a fixed threshold.

3.2 ROI detection
When users start recording a given window, the system starts a new MediaRecorder that saves the video of the window into a local file later accessible to the web application.

Once the user is done recording, the system processes the first frame, binarizes it and looks for long vertical and horizontal segments. It combines them to determine the largest rectangle as the ROI for that window, shown in Figure 2.

If the system has correctly detected this ROI, the user simply clicks over the identified region and the system proceeds to the next step. Alternately, users simply drag a rectangle to manually specify the ROI to use. Some document types such as web pages do not have clear paginated layout, making it hard or impossible for an automatic ROI detector to find the correct rectangle.

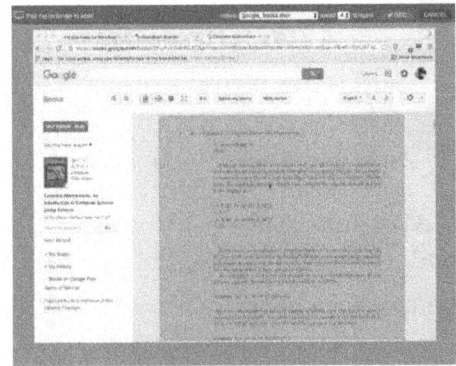

Figure 2. Detected ROI is shown in blue to the user; they can overwrite the automatic detection by dragging another rectangle

3.3 Image Stitching
Image stitching is a critical analytical step for the system. Brute force comparisons between frames to determine their vertical shift would be very CPU intensive. Instead, we borrow techniques from the image stitching literature [2] that use key point detection and matching as the basis for finding generic transformations between pairs of images and adapt it to our domain. These methods are fast and robust, making them appealing for a real-time implementation in Javascript inside a web application.

In our case, the goal of the image-stitching step is to find the amount of vertical scroll that occurred between frames. After gray scale conversion, a fast corner detector runs across the frame, yielding a set of key points. We developed a custom key point extractor that works well for textual content. For a given pixel $P_1=I(x,y)$ in the grayscale frame, we look at its three neighboring pixels $P_0=I(x-1,y)$, $P_2=I(x+1,y)$ and $P_3=I(x,y-1)$. P_1 is selected as a key point if the following condition is true:

$$|P_0 - P_1| > 32 \; AND \; |P_0 - P_2| <= 6 \; AND \; |P_0 - P_3| > 32$$

The idea is to select keypoints that have a sharp increase in contrast when scanning from left to right and top to bottom (thus a threshold of 32), while having the next pixel similar (the threshold of 6). Intuitively, it corresponds to corners of character glyphs (see Figure 3). To limit the number of key-points, if a pixel P_1 is selected we skip 128 pixels to the right on the same line.

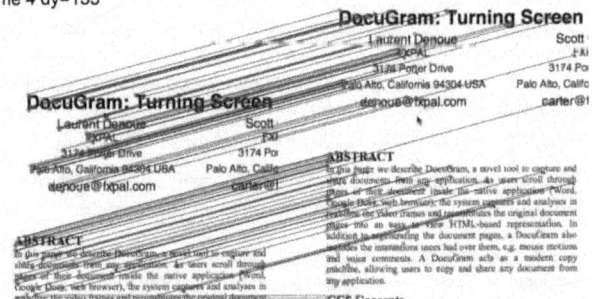

Figure 3. BRIEF vectors are matched in a vertical shift up: left previous frame, right next frame; blue lines join matching key-points; red lines show mismatches

Each key point is represented by a BRIEF descriptor, which is a binary descriptor described in [3] that represents the neighboring pixels of a given key point by a 512 dimensional vector. Vectors can be quickly assessed for similarity with a simple Hamming distance, implemented using XOR operations.

Given two images, we thus have two lists of key-points and their BRIEF descriptors. A reciprocal matching algorithm finds the closest matches, but adds a specific constraint for our domain: a match is only allowed between 2 BRIEF vectors if their corresponding key point locations have the same X coordinate. In practice, we have observed that most people view their documents without a horizontal scrollbar, thus letting us optimize the execution of the matching to finding only vertical scroll offsets. This constraint can be relaxed as needed with a corresponding loss of efficiency.

The estimated vertical scroll value ΔY between two frames is found by keeping the most popular value between pairs of matching key points.

3.4 Handling non-scrolling document viewers

Our research has shown that ΔY can erroneously be set to zero, especially on documents that have little text content such as PowerPoint slides. Another example would be an online Google Presentation where users flip through pages of a presentation, or a presentation given by a co-worker during a live web meeting.

To recover from these mistakes, we empirically found that ΔY is correct if the number of matching key points is at least 20 percent of the average number of key points found in each image. If not, the system detects that the frames correspond to entirely different pages and sets ΔY to the frame height instead of zero. When stitching all frames later, the result will be that pages will neatly be paginated as in the original document.

On the other hand, the matching step can erroneously report ΔY as non-zero. This can also happen on PowerPoint slides where letters match with the wrong key points. We also empirically found that this happens when the popular value found in the previous step is found less than three times. The algorithm determines that the document viewer is pagination (versus scrolling) if it happens more than twice.

3.5 Detecting mouse, text and voice actions

Capturing mouse and text actions performed by the user while recording is important to preserve contextual information as users markup documents [4]. An author can for example highlight specific words for revision with a co-author, or a teacher can explain a chart or figure by moving her cursor, or a lawyer can circle a whole section with her mouse cursor and ask a question verbally.

To detect these actions, it is enough to recognize when people only move their cursor and stop scrolling or paginating through the document. Conveniently, these times correspond to when the stitching algorithm yields $\Delta Y=0$. For such frame pairs, we thus compare their absolute difference and cluster the positions of their changed pixels into blobs of 64x64 pixel areas. Clustering changed pixels onto a grid allows for a nice speed up as well as suppresses noise due to other smaller changes that might occur during the recording. The winning cluster is reported as the detected changed location, used in the next section when overlaying the action on the final DocuGram.

3.6 Generating the final DocuGram

Given the set of frames and estimated shifts between them, the system generates a single composite image whose height corresponds to the sum of the deltas plus once the ROI's height.

Each frame is then copied at its corresponding Y position based on the accumulated delta offsets until that index. Special attention needs to be paid for cases when the user started recording her window at a later page and scrolls up.

Once the composite image is created, the system identifies likely page breaks. Because of the ROI step earlier, it is rather easy to identify page breaks as long horizontal lines that cross the whole ROI's width. Special attention is paid to small interrupted fragments; while recording, the mouse cursor has sometimes been found to overlap page boundaries, thus creating little discontinuities in the horizontal segments. To speed up implementation, our fast binarization step only computes the vertical gradient of the composite image so that it only detects horizontal edges.

Once page breaks have been found, the system cuts the tall image into as many smaller page images as necessary, padding the last one with white space in case the user had not completely captured it, thus giving the inferred document pages a more uniform look.

Finally, detected actions are overlaid on the corresponding page images as a DIV element that depicts a mouse pointer. When clicked, the original motion path (as recovered from the previous step) is used to play an animation of the fake mouse cursor. The corresponding voice segment is played at the same time by seeking the audio track to the start time and playing it until the end of the segment.

3.7 Editing and annotating before sharing

Unlike sharing a document as a link or by email as an attachment, DocuGrams can be edited before being published and shared. For example, an author might want feedback on slide 1 and 5 of her presentation, but during pagination all slides 1 through 5 were captured by the system. Using the edit button, she can easily delete the page images no longer desired. She can also re-record her voice, add new highlights, or record new mouse motions that she might have forgotten to produce while recording.

An optional step allows users to apply OCR on each page image of the document page images. We currently use the Javascript port of GOCR (GNU Optical Character Recognition) to perform this step. Each detected word is represented by a transparent DIV overlaid over the page image at its bounding box. It allows users to select text from the DocuGram as if it was the original document, including highlighting parts of it.

4. EXPERIMENTS

We ran two experiments to evaluate the system accuracy and speed. The first experiment tested whether document pages were correctly reconstituted by the stitching and pagination algorithms, and if the mouse actions were correctly identified. This experiment included 17 screen recordings: 5 word documents, 2 PowerPoint slide decks, 4 PDF documents (2 using smooth scrolling, 2 using normal scrolling), 2 online Office 365 Word documents, and 4 web pages, including one from Google Books.

The ROIs were correctly identified for all videos except two web pages with no obvious line separators and one PPT exported to a long PDF that contained a tall figure including all slides on a single page.

Stitching worked well on all samples. Pagination also performed well apart from three web pages which did not contain natural page breaks. The last web page (Google Books) worked correctly because the interface showed page breaks.

Mouse motion was correctly identified, but failed to handle selected text areas; this is a limitation of our current implementation that selects one winning region in the difference maps instead of looking at region shapes.

We ran a second experiment to better understand the speed of capture without the user spending time talking or moving her mouse cursor while recording. As shown in Table 1, this experiment included screen recordings of 4 PDF documents, 3 PowerPoint files, and 3 web pages. Averaging the results, PowerPoint slides can be captured at 3.4 pages per second, documents at 1.5 pages per second, and web pages at 1.08 pages per second (by counting a page as being 600 pixels tall). Again, stitching worked correctly for all recordings, but pagination failed on one web page where strong horizontals confused the page break algorithm.

Table 1. Capturing documents in popular applications

Document type	Duration of recording (seconds)	Number of pages/pixels
PDF	4.5	7
PDF	12.4	14
PDF	18.7	32
PDF	4.3	7
PPT	8.0	23
PPT	4.0	14
PPT	6.0	24
WEB	4.7	3405 (pixels)
WEB	6.2	4318 (pixels)
WEB	6.6	3644 (pixels)

5. DISCUSSION

Early experiments show that capturing a DocuGram can be fast, especially if no interactions need to be captured. For example, capturing PowerPoint slides is as fast as scrolling through all slides with a mouse scroll wheel.

Unlike sharing the original document, users can control which pages are shared (except for web pages since the system does not yet paginate them), add comments or mouse motion, and be sure their shared documents are viewable on any web browser, including mobile phones. Users can also capture documents being shared by others, e.g. slides or a PDF document shared by a colleague during a live web conference.

Compared to a pure screen-recording, DocuGrams allow the recipients to navigate the copy as if working with the original, scrolling up and down pages, even selecting text, while still being able to replay actions created while recording, such as mouse motions and voice comments. DocuGrams are also much smaller files than the video of a screen recording and can be easily exported to an image-based PDF for printing.

6. CONCLUSION AND FUTURE WORK

The algorithm runs at 20 frames per second now, meaning that it could run as the user is capturing the recording. This would dramatically improve the user experience, especially for cases where the user is viewing an online lecture and needs to use the DocuGram as it is being captured.

Real-time would however require improvements to the ROI detector. One idea is to involve the user at the beginning of the recording, another is to leverage several seconds worth of recording to determine what parts of the frames are moving. Still, more work would be required for paginated documents such as PowerPoint slides, or YouTube videos showing slides along with speaker or animated transitions [7]. Also, web pages do not have obvious page breaks: one could automatically add page breaks as when the pages are printed.

We would also like to explore the full life-cycle of DocuGrams. For example, recipients could send back comments to the original author. During a document-authoring scenario, one could imagine the DocuGram to observe the Word document in a window and synchronize its scroll to show the author the corresponding comment left by a co-author on the DocuGram, thereby facilitating document correction.

Finally, document analytics could be integrated to support awareness of use. For example, a teacher sharing a DocuGram could be shown where students have looked, what voice comments were played, what pages were read, helping them increase their awareness of student engagement, a strong problem in for online education.

7. REFERENCES

[1] Toni-Jan Keith Palma Monserrat, Shengdong Zhao, Kevin McGee, and Anshul Vikram Pandey. 2013. NoteVideo: facilitating navigation of blackboard-style lecture videos. In *Proceedings of the SIGCHI Conference on Human Factors in Computing Systems* (CHI '13). ACM, New York, NY, USA, 1139-1148.

[2] L. Zhu, Y. Wang, B. Zhao and X. Zhang, "A Fast Image Stitching Algorithm Based on Improved SURF," Computational Intelligence and Security (CIS), 2014 Tenth International Conference on, Kunming, 2014, pp. 171-175.

[3] Calonder, M., Lepetit, V., Strecha, C. and Fua, P., 2010. Brief: Binary robust independent elementary features. Computer Vision–ECCV 2010, pp.778-792.

[4] A. Adler, A. Gujar, B. L. Harrison, K. O'Hara, and A. Sellen. A diary study of work-related reading: design implications for digital reading devices. In Proceedings of ACM CHI, 241–248. 1998.

[5] T. M. Breuel. High performance document layout analysis. Proceedings of the Symposium on Document Image Understanding Technology. 2003.

[6] C. Kim, P. Chiu, S. Chandra. Dewarping Book Page Spreads Captured with a Mobile Phone Camera. Camera-Based Document Analysis and Recognition. Vol. 8357 of the series Lecture Notes in Computer Science, pp 101-12, 2014.

[7] John Adcock, Matthew Cooper, Laurent Denoue, Hamed Pirsiavash, and Lawrence A. Rowe. 2010. TalkMiner: a lecture webcast search engine. In Proceedings of the 18th ACM international conference on Multimedia (MM '10). ACM, New York, NY, USA, 241-250.

An Exploratory Study on Managing and Searching for Documents in Software Engineering Environments

Eya Ben Charrada
Institute for Informatics
University of Zurich
Switzerland
charrada@ifi.uzh.ch

Stefan Mussato[*]
Kaba AG
Rümlang
Switzerland
stefan.mussato@dormakaba.com

ABSTRACT

A large number of documents are usually produced in the software industry. In this work, we conduct a qualitative study to explore the main practices and challenges related to managing these documents. The results of this study are based on interviews with 13 practitioners from nine companies. The main findings of the study are: (1) much data is stored in e-mails and in meeting protocols, (2) practitioners like wikis, (3) when searching for documents, practitioners would rather browse the structure than use the search function and (4) searching for documents is still a challenge due to the low effectiveness of search functions and the scattering of documents over several locations and tools.

Keywords

Document management; software engineering; qualitative study; industrial study

1. INTRODUCTION

In software development projects, a large number of documents, technical and non-technical, are usually created and used by practitioners with various backgrounds and positions (managers, developers, sale, etc.). For these practitioners, managing the documents is a daily task that can be more or less challenging. In this work, we aim at exploring the practices and challenges related to document management in the software industry. Unlike previous studies and surveys that have been conducted in this field (e.g. [5, 3, 7]), this work has a special focus on how documents are searched for. Furthermore, previous studies usually focused on the use of technical software documentation by software engineers, while this work considers all documents that are produced and used by practitioners holding various technical and non-technical positions.

The results of this work are based on semi-structured interviews with 13 participants working in software development environments. The participants are from nine companies, all based in Switzerland.

[*]This work was conducted during the author's studies at the University of Zurich

DocEng'16, September 12–16, 2016, Vienna, Austria.

© 2016 Copyright held by the owner/author(s). Publication rights licensed to ACM.
ISBN 978-1-4503-4438-8/16/09...$15.00

DOI: http://dx.doi.org/10.1145/2960811.2967149

The remainder of the paper is organized as follows. In Section 2, we present the research question, design of the study, and threats to validity. We report the main results of the study in Section 3 and discuss them in Section 4. In section 5, we present related studies and surveys and we conclude in Section 6.

2. RESEARCH METHODOLOGY

To understand the practices of document management in software development environments, we conducted an exploratory study with nine companies. Since we aim at investigating new and diverse data, we chose a qualitative research approach. The study was conducted via semi-structured interviews. In the remainder of this section, we present the research question and the study design.

2.1 Research question and topics of interest

The study aims at answering the following question:

How do practitioners manage and search for documents in software environments and what challenges they face?

Through this question, we would like to investigate the following aspects. Primarily, we would like to explore how practitioners, from different positions, search for documents. By document we mean any data that is stored electronically on storages provided by the company or on the practitioners' own storages. In addition to searching for documents, we are also interested in how practitioners manage (e.g. create, store and structure) documents and how this impacts their search strategies. Furthermore, we would like to explore to what extent is the ease of search impacted by the companies' processes and guidelines for document management. Finally, we are interested in identifying the main challenges that practitioners face when searching for documents and what limitations they see in current document management tools. Practitioners from the software engineering field are likely to be fairly familiar with software tools and technologies and it is therefore interesting to find out the main problems they face.

2.2 Initial preparation

After reviewing the literature related to document management in software engineering, we defined an initial set of topics of interest. We then prepared questions that we used to conduct five pilot interviews with practitioners. The pilot interviews covered various aspects about documentation such as the type of documents that practitioners create and why, usages of documents in practice and the challenges that practitioners face with current document management practices. The output of the pilot interviews was then used for refining the topics of interest and redefining the questions to be used during the interviews. The output of the pilot interviews is not included in the results reported in this paper.

2.3 Selection of participants and data collection

Thirteen interviewees from nine companies all based in Switzerland were contacted and interviewed. The sector in which the companies are working are presented in Table 1. All interviewees are from the personal network of the second author. Since the number of participants is not too large and as we would like to get a representative picture about the practices of document management, the sampling was done towards covering various positions within software projects. The positions held by the interviewees as well as their experience are presented in Table I. All interviews were organized, conducted and transcribed by the second author, a product manager with 23 years experience in industry who was also enrolled as student at the University of Zurich during the interviewing period. The interviews took place from April to June 2015. All interviews were conducted face to face and were audio recorded after getting the consent of the interviewees. The interview language was German, which is the mother tongue of the participants.

2.4 Data transcription and analysis

The interviewer translated the interviews to English while transcribing them. The transcription was not done word to word but was a crisp reformulation of what the participants said. The analysis was mainly performed by the first author based on the transcribed data. In case of doubt during the analysis or when looking for quotes, the author used the audio recordings to check the original data. Although the collected data covered aspects related to search for information in general (e.g. in the internet), this data was excluded during the analysis so we only focused on data related to searching within documents stored electronically in the company storages or in the practitioner's own storages.

2.5 Threats to validity

Qualitative studies are subject to several threats. Below we explain the design decisions that we made to limit potential ones.

Construct Validity issues appear if the answers obtained from the participants do not accurately reflect the real practice. In order to limit this threat, we informed the participants about the anonymity of the study and we avoided judgements during the interviews. Misunderstandings between the interviewer and interviewees constitute another threat to construct validity. In order to minimize this, the interviewer explicitly explained the goal of the study in advance. Additionally, all studies have been conducted in German which is the mother tongue of both the interviewer and the interviewees. Since the person analysing the data is different form the person conducting and transcribing the interviews, there is a risk of misinterpreting the transcribed data. In order to limit this risk, the analyst listened to the audio files whenever there was doubt about the meaning or context of the transcribed data. Additionally, the interviewer was involved in checking the results that the analyst produced.

Since all participants are form the network of the interviewer, no one declined. This limits the threat of getting only participants that have a special interest in the topic, which would present an *internal validity* threat. However, getting all the participants form the same network could result in a group of participants that have similar backgrounds. To reduce this threat, we selected participants with heterogeneous positions (e.g. technical, managerial) from companies working in various sectors (e.g. manufacturing, consultancy, etc.).

Since the study is qualitative, generalizing the results beyond the settings of this study is rather difficult (*external validity*). Nevertheless, since the selected participants had diverse positions and settings that would cover the main roles in software development projects, findings that apply to the different participants of the study are likely to apply to other practitioners in software development environments.

3. RESULTS

Searching for documents and data is a daily task for software practitioners that takes much of their time. Although practitioners use and manage documents in diverse ways, some similar practices and challenges were reported by many interviewees. In the reminder of this section, we report the main findings we observed in this study.

E-mails and protocols store data

Although not primarily meant for data storage, engineers use e-mails for storing data such as agreements information, reports, documents and links. Example of data looked for within e-mails are:

"...what was done, what was already addressed and how it was addressed, what was decided." – P2

Protocols or slides of meetings are also among the frequently searched documents among managers. When asked about what kind of information he looks for, a participant answered:

"...a lot of protocols or e-mails, I know that people had sent me that and that, and I need to look again how that was..." – P1

Meeting protocols are mostly office documents, but could also be found as plain text in e-mails. To facilitate information finding within e-mails several practitioners (seven in our case) create their own, more or less detailed, structure, e.g. based on projects. However, due to the growing number of e-mails they receive, two participants mentioned giving up on e-mail categorization and switching to solely relying on the search function of the e-mail program.

"...I had a huge folder system with defined themes where I store and find e-mail in a relatively good way, but it is so that I have since long lost the fight... I receive so many e-mails..." – P1

Finding information within e-mails is usually regarded by practitioners as easy, unlike the search within other types of storages, which could be very challenging (this point will be discussed further later). One factor influencing the ease of search in e-mails is the good capabilities of the search function in e-mail clients, which participants were generally happy with. Additionally, participants usually remember data and meta-data about the e-mail such as the sender name, keywords from the e-mail subject and body or the project number. Only three participants mentioned deleting e-mails on a regular basis. One of them does it as soon as the task is done, while the two others keep the e-mail in a folder structure for some time before deleting them.

Practitioners like wikis

Wikis were mentioned in eleven interviews. Among the eleven interviewees, only one, with a managerial position, reported never having used a wiki. The other participants had different levels of experience with wikis. Wikis seem to be very liked by practitioners with technical tasks

"...[the wiki is used] for the support, for example to get information about recurrent problems and failures, and the development of course, and also the programming." – P7

Company ID	Size[a]	Sector	Participant ID	Experience[b]	Position
C1	L	Manufacturing industry	P1	26	Product manager
C1	L	Manufacturing industry	P2	30	Program Lead
C1	L	Manufacturing industry	P3	25	Technical sales manager
C1	L	Manufacturing industry	P4	25	Business owner
C2	L	Consulting and Engineering	P5	19	Consultant
C2	L	Consulting and Engineering	P6	>10	Consultant
C3	L	Banking	P7	16	IT security manager
C4	S	IT security	P8	18	Security manager
C5	L	Consulting	P9	13	Consultant/ Requirements Engineer
C6	S	IT software services	P10	20	Company owner (One person business)
C7	L	Manufacturing Industry	P11	23	Department head
C8	M	Interaction Design	P12	19	Interaction designer
C9	M	Software solutions	P13	30	System Engineer

[a] Company size: (S)mall, (M)edium, (L)arge   [b] Experience in years

"...it is thin and quick...it has surely not a great look and feel, it contains sequences of information and as a technical person I find this good" – P13

But also practitioners with less technical positions seem to prefer wikis to other content and document management systems, and this is mainly for its better structure and better search function:

"...the search function of the wiki simply provides better results..." – P9

Other cited advantages of wikis are that they allow a simple and fast way of changing the content in the same media, and that the relevant pages in wikis can be marked in the browser bookmarks which facilitates finding them later on. Only one participant mentioned not liking the wiki, and this is because of its structure:

"I don't like wikis too much; there's a large amount of data and a strange structure ... I often have the impression of document cadavers" – P12

Browsing first, then using the search function

When looking for a specific document, practitioners would rather browse the folder structure than use the search function. Therefore, to facilitate the search for data, many participants mentioned defining a good structure on their own drives and some on their e-mail clients:

"I have a clever storage [using a catalogue by topics] which makes searching obsolete" – P2

"If I do not find a document or information at the first location, I would retry in another folder. If still there is no match, I may attempt to use the search on all locations ..." – P4

When looking within a collaborative structure, finding documents by browsing becomes more challenging. Practitioners would then behave differently depending on whether they have an idea or not about the location of the document. In the former case, practitioners use browsing to find the document. In the latter case, we identified two types of behaviour. The majority of users find the search function to be unreliable and thus still try to guess where the document is and use browsing. For these users the search function is only used as a last resort if no results could be found by browsing.

"I had higher expectations with the [shared storage] tool, the search is (thinking), well, the logic is not so good, when not knowing exactly what one is looking for it is not reliable. So I try to remember in which folder and in which structure is the file." – P1

A few users, however, wouldn't mind using the search function and might even find it faster than browsing in that case.

"I don't use the catalogue [browsing] in the shared storage tool because it does not have a logic structure...I can only use the search...I am faster then" – P2

"[When looking within shared structures, I use] mostly structure browsing too, but I also use the search function more often" – P4

As browsing is the preferred way for searching, the structure of the shared data and the company processes about document management influence the efficiency and ease of the search. Regarding the search for documents within shared drives, a participant mentioned:

"Because the structure is pre-defined and each project has its structure, it is relatively simple to find..." – P12

In practice, however, only about half the participants mentioned having a more or less strict processes for document storage, while the others only have loose or no regulations.

Searching for documents: the challenges

Although searching for documents is a very common and recurrent task, it is not always easy. In fact, several interviewees mentioned having experienced problems and frustration when looking for a document:

"...I know that it exists, I have opened it once, but after that I didn't find it anymore." – P9

"That's very annoying, then depending on how important the document is, I might ask someone... I might also reproduce it again..." – P12

Several factors have been cited as negatively impacting the search for documents in practice. In some cases, companies would use more than one tool for document storage, which results in the data being scattered over multiple locations. Consequently, when not sure about the location of a document, practitioners need to try the search on each location separately. Some practitioners might even have their own storage on top of that.

"...I use Google Docs from one project and then Dropbox and now OneNote, then my computer and the company computer...I need to shortly think about which project is it, where do they work and why..." – P12

Available search tools are also considered as very limited by most participants. This is because they deliver too many matches, or in some cases, no match:

"I also experienced situations where a search function did not show the expected match even though the keyword entered was correct. Of course this disappointed me..." – P4

One participant mentioned that the search logic which is different among different tools would require more effort for performing the search. Additional factors that were mentioned to negatively influence the data search are human-errors such as the document names not matching content, or using a different spelling in the document name.

4. DISCUSSION

Morkala and Maurer [6] identified scattered documentation and limited search functions as communication wastes in globally distributed agile software projects. Our results support this finding since scattering of documents over several tools has also been reported to hinder document search. However, in our study this problem was not linked to globally distributed teams. In fact, such a problem happens when the company (or even the practitioner) uses more than one storage tool.

When browsing the structure, practitioners need to rely much on memory and/or guessing to find the location of a document. Therefore, the search would be easier if the practitioner has prior knowledge about the document location. This finding is in accordance with the results of the study of de Graaf et al. [1], which identified that prior knowledge helps in searching software documentation efficiently and effectively.

Despite the advances made in document search, current search tools do not seem to meet the expectations of practitioners. In fact, many practitioners see the offered search functionalities as limited, unreliable, and lead to all kinds of results. Consequently, many practitioners use structure browsing as the main search strategy even when the location of the document is not known for them. Since the search space is usually huge, practitioners need to guess where could the file be located, which is not always effective. There is therefore a clear need for better document management and search tools that are aligned with the users' behaviour and way of thinking.

5. RELATED WORK

Studies about the management and use of technical documentation in software projects are numerous. While some of these studies cover very specific tasks such as architectural design [8] or software maintenance [2], others are more generic and cover the use of various types of documentation [3]. Due to space limit, we restrict our focus to recent industrial studies covering aspects that overlap with the scope of this work. The work of Garousi et al. [5] explored how technical documentation is used and what factors impact its usefulness in practice. Plösch et al. [7] assessed the most important

quality attribute of software documentation via a survey. Related to search of information, Freund [4] explored what contextual factors impact the information seeking behaviour of software engineers. The focus of our work, which is storage and search for documents, is different from the previous studies. Furthermore, the scope of this work is also larger since it covers not only software documentation but also other type of documents produced in software environments.

6. CONCLUSION

In this study, we explored practices and challenges related to managing documents in software development environments. Our findings include strategies that practitioners use to structure and search for documents. We also report challenges that practitioners face when searching for documents. For future work, we plan to use the findings of this study to conduct a survey that will provide quantitative data on the topic.

Acknowledgments

We would like to thank all the participants for accepting to participate, and for their time.

7. REFERENCES

[1] De Graaf, Klaas Andries, Peng Liang, Antony Tang, and Hans Van Vliet. The impact of prior knowledge on searching in software documentation. In *Proceedings of the 2014 ACM symposium on Document engineering*, pages 189–198. ACM, 2014.

[2] de Souza, Sergio Cozzetti B., Nicolas Anquetil, and Kathia M. de Oliveira. A study of the documentation essential to software maintenance. In *Proceedings of the 23rd annual international conference on Design of communication: documenting and designing for pervasive information*, pages 68–75. ACM, 2005.

[3] Forward, Andrew, and Timothy C. Lethbridge. The relevance of software documentation, tools and technologies: A survey. In *Proceedings of the 2002 ACM symposium on Document engineering*, DocEng '02, pages 26–33. ACM, 2002.

[4] Freund, Luanne. Contextualizing the information-seeking behavior of software engineers. *Journal of the Association for Information Science and Technology*, 66(8):1594–1605, 2015.

[5] Garousi, Golara, Vahid Garousi-Yusifoglu, Guenther Ruhe, Junji Zhi, Mahmoud Moussavi, and Brian Smith. Usage and usefulness of technical software documentation: An industrial case study. *Information & Software Technology*, 57:664–682, 2015.

[6] Korkala, Mikko, and Frank Maurer. Waste identification as the means for improving communication in globally distributed agile software development. *Journal of Systems and Software*, 95:122–140, 2014.

[7] Ploesch, Reinhold, Andreas Dautovic, and Matthias Saft. The value of software documentation quality. In *14th International Conference on Quality Software.*, pages 333–342. IEEE, 2014.

[8] Rost, Dominik, Matthias Naab, Crescencio Lima, and Christina von Flach Garcia Chavez. Software architecture documentation for developers: a survey. In *European Conference on Software Architecture*, pages 72–88. Springer, 2013.

Mass Serialization Method for Document Encryption Policy Enforcement

Margaret Sturgill
HP Labs,
3390 E Harmony Rd,
Fort Collins, CO 80528
+1 970-898-8581
Margaret.Sturgill@hp.com

Steven J. Simske
HP Labs
3390 E Harmony Rd,
Fort Collins, CO 80528
+1 970-895-8580
Steven.Simske@hp.com

ABSTRACT

Analytics obtained during the creation of a database of mass serialized codes can also be used to help enforcement of encryption policy on documents. In this paper, we introduce a set of metrics which complement traditional NIST cryptography methods – 4 mass serialization and one entropy metric -- which in combination can allow a discrimination between encrypted vs. zipped files. We describe the use of these methods to identify a broad range of non-randomness in number sets, and apply them to a more mundane problem—that of automatic assessment of the encryption state of a corpora of documents.

CCS Concepts

• **Information systems~Content analysis and feature selection.**

Keywords

Mass serialization; encryption policy enforcement; classification

1. INTRODUCTION

In today's business world, the security of electronic documents is paramount, and companies often enforce a specific policy/policies on the protection of documents both within the organization and also when the documents are transferred outside of the organization by electronic means (e.g. email attachments). It is a reasonable policy to require that any such documents be encrypted.

While one way of ensuring this is to require use of encrypted email solutions like PGP, it is often not feasible as the party receiving the message might not have ability to receive encrypted email messages. Thus, a reasonable approach is to require that the email attachments themselves be encrypted, or at least salient portions of compound documents be encrypted. To evaluate feasibility of such policy enforcement, we were interested if it would be possible to determine whether a given file was encrypted or just compressed.

There are several approaches to detecting encrypted streams, especially using stream entropy [3][5][10] and statistical test suites like Die Hard or NIST Statistical Suite[2][6]. One of the problems faced by those tests is a requirement for large data sets. By combining multiple binary classifiers [9] we can use a smaller dataset using multiple classifiers that are possibly less accurate individually [8].

2. METRICS AND CLASSIFIERS

The metrics we have chosen are: Bit Equivalent Entropy (B.E.E., Equation 1, where p_i is the percentage of values at bin i), Mass Serialization Collision Analytics of 1-byte strings (initial and incremental) and Mass Serialization Collison Analytics of 2-byte strings (initial and incremental). This provides us with five metric classifiers then we can combine. All of these are largely mutually independent and thus make a good choice for meta-algorithmic classification [8].

2.1 Bit Equivalent entropy

A cryptographically secure stream of data should be mathematically indistinguishable from a stream of random data. For many data sets, the difference is huge, and so the fastest means possible of determining the cryptographic insecurity of a stream is needed. The simplest measurement of a stream is its entropy. We can, therefore, use bit-equivalent entropy to detect when a data stream is not cryptographically secure. If the entropy does not closely match random data entropy, we should assume that the data was not encrypted. It is important to note that the inverse is not true, and that simply passing the entropy test does not guarantee data safety, but instead warrants more in-depth analysis along the lines of Mass Serialization collision detection.

$$\text{B.E.E.} = -\sum_{i \in C} p_i \cdot \ln(p_i) \qquad (1)$$

Where C is the set of allowable characters and p_i is the probability of occurrence of character i.

It should be noted that this metric is sensitive to the amount of test data with results being more accurate with larger data sizes. There is also no guarantee, as with the other standards [2][4], that all forms of non-randomness are identified. Our approach is conveniently tied, however, to mass serialization, which we describe next.

2.2 Mass Serialization

Mass serialization (MS) is the process by which a list of codes for a serialized set of items is generated. Serialization means that the numbers follow one another serially, or are associated with a sequence. For a general (non-secure) mass serialization, the binary strings representing the serial numbers will be {000...000}, {000...001}, etc. However, no modern serialization of products would provide such a sequence, for at least two reasons: (1) counterfeiters will be able to predict roughly which numbers will be printed at a given time in the future, and so illicitly print their own "legitimate" numbers, and (2) since the numbers are all sequential, it will be easier for a competitor to reverse-engineer a supply chain.

As a consequence, the best mass serialization sets will produce randomly numbered sequences without repetition. In order for a mass serialization to be scalable, secure and efficient to roll out, it needs to (a) provide a mass serialization set with a specified format (byte string, bit string, alphanumeric only, numeric only, etc.) and length; (b) provide an augmented (non-colliding) set of mass serialized codes when a related set exists; and (c) be possible to perform analysis on these two mass serialization sets to determine if there is a measurable anomaly in the serialized data (indicative of an "attack surface" for someone wishing to break the cryptographic algorithm and so determine the serialization algorithm used).

The side effect of this behavior is that since encrypted data should look like a set of random numbers (just like a valid mass serialization set), we can use the same test to compare the collision statistics of the data set with the theoretical values.

In generating mass serialization sets, we noted that the number of collisions for a cryptographically secure set should be predictable and vary little between instances of the same serialization (Equation 2). This means that if the RNG of the mass serialization engine is cryptographically secure, then the odds of it generating a new byte string that already exists in the mass serialized set (MSS) should be directly proportional to the percent of possible byte strings that currently exist in the MSS[7]. Any significant deviation from this probability can be an indication of non-random subsets in the data. To test for such deviations, we consider consecutive binary sub-strings (BS) of length LB, where B is the number of bytes, with no collisions allowed. When collisions do occur, we disallow the collision and do not increment the index, but instead log the collision. The collision statistics should be governed by $f(p) = 1/(1-p)$, as shown in Fig. 1. The expected number of collisions is therefore $EC(p) = p/(1-p)$.

The hatched area in Figure 1 is given by:

$$\int_a^b \frac{1}{1-p}\,dp = \ln(1-a) - \ln(1-b) \qquad (2)$$

Thus, the expected number of collisions in moving from a to b when there are N possible characters in the string and B is the length of the string, or EC(a→b), is given by:

$$EC(a \rightarrow b) = \left(\ln(1-a) - \ln(1-b) - (b-a)\right) * \left(N^B\right) \qquad (3)$$

To calculate the Mass Serialization analytics, we process the available data as follows: we generate (or read) $N^B a$ unique strings (ignoring additional occurrences of existing strings) and then

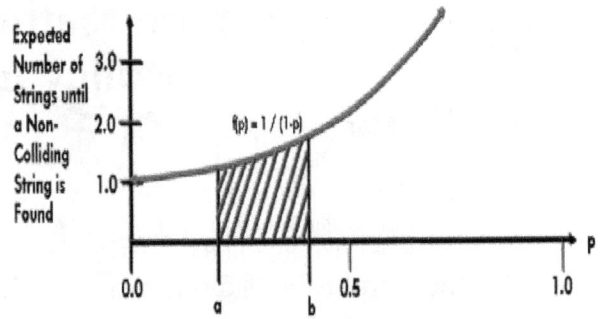

Figure 1. Probability of collision when moving from a to b (fraction of total number of possible strings)

continue until we have $N^B b$ unique strings. We keep track of collisions encountered during the generation of the $N^B a$ (EC(a)) and also the number of collisions when continuing to $N^B b$ size set (EC(a→b)). We repeat the above process until all the data is consumed (n iterations). We report mean and standard deviation of the number of collisions generated for EC(a) and EC(a→b). Only a single pass through the data is required to count the collisions by maintaining a hash set of all the unique values existing in the current iteration.

For example, given a 8-bit character set (256 possible values) we process all the data in the test set by generating as many iterations of generating $256^B*0.25$ (64 or 16,384 bytes) and $256^B*0.75$ (192 or 49,152 bytes) for B=1,2 as the data allows.

If B=2, a=0.25 and b=0.75 and given 256B=65,536, then EC(a→b)=(1.09861-0.5)*65,536=39,231. We thus expected 39,231 collisions in moving our MSS from 16,384 to 49,152 entries. For each iteration we therefore expect to consume a minimum of 49152 (unique values) + 2469 (EC(0→.25)) + 39231 (EC(.25→.75)) = 90,852 bytes of data.

2.3 Metric Classifiers

To see whether we can differentiate between compressed and encrypted files, we have taken a subset of PDF files from the ACL Anthology[1]. We started with a randomly-selected set of 200 PDF (size between 800 kilobytes and 8 megabytes) files from which we have used 50 (25%) as our training data. For each training file we generated four files: Triple DES encrypted (Using .NET *TripleDESCryptoServiceProvider*), gzip compressed, WinZip compressed and WinZip compressed with encryption (AES 128-bit).

For each of those files we have then generated the following metrics: B.E.E., Mass Serialization EC(.25) with B=1 (*MS EC(.25) B=1*), Mass Serialization EC(.25→.75) with B=1 (*MS EC(.25→.75 B=1*), Mass Serialization EC(.25) with B=2 (*MS EC(.25) B=2*), Mass Serialization EC(.25→.75) with B=2 (*MS EC(.25→.75 B=2*) Table 1 shows raw ground truth data. Note that, for example, the means of EC(.25→.75) with B=2 for both Triple DES and Encrypted WinZip are close to the theoretical value of 39,231 (as calculated in the previous section).

The Raw PDFs have highly variable metric data; for example, the B.E.E. for our 50 PDF documents have μ=7.65, σ=0.86206. After compression or encryption is applied, the data becomes a lot more uniform. For example, the B.E.E. data for WinZip compressed and Encrypted WinZip compressed files is μ=7.99788, σ= 0.00194 and μ=7.99985, σ= 0.00014 respectively.

Table 1. Metric Population Data

Data	B.E.E. μ	B.E.E. σ	MS EC(.25) B=1 μ	MS EC(.25) B=1 σ	MS EC (.25→.75) B=1 μ	MS EC (25→.75) B=1 σ	MS EC(.25) B=2 μ	MS EC(.25) B=2 σ	MS EC(.25→.75) B=2 μ	MS EC(.25→.75) B=2 σ
Raw Pdf	7.6544	0.86206	107.98	756.51	1200.5	6520.1	8049.4	3003.2	107206	47191
Triple DES	7.9998	0.00005	9.4779	0.05993	151.89	0.28541	2468.2	18.365	39232	123.30
WinZIP	7.9978	0.00194	10.201	0.37194	159.46	4.5455	2597.0	43.394	40410	730.81
Gzip	7.9979	0.00199	10.171	0.40754	158.64	3.9830	2556.7	34.443	40143	710.04
E WinZip	7.9998	0.00014	9.4825	0.05457	151.98	0.34718	2469.6	19.525	39235	119.90

Table 2. Percentage of correctly classified training files by each classifier and its corresponding weight.

	B.e.e	MS EC(.25) B=1	MS EC(.25→.75) B=1	MS EC(.25) B=2	MS EC(.25→.75) B=2
Compression	100	100	100	93	98
Encryption	98	93	96	99	99
Classifier Weight	0.204	0.197	0.2	0.196	0.203

Table 3. Number of test files out of 150 correctly classified by each classifier.

	B.E.E	MS EC(.25) B=1	MS EC(.25→.75) B=1	MS EC(.25) B=2	MS EC(.25→.75) B=2
Gzip	145	150	150	112	139
WinZip	146	150	150	129	136
Triple DES	101	138	141	145	128
EWinZip	89	127	132	142	119

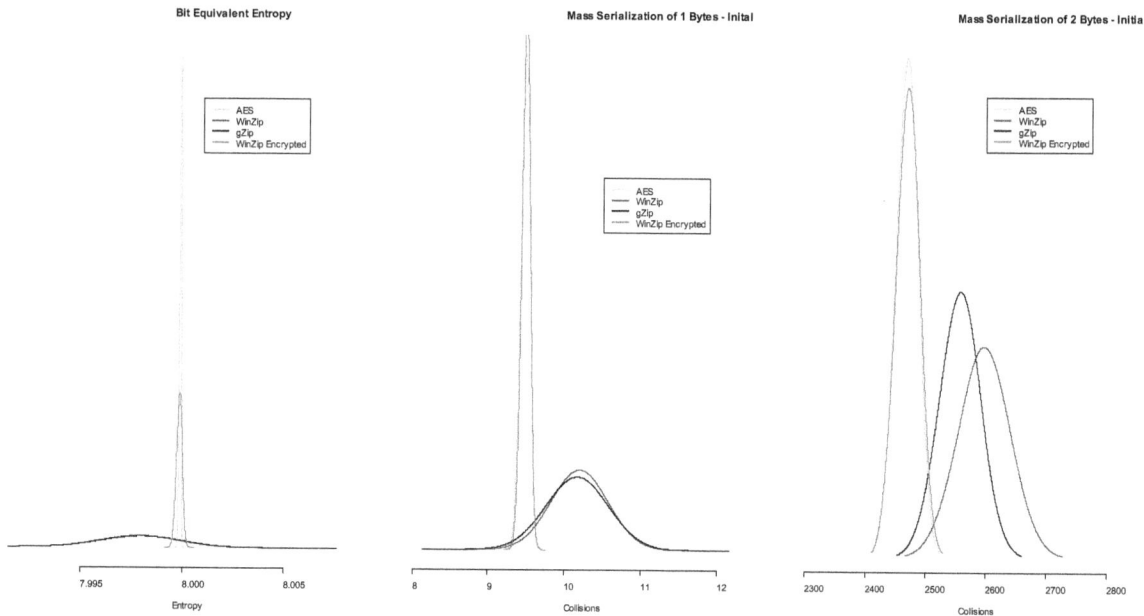

Figure 2. Metric population graphs. a) B.E.E. b) MS EC(.25) B=1 c) MS EC(.25) B=2

While entropy is usually used to detect encrypted data, it is not enough for discrimination between compression and encryption. Figure 2a shows the overlap between the two populations that can cause misclassification. Indeed in our tests the Encrypted Win Zip files were often misclassified (41% of time) by the B.E.E. metric. Additionally since entropy is very sensitive to data set size, smaller files will have higher error rates.

When looking at the population data for the metrics, we cannot distinguish between the Triple DES encrypted and Encrypted WinZip data, but there is separation between grouped compressed and encrypted data (Figure 2). In the end, we decided to combine the two encrypted files sets and the two compressed files sets into single "compressed" and "encrypted" classes giving us 100 training files in each set. As Table 2 shows, the classification of compressed files via *MS EC(.25) B=2* metric produced comparatively poorer results than the other metrics. This is probably due to the pronounced difference in the metric population between gzip and WinZip files. See Figure 2c. This distinction is not present when Mass serialization analytics are performed with B=1. See Figure 2b.

As seen in Table 2, each of the classifiers performs well on the test data with varied accuracy. But when we used a simple voting schema, we have observed an 87.3% to 100% accuracy. Individual classifiers are generally accurate for the data sets tested; the combination of 4 or 5 classifiers more so. See Tables 3 and 4.

This approach does require a training set to set up the initial classifiers. This is especially true for the B.E.E. metric as the entropy means are very close to each other for both the encrypted and compressed data. Entropy is also sensitive to the amount of data we have available. On the other hand, if ground truth data is not initially available, we can compare the number of initial and incremental collisions to the theoretical expected value. When excluding the B.E.E. classifier, weighted voting (proportional to accuracy) combination of Mass Serialization classifiers had only lower accuracy when classifying Encrypted WinZip files (87.3% vs. 90 %). Other three file types were classified with same or better accuracy.

Table 4. Number of correctly classified files out of the 150 in each training set.

	All 5 Classifiers	Mass Serialization Classifiers only
Gzip – classified as compressed	147 (98%)	150 (100%)
WinZip- classified as compressed	146 (97.3%)	150 (100%)
Triple DES – classified as encrypted	147 (98%)	147 (98%)
EWinZip – classified as encrypted	135 (90%)	131 (87.3%)

Additionally, the classification can be done very quickly requiring only a single pass through the data, and as none of the methods are dependent on position of data within the file or on the file structure, we can provide de-identification or "anonymization" of data by scrambling before the classification is performed. This is particularly useful for privacy (e.g. medical) related data.

3. CONCLUSIONS AND FUTURE WORK

While encrypted data looks and behaves like random data, usual tests for randomness require a large data set (The Die Hard team recommends 2×10^9 bytes)[2]. This is impractical for a system that quickly needs to assess the encryption state of an attachment. In practice, our approach works on data sets of 1×10^6 bytes, making it more usable in real life situations.

Future work should include investigation of possible security attack surfaces. One of the investigations could involve whether images can be modified to exhibit entropy associated with random or encrypted data but still be readable, and whether mass serialization tests would detect such tampering.

4. REFERENCES

[1] Association of Computational Linguistics, ACL Anthology http://aclweb.org/anthology .

[2] Dieharder tool (http://www.phy.duke.edu/~rgb/General/dieharder.php) based on Diehard Tests (http://en.wikipedia.org/wiki/Diehard_test .

[3] Dorfinger P., Panholzer G. and John W. 2011. Entropy estimation for real-time encrypted traffic identification. In *Proceedings of the Third international conference on Traffic monitoring and analysis* (TMA'11), Jordi Domingo-Pascual, Yuval Shavitt, and Steve Uhlig (Eds.). Springer-Verlag, Berlin, Heidelberg, 164-171.

[4] Levenson, M. Vangell, D. Banks, A. Heckert , J. Dray, S. Vo, L. E. Bassham III, A Statistical Test Suite for Random and Pseudorandom Number Generators for Cryptographic Applications. NIST, Special Publication April 2010. Special Publication 800-22 Revision 1a, http://csrc.nist.gov/groups/ST/toolkit/rng/stats_tests.html, 2010.

[5] Malhotra P. *Detection of encrypted streams for egress monitoring.* Master's thesis, Iowa State University, 2007

[6] Piccinelli M. and Gubina P. 2014.Detecting Hidden Encrypted Volume Files via Statistical Analysis. In *International Journal of Cyber-Security and Digital Forensics* 3(1) 30-37. DOI: http://dx.doi.org/10.17781/P001103.

[7] Simske, Steven J. "Mass Serialization Analytics," US. Patent 9344277, Issued May 17, 2016.

[8] Simske S, Wright D, and Sturgill M. 2006. Meta-algorithmic systems for document classification. In *Proceedings of the 2006 ACM symposium on Document engineering* (DocEng '06). ACM, New York, NY, USA, 98-106. DOI=http://dx.doi.org/10.1145/1166160.1166190.

[9] Woniak M, Graña M, and Corchado E. 2014. A survey of multiple classifier systems as hybrid systems. *Inf. Fusion* 16 (March 2014), 3-17. DOI=http://dx.doi.org/10.1016/j.inffus.2013.04.006

[10] Zhang, Han, and Christos Papadopoulos. "Early detection of high entropy traffic." In *Communications and Network Security (CNS), 2015 IEEE Conference on*, pp. 104-112. IEEE, 2015.

Appling Link Target Identification and Content Extraction to improve Web News Summarization

Rodolfo Ferreira
Rafael Ferreira
Rafael Dueire Lins
Hilário Oliveira
UFPE, Recife, PE, Brazil
rodolfoferreira@gmail.com

Marcelo Riss
HP Brazil R&D
Porto Alegre, RS, Brazil
marcelo.riss@hp.com

Steven J. Simske
HP Labs.
Fort Collins, CO 80528, USA
steven.simske@hp.com

ABSTRACT

The existing automatic text summarization systems whenever applied to web-pages of news articles show poor performance as the text is encapsulated within a HTML page. This paper takes advantage of the link identification and content extraction techniques. The results show the validity of such a strategy.

Categories and Subject Descriptors

I.2.7 [**Natural Language Processing**]: Text analysis.

Keywords

Summarization; Content Extraction; Link Identification

1. INTRODUCTION

The Internet or the World Wide Web is an important source of information today. A web page is complex HTML structure in which the text is mixed with codes, images, links to other web pages, etc. Several systems for web page summarization may be found in the literature, as example [1]. Although, those systems target the extractive summarization of the text part of web pages, they have two drawbacks: (i) They do not separate web pages with relevant information from the ones with advertising and directories; (ii) They are too general purpose, as they are not designed to a specific type of text, such as news articles.

This paper presents a new approach to automatically perform the extractive summarization of web pages of news articles. The proposed system receives as input the root link of any news site and it identifies and summarizes all news. This process is performed in four steps: Web Crawler, Link Target Identification, Content Extraction, and Text Summarization.

The experimental results obtained for web pages show that the proposed system reaches comparable results to the summarization of the plain text (with the text extracted manually) of the same web pages. This proves the efficiency of the new summarization system proposed. The link identification/ classification step achieved 96.72% and 96.70% in terms of accuracy and F-measure, respec-

DocEng'16, September 13–16, 2016, Vienna, Austria.
© 2016 ACM. ISBN 978-1-4503-4438-8/16/09. . . $15.00
DOI: http://dx.doi.org/10.1145/2960811.2967158

tively; and the proposed content extraction algorithm outperforms the state-of-the-art system by 8.35% using F-measure.

2. BACKGROUND

This section presents an overview of the main concepts associated with the proposed system.

2.1 Link Target Identification

The link analysis field studies the relationship between web pages. This research area flourished after the proposal of the page rank algorithm [12], which assesses the importance of a web page according to the number of external references (links) to it. Some other works follow the same direction [16]; none of them use the link as a way to classify the content of web pages, however.

The link analysis proposed here, called link target identification, is a completely original step. It benefits from several features extracted from the link structure in order to classify the link-target page as a "news article" or an "irrelevant page" (advertisement, non-text information, etc.).

2.2 Content Extraction Methods

The Content Extraction (CE) process tries to detect and extract relevant textual content from web pages, avoiding navigation menus, advertisement banners, and structural information.

Document Slope Curves (DSC) [13] treats a web page as a sequence of tokens, which could be HTML tags or text, looking for sections with a low number of HTML tags.

The Texto To Ratio (TTR) algorithm [14] counts the number of HTML-tags per line. Lines with a high number of text characters are considered relevant content.

Link Quota Filter (LQF) could be used as a CE algorithm and as a preprocessing step for other CE algorithms. The algorithm looks for the ratio of text which is inside the DOM-tree nodes to text outside of these nodes [4].

The Boilerplate Detection algorithm [7] uses text features, structural information and densitometry features to find the content sections of a website. Decision trees and linear support vector machines are used to classify the sections into content or boilerplate.

The drawbacks of the recently proposed content extraction algorithms [6] are: (i) They are supervised, requiring an annotated corpus to perform the extraction; (ii) They were developed to improve the printing process; thus, the images within the web page can also be selected as relevant content; (iii) They are slower than the solution proposed here.

2.3 Extractive Summarization Methods

An extractive summarization platform selects from the original text document a subset formed with the sentences considered as most relevant exactly as they appear, to form the summary. Ferreira et al. [2] evaluated the 17 extractive summarization methods described in the literature, of which reference [3] points out the six sentence scoring methods better suitable for news articles:

- **Word Frequency**: The more frequently a word appears in a text, the higher would be its score.

- **TF/IDF (Term Frequency/Inverse Document Frequency)**: Formula 1 gives scores to sentences.

$$TF/IDF(w) = (NumTS) * log(\frac{(NumS)}{(MenST)}) \qquad (1)$$

NumTS = frequency of term t in sentence S, NumS=total number of sentences, MenST = sentences with term t.

- **Lexical Similarity**: Relates sentences that employ words with the same meaning (synonyms) or other semantic relation.

- **Sentence Position**: The most important sentences tend to appear at the beginning of a document.

- **Sentence Resemblance to the Title**: the vocabulary overlap between a sentence and the document title increases its importance.

- **Sentence Length**: short and long sentences are penalized.

3. WEB NEWS SUMMARIZATION

The input of the system is a root link to some website of news articles, such as CNN[1]. The target web page is processed in four steps before reaching the final output that is the summarization of all news found in the website. The following sections describes each step.

3.1 Link Target Identification Step

The goal of the link target identification step is to classify links as "news article" or "irrelevant page". Thus, it eliminates pages containing advertising, navigation menu, videos, etc.

The proposal is to create a classification to retrieve the relevant content pages, more specifically a news article web page. Six features based on link structure are used:

- **Has Number**: This attribute checks if the link has some number in the "name" of the link. Links related to news usually have an ID in its structure;

- **Has Date**: If the link contains a date, it is more likely it to be a news article. In general, advertising and navigation menus have no date in they link structure;

- **Length**: Usually longer link structures are news. Some websites use the title of the article in the link;

- **Ends with Slashes**: The attributes responsible to divide a navigation menu usually end with a slash sign in the case of a news article web page;

- **Has reserved Word**: This attribute was chosen to filter multimedia news, as the proposed system targets text. The proposed system adopts the words *gallery, video, image, photo, slideshow, episode* and *player* as a list of reserved words indicating that the web page pointed at by such link cannot be processed;

[1]www.cnn.com

- **Slash number**: Count the number of slashes in the link address, indicating the depth of the page in the website.

Several different supervised machine learning algorithms were tested to automatically classify the proposed features of links. Further details on the classification and the training corpus are presented in Section 4.1.

3.2 Content Extraction Step

Once the link is classified as pointing at a text news article web page, the next step is to extract the relevant content from the HTML page provided by the link. Initially, the proposed algorithm processes the web page to remove the native HTML attributes that are not used for text content, some examples are *style, color, padding, margin* and *likewise*. Then the content in each tag is replaced by its number of words. In other words, it creates a new document only with the tags and the number of words inside each tag, as shown in Figure 1. After the initial processing the proposed algorithm

```
<p class="zn-body__paragraph">Five things kill more people in the United States
<p class="zn-body__paragraph">Together, these five conditions cause almost two
<p class="zn-body__paragraph">On Thursday, the Centers for Disease Control and
<p class="zn-body__paragraph">We already know how to do it -- now we need to
<p class="zn-body__paragraph">The greatest impact comes when we make the
```

```
<p class="zn-body__paragraph">18
<p class="zn-body__paragraph">41
<p class="zn-body__paragraph">92
<p class="zn-body__paragraph">27
```

Figure 1: Content Tag with Text and Numbers

creates a DOMTree based on the remaining tags. It contains the number of words of each tag, as presented in Figure 2. Once the DOMTree is completely built, the system scans every leaf in order to remove void tags or script codes. Those tags are used to: (i) detail the style of some text, (ii) group other tags inside it, and (iii) encapsulate code (program) inside the web page.

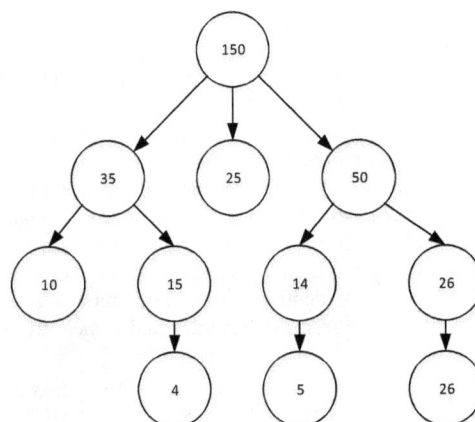

Figure 2: Initial Tree

Then, the algorithm checks the number of words inside the nodes, if it has at least ten words, then it is a possible candidate

198

to point at a news relevant content; otherwise, the system excludes the node, as presented in Figure 3. The last step is the core of the

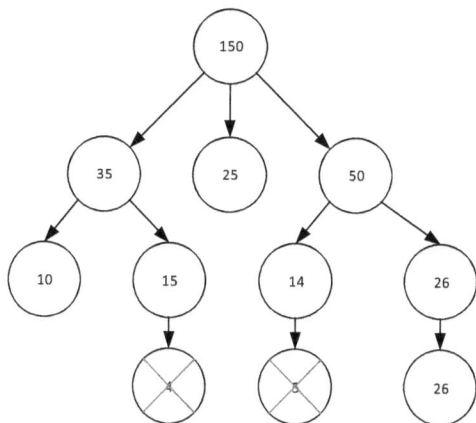

Figure 3: Eliminating nodes with less than ten words

content extraction step. It follows a bottom-up approach that calculates the sum of the number of words in children nodes and in their parent node. The sytem tests if the number of words in the parent node is less or equal to the sum of the words in its children (difference <=0). If so, its child nodes are deleted; otherwise they are kept. Figure 4 details this step.

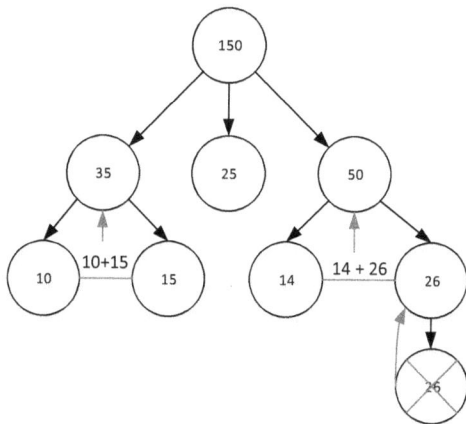

Figure 4: Final Tree

3.3 The Text Summarization Step

The proposed system creates two ordered vectors to represent the text (first step of text summarization). The vectors contain the list of sentences and words from the text that will be the input to the sentence scoring process.

The system employs six sentence scoring services that meet the specifications detailed in Section 2.3. It is important to observe that all those services provide an output score between 0 and 1 for each sentence.

The scores obtained by the summarization methods are averaged to find the most relevent sentences of each text. The sentences with the highest scores compose the summary.

4. EVALUATION

The evaluation of the proposed platform was divided in three parts as follows.

4.1 Link Target Identification

A dataset containing 1,590 instances was created. The links were collected from 10 different news websites (ABC news, BBC news, CBC news, CNN, Daily post, Fox news, Yahoo news, the New York times, the Verge, Reuters), of which 800 were tagged as news. Different machine learning algorithms were applied in order to find which one better fits the proposed PI approach. The WEKA Data Mining Software [15] was used.

Table 1 presents the results of the proposed method using the classifiers listed. The data obtained show that the worst classifier reached 93.45% of Accuracy and 93.50% of F-measure. Thus, these results confirm that the proposed set of features achieve good results in the task of identifying news article web pages by inspecting only the "name of the link".

Table 1: *Results of the proposed approach*

Algorithm	Accuracy	F-measure
Bayesian Network	93.45	93.50
MLP	96.10	96.10
C4.5	96.72	96.70
KNN	96.41	96.40

Among those algorithms, the C4.5 classifier was chosen for the following reasons: (i) It achieves better results; (ii) The output of C4.5 is human interpretable; (ii) It generates a tree that can be easily translated into a set of rules.

4.2 Content Extraction

A dataset extracted from the CNN website was used to perform the evaluation on the Content Extraction and Summarization steps.

The CNN-corpus [9] encompasses 3,000 texts in ten different subject categories, originally tagged by CNN. The CNN-corpus dataset was created to assess automatic summarization methods; however, since its source is news articles from the CNN website it was easily adapted to the content extraction task.

Gottron [5] presents four different levels of granularity of representations to evaluate CE algorithms. This work adopted the words as a set approach. Such a method provides results very similar to its competitors, but is simpler to implement and evaluate the results obtained.

Table 2 presents the results for each related work against the new approach in terms of precision, recall and F-measure. The proposed system reaches a result 17.40% and 8.35% better than its competitors in terms of recall and F-measure, respectively. In relation to the precision, the DSC + LQF algorithm achieves the best results.

Table 2: *Evaluation of Content Extraction Methods*

Algorithm	Precision	Recall	F-measure
Proposed System	50.13	**71.37**	**58.90**
Boilerplate	49.17	60.79	54.36
DSC + LQF	**58.57**	41.63	48.66
TextToRatio	08.54	05.18	06.44

The main interpretation of these results is that the proposed system retrieves 17.40% more relevant content than the others (recall), even with a lower precision than DSC + LQF. As the main goal of the system is text summarization, it is more desirable to have more text with a little noise, than losing some important parts of the text.

4.3 Text Summarization

The main goal of this evaluation is to assess the summarization results using text-only files and a complete HTML page. Thus, the results compare: (i) the text summarization system presented by [3] and (ii) the proposed system that performs the content extraction phase to identify the main content.

The evaluation of the quality of the final summaries was performed using ROUGE [8] on the CNN dataset. ROUGE-1 measure was adopted in order to show the relation among the summaries created from a simple text data and the text extracted from web pages (proposed system). It is important to notice that both systems use the same summarization method, the difference here being only the input file (simple text and HTML page).

Table 3 shows the results using ROUGE 1, in which one may see that the proposed system achieves a better precision when compared with the original web page, thus applying the process described in this paper yields summaries that contain more relevant words than the traditional summarization methods [2]. On the other hand, it achieves a lower recall which shows that some relevant words were not recovered by the system. The results of the F-measure show that the traditional system reaches less than 1% improvement, being statistically equivalent. Some conclusions may

Table 3: *Summarization Evaluation - ROUGE 1*

System	Precision	Recall	F-measure
Proposed System	47.49	55.18	51.05
Text-only Web page	46.62	58.11	51.73

be drawn: (i) The ROUGE 1 results show that the proposed system retrieves as many important concepts as the traditional summarization system. This measure assesses the number of unigrams in the generated summary that is in the gold standard summary; (ii) The results of ROUGE 1 show the equivalence between the system proposed and the traditional system.

5. CONCLUSIONS AND FURTHER WORK

This paper proposes a system to summarize news article web pages, which takes advantage of a new link target identification classifier and a new content extraction algorithm proposed here.

The link target identification classifier uses six features based on link structure to classify the HTML page as "news article" or "irrelevant page". The best classifier proposed reached 93.45% and 93.50% of Accuracy and F-measure respectively.

The content extraction algorithm proposed uses the HTML DOM tree to identify the main content of the HTML page. The evaluation in the proposed content extraction algorithm shows a result 17.40% and 8.35% better than the competitors in terms of recall and F-measure, respectively.

The assessment the summarization process showed that the proposed system retrieved as many important concepts as the same summarization methods applied to text-only files.

Currently, these following research lines are under development: (i) Evaluating the proposed system using different datasets; (ii) Creating a web crawler based on the news summaries; (iii) Extending the approach presented here to other kinds of web pages.

Acknowledgments

The research results reported in this paper have been partly funded by a R&D project between Hewlett-Packard do Brazil and UFPE originated from tax exemption (IPI - Law number 8.248, of 1991 and later updates).

6. REFERENCES

[1] N. Akhtar, B. Siddique, and R. Afroz, "Visual and textual summarization of webpages," in *Data Mining and Intelligent Computing*. IEEE, 2014, pp. 1–5.

[2] R. Ferreira *et al*. Assessing sentence scoring techniques for extractive text summarization. *Expert Systems with Applications*, 40(14):5755–5764, 2013.

[3] R. Ferreira, *et al*. A context based text summarization system. In *Document Analysis Systems*, pp. 66–70. IEEE, 2014.

[4] T. Gottron. Evaluating content extraction on HTML documents. In *International Conference on Internet Technologies and Applications*, pp. 123–132, 2007.

[5] T. Gottron. Evaluating content extraction on HTML documents. *ITA*, pp. 123 – 132, 2007.

[6] T. Hassan and N. Damera Venkata. The browser as a document composition engine. In *Symposium on Document Engineering*, pp.pp 3–12. ACM, 2015.

[7] C. Kohlschutter, P. Fankhauser, and W. Nejdl. Boilerplate detection using shallow text features. In *Web Search and Data Mining*, pp. 441–450, 2010.

[8] C.-Y. Lin. Rouge: A package for automatic evaluation of summaries. In ACL-04 Workshop, pp. 74–81,2004.

[9] R. D. Lins, *et al*. A multi-tool scheme for summarizing textual documents. In *WWW/INTERNET 2012*, pp. 1–8, 2012.

[10] E. Lloret, M. T. RomÃ¡-Ferri, and M. Palomar. Compendium: A text summarization system for generating abstracts of research papers. *Data & Knowledge Engineering*, 88(0):164-175, 2013.

[11] A. Nenkova and K. McKeown. A survey of text summarization techniques. In *Mining Text Data*, pp. 43–76, 2012.

[12] L. Page, S. Brin, R. Motwani, and T. Winograd. The pagerank citation ranking: bringing order to the web. 1999.

[13] D. Pinto *et al*. Quasm: A system for question answering using semi-structured data. In *Joint Conference on Digital Libraries*, pp. 46–55, 2002.

[14] T. Weninger, W. H. Hsu, and J. Han. Cetr: Content extraction via tag ratios. In *World Wide Web*, pp. 971–980, 2010.

[15] I. H. Witten and E. Frank. *Data Mining: Practical Machine Learning Tools and Techniques with Java Implementations*. Morgan Kaufmann Pub. Inc., 2000.

[16] Z. Zhao, *et al*. Topic oriented community detection through social objects and link analysis in social networks. *Knowledge-Based Systems*, 26:164 – 173, 2012.

Towards Cohesive Extractive Summarization through Anaphoric Expression Resolution

Jamilson Batista,
Rafael Dueire Lins,
Rinaldo Lima
UFPE, Recife, PE, Brazil
{jba, rdl, rjl4}@cin.ufpe.br

Steven J. Simske
HP Labs
Fort Collins, CO 80528, USA
steven.simske@hp.com

Marcelo Riss
Hewlett-Packard Brazil
Porto Alegre, RS, Brazil
marcelo.riss@hp.com

ABSTRACT

This paper presents a new method for improving the cohesiveness of summaries generated by extractive summarization systems. The solution presented attempts to improve the legibility and cohesion of the generated summaries through coreference resolution. It is based on a post-processing step that binds dangling coreference to the most important entity in a given coreference chain. The proposed solution was evaluated on the CNN corpus of 3,000 news articles, using four state-of-the-art summarization systems and seventeen techniques for sentence scoring proposed in the literature. The experimental results may be considered encouraging, as the final summaries reached better ROUGE scores, besides being more cohesive.

Keywords

Cohesive Summarization; Anaphoric Expressions; Coreference Resolution

1. INTRODUCTION

Automatic Text Summarization (ATS) aims at extracting the information of one or several related documents [15]. ATS methods may be broadly classified as *Extractive* and *Abstractive*. While the former selects a set of the most significant sentences from a document, exactly as they appear, to form the summary; the latter attempt to improve the coherence among sentences, and may even produce new ones [10].

Extractive summarization has been the most studied approach in the literature and may be seen as a preliminary step towards abstractive summarization. Unfortunately, the quality of extractive summaries is still unsatisfactory [4][6][16] mainly due to cohesion concerns.

Batista *et al.* [1] presents the result of assessing over twenty-two state-of-the-art extractive summarization systems on the CNN corpus [9]. The conclusion drawn is that extractive summarization systems are likely to generate summaries with cohesion problems, mainly due to the existence of dangling coreferences [11].

This paper describes the proposed solution that employs anaphoric expression resolution [13] to generate more cohesive

ACM acknowledges that this contribution was authored or co-authored by an employee, contractor or affiliate of a national government. As such, the Government retains a nonexclusive, royalty-free right to publish or reproduce this article, or to allow others to do so, for Government purposes only.

DocEng '16, September 12-16, 2016, Vienna, Austria

© 2016 ACM. ISBN 978-1-4503-4438-8/16/09...$15.00

DOI: http://dx.doi.org/10.1145/2960811.2967159

extractive summaries. The solution proposed is rooted on a heuristic-based post-processing step on summaries, replacing dangling coreferences by their most important entity in a coreference chain. The main goal here is twofold: improving the textual quality of the input summaries by solving dangling coreferences, which are typically introduced by extractive summarizers, and avoiding redundant nominal references in the summaries.

The seventeen extractive summarization techniques listed in [5] and four state-of-the-art extractive summarizers were benchmarked using the CNN corpus. The results revealed that the proposed method not only produces more cohesive summaries, but also outperforms several techniques and summarization systems proposed in the literature.

2. RELATED WORK

Orăsan and colleagues [11] used anaphora resolution to improve a term-based summarizer based on simple Term Frequency-Inverse Document Frequency (TF/IDF). It was evaluated using several versions of the CAST corpus [7] modified by six coreference resolution systems and one human coreference annotator. The experimental results, using the cosine similarity measure [3], suggest that pronominal coreference resolution improved the legibility of the final summaries.

Smith *et al.* [13] introduced the COHSUM summarizer which computes the distribution of the coreferences in the source texts. Its underlying idea is that both referencing and referenced sentences in all the coreference chains in a document should indicate the most important candidate sentences to compose the final summary. COHSUM was evaluated over the DUC 2002 corpus using two measures: ROUGE (for content coverage) and cohesion (number of broken coreference chains). Empirical results showed that COHSUM performed comparatively well in terms of content coverage, producing significantly fewer broken coreference chains compared with other summarizers.

Christensen *et al.* [2] proposed a multi-document summarization system based on the G-FLOW model that balances the coherence and salience among sentences, estimating the level of cohesiveness of a candidate summary. The system also uses coreference instances as features for ranking sentences and connecting the G-FLOW nodes (or sentences).

The systems described in [11] and [13] integrate coreference resolution with a weighting factor for ranking sentences. The present work differs from those as coreference resolution is used here to analyze anaphoric expressions and replace them by the most representative referent.

Contrarily to [2], in which the pronominal references are always bound to their first referent entity, the method proposed here performs a summary post-processing step that replaces coreference in-

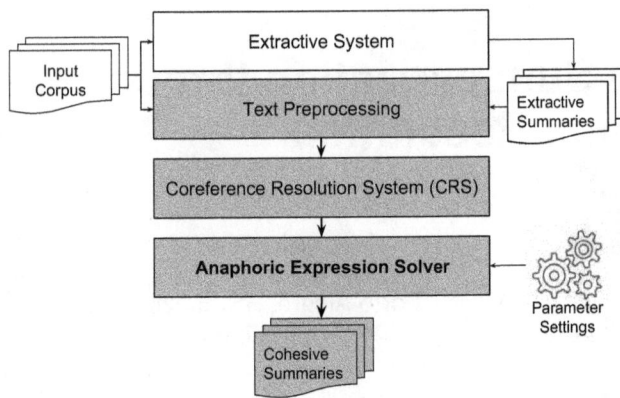

Figure 1: Architectural Components.

stances by the most important entity in each of their coreference chains. Specific criteria for such substitutions are also introduced: preventing many repetitions of anaphoric expressions in the text, as occurs in [2]. Moreover, the proposed method is independent of the extractive summarizer used, while all related work are tightly bound to a particular summarization system [11][2][13]. Finally, no related work has been conducted, providing an extensive evaluation as the one performed in this paper involving several extractive summarization techniques and systems, on a much larger corpus.

3. TOWARDS COHESIVENESS

The architecture of the proposed solution, shown in (Fig. 1), is formed by the Anaphoric Expression Solver (AES) a component that integrates a state-of-the-art coreference resolution system and constitutes the main contribution of this paper. In a broad view, after the generation of the extractive summaries by the external summarizers in Fig. 1 and the preprocessing of both complete and summarized version of a given document, the AES performs a post-processing step in which all of the sentences in the summary are mapped onto their corresponding sentences in the original text. This step enables discovering the most representative subject to replace each dangling reference in the summary. In other words, if the pronoun appears after its referents in the summary, the pronoun is kept; otherwise, the pronoun is unbound and must be replaced by the most representative subject in its coreference chain originated from the complete version of the document. Eventually, such process yields a more cohesive summary as output, with the cost of a slightly decrease in the compression rate of the summary. The components displayed in Fig. 1 are further described next.

Text Preprocessing: This component provides the morphosyntactical analysis of the input documents. Its current implementation relies on the Stanford CoreNLP, a state-art-of-the-art NLP system toolkit[1]. The Text Preprocessing component performs the following NLP substasks: sentence splitting, tokenization, POS tagging, Lemmatization, among others.

Coreference Resolution System (CRS): This module provides the coreference chains present in the input text to the AES component. It was implemented using the Stanford CRS[2] which is able to discover all relevant entities and their references (nominal and pronominal) in text. An unfolding of this work will consider ways of combining the output of multiple CRSs in order to generate more

accurate coreference chains, and even using coreference types independently to test if an approach works.

Anaphoric Expressions Solver (AES). It uses both versions of a document (original and summarized) after have been processed by the text preprocessing steps. It extends previous work in [14][11] by applying a set of rule-based heuristics for:

Task 1: Filtering out the spurious coreference chains before identifying the most representative entities (MRE) and its referents, and;

Task 2: Improving the degree of informativeness of the generated summaries. In other words, reducing the redundancy of the most representative entities in the final summaries. Such redundancy is usually due to the simple strategy of replacing every pronoun with the corresponding entity, as done in [14].

The rule-based heuristics in Task 1 are based on the notion of the Most Representative Entity (MRE) in a coreference chain, defined as the entity represented by its full name followed by the shortest of its appositions present in text. Another acceptable form for the MRE can have up to five tokens not separated by commas, e.g., multi-word entities.

Task 2 address the problem of avoiding the resolution of all the pronominal anaphoric references which would lead to redundant information by repeating entity descriptions in the document. Moreover, in order to improve summary cohesiveness, Task 2 checks the distance, in terms of the number of sentences, between the entity and its referring pronoun. More precisely, if the entity information is found in the nearest preceding sentence, then there is no need to solve the reference given by the pronoun found in the next sentence. A straightforward application of such an idea is related to the substitution of anaphoric expressions that have their contexts not present in the extractive summary.

Before performing the aforementioned tasks, AES checks if a summary has broken coreferences that are determined when there is a pronoun whose MRE to which it refers to is not contained in the candidate summary [14] [13]. For illustrating that, Table 1 shows an example of two sentences contained in an extractive candidate summary (Baseline Summary) of a news article[3] and the output of the AES method (AES Summary) after having processed the baseline summary.

4. EXPERIMENTAL EVALUATION

Experimental Setup. This section describes the experimental evaluation aiming at assessing the effectiveness of the AES method. All the experiments were performed using the full version of the CNN-corpus [9] which encompasses 3,000 news articles collected from the CNN website[4]. The documents address general themes such as sports, politics, among others. Each news article has its *highlights*, a good quality and concise abstractive summary composed of up to four sentences written by the original author of the news article. In addition, each text in the CNN corpus has a *gold standard*, an extractive summary created by human annotators who mapped each sentence of the article highlights onto one or more sentences of the original news article.

The ROUGE-1 (R1) evaluation measure [8] was employed in all the experiments reported in this section. As the golden standard summaries of the CNN corpus comprise 10% of the size of the original corpus, the same compression rate was used in the experiments.

---

[1] http://stanfordnlp.github.io/CoreNLP/
[2] http://nlp.stanford.edu/software/dcoref.shtml

[3] http://edition.cnn.com/2013/01/24/business/davos-uk-cameron/
[4] http://www.cnn.com

Table 1: AES application example

Baseline Summary	**S1:**[*He*]$_1$ sees free trade as key to that success, saying that when it isn't free, everyone suffers.
	S2:[*He*]$_1$ wants Britain to be outward-looking, [**Cameron**]$_1$ said, as [*he*]$_1$ insisted that [*his*]$_1$ referendum promise was "not about turning our backs on Europe" but about making the 27-member bloc work for everyone.
AES Summary	**S1:Prime Minister David Cameron** sees free trade as key to that success, saying that when it isn't free, everyone suffers.
	S2:_He_ wants Britain to be outward-looking, _Cameron_ said, as _he_ insisted that _his_ referendum promise was "not about turning our backs on Europe" but about making the 27-member bloc work for everyone.

Four extractive summarizers were used in the experiments: Auto Summarizer (AutoS), Aylien Text Analysis API (Aylien), HP-Functional Summarization (HP-FS), and Classifier4J (C4J) [1].

Sentence scoring [5] is one of the most employed technique in extractive summarization. For that reason, we also selected and implemented seventeen sentence scoring techniques from [5] to be evaluated in this work, namely: Aggregate Similarity (AS), Word Co-Occurrence (N-GRAM), Sentence Centrality 2 (SC), Bushy Path (BP), Sentence Length (SL), TextRank Score (TS), Cue-phrase (CP), Sentence Centrality 1 (BLEU), Sentence Position in Paragraph (SPP), Lexical Similarity (LS), Term Frequencies (TF/IDF), Word Frequency (WF), Upper ase (UC), Resemblance to the Title (RT), Inclusion of Numerical Data (ND), Proper Noun (PN), and Sentence Position in Text (SPT). More details about all the aforementioned sentence scoring techniques can be found in [5]. Summarization systems differs from Sentence scoring techniques in the sense that the former can integrate a combination of several scoring techniques, i.e., it is a specific solution with particular settings and design decisions.

4.1 Results and Analysis

Broken Coreferences. This preliminary experiment aims at determining the number of summaries with broken coreferences produced by both summarization systems and techniques. In turn, such summaries are treated by the proposed AES method in the next experiment (Tables 4 and 5).

The yielded results on the CNN corpus are summarized in Table 2 (systems) and 3 (techniques) showing: the total number of summaries (column #Summaries) with broken coreferences in the CNN corpus; the corresponding ratio with respect to the whole corpus (column %); the number of broken coreferences in the whole corpus; and the average number of broken coreferences per summary.

From the results in Table 2, one can observe that more than half (56%) of the summaries generated by AutoS had broken coreferences, while C4J was the most resilient among the evaluated systems. Indeed, such summaries have, in the mean, 46.50% of broken coreferences.

Table 3 shows that the summarization techniques had much less cohesion problems (26% in average). The AS technique, in particular, yielded the highest number of summaries, approximately 32% of the total number of summaries, while SPT was the less affected by cohesion problems.

The results in Table 3 corroborate the ones reported in [12, 5] that pointed out the importance of sentence position as, feature for extractive summarization, mainly in the news articles domain. A possible explanation resides in the fact that usually the authors introduce the most representative entities at the beginning of the article. Then, later references to such entities are replaced by pronouns along the text. Therefore, the simple heuristic of choosing the first sentences of the text, is less likely to generate summaries with broken coreferences in the news domain. On the other hand, the PN technique achieved the second best result, possibly because such a technique assigns higher scores to the sentences having proper nouns.

Table 2: Basic Statistics of the summaries with broken coreferences by systems

Systems	#Summaries	%	#Broken Coreferences	#BCoref per Summary
AutoS	1,686	56.20	3,095	1.84
Aylien	1,490	49.67	2,761	1.85
HP-FS	1,219	40.63	2,152	1.77
C4J	1,185	39.50	2,136	1.80
Average	*1,395*	*46.50*	*2,536*	*1.82*

Table 3: Basic Statistics of the summaries with broken coreferences by techniques

Techniques	#Summaries	%	#Broken Coreferences	#BCoref per Summary
AS	954	31.80	2,074	2.17
N-GRAM	935	31.17	2,087	2.23
SC	931	31.03	2,003	2.15
BP	930	31.00	1,984	2.13
SL	923	30.77	2,029	2.20
TS	811	27.03	1,529	1.89
CP	809	26.97	1,561	1.93
BLEU	784	26.13	1,433	1.83
SPP	777	25.90	1,513	1.95
LS	768	25.60	1,427	1.86
TF/IDF	750	25.00	1,373	1.83
WF	737	24.57	1,348	1.83
UC	694	23.13	1,195	1.72
RT	672	22.40	1,241	1.85
ND	656	21.87	1,207	1.84
PN	650	21.67	1,080	1.66
SPT	564	18.80	972	1.72
Average	*785*	*26.17*	*1,532.71*	*1.93*

Comparative Evaluation. Tables 4 and 5 show the comparative results, in terms of the R1 measure, between the summarization systems and techniques, respectively. Both tables show the comparisons before (column R1-Baseline) and after (column R1-AES) employing the AES method for fixing the broken coreferences of the summaries. For all the comparisons, statistical significance tests using a two-sided Wilcoxon signed-rank test with p = 0.05 were used.

Tables 4 and 5 show that, in the mean, the AES method really pays off as the overall F1 scores for almost all the systems and techniques had a statistically significant improvement over the baseline.

In particular, the Aylien, HP-FS, and C4J were the systems that benefitted most of the AES, whereas AutoS was the only system that the AES produced a tiny drop in the F1 score. Actually, a closer look at the AutoS results indicates that, on the one hand, the application of the AES boosted recall considerably, but precision also dropped (6 percent) with respect to the baseline, impacting on the F1 score. On the other hand, such a difference in performance is not important according to the significance statistical tests.

The results in Table 5 were even more encouraging as the summaries processed by the AES achieved the best F1 scores for all the techniques evaluated. However, particularly for the N-GRAM and ND techniques, the AES and the baseline achieved comparable F1 performance, since the difference was not significant.

Table 4: Comparative performance evaluation of the systems.

Systems	R1-Baseline			R1-AES		
	R	P	F1	R	P	F1
AutoS	49.87	47.02	48.40	59.26	40.59	48.18
Aylien	56.08	39.51	46.36	55.31	41.14	**47.18**
HP-FS	57.47	38.14	45.85	56.41	39.52	**46.48**
C4J	51.10	45.64	48.22	56.01	43.47	**48.95**

Table 5: Comparative performance evaluation of the techniques.

Techniques	R1-Baseline			R1-AES		
	R	P	F1	R	P	F1
AS	35.44	36.75	36.08	35.81	37.91	**36.83**
N-GRAM	41.08	35.92	38.33	41.34	37.33	39.23
SC	16.87	30.17	21.64	18.65	33.66	**24.00**
BP	35.04	36.36	35.69	35.49	37.61	**36.52**
SL	46.58	33.52	38.99	46.62	35.00	**39.98**
TS	44.28	37.04	40.34	44.11	38.55	**41.14**
CP	30.99	35.11	32.93	31.91	36.88	**34.22**
BLEU	22.77	36.15	27.94	24.13	38.82	**29.76**
SPP	30.78	35.38	32.92	31.54	37.11	**34.10**
LS	50.38	37.14	42.76	50.07	38.37	**43.45**
TF/IDF	53.08	36.84	43.49	52.59	38.15	**44.22**
WF	52.57	37.35	43.68	52.06	38.68	**44.39**
UC	44.30	35.72	39.55	44.45	37.06	**40.42**
RT	47.42	40.03	43.41	47.22	41.19	**44.00**
SPT	35.13	39.47	37.17	34.97	40.46	**37.52**
ND	38.11	37.18	37.64	38.06	38.59	38.32
PN	43.26	35.65	39.09	43.33	37.16	**40.01**

5. CONCLUSIONS

This paper presented a new method (AES) to improve cohesion in extractive summaries using anaphoric expression resolution. Preliminary experiments with 4 systems and 17 summarization techniques on the CNN corpus showed that both extractive systems and techniques in the literature can generate incomprehensible summaries to human.

The main contribution of this paper was to mitigate this problem by means of the AES method which basically applies a post-processing step on the summaries in order to eliminate the broken coreferences with respect to the original text. Experimental results also showed that not only the summaries treated by AES were more cohesive, but also presented better scores in terms of R1 (ROUGE) when compared with summaries without any treatment.

6. ACKNOWLEDGMENTS

This research work has been partially funded by a R&D project between Brazilian Hewlett-Packard and UFPE originated from tax exemption (IPI -Law number 8.248, of 1991 and later updates).

7. REFERENCES

[1] J. Batista, R. Ferreira, H. Oliveira, R. Ferreira, R. D. Lins, G. Pereira e Silva, S. J. Simske, and M. Riss. A quantitative and qualitative assessment of automatic text summarization systems. In *Proc. of the 2015 ACM*, DocEng '15, pages 65–68, New York, NY, USA, 2015.

[2] J. Christensen, S. Soderl, and O. Etzioni. Towards coherent multi-document summarization. In *Proc. of the North American Chapter of the ACL: Human Language Technologies*, NAACL, 2013.

[3] R. L. Donaway, K. W. Drummey, and L. A. Mather. A comparison of rankings produced by summarization evaluation measures. In *Proc. of the 2000 NAACL-ANLP - Volume 4*, NAACL-ANLP-AutoSum '00, pages 69–78, Stroudsburg, PA, USA, 2000. ALC.

[4] R. Ferreira, F. L. G. Freitas, L. S. Cabral, R. D. Lins, R. Lima, G. F. Pereira e Silva, S. J. Simske, and L. Favaro. A context based text summarization system. In *11th IAPR International Workshop on Document Analysis Systems, (DAS) 2014, Tours, France, April 7-10, 2014*, pages 66–70, 2014.

[5] R. Ferreira, L. Souza Cabral, R. D. Lins, G. Pereira e Silva, F. Freitas, G. D. C. Cavalcanti, R. Lima, S. J. Simske, and L. Favaro. Assessing sentence scoring techniques for extractive text summarization. *Expert Systems with Applications*, 40(14):5755–5764, 2013.

[6] Y. Graham. Re-evaluating automatic summarization with BLEU and 192 shades of ROUGE. In *Proc. of the 2015 Conf. on Empirical Methods in Natural Language Processing, EMNLP 2015, Lisbon, Portugal, September 17-21, 2015*, pages 128–137, 2015.

[7] L. Hasler, C. Orăsan, and R. Mitkov. Building better corpora for summarisation. In *Proc. of Corpus Linguistics 2003*, pages 309 – 319, Lancaster, UK, March 2003.

[8] C. Lin. Rouge: A package for automatic evaluation of summaries. In S. S. Marie-Francine Moens, editor, *Text Summarization Branches Out: Proc. of the ACL-04 Workshop*, pages 74–81, Barcelona, Spain, July 2004. Association for Computational Linguistics.

[9] R. D. Lins, S. J. Simske, L. S. Cabral, G. F. Silva, R. Lima, R. F. Mello, and L. Favaro. A multi-tool scheme for summarizing textual documents. In *Proc. of 11st IADIS International Conf. WWW/INTERNET 2012*, pages 1–8, July 2012.

[10] E. Lloret and M. Palomar. Text summarisation in progress: a literature review. *Artif. Intell. Rev.*, 37(1):1–41, Jan. 2012.

[11] C. Orăsan. The influence of pronominal anaphora resolution on term-based summarisation. In N. Nicolov, G. Angelova, and R. Mitkov, editors, *RANLP V*, volume 309, pages 291–300. John Benjamins, Amsterdam & Philadelphia, 2009.

[12] Y. Ouyang, W. Li, Q. Lu, and R. Zhang. A study on position information in document summarization. In *Proc. of the 23rd International Conf. on Computational Linguistics: Posters*, COLING '10, pages 919–927, Stroudsburg, PA, USA, 2010.

[13] C. Smith, D. Henrik, and J. Arne. A more cohesive summarizer. In *COLING (Posters)*, pages 1161–1170, 2012.

[14] J. Steinberger, M. Poesio, M. A. Kabadjov, and K. Ježek. Two uses of anaphora resolution in summarization. *Information Processing & Management*, 43(6):1663 – 1680, 2007. Text Summarization.

[15] J. M. Torres-Moreno. *Automatic Text Summarization*. Wiley-ISTE, Montréal, Canada, 2014.

[16] C. S. Yadav and A. Sharan. Hybrid approach for single text document summarization using statistical and sentiment features. *CoRR*, abs/1601.00643, 2016.

Assessing Concept Weighting in Integer Linear Programming based Single-document Summarization

Hilário Oliveira, Rinaldo Lima,
Rafael Dueire Lins, Fred Freitas
UFPE, Recife, Brazil
htao@cin.ufpe.br

Marcelo Riss
HP Brazil R&D
Porto Alegre, Brazil
marcelo.riss@hp.com

Steven J. Simske
HP Labs
Fort Collins, CO 80528, USA
steven.simske@hp.com

ABSTRACT

Some of the recent state-of-the-art systems for Automatic Text Summarization rely on the concept-based approach using Integer Linear Programming (ILP), mainly for multi-document summarization. A study on the suitability of such an approach to single-document summarization is still missing, however. This work presents an assessment of several methods of concept weighing for a concept-based ILP approach on the single-document summarization scenario. The unigram and bigram representations for concepts are also investigated. The experimental results obtained on the DUC 2001-2002 and the CNN corpora show that bigrams are more suitable than unigrams for the representation of concepts. Among the concept scoring methods investigated, the sentence position method presented the best performance on all evaluation corpora.

Keywords

Automatic Text Summarization; Single-document summarization; Concept-based ILP approaches

1. INTRODUCTION

Automatic Text Summarization (ATS) is the computer process of producing a shorter version of a single or a collection of related text documents (multi-document), keeping the essential information of the original document. Given the vast amount of textual information present on the Web, ATS systems are potentially useful to support users in the process of sieving relevant information. The recent surveys [6, 12] offer a broad overview of the field.

In recent years, concept-based approaches for summarization have gained the attention of the research community due to their good performance, especially in the multi-document summarization task [7]. In such approaches, summarization is seen as a budgeted maximization coverage problem; i.e., one has to select the most important concepts from a document using the minimum possible number of sentences, constrained by a certain length L. Although such an optimization problem has been shown to be NP-hard, approximate or exact solutions are possible using Integer Linear Programming (ILP)[10].

DocEng '16, September 12-16, 2016, Vienna, Austria

© 2016 ACM. ISBN 978-1-4503-4438-8/16/09...$15.00

DOI: http://dx.doi.org/10.1145/2960811.2967160

Two fundamental issues to be defined in a concept-based ILP model consist of finding a suitable representation for concepts and a method for estimating their weights. For representing concepts, most of the works in the literature [1, 3, 7, 8] have adopted either unigrams or bigrams. Traditionally, the weights given to concepts have been estimated in many ways: using methods based on document frequency [1] for multi-document summarization; considering the position of the sentence in which the concept is located [8]; and applying a supervised learning model [3, 8].

To the best of the knowledge of the authors of this paper, no previous work has investigated the performance of different scoring methods on the concept-based ILP approach in the context of single-document summarization on the news domain. This work provides an assessment of several methods for estimating the weights of concepts in the concept-based ILP approach for single-document summarization. Traditional statistical and graph-based methods are investigated, employing unigrams and bigrams as concepts.

The evaluation results using ROUGE evaluation measures [9] on both the well-known DUC 2001-2002 datasets and the CNN corpus demonstrate the feasibility of adopting a concept-based ILP approach for single-document summarization. The results also show that choosing bigrams as concepts can lead to a better performance than using unigrams in most cases. Among the scoring methods investigated, sentence position presented the best performance measurements on the three corpora tested.

The remaining of this paper is organized as follows. Section 2 introduces the concept-based ILP approach adopted in this work, and the statistical and graph-based concept weighting methods investigated. The experimental results are presented in Section 3. Finally, Section 4 presents the conclusions and draws lines for further work.

2. CONCEPT-BASED ILP APPROACH

The concept-based ILP approach proposed by Gillick et al. [7] can be formally described by Equation 1. In which, w_i represents the weight of the concept (c_i). Variables c_i and s_j are binary. Occ_{ij} is also a binary variable and indicates the presence of the concept c_i into the sentence s_j. The variable l_j is the length of the sentence s_j, and L is the maximum length threshold for the summary. Equations 1c and 1d represent the constraints that guarantee the consistency of the solution; i.e., if a sentence is selected, this implies selecting all the concepts it encompasses, and a concept is only selected if it is present in at least one sentence selected.

The summarization process adopted is composed of the following five steps:

1. Preprocessing: This first step processes the input document using the Stanford Natural Language Processing

$$max \sum_i w_i c_i \tag{1a}$$

$$s.t. \sum_j l_j s_j \leq L \tag{1b}$$

$$s_j Occ_{ij} \leq c_i \quad \forall i,j \tag{1c}$$

$$\sum_j s_j Occ_{ij} \geq c_i \quad \forall i,j \tag{1d}$$

$$c_i, s_j, Occ_{ij} \in \{0,1\} \quad \forall i,j \tag{1e}$$

Toolkit (CoreNLP)[1], which performs the following Natural Language Processing (NLP) tasks: tokenization, sentence splitting, Part-Of-Speech (POS) tagging, and lemmatization.

2. Concept Extraction: In this step, unigrams and bigrams are extracted as concepts. Concepts formed exclusively by stop words or containing punctuation symbols are removed.

3. Concept Scoring: This step assigns a weight to each concept extracted in the previous step. Due to their importance, the scoring methods investigated in this work are described in the next section.

4. Sentence Pruning: This step removes either the very short sentences that may not be representative enough, or the very long sentences that may contain redundant and fragments of irrelevant information. Thus, sentences shorter than 10 words or larger than 70 words were removed[2]. Besides that, duplicate sentences were also removed.

5. Summary Generation: The last step formulates the optimization problem according to Equation 1, which is solved by the ILP implementation available at the GNU Linear Programming Kit (GLPK) package[3]. A binary value is assigned to each sentence, where sentences selected to the summary are marked by 1.

2.1 Statistical Scoring Methods

In this work, the following statistical weighing concepts methods were investigated:

CF-ISF: Concept Frequency - Inverse Sentence Frequency (CF-ISF) is a variant of the traditional Term Frequency - Inverse Document Frequency (TF-IDF). This variant is applied in this work at sentence level instead of document level, using the extracted concepts. The CF-ISF of a concept c_i is computed as shown in Equation 2.

$$CF - ISF(c_i) = CF(c_i) \times log\left(\frac{S}{s_{c_i}}\right) \tag{2}$$

- CF returns the frequency of a concept c_i.
- S is the total of sentences in the document.
- s_{c_i} is the total of sentences in which c_i occurs.

Sentence Frequency: In this method, the importance of a concept is given by its coverage; i.e., the number of sentences in which it appears.

[1] http://stanfordnlp.github.io/CoreNLP/
[2] These thresholds were defined empirically.
[3] https://www.gnu.org/software/glpk/

Concept Frequency: In this method, the weight of a concept is given by the number of times it appears in the input document, normalized by the total of concepts in the document.

Sentence Position: It is well known that sentences that appear at the beginning of a document have a higher importance for ATS [4] in the news domain. To capture this assumption, in this method concepts that appear at the beginning of the document receive a higher weight than concepts that only appear at the end of the document. Equation 3 shows how the weight of a concept using this method is computed.

$$SentPos(c_i) = 1 - \frac{Index_{s_{c_i}}}{S} \tag{3}$$

- $Index_{s_{c_i}}$ returns the index of the first sentence that contains the concept c_i, with the index of the sentences starting by 0.
- S is the total of sentences in the document.

2.2 Graph-based Scoring Methods

Given a document, the first step consists in building a graph representation from its concepts. The graph-based methods investigated in this work are computed using the word graph representation [5]. Since this work uses unigrams and bigrams as concepts, from now on such a representation will be referred as a *concept graph*. A directed concept graph is created for each document, in which vertices are concepts (unigrams or bigrams) and edges consist of the adjacency relations between the concepts.

After the concept graph is constructed, several measures can be computed to assign a score to each vertex. The graph-based methods investigated in this work are briefly described:

Betweenness Centrality is the number of shortest paths between two vertices in the concept graph that includes the vertex v_i. Equation 4 shows how this measure is computed.

$$Betweenness(v_i) = \frac{Sv_i}{|SP|} \tag{4}$$

- Sv_i is the number of shortest paths connecting two vertices that pass through v_i.
- SP is the total number of shortest paths.

Degree is the number of edges incident to a vertex. In the concept graph, the degree of a concept c_i (vertex) represents the number of concepts that co-occur directly with c_i.

Closeness centrality is the sum of the shortest distances between a vertex and all the other vertices. Equation 5 shows how this measure is computed.

$$Closeness(v_i) = \frac{|V| - 1}{\sum_{i \neq j}^{V} shortestPath(v_i, v_j)} \tag{5}$$

- $shortestPath(v_i, v_j)$ returns the distance of the shortest path between v_i and v_j.
- V is the set of vertices in the graph.
- $|V|$ is the total of vertices in the concept graph.

Eigenvector centrality measures the centrality of a vertex as a function of the centralities of its neighbors. It is based on the assumption that connections to high-scoring vertices are more important than those to low-scoring ones. This method is formally defined in Equation 6.

$$Eigenvector(v_i) = \sum_{v_j \in Inc(v_i)} w_{ji} \times Eigenvector(v_j) \quad (6)$$

- $Inc(v_i)$ is the set of incident vertices to v_i.
- w_{ji} is the number of co-occurrences between v_i and v_j.

Hypertext Induced Topic Search (HITS) is a popular algorithm for link analysis between web pages. HITS classifies each web page, which is represented as a vertex in a graph, as Hub or Authority. Authority is a vertex with many in-links, whereas a hub is a vertex with many out-links. This work used a weighted version of this algorithm, in which the weight of the edges was set as the number of co-occurrences between the two vertices.

TextRank is a graph-based ranking algorithm [11] used to extract important keywords and determines the weight of these keywords within the entire document using a graph model. TextRank is based on the eigenvector centrality measure. The score of a vertex is computed as presented in 7.

$$T(v_i) = (1 - d) + d \times \sum_{v_j \in In(v_i)} \frac{w_{ji}}{\sum_{v_k \in Out(v_j)} w_{jk}} \times T(v_j) \quad (7)$$

- d is a damping factor that usually is set to 0.85 [2].
- $In(v_i)$ is the set of vertices that point to v_i,
- $Out(v_j)$ is the set of vertices that v_j points to.
- w_{ji} is the number of co-occurrences between v_i and v_j.

3. EXPERIMENTAL RESULTS

3.1 Experimental Setup

The experiments were conducted using the traditional DUC 2001-2002 datasets, and the CNN corpus. Table 1 summarizes some basic features of the test corpora.

Table 1: Basic Statistics of the Corpora.

Corpus	#Documents	#Sentences	#Words
CNN	3,000	115,649	2,628,336
DUC 2001	309[4]	11,026	269,990
DUC 2002	576[5]	14,370	348,012

Two quantitative measures are used to assess the effectiveness of the concept scoring methods evaluated.

The first evaluation measure adopted is the fully automated and widely used Recall-Oriented Understudy for Gisting Evaluation (ROUGE). ROUGE computes the content overlap between the generated summaries and the golden standard summary(ies). ROUGE-1 and ROUGE-2 recall [9] were computed for all the experiments in this section. ROUGE-1.5.5 was set with the parameters: -n 4 -m

---

[4]The 308 distinct documents were used in the experiment.
[5]The 533 distinct documents were used in the experiment.

-c 95 -r 1000 -f A -p 0.5 -t 0. On the DUC corpora, the parameter *-l N* was used to truncate all candidate summaries to *N* words.

The second evaluation measure used is the Direct Matching (DM) [4], which computes the intersection of sentences between the generated summary and the golden standard summary(ies) available. This measure can only be computed whenever there is an extractive golden standard summary available. Thus, the DM is calculated only for the CNN corpus.

For the CNN corpus, a compression rate of 10% of the number of sentences in the input document was adopted. In the DUC 2001-2002 the summarization threshold was set to 105 words.

3.2 Results and Discussion

Table 2 presents the performance of each concept scoring method described in Section 2.2 on the three summarization corpora. The two-sided Wilcoxon signed-rank test is employed to verify whether there is a statistical significance difference in performance among the assessed concept scoring methods. The results show that sentence position obtained the best performance over all the three corpora according to the ROUGE-1 (R-1), ROUGE-2 (R-2), and Direct Matching (DM) measures. On the CNN and DUC 2002 datasets, sentence position statistically outperforms all other methods in terms of R-1 and R-2 (at 95% of confidence level). On the DUC 2001 dataset, again, sentence position significantly surpasses all other methods in terms of R-1 scores, except for the sentence frequency and concept frequency scoring methods. Regarding R-2, it presents statistically better results than all other methods. On the CNN corpus, sentence position obtained the best results according to the DM measure, recognizing 25.33% of the 10,754 sentences of the golden standard summaries available.

Single- and multi-document summarization suffer slightly different influences of aspects such as sentence position and centrality. In single-document summarization, especially for news articles, sentence position has been proved to be one of the most efficient technique for sentence scoring [4], whereas, in the multi-document scenario, methods that measure the centrality and the spread of information in the documents tend to provide better performance. Such behavior was also observed in the experiments performed here, as sentence position demonstrated to be more efficient for concept weighting than the other methods based on frequency and centrality. These results show that the sentence position method is more important in single-document scenario than for multi-document summarization.

Some other conclusions may also be drawn from Table 2: (i) in general, the traditional scoring methods presented better performance than the graph-based ones; (ii) adopting bigrams in the traditional scoring methods leads to better performance in all scenarios; (iii) in most cases, the bigram concept representation decreases the performance of the graph-based methods; (iv) among the graph-based methods, Degree presented the best performance; and (v) considering all experiments, in 68.83% of the comparisons made, bigrams presented better performance than unigrams.

4. CONCLUSION AND FUTURE WORK

This paper presents an assessment of several concept scoring methods for single-document summarization. The concept scoring methods were integrated into a concept-based ILP approach using both unigram and bigram representations. The empirical results demonstrate the following findings: (i) a clear superiority of the bigram representation over the unigram one; (ii) the Sentence Position method achieved the best performance for estimating the concept weights on all the three corpora evaluated; and (iii) among the graph-based scoring methods, Degree (the simplest one), yielded

Table 2: Results (%) and standard deviation (in parentheses) of the concept scoring methods based on ROUGE-1 (R-1), ROUGE-2 (R-2) recall, and Direct Matching (DM). The overall highest performance for each corpus is marked in bold and the group of methods statistically similar is indicated by a dagger (†).

Statistical Methods	N-gram	CNN			DUC 2001		DUC 2002	
		DM	R-1	R-2	R-1	R-2	R-1	R-2
Concept Frequency	Uni	20.41	53.28 (18.33)	31.05 (23.94)	41.01 (8.76)	14.75 (9.37)	44.45 (9.20)	18.15 (9.92)
	Big	20.93	54.00 (19.31)	32.73 (25.16)	41.94† (8.68)	15.76 (9.57)	45.62 (8.73)	19.09 (9.59)
CF-ISF	Uni	19.89	53.01 (18.48)	30.64 (24.29)	39.60 (8.97)	13.79 (9.29)	43.51 (9.23)	17.48 (9.78)
	Big	20.81	53.92 (19.54)	32.42 (25.58)	41.81 (8.86)	15.67 (9.74)	45.29 (8.84)	18.89 (9.70)
Sentence Frequency	Uni	20.67	53.54 (18.43)	31.39 (24.22)	41.07 (8.87)	14.58 (9.35)	44.71 (9.03)	18.19 (9.75)
	Big	21.03	54.10 (19.32)	32.84 (25.25)	42.09† (8.68)	15.82 (9.60)	45.69 (8.81)	19.29 (9.58)
Sentence Position	Uni	20.34	52.88 (18.80)	31.10 (24.83)	38.65 (9.56)	13.97 (9.52)	43.07 (9.53)	17.37 (10.05)
	Big	25.33	**56.45** (19.52)	**37.21** (25.62)	**43.02** (9.38)	**17.50** (10.63)	**47.31** (8.86)	**21.59** (10.16)
Graph-based Methods								
Betweenness	Uni	19.66	51.42 (18.17)	29.42 (23.58)	39.98 (8.79)	13.82 (9.51)	43.53 (8.98)	17.33 (9.77)
	Big	17.96	47.51 (19.10)	26.35 (23.23)	39.86 (8.11)	13.52 (8.44)	42.76 (9.06)	16.75 (9.74)
Closeness	Uni	18.36	50.52 (20.00)	28.40 (24.65)	38.38 (9.36)	12.84 (9.42)	42.59 (9.89)	16.61 (10.20)
	Big	11.58	38.14 (18.01)	16.48 (19.59)	37.58 (9.42)	12.18 (9.41)	42.01 (9.70)	15.79 (10.10)
Degree	Uni	20.11	53.26 (18.30)	30.88 (24.24)	40.50 (8.55)	14.17 (9.05)	44.13 (9.26)	17.64 (9.86)
	Big	20.81	*53.85* (19.30)	*32.43* (25.21)	*41.47* (8.85)	*15.23* (9.98)	*45.20* (8.62)	*18.81* (9.49)
Eigenvector	Uni	20.61	50.96 (19.09)	29.70 (23.79)	40.96 (8.79)	14.19 (9.31)	44.24 (8.81)	17.86 (9.63)
	Big	17.62	44.69 (19.25)	24.70 (23.00)	39.89 (9.13)	14.20 (9.60)	42.69 (9.15)	17.16 (9.94)
HITS Authority	Uni	19.30	49.91 (18.34)	28.11 (23.35)	39.89 (8.99)	13.70 (9.53)	43.36 (9.08)	16.97 (9.35)
	Big	18.98	50.19 (19.67)	28.85 (24.65)	41.02 (9.23)	14.74 (9.59)	44.47 (9.08)	18.38 (9.86)
HITS Hub	Uni	19.10	49.71 (18.49)	27.92 (23.15)	40.42 (8.93)	14.13 (9.67)	43.24 (9.32)	16.90 (9.98)
	Big	19.51	50.49 (19.65)	29.42 (24.69)	41.13 (9.21)	15.05 (9.96)	41.13 (10.02)	16.47 (9.93)
TextRank	Uni	18.54	51.06 (18.51)	28.56 (24.25)	39.19 (9.63)	13.76 (9.69)	43.55 (9.58)	17.04 (10.16)
	Big	20.54	53.41 (19.36)	31.93 (25.27)	41.40 (9.28)	15.10 (10.41)	44.80 (9.39)	18.79 (10.14)

the best performance measurements.

Further work is being done to propose and evaluate a new concept-based approach for single-document summarization that combines sentence position and frequency methods to measure the concept weights. Such an approach will prioritize sentences at the beginning of the documents and also take into consideration the readability of the generated summary.

5. ACKNOWLEDGMENTS

This research work has been partially funded by a R&D project between Brazilian Hewlett-Packard and UFPE originated from tax exemption (IPI - Law number 8.248, of 1991 and later updates). The authors are also grateful to the Brazilian Research Agency CNPq for supporting this research.

6. REFERENCES

[1] F. Boudin, H. Mougard, and B. Favre. Concept-based summarization using integer linear programming: From concept pruning to multiple optimal solutions. In *Proceedings of the 2015 Conference on Empirical Methods in Natural Language Processing*, pages 1914–1918, Lisbon, Portugal, September 2015.

[2] S. Brin and L. Page. The anatomy of a large-scale hypertextual web search engine. *Computer Networks and ISDN Systems*, 30(1-7):107–117, Apr. 1998.

[3] Z. Cao, F. Wei, L. Dong, S. Li, and M. Zhou. Ranking with recursive neural networks and its application to multi-document summarization. In *Proceedings of the Twenty-Ninth Conference on Artificial Intelligence*, pages 2153–2159, Austin, USA, January 2015.

[4] R. Ferreira, L. de Souza Cabral, R. D. Lins, G. Pereira e Silva, F. Freitas, G. D. Cavalcanti, R. Lima, S. J. Simske, and L. Favaro. Assessing sentence scoring techniques for extractive text summarization. *Expert Systems With Applications*, 40(14):5755–5764, 2013.

[5] K. Filippova. Multi-sentence compression: Finding shortest paths in word graphs. In *Proceedings of the 23rd International Conference on Computational Linguistics*, pages 322–330, Beijing, China, 2010.

[6] M. Gambhir and V. Gupta. Recent automatic text summarization techniques: a survey. *Artificial Intelligence Review*, pages 1–66, 2016.

[7] D. Gillick, B. Favre, D. Hakkani-Tür, B. Bohnet, Y. Liu, and S. Xie. The ICSI/UTD summarization system at TAC 2009. In *Proceedings of the Second Text Analysis Conference*, Gaithersburg, USA, November 2009.

[8] C. Li, Y. Liu, and L. Zhao. Using external resources and joint learning for bigram weighting in ilp-based multi-document summarization. In *Proceedings of the Conference of the North American Chapter of the Association for Computational Linguistics: Human Language Technologies*, pages 778–787, Denver, USA, May–June 2015.

[9] C.-Y. Lin. Rouge: A package for automatic evaluation of summaries. In *Text Summarization Branches Out: Proceedings of the 42nd Annual Meeting of the Association for Computational Linguistics Workshop*, pages 74–81, Barcelona, Spain, July 2004.

[10] R. McDonald. A study of global inference algorithms in multi-document summarization. In *Proceedings of the 29th European Conference on IR Research*, pages 557–564, Rome, Italy, 2007.

[11] R. Mihalcea and P. Tarau. Textrank: Bringing order into texts. In *Proceedings of the Empirical Methods in Natural Language Processing*, pages 404–411, Barcelona, Spain, July 2004.

[12] A. Nenkova and K. McKeown. A survey of text summarization techniques. In *Mining Text Data*, pages 43–76. 2012.

Author Index